Evelyn de R. McMann retired in 1978, having been responsible for the indexing of Canadian art for the Fine Arts and Music Division of the Vancouver Public Library for fourteen years.

This detailed reference work lists, by artists, all works exhibited by the Royal Canadian Academy in its first 100 years. These include works in all media shown in the annual exhibitions, special exhibits organized by the Academy, fairs and world expositions to which the Academy officially contributed, and travelling exhibitions organized by the National Gallery of Canada.

The more than 22,000 entries embrace work in the fields of painting, sculpture, architecture, design, photography, and film, executed by approximately 3,000 artists.

Evelyn McMann's compilation includes concise biographical data on each artist, the artist's residence at the time the work was exhibited, the title and nature of each piece, and its sale price if known. A total of 134 exhibitions are listed with date, place, and number of works exhibited.

This book draws on many previously unpublished sources, presents an historic view of Canadian art, and greatly enhances a precise knowledge of Canadian artists' contributions to our heritage. It is an invaluable reference for Canadian collectors, art historians, dealers, and gallery staff.

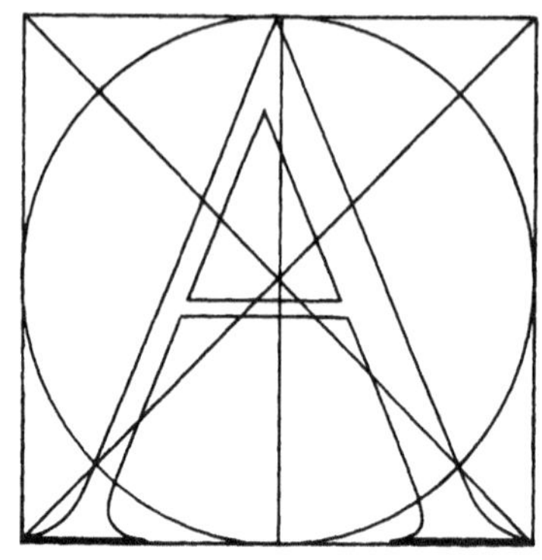

EVELYN de R. McMANN

Royal Canadian Academy of Arts/Académie royale des arts du Canada

EXHIBITIONS AND MEMBERS 1880-1979

UNIVERSITY OF TORONTO PRESS
TORONTO BUFFALO LONDON

Toronto Buffalo London
Printed in Canada
Reprinted in 2018
ISBN 0-8020-2366-5
ISBN 978-1-4875-7701-8 (paper)

Canadian Cataloguing in Publication Data

McMann, Evelyn de R. (Evelyn de Rostaing), 1913-
Royal Canadian Academy of Arts/Académie royale des arts du Canada; exhibitions and members, 1880-1979

ISBN 0-8020-2366-5

1.Royal Canadian Academy of Arts - Directories.
2.Royal Canadian Academy of Arts - Exhibitions.
3.Royal Canadian Academy of Arts - History.
4.Art - Canada - Exhibitions. I.Title.

N17.C36M45 706'.71 C81-094440-5

Contents

Preface

This book has been prepared as a centennial tribute to the Royal Canadian Academy of Arts, founded in 1880 by the Marquis of Lorne, Governor General of Canada.

It is a complete record of the ninety-two annual, and twelve special, exhibitions organized by the Academy. It records also the Academy's official participation in twelve national and international fairs and expositions, and the selections made by the Academy from annual exhibitions for eighteen travelling exhibitions organized and toured by the National Gallery of Canada.

Sets of the annual exhibition catalogues are scarce. Fewer than ten institutions in Canada have the entire series, and in most of those collections at least some of the catalogues are photocopies. Few of the other catalogues are even in the Academy's records in the Public Archives of Canada. After an extensive search photocopies of all were obtained through the generous co-operation of a number of galleries, the National Gallery of Canada and the Art Gallery of Ontario in particular.

More than 3,000 men and women contributed works to these exhibitions, from the first in 1880 to the most recent in 1976. Each contributor is listed in the following pages, with the record of works shown. Where available, brief biographical information is included. The exhibitors who were not Members were, for the most part, Canadian, but nearly 200 were American, British, or European. The Academy has had 885 Members in its first century: all are listed, though not all have exhibited (in most cases because of the suspension of annual exhibitions after 1971).

The 25,563 works noted in the catalogues provide a wide historical perspective of Canada's heritage of art, the work of her outstanding artists past and present. The entire field of the visual arts is represented in the Membership and the exhibitions; painters, sculptors, architects, engravers, etchers, graphic artists, industrial, stained glass and theatrical designers, tapestry weavers, photographers and film makers.

The information in the book is the most accurate that it has been possible to gather from many, often conflicting sources. There are discrepancies in the Academy's records, and a number of past Members' files have been discarded. Variations appear in biographical forms returned by artists to the Academy and to libraries. Newspaper obituaries disagree. Reference books supply a choice of dates and places of birth and death. The catalogues spell artists' names in several ways. For all the errors of commission, omission, and selection I claim full responsibility. I would welcome corrections where necessary.

To the President, Council, and Centennial Committee of the Academy I am deeply indebted. Only with their sanction and the privilege of full access to all necessary records could this book have been compiled. To Rebecca Sisler, RCA, Executive Secretary, and Dorothy Aitken, Secretary, countless thanks for finding time in a particularly busy year to help me with many of the details.

To the University of Toronto Press, my gratitude for turning a personal wish, to make this information readily available to libraries, into a reality. Ian Montagnes guided this amateur from first to final step in preparing the work for publication. The design skill of William Rueter, RCA, made it possible for one volume to contain the thousands of artists and their thousands of works.

To the National Gallery of Canada go my profound thanks. Charles C. Hill, Curator of Post Confederation Art, offered constant encouragement and sent answers before I asked the questions. Mrs Noel Balke and Miss Jacqueline Hunter, Librarians, gave unlimited aid and made my days of hunting the National Gallery Library files into a time of pleasure. Without the resources of the Gallery, and assistance from many of the staff, this book would have been far less informative.

The Ontario Arts Council assisted the preparation of the manuscript.

And Irma Hock proofread every figure, letter, punctuation mark, and space. I can never thank my friend adequately for her toil.

Each of the following has improved the quality of the book. Their replies to my requests for assistance have been most gratefully received, and valued.

Architects Association of New Brunswick, Freda M. Large, Executive Secretary; Architects Association of Prince Edward Island, Peter W. Hyndman, Secretary; Art Gallery of Ontario, Sybille Pantazzi, Librarian, and staff; John Bland, RCA, Emeritus Professor of Architecture, McGill University; Edmonton Art Gallery, Terry Fenton, Director; J. Russell Harper, Canadian art historian; Robert G. Hill, architect, Toronto; Robert Lemire, architectural historian, Montreal; Colin S. MacDonald, author, Dictionary of Canadian Artists; Montreal Museum of Fine Arts/Musée des beaux-arts de Montréal, Juanita Toupin, Libraryan; Musée d'art contemporaine, Isabelle Montplaisir, Librarian; Nova Scotia Association of Architects, Kaw Worsley, Executive Secretary; Onondaga County Public Library, Local History and Genealogy Department, Gerald J. Parsons, Head; Ontario Association of Architects, Jeanne Arnold, Registrar; Public Archives of Canada, Government Cartographical and Architectural Records Section, Dorothy Ahlgren, Head; Public Archives of Canada, Social/Cultural Archives Manuscripts, Anne Goddard, Archivist, and Joan Kennie, assistant; Public Archives of Nova Scotia, Margaret Campbell, Picture Archivist; Humphrey Toms, Vancouver; University of British Columbia, Melva Dwyer, Librarian, and Diana Cooper, Assistant Librarian; Vancouver Art Gallery, Jean Martin, Librarian, and Nora Blair, assistant: Vancouver Public Library, Administration and the seven Reference Divisions, for enthusiastic assistance in research, and interest in every aspect of compilation.

Evelyn de Rostaing McMann
Vancouver
December 1980

Guide to Entries

Works exhibited are listed under the name of the artist. The entries contain the following information, as in this sample:

DOE, JOHN
23 Feb 1901, Winnipeg 19 May 1972,
Ottawa AGO CC2 CWW64 M NGC WWA47
ARCA 1949 RCA 1957 Sr 1970 Council
Painter
Addr: 1929-36, 9 Glen Rd, Winnipeg;
1950-71, Ottawa
1926 23 Days past $50 1927-36 $60
1929 28 Sunlight wc 18 x 22 illus
      $45 F9-35 S7-42
1933 37 Winter $75 T34-12 nfs
1935 30 Rideau Canal Radeau, mispr
1936 40 Quebec (Mr N.K. Harris)
1943 19 Harvest aqua ∅NGC∅
1956 33 Flowers DW 1957 36 x 48

Name of artist

Biographical data

Date and place of birth, when available

Date and place of death, when available

Sources of biographical information. Each source work is identified by an abbreviation, see pp xv-xvi

Status in Royal Canadian Academy of Arts

ARCA. Associate Member, 1880-1972-3. A Member remained ARCA until presentation of a Diploma work.

RCA(e). Member elect. In 1973, a revised constitution designated all Members RCA. A Member remains elect until presentation of a Diploma work.

RCA. A Member who has received the Diploma of Academician on presenting a work for deposit in the National Gallery of Canada. The RCA date is that which is on the Diploma.

RCA Hon Non-Res. Honorary Non-Resident members were elected to the Academy but were not required to present a work on receiving the Diploma of Academician. Several of the artists gave a work to the Academy for presentation as a gift to the National Gallery of Canada; these works are entered as gift.

RCA/ARCA Non-Res. Members residing for a length of time outside Canada, but retaining membership.

RCA Medal. To honour persons who have made notable contributions to the fine or applied arts in Canada. First awarded in 1962. List of recipients in the catalogues 1968-71 and Special #12, 1976.

Ret. Retired Member

Sr. Senior Member. A by-law in November 1936 established the status of Senior RCA/ARCA and exempted Seniors from payment of annual dues. In 1968 the transition to Senior was set at age 70, to be reduced each year to 60 by 1978. Catalogues 1937-71 list Seniors. Current membership lists do not indicate Seniors, although the membership category remains.

Council. Members of Council are from the catalogues, 1880-1971, and from the minutes, 1972-9. Errors appear in the catalogues; these have been corrected from the annual reports. Detailed list of Members serving, pp 441-4.

Discipline of Membership

The discipline within which the Member has been elected to the Academy.

Addresses

City addresses of Members are listed in the catalogues, 1881-1971. 1880 addresses are from the minutes, 1979 addresses from the membership list. Exhibitors' addresses are in the catalogues 1881, 1883-4, 1887, 1893-1937, and Special #12, 1976.

Year and nature of exhibition
Unless other notification appears, works were exhibited in the annual exhibition of that date.

F1-F11. Fairs and expositions to which the Academy officially contributed, and selected the works. The Academy was represented on the Selection Committees for the exhibitions in London, 1886, and Chicago, 1893.

S1-S12. Special exhibitions organized by the Academy.

T34-T56. Travelling exhibitions, 1934-56, organized and circulated by the National Gallery of Canada to galleries across Canada. The Academy selected the works from the annual exhibition preceding the year of the tour.

A detailed list of the exhibitions appears on pp 445-8.

Works exhibited

Catalogue number. Numbers followed by a letter indicate the separately numbered sections in some catalogues: A architecture; G graphic design; I industrial design; S sculpture; W water color. Films were unnumbered in the 1970 and 1971 catalogues.

Title. Titles are entered as listed in the catalogues. In some cases works apparently have been listed with full title in one catalogue and a shorter title in another; in such cases, as a precaution, both titles are entered. When precisely the same title and medium are shown in more than one catalogue, the later exhibition date and catalogue number are added to the first entry, with any change in price, or note of illustration. Sometimes artists painted two, or more, works with the same title; where this is clearly the case, each work is entered.

Medium. Painting without medium noted is oil. The catalogues of 1905-6 and 1908-10 do not indicate the media of works. List of abbreviations, pp xvii.

Size. Where noted in the catalogue.

Illus. Illustrated in the catalogue.

Price. All prices in the catalogues are entered, also any change in price of the same work in a later exhibition.

Nfs. Not for sale, where noted in the catalogue.

Mispr. Misprint, or error in spelling of place name in title, or in artist's name; the error has been corrected and the misprint is noted.

DW. Diploma work, required of a Member to receive the Diploma of Academician. Diploma works are deposited in the National Gallery of Canada. The 1880 Diploma works formed the nucleus of the Gallery's collection. The DW date is the year in which the work was entered in the Gallery's acquisition record; in some cases it is a year, or more, later than the date of the Diploma.

Name of lender. Shown in parentheses (Mr N.K. Harris).

Present location in a public gallery. The name of the gallery holding the work in its permanent collection is shown in double parentheses ((NGC)). Many works now in permanent collections lack this notation because of title changes during the intervening years; these could not be positively identified by the published catalogues of gallery collections. List of gallery abbreviations, p xvii.

Not included

The lengthy poems accompanying titles of eight paintings in the catalogues for 1880, 1882 and 1884; and the Honorary Members listed in the catalogues for 1880-90. These were not elected Members, but simply donated $1 or more to the Academy.

Biographical Sources

AAA American art annual. Washington, DC, American Federation of Arts. Checked 1924, 1928-35

AGO Art Gallery of Ontario. The Canadian collection. Toronto, McGraw-Hill Company of Canada Limited, 1970

B Bénézit, Emmanuel. Dictionnaire critique et documentaire des peintres, sculpteurs, dessinateurs et graveurs. Paris, Librarie Grund, 1976 ed.

CC1
CC2 Creative Canada: a biographical dictionary of 20th century creative and performing arts. Compiled by the Reference Division, McPherson Library, University of Victoria. Toronto, University of Toronto Press. Vol 1, 1971; Vol 2, 1972

CNS Canadian Newspaper Service Reg'd. Reference book. Biographical reference data and other general information. Montreal, Canadian Newspaper Service Reg'd. Checked 1927 and later editions

Co Colombo, John Robert. Colombo's Canadian references. Toronto, Oxford University Press, 1976

CWW Canadian who's who, Kieran Simpson, editor. Toronto, University of Toronto Press, 1979. Previous editions, The Times, London, 1910, Toronto, Musson Book Co; Arthur L. Tunnell, editor, 1936-75, Toronto, Trans Canada Press, 1936-8 to 1964-6; Toronto, Who's who Canadian Publications, 1967-9 to 1973-5

DBA Dictionary of British artists 1880-1940. Jane Johnson and A. Greutzner, editors. Woodbridge, Sussex, Antique Collectors Club, 1976

DBW Dictionary of British watercolour artists up to 1920, H.L. Mallallieu. (n.p.) Antique Collectors Club, 1976

DCB Dictionary of Canadian biography. Toronto, University of Toronto Press, 1966; in progress

DIA Dictionary of Irish artists, Walter George Strickland. Shannon, Irish University Press, 1969

DMS New dictionary of modern sculptors, Robert Maillard, general editor. New York, Tudor Publishing Co, 1970. Original edition, Nouveau dictionnaire de la sculpture moderns. Paris, Fernan Hazen, 1970

DVP Dictionary of Victorian painters, Christopher Wood. Woodbridge, Sussex, Antique Collectors Club, 1978 ed.

EC Encyclopedia Canadiana. Toronto, Grolier Society of Canada, 1972 ed.

ED Directory of Eskimo artists in sculpture and prints, Philip Howard Gray. (Montana State University) Box 177, Boseman, Mont, 59715. c1974

F Fielding's dictionary of American painters, sculptors and engravers, Mantle Fielding. Addendum compiled by James F. Carr. New York, James F. Carr Publisher, 1965

G Graves, Algernon. The Royal Academy of Arts: a complete dictionary of contributors and their work from its foundation in 1769 to 1904. London, Henry Graves & Co, Limited, and George Bell & Sons, 1905

Gr Groce, George G. and Wallace, David H., editors. New York Historical Society's dictionary of artists in America 1564-1860. New Haven, Yale University Press, 1957

H Harper, J. Russell. Early painters and engravers in Canada. Toronto, University of Toronto Press, 1970

IO Index of Ontario artists, Hennie Wolfe. Toronto, Visual Arts of Ontario and Ontario Association of Art Galleries, 1978

M MacDonald, Colin S. Dictionary of Canadian artists. Ottawa, Canadian Paperbacks, 17 Gwynne St, Ottawa, K1Y 1X1. A-Perri, in progress

Mo98 Morgan, Henry James. Canadian men and women of the time. Toronto,
Mo12 Briggs, 1898 and 1912 editions

NGC National Gallery of Canada. Catalogue of paintings and sculpture. Vol 3, Canadian school, R.H. Hubbard. Ottawa and Toronto, published for the Trustees by University of Toronto Press, 1960 (Diploma works are illustrated pp 363-423)

PMC Prominent men of Canada 1931-1932, Ross Hamilton, editor. Montreal, National Publishing, 1932

R1 Roberts, Charles G.D. and Tunnell, Arthur L., editors. A standard dic-
R2 tionary of Canadian biography: the Canadian who was who. Toronto, Trans Canada Press. Vol 1, 1875-1933, 1934; Vol 2, 1875-1937, 1938

RA Royal Academy. A dictionary of artists and their works in the annual summer exhibitions of the Royal Academy of Arts, 1905-70. East Ardsley, Wakefield, Yorkshire, E.P. Publishing Limited, 1973. A-L, in progress

RSA Royal Scottish Academy. A complete list of the exhibited works by Raeburn and by Academicians, Associatiates and Honorable Members: giving details of those works in public galleries. Compiled under the direction of Frank Rinder. Glasgow, James Maclehose & Sons, 1917

RSBA Royal Society of British Artists. Members exhibiting 1824-1962, Maurice Bradshaw. Leigh-on-Sea, England, F. Lewis Publishers, 1973-77

TB Thieme, Ulrich und Becker, Felix. Allgemeins Lexikon der bildenden
TB2 Kunstler von der Antike bis zur Gegenwart. 37 vols 1907-50. (2) Voll-
TB3 mer, Hans, Allgemeines Lexikon der bildenden Kunstler der XX Jahrhunderts. Vols 1-5, 1953-61. (3) Vollmer, Hans, Vols 5-6, 1961-2. Leipzig, E.A. Seeman, 1907-62

W78 Wallace, W. Stewart, editor. Macmillan dictionary of Canadian biography. Toronto, Macmillan of Canada, 1978. Also checked 1963 edition

WBA Waters, Grant G. Dictionary of British artists working 1900-50. Eastbourne, England, Eastbourne Fine Arts, 1975

WWA Who's who in American art. Washington, DC, American Federation of Arts, 1936-47. New York, R.R. Bowker, 1953 to date. Checked to 1978 edition

WWB Who's who in art: being a series of alphabetically arranged biographies of the leading men and women in the world of art to-day. London, Art Trade Press Limited. Checked 1927 and later editions

WWC Who's who in Canada, B.M. Greene, editor. Toronto, International Press Limited. Checked 1922 and later editions

Y Young, William. Dictionary of American artists, sculptors and engravers from the beginnings through the turn of the 20th century. Cambridge, Mass, William Young Company, 1968

Abbreviations

MEDIA

acry	acrylic
alum	aluminum
aqua	aquatint
arch	architectural
b&w	black and white
cal	calligraphy
cart	cartoon
carv	carving
cer	ceramic
charcl	charcoal
col	color
coll	collage
dec	decorative
des	design
drwg	drawing
dry pt	dry point
engr	engraving
etch	etching
gr	graphic
illum	illumination
jwlry	jewelry
lacq	lacquer
lino	linoleum
litho	lithograph
m med	mixed media
m tech	mixed techniques
medln	medallion
mezz	mezzotint
min	miniature
monoc	monochrome
monog	monograph
monot	monotype
pr	print
rel	relief
sculp	sculpture
sergph	serigraph
st gl	stained glass
tap	tapestry
temp	tempera
ter cot	terra cotta
text	textile
wc	water color
wd	wood
wld	welded

GALLERIES

AGH	Art Gallery of Hamilton
AGO	Art Gallery of Ontario
BAG	Beaverbrook Art Gallery
CAG	Coburg Art Gallery
CON	Confederation Centre Art Gallery and Museum
EAG	Edmonton Art Gallery
LAG	London Public Library and Art Museum
MMFA	Montreal Museum of Fine Arts/ Musée des beaux-arts de Montréal
MQ	Musée du Québec
NGC	National Gallery of Canada
UBC	University of British Columbia
VAG	Vancouver Art Gallery

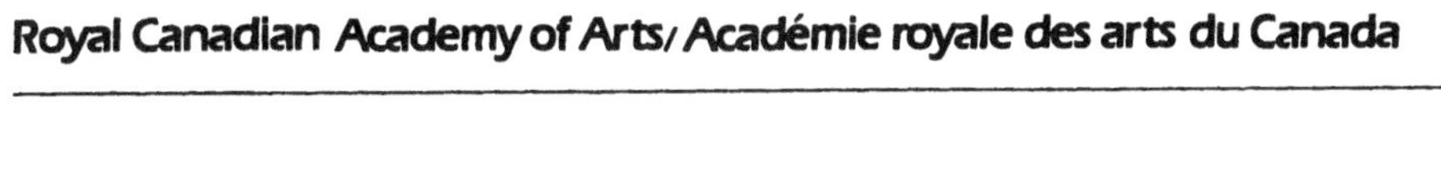

Royal Canadian Academy of Arts / Académie royale des arts du Canada

Exhibitions and Members

A

ABBOTT, ISABELLA M.
Addr: 1922-3, 299 Pine Ave, Montreal
1922 1 Rocks, Kennebunk, Maine wc
1923 1 The poplars

ABBOTT, JOHN BETHUNE
1851, Montreal 1929, Montreal B
H Mo12
Addr: 1902, 412 Guy St, Montreal;
1903-10, Art Association Montreal
1902 168 Isle St Geneviève, early
morning wc
169 A lonely marsh wc
1903 134 Dawn wc
1904 186 Drifting snow wc
187 The ravine wc
188 The old fort wc
1905 4 Early June
5 A cold evening, October
6 Evening
1907 205 Shadowy night wc
206 Moonlight wc
1909M 1 Moonlight
1910 1 Moonlight in the birchwood

ABRAHAM, MARY B.
Addr: 1923, 356 Victoria St,
Chatham, Ont
1923 2 Harvest time

ADAM, CAMIL
1971 Au plus petit d'entre nous
film screened 31 Mar

ADAM, PETER
Addr: 1976, Toronto
1976 S12, Montreal
112 Festival Ontario pamph-
lets/dépliants illus
113 Fact sheet booklets, Ministry of Education, Ontario
4 illus

ADAMS, JAMES M.F.
fl 1891-3 H
Addr: 1893, Toronto
1891 94 Study of an old man
98 Work wanted
1893 1 In the studio $45 F1-1

ADAMS, LILY OSMAN
1865, Toronto 1945, Toronto AGO H
Addr: 1904-7, Toronto; 1918A, 27
Irwin Ave, Toronto; 1918N-19, 10
Elmscourt Apt, Toronto; 1923-36, 27
Irwin Ave, Toronto
1904 189 Rainy day wc
1907 207 Pines wc
208 Poppies wc
209 A study in green wc
1918A 1 An Ontario valley O.Adams,
mispr
1918N 1 Canadian valley
2 Cottage among pines
1919 1 Red roof
1923 3 A Canadian valley
1925 1 Little peach trees
1928 1 Poppies pastel $100
2 Trilliums pastel $75
1930 1 An October bouquet $125
1931 1 Autumn garden flowers
pastel $60
2 Trilliums pastel $50
1932 1 Blue and gold pastel $50
1933 1 Gladioli pastel $100 1934-1
1934 2 Trillium pastel $50
1936 1 Phlox pastel $50

ADAMS, WAYMAN American
23 Sep 1883, Muncie, Ind 8 Apr
1959, Austin, Tex F WWA36
Addr: 1927-30, 200 W 57th St, New
York
1927 1 Archibald Browne, RCA illus
1929 1 Mrs Alexander Cameron
$2,500
1930 2 Glenn Cooper Henshaw $2,500
3 Prof Leopold Auer $2,500

ADAMSON, CHARLES
1880, Scotland 13 Feb 1959, Toronto
Addr: 1928, 14 Elm St, Toronto;
1930, 1A Hogarth Ave, Toronto; 1931,
106 Richmond St W, Toronto
1928 160 Franz Johnston, ARCA sculp
1930 183 Portrait bust

1931 301 Frederick S. Challener, RCA bronze $900

ADAMSON, GERALD JAMES
12 Mar 1937, Galt, Ont
RCA(e) 1979 Industrial designer
Addr: 1979, Toronto

ADAMSON, GORDON SINCLAIR
19 May 1904, Orangeville, Ont
CNS59 Co CWW79 NGC
ARCA 1950 RCA 1956 Council Architect
Addr: 1949-71/79, Toronto
1949 100 Office wing of Canadian Nashua Paper Co, Limited, Peterborough, Ont
101 Studio for Mr Cleeve Horne, Toronto
1952 98 Lawrence Park Community Church photos illus DW 1956 photo 19 1/4 x 14 1/2
1953 94 Crystal Glass and Plastics photo illus
95 Apartment, 130 Old Forest Hill Rd, Toronto photo
1954 114 Township of Toronto Municipal Offices, Cooksville, Ont photo illus
1957 93 Laboratory for Canadian Oil Companies, Ltd, Sarnia
1958 Gordon S. Adamson & Assoc
97-8 Jordon Wines Limited. Store and office buildings. View of reception room
1959 95 G. Tamblyn Limited, head office, Toronto
96 Margaret Addison Hall, Women's Residence, Victoria University, University of Toronto illus
1960 93 New York Life Insurance Building, Toronto photo
94 Margaret Addison Hall, Victoria University, Toronto photo
1961 91 Young Men's and Young Women's Hebrew Association, North York Branch
92 Canada and Dominion Sugar Company, Toronto
1963 110 Royal Conservatory of Music, University of Toronto photo illus
1964J 95-8 William Wrigley Jr Bldg. South west view. Detail of exterior wall. Offices. Landscape plan
99 R.S. McLaughlin Collegiate and Vocational Institute, Oshawa. Main entrance, sculpture by Leonhard Oesterle
1965 105-6 Laurentian University, Sudbury. Library Podium Bldg. Library Podium dining assembly building
107-8 Kingsmill Vocational School. Front of building, from Royal York Rd. School from playfield at south. Des in association with Dr. T Howarth
1966 91-5 London Free Press Bldg, London, Ont. Beginning of ramp at main entrance. Entrance foyer. Centre court looking towards cafeteria. View from main entrance canopy to northwest, 1st floor plan
1967 86-9 CUNA Mutual Insurance Society. A.Building looking from southeast. B.Corner detail. C.West elevation D. Model
see also McInnes, Garfield, 1968; Spratley, Keith, 1971

ADAMSON, MABEL CAWTHRA (Mrs)
Addr: 1903, 121 Nepean St, Ottawa
1903 219 Rising mist enamel on copper
port: by E.W. Grier, 1893-63

ADASKIN, GORDON
7 Jun 1931, Toronto M
RCA(e) 1976 Painter
Addr: 1979, Winnipeg

ADNEY, EDWIN TAPPAN American
13 or 23 Jul 1868, Athens, Ohio
10 Oct 1950, Woodstock, NB B M TB
Addr: 1922, 14 Phillips Sq, Montreal; 1923, 364 Dochester St W, Montreal
1922 242 Decorative heraldic panel
243 Design for heraldic panel
1923 200 Panel of arms of Struan Robertson
201 Panel of arms of McLean of Dowart

AFFLECK, RAYMOND TAIT
20 Nov 1922, Penticton, BC
ARCA 1958 RCA 1966 Council Architect
Addr: 1959-71/79, Montreal

1964J Affleck, Desbarats, Dimakapoulis, Lebensold, Michaud & Sise, to 1968
91 St Gerard Magella Church, St Jean, Que. Bapistry
92-4 Place des Arts. Model. Grand Salle, interior. Foyer
1964N 97-101 Church of St Gerard Magella, St Jean, Que. Front view, exterior. Side view, exterior. General view, exterior. Main floor plan. Model
1965 98-101 Georges P. Vanier Library, Loyola College. Main entrance. Reading room. Exterior
102-4 Chomedy Civic Centre. Rear view of City Hall. Council Chamber. Alley and ramp on the Plaza. 104 illus
1966 96-103 Confederation Centre, Charlottetown. Art Gallery looking south, illus. Concourse corridors, around large sculpture court, mural by Jean Paul Lemieux. Night view from northwest. Memorial Hall in its setting. Restaurant overlooking Sculpture Court. Interior Confederation Memorial Theatre. Larger Sculpture Court, looking south. Sections through Memorial Hall and Theatre. Terrace level plan
104-12 Stephen Leacock Building, McGill University, Montreal. Hallway connecting Leacock Building with old Arts Building. West elevation. Principal stair to mezzanine. Tower of Leacock Building and connecting element. Staff member's office. Concourse, east side. Large Auditorium. Auditorium detail. 1st floor plan
DW 1968 Stephen Leacock Building, McGill University photo 14 x 18
1967 90-4 Georges Vanier Library, Montreal. A.Staircase to entrance. B.Interior staircase. C. Detail, exterior. D.Exterior. E.First floor plan
95-8 McGill University Centre, Montreal. A.Exterior view B. Stairway C.Interior D.Third floor plan
1968 66-71 Place Bonaventure, Montreal. A.Hotel staircase B. Hotel garden C.University St detail D.La Gauchetière St detail E.Better Living Centre stair F.Concordia Hall
72-5 Eglise St Thomas d'Aquin, St Lambert. A.View of nave, illus B.View of steeple, and entrance from south C.View of steeple and entrance from southwest D.View of choir
see also Lebensold, F, 1970

AHRENS, CARL HENRY VON
15 Feb 1863, Winfield, Ohio 27 Feb 1936, Toronto B CC1 H M Mo12 NGC TB3
ARCA 1891-9 Painter
Addr: 1892, Toronto; 1893, 48 Caroline Ave, Toronto; 1894-5, Doon, Ont; 1896-7, Toronto; 1898, Yonge St, Toronto; 1922, 278 Bloor St W, Toronto; 1923, 117 King St W, Toronto
1891 111 At the close of day
113 Evening
114 Breaking wave
1892 16 Cradled in the net $300
1893-2 $250 F1-2
1894 2 Goose girl (O.H. Howland, Toronto)
3 Building the fleet
4 Grey evening (C.E.L. Porteous, Montreal)
5 Dutchman and sheep (Miss Lackner, Berlin, Ont)
6 Dutch rag pickers
1895 1 Ripe corn time
2 Moon and meadow
3 Nearing the night
4 One day
4a Sunset
1898 2 The lane
3 Wet evening
4 Smoky weather
5 A lonely shore
6 The coming storm
7 The stream
1922 2 Night time
1923 4 Summer
5 Spring
port: bust by F.E. Elwell, 1893-280

AIKMAN, GEORGE W. Scottish
1830, Edinburgh 1905, Edinburgh

B DBA H RSA TB
1880 23 Kelp burning, Iona (Sandford Fleming)

AIMERS, JEFFREY J.F.
see BOLTON, RICHARD, 1964

AIROLA, PAAVO
16 Apr 1915, Karelia, Finland M
TB3 WWA59
ARCA 1962 Painter
Addr: 1963-4J, Colborne, Ont; 1964N, USA; 1965-71/79, Phoenix
1953 1 Down town $400
1954 1 Studio interior 32 x 26 $400
1956 1 Down town #2 illus $400 T56-1
1957 1 Le Havre harbour $600
1958 1 Flowers in blue vase $400
2 Le port de Le Havre $400
1959 1 Notre Dame de Paris 40 x 32 $400
1961 4 Still life with water melon 48 x 30 illus $350
5 Still life with black bottle 55 x 24 $400

AITCHISON, GEORGINA
1871, Ottawa
Addr: 1924-5, 88 Argyle Ave, Ottawa
1924 1 Garden flowers
1925 4 Phlox $100

AITKEN, JAMES ALFRED Scottish
1846, Edinburgh 21 Dec 1897, Glasgow B DBA DVP DWC G H TB
1887 99a A glen in the Selkirks

AITKEN, MELITA (Mrs R.J. Aitken)
1866, Drumbo, Ont B H
Addr: 1931-2, 316 Cook St, Victoria; 1933, 424 Linden Ave, Victoria
1931 3 Zinnias wc $300
4 Poppies wc $250
1932 2 A large bowl of peonies wc $300
1933 2 The mermaid rose wc $75

AITKEN, W. DESMOND
see DUNLOP, DANIEL, 1970

AITTAUQ, SILAS
Addr: 1976, Baker Lake, NWT
1976 S12, Montreal
53 Family with musk ox stone/pierre 11 1/2 x 5 1/2 illus

AKATSIAQ
Addr: 1976, Igloolik, NWT
1976 S12, Montreal
54 Two standing figures soapstone/saponite 8 1/2 x 5 x 3 illus

AKED, ALLEN
1938 1 The brass bowl nfs

AKSALIK, NELSON
Addr: 1976, Gjoa Haven, NWT
1976 S12, Montreal
56 Figure with arm raised soapstone/saponite 7 x 5 x 2 illus

ALDWINCKLE, ERIC
22 Jan 1909, Oxford, Eng Jan 1980, Toronto CWW79 M NGC WWA47
RCA(e) 1975 Graphic designer
Addr: 1936, 82 Broadway Ave, Toronto; 1937, 80 King St W, Toronto; 1979, Toronto
1936 2 Berwyn Range, Wales $300
3 Brecon Beacons, Wales $300 T37-1
1937 1 Georgian Bay wc $50
1938 2 The magic carpet nfs
1938 S8, Toronto
1-3 Willard's window posters caddy, diver, skier
4 Display card Shiffer Hillman figure
5 Brell Shirt display
6 Leishman Clothing display card
7 Maurice Advertising direct mail folder
8-10 Trade magazine cover Fashion, 1934, 1935, 1936
11 Newspaper advertisements, 3, Tip Top Tailors scientific tests
12 Package design Bay Rum shaving cream
13 Package design Buckingham shaving cream
1939 F11, New York
1 Welsh landscape 24 x 32 $350
1940 1 Sturgeon Lake $350 T41-1
1941 S9, Toronto
1 Vermont valley $75

ALEXANDER, CHARLES (b Charles Alexander Smith)
2 Nov 1864, Galt, Hamburg or London

Ont Jun 1915, London, Eng B H Mo12 TB2
ARCA 1896-01 Painter
Addr: 1887, Montreal; 1893, Galt, Ont; 1897-02, London, Ont
1887 C.A. Smith
52 La jeune cuisinière $150
82 Un garde champètre $150
1893 Charles Alexander
3 Gathering plums $1,200
4 A peasant girl drinking $1,000

ALEXANDER, HAROLD RUPERT LEOFRIC GEORGE, 1st Earl of Tunis, Governor General of Canada 1946-52
10 Dec 1891, London, Eng 16 Jun 1969, Windsor Forest, Berks, Eng
RCA Hon Member 1948
Addr: 1946-52, Rideau Hall, Ottawa
1947 1 Landscape nfs T48-1
2 Farm on the Gatineau River illus nfs T48-2
1949 1 View from my studio window, Rideau Hall nfs
2 Houses of Parliament, Ottawa nfs
port: by L.T. Newton, 1952-68

ALEXANDER, J.W.
1894 205 Carved panel

ALEXANDER, LOUISE (Louie, Mrs F.H. Alexander)
2 Sep 1880, Owen Sound, Ont
Addr: 1924, 272 Main St, Winnipeg
1924 2 A portrait

ALEXANDER, M. (Mrs)
Addr: 1928-36, 176 Hughson St S, Hamilton
1928 3 Bowl of dahlias $75
4 Bowl of gillardia $50
1929 2 Phlox $75
3 Bowl of hydrangea $125
1930 5 Still life, zinnias $100
1931 5 Peonies $100
6 September flowers $100
1936 4 Sunflowers $100

ALEXANDER, ROBERT SAMUEL
25 Aug 1916, Vancouver 20 Apr 1974, North Vancouver M
1941 1 Self portrait $75
1954 2 Tahltan chief 22 x 38 $250

ALEXANDER, WILLIAM WALKER
9 Aug 1869, Toronto 3 Apr 1948, Toronto AGO M
Addr: 1912, 114 King St W, Toronto; 1918A-27, 116 King St W, Toronto
1912 253 Brock's Monument, Queenston etch
254 Sous le Cap, Quebec etch S3-153
255 Book plates engr on copper
1912 S3, Winnipeg
152 A northern Ontario river b&w
154 Old ferry road, Queenston etch
1918A 206 Book plate, Sir John Eaton engr
1922 244 Bridge at twilight aqua ◊AGO◊
1927 279 The river road dry pt
280 In harbour, Gloucester etch

ALFRED, PAUL (b Paul Alfred Ernest Meister)
10 Apr 1892, Hanley, Staffs, Eng
6 May 1959, Ottawa M NGC WWA47
Addr: 1921-34, 144 Concord St, Ottawa
1921 1 Evening on the Ottawa River wc
1922 3 Moonrise in May wc
4 A group of elms wc
1924 3 A Laurentian village wc
251 Notre Dame de Bonsecours pencil
252 Parliament Hill, Ottawa, winter drwg
1925 2 Winter wc
3 Winter market, By Ward temp ◊NGC◊
280 Bank of Montreal, Montreal pencil
281 The Murailles, Percé, Quebec pencil
1926 1 By Ward Market, Ottawa illus S7-1 $300
1927 2 The quarry pool
3 Winter landscape on the Ottawa temp
1929 4 Red maple wc $150
1932 3 Gatineau woodland wc $150
1934 3 Hay Market, By Ward, Ottawa temp $200 T35-1

ALFSEN, JOHN MARTIN
23 Dec 1902, Alpena, Mich 30 Nov 1971, Toronto AGO CC2 M NGC WWA47
ARCA 1942 RCA 1959 Sr 1971 Council Painter

Addr: 1928-35, 111 Dunn Ave, Toronto; 1936, 218 John St, Toronto; 1943-60, Toronto; 1961-71, Markham, Ont
1928 190 Head of a woman drwg $25
191 Head of a child drwg $25
1930 199 Woman sleeping charcl
1936 5 Portrait, S. Tody $400
1938 3 Portrait $150
1939 1 The evening paper $200
1939 F11, New York
2 Portrait 43 x 36 $500
1940 2 The reader $500 T41-2
3 Portrait illus $150
1941 2 The blonde model $100 T42-1
1941 S9, Toronto
2 Child study $35
1942 1 Portrait $500
2 Eleanor illus $300
1944 1 Lieut Haakon Aass $500 T45-1
2 The mill at Kettleby $500 T45-2
3 Willows, Kettleby $500
4 Andrew and Karen $500
1945 1 The wanderer $1,000
1946 1 Self portrait $200 T47-1
1948 1 Self portrait
1951 1 E.W. McNeil, Esq nfs
1952 1 Mother and child $1,000
2 Self portrait $800
1953 2 Head $200
1954 3 Portrait 34 x 25 $300
1955 1 Marie $600
2 Portrait $400
1957 2 Dickson Kenwin, Esq $1,500 1958-4
3 Lynn $1,000
1958 3 Larissa $1,000
1960 1 Portrait of a woman 36 x 46 $1,200
1961 1 Maureen 36 x 30 $800
1963 1 Dr E.H. Botterell $2,000
1966 S10, Charlottetown
1 Mrs Claude Bissell nfs
DW 1960 Portrait of Helen 26 x 18

ALFSEN, MARION SCOTT (Mrs John Martin Alfsen)
b 1902
Addr: 1930, 245 Howland Ave, Toronto
1930 191 Dr Newell Beattie sculp $125
1951 2 Ringling Bros, Barnum & Bailey Combined Shows $150

ALLAN, MARGUERITE I. (Mrs Marguerite Buller Allan) see also, Buller, M.
Addr: 1910, 147 Bishop St, Montreal; 1914-15, 154 Drummond St, Montreal; 1916, 147 Bishop St, Momtreal
1910 2 Sketch
1914 1 Still life
1915 1 Still life
1916 1 Still life
2 Poppies

ALLAN, MARJORIE L.
Addr: 1922-4, 386 Sherbrooke St W, Montreal
1922 5 Still life wc
1924 4 Still life wc

ALLAN, MARVIN FRANCIS
d 22 Jun 1964, NB
see MARANI, FERDINAND, 1959-64J

ALLAN, WILLIAM GEORGE
6 Apr 1929, Ottawa
Addr: 1976, Toronto
1976 S12, Montreal
58 Construction #6 PVC plastic & wood 60 x 96 x 48 illus
175 Series 9 #1 photo 11 x 14 illus

ALLEN, NEWSTEAD A.
fl 1913-35
Addr: 1913, 1949A Christopher Columbus St, Montreal
1913 335 Design for city hall, Winnipeg

ALLEN, RALPH
6 Dec 1926, Raunds, Northants, Eng
AGO CC1 M WWA62
ARCA 1967 Council Painter
Addr: 1968-71/79, Kingston
1958 5 James $200
1959 2 Fall study V $250
1961 2 Portrait of a woman 30 x 34 illus $400
3 Night coast 24 x 36 $300
1963 2 Coast edge in air $400
1964N 1 Untitled #8 44 x 44 $400
1970 S11, Halifax
1 Landscape forms. 1969 acry 58 x 36 $500
2 Snow landscape. 1969 acry 36 x 58 $500

ALLEN, W.A.
1938 S8, Toronto
214 Sermon on the Mount wood

carv, by Mr W.A. Allen
Limel Rawlinson Ltd, Toronto

ALLEYN, GEORGE EDMUND
9 Jun 1931, Quebec AGO CC2 M NGC
1964J 1 Afternoon on the island
51 1/4 x 63 illus $1,000

ALLIE
Addr: 1976, Belcher Island, NWT
1976 S12, Montreal
57 Spirit figure soapstone/saponite 8 x 2 x 6 illus

ALLISON, FRANK DRUMMOND
29 Mar 1883, Saint John 1951, Saint John
Addr: 1915, Joyce's Chambers, Phillips Sq, Montreal; 1931, 43 Carleton St, Saint John
1915 2 Gray day, Rideau River wc
1931 7 Court of Fez $250
8 St Cerq de Popie $250
1938 4 Lifting fog $175
5 Sou'easter $175 T39-1
1939 2 Gray day on Baldhead $150
1941 3 Near Fundy's tides $175

ALLWARD, HUGH LACHLAN
25 Dec 1899, Toronto 30 Dec 1971, Toronto NGC
ARCA 1941 RCA 1945 Sr 1969 Council
Architect
Addr: 1941-71, Toronto
1941 200 Residence, Mr and Mrs A. H.C. Proctor. DW 1946 crayon drwg 12 1/2 x 21 1/2
201 Residence, Maj James Hahn photos
1949 Allward & Gouinlock, to 1963
102 Sunnybrook Hospital photo
103 Mechanical Bldg, University of Toronto photo
1955 86 East building of Veterans' Memorial Bldg, Ottawa. From northwest photo illus
1957 94 Ontario Cancer Institute, Toronto photo
1959 97 School of Dentistry, University of Toronto
1963 109 Ford Motor Company of Canada, head office bldg, Oakville, Ont

ALLWARD, WALTER SEYMOUR CMG LLD
18 Nov 1876, Toronto 24 Apr 1955, Toronto CC1 CWW49 EC M NGC WWA47
ARCA 1903 RCA 1920 Sr 1947 Council
Sculptor
Addr: 1901, 28 Toronto St, Toronto; 1904-20, Toronto; 1921, 76 Walker Ave, Toronto; 1922-4, Toronto; 1925-6, London, Eng; 1927-37, Toronto; 1938-55, York Mills, Ont
1901 254 Sir George Burton, Chief Justice of Ontario bust F2-87
255 Sir Wilfrid Laurier, Prime Minister of Canada bust F2-88
1921 175 Canadian Battle Fields Memorial, for Hill 62 in Flanders photo
1955 Memorial Sec. Photo of the sculptor, biography
#1-19, photos; 20 sketches; 21-9 pen & wash drwgs
1 William Lyon Mackenzie
2 South African War Memorial, figure
3 North West Rebellion Memorial, figure
Vimy Memorial #4-18
4 Final perspective
5-7 Three views
8 Mourners on stairway, group
9 Breaking the sword, group illus
10 The defenders, group
11 Canadian sympathy for the helpless, group
12 Faith, figure
13 Peace, figure
14 Torch bearer, figure
15 Honour, figure
16 Two angels, group
17 Justice, figure
18 Canada, figure
19 Composition in low relief
20 Group of sketches in plaster
21 Death and the artist
22 3 figures, with iron grill
23-4 Suggestion for memorial on the St Lawrence
25 Mourning figure at door
26 3 figures on road
27 Figure on pedestal
28 Weeping figures at wall
29 Group of war cartoons, 1938-45
War Memorial, Stratford, Ont illus
DW 1921 The storm bronze 13 1/4h

ALMOND, PAUL
26 Apr 1931, Montreal WWA76
ARCA 1972 Film maker
Addr: 1979, Montreal

ALSTON, T.H.
Addr: 1925, 12 Grenville St, Toronto
1925 4 Fisherman's Cove, Portland, Maine

ALSTYNE, THELMA see VAN ALSTYNE, THELMA

ALTWERGER, LIBBY DEBORAH (Mrs)
13 Jul 1921, Toronto WWA62
1959 3 Francesca 29 1/2 x 21 1/2 $125

AMOS, LOUIS A.
c 1869, Montreal 20 Aug 1948, Montreal
Addr: 1893, 17 Place d'Armes Hill, Montreal
1893 Cox and Amos
275 Proposed government buildings, Victoria, BC des

ANDERSON, (Mrs)
1881 224 Girl and candy (W.C. Silver)

ANDERSON, HELEN VIOLET
1882, Brockville, Ont
Addr: 1906-9, 146 Wellington St, Ottawa; 1910, Montreal; 1912, 292 Daly Ave, Ottawa
1906 1 A Suffolk common
2 Landscape
3 Fritton Lake
1907 1 A model F6-1 $75
2 Dark trees
3 The house on the hill
4 Madame Veiseneuve's garden F6-2 $50
1909M 5 A Rockcliffe byway
5a A country road
1910 3 L'éventail
4 Normandy landscape
1912 1 A Beaupré road
2 House on the hill
3 A Beaupré sugar bush

ANDERSON, MILLICENT see GORE, MILLICENT

ANDERSON, WALLY
b Toronto
1971 1G Studio promotion, Sherman Laws Limited

ANDRE, FRANCOIS MARISE SYLVIANE
(Mrs Charles Stegeman)
1926, Les Sables d'Olenne, France M
1963 2 Urban nuptial $700

ANDREW, PAUL SINCLAIR
16 Feb 1908, Antigonish, NS
Addr: 1936, 1158 Beaver Hall Sq, Montreal; 1937, 3531 Ste Famille St, Montreal
1936 6 Still life nfs T37-2
1937 2 Interior $125
3 Interior with figure $100
1938 6 Miss Janet Cormack $250
7 Studio interior $100
1947 3 Flower piece $250 T48-3
4 Near Côte des Neiges $150

ANDREWS, GEORGE HENRY English
1816, Lambeth, London 1898, Hammersmith, London B G H TB
1880 326 Oyster dredging wc (Thos. Reynolds)
331 Falls of the Chaudière, Quebec wc (Thos. Reynolds)
334 Honfleur wc (Thos. Reynolds)

ANDREWS, JOHN HAMILTON
29 Oct 1933, n Sydney, Australia
Co CWW79
1971 1A-4A Miami passenger terminal. A single node. Passenger conduit. Baggage area. Passenger terminal
5A-8A Mirvish Gallery, Toronto. Main gallery. Sculpture court. Street front and entrance, illus. Plan main floor

ANDREWS, STEPHEN JAMES
16 May 1922, Saskatoon M
RCA(e) 1977 Painter
Addr: 1979, Winnipeg

ANNAND, ROBERT WILLIAM
5 Nov 1923, Truro, NS CC1 M NGC
Addr: 1976, Halifax
1976 S12, Montreal
1 Crucifixion 20 x 24 illus

ANNAU, ERNEST
24 Dec 1931, Hungary
1971 1I Telephone kiosk, Design Craft Limited

ANNIE
Addr: 1976, Lake Harbour, NWT

1976 S12, Montreal
55 Mother and child soapstone/ saponite 16 1/2 x 10 x 6 illus

ANTIGNA, MARC
b Paris fl 1890-1910 B H
Addr: 1902, 2714 St Catherine St, Montreal
1902 1 Mr Paul Beau
2 Miniatures
289 Applique bronze for electric light, women and flowers. Marc Antigna and Paul Beau

AOUTHET, RICKSON see OUTHET, RICKSON A.

APTER, SONIA
28 Nov 1906, New York
Addr: 1931, 3647 Durocher St, Montreal; 1933, 1235 Bernard Ave W, Montreal
1931 302 Portrait sculp
1933 249 Head of a woman sculp

ARBUCKLE, FRANCES see JOHNSTON, FRANCES ANN

ARBUCKLE, GEORGE FRANKLIN
17 Feb 1909, Toronto AGO CC2 CWW79 M NGC TB2/3 WWA70
ARCA 1936 RCA 1945 Council Painter
Addr: 1932, 1104 Bay St, Toronto; 1933, 4 Spadina Rd, Toronto; 1934, 436 Avenue Rd, Toronto; 1936, 64 Grenville St, Toronto; 1937, 428 Lake Front, Toronto; 1938-40, Toronto; 1941-2, Thornhill, Ont; 1943-57, Montreal; 1958-71/79, Toronto
1932 4 October $275
228 Mural sketch
1933 3 The picnic $500 T34-1
1934 4 By the moon, the reaper weary $500
5 Jennifer illus $350
1936 7 Summer morning $350
8 Trolley car madonna illus $200
1937 4 Private view and interview $500
1939 F11, New York
3 Saturday night 36 x 40 $500
1941 S9, Toronto
3 Spring $100
1945 2 Mi-carême, Charlevoix. Mid-lent celebration in masks, Charlevoix County, Quebec nfs DW 1945 30 1/4 x 40 1/4 T51-1 1954 Retro Sec 53
3 Grist mill, Baie St Paul illus $600
1947 5 Land of the Nootkaas $800 T53-1 $900
6 St Jovite $600
1949 3 True Lover's Leap, Newfoundland illus $900
1950 1 Portuguese Cove, NS 30 x 40 $1,000
1951 3 Barn with hay press illus $900
1952 3 Portuguese Cove, NS illus $800
1953 3 Sunday, Cap à l'Aigle illus $900
1954 4 St Lawrence barn 30 x 40 illus nfs ◊AGO◊
1957 4 Lunenburg, NS illus $800 1958-6
1959 4 Catalpa cat 40 x 40 illus $1,000
1960 2 Procession 36 x 45 illus $1,200
1961 6 La chatte 35 x 40 illus $1,000
1963 4 Pingo in tundra near the Beaufort Sea 40 x 60 illus $1,500 1964J-2
1964N 2 Indian houseboat, Aklavik 32 x 48 $1,000
1965 1 Autumn bouquet 32 x 48 illus $1,000 S10-2 illus
1966 1 Rara avis 48 x 36 illus $1,000
1966 S10, Charlottetown
3 St Lawrence River Basin 30 x 40 illus

ARCHAMBAULT, FRANCOISE
1941 4 Première neige $50

ARCHAMBAULT, LOUIS DE GONZAQUE PASCAL
4 Apr 1915, Montreal AGO CC1 CWW79 M NGC TB3 WWA53
ARCA 1966 RCA 1969 Sculptor
Addr: 1967-71, Montreal; 1976/79, St Lambert, Que
1955 99 Seated woman combing her hair sculp $300 ◊NGC◊
1970 77 Prototype pour une sculpture devant être réalisée en metal 48 x 48 x 144
1976 S12, Montreal
59 Etude préliminaire pour une châsse monumentale/Preliminary study for a monu-

mental tabernacle cédre canadien/Canadian cedar 46 1/4 x 38 1/2 x 24 1/2 illus
DW 1969 Fécondité bronze 24h

ARCHAMBAULT, RICHARD BENSON
26 Jan 1931, Vancouver
RCA(e) 1978 Architect
Addr: 1979, Vancouver
1964N Archambault, MacDonald & Downs
93-6 Ladner Pioneer Library, Ladner, BC. Entry court, exterior. Library, interior. View of court, exterior. Ground floor plan
see also, Downs, Barry, 1976

ARCHERY CRAFT COMPANY LIMITED
1970 109 Mk 2, pro target bow

ARCHIBALD, JOHN SMITH
14 Dec 1872, Inverness, Scot 1934, Montreal CNS27
Addr: 1899, 79 Imperial Bldg, St James St W, Montreal; 1916, 314 Dorchester St W, Montreal
1899 Archibald & Saxe
240 Prospective of apartment house, Metcalfe Street
241 Prospective of semi-detached residence, Westmount
1916 259 Residence, Mrs E.C. Walker, St Andrews, NB
260 Farm buildings, Wm. Lyall, Magog, Que
see also Saxe, Charles, 1902

ARCHIBALD, MARY
fl 1881 H
Addr: 1881, Halifax
1881 153 Primroses wc
154 Primula wc
155 Dead bird wc

ARISS, HERBERT JOSHUA
29 Sep 1918, Guelph AGO CWW79 M WWA56
RCA(e) 1978 Painter
Addr: 1979, London

ARKACRONA
1880 13 On the desert boundaries of Morocco and Algiers (Allan Gilmour)

ARMINGTON, FRANKLIN MILTON
28 Jul 1876, Fordwich, Ont 23 Sep 1941, New York AGO CWW49
Addr: 1904, Winnipeg; 1921, 70 Blvd Montparnasse, Paris
1904 1 Mammy Nix and Miss Becky Sharp
1921 2 Brittany cottage

ARMITAGE, ARTHUR S.D.
1939 3 The reader

ARMOUR, PHYLLIS (Mrs Hertzberg)
c 1885, Toronto d 1975
Addr: 1920, 25 Severn St, Toronto; 1921, 103 Avenue Rd, Toronto; 1922, Studio Bldg, 25 Severn St, Toronto; 1926, 47 Boswell Ave, Toronto; 1928-9, 246 Brunswick Ave, Toronto; 1935, Bowmanville, RR4, Ont
1920 1 Study of an old woman
2 Cottages
1921 3 The Russian scarf
1922 245 Decoration temp S6-117
1926 2 and 3 In the woods
171 The cedar grove etch
1928 192 Fishing flakes, St John's, Newfoundland dry pt $20
1929 5 Studio study $100
253 Fish flakes, in Newfoundland dry pt $15
1935 Hertzberg
322 An old man dry pt $15

ARMSTRONG, EVELYN A.
Addr: 1976, Vancouver
1976 S12, Montreal
153 Sidewalk #1 litho 18 x 24 illus

ARMSTRONG, THOMAS WILLIAM
11 Feb 1908, Ovington-on-Tyne, Newcastle, Eng
1947 7 Mount Elephantis, Lake Memphremagog $65
1948 2 Lake Memphremagog $125

ARMSTRONG, WILLIAM
28 Jul 1822, Dublin 8 Jun 1914, Toronto H NGC
ARCA 1880-7 Painter
Addr: 1880-7, Toronto
1882 177 Yacht Oriole, RCYC wc
1885 309 Hudson Bay post wc $40
312 Miss Delaronde wc $20

ARNOTT, JOHN
1971 2I Television set, Canadian General Electric Co Ltd

ARSENAULT, REAL
19 May 1931, Quebec
1964N 3 Ardoise

ARTHUR, ERIC ROSS LLD
1 Jul 1898, Dunedin, NZ Co CWW79
ARCA 1956 RCA 1964 Sr 1969 Council
Architect
Addr: 1957-71/79, Toronto
1957 Fleury & Arthur
96 Residence, Valecrest Dr, Toronto
DW 1965 Victoria College Student's Union photo 14 3/4 x 19 1/4

ARTHUR, PAUL RODNEY
20 Dec 1924, Liverpool
ARCA 1972 Graphic designer
Addr: 1979, Toronto

ARTHURS, ANNIE J. (Mrs George Arthurs)
Nov 1845, Toronto d 1927 H
1880 102 Five o'clock tea

ASH, STUART BRADLEY
10 Jul 1942, Hamilton CWW79
RCA(e) 1975 Graphic designer
Addr: 1976/79, Toronto
1970 115-16 Magazine covers, Science Affairs, 1/67, 2/67
117 Annual report Canada Council 1967-68
1976 S12, Montreal
115 Metric Commission, corporate image 2 illus

ASHBY, HERBERT WILLIAM
Addr: 1910-12, 6 Lorne Ave, Montreal; 1918N, Lakeview, Argenteuil Co, Que
1910 5 Study in charcoal
1912 4 Mrs Ashby
1918N 3 Study of asters
4 Study of stocks

ASHTON, RALPH HERBERT
7 Aug 1912, Bowmanville, Ont
1951 4 August light wc $45

ASKIN, H.H.
H
Addr: 1886, London, Ont
1886 Fla, London, Eng
1985, artist number
Dead mallard

ASTMAN, BARBARA ANNE
12 Jul 1950, Rochester, NY IO WWA78
Addr: 1976, Toronto
1976 S12, Montreal
174 Carol col xeroxography 11 x 14 illus

ATKINS, ALBAN F.T. (Mrs) English
fl 1928-41 DBA
1941 230 Cotswold farm drwg $20
231 Scene near Burford drwg $20

ATKINS, GORDON LEE
5 Mar 1937, Calgary WWA76
ARCA 1970 Architect
Addr: 1971/76/79, Calgary
1968 76-9 Alberta Government Telephone, Elbow Park Exchange A.North stair B.Path C.Entry D.Exterior
80-3 Drahanchuk Studios A.Spiral stair B.South elevation C.The tower D.Plan main floor
1971 S12, Montreal
96 Pinebrook Golf and Winter Club, Calgary 2 illus

ATKINSON, ERIC NEWTON
23 Jul 1928, West Hartlepool, Durham, Eng WWA76
RCA(e) 1978 Painter
Addr: 1979, London

ATKINSON, SOPHIA M.
Nov 1876, Newcastle, Eng flg 1965, Revelstoke, BC
Addr: 1927, 318 Sherbrooke St W, Montreal
1927 4 Autumn, Sainte Marguerite wc

ATKINSON, WILLIAM EDWIN
22 Mar 1862, Toronto 31 Jul 1926, Toronto AGO B H M NGC TB
ARCA 1894-14, 1918 Painter
Addr: 1893, Toronto; 1894-01, 203 Crawford St, Toronto; 1902-3, 207 Crawford St, Toronto; 1904, Toronto; 1905, 2 Durie St, Toronto Junction; 1906-8, 20 Durie St, Toronto Junction; 1909N-12, 364 Durie St, West Toronto; 1913, 565 Annette St, West Toronto: 1914-18A, 3 Baby Point Rd, West Toronto; 1919, 64 Baby Point Rd, West Toronto; 1920-3, 207 Crawford St, Toronto; 1924-5, Toronto

1893 5 Moonlight $40 F1-5
6 Autumn evening, Bretagne $100 F1-6
1894 1 Solitude
1895 5 The sun retires and twilight with murmuring breezes lulls in the solitude of night
1896 1 Old stage days, Ontario
2 November evening, Ontario
3 Autumn evening, Ontario
4 November, Ontario
5 Old saw mill, Ontario
1897 1 Cloudy moonlight
2 Woodland
3 Old French Canadian mill, below Quebec
1898 1 Bit of woods near the Moor, Devonshire
130 Lane, Devonshire wc
131 Plymouth harbour, misty moonlight wc
132 Clovelly wc
1899 1 Evening
2 After the rain, Dolgelly, Wales
3 Frosty morning, Dartmoor
4 Old street in Sluis, Holland
5 Threatening, Holland
6 Church of St Mary, Tavy, Devon
151a Old mill, Dartmoor, Devon wc
152 Moonlight, Dort, Holland wc
153 Solitude, Exmoor, Devon wc
1901 1 Threatening weather
140 Freshets on the moor, Devonshire wc F2-1
141 Sheep shelter on the moor, Devonshire wc
142 Autumn wc
1902 2 Group of sheep on the moor
170 Freshet on the moor, Devon wc
171 Bit of the New Forest wc
1902 F3, Rochester
3 Edge of woods, November $120
1903 1 Autumn
2 Cloudy day
3 Threatening weather, Holland
4 After the rain
135 The shelter wc
136 Twilight wc
1904 2 Indian summer F4-1
3 Woodland F4-2
4 Autumn shadows
5 Moonlight
190 French Canadian village wc
1905 1 Misty moonlight
2 Church of St Mary, Devon
3 Old houses near Manchester
1906 4 The October moon F5-1 $200
5 The departure F5-2 $100 illus F6-5
6 Grey moonlight
7 Old West Gate, Southampton, England
1907 5 Grey morning
6 Dutch sunset
210 Homewards wc
211 Dutch moonlight wc
212 Thatch cottage, Devonshire wc
1907 F6, Sherbrooke
3 The Groote Kerke, Dordrecht $300
4 Autumn moonrise temp $250
6 Misty harbour, Brittany $500
1908 1 Early morning
2 Showery weather
3 Breton mill
1909M 2 November
3 Willows, evening ≬NGC≬
4 Subsiding flood
4a Field at rest
1909N 1 The Groote Kerke, Dordrecht, Holland S3-1
2 Solitude
3 The golden hour
1912 5 Dispersing clouds
6 Iron workers home
7 Freshet on the Humber River, spring
8 Sand cart
9 Breton barn, Finistère, France
10 Return of the flock, silvery moonlight wc
1912 S3, Winnipeg
2 Moonrise
1913 1 November
2 Grey autumn evening S4-1 $200
3 October day
4 Autumn field
5 The lane
6 Grey day, Holland S4-2 $300
1914 2 Gloaming
3 Clearing sky, autumn evening
4 Across the valley
1914 S5, Patriotic Fund
16 Misty day in Normandy illus
1916 3 The afternoon thaw ≬AGO≬

4 April showers
1918A 2 Spring in the hills
3 First snow fall
1919 2 The ravine
3 The landmark 1920-4
1920 3 Snow on the hill
1921 4 Afternoon sun illus 1922-6 S6-1
5 The changeful season
6 Early spring
1922 6 Afternoon sun
1923 6 Spring morning wc
7 Evening in the pasture

AUERBACH, MALCA ROSE
fl 1891-13 B
Addr: 1893, Montreal; 1896, 151 Hutchison St, Montreal
1891 221 Basket of flowers
222 Marguerites and buttercups
223 Field flowers
1893 7 Wild roses $30
1896 6 Roses and violets

AULD, GEORGE E.
see WILSON, PERCY ROY, 1937 #269-70, 1939 #287-8

AUSTIN, ROY
b England
1946 2 Totem, Prince Rupert, BC $350
1948 3 The 8.20 ferry $200

AYKROYD, WOODRUFF KERR
3 May 1904, Toronto
Addr: 1935, 40 Concord Ave, Toronto
1935 306 The bridge etch $10
307 Rain, Yonge Street, Toronto etch $10

AYRE, AGNES MARION (Mrs)
2 Feb 1890, St John's
Addr: 1937, 120 Military Rd, St John's
1937 5 Portugal Cove wc nfs

AYRES, CHARLES HAROLD
17 Jan 1894, Toronto
Addr: 1931, 58A Astley Ave, Toronto
1931 5 Rugged shore wc $60

B

BABICKI, BOGUSLAW BLAZEJ (BOGUE)
2 Feb 1924, Warsaw
RCA(e) 1979 Designer
Addr: 1979, Vancouver

BACHINSKI, WALTER JOSEPH GERARD
6 Aug 1939, Ottawa IO WWA78
Addr: 1976, Guelph
1976 S12, Montreal
60 Running mother and child cement fondu 51 1/2 x 34 1/2 illus

BACK, FREDERIC HENRI
8 Apr 1924, Saarebruck
RCA(e) 1978 Graphic designer
Addr: 1979, Montreal
1950 2 Kitwancool, Indian village in the spring, BC 30 x 40 $180

BAGLEY, D. MARY (Mrs Geoffrey Spink Bagley)
Addr: 1931, 4982 Queen Mary Rd, Montreal; 1932-5, 5245 Côte St Luc Rd, Montreal
1931 9 Rapids on the Ouareau wc $100
10 June in the bush wc $45
1932 6 Laurentian rapids wc $50
7 Mont St Pierre, Gulf of St Lawrence wc $50
1933 4 The hills in March $50 T34-2
1934 6 The Saguenay cliffs wc $75 T35-2
7 After the snowfall wc $40
1935 1 November, Sault au Recollet wc $45
2 Cleaning day wc $75

BAGLEY, GEOFFREY SPINK
3 Nov 1901, Pontefract, Eng
Addr: 1930, 1203 Blvd Mount Royal, Montreal; 1931, 4982 Queen Mary Rd, Montreal; 1932-4, 5245 Côte St Luc Rd, Montreal; 1937, Beloeil, Que
1930 6 Bonne espérance $250
7 Notre Dame, Bruges wc $100
1931 11 Labrador, morning $250
379 Impromptu drwg $60
1932 8 The St Lawrence at l'Islet $200
229 On the lower St Lawrence linocut $6 unfrmd
230 The ceinture fléchée wd cut $6 unfrmd
1933 5 Baie St Paul, morning $300 T34-3
278 The mill at Repentigny wd cut $6 unfrmd

1934 8 Labrador shore $350
9 Laurentian lake wc $150
T35-3
1937 6 The deserted house wc $50
1938 S8, Toronto
Howard Smith Paper Mills Ltd
146 Two calendars
147 House magazine, 'Paper on parade'
148 Miscellaneous mailings
149 Trade paper advertisements
150 Page layout for 'Paper on parade'
151 Calendar pages
152 Letterheads
153 Folders

BAGOT, JOSCELINE (Hon)
fl 1883 H
1883 256 Old monastery at Santa Barbara, Calif wc

BAIGENT, ROBERT RICHARD
1830, Winchester, Eng 1890, Toronto H
ARCA 1880-5 Painter
Addr: 1880, Toronto; 1881, Sherbourne St W, Toronto; 1882, Toronto; 1883, 465 Sherbourne St, Toronto; 1884-5, Toronto
1880 90 Stonehenge
96 Canadian lynx
171 Canary wc
1881 146 Dead shrike (T. Mower Martin, RCA)
1883 111 Falls, Bracebridge $100
236 Duffin's Creek, Pickering wc $15
237 An English lane, Curdridge Common, Hants wc $20
314 Botley Common, Hampshire wc $20
1884 S1, Saint John
151 Indian River, Owen Sound $100
154 Potowandsa Falls $120
1888 180 Pigeon Lake, Bobcaygeon $40

BAILEY, DAISY (Mrs Robert L. Bailey)
15 Mar 1921, Toronto d 1972
1960 3 Mirror by moonlight 40 x 36 $350
1961 7 The blue period $350

BAILLARGE, CHARLES P. (Chevalier of St Sauveur, Italy)
27 Sep 1825 or 1826, Quebec 10 May 1906, Quebec Co EC Mo98 W78
ARCA 1880-4 Architect
Addr: 1880-4, Quebec

BAILLEUL, JAN
Addr: 1925, 37 St Joachim St, Quebec
1925 252 Hon L.A. Tachereau médln bronze
253 Monument au naturaliste N. Comeau bas rel plâtre

BAILLIE, HELEN PHOEBE AIRD (Mrs John R. Baillie)
16 Nov 1916, London, Eng IO
1970 1 Abandoned fish house 20 x 28 $200
1971 1 Is anyone listening? 22 x 30 $200

BAIN, DONALD
Addr: 1934, 2036 Northcliffe Ave, Montreal
1934 211 Nude wd cut $7.50

BAIN, MABEL A.
1880, Prince Edward Island M
1940 4 Desolation Valley, BC wc $60
1941 5 Peaks at Jasper, BC wc $150

BAINBRIDGE, UNITY (Mrs Leslie William Brewster)
6 Jul 1916, Victoria
1938 8 Ennui $150

BAIRD, RONALD ARNOTT
29 Mar 1940, Toronto
RCA(e) 1973 Council Sculptor
Addr: 1979, Stouffville, Ont
1964J 68 Raven sculp 84 x 36 $1,150

BAKER, FRANCIS SPENCE
21 Aug 1867, Kilbride, Ont 3 Jan 1926, USA Mo12
Addr: 1911, Traders Bank Bldg, Toronto
1911 191 The Graphic Arts Bldg, Toronto. Interior
192 Office building, Toronto
193 Residence, Admiral Rd, Toronto
see also Siddall, John, 1895

BALBONI, CARLO
B
Addr: 1927, 566 Dorchester St E, Montreal; 1931, 1173 St Timothé St,

Montreal
1927 253 Benito Mussolini bust and column plaster
254 Capt V.V. Restaldi bust plaster
1931 303 Giovanni Cabot bust

BALFOUR, A.B.
1882 125 Sunset on the Gairloch wc

BALFOUR, E.
H
1882 121 The Sound of Mull wc

BALFOUR, JAMES
1852, Hamilton 10 Apr 1917, Hamilton Mo98/12
ARCA 1880-09 Architect
Addr: 1880-09, Hamilton
1882 236 Hospital buildings des
238 A house under the mountain des
1887 188 Toronto Court House des
1888 317 City Hall, Hamilton
318 Detroit Museum of Art
1892 168 Two residences, Bay St S, Hamilton

BALL, DOUGLAS
9 Aug 1935, Peterborough, Ont
RCA(e) 1975 Industrial designer
Addr: 1979, Ste Anne de Bellevue, Quebec
1971 31 Work table, Sunar Industries Limited illus

BALLANTYNE, JOHN Scottish
1815, Kelso, Scot 12 May 1897 B
DBA G H RSA TB
1881 213 Interior, John Phillip's studio (W.H. Harrington)

BALLON, IRIS SHKLAR (Mrs Ian Ballon)
11 May 1931, Montreal
1968 1 Maiden appearing 8 x 7 $40
2 Death of Dadon 8 x 7 $40

BALTHAZAR, EDWARD
Addr: 1907, St Hyacinthe, Que
1907 7 Portrait of anonymous

BANKS, J. LISNEY
B
Addr: 1901, 32 Adelaide St E, Toronto; 1906, 310 Jarvis St, Toronto; 1907, Toronto; 1908, 304 Jarvis St, Toronto
1901 245 Hon Justice W.G. Falconbridge, Justice of King's Bench, Ontario bust F2-81
1906 F5, Halifax
3 The round-up bas rel $100
1907 360 Athlete plaster
361 Round-up plaster
1908 171 Reverie sculp
172 Athlete sculp

BANNERMAN, FRANCES see JONES, FRANCES

BANTING, BEATRICE ALINE MYLES (Mrs J. Maitland Banting, signs Myles)
29 Jul 1911, Hamilton M
1944 5 Corp Jimmy Morrow $150
1945 4 Marie sketch $135
1946 3 Young girl $150 T47-3

BANZ, GEORGE
21 Dec 1928, Lucerne WWA76
ARCA 1970 RCA 1977 Architect
Addr: 1971/79, Toronto
1968 Banz, Brook, Carruthers, Grierson & Shaw
84-8 Mimoco Centennial Library A.Ground floor plan B. Exterior C.Approach D.Interior E. Interior
89-93 Lake Huron Water Supply System, Grand Bend A.Plan B.Exterior C.Exterior D.Entrance E.Interior
DW 1977 Buildings and architectural projects, 1957-73 35mm slides

BARBEAU, CHARLES MARIUS
5 Mar 1883, Ste Marie de Beauce, Que 27 Feb 1969, Ottawa CC2 Co CWW48 W78
1938 S8, Toronto
180 'Quebec', Marius Barbeau, Hugh Eayrs, pub by Macmillan
181 'Romancero du Canada', Marius Barbeau, Hugh Eayrs, pub by Macmillan
port: bust, by L. Mol, 1967-79

BARBEAU, CHRISTIAN MARCEL
18 Feb 1925, Montreal CC2 CWW79 M
Addr: 1976, Montreal
1964J 3 Tonquilène 50 x 76 $900
1976 S12, Montreal
2 L'adroverlulle acry 72 x 80 illus

BARBER, VICTOR

1938 S8, Toronto
167 Sanctuary window des, by OCA students, assisted by Rowley Murphy

BARFOOT, GERTRUDE OLIVE GRACE (Mrs Joseph W. Barfoot)
7 Dec 1894, Co Carlow, Ire
1958 85 Owl sculp $40
1964N 66 Night watcher ter cot 8 x 10 $100

BARFOOT, T.
1880 289 Wall paper, adpt from maple leaves
290 Wall paper, adpt from cactus
302 Jewel casket des

BARKER, ERNEST CONYERS
18 Mar 1909, Toronto IO WWA47
Addr: 1932-6, Price St, Toronto
1932 9 Self portrait $200
1936 9 Flower piece $75

BARKER, HERBERT JACKSON
Addr: 1936, 535 Osborne Ave, Verdun, Que
1936 10 Montieth's farm, Verdun wc $30
11 The old trading post, Ville La Salle wc $30

BARNARD, JULIA (Mrs H.J. Barnard)
1900, London, Eng M
1944 6 Peonies $75 T45-3
1953 3 Fungi $100

BARNES, ARCHIBALD GEORGE
19 Mar 1887, London, Eng Nov 1972, Toronto AGO CC1 CWW64 M NGC TB2 WWA47
ARCA 1933 RCA 1936 Sr 1958 Council Painter
Addr: 1930, 66 Grenville St, Toronto; 1931, 64 Grenville St, Toronto; 1932-6, 80 St Clair Ave, Toronto; 1937, 57 Bloor St W, Toronto; 1938-71, Toronto
1930 8 The grey veil illus
1931 12 The room at Black Rivers $1,500
1932 10 Miss Myers
1933 6 Miss Allison $2,000
1934 10 The artist's wife
11 Charles Watson, Esq
12 Master Joe Wright
1935 3 Braheen Urban nfs
1936 12 Portrait in a mirror illus $750
1937 9 Havana nfs
10 Portrait of a lady nfs
11 Miss Rowcliffe nfs
12 Decoration $600
1939 F11, New York
4 Havana 50 x 40 $2,500
1940 5 Renaissance nfs
1941 S9, Toronto
4 Summer $200
1942 3 Miss Goodwin nfs
4 Cadet Sergt Sinclair illus nfs 1943-1
1944 7 Dr. W.E. McNeil, LLD, VPrin Queen's University
8 Anna $750
1946 4 Maj Gen Charles D. Fenwick, RCAMC ED nfs
5 Mary Alice nfs
1948 4 Hon R.S. Robertson, Chief Justice of Ontario (Law Society of Upper Canada)
5 Miss Patricia Elliott nfs
6 Miss Barbara Ferguson nfs
1950 1 June 57 x 47 nfs
1951 5 W.G. Scoon, Esq illus nfs
1951 Travelling exhibit
2 Interior DW 1936 30 x 40 1954 Retro Sec 36
1952 4 Mrs George Cooper nfs
1953 4 Rt Hon Lord Braintree illus nfs 1954-5 illus
1955 4 S.E. Weir, Esq, QC nfs
1957 5 June and Robin illus nfs

BARNES, WILFRED MOLSON
10 Oct 1882, Montreal 14 Feb 1955, Montreal CC1 CNS36 M NGC PMC TB3
ARCA 1920 RCA 1947 Sr 1951 Council Painter
Addr: 1904, Montreal; 1910-14, 571 St Catherine St W, Montreal; 1915-27, 747 St Catherine St W, Montreal; 1928-37, 1501 St Catherine St W, Montreal; 1938-55, Montreal
1904 316 Figure study for illustration b&w
317 Beatrice b&w
318 Out shopping b&w
319 Portrait study b&w
1910 6 Vanity
7 Dancer
1913 8 Hillside
1914 5 Wood interior
1915 3 Sunset hill
4 Over the hills
1916 5 A day begins

6 A day ends
270 A Canadian officer pencil
1918A 4 The wings of night
5 A summer storm ◊NGC◊
1918N 5 Lake Massiwippi
6 Daybreak after frost
1919 4 The hooded clouds
5 The golden hour
1920 5 The day turns ghost ◊NGC◊
6 The hill beyond
1921 7 Where the river dreams
8 Then came still evening on
9 The lure of the morning
1922 7 The river, like a cup, is full of sky S6-2
8 The flaky darkness breaks within the east
1923 8 The glowing bow that smiled the clouds away
9 The warm west winds are hung with rain
10 When evening shuts the gates of day
1924 5 The last glow of day
6 Iceberg
1925 5 The mountain road at dusk
6 The fall meadow
1926 4 Golden morning
1927 5 Grounded berg off Quirpon, Newfoundland
6 Brickyards on the Hudson River
1928 5 The cloud shadow $300 S7-3
6 The last glow $160
1929 6 Ames Hill, Brattleboro, Vermont $300
7 After the shower nfs
1929 S7, Calgary
2 Evening $300
4 The west wind burden $70
1930 9 Golden gates of morning $175
1931 13 Summer clouds $150
14 The brook pastel $300
1932 11 Hill at sunset $150
1933 7 Evening $500 T34-4
8 Summer clouds pastel $300
1934 13 The lake $300
1935 4 The meadow $500
5 Grounded berg, Newfoundland $400 T36-1
1936 13 The hilltop $500
1937 7 Ascutney Mountain $350 T38-1
8 Along the river $150
1938 9 Meadow, afternoon $250 T39-2
1939 4 Sun after rain $150
5 Woodland pool $150
1939 F11, New York
5 New England village 30 x 22 $500
1940 6 The valley $100
1941 6 Silver morning $125 T42-2
7 The golden afternoon $125
1942 5 The brook $200
1943 2 The yellow house nfs
1945 5 Meadow brook after rain pastel $200
6 A day ends $300 T46-1
1946 6 Afternoon shadows $350 DW 1948 26 1/4 x 36 1/4 T51-3 1954 Retro Sec 36
1947 8 Evening sky pattern $500
1948 7 The valley $200

BARNETT, MADELEINE LORIMER JORDAN
(Mrs Leonard R. Barnett)
b Manchester
Addr: 1937, 11 Old Fellows Hall, Saskatoon
1937 271 A prairie mother sculp nfs
1939 241 Jack Proctor sculp $100
1941 202 Rex Hooten bronze plaster nfs
203 Refugee plaster $50

BARNSLEY, JAMES MACDONALD
20 Feb 1861, West Flanboro, n Dundas, Ont 25 Feb 1929, Verdun, Que B EC H M NGC TB2
Addr: 1887, Montreal; 1893, c/o Art Association of Montreal; 1894, 31 Bleury St, Montreal; 1895-7 Art Association of Montreal; 1899, Hudson, Que; 1902, Montreal; 1903-6, c/o Scott & Sons, Montreal; 1907-9, Montreal; 1910-11, Art Association of Montreal, 23 Phillips Sq; 1912, c/o Scott & Sons, Montreal; 1913, Art Association of Montreal; 1915-20, c/o W. Scott & Sons, 99 Notre Dame St W, Montreal
1886 126 Scene in France
1887 139 On the Maine wc $100
1890 1 When winter winds are piercing chill $125
117 An inlet of the Seine, near St Ouen wc $75
118 Late autumn wc $25
119 End of a winter's day wc $25
1893 8 The phantom ship $150
160 The life boat wc $100 F1-118
161 East Gloucester, Maine wc $40 F1-119 nfs
162 Shipping wc $35 F1-120 nfs
1893 F1, Chicago
7 A calm evening

1894 7 Dieppe harbour ≬NGC≬
8 Bass Rocks, Gloucester ≬NGC≬
156 Rocky Point, Mass wc
1895 9 Landscape near Montreal
10W Windmill at Dordrecht wc
11W Scene in Ireland near Killarney wc
12W Rock Point, Gloucester, Mass wc
13W Fish houses, Gloucester wc
1896 7 Misty moonlight
8 Landscape in Holland
9 Sunset in Holland, Mauve's trees
10 A quiet evening
1897 15 Autumn landscape in Holland
16 French landscape
6W Winter in Central Park wc F.M. Barnsley, mispr
7W Scene on the Richelieu River wc
1899 19 and 20 Landscape, France
21 Marine
22 Cliffs at Havre
158 The wreck wc
159 Gossips wc
1902 3 In the woods, Turey, France
4 On the Seine, Courbevoie
5 Near Beauvie, France
6 Affaurgie, France
1903 19 Landscape, Holland
1904 6 Landscape, Hautaineville
7 Thury
8 Fort, St Malo
9 Phantom ship
1905 9 Fort, St Malo, and sea
10 Landscape in Normandy
11 Night scene in Holland
1906 15 On the Seine
16 Near Rouen
17 Near Havre
1906 F5, Halifax
4 Cliffs at Havre $125
5 St Malo $125
6 Eastern Point, lighthouse $200
7 Rocky Point, Gloucester, Mass $200
1907 8 St Malo
9 Sunset
10 On the Channel
11 A french hillside
1907 F6, Sherbrooke
7 Eastern Point $150
8 Rocky Point $100
9 Haystacks $125
10 Sunset on the coast
1909M 16 Dieppe
1910 8 On the Thames
9 Farm, Normandy
1910 S2, Liverpool
1 Breaking clouds
1911 1 Rothesay Castle S3-6
2 Dutch landscape
3 French landscape
4 Haystacks
1912 11 On the Seine, Paris
12 French farm, near Dieppe
256 Seascape pen & ink
257 Sketch pen & ink
1912 S3, Winnipeg
3 The quay, Dieppe
4 Sunset in France
5 Bass Rocks
1913 9 Mont St Michel
10 Farm at Thury
11 Moonlight on the Seine
12 The orchard
1915 5 The old farm, Thury
6 The bay, St Servan
1916 7 The derelict
8 Autumn
271 The lifeboat b&w
272 Too late b&w
1918N 7 Old chateau, near Paris illus
8 French farm
1919 6 French landscape
1920 6 and 7 Landscape
297 Ships drwg
298 Moonlight drwg

BAROTT, ERNEST ISBELL
25 Mar 1884, Canastota, NY 15 May 1966, Montreal CWW64 NGC
ARCA 1930 RCA 1937 Sr 1954 Architect
Addr: 1930-6, Montreal; 1937, Canada Cement Bldg, Montreal; 1938-66, Montreal
1937 Barott & Blackader
231-4 Residence, C.G. Greenshields, Esq, Hill Park Rd
DW 1939 Aldred Building, Montreal des wc drwg 20 1/2 x 11 1/2

BARR, ROBERT ALLAN
10 Jan 1890, London, Eng 15 Aug 1959, Toronto AGO CWW55 M NGC TB3 W78 WWA47
ARCA 1928 Painter
Addr: 1923, 117 King St W, Toronto; 1926-7, 78A Howard St, Toronto; 1928-30, 31 Summerhill Gardens, Toronto; 1931-2, 98 Walmer Rd, Toronto; 1933, 63 Gormley Ave, Toronto;

1934-7, Chicora Ave, Toronto; 1938-59, Toronto
1923 11 Rt Rev Dr Bidwell, Bishop of Ontario
1926 5 Charles G.D. Roberts, MA, LLD illus ◊NGC◊
1927 7 Professor de Champ
1928 7 Mrs Dean
8 Miss Molly Bucknill $600
1930 10 The swordsman $1,500
11 Miss Jean MacPherson illus
1931 15 Doreen $1,000
1932 12 Gordon Tamblyn, Esq
1933 9 The toast $1,000 T34-5
1934 14 The silver jug $200
15 Flower piece $200
16 The convex mirror $150 T35-4
1936 14 Mrs Basil G. Morgan nfs T37-3
1937 13 Autumn flower piece $250
1939 6 Dr Wm. Perkins Bull, KC, daughter and grandsons nfs
1939 F11, New York
6 Mrs Joseph Sheard 42 x 34 nfs
1940 7 Contemplation $300 T41-3
8 Spring fantasy
1941 8 Black and gold $1,000
1941 S9, Toronto
5 Flower piece $100
1942 6 Mrs Walter Morgan nfs
7 Beaufort Belcher nfs
1943 3 Lieut Col Alan Cockram nfs T44-1
1944 9 Mrs Charles Sheard, jr nfs
10 View of Ironside, Ont $300
1947 9 Miss Margaret Barr nfs
1948 8 Mrs Allan Barr nfs
1949 4 Portrait of the artist nfs
1950 4 Self portrait 38 x 34 nfs
1952 5 Mrs Carol Telfer nfs
1957 6 Mrs Robert Hartman nfs

BARR, RUTH L.
Addr: 1907, Montreal
1907 12 Sketch

BARRAUD, CYRIL HENRY English
1877, Eng AGO DBA
Addr: 1913-14, 43 Barry St, Norwood, Winnipeg
1913 7 The ultimatum S4-3 $100
349 Houses of Parliament, Westminster etch S4-145 $32
350 Tower Bridge, London etch S4-146 $12
351 Union Station, Winnipeg etch S4-147 $9
1914 6 The end of a winter's day
7 A summer day wc

BARRE, RAOUL
29 Jan 1874, Montreal 21 May 1932, Montreal W63
Addr: 1899, 319 Rachel St, Montreal; 1929, 990 Cherrier St, Montreal
1899 162 The bath wc
1929 8 L'etang
9 A l'Oiseau Bleu

BARRY, FRANCIS LEOPOLD (FRANK)
16 Apr 1913, London, Eng WWA76
RCA(e) 1974 RCA 1975 Painter
Addr: 1976/79, Montreal
1976 S12, Montreal
3 Babel acry on shaped plywood/acry sur contre-plaque taillé 72 x 36 illus
DW 1975 Slow division. 1973 3 panels acry, wood, hardboard 84 x 36 x 3 1/2

BARRY, JOHN JOSEPH
21 Jun 1885, Hamilton, Ont d 1952
CWW49 WWA36
Addr: 1920, 411 Mackay St, Montreal; 1931-7. 18 Grenville Ave, Toronto
1920 299 Low tide, Tiburon soft ground etch
300 A Quebec street etch
1931 380 Drying the nets etch $15
381 Evening, Gloucester etch $7.50
1932 231 In the harbour etch $6
232 Old building, Rouen drwg $35
233 Rome, from my window drwg $35
1933 279 Holland scene etch $12
280 Lion d'Or etch $15
281 Leaning willow drwg $15
1935 308 Martigues etch $10
309 Early morning etch $10
1937 299 Italian fishing boats etch $8
300 Landscape etch $8
1940 166 Chartres, France dry pt $8
1941 232 Fishing craft etch $12

BARRY, LILLIE EMILY FRANCES
1863, Montreal d 1955 CNS36 Mo12
Addr: 1910, The Richmond, Union Ave, Montreal
1910 10 Patience

BART-GERALD, ELIZABETH (Mrs)
8 Sep 1907, Cleveland WWA36
Addr: 1931, 119 Cumberland St, Toronto
1931 16 Portrait of a young girl $2,500
17 Antimo Beneduce $750

BARTHOLOMEW, DAVID
1970 118 Letterhead, Flick Record Corp, Limited
1971 2G Art auction program Works of Art Committee, University of Waterloo
3G Poster, Counselling Services, University of Waterloo
4G Poster, Staff Association, University of Waterloo

BARTKIW, ROMAN
8 Mar 1935, Montreal IO
RCA(e) 1979 Ceramist
Addr: 1979, Beamsville, Ont

BARTLETT, JOHN LAWRENCE
9 May 1907, Toronto
1944 11 Eng Chow's market $100 T45-4
12 Scene in the woods $100 T45-5
1945 7 The dance of the old men $250
8 Cloudy day in April $150
1947 10 The town of Paris, Ont wc $150
11 Summer wood interior wc $150
1948 9 Spring landscape wc $100
1950 5 The town 30 x 40 $300

BARTRAM, EDWARD JOHN
21 Mar 1938, London, Ont
RCA(e) 1976 Print maker
Addr: 1979, King, Ont

BARWICK, JOHN ALFRED
22 Dec 1912, Toronto
1955 5 Rhapsody in pink $200

BATES, MAXWELL BENNETT
14 Dec 1906, Calgary 14 Sep 1980, Victoria AGO CC2 CWW79 M NGC TB3 WWA59
ARCA 1961 RCA 1971 Painter
Addr: 1961-71/79, Victoria
1959 5 Summer landscape 20 x 24 $200
1960 4 Boulevard St Martin, Paris 24 x 30 $300
1961 8 Grove of trees 24 x 30 $250
9 Autumn still life 24 x 30 $275
1963 5 West Indian puppets $250
1964J 4 Figure with flag 48 x 36 $450
1965 2 Crucifixion 32 x 40 illus $350 S10-4 illus
1968 3 Saanich landscape 24 x 30 $225
1970 2 Beach 24 x 30 illus $250
1971 2 View of Grasse, south of France 24 x 30 $250 DW 1971

BATES, PATRICIA MARTIN (Mrs C.A. Bates)
5 Jun 1927, Saint John B M
RCA(e) 1975 Print maker
Addr: 1976/79, Victoria
1976 S12, Montreal
154 Shape of speaking stars cut from misbegotten moon. perforated drwg/dessin perforé 36 x 48 illus

BATSCH, BRIAN G.
Addr: 1976, Calgary
1976 S12, Montreal
4 One, two, three acry 57 x 142 illus

BAUER, W.C. American
fl 1882-98 B F H TB
1882 17 In pasture $125
32 A day in October $100

BAXTER, ADELINE
Addr: 1914, Winnipeg
1914 S4, Winnipeg
165 Ruth, daughter of W.A. Briggs, Esq

BAXTER, INGRID (Mrs J.W. Iain Baxter)
10 Feb 1938, Spokane, Wash WWA76
RCA(e) 1978 Painter
Addr: 1979, North Vancouver

BAXTER, JOSEPH WILSON IAIN
16 Nov 1936, Middlesborough, Eng M WWA76
ARCA 1971 Painter
Addr: 1979, North Vancouver

BAXTER, RICHARD
Addr: 1923, 52 Mortlake Ave, St Lambert, Que

1923 12 Rural Quebec

BAYEFSKY, ABA
7 Apr 1923, Toronto AGO CCI CWW79
IO M NGC TB3 WWA47
ARCA 1958 Council Painter
Addr: 1958-71/79, Toronto
1953 5 Paul Bunyan and Babe $350
1955 6 Market with Mennonites $450
1957 7 Market group illus $800
1958 7 Market place, November illus $700
1960 5 An Indian theme 40 x 40 $700
1964N 4 The pensive sitter $600
see also Dorn, P, 1970-158

BAYLEY, E. UNIACHE
Addr: 1904, Toronto
1904 10 My German friend

BEACH, ELIZABETH see KNOWLES, ELIZABETH

BEAMENT, THOMAS HAROLD
23 Jul 1898, Ottawa AGO CC2 CWW79
M NGC TB3 WWA47
ARCA 1936 RCA 1947 Sr 1968 Council
Painter
Addr: 1922-4, 28 Nepean St, Ottawa; 1925, 78 Sparks St, Ottawa; 1926-7, 725 St Catherine St W, Montreal; 1928-31, 1475 St Catherine St W, Montreal; 1933-4, 3419 Drummond St, Montreal; 1935-7, 1894 Mackay St, Montreal; 1938-47, Montreal; 1948-51, Rosemere, Que; 1952-71/79, Montreal
1922 9 Cascade
10 The pavillion
1924 7 The bridge
8 The second burning
1925 7 The mountain illus (NGC)
8 At sundown pastel
282 Chateau Laurier, Ottawa drwg
283 Arundel Castle drwg
1926 7 Laurentian autumn
8 Still life
1927 8 Welders
281 Clearing burnt land drwg
282 The mountain drwg
1928 9 Rocky headland $350 1929-10
10 Snow blanket $75
193 Aurora borealis drwg $25 1929-254 $35
194 Thaw drwg $25
1929 255 Wind and rain drwg $35
1931 382 Demolition drwg $75
1933 10 Sponge trimmers, Nassau $1,200 T34-6
282 Mountain torrent drwg $40
1934 17 Growth and demolition $500 T35-5
212 Porto Rican rhythm drwg $75
1935 6 Hillside harvest $200 T36-2
1936 15 Dawn illus $500 T37-4
16 Laurentian valley $250
1937 14 Utakijut, the waiting ones $1,500
15 Huberdeau $250 T38-2
301 Arctic madonna drwg $75
302 Alone drwg $35
1938 10 Silent northland $500 T39-3
11 Labrador trading post $150
1939 F11, New York
7 Departure for the hunt 40 x 26 $750
1942 Lt Comm Harold Beament
8 Mother ship and submarine $250 T43-1
1945 Comm Harold Beament
9 Passed $250 T46-2
10 Atlantic convoy $300
11 Running fight in Channel $250
12 Rescued $450
1946 7 Fire on board during action (NGC)
8 Souvenir of Greece, Nov 1944 (NGC) T47-4
1947 12 The straggler $750 T48-4
13 Sunday at the sawmill $250
14 March sunshine, Laurentians $325
1948 10 A sealer sets out $450
1949 5 Something in sight $850 1950-6 36 x 42
6 She has new clothes $400
1950 7 Still water 36 x 40 $800
1951 6 Autumn $800
1951 Travelling exhibit
4 Lighthouse DW 1948 63 x 41 1954 Retro Sec 49
1952 6 Northland solitude illus $850 T53-2
1953 6 Gossips illus $750
1954 6 Kayak race 40 x 40 illus $750 1955-7
1955 8 Eskimo berry pickers illus $800
1956 2 Eskimo camp $850 T56-2
3 Eskimo fish trap illus $500 T56-3
1957 8 Eskimo hauling illus $850 1958-9

1958 8 Eskimo mother $850
1959 6 Lava below Mount Teide, Tenerife 36 x 42 illus $900 1960-6
1960 7 Portuguese fishermen 30 x 40 illus $900 1961-11
1961 10 Moving the net, Portugal 18 x 72 illus $1,200
1964J 6 Arrangement 62 24 x 30 illus $500
1964N 5 Lava forms, night, Tenerife 48 x 60 illus $2,000 1965-4 S10-5 illus
1965 3 Sun, wind and tidal streams 48 x 60 illus $2,000
1966 2 Castellated lava, Tenerife 48 x 60 illus $2,000 1967-1 illus
1966 S10, Charlottetown
6 Portuguese 30 x 40 $900

BEAMENT, THOMAS HAROLD (TIB)
17 Feb 1941, Montreal M WWA73
RCA(e) 1976 Council Print maker
Addr: 1979, Westmount, Que
1964J 5 Happee 60 x 36 $400
1965 5 Pink landscape 36 x 40 $400
6 Mykonos at night 27 x 36 $325
1966 3 Midnight garden 27 x 36 $350
1967 2 Pour le merit, the blue max 48 x 36 $575
3 The Wright Bros. at Kitty Hawk 2 36 x 48 illus $575
1970 3 Barn own #2 15 x 18 1/2 $200

BEANLANDS, SOPHIE see PEMBERTON, SOPHIE

BEAR, GEORGE TELFER
Oct 1874, Greenock, Scot flg 1958
DBA TB2 WWA50 WWB29
Addr: 1913, 335 Langside St, Winnipeg
1913 13 Langside Street, Winnipeg S4-4 $100
14 The black hat S4-5 $75

BEATTIE, JESSIE
Addr: 1925, 309 Stanley St, Montreal
1925 9 Old house, Beaurepaire, Que wc

BEATTY, JOHN WILLIAM
30 May 1869, Toronto 4 Oct 1941, Toronto AGO B CC1 EC M NGC TB2/3 W78
ARCA 1905 RCA 1913 Sr 1940 Council Painter
Addr: 1898, 54 Yorkville Ave, Toronto; 1903-6, 43 Adelaide St E, Toronto; 1906 36 1/2 King St E, Toronto; 1908, 74 Roxborough St, Toronto; 1909M-11, 36 Toronto St, Toronto; 1912-13, 32 Adelaide St E, Toronto; 1914-37, Studio Bldg, 25 Severn St, Toronto; 1938-41, Toronto
1898 16 Lombard plums
132a On the Humber River wc
1903 16 October landscape
17 At Churchville, Ontario
1904 11 Early moonrise F4-3
12 October
1905 24 Early autumn
25 Homeward 1906-12 F5-9 $200
26 Harvest field
1906 11 In the Laurentians (Ontario Government) F5-8 illus
13 Evening
14 Showery weather, Quebec
1907 F6, Sherbrooke
11 Early evening $50
12 Early autumn $75
13 Landscape $50 nfs
1908 5 October day, Meadowvale
6 After rain, Quebec
7 Evening
1909M 24 At Kortenhoff, north Holland
25 Old Dutch farmhouse
1909N 18 In Holland
1910 11 After rain, the Seine
12 Autumn S2-4 1912-14
13 Dutch interior
14 Fishing boats, Katwyk
1910 S2, Liverpool
2 The prospectors 1912-13
3 The evening cloud of the north land ≬NGC≬
1911 9 Early morning, Rag Market, Bruges
10 Wood interior
1912 15 The Rag Market, Bruges 1913-16 S4-6 $500 (purchased by NGC)
16 Fishing boats, North Sea
17 Night, Toronto harbour
1912 S3, Winnipeg
7 Dutch peasant ≬AGH≬
8 In the north of Holland
9 Emnes harbour, Holland
#156-9 b&w illustrations
156 Firemen

157 Ship deck
158 Studio
159 Church
160 The Seine, Paris etch
161 Gipsy van, Holland etch
1913 15 Mount Orford, Quebec
17 The passing shadow
18 Between showers S4-7 $400 DW 1914 27 3/4 x 39 3/4 T51-5 1954 Retro Sec 16
19 Across the valley S4-8 $200
1914 8 Winter morning, Algonquin Park
9 Lake Lucerne, Canadian Rockies 1915-10
10 Hillside, Algonquin Park
11 Across the valley
1914 S5, Patriotic Fund
32 Cloud shadows illus
1915 7 The yellow tree illus
8 Morning, Algonquin Park ◊NGC◊
9 A hillside, Algonquin Park
1916 9 Early spring illus
10 The edge of the woods
1918A 6 Canoe Lake, Algonquin Park illus
7 Windsor landscape
1919 7 Canadian Cavalry bivouac, France, 1918 illus (Canadian War Memorials)
8 Birch trees, Algonquin Park
1920 9 The towers of Mont St Eloi
10 A camp behind Amiens, 1918
11 A stream in winter illus
12 A hill, Algonquin Park
1921 10 Algonquin Park illus
1922 11 Masquerade costume S6-3
12 The fortune teller illus
13 Mandolin player
14 Summer landscape S6-4
1923 13 The coming storm
14 Northland
1924 9 The north country
10 Gibralter Point, Joe Lake
11 Cache Lake, winter
1925 10 The Madawaska Valley illus 1926-9 illus
11 Cache Lake, Algonquin Park
1926 10 Early autumn
11 Winter morning F8-102 $450
1928 11 A country road $500
12 Early spring $500 F9-188 $510
13 The rapid autumn $500 1929-12
14 Winter, Meadowvale $200
1929 11 Winter, Bowen Island, BC $1,000
1929 S7, Calgary
5 Bowen Island, BC, $1,000
6 A country road, Ontario $500
7 Baie St Paul, Quebec $75
1930 12 Laurentian hills, winter illus $600
13 In the woods $500
14 Autumn reflections $600
1930 F10, London, Eng
159 A Canadian country road $515
1931 18 Waterfall, Kearney, Ontario $750
19 In the Laurentians, winter $650
1932 13 Brooks Falls, Magnetawan River illus $750 1933-11
14 Winter stream, Kearney, Ontario $450
15 Winter, Humber Valley $250
1933 12 Autumn, Beaver Lake $500 1934-19
13 Winter, Kearney, Ontario $450 T34-7
14 Stream in winter $450
1934 18 Wood interior illus $600 1935-7 T36-3
20 The bridge $400 1935-8 T35-6
21 Birch and spruce $250
1935 9 The new roof $250
1936 16a A fall on the Magnetawan $1,000
17 The red canoe $500 T37-5
18 Winter, Kearney, Ontario $400
1937 16 Across the valley, autumn $500
17 Rock, beech and maple $500
18 Rampikes Canoe Lake $300
19 The road to the lake $300
1938 12 Pickerel Lake $300 T39-4
13 Lake Ontario at Port Granby $250
1939 7 Barns, Burks Falls, Ontario $500
8 Old bridge, Port Hope $400
9 Road to Pickerel Lake $300
1939 F11, New York
8 Brooks Falls, Parry Sound $500
1940 9 Old bridge, near Port Hope $500
10 Brooks Falls, Magnetawan $300

11 Kearney, Ontario $300
T4 1-4
1941 S9, Toronto
6 French village, Province of Quebec $200
1941 The late John William Beatty
9 Winter, Bowen Island illus $1,200

BEATTY, OTTILLIE
1938 S8, Toronto
380 Wallpaper design. Hon mention, Canadian Wallpaper Manufacturers Limited

BEAU, HENRI
27 Jun 1863, Montreal 15 May 1949, Paris B H Mo12
Addr: 1896, 2336 St Catherine St, Montreal; 1899, Paris; 1901, 9 University St, Montreal; 1902, 2418 St Catherine St, Montreal; 1904, Montreal; 1910-14, 291 Mountain St, Montreal; 1925, 116 rue de Vaugirard, Paris
1896 186 Winter scene wc
187 Marine wc
1899 18 Landscape
1901 11 Spring F2-10
12 Heather at sunset
13 and 14 Landscape
1902 7 Portrait of a little girl
8 Portrait
9 Sketch from mountain top
1904 13 Landscape
14 Dr Villeneuve F4-4
15 Madame F.
16 Mother and child F4-5
1910 15 La rue du village
16 Sous-bois
1914 12 Bords de la Seine
13 Coucher de soleil, Bretagne S5-22 illus
1925 12 Port de Honfleur, France (Dominion Archives)
1945 13 Listening to a fairy tale nfs
14 The little seamstress nfs

BEAU, PAUL
Addr: 1902, 2714 St Catherine St, Montreal; 1910/38, Montreal
1902 289 Applique bronze for electric light, women and flowers Paul Beau and Marc Antigna
1910 223 Jardiniere bronze
224 Jewel case bronze
1938 S8, Toronto
14 Book ends, totemic des, wrought iron & brass
15 Cigar box, illus
16 Photograph frame
17 Pipe bowl #18 not in cat
19-20 Pair of fire dogs and fire basket. Paul Beau craftsman, W.S. Maxwell, designer
port: by M.Natigna, 1902-1

BEAUCHEMIN, MICHELINE
24 Oct 1930, Longueuil, Que CWW79 M TB3 WWA73
ARCA 1968 Council Textile designer
Addr: 1970, Outremont, Que; 1971/76/79, Les Grondines, Que
1970 29A National Arts Centre, Ottawa. Interior with tapestry. Lebensold, architect
1976 S12, Montreal
137 Le fleuve tapisserie/tapestry 96 x 48 illus

BEAUDIN, JEAN PIERRE
18 Feb 1935, Montreal
RCA(e) 1978 Photographer
Addr: 1979, Montreal

BEAUDOIN, PHILIPPE
Addr: Montreal
1938 S8, Toronto
21 'Le grand silence blanc' white levant morocco with cover & case, des in mosaic
24 'L'Ile d'Orléans' maroon levant morocco with des

BEAUGRAND-CHAMPAGNE, ARISTIDE
fl 1913-50
Addr: 1916, 409 Durocher St, Outremont, Que
1916 261 Project d'église des

BEAULIEU, CLAUDE
14 Oct 1913, Ste Rose de Laval, Que
RCA(e) 1978 Architect
Addr: 1979, Montreal

BEAULIEU, LOUIS JACQUES see JACQUE, LOUIS

BEAULIEU, PAUL VANIER
24 Mar 1910, Montreal B M TB3
RCA(e) 1979 Painter
Addr: 1979, St Sauveur des Monts, Que

BEAUPRE, ALFRED
Addr: 1907, Montreal
1907 14 Au souffle de la brise

BEAUPRE, E.L.
Addr: 1912, Toronto
1912 S3, Winnipeg
155 A day with the baby b&w

BEAUPRE, GEORGES
14 May 1937, Quebec
1970 119 Catalogue cover, Cinémathèque de films touristique canadiens
120 Catalog cover, National Film Board of Canada, Films 1968-69, available for rental and purchase in the United States
121 Symbol, National Film Board
122 Poster, Jusqu'au coeur

BECHMAN, FREDERICKA
Addr: 1933, 4862 Sherbrooke St W, Montreal
1933 15 Portrait of a lady pastel

BECHTEL, JOHN HOWARD
7 Jun 1923, Kitchener, Ont 13 Sep 1966, Kitchener, Ont
1951 7 Cliff dwellings $65
1953 7 Banana plant $85
1954 7 Infinity 22 x 24 $80
1955 9 Red fish house $125
1956 4 Ruins by night $80 T56-4
1958 10 Hidden lake $175
11 Corn stalks $175
1959 7 Hillside 24 x 36 $150
1965 7 Destination unknown 24 x 32 $250
8 Mexican memory 32 x 24 $250

BECKER, A.
H
1880 44 Dhu Lock, Balmoral (HRH Princess Louise)

BECKWITH, JAMES E. American
21 Dec 1907, Mount Pleasant, Iowa WWA38
Addr: 1934-5, 4864 Côte des Neiges Rd, Montreal
1934 22 The harbour wc $60
23 The square wc $60 T35-7
1935 10 The discussion wc $75
11 L'habitante wc $45 T36-4

BEDDOE, ALAN BROOKMAN
1893, Ottawa d 1975 M
1938 14 Spring is coming, Gatineau pastel $75

BEDER, JACK
14 Mar 1910, Opatow, Poland
Addr: 1937, 74 Prince Arthur St E, Montreal
1937 20 Across the streets temp nfs
1938 15 Gray day $175 T39-5
1966 4 Rock face print 16 x 16 $100

BEECH, ARTHUR B.
8 Sep 1876, Oldham, Lancs, Eng
1948, Winnipeg
Addr: 1923-9, 602 Rathgar Ave, Winnipeg
1923 202 Buffalo and staircase, Parliament Buildings, Winnipeg drwg
1925 11 Landscape wc
1927 283 Peace col print
284 The breakwater col print
1929 12 The Mississippi at Brainherd wc $40

BEECHEY, WILLIAM (Sir) English
12 Dec 1753, Burford, Oxfords, Eng
23 Jan 1839, Hampstead, Eng B G TB
1881 329 His Majesty William IV (loan) artist not listed

BEEVOR, A.F.
fl 1882-8 H
1882 10 The artful dodger

BELAND, LUC
1951, Lachine, Que
Addr: 1976, Montreal
1976 S12, Montreal
5 Monochrome eurythmique #9 acry 60 x 84 illus

BELANGER, FERNAND
1971 Initiation film screened 14 Apr

BELANGER, LOUIS JOSEPH OCTAVE
20 Jun 1886, Montreal 1972, Montreal B CN336
Addr: 1925, 1117 St Hubert St, Montreal; 1929, 53 Côte St Catherine Rd. Outremont, Que
1925 14 La glycine
1929 14 Quebec from Lévis $350
1952 7 The bookworm nfs

BELIVEAU, C. RENE
Addr: 1907, Montreal
1907 15 A l'ombre
16 Sur l'ecluse

BELK, M. ELIZA
Addr: 1922, 608 Royal Alexander Apt, Vancouver
1922 15 The woman in red min
16 The old Londoner min

BELL, ALISTAIR MACREADY
21 Oct 1913, Darlington, Eng CC2 M TB3 WWA73
ARCA 1965 Print maker
Addr: 1965-71/79, West Vancouver
1968 4 Trees in sand dunes VIII 22 1/2 x 15 1/2 $150
5 Trees in sand dunes IX 16 x 22 $150
1970 S11, Halifax
3 Trees in sand dunes XI 1968 ink & wc 16 1/2 x 22 3/4 $175
4 Trees in sand dunes XV 1969 ink & wc 16 x 22 $175

BELL, MARY see EASTLAKE, MARY

BELL-SMITH, FREDERIC MARLETT
26 Sep 1846, London, Eng 23 Jun 1923, Toronto AGO CC2 EC H M Mo98 NGC R2 TB3 W78
ARCA 1880 RCA 1886 Council Painter
Addr: 1880-1, Hamilton; 1882, St Thomas, Ont; 1883, London, Ont; 1884, Colborne St, London, Ont; 1885-6, St Thomas, Ont; 1887-8, London, Ont; 1888-92, Toronto; 1893-23, 336 Jarvis St, Toronto
1880 71 Study of a child's head
161 A tobogganing party wc
1881 36 Our national game wc $50
56 Tobogganing wc $15
57 Snow-balling wc $20
69 The Hanlan Race, Toronto Bay wc $50 T.M.Bell-Smith mispr
97 Tobogganing wc $50
301 The ferry $100
319 Stepping stones $100
1882 89 Break, break, on thy cold grey stones, O sea! $200
108 Stepping stones, Dundas Ravine $125
119 A passing shower wc $25
144 Great Head, Mabou, Cape Breton wc $50
148 Cliffs at Mabou wc $60
158 Under the cliffs wc $70
181 Mist clearing, Nova Scotian coast wc $60
193 Cape Porcupine wc $25
203 Study of rocks, from nature wc
1883 106 and 107 Study $15 each
137b Saco Valley $300
137c Path down the Gorge $100 (138c misprt for 137c)
171 Fall wc $20
172 Foggy morning, Casco Bay wc $60
199 Great Head, Mount Desert wc $50
207 Frenchman's Bay wc $25
208 Noon at Conway wc $40
217 The path by the brook wc $25
226 Eagle Lake, Mount Desert wc $60
252 A bit in the Thousand Islands wc $25
261 Going to school wc $20
263 A mountain path wc $25
264 Regatta, Toronto Bay wc (loan) S1-46
273 Fresh breeze on Peak's Island wc $35
307 Eagle's Crag, Lake Rosseau wc $30
311 On the Saco, Mount Washington in the distance wc $25
1884 2 Heart of the White Mountains $300
4 A breeze on the Jersey coast $25
15 Portrait of the artist from a mirror nfs
20 Art students $100 S1-111
29 Daughters of Canada $750
52 and 62 Portrait
100 A cool spot wc $25
111 Trout stream in the White Mountains wc $25
151 Rapids above Montmorency wc $25
171 In the woods wc $25
1884 S1, Saint John
2 On the Hudson wc $25
5 In the woods, North Conway wc $20
6 A White Mountain stream wc $20
21 White Mountains, from North Conway wc $25
26 Misty morning, Toronto

Bay wc $25
28 Mounts Adams and Madison from Mount Washington wc $60
38 Tobogganing wc $25
59 Study of rocks wc $15
64 Rocks at Nantasket wc $15
88 The return from school $400
96 Rocks, near Nantasket $20
115 Fog on the rocks (L.R. O'Brien)
120 Woodland stream $25
128 Path by the brook wc $25

1885 46 In the spring time when all is green $65
72 The laughing eye expresses the merry thought $125
217 Spring freshet wc $20
224 Saint John harbour wc $40
233 Low tide, Bay of Fundy wc $40 1886-94 $65
238 Warm day, Mount Washington wc $60 1886-81 $100
259 Lifting fog, Bay of Fundy wc $40
268 On the beach wc $65
271 On the Bay Shore, Saint John, NB wc $30
290 Overflow, Saint John River wc $40
295 Rainy day, Saint John River wc $40 1886-63 $50
304 A fisherman's landing wc $40
316 After a snow storm wc $125 1886-70 $100

1886 21 Toronto Bay, sunrise $50
32 Study of a head $55
53 A fisherman's landing, Saint John, NB wc $50
59 Fog clearing wc $20
69 Lake Rosseau, Muskoka wc $25
93 Boat race wc $25
98 Owl's Head, Memphramagog wc $50
138 A bye-path, Nova Scotia $35
140 Lifting fog, Bay of Fundy $50
167 Art students $100

1886 Fla, London, Eng
2019, artist's number
Laughing eyes
Fog clearing off at low tide
Last rays
Bay of Fundy (L.R.O'Brien)
Rainy day, Saint John River

1887 2 Fog clearing off at low tide, Bay of Fundy $125
20 White Head $250 DW 1887 White Head, Portland, Maine 34 1/2 x 60 1954 Retro Sec 7
30 Last rays of parting day, Bay of Fundy $400
142 Mount Madison wc $25
144 Washed by the Atlantic waves wc $75
147 On the Restigouche wc $25
165 Market morning, Jacques Cartier Square, Montreal wc $40
170 Mount Washington, from the east wc $25
172 On the Metapedia wc $40
179 Trout stream in the White Mountains wc $40

1888 10 Cheops from the road to the glacier, BC wc $100
24 Morning mists, Ross Peak Valley wc $125
29 Beaver Foot Mountains, Leanchoil, BC wc $50
38 Hazy day, summit of the Rockies wc $100
42 Mount Carrol, Rogers Pass, BC wc $200
50 Painting wc
55 The days decline wc $100
56 A breeze, Casco wc $50
87 Sunset in the Selkirks $300
162 Ross Peak, Valley of the Glacier, BC $175
243 Ross Peak, from the 'Loop' wc $150
258 Valley of the Otter Tail wc $200

1889 117 Wet day, Fraser Canyon wc $50
118 Sunset on Mount Carrol, Rogers Pass wc $75
123 Ross Peak Glacier, Selkirks, BC wc $150
140 Junction of two glacial streams, Selkirks, BC wc $150
148 Looking across the valley of the north fork of the Illecillewaet, from an elevation of over 7000 feet wc $75
153 Clearing after a storm in the Selkirks, BC wc $75
156 English Bay, Vancouver, BC wc $125

157 Burrard Inlet, Vancouver, Bc wc $40
1890 5 Siwash canoes, Lake Harrison $100
120 Canyon of the Illecillewaet, BC wc $250
121 A reminiscence of the Rockies wc $200
122 A cascade near the glacier wc $175
123 Asulkan Glacier wc $175
124 In the forest, BC wc $100
125 A glacial torrent wc $100
126 Rainbow Falls, near Lake Harrison, BC wc $75
127 On the Fraser River, near Yale wc $75
128 Mountain gloom, Selkirks wc $50
1891 49 Indian summer, in the Canadian Rockies 1892-55 $250
142 Mount Angus at sunset wc
144 Snow clad monarch of the Rockies wc
145 Lake Louise wc
147 Emerald Lake wc
149 Evening in Trinity Bay wc
150 A valley in gloom wc
168 Cape Trinity wc
190 Rocky Mountain valley wc
199 Break, break, break on thy cold grey stones, O sea! wc
1892 107 Rocky Mountain canyon wc $200
111 On the Cornish coast wc $50
118 Street scene, Paris, near Notre Dame wc $30
140 Chepstow Castle wc $60
141 Kiosk, Pont St Michel wc $30
143 St Germaine, Paris wc $30
147 In St James' Park, London wc $30
151 Avenue in the Luxembourg, Paris wc $30
163 Au jardin de Luxembourg, Paris wc $50
1893 12 Le soir $350 F1-11
12a Landscape $300 F1-12
12b Evening, Holland $40 F1-13
163 Bank of Montreal, Montreal wc $75 F1-121
164 Feeding the pigeons, St Paul's Church Yard, London wc $65 F1-122
165 Evening, Hyde Park Corner wc $75
166 After rain, Place de la Concorde, Paris wc $75 F1-123
167 The morning milking hour, Holland wc $100 F1-124
168 The Thames, at London Bridge wc $125 F1-125
169 Cape Trinity wc F1-127 nfs
1894 14 London Bridge
15 Dutch interior, making wooden shoes, 'clumpers' worn by the peasantry
16 Portrait sketch
17 Study of a head
18 Rocks at low tide
19 October
152 Pont Neuf, Paris, evening after rain wc
153 Westminster wc 1895-4W
154 Mount Carrol (MacDonald) Selkirks wc
155 Chepstow Castle, in the Wye wc
1895 18 Chrissie, a sketch
19 Violet
20 A quiet pipe
20a A cavalier
5W The Strand wc
1897 17 Lights of a city street
18 On London Bridge
19 Island Park, Toronto
20 On Westminster Bridge
21 Feeding pigeons, St Paul's Church Yard, London
22 Grey day on the Thames
23 Surf
24 Forgotten melody
25 Breezy day, Holland
1898 13 A.D. Benjamin
14 Mrs R.S. Williams, Jr
15 Mrs T.A. Gale
137 Sunset at sea wc
138 On the Saguenay wc
139 Piccadilly, London wc
140 The Row, Hyde Park, London wc
141 The Queen's Diamond Jubilee, 1897 wc
142 Mountain solitude wc
1899 7 Rogers Pass, BC
8 Valley of the Selkirks
9 Farm in the Pitt Valley
10 Mount Baker, from Oak Bay, Victoria, BC
11 The Chancellor, Leanchoil, BC illus
12 Yale, BC
13 Rotten Row

14 Jubilee procession on Ludgate Hill
160 Gorge in the Fraser Canyon, BC wc
161 St Martin's in the Fields wc
1900 5 Hyde Park Corner, evening after rain
6 Farm in the Pitt Valley, the Golden Ears in the distance
7 Morning milking, Holland
8 Piccadilly
123 Rainy day in the Selkirks, BC wc
124 Above the clouds, view from Summit Avalande, Selkirks wc
125 Cloud girt peak in the Selkirks, Mount McDonald wc
126 The Hermit Range wc
127 Smoky weather on the Fraser, near Yale, BC wc
1901 2 London Bridge (Canadian Club, Hamilton) F2-2
3 Strawberry pickers, Oakville, Ontario F2-3
143 Above the clouds, Mount Aberdeen, Canadian Rockies wc F2-4
144 Smoky weather in Selkirks wc
1902 10 Queen Victoria. Original sketch from life
11 One of the 600, how we charged at Balaclava
12 Grandmother
13 Dozing
14 Near Land's End, Cornwall
15 Twilight on the Thames
172 Tintern Abbey wc
173 Montreal market, Jacques Cartier Square wc
174 Hyde Park Corner wc
175 St Paul's from the river wc
1902 F3, Rochester
4 Le soir $420
1903 6 The news of the day
141 Piccadilly, evening after rain wc
142 St Paul's from the Thames wc
143 Melrose Abbey wc
144 Moonrise, Putney Bridge wc
145 Charles I statue, Charing Cross wc
146 Ludgate Hill wc
147 Chingford Old Church wc
1904 17 Lights of a city street
18 At the threshold
19 A forgotten melody F4-6
20 St Paul's from the river
192 Hyde Park Corner, after a shower wc
193 Winter afternoon, Luxembourg wc F4-89
194 An old street, Coventry wc F4-90
195 In the park wc
195a Fraser River, near Yale, Siwash Indian salmon fishing wc F4-7
1904 F4, St Louis
91 In the park, a thirsty afternoon wc
1905 18 Fraser River, near Yale, Siwash Indians catching salmon (#19 not in cat)
20 Westminster Abbey, evening after rain
21 Canadian fishing boats at sea
22 Parting day
23 The lakes in the clouds
1906 18 A street in London
19 Waiting
20 London, Ludgate Hill
21 Yoho Valley
22 Chepstow Castle
23 Early morning, Holland
24 Fraser River, near Yale
1906 F5, Halifax
10 State funeral of Sir John Thompson, Premier of Canada. This picture, which contains portraits of many distinguished representatives of church and state, represents the scene in St Mary's Cathedral, Halifax, Jan 3 1895 $2,000 F6-14 (#11 not in cat)
12 London, looking up Ludgate Hill to St Paul's illus $300
13 Evening glow in the Selkirks $50
14 The Coast Guard Station, Cornwall, Eng illus $50
1907 17 October on the Fraser River
18 Albion's rockbound coast
213 Grey day, Fraser Canyon wc
214 Sunset on the Hermit wc
215 A bit of old Chiswick wc
216 Oldtime tobogganning wc

1907 F6, Sherbrooke
15 Sunrise on the Olympians $1,000
16 Making wooden shoes, 'klumpers', Holland $200
17 Grandma's miniature $200
18 Indian trail, Rockies $200
19 Sunset, Hermit Range $50
1908 14 An Indian trail in the Rockies
15 Mountain solitude
16 Eventide, Warwickshire
17 White Hall
1909M 6 October on the Fraser River
7 Heart of the Empire. Awarded Dow Prize, Art Association Montreal, 1909
8 Evening, Westminster
9 The source of the Illecillewaet
1909N 5 A glacier tarn in the Canadian National Park
6 Moonlight, Indian village, Pacific coast
1910 S2, Liverpool
5 Fraser Canyon, Siwash Indians catching salmon
1910 17 Hazy morning on the Thames
18 Tintern Abbey
19 Afternoon sunlight, Lake Louise
20 Pointe à Pic
1911 11 Cloud-girt glaciers of the Selkirks ◊NGC◊
12 Smoky London
13 Tower of London
14 Ludgate Hill
15 The Strand, London
16 Limehouse
1912 18 Victoria Glacier, Lake Louise
19 Lake O'Hara, summit of the Canadian Rockies
1912 S3, Winnipeg
10 The Great Divide, Canadian Rockies
11 The Olympians, from Victoria, BC
12 Bow Echo Rock, hazy morning
13 Lake Louise
1913 20 A glacier tarn
21 Mount Victoria, Lake Louise
22 'Where the lamps quiver so far in the river' Hood
23 Where snow fields gleam 'neath a summer sun S4-9 $600
24 In the Selkirks wc S4-10 $50
25 Old Curiosity Shop wc S4-11 $50
1914 14 Heart of the Selkirks, BC
15 Late summer
16 In a Canadian forest
17 In the Tête Jaune Pass, BC
1914 S5, Patriotic Fund
2 Glaciers of the Great Divide illus
1915 11 Deserted camp, Canadian Rockies, GTPR
12 A breezy upland, Surrey
13 Sunshine after rain, London
14 New Tower Bridge illus ◊AGO◊
1916 11 The 'Tattoo', Camp Borden
12 Cloud girt glaciers, Burgess Pass, BC
13 St Mary le Strand illus ◊NGC◊
14 King William Street, London wc
1918A 8 Britain's bulwarks, Land's End illus 1918N-9 illus
9 On the Thames, off Greenwich
10 Study of a head, the old tam
11 Coming storm in the Rockies 1918N-10
1918N 11 Thames barge off Greenwich
12 Trafalgar Square
1919 9 Meeting of the waters, Glacier, BC
10 Golden sunlight, Lake Louise illus
10a Mount Sir Rider, Fraser River, BC
1920 13 The Thames, near Westminster illus
14 The trackless forest, BC
15 Barges on the Thames, near Greenwich ◊AGO◊
16 Lake Louise wc
1921 11 Parting day, Canadian Rockies
12 Theatre hour, Leicester Square
13 Twilight, Holburn wc
14 Waterloo Bridge wc
1922 17 Mount Robson, BC
18 Surrey Hills, Reigate
19 Approach to Waterloo Bridge, London wc
20 Wet day, Trafalgar Square wc

port: by W.A. Sherwood, 1891-102

BELL-SMITH, JOHN
27 Dec 1810, Rotherhithe, Kent, Eng
30 Dec 1883, Toronto H M NGC R2 W78
1880 58 The rest by the way
88 The billet doux
1883 76 Woodland spring $400
294 View on St Helen's Island wc $50

BELLE, CHARLES ERNEST DE
17 May 1873, Budapest 3 Sep 1939, Montreal AGO CWW36 M NGC PMC TB2/3 ARCA 1919 Painter
Addr: 1914, 1059 Decarie Blvd, Montreal; 1915-18A, 1129 Decarie Blvd, Montreal; 1918N-27, 202 Dupuis Ave, Montreal; 1928, Montreal; 1929, Medical Arts Bldg, Montreal; 1930, 1538 Sherbrooke St W, Montreal; 1931, 202 Dupuis Ave, Montreal; 1932-7, 3602 Northcliffe Ave, Montreal; 1938-9, Montreal
1914 S5, Patriotic Fund
64 The mysterious wood illus
1915 58 His last day
59 Children's joy illus ◊NGC◊
1916 55 Depression
56 The last flowers pastel illus ◊NGC◊
1918A 44 The sisters ◊NGC◊
45 Madonna pastel illus
1918N 40 1919 illus ◊AGO◊
41 A bleak day pastel ◊NGC◊
1919 36 The first Communion
37 O Canada illus
1920 63 Mrs Pitcher
64 Mrs Edward Maxwell, and daughter illus
65 Re-united pastel
66 Sinless pastel
1921 40 Young Canada pastel
41 The eleventh of November pastel
42 Homeless pastel
43 Eva, 'Uncle Tom's cabin' pastel
1922 48 Dr Joseph Kaufmann
49 Music illus
50 The little orphans pastel
51 Christianity pastel S6-16
1924 40 The dancers pastel
41 The little dreamers pastel
42 Joyous
1925 48 The nightingale pastel
49 In the light
50 Heavenly love
51 Summer
1926 34 The dancers pastel $500
35 Symphony pastel
36 In the clouds pastel
37 Opal pastel
1927 45 Hon Judge R. Stanley Weir (Dr J.R. Goodall)
1929 44 The dancer pastel
45 The little Irish emigrant pastel $1,200
46 At the river pastel $400
47 Blossom time pastel $1,500
1930 39 The dancers pastel $600
40 The fairies pastel $600
41 The storm pastel $350
1931 59 Going to school pastel
60 The village pastel
61 Homewards pastel
62 The pool, winter pastel
1932 45 Trio pastel $300
46 Love pastel $300
47 Alone pastel $150
1933 47 Symphonie pastel $350
48 Music pastel $400
1937 55 When nature sleeps pastel $500
56 Purity pastel $350
1938 54 The dancer pastel $500
55 Sinless pastel $450

BELLEFLEUR, LEON
8 Feb 1910, Montreal AGO CC1 M NGC TB3 WWA70
1963 6 Métamorphose $900
1964N 6 Double croissant 45 x 34 illus $900

BELLEMARE, RAYMOND
25 Oct 1942, Nicolet, Que
RCA(e) 1976 Graphic Designer
Addr: 1979, Montreal
1970 123 Poster, Francine Vandelac Tricots
124 Poster, Il ne faut pas mourir pour ça/Don't let it kill you
#250-3 Raymond Bellemare & Gilles Robert
250 Book cover, Refus de la femme
251 Letterhead, Youville Stables
252 Letterhead, Théâtre de Capricorne
253 Poster, Design Canada, Concrete awards 1967
1971 Raymond Bellemare & Gilles

Robert
63G Symbole, Secrétariat d'Etat, Gouvernement du Canada
64G Symbole, une maison d'édition, Didier International
65G Symbole, manufacturier de vêtements féminis, Joseph Ribkoff Ltd
66G Carte du nouvel an, Gilles Robert & Associés Inc
67G Affiche pour un cinéma, Société Mirco-Film Inc

BENAZON, OPHRA (Mrs Michael Benazon)
22 May 1932, Israel
1970 3 Trip to Mars 90 x 30 $500

BENDER, E.P.
fl 1877-80 H
1880 372 Ship dock elevator, original des

BENGOUGH, WILLIAM
1857, Whitby, Ont 25 Sep 1932, Kiamesha Lake, Monticello, NY
AAA33 B H
ARCA 1880-1 Designer
Addr: 1880-3, Toronto
1883 289 Italian woman wc $20

BENJAMIN, GERSHON
Addr: 1915, 25 Drolet St, Montreal; 1919, 747 St Catherine St W, Montreal; 1920, 906A City Hall Ave, Montreal
1915 269 Childhood crayon
1919 196 Zylda drwg
1920 17 St Vincent de Paul
18 Trees and twilight
301 French Canadian girl drwg
302 Self portrait drwg

BENNET, GEORGE
1880 266 Cabinet des
278 Sideboard des

BENNET-ADLER, BENJAMIN
1897, England
Addr: 1919, 4410 St Catherine St W, Westmount, Que
1919 15 Miniature

BENNETT, JOHN ALFRED EVEREST
29 Mar 1919, Diss, Norfolk, Eng
CWW61 IO M
1948 11 Electra temp $150
1950 8 Flowering cactus 15 1/2 x 27 nfs
1951 8 Pineapples $180
1952 8 Tapestry in autumn wc $80
1953 8 Coffee table $100
1954 8 Flowering cactus 28 x 16 $500
1955 10 Bridge of Silence $150
1956 5 Still life 18 x 36 illus $150 T56-5
1957 9 Sombre bright $250
1959 8 Glint of thorn 46 x 28 $300
1964J 7 Rock 48 x 48 illus $300
1968 6 Jump suit 48 x 60 illus $600

BENSA, FRANCESCO Italian
c 1830, Nice B DBA G TB
1889 114 The Gorge of the Lima, Bagni de Lucca wc $100
139 View from Casa Zanetta, Bagni de Lucca wc $100

BENTHAM, DOUGLAS
1947, Rosetown, Sask WWA73
RCA(e) 1976 Sculptor
Addr: 1979, Dundurn, Sask

BENTLEY, WINIFRED K.
Addr: 1924, 33 Cooper St, Ottawa; 1929, 29 Robert St, Ottawa; 1933, 3 Hartington Pl, Ottawa
1924 229 Study plaster
1929 236 On the trail sculp $12
256 Day dream etch $5
1933 283 Companions of the mountain drwg $15

BENTON, MARGARET MAUD PEAKE
24 May 1907, South Orange, NJ
d c 1977 WWA53
Addr: 1934, 205 Madison Ave, Toronto
1934 24 Portrait miniatures wc
1938 16 Portrait nfs
1939 10 The Swiss costume wc $25
11 Miniatures wc nfs
1940 12 Rev George E. Hartwell, BA BD nfs
1942 9 Portrait miniatures nfs
1948 12 My mother
1949 7 Miss Lakshmi Rao, India nfs

BENY, WILFRED ROY ROLOFF
7 Jan 1924, Medicine Hat, Alta
AGO CC2 CWW79 M NGC TB3 WWA47
RCA(e) 1973 Photographer
Addr: 1979, Rome

BERCOVITCH, ALEKSANDER
15 Mar 1893, Cherson, Russia

Jan 1951, Montreal AGO TB3
Addr: 1933, 4480 de Bullion St, Montreal; 1935-7, 4264 St Dominique St, Montreal
1933 16 Ninelle, Sylvia and the rabbit T34-8
1935 12 St Dominique Street $150
1936 19 Still life $350
1937 21 Cliffs on Bonaventure Island $150 T38-3

BERGERON, SUZANNE (Mrs Jean Claude Suhit)
23 Jun 1930, Causapscal, Que AGO CC1 M NGC TB3
1964J 8 Cyclone noir 48 x 70 $800

BERGMAN, HENRY ERIC
10 Nov 1893, Dresden 8 Feb 1958, Winnipeg AGO CC2 M TB2/3
Addr: 1931, 368 Baltimore Rd, Winnipeg
1931 20 My cactus $125
383 Castle Mountain wd engr $12
1940 167 Ontario wd engr $12
168 Vine and willow wd engr $10
1941 10 Hail clouds $150 T42-3
233 Celastrus scandens wd engr $11

BERKOVITZ, MARTIN
12 Nov 1945, Toronto IO
1964J 7 Remembered beach figure 25 1/2 x 18 $90

BERLIN, EUGENIA
30 Apr 1905, Kharkov, Russia M NGC TB3 WWA47
1942 159 Carol, portrait study sculp nfs
1956 46 Aspiration sculp $300

BERRINGTON, ADRIAN
c 1887, England 4 Apr 1923, London, Eng
Addr: 1921, 97 Avenue Rd, Toronto
1921 191 Thirlstane etch

BERSUDSKY, SID
1913, NB
RCA(e) 1974 Industrial designer
Addr: 1979, Toronto

BERTHON, GEORGE THEODORE
3 May 1806, Royal Palace, Vienna 18 Jan 1892, Toronto AGO B EC H M R2 W78
ARCA 1880-1 Painter
Addr: 1880-1, Toronto

BERWICK, ROBERT A.D.
see THOM, RONALD, 1964N
THOMPSON, CHARLES, 1964N
PRATT, CHARLES, 1966

BESANT, DEREK MICHAEL
15 Jul 1950, Fort Macleod, Alta
RCA(e) 1978 Print maker
Addr: 1979, Midnapore, Alta

BETHUNE, DEBAY (Miss)
Addr: 1916, 23 Lincoln Ave, Montreal
1916 15 Before rain
16 Landscape

BETHUNE, EDWARD R.C. (TED)
b Kamloops, BC
1970 125 24-sheet poster, Bapco paints are hip
126 24-sheet poster, Just add Bapco
127 Birth announcement, Mr Milkman
128 Symbol, British Columbia Hydro & Power Authority
129 Annual report, British Columbia Hydro & Power Authority

BETTERIDGE, LOIS ETHERINGTON (Mrs Keith J. Betteridge)
6 Nov 1928, Drummondville, Que WWA78
RCA(e) 1978 Gold & silver smith
Addr: 1979, Ottawa

BETTINVILLE, HENRI
1938, Belgium
Addr: 1976, Montreal
1976 S12, Montreal
155 Phase III nore seragraphie/serigr 24 x 24 illus

BETTS, M.D. (Miss)
Addr: 1913, 536 Queen's Ave, London, Ont
1913 26 Danseuse, Miss Norah Blake, Miss Kitty Betts ivory
27 Jeune italien ivory

BICE, CLARE CM LLD
24 Jan 1909, Durham, Ont 18 May

1976, St John's CWW64 M WWA47
ARCA 1940 RCA 1966 Council Painter
Addr: 1936, 135 Inkerman St, London; 1941-71, London

1936 20 Gloucester fishing boats $100
1938 17 Morning mist, Cornwall $125
18 Miss Elizabeth Inksater illus nfs F11-9 34 x 28
1939 12 Building the new wharf, Nova Scotia $350
13 A girl from Wales $300
1940 13 James Michael McCormick nfs
1942 10 Fifteen, almost $250
1946 9 Dr Mary Wong nfs T47-5
1948 13 Miss Ida Oya $300
14 A northern landscape $350
15 Still life $250
1949 8 Winter, Laurentians $200 T50-2
1950 9 Setting for a sea piece 20 x 24 $125
1951 9 The little cove, Newfoundland $250
1954 9 Horseback in the Bois 40 x 50 $500 ≬LAG≬
1955 11 The Tuileries, March $250
1957 10 Place Furstemburg, Paris $350
1958 12 Concerto for October nfs S11-5 (Sarnia Public Library and Art Gallery)
1959 9 Canadian wilderness 36 x 48 illus $600 S10-7 nfs
1960 8 Grey music 36 x 48 illus $700
9 Bright glamour of October 34 x 42 $500
1964N 8 Interior with figure 40 x 50 illus $650
1967 4 Blue pool 30 x 40 illus $700
1970 5 On the terrace 40 x 50 illus nfs DW 1970 oil & lucite on canvas S11-6

BIELER, ANDRE CHARLES LLD
8 Oct 1896, Lausanne ACO CC2 CWW79 IO M NGC WWA47
ARCA 1942 RCA 1959 Sr 1966 Council Painter
Addr: 1927-9, Ste Famille, Ile d'Orléans, Qué; 1930, 1100 Beaver Hall Hill, Montreal; 1933, 2039 Peel St, Montreal; 1935, 3745 ave de l'Oratoire, Montréal; 1936, 12 Dundas St, Kingston; 1942-71/79, Kingston

1927 9 Femme d'en bas de Québec temp
10 Le vieux cultivateur fresque
1928 15 Procession à Ste Famille $300
16 Soir d'automne, Ile d'Orléans $300
1929 16 Labour du printemps $430
1930 15 Pêcheur gaspésien $350
1933 17 La fournée de pain $300 T34-9
1935 13 Sweet corn $260
310 La laine des moutons print $12
1936 21 Settler's first crop $350
1940 14 Gatineau madonna illus $325 T41-5 ≬NGC≬
1941 11 Le batême, Charlevoix County $180
1942 11 Canadians at Dieppe oil & temp $175 T43-2
1943 4 Ceux de la Gatineau $180 T44-2
1950 10 The arrow maker 24 x 30 $400
1955 12 Tout en cherchat $350
1956 6 Art and society, the private view illus $800 T56-6
1958 13 Flowers for Hotel Dieu
1960 10 Classic figures 24 x 30 $280
1961 12 Classic landscape 24 x 28 illus $500 S10-9
1964J 9 Spadina Avenue 48 x 72 illus $1,000
1964N 9 Is it really true? 48 x 72 illus $1,000 1965-9 S10-8
1970 6 Le trésor 36 x 48 $1,200
DW 1960 Art and society, the studio group oil on board 48 x 60
port: bust, by M. Winslow, 1944-154

BIELER, ANDRE CHARLES THEODORE (TED)
23 Jul 1938, Kingston B CC1 CWW79 IO M WWA76
RCA(e) 1973 Council Sculptor
Addr: 1979, Locust Hill, Ont

1963 78 Inside out figure laminate $1,700
1966 123 Menorah, Beth Israel Synagogue, Peterborough. maquette Craig, Zeidler & Strong architects

BIERSTADT, ALBERT American
7 Jan 1830, Solingen, n Dusseldorf
19 Feb 1902, New York B F Gr H TB
Addr: 1886, 1271 Broadway, New York
1886 Fla, London, Eng
1986, artist number
Montmorenci Falls, Quebec
(Marquis of Lorne)
Quebec Citadel
(Marquis of Lorne)
View from Government House,
Ottawa (HRH Princess Louise)

BILLAUX, MARY JANE HELENE (Mrs Hugh
Clifford)
b 1903
1954 10 Woman with red hair 24 x
30 $300

BINNING, BERTRAM CHARLES
10 Feb 1909, Medicine Hat, Alta
16 Mar 1976, West Vancouver AGO
CCI M NGC WWA47
ARCA 1954 RCA 1966 Painter
Addr: 1955-61, Vancouver; 1961-71,
Hollyburn, BC
1950 11 Seaside facade 21 x 48
$400
1965 10 Summer sea 28 x 35 $450
S10-10
1967 6 St Elmo's shield 35 x 35
$600
DW 1967 The shield of Electra 36 x 36

BIRD, JOHN ALEXANDER HARRINGTON
23 May 1846, England 3 Jan 1936,
Hammersmith, London B DBA DVP G
H TB1/3 WBA
ARCA 1880-8 Painter
Addr: 1880-3, Montreal; 1884, St
Catherine St, Montreal; 1885-8,
Montreal
1882 143 Approaching storm on the
St Lawrence wc $30
176 Study of a tiger wc $40
1883 28 Troubador $125
1884 40 Going to the meet $100
S1-147 $80
101 The dicers wc $100 S1-69
$75

BIRIUKOVA, YULIA
21 Feb 1897, St Petersburg
Addr: 1930-7, 25 Severn St, Toronto
1930 16 Countess Fersen
17 Madame G. pastel 1933-18
1932 16 Signora G.B. Ambrosi
1936 23 A prairie settler $400
T37-6
1937 22 Ontario farmer $200 T38-4

BIRKS-ELLIS-RYRIE, LIMITED
Addr: 1938, Toronto
1938 S8, Toronto
25 Fluted bowl
26 Grape chased bowl
27 Hammered bowl
28 Georgian bowl
29 Fancy border bowl
30 Comport
31 Candelabra
32 4 piece Ebon Coker
33 Hot water Ebon Coker
34 Tea service and kettle,
Chantilly
35 Waiter-gadroon and shell
36 Brentwood tea pot
37 8 pieces showing the oper-
ation of Brentwood tea pot
38 Smoker's companion
39-41 3 piece toilet sets,
Duchess, Alexandra, Lucille
42 Saxon desert spoon
43 4 pieces showing the oper-
ation of Saxon desert spoon
44 George II desert fork
45 5 pieces showing the oper-
ation of George II desert
fork
46 Cabinet of 16 spoons,
sterling one illus

BISSON, HENRI
b Ste Marie, Beauce Co, Que CNS36
1941 204 Nudy study plaster $200

BITTORF, DONALD GEORGE
13 Aug 1926, Edmonton
RCA(e) 1975, Architect
Addr: 1979, Edmonton

BLACHFORD, BERNICE MABEL
31 Aug 1923, Montreal
1961 13 The city 39 x 23 $350

BLACK, BARBARA see FLOOD, LOUISE B.

BLACK, BETTY (Mrs Stokvis)
b 1928
1967 5 Untitled #2 30 x 24 $150

BLACK, FRANK CHARLES
18 Dec 1892, Southall, Eng flg 1976
1944 13 Back street, Bermuda $350
14 Ground swell $400 T45-6

1945 15 Moonlight, Bermuda $125
T46-3
16 Gloucester harbour $125

BLACK, LOUISE see FLOOD, LOUISE

BLACK, SAMUEL
5 Jun 1913, Ardrossan, Scot M
RCA(e) 1977 RCA 1978 Painter
Addr: 1979, Bowen Island, BC
DW 1978 Three gulls. Nov 1977
wc 29 1/2 x 22 1/2

BLACKADER, GORDON HORNE
see BAROTT, ERNEST, 1937

BLACKSTOCK, HARRIET
Addr: 1927, 216 Prince Arthur St W, Montreal
1927 255 The sea farer plaster
1928-161

BLACKWELL, ANNE
fl 1868-90 H
Addr: 1883, 78 1/2 King St E, Hamilton
1883 119 Fruit with foliage $30

BLACKWOOD (Mrs)
H
1882 42 Dead ducks
83 Dead game

BLACKWOOD, DAVID LLOYD
7 Nov 1941, Wesleyville, Bonavista Bay, Nfld IO M WWA73
RCA(e) 1975 Council Print maker
Addr: 1979, Port Hope, Ont
1965 11 The messenger etch 20 x 25
ØLAGØ
1970 7 Capt Edward Bishop with officers on the bridge of the SS Eagle. Lost party series 20 x 30 $300

BLADEN, GEORGE W.
Addr: 1918N-20, 84 St François Xavier St, Montreal
1918N 13 The checkered coat
1920 19 Summer reverie

BLAIN, SUZANNE
Addr: 1976, Montreal
1976 S12, Montreal
61 Torsion #1 marble 8 1/2 x 22 1/2 illus

BLAIS, ROGER (Mrs)
1939 14 Bertholot Tower, Quebec
$100

BLAKSTAD, RALPH KENNETH
24 Aug 1929, Vancouver
1963 7 The picnic $1,500

BLAND, JOHN
13 Nov 1911, Lachine, Que CWW79
ARCA 1959 RCA 1967 Architect
Addr: 1959-71/79, Montreal
1964N Bland, LeMoyne, Edwards & Shine
102-4 Northern Electric Research and Development Laboratories, Ottawa. General view, exterior. Detail of corner, illus. Overall plot plan
DW 1968 Northern Electric Research and Development, Ottawa photo 23 1/4 x 19 3/4
port: bust, by O. Wheeler, 1951-127
see also LeMoyne, Roy, 1963-113

BLANKSTEIN, MORLEY
30 Mar 1924, Winnipeg
RCA(e) 1975 Architect
Addr: 1979, Winnipeg

BLASCHKE, ELSIE (Mrs Ernest Blaschke)
b Vienna
1965 12 Arctic's Eden wd cut 16 x 17 $80
1966 5 Palazze Franchetti, Venezia print 12 x 20 $80

BLASER, HERMAN
25 Jul 1900, Thun, Switzerland
1939 15 The high fence wc $35
1941 12 Envy wc $150
13 Summer chitchat wc $150

BLATCHLEY, WILLIAM DANIEL
1838, Bristol, Eng 1903, Toronto
B H
Addr: 1895, Toronto; 1896-9, 119 Rose Ave, Toronto; 1900, Brook Cottage, Doncaster, Ont; 1901, 119 Rose Ave, Toronto; 1902, King St, Toronto; 1903, York Chambers, Toronto
1885 239 Pastoral wc $75
1891 162 Path through the ferns wc
172 Sunset wc

196 Vale of Avoca, Rosedale wc
1895 1W A cold and dull day wc
2W A warm afternoon wc
3W Mimico Grove station wc
1896 188 The glow of autumn wc
189 The decline of summer wc
190 A quiet corner wc
1897 2W The model wc
3W Spring on the hill wc
1898 135 In the woods wc
136 A breezy day at the island wc
1899 154 The path to the mill race wc
155 Anxious moments wc
156 Morning light wc
1900 128 A breezy day wc
129 The turkey wc
130 A Canadian pastoral wc
1901 145 Declining day wc F2-12
146 A Canadian homestead wc
1902 176 Solitude wc
177 October wc
178 Summer time wc
1903 152 Fading summer wc
153 Passing storm

BLATHERWICK, K.R.
see CHAPMAN, ALFRED, 1946

BLAZEJE, ZBIGNIEW
2 Jun 1942, Barnaul, Siberia AGO IO WWA73
RCA(e) 1976 Sculptor
Addr: 1979, Toronto
1966 71 Contrapuntal #2 sculp 30 1/4 x 13 x 13 $400

BLOOMFIELD, EDGAR
Addr: 1919, 3001 Point Grey Rd, Vancouver
1919 11 An old sealer volunteers

BLOUIN, ANDRE
17 May 1920, Nantes, France
ARCA 1970 Architect
Addr: 1971/76/79, Montreal
1967 André and Patrick Blouin
99-07 Place des Nations, Expo 67 Montreal. A.Vue aérienne C.Vue en diagonale de la Place vers l'entrée principale D.La tribune des invités de marque et le mur emblème G.Approches des restaurant sud-est par un accès secondaire H.Tribune de Presse et Place vues de l'entrée principale à travers les sculptures de Jordi Bonet I.Vue générale montrant restaurant-terrasse, scène, place et gradins L.Place et restaurant sud-est vue de la terrasse du restaurant nord-ouest R.Rencontre à angle droit de deux passerelles V. Détails des supports des passerelles aux coins extérieurs
1968 Beaulieu, Lambert & Tremblay
94-7 Expo 67, Expo Express station. A.General view Notre Dame station B.Aerial view of Notre Dame station expressing the principle of the roof system, Place des Nations station in background C. Notre Dame station, view of suspended ramp, pedestrian bridge and stairs D.Interior view showing the canvas roof system
1976 S12, Montreal
Blouin & Blouin
97 Maison BGL, Ste Adèle, Que 2 illus

BLOUIN, PATRICK
see BLOUIN, ANDRE, 1967, 1976

BLUMENFELD, HANS
18 Oct 1892, Osnabrueck, Germany CWW79
RCA(e) 1975 Architect Town planner
Addr: 1979, Toronto

BOBAK, BRUNO JOSEPH (Bronislaw)
23 Dec 1923, Wawelowski, Poland AGO CC1 M NGC WWA47
ARCA 1959-63 RCA(e) 1973 Painter
Addr: 1969-61, Vancouver; 1962-3/79, Fredericton
1963 8 The white chemise $800

BOBAK, MOLLY JOAN LAMB (Mrs Bruno Joseph Bobak)
25 Feb 1922, Vancouver AGO CC2 M NGC WWA47
RCA(e) 1973 Painter
Addr: 1979, Fredericton

BOILARD, RAPHAEL
Addr: 1933, 4222 De Lorimier Ave, Montreal
1933 240 Petit château, style

mauresque arch photo

BOISSEAU, ALFRED
23 Feb 1823, Paris 1901, Buffalo, NY B Gr H
ARCA 1885-9 Painter
Addr: 1883, Montreal; 1884, 212 Notre Dame St, Montreal; 1885-6, Montreal; 1887, 1613 Notre Dame St, Montreal; 1888, Ottawa
1882 93 Old French apple peddler $65
111 Mr Barron, portrait
1883 2 A Montreal butcher's shop $175
104 Salut, a study from life, a Montreal carter $150
1884 8 The grandmother $150
43 Montreal cabbies, a rush for a fare $300
47 "Witness and Star, sir?" $75
68 A Caughnawaga squaw $75
78 Mme Adelina Patti $200
1885 30 A poor old man $30
184 Italian selling plaster figures $125
190 Under a cloud $30
1887 80 T.B. Durocher

BOLLEY, ANDREA
1949, Guelph, Ont
Addr: 1976, Toronto
1976 S12, Montreal
6 Marks acry 60 x 84 illus

BOLTON, MURIEL see BOULTON, MURIEL

BOLTON, RICHARD ERNEST
18 Mar 1907, Montreal CNS40 CWW79
ARCA 1963 RCA 1968 Architect
Addr: 1937, 1178 Phillips Pl, Montreal; 1964-71, Montreal; 1979, Westmount, Que
1937 235-6 House, J. McFetrick, Esq, Pointe Claire, Que
1964N Bolton, Ellwood & Aimers, to 1966
105-7 Presbyterian College, Montreal. Chapel exterior, view. Interior view looking into garden. General plan
1965 110-11 Miss Edgar's and Miss Cramp's School, Montreal. Main entrance. Building, front view illus
112-13 McGill University, Royal Victoria College, Roscoe Wing. Room interior. Front of building
1966 176 St Bride's College, St John's, Nfld. A.T. Galt Durnford, consultant model
DW 1969 St Bride's College photo 23 3/4 x 39 3/4
see also Fetherstonhaugh, H. 1947-1954; Durnford, A.T.G, 1957-1963

BOND, CHARLES HERBERT ACTON
Jun 1869, London, Eng 29 Apr 1924, Toronto H
Addr: 1909, 19 Wellington St, Toronto
1909M 144 Bank and office building
1909N 7 Sketch, entrance hall, steamer 'Toronto'
8 Refectory, Queen Victoria, Niagara Falls Park

BOND, MARION
b Antigonish, NS M
1938 19 Modesty Cove $75
1944 15 Five and ten $100
1945 17 And then such an earth $100 T46-4

BOND, WILLIAM J.
Addr: 1918A, 193 1st Ave, Toronto
1918A 12 The edge of the cliff
13 September

BONET, JORDI
7 May 1932, Barcelona 25 Dec 1979
M TB3 WWA73
ARCA 1966 Sculptor
Addr: 1966-71, Montreal; 1979, Mont St Hilaire, Que
1967 103 Place des Nations, Expo 67 Montreal, sculptures Blouin & Blouin architects
1970 78 Lieu sculp 48 x 96 x 48
31A National Arts Centre, doors. Lebensold architect

BONHAM, DONALD
9 Nov 1940, Oklahoma City
RCA(e) 1975 Sculptor
Addr: Montreal (1978)

BONIN, PAUL
Addr: 1938, Montreal
1938 S8, Toronto
47 Three display cards for Coty

BONNET, A.L.
Addr: 1938, Toronto

1938 S8, Toronto
380 Wallpaper design. Prize award $100. Canadian Wallpaper Manufacturers Ltd

BONNYCASTLE, MURRAY CARLOW
18 Aug 1909, Campbellford, Ont
WWA47
Addr: 1934-6, 86 Lowther Ave, Toronto; 1937, 80 Lowther Ave, Toronto
1934 25 Lou with bangs $85
26 Ross $70
1935 14 Benny, summer morning $135
1936 23 1935 $250 T37-7
1937 23 Snow at midnight $150
1938 20 Victoriana $175
1940 15 Aoife $150 T41-6

BORDEN, MARJORIE MARY
13 Feb 1911, Montreal
Addr: 1931, 8 Tormey St, Ottawa
1931 21 Bianca $100

BORDUAS, PAUL
b 1940
1965 72 Building #1 sculp 24h illus $300

BORDUAS, PAUL EMILE
1 Nov 1905, St Hilaire, Que 22 Feb 1960, Paris AGO B CC1 CWW58 M NGC TB3 WWA47
RCA Posthumous 1975 Painter
'Homage à Borduas', by G. Molinari DW 1969

BORENSTEIN, SAMUEL
15 Jan 1908, Suwalkie, Poland 15 Dec 1969, Montreal W78
Addr: 1935, 1100 Beaver Hall Hill, Montreal; 1937, 3543 Ste Famille St, Montreal
1935 311 St James Street drwg $50
1937 24 Canadian National Station wc nfs
1941 14 Street scene wc nfs
1964N 10 Street scene 36 x 48

BOSWELL, HAZEL
1882, Quebec City
Addr: 1911, 24 St Ann St, Quebec; 1924, 19 St Geneviève Ave, Quebec
1911 17 Woman's head
1924 12 The potato gatherers wc

BOUCHARD, GEORGE LORNE HOLLAND
19 Mar 1913, Montreal 26 Apr 1978, Montreal M WWA47
ARCA 1943 RCA 1965 Council Painter
Addr: 1931, 71 Laurier Blvd, L'Abord à Plouffe, Que; 1937, c/o Dennison, Drummondville, Que; 1944-50, Drummondville, Que; 1951-7, Verdun, Que; 1958-71, Montreal
1931 22 Quinze River, northern Ontario $125
1937 24 Gaspé landscape $375
1938 21 Sunny headland $50
22 Malbaie mist $50
1939 16 Le boulanger du coin $100
1941 15 Souvenir $350
1942 12 March at Mechins, lower St Lawrence $450
13 Barnston's Pinnacle, Eastern Townships gouache $150
1943 5 Barn interior $75
6 View, Baie St Paul $75
1945 18 Scene near Douglastown, Gaspé $200 T46-5
1947 15 Evening vespers, Douglastown, Gaspé $500
1948 16 Boyhood days, Gaspé coast wc $150
17 Meurling Refuge, Montreal nfs
1949 9 Scene at Barachois, Gaspé coast gouache $200
1950 12 Northern twilight 24 x 30 $300
1951 10 East coast $450
1954 11 In Quebec, March 20 x 26 $350
1955 13 Sous le Fort, Québec $350
1956 7 Fisherman's landing illus $500 T56-7
1957 11 Winter harbour $750
12 Canal $600
1958 14 St Lambert Lock, St Lawrence Seaway illus $900
15 Charles Dickens Street, Montreal nfs
1959 10 Le Tunner de Mont Royal 25 x 40 $800
11 Le travers, Québec-Lévis 20 x 36 illus $600
1960 11 Spring 24 x 48 illus $900
1961 15 Season's rest 24 x 52 illus $1,000
1963 9 Winter's rest $1,000
1965 13 Dégel d'avril 18 x 30 illus DW 1966 S10-11
1966 6 April fields 32 x 48 $1,200
1967 7 La quete 50 x 65
port: by L.P. Panneton, 1947-134

BOULTBEE, ALFRED E.
1863, Toronto 7 Dec 1928, Toronto
H
Addr: 1895, 224 Carlton St, Toronto; 1897, Toronto
1891 157 A sketch at Guelph wc
171 In old Quebec wc
1895 6W The gates of Carisbrook Castle, Isle of Wight wc
7W Near Penzance, Cornwall, England wc
8W Treguainton Cairn, Cornwall, England wc
9W Porchester Castle, near Portsmouth, England wc
1897 8W Morning on the Thames, near Kew wc
9W Pont Neuf, Paris wc
10W The fountain of Villeneuve wc

BOULTBEE, CONSTANCE M.
fl 1890-7 H
Addr: 1897, Toronto
1897 11 Portrait
5W Carisbrook Castle, Isle of Wight wc

BOULTBEE, HESILL (Mrs)
17 Nov 1913, Kennilworth, Eng
d May 1966
1945 19 Houses on the hill, La Malbaie $75
20 Up the mountains nfs
1961 16 Cathedral wc 19 x 25 $85

BOULTON, MURIEL CAMERON WELSH
13 Feb 1881, Charlottetown d 1957, England M NGC
Addr: 1908, 25 Lewis St, Quebec; 1909M, 18 St Ann St, Quebec; 1910, 57 d'Artigny St, Quebec; 1911-12, 130 St Augustine St, Quebec
1908 4 The chess problem ◊NGC◊ Bolton mispr
1909M 25a Yvonne Bolton mispr
1910 21 La petite laveuse
1911 18 A studio interior, Paris
1912 10 A corner of my studio
258 Marguerite pencil study

BOURASSA, NAPOLEON
21 Oct 1827, L'Acadie, Que 27 Aug 1916, Lachenaie, Que CWW10 EC H M Mo98/12 NGC R1 TB3 W78
RCA 1880 Ret 1892 Council Painter
Addr: 1880-91, Montreal; 1892-10, Monte Bello, Que; 1911-16, Montreal
1880 160 Deborah cart wc
169 God blessing Abraham cart wc
173 Death of Jacob cart wc
185 Judith cart wc
195 God blessing Isaac cart wc
226 Esther cart wc
249 Anna cart wc
250 The Virgin's coronation (Legend) Sketch of painting executed in Notre Dame de Lourdes Chapel
251 Various sketches
1881 245 Légende de Berceau. L'Enfant courit aux anges $200 1882-68 DW 1883 11 1/4 x 10 1/2 arched at top
1882 185 Proclamation of the dogma of Immaculate Conception. For cupola of Notre Dame de Lourdes wc
186 Coronation of Holy Virgin. For church of Notre Dame de Lourdes wc

BOURKE, RICHARD DAVID
22 Oct 1931, Montreal
ARCA 1970 Architect
Addr: 1971/79, Montreal

BOUSFIELD, ROBERT WILLIAM GAMBIER
see TAYLOR, ANDREW, 1886
Bourfield mispr

BOWIE, THOMAS TAYLOR
11/8/1905, Linlithgow, Scot DBA DVP M
1954 101 Lion sculp 20 x 28 $200
1955 100 Torso sculp $1,000

BOWMAN, J.M.
Addr: 1938, Toronto
1938 S8, Toronto
E.W. Reynolds Co, Limited
218 Cylinder carton for Simms lather brush. J.M. Bowman, H.M. Hassell

BOYD, EDWARD FINLEY
1878, Montreal
Addr: 1902, 247 Mountain St, Montreal; 1907, Montreal; 1908, 153 Bleury St, Montreal; 1909, 255 Bleury St, Montreal; 1920, 247 Mountain St, Montreal
1902 16 Snow
17 A garden
1907 19 The old farmstead

20 Evening dec panel over mantle
217 The wheelright's yard wc F6-20 $35
1907 F6, Sherbrooke
21 French homestead $60
1908 20 Misty morning, France
21 Old street, Pont de l'Arche, France
1909M 22 Going to the bull fight, Seville 1909N-9
1909N 10 Red autumn S2-6
1920 20 Greenfarms road

BOYD, JAMES HENDERSON
16 Dec 1928, Ottawa AGO M WWA59
RCA(e) 1978 Print Maker
Addr: 1979, Ottawa
1971 15A Carved door in Conference Centre, office building for PSAC Holdings Ltd, Ottawa. S. Havor architect

BOYLE, JOHN BERNARD
23 Sep 1941, London, Ont
RCA(e) 1974 Painter
Addr: 1979, Allenford, Ont

BRADFORD, JOHN LOCKE
1 Apr 1897, Windsor, NS
1947 197 Deep sea wd sculp nfs

BRADSHAW, EVA THERESA
1871, London, Ont 29 Aug 1938, London, Ont
Addr: 1902-3, 346 Dufferin Ave, London; 1904, Toronto; 1906, 346 Dufferin Ave, London; 1907, London; 1920, 491 Richmond St, London
1902 18 Violets
19 Roses
1903 18 Roses
18a Daisies
1904 21 Roses
22 Violets
1906 8 Pink roses
9 Yellow roses
10 Grapes
1907 21 Study of cherries E.J. mispr
1920 21 and 22 Still life Eva J. mispr

BRADY, CYRIL PATRICK
12 Mar 1894, Toronto
Addr: 1915-18, 413 Palmerston Blvd, Toronto; 1920-2, 510 Bloor St W, Toronto
1915 15 The derelict
16 Portrait of a Spaniard
1918A 14 Mr H.S. Palmer, ARCA
15 Miss Marie Halloran
1920 23 The black cat
24 Girl in smock
1921 15 Sketch of a Mounty
1922 21 The yellow shawl

BRAITSTEIN, MARCEL
11 Jul 1935, Charleroi, Belgium
AGO CC2 M WWA62
ARCA 1971 Sculptor
Addr: 1979, Hudson Heights, Que
1964J 69 Insects sculp 24 x 35 $600
1966 72 Three warriors steel 32h $750
73 Diplomat steel 32h $600
1970 79 Contestation sculp 32 x 12 1/2 x 7 $900

BRANDES, RALPH
1970 133 Book, Ontario

BRANDTNER, FRITZ
28 Jul 1896, Danzig 7 Nov 1969, Montreal AGO CC2 M NGC W78 WWA47
Addr: 1935, 1255 Fort St, Montreal
1935 15 Corner Fort Street and Tupper $90 T36-5
312 The tempest stilled des st gl window $100
1938 S8, Toronto
48 Folder and magazine
1950 13 The truth shall make you free. In two parts, each 45 x 25 $1,000

BRANGERS, ERNEST MAURICE
23 Dec 1928, Toronto
1950 14 Carnival 21 x 32 $75

BREEZE, CLAUDE HERBERT
9 Oct 1938, Nelson, BC AGO M
RCA(e) 1974 Painter
Addr: 1979, Toronto

BRENDER A BRANDIS, GERARD WILLIAM
13 May 1942, Maarn, Netherlands
IO WWA78
1970 8 Engraver's sketch book #1 9 1/2 x 12 1/4 $75
1971 3 Forage corn 14 x 9 $85

BRETT, CARL
17 May 1928, Cork, Eire
RCA(e) 1974 Graphic designer
Addr: 1979, Toronto

1970 130 Symbol, Lawron Industries
131 Symbol and application, Canadian Conference of the Arts
132 New Year card
1971 5G Book, Poetry of relevance 2. Methuen
6G Corporate image, Hickling-Johnstone
7G Letterhead, Ecologistics Limited

BREWSTER, WENDELL MOORE
1938 23 Twilight birches pastel $100

BREWSTER, ZILLA RUTH (Mrs Wendell Moore Brewster)
26 Aug 1914, Toronto
1944 16 By the path wc $50

BRIANSKY, RITA (Mrs Joseph Prezament)
25 Aug 1925, Grajewa, Poland M WWA59
1961 17 Discovery etch 6 x 11 $25
18 The stargazer etch 8 x 11 $25
1964N 11 Adolescence etch 7 x 11 $34
1967 8 Midsummer 22 x 36 $350

BRICE, ED. E. English
fl 1912-24 DBA
Addr: 1912, 144 Nepean St, Ottawa
1912 21 Sketch at Reading, England wc

BRIDGMAN, GEORGE BRANDT
5 Nov 1864, n Byng, Ont 16 Dec 1943, New Rochelle, NY H Mo12 WWA 36
ARCA 1891-2 Painter
Addr: 1891-2, Toronto
1891 6 Winter
9 M. le Curé, quietude
10 The turnpike
11 Young musician

BRIGDEN, CORRY WILLIAM
29 Sep 1912, Toronto AGO
Addr: 1936-7, 55 Gormley Ave, Toronto
1936 24 Fishermen wc $50
1937 303 Children of Quebec dry pt $10
304 For the old is the mending of the nets block pr $10
1938 24 Twisted silo $200
1938 S8, Toronto
380 Wallpaper design. Hon mention, Canadian Wallpaper Manufacturers Limited
1939 17 Edge of the town wc $50
18 Early winter snowball wc $50
1940 16 Road from Trout Mills $175

BRIGDEN, FREDERICK HENRY
9 Apr 1871, London, Eng 4 Mar 1956, Bolton, Ont AGO EC CNS40 M NGC PMC TB2 WWA47
ARCA 1934 RCA 1939 Sr 1943 Council Painter
Addr: 1896, Toronto Engraving Co, Toronto; 1898-05, 92 Bay St, Toronto; 1906-8, 103 Rose Ave, Toronto; 1909-11, 92 Bay St, Toronto; 1912-13, 164 Richmond St W, Toronto; 1914, 160 Richmont St W, Toronto; 1915, 190 Richmond St W, Toronto; 1920-37, 160 Richmond St W, Toronto; 1938-56, Toronto
1896 191 Meadowvale Bridge wc
192 A river study wc
1898 17 Valley of the Don, evening
133 On the way to Bradford wc
134 Goldenrod wc
1901 154 A pool in the meadow wc F2-13
155 Early September wc
156 Study at sundown wc F2-14
1902 179 Evening over the hills wc
180 A hillside pasture wc
181 In September wc
1902 F3, Rochester
5 The valley $120 1903-137 wc
1903 138 Pasture on the hill wc
139 Moonrise wc
140 Evening over the hills wc
1904 196 Sunset glow wc F4-92
197 Ayrshires wc F4-93
198 The heart of the valley wc F4-94
199 The winding stream wc F4-95
1905 15 The sunlit headland (Mr C. R. Mitchell)
16 Fundy's rockbound coast
17 Lengthening shadows
1906 27 The silver stream F5-15 illus $100
28 Nova Scotia valley
29 In the valley of the Kennebecasis
30 Autumn on the hills F5-16

$75
1906 F5, Halifax
17 Moonrise $30
1907 218 The brook wc
219 By the river wc
220 At low tide wc
1907 F6, Sherbrooke
32 In the Eastern Townships $100
33 Sunset $50
34 An Ayrshire herd $40
35 Thistledown $40
36 Moonrise $35
37 A trout stream $25
1908 13 On a New Brunswick farm
1909M 17 Sunset, north Ontario
18 Coast of Lake Superior
1909N 11 Among the hills, Nova Scotia
12 In Greville Bay, NS
1910 22 Fundy's coast
23 The lumber road
24 Coast scene
1910 S2, Liverpool
7 Bay of Fundy coast wc
8 The silver stream wc
1911 19 The golden hour wc 1912-115 S3-15
20 In the north country wc
21 A Quebec pastoral wc
1912 22 Summer afternoon
23 After the rain
1912 S3, Winnipeg
14 Canadian waterfall wc
162 Old stage coach b&w
163 Rock bound coast b&w
164 Market place, Toronto b&w
1913 28 In the hardwood bush
29 Early morning in the valley
1914 S5, Patriotic Fund
27 Waterfall of the northland illus
1915 17 Muskoka highlands wc
18 Winter solitude wc
1920 25 Morning light wc
26 A northern river wc
1923 15 Spring hillside wc
16 Northern stream wc
1924 13 A Devonshire valley wc
14 The north Devon coast wc
1925 15 A Lake Superior port
16 Passing storm, Algoma wc
1926 12 Northern waters wc
13 Rapids on the Michipocoten wc ØNGCØ
1927 11 Dawn in the valley
12 Winter at the old mill wc F7-32 $150
1928 17 Looking towards Lake Superior wc $125 F9-39
18 The stream in winter wc $125
1929 18 The Schreiber Coast, Lake Superior $500
19 Stream in winter wc $150
1929 S7, Calgary
8 The mill in winter $300
9 Northern lake wc $150
10 Sketch on the Don wc $75
1930 F10, London, Eng
95 Winter stream wc $130 1931-24 $125
1931 23 Canyon of the Agawa $500
1934 27 Along the shore, Lake Superior wc $125 T35-8
28 Gull River, winter wc $125
1935 16 Mount Assiniboine wc $150
17 Cerulean Lake, Assiniboine District wc $150
18 Chrome Lake, Jasper Park $500
19 Autumn landscape $500 T36-6
1936 25 Afternoon light wc $150 T37-8
26 Fishing cove, Lake Superior wc $150
1937 26 Farthest north, Cape Breton wc $200 F11-10 $400 DW 1939 34 x 40 T51-6
27 Midsummer, valley of the Don wc $150
1938 25 Twin Falls on the Agawa $300
1939 19 St Lawrence Bay, Cape Breton wc $150
20 Wonder Pass, Canadian Rockies wc $100
21 Spring at Newtonbrook illus $400
22 Autumn in Haliburton wc $250
1940 17 Winter morning wc $100
18 Northern lumber town wc $100
19 Finlander's Ontario home $300 T41-7, Finlander's Canadian home, mispr
1941 16 In the Michipocoten country $300 T42-4
17 In the Bow Valley wc $100
18 March in the Laurentians wc $100
1941 S9, Toronto
7 Winter in Muskoka $100
1942 14 Down the river, Algoma

$250 T43-3
15 Lake in the hills $200
1943 7 Spring at Newtonbrook illus $200
8 Valley of the Illecillewaet $300
1944 17 Muskoka farm wc $125
18 Gray weather, Lake Kootenay wc $125
19 Evening at Newtonbrook $200
1945 21 Sungleams, Okanagan $500
1946 10 Sunrise, Alpine Club of Canada, 1946 camp $300 T47-6
11 October in Haliburton wc $250
1947 16 Government post-war housing $400 T48-5
1948 18 Storm clouds and sunshine over the mountains $500
19 Newtonbrook pastures $250
1949 10 Storm clouds over the mountains $500
1950 15 Fisherman's home, Humber Mouth, Nfld 23 x 26 $300
1951 11 March in the Eastern Townships, Quebec $300
1953 9 In the Lake Superior country illus $300
1954 12 Moving clouds, Jervis Inlet, BC 29 1/2 x 35 $500
27 Retro Sec. Rainy weather, Okanagan Lake, BC
1955 14 At the top of Jervis Inlet $300

BRIGDENS LIMITED
Addr: 1938, Toronto
1938 S8, Toronto
49 Sunworthy Wallpapers, Book
50 Nassau and the treasure islands, book
51 Pontiac autumobiles, book
52 McLaughlin-Buick automobiles, book
53 Duplate Safety Glass Co, Ltd, book
54 Stevens-Hepner Co, Ltd, book
55 Sun Life Assurance Company of Canada, book
56 General Motors of Canada, Ltd, newspaper advertisement
57 Machine Shop 2 drwg
58 Pontiac automobiles 2 drwg
59 Sun Life Assurance Company of Canada, 2 photomontages

BRIGGS, LILY
Addr: 1905, Doon, Ont
1905 13 Woodland landscape
14 Pasture lands

BRISLEY, ROSS
see SOMERVILLE, WILLIAM, 1951

BRISSENDEN, MARION
1939 27 Gramps nfs

BRITTAIN, DONALD
10 Jun 1928, Ottawa
RCA(e) 1978 Film maker
Addr: 1979, Westmount, Que

BRITTON, HARRY
23 Sep 1878, Cambridge, Eng 23 Jul 1958, Toronto AGO CC1 CWW55 M NGC TB2 WWA47
ARCA 1908 RCA 1934 Sr 1948 Painter
Addr: 1905, Deer Park, Toronto; 1906, 279 Markham St, Toronto; 1906-8, 229 Howland Ave, Toronto; 1909M-11, 340 Bloor St W, Toronto; 1912-13, 278 Bloor St W, Toronto; 1914, 425 Sherbourne St, Toronto; 1915-20, 67 Wellesley St, Toronto; 1922, Newlyn West, Penzance, Eng; 1923, Tintagel, Cornwall, Eng; 1925-6, P O Box 466, Canning, NS; 1927-32 61 Havelock St, Amherst, NS; 1933, Parrsboro, NS; 1934-7, 836 Dovercourt Rd, Toronto; 1938-58, Toronto
1905 12 The drinking place
1906 40 October evening
41 The evening meal
42 The coming of winter
43 The end of day
1906 F5, Halifax
18 Spring $150
1907 22 In the meadow
23 Marguerita
1907 F6, Sherbrooke
38 Cape Diamond, Quebec $30
39 Evening $30 1908-18
40 Wolfe's Cove, Quebec $30
1908 19 Departure of day ≬NGC≬
1909M 10 Ploughing 1909N-15
11 The goat herd
12 Marguerite ≬NGC≬
13 Twilight
1909N 13 St Paul's in winter S2-9
14 Spring
1910 25 Misty evening, St Ives
26 Eventide
27 Fishing boats, St Ives

28 The drinking place S2-10
1911 22 Cornish fishing boats
23 Cornish fishers
24 Interior of a sail loft 1913-30 (NGC)
25 Evening clouds
26 Boats at evening
27 The quay at St Ives
1912 S3, Winnipeg
17 Cornish fishermen
18 The mill pond
1913 31 The fisherman's wife S4-12 $750
32 Cornish landscape
33 Fishing boats S4-13 $250
34 Rocky coast towards sunset
35 The end of a breezy day
1914 18 Faraglioni Rocks, Capri
19 Cornish landscape
20 An Italian fruit stall
21 Cloud shadows, Cornwall wc
1914 S5, Patriotic Fund
19 A rocky coast illus
1915 19 Rock and sea, Capri
20 Evening, Capri
21 Early morning, Capri
22 Fruit stall, Amalfi illus
1916 17 Harbour of St Ives illus
18 The Cornish coast
19 Calm weather, Cornish coast
1918A 16 Miss Drew-Brook
17 Frank S. Weston, MA
18 Capt Fred Hancock
19 Winter 1918N-15
1918N 14 Gossip illus
1919 12 The Isle of Capri
13 The shallow cove
1920 27 Near Land's End illus
28 Dutch boats wc
29 Mild weather wc
30 Cloud shadows wc
1922 22 French fishing smacks S6-7
23 Mount's Bay, Cornwall illus
1923 17 Sunlight and sea
1925 17 Squalls
18 Moonrise
19 The old mill
20 Newlyn harbour
1926 14 Winter weather off the Cornish coast
1927 13 Rev D.A. Steele, DD 1930-18
14 Sunset
15 On the Atlantic coast
16 Turbulence
1928 19 In Lunenburg harbour, Nova Scotia $500 F9-183
20 Entrance to the cave $500
1929 S7, Calgary
11 At Lunenburg, Nova Scotia $200
12 The cove $200
13 Sunset $100
1930 19 Moonlight $400 1931-26
1931 25 In Lunenburg harbour, Nova Scotia $600
1932 17 A Nova Scotian and her goats $600
18 Italian woman washing $400 1933-20 DW 1935 25 1/2 x 28 1/2
1933 19 The goat farm $600 T34-10
1934 29 In harbour $350 T35-9 1935-21 T36-7
30 The old back road $350 1935-22
31 Winter in Parrsboro, NS $200 1935-23
1935 20 Evening $800
1936 27 Old houses wc $300 T37-9
28 Winter #1 wc $75
29 Winter #2 wc $75
30 Twilight wc $75
1937 28 Early morning $400 T38-5
29 In harbour, Bay of Fundy wc $300
1938 26 Summer weather $1,000 1939-23 F11-11 43 x 50
27 Showers $300
1939 24 Off the coast of Nova Scotia $600
1940 20 A glimpse of the sea wc $200
21 Turmoil wc $200
1941 19 Somewhere in England $600
20 Snow in October, Nova Scotia $400 T42-5
1941 S9, Toronto
8 In Lunenburg harbour, Nova Scotia $200
1942 16 In harbour $600 T43-4
1943 9 On the Atlantic illus $1,000 1944-20 T45-7
10 Sunset $250 T44-3
1945 22 Drying sails $800
23 Market day near Lunenburg, NS illus $500 T46-6
1946 12 Early morning $800 T47-7

BRITTON, HENRIETTA HANCOCK (Mrs Harry Britton)
20 May 1874, Ealing West, Eng 27 Jul 1963, Toronto
Addr: 1905, Bishop Strachan's School, Toronto; 1916-21, 67 Wellesley St, Toronto; 1922, Newlyn West, Penzance,

Eng; 1923, Tintagel, Cornwall, Eng; 1926, P O Box 466 Canning, NS; 1927-32, 61 Havelock St, Amherst, NS; 1934-7, 836 Dovercourt Rd, Toronto
1905 98 Beaupré, Quebec. Hancock
1916 20 A shady grove
1918A 20 The life class 1918N-16
1919 14 Bristle and brustle 1920-32
1920 31 Evergreens
1922 24 Old houses, England
1923 18 Quietude
1926 15 Clay pits, Nova Scotia 1927-18 S7-14 $300
1927 17 Early winter, New Brunswick 1928-22 $300
1928 21 Gypsum quarries, Nova Scotia $500
1930 20 Carpet rags $500 1931-27
1932 19 Chisels and wood $600 1933-21
1934 32 Near St Martin's, NS $400
1935 24 Evergreens $600 T36-8
25 Under the light of the moon $300 1936-31 T37-10
1936 32 Evening $300 1937-31 T38-6
1937 30 Ice and snow, New Brunswick $600
1938 28 Behind the scene $200 1939-26
1939 25 In the Wentworth Valley, NS $350
1940 22 Gypsum industry pastel $300 1941-22 $250
1941 21 Near Parrsboro, NS $400
1941 S9, Toronto
9 Nova Scotia coast scene $300
1942 17 Near Parrsboro, NS $400
1944 21 Portrait study pastel nfs 1945-25
1945 24 The prodigal $400 T46-7 1948-20
1946 13 An old mill pond $175

BROADHEAD, W.S.
Addr: 1912, Toronto
1912 S3, Winnipeg
165 Titanic disaster b&w cart
166 Girl's head, cover design col drwg
167 Illustration, Christmas b&w
168 Illustration, burglar b&w

BROCK, GUY N.
Addr: 1916-18, 4282 Sherbrooke St W, Westmount, Que
1916 21 In harbour
1918A 21 The tow boat

BRODEUR, ALBERT SAMUEL
1862, Montreal H
Addr: 1904, Montreal
1904 200 In the woods wc

BRONFMAN, PHYLLIS see LAMBERT, PHYLLIS

BROOK, PHILIP R.
7 Feb 1918, Salmon Arm, BC CWW79
RCA(e) 1978 Architect
Addr: 1979, Toronto
see also Banz, George, 1968

BROOKE, JOHN D.
1970 134 Promotion piece, E.B. Eddy Company. Fish and bee
135 Poster, Art Directors Club of Toronto. Graphics 68
1971 8G Booklet, Carpet buying without fear, Wool Bureau of Canada
9G Billboard, Last word in miracle fabrics, Wool Bureau of Canada
10G Planning booklets, North American Life Assurance Co

BROOKER, BERTRAM RICHARD (pseuds Richard Surrey, Huxley Hearne)
31 Mar 1888, Croydon, Eng 21 Mar 1955, Toronto AGO CC1 CWW49 M TB3 WWA47
Addr: 1930-6, 107 Glenview Ave, Toronto
1930 21 Miss Rosa Hermannsson
1932 20 Still life $150
1936 33 Ski poles $150 T37-11
1938 S8, Toronto
179 Book, Yearbook of the arts in Canada. Macmillan
1950 16 Abundance 30 x 24 $400
17 The bitter cup 30 x 24 $400

BROOKS, FRANK LEONARD
7 Nov 1911, Enfield, London, Eng
AGO CWW79 M WWA47
ARCA 1939 Non-res 1956 Painter
Addr: 1936, 677A Spadina Ave, Toronto; 1937, 380 Roehampton Ave, Toronto; 1938-55, Toronto; 1956-68, USA; 1969-71/79, Mexico
1936 34 Maple sugar bush, Haliburton $200 T37-12
35 The Sussex coast wc $50

1937 32 Muggy January $200 T38-7
33 Nipissing boat house $100
1938 29 Before snow illus $400
30 Still life $250 T39-9
1939 28 October $300
29 Grist mill, Meadowvale, Ont $500
1939 F11, New York
12 The yellow house, Burks Falls 40 x 50 $500
1940 23 Winter evening, Unionville $300 T41-8
24 North Bay homes wc $75
1941 23 Northern lake, winter $500
24 Old Ontario house, January illus $200 T42-7
25 Wet evening, Whitney Village $175
26 Scrap iron wc $50
1941 S9, Toronto
10 North Bay homes $100
1942 18 Gas phantasy oil & temp nfs
19 Blast furnace wc nfs
20 Unloading iron ore wc nfs T43-5
21 Flood-torn willows nfs
1948 21 Street in San Miguel wc $125

BROOKS, MARIA English
b England fl 1869-90 B DBA DVP G H RSBA TB
1885 50 Ready for a bowl $300 1886-129 $400
54 Ready for a tramp $200 1886-206
83 Edith $125
111 A moment's rest $75 1886-113 $100
124 Un désir $100 1886-124 $125
138 Missionaries $300 see also 1886-209
148 The broken string $125 1886-137 $150
151 The old, old story $800
154 Laura $50 1886-169 $20
180 Down Piccadilly $1,000
1886 123 Ready for bed $200
127 Lilies $400
132 Little Fatty $75
151 Down Piccadilly, returning from Covent Garden Market $1,250
168 Our nurse $60
205 The Ice Palace, Montreal, 1885
206 Ready for a walk
209 Missionaries explaining the doctrines of Christianity to a pagan British family, 2nd century $400
#205, 206, 209 selected for Fla, not in Fla catalog

BROOMFIELD, ADOLPHUS GEORGE
26 Aug 1906, Toronto CWW64 M WWA47 ARCA 1944 RCA 1975 Sr 1973 Painter
Addr: 1932, 31 Eastbourne Cr, Mimico, Ont; 1934-5, 932 King St E, Hamilton; 1936, Burlington, Ont; 1937, 930 King St E, Hamilton; 1945-6, Mimico, Ont; 1947, Long Branch, Ont; 1948-71, Cooksville, Ont; 1979, Mississauga, Ont
1932 21 Windblown pines $500 George R. Broomfield, mispr
1934 33 Open water $100 T35-10
1935 26 Approaching storm $75
27 February afternoon $40
1936 37 Morning $300 T37-14
38 Fallen leaves $300
1937 34 Blue sky $150
1939 30 Moonlight $150
1940 25 Railroad rock cut, Bracebridge, Ont $150
1941 27 Spring near Ravenscliffe, Ont $150 T42-8
1941 S9, Toronto
11 Northern waterfall $50
1942 P/O George Broomfield
22 Rear gunners $100 T43-6
1945 26 St Paul's, London, England, 1943 $100 T46-8
27 Hurricane balloon barrage, 1943 $100
28 Weather closes down at Eindhoven, Holland, 1944 $100
29 Mechs work on Typhoon Fighter, Eindhoven, Holland, 1944 $100
1947 17 After school in winter, Ontario $300
1948 22 Gaspé road, Grande Vallée $500
23 Chaleur Bay farm $500
1949 11 Dagmar farm, Ontario $500
1960 12 Mazinaw portage 30 x 36 $400
1961 14 Port Credit, 1868 36 x 36 $450
DW 1975 Memories of 1913

BROOMFIELD, ISOBEL COOK (Mrs

Adolphus George Broomfield)
Addr: 1936, St Paul St, Burlington, Ont
1936 36 George nfs T37-13
1939 31 Gordon A. Kidder nfs
1940 26 Max Pembleton nfs
27 Sunday, Coldwater, Ont wc $35
1941 28 Patrick O'Lee nfs

BROWN, ALEXANDER KELLOCK Scottish
1849, Edinburgh 9 May 1922, Glasgow
B RA RSA TB1/3
Addr: 1902, 96 Washington St, Boston
1902 182 Ludlow, England wc
183 Shrewsbury, England wc

BROWN, ANNORA
1899, Fort Macleod, Alta
1938 31 Fire weed wc $40
32 Mountain columbine wc $40
1939 32 Glacier lillies wc $75
33 Forest floor wc $75

BROWN, ARCHIBALD see BROWNE, JOSEPH ARCHIBALD

BROWN, DAVID L. ROBERTSON
28 Aug 1869, Montreal 28 Mar 1946, Montreal CNS27 CWW38 Mo12 PMC
Addr: 1893, 38 Mechanics Hall, Montreal
1893 273 Westminster Church, Atwater Avenue
274 Sketch for a city residence

BROWN, FRANCIS BRUCE
see SOMERVILLE, WILLIAM, 1951

BROWN, HENRY HARRIS English
29 Dec 1864, Northants, Eng 27 Aug 1948, London, Eng B DBA G H TB WBA
Addr: 1919, Canada Life Assurance Co, King St, Toronto
1919 15 Frank Darling, Esq, RCA FRIBA
16 Prof Pelham Edgar, PhD illus

BROWN, HUNTLEY
12 May 1932, Lethbridge, Alta
RCA(e) 1976 Illustrator
Addr: 1979, Markham, Ont

BROWN, JEAN
Addr: 1911, 45 Avenue Rd, Toronto
1911 24 Across the valley

BROWN, JOHN FRANCIS
1866, Lévis, Que May 1942, Toronto
Addr: 1895, Board of Trade Bldg, Toronto
1895 1A Legislative and administrative buildings, Victoria, BC
2A Residence, Edgar A. Willis, Esq
3A Residence, Walter Davidson, Esq
4A Chester Mission of Jarvis Street Baptist Church
5A Residence, Arthur Thompson, Esq, Rosedale

BROWN, JOHN GEORGE (or BROWNE)
1831, Durham, Eng English
1913, New York B DVA DVP H
1882 63 Country children watching the ball match $1,500

BROWN, LILY MCENTEE
fl 1887-91 H
Addr: 1887, 85 Union Ave, Montreal
1887 60 Twilight $25
115 Sheepfold wc nfs
146 Twilight wc $40
178 By the creek wc $40
1890 6 November $50

BROWN, LOUISE
Addr: 1918A, 600 Sherbourne St, Toronto
1918A 184 Study of a girl's head plaster

BROWN, MURRAY
10 Nov 1884, Broughty Ferry, Scot
1 Apr 1958, Toronto NGC
ARCA 1943 RCA 1947 Sr 1955 Council
Architect
Addr: 1943-58, Toronto
1957 Brown & Elton
97 Knob Hill Public School
DW 1948 Postal Station K, Toronto temp drwg 13 x 22

BROWN, UNA
Addr: 1916-18, 175 Indian Rd, Toronto; 1918N-19, 175 Keele St, Toronto
1916 22 The orchard cottage
1918A 207 Vanity des
1918N 17 A riverside rookery
18 Elms
1919 17 Shetter Valley

BROWN, WINIFRED L.
1941 29 Haystacks near Knowlton nfs

BROWNE, JOHN GEORGE see BROWN, JOHN GEORGE

BROWNE, JOSEPH ARCHIBALD
28 Feb 1862, Liverpool 7 Nov 1948, Cornwall, Ont AGO H M Mo12 NGC PMC ARCA 1898-01, 1913 RCA 1919 Ret 1932 Council Painter
Addr: 1895, Toronto; 1897, Imperial Loan Bldg, Toronto; 1898, 423 Yonge St, Toronto; 1899, Brook Cottage, Duncaster, Ont; 1900, Toronto; 1901, 34 Victoria St, Toronto; 1905-11, 5 King St W, Toronto; 1913, 36 Toronto St, Toronto; 1914-20, 54 Adelaide St E, Toronto; 1921-2, Lake Placid, NY; 1923,781 University St, Montreal; 1924-5, 815 University St, Montreal; 1926-35, Lancaster, Ont
1895 14 Midsummer Brown mispr
15 Autumn
16 A sunny glade
17 In the farm, in winter
1897 12 Blowing over
13 There's a storm brewing
14 A distant gleam
1898 8 Moonrise
1899 16 The clearing
1900 9 Sundown
10 Evening
1901 6 The miller's home F2-8
7 The ravines
1902 F3, Rochester
13 Summer evening, Canadian landscape illus
1905 31 Canadian pastoral
32 Misty moonrise
33 Woodland (A. Sharp, ARIBA)
34 Moonrise (A. Sharp, ARIBA)
1906 25 The anchorage
26 Nocturne, #5
1908 22 Nightfall
1909N 16 Bewitchment
17 Lake Couchiching
199a and 199b Moonlight
1910 S2, Liverpool
11 Spring song
12 Slumbering waters
13 The little white sail
1911 25 October evening
1913 36 The risen moon
37 Summer eve
38 Annapolis, NS S4-14 $350
39 After the shower, Crosby Sands, near Liverpool S4-15 $400
1914 22 Summer idyl
23 Silvery twilight S5-45 illus
24 Silver birches ◊NGC◊
1915 23 Sundown illus (Norman MacKenzie, Esq, KC, Regina)
24 Lake Ontario, stonehookers
25 A symphony
1916 23 Ben Lomond, Nova Scotia
1919 18 Benediction DW 1920 61 x 42
1920 33 The church on the hill
34 The opal
35 A summer day
36 Across the bay
1921 16 Early twilight on the St Lawrence
17 Harmony in blue and silver, Fairy Lake illus
18 Harmony in russett and green, Hunters Bay
19 Night fall
1922 25 Harmony in gold and amethyst, evening in the Adirondacks
1923 19 Winter in the Adirondacks
20 After the shower
1924 15 Afterglow illus
16 Mid-winter
1925 21 The end of the day illus
1926 16 The frozen lake
17 The little red barn
1927 19 Mountain hamlet
20 The frozen lake (C.E. Stone, Esq)
1927 F7, London, Eng
160 In the gloaming $575
1928 23 Winter moonrise $600 ◊NGC◊
1932 22 Evensong
23 March day
1933 22 The day's ending $1,000
23 The risen moon $800
24 Nocturne $600
1934 34 The blush of sunset $1,500 T35-11 1935-29
35 The golden cloud $1,500
1935 28 Gold, purple and silver $1,500
1941 S9, Toronto
12 The head of the lake $250
ports: by J.W. Russell, 1909N-129; A.C. Williamson, 1910-110; W. Adams, 1927-1

BROWNELL, PELEG FRANKLIN
27 Jul 1857, New Bedford, Mass 13

Mar 1946, Ottawa AGO CC2 H M Mo98/12 NGC PMC TB3 W78
ARCA 1894 RCA 1895 Ret 1915 Council
Painter
Addr: 1893, c/o J. Wilson & Co, Ottawa; 1894-8, 660 Rideau St, Ottawa; 1899-03, 177 Sparks St, Ottawa; 1904-5, Ottawa; 1906, 124 Wellington St, Ottawa; 1907-11, Ottawa; 1912-15, 307 Wilbrod St, Ottawa; 1918A, 177 Sparks St, Ottawa

1889 27 A study, Squituscket, M V $50
28 Roses
50 A village notary $150
51 A study $50
72 Summer sea, a study $25
1892 43 Low tide, north east $50 ◊NGC◊
46 The stepchild $100
52 Corner of pasture
1893 13 Satyr and Bacchante $200
14 Lamplight $100 F1-14 nfs ◊NGC◊
15 Anderson's garden $100 F1-15
1894 22 Portrait
23 Going gishing
24 Wilfred Campbell
25 Landscape
1895 6 Autumn dec panel
7 Winter, waining snow
8 Portrait
1896 12 The photographer DW 1896 23 1/2 x 19 1/2 T51-7
13 Barren lands
14 Autumn woods
1897 4 A portrait
5 Plum trees, winter
6 Budding genius
7 Sand dunes
8 Study of an actor
9 Head, decorative sketch
10 Costume du bal
1898 9 The reader
10 A Gatineau sketch
11 New England coast sketch
12 A Rideau sketch
1899 17 A tea party, children of Robert Allan, Esq
1900 1 Day in June
2 A trout pool
3 Midsummer, Quebec
3a The man in grey
1902 20 Salome
1903 11 Souvenir
12 Northern flowers
13 The log cabin
14 Childhood
15 Autumn
1904 23 Rev Thomas Wardrope
24 Motherhood
25 Rainy day, Little Saguenay
1905 7 The blue kimono 1906-46
8 Idyll, doux pays
1906 44 "Paper, sir."
45 Reverie F5-19 $500
47 Violets
1906 F5, Halifax
20 The romance $100
21 Fog lifting, Baie St Paul $110
1907 24 Sandalphon F6-22 $150 Sanddalphur
25 October morning
26 The grey mill
27 October wood
1907 F6, Sherbrooke
23 Solitaire $100
24 Idling $75
25 and 26 Landscape $50 each
1908 8 Lois
1909M 18 Autumn hillside
19 Fish wife of Calvados
20 Mount Field, evening glow
21 Reading
1912 28 and 29 Landscape
30 Cockfighting, Costa Rica (Hon W.C. Edwards)
1912 S3, Winnipeg
19 Sea at Porto Rico
20 Porto Rico landscape
21 Street in St Thomas, WI
1913 40 On the beach, St Kitts, BWI ◊NGC◊
1914 25 On the beach, Basseterre, WI ◊NGC◊
26 Moonrise, Bonaventure Island
1914 S5, Patriotic Fund
43 A nor'easter, Bonaventure Island illus
1915 26 Boat landing, Island of St Thomas, DWI illus
27 By Ward Market, Ottawa ◊AGO◊
28 Trout water, Algonquin Park
1918A 22 The Nevis packet illus
23 Summer landscape, Fitzroy, Ont
port: by E.G. Fosbery, 1924-52

BROWNLEE, CECIL L.
Addr: 1931, 393 4th Ave, Verdun, Que

1931 28 Portrait

BRUCE, ADA MILDRED (Mrs Thomas L. Torrance)
1903, Grand Valley, Ont
Addr: 1934-6, 56 Davisville Ave, Toronto
1934 36 Tobermory wc $45
1936 39 Still life $75
40 Marsh calla lillies wc $50
1938 Torrance
218 Apples $39 T39-54
1938 S8, Toronto
380 Wallpaper design. Hon mention. Canadian Wallpaper Manufacturers Limited
1939 232 Autumn woods wc $45
1942 141 Sun flowers $150 T43-46

BRUCE, WILLIAM BLAIR
8 Oct 1859, Hamilton, Ont 17 Nov 1906, Stockholm AGO B DBA DVP G H M Mo98 NGC R2 TB W78
Addr: 1883, Hamilton, Ont; 1901-2, c/o William Bruce, Hamilton, Ont
1883 47 Summer afternoon (Henry Martin, ARCA, Hamilton)
1901 10 The bathers F2-9
1902 31 Bathers at Capri, Italy
1910 S2, Liverpool
late W.B. Bruce
14 Seascape in the Baltic

BRUEMMER, FRED
26 Jun 1930, Riga
RCA(e) 1975 Photographer
Addr: 1979, Montreal

BRUENECH, GEORGE ROBERT
1851, St Malo, France 22 Jul 1916, Toronto B H Mo12
ARCA 1891 Painter
Addr: 1887, 28 Toronto St, Toronto; 1891-2, Toronto; 1893, 32 Bismark Ave, Toronto; 1894-5, Toronto; 1896, 95 Yonge St, Toronto; 1897-9, 28 Yonge St, Toronto; 1900-1, Toronto; 1902, 95 Yonge St, Toronto; 1903-16, Toronto
1882 187 A November day on the coast Bruenich, mispr
1883 246 Entrance to the bush wc $20
1885 241 On the sea shore wc $20
248 Before sunrise, Lake Rousseau wc $20
276 Ottawa wc $30
318 Road in Lower Canada wc $50
1886 75 On the brow of the ravine wc $30
90 Autumn of the Indian River wc $40
1886 F1a, London, Eng
1987, artist number
Autumn on Shadow River, Muskoka
Indian camp on the Ottawa River
1887 180 In the Sveningdale Valley, Norway wc $75
1889 110 Leer Foss, near Trondhjem, Norway wc $75
132 Mouse-hole Harbour, Cornwall wc $75
1890 129 The North Cape, Norway wc $50
130 Elizabeth Castle, Jersey, Channel Islands wc $50
1891 143 On the coast, Maine wc
148 Near Wolfe's Cove, Quebec wc
158 White Head, Cushing Island, Maine wc
189 The toilers of the sea wc
1892 101 Summer afternoon, Vermont wc $40
1893 170 A Norwegian fjord wc $100
1896 193 Svorholt Klubben, near North Cape, Norway, midnight wc
194 Gjata Mountain, Svolvarhofoten Islands, Norway wc
1897 1W The North Cape, early morning wc
1898 148 Under the sandstone cliffs, Gulf of St Lawrence wc
1899 157 Foggy weather on the Arctic Ocean wc
1902 184 Lake Ontario at Bronte wc
1902 F3, Rochester
14 Hopis Mountain, Lafolin Islands, Norway $90
1907 221 At Placentia, Nfld wc
1912 S3, Winnipeg
22 Cockington forge and cottages, Devonshire wc

BRUNEAU, CLAIRE B. (MRS)
1945 30 Dr Y.K. Wu, Chief Surgeon, Chungking State Hospital nfs
31 Flowers nfs

BRUNEAU, KITTIE (Mrs Serge Gilbert)
12 Oct 1929, Montreal CC1 M WWA73
1964J 10 Oiseaux du coucher du soleil 42 x 36 $175

1967 9 Les baleines electrique 17 x 44 1/2 $450

BRUNET, JEAN EMILE
18 Mar 1899, Huntington, Que 11 Jan 1977, Montreal B M
Addr: 1915-16, 654 Côte des Neiges Rd, Montreal
1915 227 Sketch for a fountain
228 Sketch for a building
1916 241 Mme J. Narcisse Dupuis bas rel

BRUNI, UMBERTO
24 Nov 1914, Montreal M
RCA(e) 1977 Painter
Addr: 1979, Duvernay, Laval, Que
1939 242 Joseph Giunta, painter sculp nfs
1947 18 Still life $150

BRYAN, EUGENE LORNE MACDONALD
b 1919
1944 22 Autumn in the suburbs wc $50
1945 32 Time and a half wc $75
1946 14 Purple house wc $75
1947 19 Still life $100

BRYDALL, ROBERT Scottish
fl 1874-96 d c 1908 DBA DVP H
1880 10 Interlacing boughs (Sandford Fleming)

BRYDONE-JACK, KATHARINA SYBIL (Mrs)
1 Dec 1895, Sackville, NB 29 Nov 1945, Montreal
Addr: 1929, Nipawin, Sask; 1935-7, 3488 Côte des Neiges Rd, Montreal
1929 20 Bridging the Saskatchewan $200
1935 30 White flowers pastel nfs
31 Zinnias pastel nfs
1937 35 Mitchie and Ann pastel nfs
1939 34 Miss Suzon Mathieu nfs

BRYMNER, WILLIAM CMG
14 Dec 1855, Greenoch, Scot 18 Jun 1925, Wallasey, Ches, Eng AGO B CC2 CNS36 Co EC H M Mo12 NGC R2 TB1/3 W78
ARCA 1883 RCA 1886 Ret 1920 Council Painter
Addr: 1883, Ottawa; 1884, c/o D. Brymner, Esq, Ottawa; 1885-6, Ottawa; 1887, St John St, Montreal; 1888-9, Montreal; 1890-04 c/o Art Association Montreal; 1905, 67 St James St, Montreal; 1906-9M c/o Art Association Montreal; 1909N-18, 255 Bleury St, Montreal; 1920, 16 Lorne Ave, Montreal; 1921-5, Montreal
1882 9 Day $60
13 An unwelcome guest
38 Night $60
95 Reading made easy
107 Forbidden fruit $300
1883 315 Study of an Italian piper drwg
316 A caleche drive at Murray Bay drwg $15
317 Pen and ink drawing from painting by D. Teniers $10
322 Scraps drwg $10
323 Study drwg $10
324 Pen and ink drawing from painting by Adrian Van Ostado $10
325 High tide, lower St Lawrence drwg $10
1884 33 With Dolly at the sabot maker's $90 (NGC)
85 Asleep at the church door $75
94 Preparing to spin $75 S1-129
1884 S1, Saint John
103 The smithy $25
121 At the church door $75
146 Village store $50
1885 13 One summer's day $60
66 Home brewed ale
79 Near Hinderwell, Yorkshire $60
92 In a garden $40
103 A wreath of flowers $400 DW 1886 47 1/4 x 55 1886-213 Fla-1988
106 For His sake $120
1886 18 The day is done $40 Fla-1988
158 Early summer $40 Fla-1988
159 Baie St Paul on the St Lawrence $100 Fla-1988
160 Sad memories nfs
166 Wild berries $50 Fla-1988
170 Crazy patchwork $85 Fla-1988 (NGC)
173 The books they love they read in running brooks. sold
178 Portrait
1886 Fla, London, Eng
1988 artist number
Portrait
1887 27 Giving out rations to Blackfoot Indians NWT $200

33 Along the Bow River, NWT $40
42 Blackfoot Indian ready for the sun dance $100
44 Dreams $40
67 Reflections $40
79 Morning at Yale, BC $125
109 Winter on the edge of the forest, Fontainebleau $125
1888 123 Par derrière, chez mon père $200 1889-49 $150
136 Un jour de fête
1889 6 Spinning wheel $75
32 The smithy $150
39 The swing $750
76 A summer morning $100
79 Spring, Baie St Paul $200
91 In a French parish $60
99 Where the road dips to the valley $35
1890 7 An August afternoon, Fontainebleau $80
8 Evening, Sorgues, France $80
9 A by-way, Baie St Paul $75
10 Wintry day, Bord à Plouffe nfs
1891 73 Low tide, Baie St Paul $75
76 August afternoon, Sorgues, France
77 Haying time, Valois, near Montreal
78 The oven, French Canadian village
79 Blackfoot Indian ready for sun dance
80 Summer eve, Sorgues, France
81 Sad memories
82 Schooner at low tide
1892 11 Summer clouds $75
20 Champ de Mars, Winter $250 {MMFA}
30 Near Killarney, Ireland $75
44 In the County of Cork, Ireland $400
65 Carpenter's shop $75
1893 16 In County Cork, Ireland $350 F1-16
17 Lake Louise, Rocky Mountains $350 F1-17
18 Lake Agnes, Rocky Mountains $350 F1-18
19 Old bridge, Bord à Plouffe, winter nfs
20 Border of the forest of Fontainebleau nfs F1-20
1893 F1, Chicago
19 Entr'acte
1894 9 Hell's Gate
10 Wood interior, near Emerald Lake
11 Great Illecillewaet Glacier
12 The Black Canyon, Thompson River
13 Mount Baker at sunset {MMFA}
1895 10 Isabella, or 'The pot of basil', from Keats
11 Winter
12 The Groote Kerk, Dodrecht
13 Memories, France
1896 15 Portrait
16 Old building, Lower Lachine Road
17 Study of a boy's head
18 Girl's head
195 Francie wc 1901-149 F2-7 (James Ross, Esq)
1897 4W The grey girl wc 1901-147 F2-6 (C.E.S. Porteous, Esq)
1898 18 The lode star
143 Sisters wc {NGC Two girls reading} see 1900-117
144 Old canal, Bruges, Belgium wc
145 In County Kerry, Ireland wc
146 An Irish cottage, Gap of Dunlow wc
147 London Bridge wc
1899 15 Early morning in September illus 1900-4 Early moonrise in September F4-12 1908-9 {NGC} 1899 'morning' mispr
1900 117 The picture book wc {NGC Two girls reading} see 1898-143
118 The black schooner wc
119 Cap Tourment wc
120 An old orchard wc
121 A corner in oats wc
122 Wheat stocks wc
1901 4 Clearing weather F2-5
148 A habitant wc
150 At the spring wc
151 September, old Canada wc
152 July, lower St Lawrence wc
1902 22 The thunder cloud F3-22 $420
23 Haymaking, lower St Lawrence, evening
24 Girl in eastern costume 1903-8

25 Drying sails
26 A schooner captain, study of a head
27 Head of old woman
185 Jacques Guay wc
186 Marguerite Poulin wc
187 Marie Louise Létourneau wc
188 Léon Pichette wc
1902 F3, Rochester
22 The thunder cloud $420
1903 7 Haymaking, lower St Lawrence
9 Summer morning
10 Road to church
148 A corner of Venice wc
149 Canal, Venice wc
150 Autumn day wc
151 The horse of all work wc
1904 26 Cloud shadows F4-11
27 Comrades
28 Calves drinking, evening F4-13
201 Cool shade wc F4-96
202 The old apple tree wc
203 The young hunter wc
204 Daisies wc
205 The garden wc
1905 27 Clearing weather, lower St Lawrence
27a The habitant
28 The seiners
29 September sunshine
30 The red girl
1906 35 Prelude
36 Early morning
37 In cool glades F5-24 $200 F6-31
38 Under the apple tree 1910-17
39 Clouds and sunshine F5-22 $300
1906 F5, Halifax
23 Little girl in red $250 1911-26
25 Summer $50
26 Old mill $75
1907 28 October
29 Summer evening, Ste Famille, Isle of Orleans
30 The farm
31 Harvest field
1907 F6, Sherbrooke
27 Summer evening, Ste Famille $500
28 In the shade of the apple tree $500 1908-11
29 At sunset $200
30 Comrades $150
1908 10 Shades of evening
1909M 14 The letter 1909N-19
15 Miss Buller, Montreal
1909N 20 Portrait
21 Autumn landscape
1910 29 Summer
30 Sea foam 1912-34
31 Autumn
32 A village garden
1910 S2, Liverpool
15 Miss Dorothy and Miss Irene Vaughan S3-23 (Victor E. Mitchell, Esq) ◊AGH◊
16 October in Canada
18 Blackfoot Indian
1911 27 Late September (#28 not in cat)
29 Elm trees, October
1912 31 Frontenac receiving Sir William Phips' envoy dec panel (Sir Edward Clouston, Bart)
32 Summer (Robert Lindsay, Esq)
33 Feeding chickens ◊MMFA◊
35 Elm trees at sunset
1912 S3, Winnipeg
24 Portrait of a girl
25 Golden autumn
1913 41 Afterglow S4-16 $1,000
42 Nightfall
43 Late afternoon S5-1 illus
1914 27 October
28 By the light of the lantern
1914 S4, Winnipeg
17 Old cottages $500
1915 29 Nude figure illus ◊NGC◊
30 A child
31 Incoming tide, Louisburg, Cape Breton
32 Coast at Louisburg, Cape Breton ◊NGC◊
1916 24 Sunset, Louisburg, NS illus
25 A lonely grave, Louisburg, NS
26 Sunset
27 Sea coast, Louisburg
1918A 24 Late K.R. Macpherson, Esq, KC illus
1918N 19 October at Ste Famille illus
1920 37 Bridge at Nemours, France illus
38 Evening light, Portneuf, Quebec
1927 Late William Brymner
21 Old Certosan Monastery, Capri

22 View of Capri
1929 S7, Calgary
15 St Francis valley $750
16 Lower St Lawrence $750
1954 10 Retro Sec Jeune fille au jardin (Musée du Québec)
port: bust, by G. Hill, 1918A-191

BUCKHAM, ROBERT MARSHALL
b 1918
1947 20 Minogue's farm wc $75
1948 24 Sawmill, Mont Tremblant $150
1956 8 Self portrait nfs T56-8
9 Marionettes illus $150

BUDAY, LAZLO
b Hungary
1965 14 Still life 30 x 25 $300

BUELL, KATRINA S.D.
b Brockville, Ont fl 1890-26 B H
1890 11 Dear little girl $65
1891 232 Girl's head

BULLER, CECIL TREMAYNE (Mrs John Murphy)
1888, Montreal 29 Sep 1973, Montreal M NGC WWA62
Addr: 1913, 5 rue Nouvelle Stanislas, Paris; 1915, 154 Drummond St, Montreal; 1916-18, 147 Bishop St, Apt B6, Montreal
1913 44 Verdure S4-18 $50
1915 33 Le marché
34 Breton house wc ◊NGC◊
1916 273 Notre Dame aqua
274 Little houses, Chelsea etch
1918N Murphy
140 Fishing fleet
141 A grey day
245 Summer afternoon wd cut

BULLER, MARGUERITE (Mrs Marguerite Buller Allan)
Addr: 1906, 111 Drummond St, Montreal; 1907, Montreal
1906 31 The promenade
32 Audrey
33 In the Tuileries
34 Neighbourly curiosity
1907 222 The three of us wc
223 The tea party wc
224 In the garden wc
see also Allan, Marguerite Buller (Mrs Allan)

BULOW, KAREN
8 Nov 1899, Skanderborg, Denmark
RCA(e) 1976 Textile designer
Addr: 1979, Ottawa

BULOW-HUBE, SIGRUN
31 Jan 1913, Linkoping, Sweden
RCA(e) 1973 Industrial designer
Addr: 1979, Ottawa

BUNNER, ANDREW FISHER American
1841, New York 19 Apr 1897, New York B H TB
1882 302 Looking off from Venice towards Sal Lazzaro (loan)

BUNNETT, HENRY RICHARD S. English
b England fl 1881-9 H
Addr: 1887, Montreal
1887 4 Old Grey Nunnery, Montreal $50
1888 199a View on Richelieu River
209 Old mill at St Marie, Richelieu River Burnett, mispr

BUNYARD, RICHARD G.
b 1900
Addr: 1936, 2043 Pendrell St, Vancouver
1936 232 Buffalo linocut $5 unfrmd $10 framd

BURGOYNE, LORNA HEYWOOD (Mrs von Ritschl)
25 Oct 1894, Plympton, Devon, Eng
3 Apr 1961, Toronto B DBA RA WBA
Addr: 1937, RR 2, Port Perry, Ont
1937 36 Harebells min $25
37 Autumn bush min $30

BURGOYNE, SAINT GEORGE
7 Aug 1882, England Nov 1964, Montreal M NGC W78
Addr: 1912, P O Box 212, Montreal; 1913-15, 2588 Park Ave, Montreal; 1916-19, 2584 Park Ave, Montreal; 1920-4, 2198B St Denis St, Montreal; 1925-37, 6636 St Denis St, Montreal
1912 36 Autumn landscape
1913 45 Tide coming in, Orrs Island, Maine
1914 29 Over the shallows, Orrs Island, Maine
1915 35 October afternoon
1916 28 A Laurentian brook
1918A 25 Barns under snow wc 1918N-20

1919 19 Autumn afternoon, Boule River, Laurentians wc
1920 39 The edge of the clearing
1921 20 The hillside under snow wc
21 Autumn afternoon
1922 26 A northern stream, autumn wc
1923 21 Winter landscape wc
1924 17 Outlet, Lac Supérieur, Quebec wc
1925 22 Laurentian logging road
1929 21 A Laurentian stream wc $100
1931 29 A northern stream $100
30 Laurentian hillside wc $50
1933 25 Frozen falls, Archambault Creek, Quebec $100
1935 32 Two bridges, winter $100 T36-9
1937 37a Sundown, Devil River, Lac Supérieur, Quebec $100
1945 33 Laurentian bush, March wc $100
1947 21 Lac Supérieur from Ridge at Bear Lake wc $75

BURKE, EDMUND
31 Oct 1850, Ireland 1919, Toronto
Co Mo98/12
ARCA 1880-90, 1908-14 Architect
Addr: 1880-90, Toronto; 1908-10, 28 Toronto St, Toronto; 1911-14, Toronto
1895 Burke & Horwood, 6A-9A
6A Designs for Saturday Night Building
7A Business building, Toronto
8A Foresters' Building, Toronto
9A Globe Building, Toronto
10A Walmer Road Baptist Church
11A Art Institute, Sackville, NB
12A Houses on Wellesley Crescent, A.E. Kemp's
13A Hall of A.E. Kemp's house
14A C.J. Holman's house, Lowther Avenue
15A Summer cottages, Toronto Island
16A Summer cottage, Lorne Parke
17A House in Erie, Pennsylvania
18A House, Queen's Park
19A Simpson Building
1907 302 Residence, A.E. Kemp, Esq
302 Residence, Mrs T.H. Harris, Toronto
304 Bible Training School, Toronto
305 McMaster University, Chapel, Toronto
1908 167 Country house near Oakville photo
1909N 22 Royal Astronomical Observatory, Toronto
1910 207 Meteorological Observatory, Toronto
208 Design for church

BURNETT, HENRY see BUNNETT, HENRY

BURNS, WILLIAM HALL
1880 144 Sir John A. Macdonald bust plaster

BURRELL, LOUIE H. (Mrs Louise H. Luker) English
fl 1901-24 DBA
Addr: 1912, 215 Metcalfe St, Montreal
1912 37a A sketch wc
38 The fountain, Kensington Gardens wc
39 Villars, Switzerland wc
40 A case of miniatures

BURRIDGE, RAY ELEANOR
1946 158 The roomer litho $85

BURRILL, BLAKE (Mrs)
Addr: 1936, 32 Inglis St, Halifax
1936 41 Vesuvius Point, BC pastel nfs

BURTON, DENNIS EUGENE NORMAN
6 Dec 1933, Lethbridge, Alta AGO
B CWW79 IO M
1959 12 Close-in 48 x 48 $400
1960 13 Totem I 48 x 60 $500
1964J 11 Painting 40 x 40 $300

BURY, JEANNE VISART DE
31 Jan 1871, Portland, NB H Mo98
Addr: 1897, Saint John
1897 26 Old fisherman

BUSCH, HENRY FREDERIK
6 Jan 1826, Hamburg 28 Jan 1902, Halifax
ARCA 1880-8 Architect
Addr: 1880-8, Halifax

BUSH, CHARLES ROBERT (also signs Charles Robb)

28 Jun 1938, Toronto WWA78
1960 15 Mediterranean 40 x 54 $200
1961 19 Flight 32 x 54 $165

BUSH, JOHN HAMILTON (JACK)
20 Mar 1909, Toronto 23 Jan 1977, Toronto AGO B CC1 CWW64 M TB3 WWA47
ARCA 1946-63 Painter
Addr: 1930, 42 Barton Ave, Toronto; 1936, 43 Chudleigh Ave, Toronto; 1947-63, Toronto
1930 22 La vielle maison $200
1936 42 Children playing $100 T37-15
1938 S8, Toronto
MacLaren Advertising Company
167 Booklet, Canada, your friendly neighbour invites you. Jack Bush, and others
1942 23 March snow wc $75 T43-7
1946 15 Harold W. James, artist nfs
16 Winter morning $200
1947 22 Winding road wc $100 T48-6
23 Market place wc $75
1949 12 The new road wc $125 T50-2
1950 18 Spring song 40 x 60 $800
1951 12 Summer, Deer Lake wc $100
1952 9 Summer afternoon $300 T53-3
1953 10 Before spring illus $400
1954 13 The sleeper 23 x 48 illus $400
1956 10 Desert dream illus $400 T56-10
11 Quiet day, desert $300 T56-11
1958 16 Summer #4 illus $500
1959 13 Fire 48 x 53 $800
1960 14 Rose #2 63 x 34 $500
1963 10 Spain #1 $1,200

BUSH, ROBIN BEAUFORT
18 May 1921, Vancouver
RCA(e) 1974 Industrial designer
Addr: 1979, Mississauga, Ont

BUSSCHAERT, IRENE
c 1953
Addr: 1976, Toronto
1976 S12, Montreal
7 Untitled/Sans titre 65 x 94 illus

BUSTIN, FREDERICK J.
Addr: 1918A, 38 Alcina Ave, Toronto
1918A 26 Dawn of tribulation, St Matt 12:21 wc

BUTLER, BERYL
1939 35 Across the roof tops $50

BUTLER, KENNETH JOHN
23 Apr 1937, Pittsburgh M
RCA(e) 1976 Painter
Addr: 1976/79, Winnipeg
1976 S12, Montreal
8 Shaman gouache 30 x 31 illus

BYERS, JOHN ROBERT MONK
2 Apr 1905, Brockville, Ont M
Addr: 1930, 113 Roncesvalles Ave, Toronto
1930 184 Mr Frank Sperry bronze $400

BYNNES, MURIEL
1904 29 Reverie

CAHEN, OSCAR
8 Feb 1916, Copenhagen 26 Nov 1956, n Oakville, Ont AGO CC2 M NGC WWA56
RCA Medal 1975
1949 13 Christus $500
1950 19 The Adoration 48 x 52 nfs
1951 132 Cockfight drwg $45 oil $150
1953 11 Object d'art $650
1955 15 Austin-Healy 100 engine $600

CAISERMAN, GHITTA (Mrs Maxwell W. Roth)
2 Mar 1923, Montreal AGO CC1 M NGC WWA56
ARCA 1956 Council Painter
Addr: 1956-71/79, Westmount, Que
1950 21 Mending shop 23 x 46 $200
1952 114 Reclining figure litho $25
1954 14 Still life 32 x 48 $250
1955 16 Still life, with music stand $225
1957 13 Family $450
14 Hide and seek illus $450
1959 14 Still life with lovers 48 x 36 illus $600
1960 16 Crowned harlequin 36 x 48 illus $650
1964N 47 Interior 48 x 36 $650
48 Memory 36 x 24 illus $400
1966 7 Riot #10 48 x 60 illus $900

1966 S10, Charlottetown
12 The nest $400 S11-8 32 x 48 $600
13 Sunflower $750 S11-7 36 x 48 $700
1967 10 Aftermath 48 x 60 1/2 illus $900
1968 7 Memory 37 x 61 $900
8 Riot 15 24 x 28 $700
1970 9 Dream puzzle 48 x 36 illus $850
1976 S12, Montreal
9 Presence, deck chairs acry 35 x 39 illus

CALDWELL, ATHA HAYDOCK (Mrs William Caldwell)
fl 1904-21
Addr: 1904-10, Montreal
1904 30 Spring in Yokohama
1907 32 The retreat
33 In the fields
34 Haymaking
35 Learning to milk
36 On the farm
1910 S2, Liverpool
19 Milking time pastel

CALDWELL, ELIZABETH A. (Mrs)
fl 1894-04 H
Addr: 1902, 213 Peel St, Montreal; 1904, Montreal
1902 257 Miss Redmond min
258 Baby Phillips min
259 Baby Feron min
260 A lady min
261 A fancy head min
1904 310 Portrait of a lady min

CALLEJA, JOSEPH JOHN
21 Dec 1924, Gozo, Malta IO M
1964J 12 Metamorphosis monog 16 x 13 $75

CALLOW, WILLIAM English
28 Jul 1812, Greenwich, Eng 20 Feb 1908, Great Missenden, Bucks, Eng
B DBA G TB
1881 93 Street in Rouen wc (Lady Macdougall)

CALVERT, EDWIN SHERWOOD English
1844, Edinburgh flg 1898 B DBA DBW DVP G H TB
1884 64 Toilers of the shore (J.W. L. Forster)

CAMERON, ALLAN ARCHIBALD
19 Feb 1905, Chicago
Addr: 1931. 1207 Bleury St, Montreal; 1933, 561 Victoria Ave, St Lambert, Que; 1935-6, 1207 Bleury St, Montreal; 1937, 561 Victoria Ave, St Lambert, Que
1931 304 Charioteer bronze $50
305 Study of a pioneer woman plaster
1933 250 Begg Memorial Fountain, Orillia, Ont scale model
1935 270 Mother and child full size model for granite, Begg Memorial Fountain
271 Bathing scene sculp $50 each
1936 214 Study sculp $50
1937 272 Fountain sculp $100
1948 25 Sto PO G.T. Barrett

CAMERON, D.R. (Maj Gen) CMG
1889 120 In the valley of the Arno wc $150
131 In the valley of the Lima wc $75

CAMERON, JEAN PARK
11 Nov 1905, Paisley, Ont
1942 24 Lilies $125
1943 11 Sunflower $125 T44-4
1948 26 Rubrum lillies $125

CAMPBELL, ALFRED WILLIAM
1875, Albion, Peel Co, Ont
Addr: 1933-4, 37 O'Hara Ave, Toronto
1933 26 Winter in the woods $60
1934 37 A touch of autumn $100

CAMPBELL, NORMAN
1924, Los Angeles
RCA(e) 1975 Film maker
Addr: 1979, Willowdale, Ont

CANADIAN INDUSTRIES LIMITED
Addr: 1938, Montreal
1938 S8, Toronto
60 Illustrated map, A. Cloutier
61 8 display cards, CIL, A. Cloutier
62 4 packages, CIL Advertising Department
63 Booklet, ABC of CIL, A. Cloutier, C. Mangold
64 3 folders, CIL
65 16 page magazine insert, Ronalds Advertising Agency

CANADIAN THERMOS PRODUCTS LIMITED
1970 110 Insulated drink server

CANADIAN WALLPAPER MANUFACTURERS LIMITED
Addr: 1938, Toronto
1938 S8, Toronto
65a Framed designs of wallpaper one illus
380 Wallpaper competition. Winning design, prize award $100, A.L. Bonnett. Hon mention: Ottillie Beatty, Corry Brigden, Ada M. Bruce, Jean Carson, Norma Droye, Velma Elliott, Donald Forbes, Charlotte Freyvogel, Lucy Johnston, Ian Lindsay, Clifford Logan, Gabrielle Lomax, Mrs R.R. Macaulay, Percy E. Nobbs, Yvonne Noice, H.R. Perrigard, Walter N. Phillips, Barbara Rae, Mary Storms, S. Truster, Orma Wainwright, Grace Whitton

CANADIAN WILLIAM A. ROGERS LIMITED
see WILLIAM A. ROGERS LIMITED

CANN, ELIZABETH LOVITT (Mrs)
6 Oct 1901, Yarmouth, NS M
Addr: 1929, 23 McGill College Ave, Montreal; 1930, 87 King St E, Toronto; 1936, 36 Vancouver St, Yarmouth, NS
1929 257 A cottage in the Bourbonnais $5
1930 23 Portrait of a model $100
1936 43 Falmer $125
1939 36 At the end of the day $100
1942 25 A country girl $125
1944 23 Miss Grace H. nfs
1945 34 Restlessness $300 T46-9

CANTWELL, WILLIAM
9 Jun 1845, Toronto H
Addr: 1895, 143 Cumberland St, Toronto
1895 31 Sunset after the shower
14W Afternoon on the Speed wc
15W Etobicoke Creek wc
16W Near Burlington wc

CAPELLO, LUIGI G.
b Italy fl 1874-88 H
Addr: 1887, Montreal
1880 27 Maison greque au temps de Sapho Cappello mispr
1882 16 Sappho in a holiday at Athens $200
22 St Jerome $100
39 Scene on the prairies
115 Genoese woman $80
1887 53 Idea $50
65 The evening $60

CAPES, ALFRED
H
1890 131 Old cottages, Hampstead Heath wc $75
132 Sand banks, Hampstead Heath wc $50
133 End of summer, Hampstead Heath wc $175

CAPPER, STEWART HERBERT
15 Dec 1859, Douglas, Isle of Man
Jan 1925, Cairo Mo98
ARCA 1897 RCA 1898 Ret 1906 Council
Architect
Addr: 1897-01, McGill University, Montreal; 1902-3, Montreal; 1904-23, England; 1924-5, London, Eng
1897 69A Building for University Hall, extension, Edinburgh, and competitive design for golf club house, Barnton, Edinburgh
70A Orphanage, Whiteinch, Glasgow
71A Robbie Burns' land, Lawn Market, Edinburgh
72A Doorway of Whiteinch Orphanage 1898-238
73A In St Mark's, Venice 1898-240
1898 237 New orphanage for girls, Whiteinch, Glasgow
239 Club house at Barnton
1901 241 University Hall, extension, Castle Hill, Edinburgh DW 1900 not recorded in National Gallery DW coll

CARDINAL, DOUGLAS JOSEPH HENRY
7 Mar 1934, Calgary WWA78
RCA(e) 1973 Architect
Addr: 1976/79, Edmonton
1976 S12, Montreal
98 Grande Prairie College, Grande Prairie, Alberta photos 2 illus

CAREY, HENRY (or CARY) American
fl 1879-99 F H
1882 25 Mme Lamothe

33 Dr P.P. Chapelle

CARLILE, WILLIAM see CARLISLE, WILLIAM

CARLISLE, MARY HELEN English
1869, Grahamstown, S Africa 19 Mar 1925, New York AAA28 B DBA DVP G RA TB1/2
Addr: 1918N, c/o W. Scott & Sons, 99 Notre Dame St W, Montreal
1918N 21 The courtyard of Haddon Hall at dusk pastel
22 Hon Robert Mackay's place at St Andrews pastel

CARLISLE, WILLIAM OGLE(Maj) English
fl 1870-96 H
Addr: 1886, 54 The Common, Woolwich, Kent, Eng
1886 F1a, London, Eng
1989, artist number
Route marching in Canada
Carlile, mispr

CARLYLE, FLORENCE
1864, Galt, Ont 7 May 1923, Crowborough, Eng B CC2 DBA DVP G H M Mo98/12 NGC R2 TB3 W78
ARCA 1897-08, 1912 Painter
Addr: 1895, Paris; 1897-12, Woodstock, Ont; 1913-15, Sweet Haws, Crowborough, Sussex, Eng; 1916, Queen Mary's Hospital, Abbywood, Woolwich, Kent, Eng; 1917-22, Crowborough, Eng
1895 24a La vieille Victorine
1897 34 Portrait of a Dutch lady 1898-33
35 Sketch, darning stockings
36 Portrait
1898 27 Portrait of my brother Carlisle, mispr
28 Portrait of my mother
29 Day of works
30 Reading to mother
31 Peeling potatoes
32 Road through the fields
1900 20 Portrait
21 We beseech Thee to hear us, O Lord
22 The garden
23 June 1902-30
1901 27 Panel picture of self
28 Coal schooner waiting for the tide
29 The willows
30 Grace before bread
31 Golden rod F2-19
32 Harvest moon, Barbizon
1902 28 Mr Edwin S. Carlyle
29 Mrs Ernest Smith
31 The threshold
32 Bye-and-bye
33 Thoughts
1902 F3, Rochester
23 My lady Anne $90
1903 30 Before her first Communion
31 The studio
32 Iris
33 The little housewife
1904 31 Reminiscences
32 The tiff F4-14 F5-27 (Ontario Government) S2-22
1906 F5, Halifax
27a Like unto a flower $300
1910 33 Mother and child S3-28
1910 S2, Liverpool
20 Grey and gold ◊NGC◊
21 Joy of living
1912 41 The critic 1913-51 S4-22 $500
42 White flower
43 The story
1912 S3, Winnipeg
26 The spring song S5-3 illus
27 The threshold
1913 46 Afternoon, Venice S4-19 $175 ◊NGC◊
47 The guest, Venice S4-20 $250
48 Summer morning
49 Via Roberto Browning, the little street in Asolo where Pippa worked and sang S4-21 $150
50 A byway, Venice
1916 29 Roses and copper
30 Nasturtiums

CARMICHAEL, FRANKLIN
4 May 1890, Orillia, Ont 24 Oct 1945, Toronto AGO CC2 EC M NGC PMC W78
ARCA 1935 RCA 1938 RCA medal 1969, Group of Seven Council Painter
Addr: 1918A, Thornhill, Ont; 1920-1, Cameron Ave, Lansing, Ont; 1927, 11 Cameron Ave, Lansing, Ont; 1935-7, 21 Cameron Ave, Lansing, Ont; 1938-41, Toronto; 1942-5, Lansing, Ont
1912 S3, Winnipeg
169 and 170 Decorative illustration col 2
1918A 27 Early autumn
28 The poplars

1920 40 An autumn hillside
1921 22 Wood interior
23 Autumn sunlight
1927 23 A northern village
1929 S7, Calgary
17 North shore, Lake Superior $850 ØLAGØ
18 The sand hill of Oro $350
1935 33 Showers $600
34 Stormy weather $200 T36-10
1936 44 Sombre valley $300 T37-16
1937 38 Hilltops $350 T38-8
1938 33 Snow clouds $650 T39-10 DW 1940 37 3/4 x 47 3/4 T51-8 1954 Retro Sec 23
34 Wild cherry $300
1938 S8, Toronto
Ryerson Press
266 Book, Snobs and spires
270 Book, This is Ontario. Frank Carmichael; map by Stanley Turner
1939 37 Frood Lake illus $650
1939 F11, New York
13 Light and shade 38 x 48 $600
1940 28 Spring $350
29 Late evening $350 T41-9
1941 30 Autumn T42-9
1941 S9, Toronto
13 Jack pines $50
1942 26 A Haliburton farm temp $325 T43-8

CARMICHAEL, ROBERT RALPH
20 Dec 1937, Sault Ste Marie, Ont
1968 9 Expecting to fly 30 x 24 $500

CARON, PAUL ARCHIBALD OCTAVE
4 Sep 1874, Montreal 17 Feb 1941, Montreal CC1 CNS36 M NGC TB3 ARCA 1939 Painter
Addr: 1904-8, Montreal; 1910, 49 Durocher St, Montreal; 1914-23, Ste Anne de Bellevue, Que; 1924-7, 161 Beaver Hall Hill, Montreal; 1928, 1029 Beaver Hall Hill, Montreal; 1929-37, 1117 St Matthew St, Montreal; 1940-1, Montreal
1904 206 Birches wc
207 Twin birches wc
1908 291 A portrait b&w
292 It b&w
1910 34 Study of a child
1914 30 Cement workers
1915 36 The river
37 The old canal
1916 31 Concrete
1918N 23 Old French house, Lachine
229 Knitting chalk
230 Cicely, portrait study chalk
1919 20 The river road wc
21 In winter quarters wc
1920 41 The pool wc
42 The hillside wc
1921 24 December
1923 22 Old courtyard, St Vincent Street, Montreal wc
1924 18 Court House Corners, Montreal
1925 23 Rue St Maurice, Montreal wc
24 Rue St Vincent, Montreal wc
1926 172 Rasco, old courtyard, St Paul Street, Montreal wd cut
173 Gateway to the Silver Dollar Inn, Montreal wd cut
1927 24 Below zero wc
25 Midi wc
285 Mme de Péan cottages, Quebec wd block
286 Mountain Hill, Quebec wd block
1928 24 The habitant wc $70 S7-21 $75
25 Market day wc $70 S7-20 $75
1929 22 Politics wc
23 Well known Montrealers wc
1929 S7, Calgary
19 Les habitants wc $100
1930 24 At Bonsecours Market, Montreal wc $150
25 Old courtyard, Montreal wc $150
1931 31 Ancient gate in Quebec wc $200
32 Old court wc $200
1933 27 18th century house, St Vincent Street, Montreal wc $100 T34-11
1934 38 Old courts, Craig Street, Montreal wc $100
39 Champlain Street, Quebec wc $100
1935 35 The hills of Baie St Paul wc $200 T36-11
36 Early April, Baie St Paul wc $200
1936 45 In the Laurentians wc $250
46 A Laurentian village road wc $250 T37-17
1937 39 A hillside, Baie St Paul wc $300
40 At St Hilarion, Quebec wc $300

1938 35 In the Chinese quarter, Montreal wc $200
36 XVIIth century houses, Dorchester Street, East, Montreal wc $200
1938 S8, Toronto
188 Book, Saguenay. Paul Caron and others. McClelland & Stewart
1939 38 Mid-summer, Bonsecours, Montreal wc $250
1940 30 Notre Dame Street key shop wc $150

CARR, EMILY
13 Dec 1871, Victoria 2 Mar 1945, Victoria AGO B CC1 M NGC TB2
RCA medal 1978

CARR-HARRIS, IAN REDFORD
12 Aug 1941, Victoria WWA78
RCA(e) 1976 Sculptor
Addr: 1979, Victoria

CARREAU-KINGSWELL, ARLETTE (Mrs J. Kingswell)
1917, Montreal
1971 1S Scalp wall hanging 18 x 38 illus $300

CARRIERE, MARCEL
1970 Avec tambours et trompets film screened 20 Feb

CARRINGTON, F.R.
Addr: 1938, Toronto
1938 S8, Toronto
67 Radio cabinet
68 Commode
69 2 armchairs, English oak, natural finish

CARRUTHERS, ELEANOR RUTHWELL
29 Nov 1908, Peterborough, Ont
1954 15 Coach house 24 x 18 $75
1955 17 Hen house $100
1960 17 They follow 20 x 32 $150

CARRUTHERS, WILLIAM E.
see BANZ, GEORGE, 1966

CARSON, JEAN
1938 S8, Toronto
380 Wallpaper design. Hon mention. Canadian Wallpaper Manufacturers Limited

CARSWELL, KATHLEEN
Addr: 1935, 710 Roslyn Ave, Westmount, Que
1935 37 Elizabeth wc nfs

CARTER, ALEXANDER SCOTT
7 Apr 1880, Harrow, Eng 30 Dec 1968, Toronto CNS40 CWW36 M NGC PMC
ARCA 1922 RCA 1928 Sr 1951
Designer
Addr: 1920-37, 1 Breadalbane St, Toronto; 1938-68, Toronto
1920 303 Illumination on vellum, King Ryence's challenge to King Arthur, composed and sung before Queen Elizabeth at the grand entertainment at Kenilworth Castle, in 1575
1921 192 Presentation casket, in gilt and painted gesso, containing an illuminated book on vellum, bound in velvet, with gold covers, chased and enriched with jewels and enamels. Goldsmith work by A.M. Doret (Sir Edmund Walker)
193 Presentation tablet in gold, chased and enriched with enamels. Goldsmith work by A.M. Doret (Sir John and Lady Eaton)
1922 246 Illumination on vellum
1923 203 Memorial casket, silver work and jewel setting by A.M. Doret (Lady Eaton)
1927 287 Illuminated address on vellum (Sir Vincent Meredith, Bart)
1928 195 Illuminated page on vellum
196 Illuminated coat of arms on vellum
1934 213 Book plage, Art Gallery of Toronto
214-15 Book plates
1935 313-15 Book plates nfs
1936 233 Ceiling decoration nfs
234-5 Book plates nfs
1937 305 Ceiling decoration des wc nfs
306 Decorative map of University of Toronto photo nfs
307 Heraldic painting on vellum wc nfs
1939 292 Illuminated page nfs
1940 169 Illuminated page nfs
DW 1929 Illuminated page vellum 10 1/2 x 6 1/4

CARTER, DENNIS HAMPTON
see SMITH, ERNEST, 1964J-67

CARTER, DOROTHY FRANCES COLLEY (Mrs A.M.W. Carter)
31 Aug 1903, Stevenage, Herts, Eng
1944 24 Market garden workers, Manitoba wc $85
1945 35 Winter sunshine wc $85
36 Children playing wc $60

CARTER, E.
fl 1888-9 H
1888 232 Bermuda wc
236 Flowers wc $12
238 Palm grove, Bermuda wc $15

CARTER, ELIZABETH A.
fl 1880-98 H
1880 151 Interior of Trinity Church, Boston wc
157 Interior of Henry VII Chapel, Westminster Abbey wc

CARTER, H.J. (Mrs)
H
1885 49 Roses $30
69 Marsh reeds and grasses panel $30
70 Nasturtiums panel $30
117 Still life $50
143 Azalias $15
144 Yellow roses $15
155 Rose $20

CARTER, HARRIET ESTELLE MANORE (Mrs John G. Carter)
22 Mar 1929, Grand Bend, Ont
RCA(e) 1977 Painter
Addr: 1979, Hamilton

CARTER, HENRY THOMAS
1850, Belfast 19 Dec 1931, Falmouth, Eng B H
Addr: 1887/1896-07, Montreal; 1910-13, 392 Dorchester St, Montreal; 1916, 303 St James St, Montreal
1887 173 Pointe Claire, Lake Saint Louis wc $15
1888 1 Home of the Pigeons, Port Clair wc $15
1896 196 The Iron Mountain, Knowlton wc
1907 225 Old haunted château of La Tortue, XVIII century wc
1910 35 Lane, Montreal West
1913 52 Outremont Golf Links, Montreal wc
53 Richelieu wc
54 Chambly, the old order changeth wc
1916 32 Ere the waning light decay wc

CARUSO, BARBARA ANN
27 Jul 1937, Kincardine, Ont IO
1966 8 Town image #2 19 x 24

CARUSO, IRVING
see ROSEN, BERNARD, 1964N

CARY, HENRY see CAREY, HENRY

CASINI, GUIDO
Addr: 1927, 1048 Sherbrooke St E, Montreal; 1931, 1274 Papineau Ave, Montreal
1927 256 Mme Casini plaster
257 Monument aux mort de la Guerre, érigé à Firenzulo, Italie photo
1931 306 Maquette de la statue de Giovanni Caboto, ériger à Montréal plaster $200
307 Buste de feu de Député Plante plaster $250

CASSILS, M. GILMOUR (Mrs)
1947 24 Mrs Hazen Hansard nfs

CASSON, ALFRED JOSEPH LLD
17 May 1898, Toronto AGO B CC2 CWW79 EC IO M NGC TB2/3 WWA47
ARCA 1926 RCA 1940 Sr 1968 RCA medal 1969, Group of Seven Council Painter
Addr: 1922-3, 806 Bloor St W, Toronto; 1925-7, 22 St Hilda's Ave, Toronto; 1928-31, Toronto; 1932-7, 43 Rochester Ave, Toronto; 1938-71/79, Toronto
1922 27 Smoke haze
247 Oriental poppies block pr ◊AGO◊
1923 23 Grey day, Lake Kushog
24 Early morning
1925 25 A northern lake
26 Summer landscape ◊NGC◊
284 The old willow block pr
1926 18 Sunrise illus 1927-26
19 Birches wc
1929 S7, Calgary
22 Ontario village $350
1932 24 Old farmhouse near Maple wc $125 1933-28 T34-12
1933 29 Mill in winter wc $125

1934 40 Mill town $250 T35-12 1935-39
1935 38 Old store at Salem $250 T36-12 T41-10
1936 47 Fire haze $225 T37-18
1937 41 The village mill $350 T38-9
42 Passing storm, October $75
1938 37 Street in Glen Williams $350 T39-11
1938 S8, Toronto
Sampson Matthews Limited
277, 279, 282 Wampoles bottle labels and cartons
289, 291 McCormick's Fiddle sticks and Bix cartons illus
294 Rose brand marmalade tin label
299 Fancy free carton
301-8, 310 Tuckett cigarette and tobacco cartons illus
313, 315, 317 Neilson chocolate boxes illus
319 Neilson Bitter sweet, Butter toffee, Jersey milk
320 Birks-Ellis-Ryrie booklet
321 Buntin Reid folders
326 Provincial Paper, Supertext folder
328 Provincial Paper blotter
329 Canada Life 2 folders
330 Terminal Warehouse booklet
331 Shirriff, Lushus showcard
332 Shirriff, Lushus and Fancy free magazine advertisements, produced for Cockfield Brown & Company
334 Canada Packers, Biscot shortening tin
1939 39 Golden October $350
1939 F11, New York
14 The white village 34 x 45 $300
1940 31 Winter's end illus $350
1941 31 The little bay $300
1941 S9, Toronto
14 Passing storm $75
1942 27 Sunshine and showers $300 T43-9
1943 12 Thunder weather illus $300 T44-5
1944 25 Aftermath illus $300 T45-9
1945 37 Whitney illus $400 T46-10
1946 17 Sunshine after rain $350 T47-8
1947 25 Box period $350 T48-7
1948 27 Midwinter $300
1949 14 La Cloche Channel, Georgian Bay illus $700 1950-20 38 x 48
1951 13 Calm after storm illus $500 1952-10
1951 Travelling exhibit
9 Summer sun DW 1940 30 x 36 1954 Retro Sec 48 S11-9
1952 11 Frosty morning illus $350
1953 12 Crescendo illus $350 1954-16 30 x 36 illus
1953 Travelling exhibit
4 Village in winter $350
1955 18 Summer sky illus $350
1956 12 Old Ontario illus nfs T56-12
1957 15 The blue heron illus (J.A. Scythe, Esq)
1958 17 Old boarding house, lumber village illus $350
1959 15 Ukranian farm on the Madawaska 30 x 38 illus $800
1960 18 Bedard Pond 30 x 36 illus nfs
1961 20 Winter sun 20 x 40 nfs
1963 11 Morning on Main Street, 1962 $750
1966 S10, Charlottetown
14 Country store 30 x 36 nfs ◊AGO◊
15 Rock, spruce and poplar 30 x 36 illus nfs

CASTLE, MONTAGUE American
fl 1888-96 F H
Addr: 1896, 55 E 59th St, New York
1896 19 Purity

CATTELL, RAYMOND VICTOR
5 May 1921, Birmingham, Eng IO
WWA73
ARCA 1967 RCA 1979 Council Painter
Addr: 1967-71/79, Toronto
1963 12 At the end of the fountain $470
1964N 13 Morning orbit 24 x 36 $500
1965 15 The great seal of Nautilus Rex 60 x 62 $850
16 The fire of Nautilus Rex 50 x 48 $550
1966 9 From across the lake 60 x 48 $800
10 The wooded journey 51 x 40 $500
1967 10 The blooded sound of October's breath 40 x 45 $700 ◊LAG◊

1968 10 Reliquary for day-starts 50 x 39 $750
11 Day-makers mantle 50 x 39 illus $750
1970 10 Tapestry of morning breath 72 x 120 illus $2,500
11 Rain-folded October 72 x 60 $1,500
1970 S11, Halifax
10 River tracked silence. 1970 acry m med 36 x 48 $850
11 Morning moved time shift. 1970 acry m med 36 x 48 $850
DW 1979 Fallow time tracks wc

CAUDLE, NANCY MARY
16 Apr 1908, Cam, Glos, Eng
1944 26 Deserted house wc $75
27 Potted plant wc $50
1946 18 Dr B.R. English nfs T47-9
19 Rev V.R. Browne nfs
1953 13 Markham house $100

CAWTHRA, MABEL see ADAMSON, MABEL

CHABAUTY, CHARLES E.
Addr: 1933, 9006 Routhier St, Montreal
1933 30 Soir de septembre, Laurentides $300

CHADWICK, RICHARD
see FETHERSTONHAUGH, HAROLD, 1947-54
DURNFORD, ALEXANDER, 1957-63

CHADWICK, ROBERT LEE
10 Oct 1903, Heywood, Lancs, Eng
1940 32 Valley of the Holland River, March $150
1941 32 Road to Ste Adèle, Laurentian Mountains $150
1942 28 Ontario barns, winter $150
1943 13 Rural Ontario grist mill $125
14 Local grist mill, Millbrook, Ont $125 T44-6
1945 38 Old house by the creek, March $150 T46-11
39 Main Street, Markham, Ontario $200

CHALLENER, FREDERICK SPROSTON
7 Jul 1869, Whetstone, Eng 30 Sep 1959, Toronto AGO B CC1 CWW55 M Mo12 NGC PMC TB W78 WWA47
ARCA 1891 RCA 1901 Sr 1938 Council
Painter
Addr: 1891-2, Toronto; 1893, Mail Bldg, Toronto; 1894-00, 87 Garden Ave, Toronto; 1901-3, 43 Adelaide St E, Toronto; 1904-5, Adelaide St, Toronto; 1906, Old Court House, Toronto; 1907-8, Toronto; 1909M-10, Conestogo, Ont;1912, Winnipeg; 1913-16, Conestogo, Ont; 1918A-18N, 2 Bloor St W, Toronto; 1919, Conestogo, Ont; 1920-3, 1 Breadalbane St, Toronto; 1924, 513 Church St, Toronto; 1925-6, 112 Roehampton Ave, Toronto; 1927, 1158 Bay St, Toronto; 1928, 610A Jarvis St, Toronto; 1930-7, 1 Breadalbane St, Toronto; 1938-59, Toronto
1891 35 Waiting for a bite
87 Reflections
96 Dreamer
100 Old lady
1893 21 Forty winks on a Sunday afternoon $50 F1-21
22 Maréchal Niel roses $35 F1-22
23 A sweet penitent $20 F1-23
24 Where the mistletoe grows $25 F1-24 nfs
25 Showery weather $20 F1-25 nfs
1894 30 Golden October
31 A song of twilight
32 The hay field
33 The morning lunch
34 Forty winks
35 The boys' bathing place
36 Brunita
157 A grey autumn day wc
158 An autumn reverie wc
1895 27 A sunny morning
28 Study
1896 20 A brunette
1897 43 The milk maid
44 A sewing lesson
45 Henry Simpson, Esq
46 Blossom time
47 A blonde
48 Departing day
49 An old English inn
13W Golden October wc
1898 34 A relic of the past
1899 28 Rachel's tomb illus
29 When the lights are low
30 Conscience makes cowards of us all
163 The Virgin's spring, Nazareth wc
164 The tomb of Samuel, Mizpah wc
164a A minaret at Jaffa,

Palestine wc
239 Richelieu & Ontario Navigation Company, low rel panel cart
1900 16 In a Nazareth garden
17 Ida (S.M. Wickett, Esq)
18 A singing lesson 1901-21 F3-24 $105 illus
19 Where the lake and river meet
131 On a country road wc
1901 19 A relic of the past
20 Workers of the field F2-5 (RCA)
1903 21 Richelieu & Ontario Navigation Company's steamer 'Montreal', grand salon ceiling, large panel
22 Figure 'The toilet' sketch
23 Figure 'Repose' sketch
24 Figure, same ceiling, small panel pastel sketch
25 McConkey's Café, Toronto, ceiling, figure study pastel
26 R & O steamer 'Kingston', mural painting figure sketch
27 Ceiling panel for café, figure sketch
28 Decorative panel for over mantel
1904 33 The milkmaid F4-15
1905 35 Haying
1906 48 Indians spearing fish by torchlight F5-29 $400 1907-37 S2-23
49 An old Ontario farm
50 In pastures green
51 A hay maker F5-30 $150
52 A pagan dancer
53 When the long day's work is over (#54 not in cat)
55 A jolly little girl crayon
56 Gold and green pastel
57 Juliet crayon
1906 F5, Halifax
28 Milking (Ontario Gov't)
32 The farmer's daughter $50 (#31 not in cat)
1907 38 Eventide
39 Putting up haycocks
226 Mural dec pastel sketch
227 A garden party pastel
1907 F6, Sherbrooke
45 Greenland gold $100
46 Girl sewing $150
47 In the hayloft $100
48 The miniature $100
49 Rachel's tomb $100
50 Golden October $250
51 Mid-day lunch $75
52 The haymaker $75
1909M 33 Evening, twilight and night
1909N 23 Stars of the evening
24 The enchanted wood
25 Girl with rabbits S2-25
26 Girl with miniature S2-24, The miniature
1912 S3, Winnipeg
240 Mounted Cree Indian fighting
241 Mounted Sioux Indian fighting
242 Theatre mural decoration pastel
243 Mother love
1913 55 The trapper S4-23 $100
56 The refugees S4-24 $100
352 and 353 Mounted Indian, Cree crayon
354 Large mural decoration pastel sketch
1914 31 A stop for water
32 Wild steeds of the prairie ◊NGC◊
33 The great fall buffalo hunt
34 Over an old trail
1914 S4, Winnipeg
25 Woodland landscape wc $20 nfs
26 Squaws gathering firewood wc $20
27 Northern travellers wc $20
1914 S5, Patriotic Fund
12 Her treasure illus
1915 38 A Selkirk pioneer ◊NGC◊
39 Stepping stones wc
40 An Indian village wc
1916 33 Girls and ducks
34 The enchanted wood
35 Summer afternoon
36 In winter dress
275 Prof James Mavor crayon
276 Drapery study crayon
277 Mrs Albert Jordan crayon
1918A 29 Returning troopships nearing Quebec 1918N-24
30 St François, Ile d'Orléans
31 With wind and tide illus 1918N-25 illus
32 A misty morning
1918N 26 In my orchard
27 Near Baie St Paul, St Lawrence River

1919 22 H.S. Palmer, ARCA illus
23 Miss Edith Fulton
1920 43 In lilac time
44 The swimming place
45 A riverside home
46 St Lawrence River fishermen
1922 28 Happy moments S6-8
29 The Grand River at Conestogo, Ont illus S6-9
30 The blue hat
31 Studio interior
1924 19 Passing the lighthouse
20 French Canadian fisherman
21 In winter furs
22 In pensive mood
253 Mounted Indian crayon
254 An old Scotsman crayon
255 Barbara crayon
256 Man smoking pencil
1925 27 Child and grandfather
28 Girls and ducks
29 Bedtime
30 Sea shells
1926 20 The evening breeze dec panel illus 1927-27 (NGC)
1928 26 Fort Rouillé. A French trading post at Toronto, built 1749, abandoned and burnt 1759 $4,000
27 News from home $350 S7-23 $400
1929 S7, Calgary
24 The scout story $175
25 An old timer $100
26 Ontario rustic $100
1930 26 The Grand River at Conestogo $250
27 Gaspé skipper $80
28 An after supper smoke $80
1931 33 Vacation days $300
34 A lumbering alligator $250
35 Franciscan patriarch $125
36 Early settler $125
1932 25 The road to Mattawa $500 1933-31 $400 T34-13
26 Making the Trans-Canada highway $600
27 Sylvan solitude $100
1933 32 The blue punt $400
1934 41 Rev John S. Humphreys
42 Feeding the pigeons $100 T35-13
1935 40 Queen's Park, Toronto, autumn $100
41 Autumn days $100 T36-13
42 A cottage patriarch $100
43 Playmates $75
1937 43 In the days of Paul Kane $300 T38-10
1938 38 The star fish $250
39 A fairy's child $250
1939 40 Miss Margaret Ethelreda Wilson and Qwan Yin, Queen of Heaven nfs
41 Waiting for the stage coach $150
1939 F11, New York
15 Egbert C. Reed as a Bedouin 36 1/2 x 28 1/2 $1,000
1940 33 Pioneers $150
1941 S9, Toronto
15 Haying time $100
1948 28 On the Athabaska $400
DW 1902 Harvest 31 1/2 x 63 1/2
port: bust, by C. Adams, 1931-301

CHALMERS, ROLAND JOHN ANDERSON
12 Nov 1884, Rochester, Kent, Eng
Addr: 1921, 159 Villeneuve St W, Montreal; 1925-34, 105 51st Ave, Dixie, Lachine, Que
1921 194 Nelson's Monument, Montreal pencil
195 Back yard, St Vincent Street, Montreal pencil
1925 285 Lower town, Quebec drwg
1927 288 Victory Tower, Ottawa pencil
289 Rue Champlain, Quebec pencil
1928 197 Victory Tower, Ottawa etch $35
198 Rue des Carrières, Montreal etch $30
1931 384 Mallards rising etch $25
385 Canadian geese etch $25
1933 284 Old homestead, Lakeside, Que etch $25
285 Daybreak etch $25 1934-216
1934 217 Mallards rising etch $25

CHAMBERLAND, CLAUDE
1971 Tabarnak film screened 14 Apr

CHAMBERS, FRANK PENTLAND English
Nov 1900, England B DBA RA TB2 WWB29
Addr: 1931, McGill University, Montreal
1931 308 Ramsay Traquair, Esq sculp

309 Comus sculp

CHAMBERS, JOHN RICHARD (JACK)
25 Mar 1931, London, Ont 13 Apr 1978, London, Ont AGO CC2 IO M WWA70
ARCA 1972 Council Painter

CHAPDELAINE, W.
H
Addr: 1894, North Nicolet, Côte Nicolet, Que
1894 27 Peeling potatoes

CHAPMAN, ALFRED HIRSCHFELDER
8 Dec 1878, Toronto 12 Nov 1949, Toronto CWW48 PMC
ARCA 1925 Sr 1947 Architect
Addr: 1925, 1068 Northern Ontario Bldg, Toronto; 1926, 33 Bay St, Toronto; 1927, 330 Bay St, Toronto; 1928-49, Toronto
1925 235 Knox College, Toronto. East elevation
236 Sunnyside Bathing Pavilion, Toronto
1926 148 Ontario Government Bldg, at CNE, Toronto. Northeast entrance photo
149 Model of entrance, feature proposed to be erected at eastern end of Canadian National Exhibition grounds photo
1927 234 Princes' Gate, CNE
1946 Chapman, Oxley & Facey
151-3 Bank of Montreal, Toronto. Perspective study. Perspective study of main banking room. Perspective study of lower floors. Marani & Morris, K.R. Blatherwith associate architects

CHAPMAN, CHARLES
1827, Norfolk, Eng d 1887 H
1880 22 Study of a hollyhock

CHAPMAN, CHRISTOPHER
25 Jan 1927, Toronto CC1
ARCA 1970 RCA 1973 RCA medal 1965 Council Film maker
Addr: 1971, Markham, Ont; 1979, Sunderland, Ont
DW 1974 A place to stand. 1967 16mm 18 mins col

CHARBONNEAU, MONIQUE
25 Jun 1928, Montreal
1964J 13 Nuit acceptée 60 x 45 $450

CHARETTE, JACQUES F.
1970 136 Booklet, Carleton University, School of Art Literature
137 Symbol, Society of Graphic Designers of Canada
138 Symbol and application, Canadian Conference on Housing

CHARLEBOIS, JOSEPH CHARLES THEOPHILE
1872, Montreal 21 Oct 1935, Montreal
Addr: 1931-3, 1220 Drummond St, Montreal
1931 386 Book of wedding gouache
387 Ballade des pendus de François Villon gouache $150
1933 286 Acte d'Incorporation de Montréal

CHARLEBOIS, R.H.
Addr: 1938, Montreal
1938 S8, Toronto
23 'Maria Chapdelaine' dark grey levant morocco, des in mosaic

CHATFIELD, EDITH (Mrs R.S. Gossage)
1906, New Haven, Conn
1947 26 Rob nfs
1955 19 Frugal lunch $250

CHAVIGNAUD, GEORGES
24 Sep 1865, Finistère, France
3 May 1944, Meadowvale, Ont AGO H M Mo12 NGC TB3
Addr: 1898, 69 McGill St, Toronto; 1901, 43 Adelaide St E, Toronto; 1903, Toronto; 1904, Montreal; 1905-6, c/o Henry Morgan Co, Montreal; 1908, Meadowvale, Ont; 1909 c/o McKenzie & Co, Toronto; 1909N, Lambton Mills, Ont; 1914, Victoria School of Art, Halifax; 1918, Kleinburg, Ont
1898 151 Pastoral, Meadowvale wc
152 Refitting the fleet, Port Credit wc
153 Grey day, Humber Valley wc
1901 158 The old town hall wc
159 Dutch boats wc
160 On the sands near Heyst wc

1903 156 The Quai of the Augustine, Bruges wc
157 The old sluice port, Simsking, evening wc
158 Marine wc
159 Landscape wc
1904 208 Evening, Bruges wc F4-97
209 In the Campine wc
210 A bit of snow wc
211 Claire de lune wc F4-98
1905 51 Canal boat
52 Moonlight 1906-67
1906 68 Interior
69 Morning
70 Cornwall coast
1906 F5, Halifax
33 A Brittany lane $50
34 Fishing boats $65
1907 F6, Sherbrooke
41 Dutch village wc $125
42 Dutch windmill wc $250
43 Le soir $400
44 Petit Pierre $150
1908 35 The willows, morning light
1909M 29 Christine dec port
1909N 27 The rain
28 Bridge over the Etobicoke
1910 S2, Liverpool
26 Grand Canal, Bruges wc
1914 S5, Patriotic Fund
71 Dutch fishing boats illus
1918A 33 Dreamland wc
34 River landscape wc
1918N 28 Summer day, the bridge wc

CHECKLEY, FRANK
fl 1893-6 H
Addr: 1894, Ottawa; 1895-6, 8 Cooper St, Ottawa
1894 28 Portrait of my mother
29 Portrait of an old lady 1895-26
1895 25 Study of an old man 1896-23
1896 21 Girl knitting
22 Study of a girl's head

CHENEY, ANNA GERTRUDE LAWSON (NAN)
(Mrs Hill Cheney)
22 Jun 1897, Windsor, NS
Addr: 1928-33, 55 Sunset Blvd, Ottawa; 1934, 3610 Lorne Cr, Montreal
1928 28 Low tide $100
1931 37 The hill, Trail, BC $50
1932 28 The deserted quarry $100
1933 33 The slasher mill $100 T34-14
1934 43 Yuki $50

CHERRY, AILEEN ALMA
1896, Brockville, Ont
Addr: 1924-5, 83 Hyland Ave, Belleville, Ont
1924 23 The Niagara
1925 31 Harvest days

CHESLEY, J.L.
Addr: 1906, 7 Victoria Rd, Halifax
1906 F5, Halifax
35 King Edward VII
36 Miniatures
37 Portrait crayon

CHESTERTON, WALTER
1845, London, Eng 13 Nov 1931, Ottawa H
ARCA 1880-8 Architect
Addr: 1880-2, Ottawa; 1883, Winnipeg; 1884-8, Ottawa
1880 357 Proposed legislative buildings, Fredericton des
1881 195 Church (Metropolitan) Ottawa
1883 348 St Andrew's Church, Winnipeg.
357 Hall. Chesterton & McNichol
363 Residence, A.W. Ross, Esq, MP
364 Residence, Kildonan, near Winnipeg
371 Trinity Church, Winnipeg

CHETWYND, ARTHUR RALPH TALBOT (Sir)
28 Oct 1913, Walhachin, BC CWW79
1970 The final gun. Archur Chetwynd, Ross McConnell, William Street film screened 20 Feb

CHEWETT, ALBERT R. English
fl 1905-15 DBA RA
Addr: 1905, rue de Grenelle, Paris
1905 54 Jeanette

CHIARANDINI, ALBERT
30 Sep 1915, Udine, Italy WWA56
1948 29 Old man nfs
1963 12 Black shawl 40 x 29 illus $1,000
1968 12 Hippie from Yorkville 48 x 40 $1,000 illus
13 Hippie from Yorkville 48 x 34 $1,000

CHIASSON, IRENE
b Senneterre, Que

1971 2S Participez à la culture
sculp 28 x 120 $1,000

CHICOINE, RENE
1905, Montreal WWA47
1939 42 In the sun $150

CHILD, MARJORIE L. (Mrs Marjorie Thompson Child)
1947 27 Silver and blue nfs
1951 14 Joan
1952 12 Giselle $500

CHIPMAN, N.I.
Addr: 1927, 45 Lincoln Ave, Montreal
1927 290 Miss Ruth Carsley chalk

CHIPMAN, NOEL
fl 1925-63
Addr: 1937, 1474 Drummond St, Montreal
1937 237 Interior views, residence, V.M. Lynch-Staunton, Esq
238 Doctor's office, The Sherbrooke Apartments

CHISHOLM, FLORENCE MARY HELEN
b 1918 d 1975
1938 S8, Toronto
167 Design for sanctuary window. OCA students, assisted by Rowley Murphy

CHISHOLM, MADELEINE
1934, Halifax
Addr: 1976, Vancouver
1976 S12, Montreal
139 Mattel hand dyed knitted chenille 45 x 45 x 3 1/2 col illus

CHOLAKIAN, VARTKES
Addr: 1976, Montreal
1976 S12, Montreal
167 The cage 35mm b&w 17 min one illus

CHOQUETTE, MARCEL
1941 206 Winston Churchill sculp $300
1945 217 Jean plaster nfs
1947 198 Etude sculp nfs

CHRISTIE, E.L.
H
1890 134 A quiet bit of the Catskills wc $25

CHRISTY, ROBERT B.
Addr: 1914, 245 Leslie St, Toronto; 1915, 710 Rhodes Ave, Toronto
1914 35 Buckhaven, east coast of Scotland
36 Out Scarboro way
1915 41 Flowers
42 A break in the storm

CHURCH, FREDERICK STUART American
1 Dec 1842, Grand Rapids 18 Feb 1923, New York AAA29 B F Gr TB1/3 Y
1882 307 A fog on the beach (loan)

CICCIMARA, RICHARD MATTHEW
12 Jul 1924, Vienna 19 Jun 1973, Greece
1964J 14 The young dignitary wc 29 1/2 x 23 1/2 $250

CLAPP, WILLIAM HENRY
29 Oct 1879, Montreal 21 Apr 1954, Oakland, Cal B F M NGC TB2/3 WWA 36
ARCA 1911-19 Painter
Addr: 1904, Montreal; 1908, 153 Bleury St, Montreal; 1909, 255 Bleury St, Montreal; 1910, 172 E 75th St, New York; 1911, c/o Johnson & Copping, Montreal; 1914, 314 St Catherine St W, Montreal; 1915-16, McKinley, Isle of Pines, Cuba; 1918A, Oakland, Cal
1904 34 The cloud
35 Apple trees F4-16
1908 27 Autumn morning, France
28 Morning in Spain ◊NGC◊
1909M 41 The village of Corsenca, Spain
42 Waders, Canada
1909N 29 Bird nesting
30 Loading lumber
1910 36 A Canadian orchard
1911 30 Satisfaction
31 Portrait study
1912 44 Afternoon
45 Morning
46 Kitchen garden
47 Grey autumn
1912 S3, Winnipeg
29 Under the arbour
30 A rainy day
31 and 32 Landscape wc
1913 57 and 62 Landscape
58 Decorative landscape
59 Autumn mist
60 Philipsburg S4-29 $125
61 Country road

1914 37 Afteroon, St Sulpice
38 Sunset, St Sulpice
39 Summer landscape, St Sulpice ‖NGC‖
1914 S4, Winnipeg
28 Decorative landscape $500
29 Afternoon, Philipsburg $125
30 Country road $125
1914 S5, Patriotic Fund
61 Sunset, in-coming tide illus
1915 43 Rio Nuevas, Cuba illus ‖NGC‖
44 Nueva Gerona, Cuba
45 A Cuban river
46 A river through the jungle, Cuba
1916 37 The three bathers, Cuba illus ‖NGC‖
38 Misty morning
39 A sunny day
40 Rio Nuevas, Isle of Pines
1918A 35 Bathers, Cuba illus
36 Filling parongs, Cuba

CLARE, OLIVER English
c 1853 d 1927 DBA H WBA
Addr: 1884, c/o J. Penfold, Bank of British North America, Montreal
1884 55 Fruits
57 Flowers

CLARK, A.J.
Addr: 1914-19, 159 Springhurst Ave, Toronto; 1920, 435 Spadina Ave, Toronto; 1924, P O Box 2, Maple, Ont
1914 200 E. Pauline Johnson bronze
1916 242 Sir William Van Horne bronze bas rel
1918A 185 Sir Charles Tupper, Bart bronze
1918N 208 Memorial plaque design bas rel
209 Prescott Memorial photo
1919 173 Sir James Whitney bronze
1920 263 Bank of Toronto, War Memorial mural panels in bas-rel, detail
1924 230 Sir Henry Irving bas rel

CLARK, ALSON A.
Addr: 1907, Quebec
1907 40 Solitude
41 From Hope Hill
42 The Champlain Market Quebec
43 The market day

CLARK, H.M.
Addr: 1902, 1830 Notre Dame St, Montreal
1902 190 Cemaes Bay, Angelsea wc

CLARK, PARASKEVA PLISTIK (Mrs Oreste Allegre) (Mrs Philip Clark)
28 Oct 1898, St Petersburg AGO CCI IO M NGC TB3 WWA47
ARCA 1956 RCA 1966 Sr 1968 Council Painter
Addr: 1932, 315 Lonsdale Rd, Toronto; 1956-71/79, Toronto
1932 29 Self portrait
1948 30 The red church, Perkins, Quebec $225
1949 15 Road builders $175
1950 22 Midwinter in Rosedale 20 x 24 nfs
1951 15 Bridge on Canoe Lake $125
1952 13 Leaside, still life $85
1953 14 Woods by the end of August $250
15 Still life with mask $225
1955 20 Three roses, Jules Bouche illus $300
21 After breakfast, still life $200
1956 13 Woods by the lake illus $200 T56-13
1957 16 Muskoka evening $400
1958 18 Boston marigolds $225
1959 16 Noon at Tadoussac 32 x 40 $400
1960 19 Trees at sunrise 24 x 20 $225
1961 21 Nasturtiums 34 x 22 $300
22 By the lake 20 x 24 $150
1963 14 White platycodon 30 x 20 illus $300 S10-6 illus nfs
1966 11 Brandy Creek reflections, #2 22 x 40 $325
DW 1967 Sunlight in the woods 33 1/2 x 29 3/4

CLARKE, B. STANLEY
fl 1897-02 H
Addr: 1897, 15 Toronto St, Toronto; 1902, 79 Admiral Rd, Toronto
1897 50 Hope on, hope ever, brave mariner
1902 189 Coast scene wc

CLARKE, EDITH GRAEME
Addr: 1918A-19, 386 Berkeley St, Toronto
1918A 208 Design for a panel
1919 24 Still life

CLARKE, EMMA
d 31 Dec 1946, Belleville, Ont
Addr: 1910, Corner of Bridge & Anne Sts, Belleville, Ont
1910 37 Maskinonge
38 Black bass

CLARKE, PEGGY
Addr: 1937, 64 Oakwood Ave, Toronto
1937 308 Philip and Miguel brush drwg nfs

CLARKES, GERARD LUTHER
1934, Winnipeg
1964J 15 The promise 36 x 48 $350

CLAY, MARY see EWART, MARY CLAY

CLAYS, PAUL JEAN Belgian
27 Nov 1819, Bruge 9 Feb 1900, Brussels B H TB
1882 308 Calme dans l'Escant (loan)

CLEAVER, ELIZABETH ANN (Mrs Mrazik)
19 Nov 1939, Montreal WWA76
RCA(e) 1974 Illustrator
Addr: 1979, Montreal

CLEGHORN, WILLIAM HENRY EDWARD
1902, Montreal Mar 1962, Montreal
1939 43 Percé Rock wc $25

CLELAND, MARY ALBERTA
1876, Montreal d 1960 M NGC TB3
Addr: 1899, 244 Guy St, Montreal; 1902-27, 15 Souvenir Ave, Montreal; 1929-35, 2211 Souvenir Ave, Montreal
1899 23 St Ann's Market, Montreal
24 Little Champlain Street, Quebec
25 Overlooking St Charles River
1902 34 Moonrise
273 Drawing charcl
1904 36 St Ann's Market
296 Sketch in clay sculp
1905 36 Portrait
1906 71 Miss Elsie Michaels
72S Sketch in clay sculp
1906 F5, Halifax
38 Elsie pastel $60
1907 228 Portrait of a boy pastel
229 Baby's head pastel
1907 F6, Sherbrooke
53 Head of a young girl pastel $40
54 Baby's head pastel $25
1908 34 Study of a child pastel
1909M 27 Sketch, Naples
28 Sketch, Rome
1910 39 On the North River, St Andrews, Quebec
40 Sketch
1910 S2, Liverpool
27 Wilhelmina pastel
1912 48 Sketch
49 Barbara pastel
1912 S3, Winnipeg
33 Elsie pastel
1913 63 Evening
1915 47 On the neach, Notre Dame du Portage ǁNGCǁ
48 Sketch, Notre Dame du Portage
1916 41 Little friends pastel
1918A 37 Portrait of a boy pastel
1918N 29 The kiddie-kar
1919 25 An interior wc
1920 47 Maine coast, sketch
1922 32 Wilhelmina pastel
1923 25 Selby pastel
1924 24 Valerie
1925 32 A breezy day
1926 21 A convent, Montreal, built 1698
1927 28 Gathering sea weed
1929 24 Mills near the canal $75
25 Calendulas $35
1929 S7, Calgary
27 On the way to Carillon $200
28 Zinnias $100
29 Cordwood $200
1931 38 Country store $150
1935 44 Zinnias $100
272 Brian, son of Mr and Mrs A.D.P. Heney clay
1941 33 Single peonies $150
1947 28 Phlox $100

CLEMENTS, WILLIAM ALBERT
5 Oct 1921, Toronto M
1953 114 Mary sculp illus nfs
1955 101 In the garden sculp $250

CLEMES, EMILY (Mrs)
H
Addr: 1896, Revere House, Brockville
1896 197 Sunflowers wc

CLEMMER, SHIRLEY
1938, St Catharines, Ont
Addr: 1976, Toronto
1976 S12, Montreal
138 Fat Albert rope/corde 54 x 42 x 36 illus

CLERK, PIERRE JEAN
26 Apr 1928, Atlanta, Ga TB3 WWA78
Addr: 1976, New York
1976 S12, Montreal
10 Nichicun acry 72 x 72 illus
62 Soho welded alum 48 x 66 x 14 illus

CLIFF, DENIS ANTHONY
8 Aug 1942, Victoria IO
RCA(e) 1976 Painter
Addr: 1979, Toronto

CLIFTON, JOHN TERRENCE
26 Jul 1933, Peterborough, Ont
RCA(e) 1979 Industrial designer
Addr: 1979, Don Mills, Ont

CLOUTIER, ALBERT EDWARD
12 Jun 1902, Leominster, Mass 9 Jun 1965, St Hilaire, Que CC2 CNS40 CWW64 M NGC W78 WWA47
ARCA 1951 RCA 1958 Council Painter
Addr: 1932-3, 1801 University Tower, Montreal; 1935, 660 St Catherine St W, Montreal; 1936, 522 Pine Ave, Montreal; 1952-65, Montreal
1932 30 Moulin de Gaspé, near l' Islet wc $45
1933 34 From Malté's Hill, Murray Bay $200 T34-15
35 The old tannery, Murray Bay wc $50
1935 45 The hill, south shore, lower St Lawrence $350
46 April motive, Quebec $350 T36-14
1936 48 The tannery by the clay bank, $600
1938 40 Cap à l'Original, winter $300 T39-12
41 North shore road $275 F11-16 28 x 24
1938 S8, Toronto
60 Illustrated map, CIL
61 8 display cards, CIL
63 Booklet, The ABC of CIL A. Cloutier, C. Mangold
70 2 catalogue covers
71 Menu illustration
72 6 original illustrations for CIL
1951 16 Wasted wilderness $800
1952 14 Wasted wilderness #2 $800 T53-5
15 Boats in port illus $700
1953 16 Ste Adèle, Quebec, winter $800
1954 17 Antiques 24 x 30 illus $500
18 Cliff at Gay Head 24 x 30 $500
1955 22 Pueblo, Taos, NM illus $600 1956-14 illus T56-14
1956 15 Dimanche en ville $700 T56-15
1957 17 Skaters at Ste Marguerite illus $500
1958 19 Wash day at the cross roads $500
20 By the old mill stream illus $400
1959 17 Les bouleaux, Petite Rivière, Quebec 30 x 40 illus $650
18 Grisaille du printemps 26 x 32 $500
1960 20 The break-up, St Hilaire 30 x 40 $700 1961-23 $800
21 Forest elevation 30 x 40 illus $700
1964N 14 View of Assisi 30 x 40 illus $1,200 S10-7 illus 1965-17a, in memoriam
DW 1958 Défrichement, Comte Charlevoix 32 x 40

CLUSE, ZILLAH MARY
7 Jan 1916, Toronto
Addr: 1935, 239 Percival Ave, Montreal West
1935 273 Venite ad me bronze rel $50

CLYMER, JOHN FORD
29 Jan 1907, Ellensburgh, Wash M
ARCA 1935 Non-res, 1956 Painter
Addr: 1933, 69 Donwoods Dr, York Mills, Ont; 1934-5, 290 Jedburgh Rd, Toronto; 1936-40, Toronto; 1941-55, Westport, Ont; 1957-71 USA
1933 36 The river dwellers, BC $500 T34-16
1934 44 She who talks with the spirits $400 T35-14
1935 47 Thunder Mountain $300 T36-15
48 Autumn trail $250

COATES, FREDERICK
27 Sep 1890, Nottingham, Eng
Addr: 1916, Toronto, AMC Overseas; 1919, RR 2, West Hill, Ont
1916 243 Portrait bust plaster
1919 174 Capt Walter R. Duff plaster

COBB, ANDREW RANDALL
13 Jun 1876, Brooklyn, NY 2 Jun 1943, Halifax
ARCA 1941 Architect
Addr: 1941-3, Halifax

COBERWEIN see KOBERWEIN

COBURN, FREDERICK SIMPSON
18 Mar 1871, Upper Melbourne, Que
25 May 1960, Upper Melbourne, Que
AGO CC2 CNS36 CWW58 M Mo12 NGC TB3 W78 WWA47
ARCA 1920 RCA 1928 Sr 1941 Council
Painter
Addr: 1904, Antwerp; 1906-7, Henry Morgan & Co, Montreal; 1913, 39 Rempart des Béguines, Antwerp; 1916-18, Upper Melbourne, Que; 1919, 39 Rempart des Béguines, Antwerp; 1920-1, 79 Mansfield St, Montreal; 1922 c/o Ch. Edlington, 146 Mansfield St, Montreal; 1923-4, 52 St Matthew St, Montreal; 1925, c/o Scott & Sons, Montreal; 1926, 52 St Matthew St, Montreal; 1927-37, 1258 St Matthew St, Montreal; 1938-50, Montreal; 1951-60, Upper Melbourne, Que
1904 37 Flemish fire place F4-17
38 The cow kettle F4-18
212 Le pot au feu wc F4-99
1906 F5, Halifax
39 Dutch interior $300
1907 F6, Sherbrooke
55 Dutch interior $250
56 Dutch peasant $100
1913 64 The letter S4-31 $500
65 Haymaking, afterglow S4-32 $500
1916 278 A Venetian waterway wax drwg
279 Relics wax drwg
280 Winter etch
1918A 38 The river road
39 Wind in March
1918N 30 Logging, a windy day in March
1919 26 March morning
27 The grey barn, haying
1920 48 Logging, sunlight and shadows in the woods illus
49 April morning, Melbourne
1921 25 Danville roses
26 L'habitant illus
27 Logging, a heavy load
28 Over the hill
1922 33 Winter morning at Melbourne S6-10 ǂNGCǂ
34 Logging
35 Oxen in the woods S6-11
1923 26 The blue pung
27 The sun-tipped mountain
28 A fine winter morning
204 The Danville Road col etch
1924 25 The red cariole
26 Blue Montmorency
27 Cloud shadow, plowing
1925 33 Autumn, Eastern Townships, Quebec
34 Indian summer, Quebec
1926 22 The rollway
23 Two loads of cordwood
1927 29 The pasture hill, Healey Valley illus
30 Woods at Melbourne
31 The Healey Valley
32 The Trenholmville Road
1927 F7, London, Eng
127 Logging, winter, Quebec $315
1928 29 Houses at Lac Mercier $600
30 Warden Bridge $600 F9-190 $715
31 Wood interior $500 S7-30
32 The Melbourne Notch DW 1929 25 x 31 T51-10
1928 F8, London, Eng
122 Winter in the Laurentians, Quebec $470
1929 26 The hills at Valcourt $1,000
27 Oxen in the woods $800
1929 S7, Calgary
31 Laurentians $600
1931 39 Frosty morning $600
40 Noon $600
41 L'abreuvoir $400
1933 37 Rollway $600
38 The lake road
39 Winter evening $300
40 Winter road $400 T34-17
1934 45 Nude study $300 T35-15
46 The red cariole $250 1936-51
47 Wood interior illus $300
1935 49 River road, Richmond $500
50 Still life, roses $250
51 Portrait sketch nfs
52 Nude study $500 T36-16
1936 49 Grey winter $500
50 Blueberry Hill, Richmond $500 T37-19
1937 44 Winter evening $1,000
45 Chinoiserie $500 T38-11
46 Carlotta nfs
1938 42 Gipsy $500

43 March morning $500 T39-13
1939 44 Winter sunlight $1,000
45 Somewhere in Quebec $400
1939 F11, New York
17 The red cariole 32 x 20 $500
1940 34 Penfold's Hill $500 T41-11
1941 34 Rollway $500 T42-10
35 Bucking firewood $500
36 Winter afternoon $500
1943 15 Retour du baptême $500 T44-7
16 Mill logs $500 T44-8
1949 16 Noon $800
1954 28 Retro Sec. Winter landscape with oven. 1929 ◊MMFA◊

COBURN, MALVINA SCHEEPERS (Mrs Frederick Simpson Coburn)
b Belgium d 1933
Addr: 1916, Richmond, Que; 1918N, Upper Melbourne, Que; 1919, 39 Rempart des Béguines, Antwerp; 1920-1, 79 Mansfield St, Montreal
1916 Scheepers, to 1919
208 and 209 Roses
1918N 170 Chaumières en Flanders 1919-143
1919 144 Sheepfold in Flanders
1920 50 La rentrée du troupeau
51 Early morning
1921 29 Sheepfold, Flanders
30 Sheep going to pasture

COCHRANE, BERTHA L.
fl 1891-08 AAA1900 H
Addr: 1898-02, Hillhurst, Que; 1906-08, 265 University St, Montreal
1898 149 Shady road wc
1901 161 A quiet spot wc
1902 191 Pathway by the willows wc
1906 F5, Halifax
40 Sketch at North Hatley
1907 44 Sketch at Stowe, Vermont
1907 F6, Sherbrooke
57 View of St Andrews, Quebec pastel $25
1908 29 Frances

COCKFIELD, BROWN & CO, LIMITED
Addr: 1938, Toronto
1938 S8, Toronto
73 6 proofs of newspaper advertisements, International Nickel Company of Canada Limited. Charles Comfort
74 Newspaper and magazine advertisements, Tea Market Expansion Bureau

COGILL, ZEMA see HAWORTH, ZEMA

COGSWELL, THOMAS FREDERICK BARRY
20 Feb 1939, London, Eng
RCA(e) 1978 Sculptor
Addr: 1979, North Vancouver

COHEN, JEAN (Mrs)
Addr: 1919, 31 Parkwood Ave, Toronto
1919 28 Still life

COHEN, SHELDON
24 Sep 1935, Kitchener, Ont
1965 17 6H/13 40 x 52 $250
1966 12 6K/34 33 x 57 $300
1967 12 6L/59 49 x 56
13 6L/60 52 x 60

COHEN, SOREL
Addr: 1976, Montreal
1976 S12, Montreal
63 Grid #2 detail cotton & polyester 48 x 96 illus

COLE, PHILIP TENNYSON English
c 1862, England 15 Sep 1939, England B DBA RA TB
Addr: 1922, c/o Johnson Art Galleries, Montreal
1922 36 Comtesse de Vannes wc

COLEMAN, ARTHUR PHILEMON
4 Apr 1852, Lachute, Que 1939, Toronto H Mo12
Addr: 1881, Cobourg, Ont; 1884, Victoria College, Cobourg, Ont
1881 12 The old canoe wc $30
95 Snowdon, north Wales wc $35
1882 123 Fladmark, Romsdal Horn, Norway wc $25
127 Bird Rock, coast of Norway wc $20
149 Old church and parsonage wc $20
153 Old barn, Silesia wc $25
1883 225 Vesuvius wc $20
243 Tromso harbour wc $25
247 Skjolden, Norway wc $12
248 Castle Ovo wc $15
249 Hazy afternoon on the Mediterranean wc $20
262 Winter in Silesia wc $25
271 At Naples wc $15
279 Evening at Venice wc $15
290 On the Campagna wc $25

1884 105 A leaning tower, Venice wc $15
131 Waterfall, Romsdal, Norway wc $25
139 In the Thousand Islands wc $25 S1-30 $20
165 Near Arnsteg, Switzerland wc $26 S1-18 $20
1884 S1, Saint John
9 In southern Italy wc $20
1885 215 A memory of Florida wc $20
220 Camp in the Selkirks wc $40
235 Among the Rockies wc $20
252 Pensacola Bay wc $15
272 Near Whiteman's Pass wc $20
313 Bow Pass wc $40
1886 80 Wreck, Presquile wc $20
92 Mount McDonald, Big Bend of Columbia River wc $20
1888 239 Vase and flowers wc $25
260 Tide out wc $30
285 Amstig, Switzerland wc $40
290 Storm on the lake wc $40

COLEMAN, DIANE
1970 139 Wall painting. Lightsound sensorium
140 Wall hanging

COLES, DOROTHY RHYNAS
fl 1916-37
Addr: 1918N-26, 174 Mance St, Montreal; 1929, 3466 Mance St, Montreal
1918N 31 Harvest
1926 24 Low tide, Concarneau, Brittany
1929 28 John pastel
29 Pendennis Point, Cornwall

COLLIER, ALAN CASWELL
19 Mar 1911, Toronto AGO CC1 CWW79 IO M NGC TB3 WWA70
ARCA 1956 RCA 1960 Council Painter
Addr: 1957-71/79, Toronto
1948 31 The footbridge, winter afternoon $150
32 The east wind hath broken thee $400
1951 17 Ore car on the 2875, Delnite Mine m med illus $300 ◊NGC◊
18 Underground hoist room, Delnite Mine m med $175
1952 16 Shrinkage stope drillers, Delnite Mine $400 T53-6
1953 17 Draft doors, New Calumet Mine $200
1954 19 Sawmill 24 x 32 $250
1955 23 Constance at Meaford $250
24 Ian nfs ◊AGH◊
1956 16 262,000 gallons of butane-butylene, Edmonton illus $450
1956 Travelling exhibit
16 Smelter smoke at Copper Cliff $600
1957 18 Grande Grêve fish house illus $600
1958 21 The guitar player $750 DW 1961 30 x 40 S11-12
1959 19 Splintered stump 30 x 50 illus $700
1960 22 Mountain road 30 x 40 illus $600
1961 24 And I, where shall I go? 70 x 40 $1,000
1963 15 The field of August 24 x 36 illus $450
1964N 15 They are gone and unreturning 50 x 30 illus $900 S10-18 $1,000
1965 18 The shore is an ancient world 30 x 50 illus $1,000 S10-19 illus
1966 13 Grey sands curve 30 x 50 $1,000
1967 14 Ian at sixteen 50 x 30 illus $1,200
1968 14 Cape North 30 x 50 illus $1,000
1970 12 Alberta sky 40 x 60 illus $1,600

COLLINGS, CHARLES JOHN
1848 or 1849, Devonshire, Eng 7 Aug 1931, Seymour Arm, Shuswap Lake, BC B H M NGC TB1/3
Addr: 1897, Chudleigh, Devon, Eng
1897 31 Woodland rambles Collins, mispr
32 Near the old village
33 A Devon glen
12W Autumn wc

COLLINS, JOHN ALTON
7 Oct 1917, Washington, DC CWW79
1941 37 Coffee and rum 5 a m wc $35
38 5 o'clock wc $35
1943 17 Shadows wc $50
18 House in the rain wc $50
1945 40 Two tugs wc $75
41 Rainy Saturday, Snowdon wc $75

1947 29 Misty morning, South Street, New York wc $75 T48-8
30 Boats on Lake St Louis wc $75
1948 33 Loading at Market Basin wc $75
1949 17 Along the canal wc $75

COLLINS, WARREN
1970 Musical chairs film screened 12 Feb

COLLYER, NORA FRANCES ELIZABETH
7 Jun 1898, Montreal
Addr: 1922-37, 4029 Dorchester St W, Westmount, Que
1922 37 Jack
1923 29 Autumn
1924 28 Portrait
29 Autumn morning
1925 35 Brome Lake
1926 25 Lisieux
1927 291 Street, Quebec drwg
292 Sketch drwg
1928 33 Windy day, Brome Lake $100
1929 30 Winter, Eastern Townships $200
1937 47 Farm, St Fidèle, Quebec $100
1938 44 Village on the St Lawrence $100 T39-14
1939 46 The creek $100
47 Village on the St Lawrence River $150
1942 19 The creek, Foster, Quebec $100

COLONNA, EUGENE
TB
1890 12, 13 and 14 A bit of colour nfs
214 A hall in a modern house
215 Mantel piece arch drwg
216 and 217 Memorial window drwg
218 Interior of sleeping car arch drwg
219 Interior of parlour car arch drwg
220 Cabinet drwg
221 Designs for jewellry

COLSON, FREDERICK
23 Jul 1854, Shedfield, Hants, Eng
d 1924 H
Addr: 1903-14, Ottawa
1903 155 Among the hills wc
1904 213 An old sugaring bush wc
214 The naked trees at evening sough wc
1905 37 In the land of the habitant
38 Habitant homestead, St François, d'Orléans, Quebec
39 October morning, Green Mountain country
1906 58 Winter reigneth o'er the land
59 Habitant homestead, Ile d'Orléans
1907 230 Winnoski willows wc F6-58 $25
1907 F6, Sherbrooke
59 In the Green Mountains wc $20
1909M 26 Elmsdale farm
1912 50 In the Gatineau country wc
51 October, Rockcliffe Park, Ottawa wc
1913 66 A Hampshire homestead wc
67 Evening at Liverpool wc
68 A Vermont vista
1914 40 Evening at Cobourg, Ont wc
41 Afternoon at Cobourg, Ont wc

COLVILLE, DAVID ALEXANDER
24 Aug 1920, Toronto AGO B CC1 M NGC TB3 WWA47
1940 35 Rocks and sea $100
1941 39 September morning $125 T42-11
40 Self portrait $60
1942 29 Old woman $40 T43-10
30 Colored boy temp $30
1946 20 Three horses $125 T47-10 ◊AGO◊

COMFORT, CHARLES FRASER OC LLD
22 Jul 1900, Edinburgh AGO B CC2 CWW79 M NGC TB3 WWA47 WWB52
ARCA 1936 RCA 1942 Sr 1969 Council
Painter
Addr: 1925-6, 87 St Clair Ave E, Toronto; 1927-8, 12 Hudson Dr, Toronto; 1929, 407 St Clair Ave E, Toronto; 1931-2, 48 Sheridan Ave, Toronto; 1936, 165 Crescent Rd, Toronto; 1937, 25 Severn St, Toronto; 1938-59, Toronto; 1960-5, Ottawa; 1966, Hull, Que; 1967-70, Ottawa; 1971/79, Hull, Que
1925 36 Out west
37 Prairie sunlight wc
1926 26 Quebec landscape

27 Autumn wc
1927 33 The Ogilvie
34 Autumnal
1928 34 Portrait of a young man
1929 31 The late Will O. Staples
1929 S7, Calgary
32 A great rock $800
33 Elizabeth wc $250
1931 42 Brothers $600
43 Chuhaldin wc $300
1932 32 John H. Creighton, Esq $500
234 Design for mural decoration
1936 52 Smelting stacks, Copper Cliff $600 T37-20 ≬NGC≬
53 Louise nfs
1937 48 Ballerina wc nfs
49 Ballerina resting wc $125
309 Tinted drawing #2 $10
310 Tinted drawing #3 $10
1938 45 Pioneer survival $600 DW 1945 40 1/4 x 48 1/8 1945-43 nfs T51-11 1954 Retro Sec 50
1938 S8, Toronto
73 6 proofs for newspaper advertisements for International Nickel Company of Canada. Cockfield, Brown Co, Limited
275 3 original working drawings for posters, Salada Tea Company
1940 36 Ontario, summer 1940 illus $600
1941 S9, Toronto
16 Promontory $150
1945 Major Charles Comfort
42 Canadian guns firing near Ortona (Loaned by kind permission of the Chief of the General Staff, Lieut Gen Charles Faulkes, CB CBE DSO) illus
1946 21 Italian landscape illus $250
1947 31 Abruzzi village $300
1948 34 Flt Lieut Carl Schaefer, RCAF illus ≬AGO≬
1952 17 Promontory $800 T53-7
1953 18 Becalmed $500
19 Horned cloud illus $400
1954 40 Brig Sherwood Lett, CBE DSO MC QC BA LLD 48 x 56 (University of British Columbia)
1957 19 Wherewhen 30 x 60 illus $850 1958-22
1958 23 Pre-Cambrian legend illus $500
1959 20 Stonehenge 50 x 60 illus $1,200 S10-20 $1,500
1966 14 Epic theme 67 x 50 illus $1,200
1967 15 Topstep I, Newspeak series 50 x 40 illus $1,000
1968 15 Hommage 50 x 72 illus $4,500
1970 13 Carl Schaefer, at Bond Head 67 x 50 illus $5,000
1970 S11, Halifax
13 Heritage 23 x 72 1/2
14 Legacy 23 x 72 1/2
13 and 14, oil on canvas. Working colour sketches for mural paintings in National Library and Archives Building, Ottawa
port: bust, by E. Holbrook, DW 1975

CONDE, KENT L. DE
Addr: 1935-6, 864 Bloomfield Ave, Outremont, Que
1935 62 Enclosure wc $100 T36-20
63 Autumn gold wc $75
1936 60 Sunlit hills, Morin Heights wc $100
1938 56 Summer days, Otter Lake wc $100 T39-17

CONNAUGHTON, ALICE
Addr: 1907, Montreal
1907 45 Still life

CONNER, RALPH
1895, Birkenhead, Eng d 1951
1945 44 Spring sunlight $300
45 Landscape $50
1946 22 The shower $50
1947 32 Back yard $50
33 Church of Our Lady $75

CONNOLLY, JOSEPH
c 1839, Limerick 13 Dec 1904, Toronto Co
ARCA 1880 RCA 1886-94 Council
Architect
Addr: 1880-2, Toronto; 1883, Church St, Toronto; 1884-94, Toronto
1880 340 Mozart Music Hall, Lombardo Romanesque, side elevation
343 Mozart Music Hall, front elevation
358 Alternative design for residence
362-3 Church of Our Lady,

Guelph. Perspective. Front elevation
364 Church of St Mary, Ontario. Northwest view
368 Consumers Gas Co, Toronto, offices
369 Convent and orphanage of St Joseph, London. Perspective view
373 Mozart Music Hall, geometric pointed, front and side elevations
374 Church of St Patrick, Hamilton, Ont
1883 350 St Peter's Cathedral, London, Ont
1887 185 Church of St Mary, Cushendall, diocese of Kingston, Ont des
186 Thorne des
no record of DW

CONSTANTINEAU, FLEURIMOND
27 Aug 1905, St Leonard de Port Maurice, Que
1945 46 Les pays d'en haut $250
47 L'entrée du village $250

CONTANT, EDGAR
Addr: 1920, 1922 St Denis St, Montreal
1920 52 Self portrait

COOKE, EDWY FRANCIS
10 Mar 1926, Toronto AGO IO M WWA53
1944 28 Winter port wc $75
1945 48 Urban desolation wc $150
1946 23 Interior in blue gouache $100

COOMBS, EDITH GRACE (Mrs James Sharp Lawson)
22 Dec 1890, Hamilton CCI CNS36 CWW49 M WWA47
Addr: 1924-5, 99 Gloucester St, Toronto; 1928-32, 648 Ontario St, Toronto; 1934-7, 64 Grenville St, Toronto
1924 30 Desert sands and Green River, Utah
1925 38 Saunder's farm, Neighick Lake, northern Ontario
1928 35 Wind $125
1929 32 From my studio roof $250
1930 200 Head of a negro, #2 crayon $10
1931 44 The sky woman. They shall come to me on their journey to the Land of the Little People $400
1932 33 Neighick Lake, December $200
1934 48 Wylie's farm, northern Ontario $200 T35-16
1937 50 Solomon's seal wc $50
1938 46 Viburnum wc $50 T39-15
1939 48 Christmas morning $300
1940 37 Jacks wc $150
38 Iris wc $150
1941 41 Spring woods wc $60
1941 S9, Toronto
17 Cardinal $70
1950 23 May time 20 x 24 $125

COONAN, EMILY
1885, Montreal NGC
Addr: 1910-27, 13 Farm St, Montreal; 1930, 627 Farm St, Montreal
1910 41 The black cat
1913 72 The girl with a rose S4-35 $150
73 Girl in green S5-73 illus
1914 44 Two Spanish girls
45 The canal
1916 43 Girl with baskets
44 The orphans illus
1918N 32 Girl in red
1919 29 The green balloon 1920-53 ◊NGC◊
30 Spanish dancer illus
1921 31 Girl and car
32 Ponte Vecchio, Florence ◊NGC◊
1922 38 Interior
1923 30 Carmelita 1924-31
1925 39 San Frediano Gate, Florence ◊NGC◊
1927 35 A villa outside Florence
1930 29 The blue armchair $300

COOPER & BEATTY LIMITED
Addr: 1938, Toronto
1938 S8, Toronto
William E Trevett
75 Foundry type specimen books
76 Proof envelope

COOPER, A.T.
1971 11G Magazine advertisement. Province of New Brunswick

COOPER, ANTHONY
Addr: 1932, 156 Edgmont St, Toronto
1932 34 Chinese girl $75

COOPER, EMMA see LAMPERT, EMMA

COOPER, H.J.
1938 47 Trees wc $100
1939 49 Zinnias wc $100

COOPER, HEATHER
16 Mar 1945, Louth, Lincs, Eng
RCA(e) 1976 Illustrator
Addr: 1979, Toronto

COOPER, REED TALMADGE
b 1931
1970 14 Ancient screen 51 x 89 $450

COOPER, STANLEY SMITH
1 Apr 1906, Leeds, Eng
1946 24 Evening practice $250 T47-11
1947 34 Easter lily man $350
1948 35 Fish house paraphernalia $150
36 Rocks, Nova Scotia $200
1949 18 Burnt mill, Cos Cob, Conn $500
1950 24 Headland, Indian Harbour, NS 36 x 45 $300

COPELAND, ALFRED BRYANT American
1840, Boston 30 Jan 1909, Boston
AAA28 B F H TB
1882 20 An afternoon's nap $100
57 Arch of Thermes at Musée Cluny $125
267 Outward bound monoc $75

COPLEY, JOHN SINGLETON American
3 Jul 1738, Boston 9 Sep 1815, London, Eng B F G Gr TB
1881 215 Mrs Franklin (Rev Jas. Uniacke)
216 Lieut Gov Franklin (Rev Jas. Uniacke)

COPPOLD, LESLIE GEORGE MURRAY
22 Jun 1914, Montreal
ARCA 1950 Council Painter
Addr: 1951-71/79, Montreal
1943 20 Lesage wc $100
21 Farm wc $100
1944 29 Terrebonne $175
30 Wagon wc $200
1945 49 Boathouses wc $250
50 Tree $200
1946 25 Pump wc $175
1947 35 Island wc $400
36 Quebec farm wc illus $400 T48-9
1948 37 Ste Lucie de Doncaster wc $400
38 Quebec oven wc $300
1949 19 Waterfall wc $300
20 Buggy wc nfs T50-3
1951 19 The Asia $200
1952 18 Gate Tower illus $600 T53-8
1954 21 Rooms 35 x 35 illus $600 S10-21

CORBETT, HELENA MAE
6 Sep 1885, Windsor, N Dak
Addr: 1925, Brownville, Ont; 1927, 666 Spadina Ave, Toronto
1925 40 The field path
41 Birches on Georgian Bay
1927 36 Wayside cottage

CORBOLD, CAROLINE (Mrs)
Addr: 1929-31, 331 Clarke Ave, Westmount, Que
1929 33 Zinnias $50
1931 45 Phlox $90

CORMIER, ERNEST
5 Dec 1885, Montreal 1 Jan 1980, Montreal CNS36 CWW58 NGC
ARCA 1925 RCA 1932 Sr 1956 Council Architect
Addr: 1914-15, 52 Sherbrooke St W, Montreal; 1918N, New Birks Bldg, 10 Cathcart St, Montreal; 1922-5, 52 Sherbrooke St W, Montreal; 1927-32, 2039 Mansfield St, Montreal; 1933-71/79, Montreal
1914 46 Portail de St Gilles du Gard, France wc
47 Abbaye de Montmajour, près Arles, France wc
1915 250 Porta del Popolo, Rome
251 Temple d'Antonin et Faustine, Rome
1918N 33 Vieux portail au soleil wc
34 Cyprès, Villa Falconiere à Frascati wc
1922 39 A fountain in Rome wc S6-12
40 A bridge in Venice wc S6-13
1924 220 La colonnade de Trianon, Versailles
1925 42 Amalfi wc illus
43 Cloitre à Amalfi wc
1927 37 Jardins de St Cloud wc
235 Vitrail pour un architecte
1931 46 Fontaine wc

47 Patio des Evangélistes, l'Escurial, Espagne wc
48 Barques en Espagne wc
1932 201 Université de Montréal DW 1932 arch drwg pencil & wc 24 3/4 x 35 3/4

CORNEIL, CARMEN STEWART
19 Dec 1933, Niagara Falls, NY
RCA(e) 1973 Architect
Addr: 1979, Toronto

CORNELL, BETTY see GALBRAITH, ELIZABETH ROBERTA

COSGROVE, STANLEY MOREL
23 Dec 1911, Montreal AGO CC2 M NGC WWA47
ARCA 1951 Council Painter
Addr: 1951-71, Montreal; 1979, Hudson, Que
1950 25 The two sisters 48 x 36 nfs
26 Landscape with road 42 x 48 $950
27 Still life 24 x 36 nfs
1951 20 Trees $600
21 Nude nfs
1954 22 Trees by the road, France 32 x 25 illus $475
23 Still life with red milk jug 24 x 36 $500

COSGROVE, THERESA LENORE
27 Dec 1934, Port Arthur, Ont IO
1963 16 Painting #7 $350

COTE, MARC AURELE SUZOR see SUZOR-COTE, MARC AURELE

COTE, PAUL MARIE
see DESGAGNES, LEONCE, 1964N

COTTINGHAM, MURIEL HARTLEY (Mrs W. Randolph Cottingham)
15 Jun 1889
Addr: 1931, 220 Wellington Cr, Winnipeg
1931 49 'Seven Sisters', Winnipeg River wc $50

COTTON, JOHN WESLEY
29 Oct 1869, n Dundas, Ont 24 Nov 1931, Toronto AGO
Addr: 1912-19, 327 Huron St, Toronto; 1930-1, 760 Spadina Ave, Toronto
1912 259 The tryst col aqua
260 Between tides col aqua
261 The first homestead aqua
262 St Ives harbour line etch S3-173
1912 S3, Winnipeg
171 On Hampstead Heath aqua
172 Foreshore, St Ives etch
173 St Ives harbour, Cornwall etch
1914 48 The étude wc
49 The forest clearing wc
1914 S5, Patriotic Fund
65 Evening in the northland illus
1915 270 Old butter house, Bruges col etch
271 Nocturne col etch
1916 281 Before the strife aqua
282 Belfry of Bruges aqua
1919 197 Great tower, Cathedral of Bourges, France etch
198 Notre Dame Cathedral, Paris etch
1930 30 Across the valley $300
31 Triponti, Venezia wc $200
1931 50 Beneath the walls of Rothenberg $400
51 Snug Harbour, Georgian Bay $400

COUCILL, WALTER JACKSON
22 Jun 1915, Camden, NJ AGO
RCA(e) 1978 Painter
Addr: 1979, Toronto

COUGHTRY, JOHN GRAHAM
8 Jun 1931, St Lambert, Que AGO CC1 IO M NGC WWA59
1963 16 Two figures #5 $1,300
1964J 17 Two figures 72 x 60 $1,800

COURTENAY, L. CAMERON
Addr: 1922-4, 189 Metcalfe St, Ottawa
1922 41 August sunshine
1924 32 Gatineau country
257 Cover design for magazine drwg

COURTICE, RODY KENNY HAMMOND (Mrs Andrew Roy Courtice)
30 Aug 1895, Renfrew, Ont 6 Dec 1973, Toronto AGO CWW66 M WWA47
ARCA 1956 Sr 1965 Painter
Addr: 1925, 64 Fallingbrook Rd, Toronto; 1929-34, 90 Balsam Ave, Toronto; 1936, RR 1, Markham, Ont; 1956-71, Toronto

1925 99 Monkey Mountain, Port Hope
100 St Jean de Luz, France
291 Edward Street, Toronto aqua Hammond, 1925
1929 34 Firerangers' Hill, Gowganda $150
258 Snow aqua
259 Old house near St Patrick's Church aqua
1934 49 Pink house, St Hilarion, Quebec $35 T35-17
1936 54 Lowrey's cauliflowers, Markham $50
236 St Hilarion, Quebec scratch bd $10
1938 48 Vera, Maida and I $100 T39-16
1941 S9, Toronto
18 A Quebec village $25
1950 28 Weather vane 30 x 33 $150
1951 22 Crows on fall wheat $100
1952 19 Country mousers $75
1955 25 Of the sea $350
26 Sea horse ballet illus $250
1956 17 In Florida surf $250 T56-17
1957 20 Young spruce, winter $150
1958 24 Sea shell market $250
1959 21 Northern channel 30 x 24 $200
1964N 16 Totem variation 38 x 18 $200
'Conversation piece of Rody Kenny Courtice' by Dorothy Stevens, F11-65

COUVREUR, DANIEL
1944, Colombes, France
1971 4 Cancelled 96 x 60 illus $550
5 This is an American painting 78 x 48 $400

COWAN, ROBERT (BOB)
1971 Earth song film screened 31 Mar

COWAN, ROBERT BRUCE
8 Apr 1930, Toronto
1953 20 Catharine $200

COWIE, VICTOR
1970 And no bird sings film screened 12 Feb

COWLEY-BROWN, PATRICK GEORGE
21 Oct 1918, Singapore M WWA47
1950 29 Somnolism 36 x 42 $250

COX, ALFRED ARTHUR
see AMOS, LOUIS A.

COX, AMY E.
H
1889 30 Still life $15

COX, ARTHUR W.
1840, England Aug 1917, Nottingham, Eng H TB W78
ARCA 1883-14 Painter
Addr: 1883, 88 St Mary St, Toronto; 1884-6, Toronto; 1887, GNW Telegraph Co, Toronto; 1888-93, Toronto; 1894-00, 39 Huntley St, Toronto; 1902, 84 Homewood Ave, Toronto; 1903-4, Toronto; 1905, 8 Admiral Rd, Toronto; 1906-9, Toronto; 1910, England; 1911-14, Gelding, Notts, Eng
1880 21 On the silvery Trent (Sandford Fleming)
1883 24 The summer holiday $25
29 Where the deer drinks $20
58 A summer sea, Cape Elizabeth $50
64 Amongst the rocks $25
72 A rocky headland, Cushing's Island $75
112 The Spindles, Portland harbour $50
214 Edge of the woods, Don Flats wc $20
1884 S1, Saint John
97 La Salle trading post $30
1885 57 and 185 Muskoka solitude $50 each
81 The trysting tree $25
121 Father's boat $60
122 Dawn $75
139 Dwight-Wiman Club House
187 A Canadian valley, Ancaster $125
193 Disappearing mists $25
203 A cottage home of Canada wc $75
1887 21 The Island of Arran from the Kyles of Bute $50
1888 76 The ford $50
221 Birches $50
1890 15 Isle of Arran $100
1891 216 Silurian Gates of Elora
1892 25 Vale of Gilead, Maine $35
1894 37 Crossing the bar
1895 24 Across the St Lawrence from Cape Langlier to Rimouski
1896 27 Emancipation Oak

1897 11 Breakers wc
1898 19 October sunshine
1900 12 The brook's song to the sunset
1902 38 Oat harvest
1905 50 Shelley's tomb by the Walls of Rome
1912 56 Moorland sunset 1913-74

COX, EDWIN JAMES
1850, Montreal d c 1930 H
Addr: 1907, Montreal; 1916, 114 St François Xavier St, Montreal; 1918A, Mappin & Webb, Bldg, Montreal
1907 306 Illumination, scripture text
1916 283 Illuminated work
1918A 209 Illuminated work
210 Illuminated address

COX, EDYTHE C.
Addr: 1937, 530 Mount Pleasant Ave, Westmount, Que
1937 51 Habitant chair $30
1939 50 Still life with artichokes $75

COX, ELFORD BRADLEY
16 Jul 1914, Botha, Alta AGO CC2 IO M WWA47
ARCA 1960-72 Sculptor
Addr: 1960-71, Willowdale, Ont
1955 102 Torso sculp $350
1958 86 Head sculp $750
1960 74 Head sculp illus $800
1963 79 Blue figure sculp $2,500

COX, HAROLD
Addr: 1918A, 94 St George St, Toronto
1918A 211 Miss Renalde Begin chalks

COZIC, YVON
4 Aug 1942, St Servan, France B
1971 6 Chenile vert 72 x 72 $800

CRABTREE, ELVINA KENNEDY GREENHAM
(Mrs Charles Archibald Crabtree)
1878, London, Eng d 1943
Addr: 1924-8, 53 McKinnon Rd, Ottawa; 1932, 95 McKinnon Rd, Ottawa
1924 33 Elizabeth
1927 38 The story book
1928 36 Mass of bloom $100
1929 S7, Calgary
34 Peonies $75
1932 35 Portrait of my daughter $50

CRABTREE, GRAHAM
1944 31 Dyeing the nets, Nova Scotia $75

CRABTREE, JOHN G.
b Ottawa
1950 30 Blue stream 17 7/8 x 21 1/2 $200

CRAIG, GEORGE HENRY H.
fl 1871-94
1889 65 Grapes and peaches $30

CRAIG, GRACE MORRICE
20 Feb 1891, Pembroke, Ont
1953 21 Unreal city nfs

CRAIG, JAMES S.
17 Dec 1912, Moose Jaw, Sask CWW61
1965 Craig, Zeidler & Strong, to 1967
114-16 Ajax and Pickering General Hospital. Courtyard, illus. General view. Model
1966 113-18 Willow Park Public School, Scarborough, Ont. Main entrance and corridor. School exterior. West entrance, detail. Interior courtyard. 1st & 2nd floor plans. Model
119-24 Beth Israel Synagogue, Peterborough, Ont. Main entrance and front elevation. Interior, illus. Floor plan. Menorah, maquette by Ted Bieler. Tapestry for the Ark, by Grace Svarre
1967 108-110 Pickering Municipal Building. A.Main entrance, illus. B.General view C. Council Chamber
111-15 Scarborough Centennial Recreation Centre. A.Main entrance B.General view C. Exterior detail D.Interior pool from gallery E.Ground floor plan

CRANE LIMITED
Addr: 1938, Toronto
1938 S8, Toronto
77 Bathroom

CRANSTON, DULCIE
Addr: 1924, 21 Dalhousie St, Ottawa
1924 34 Still life

CRAWFORD, A.W. (Mrs)
Addr: 1914, Winnipeg
1914 S4, Winnipeg
165a Ruth Kent min (A.B. Kent)

CRAWFORD, EDMUND THORNTON Scottish
1806, Cowden, Scot 27 Sep 1885, Lasswade, Scot B H RSA TB
1880 18 Dutch shipping (Sandford Fleming) T. Crawford mispr

CRAWFORD, WALTER JOHN
1911, Toronto
Addr: 1934, 324 Quebec Ave, Toronto
1934 50 Study $75 T35-18

CRAWLEY, ALICE MARION FINNIE (Mrs Crawley)
14 Mar 1915, Peterborough, Ont
1954 24 Carriage house 18 x 24 nfs

CRENNELL, W.N. see CRESSWELL, WILLIAM NICHOL

CRESSWELL, WILLIAM NICHOL
1822, Devon, Eng 1888, n Seaforth, Ont AGO H NGC W78
RCA 1880 Council Painter
Addr: 1880-6, Seaforth, Ont
1880 164 The last of the Brig, Mount Desert, Maine wc 1881-75 $50 DW 1882 12 x 20
165 Lobster fishing, Mount Desert wc
166 Ogden's Point, Mount Desert wc
174 The Pinnacles, Mount Desert wc W.N. Crennell, mispr
225 Old Hulk, Mount Desert wc
248 Reef off Porcupine Island wc
1881 52 Bishop Rock, Grand Manan wc $90 1883-201 $75
64 Fish cleaning, Flagg's Cove wc $55
85 Fish Head Bay, Grand Manan wc $50 1883-166 $60 S1-22 $75
235 Fish Head, Grand Manan $350
1882 134 The wreck off Tower Rock wc $60
154 Bald Porcupine Island, from Pulpit Rock wc $40
157 Low tide, Indian Beach, Mount Desert wc $40
159 The Pinnacles, Mount Desert wc $70
195 Eel Brook Point, Grand Manan wc $80 1883-143
1883 168 On the Arkansas River, Colorado wc $70
174 In Colorado wc
179 Otter Cliffs, Mount Desert wc $50
185 Pike's Peak Trail, Iron Spring, near Manitou, Colorado wc $75
189 Pike's Peak from the Garden of the Gods wc
195 Porcupine Island wc $50
210 Ashburton's Heads, Grand Manan wc $90
216 Amethyst Cove, Grand Manan wc $65
224 A Colorado cascade wc
230 Falls on Pike's Peak Trail wc
291 Indian Beach, Grand Manan wc $50
298 Sketch in the Garden of the Gods wc $50
306 Toltee Gorge, Colorado wc $60
308 The Spanish Peaks, western Spain wc $60
309 Head of the Toltee Gorge wc
1884 109 Fishing house, Castine, US wc $50
112 Evening on the St Lawrence wc $35
125 Wood boat, near Brockville wc $35
136 Berry gatherers, Fish Head Bay, Grand Manan wc $75
159 A roadside sketch wc $36
166 Towing, off Goderich wc $20
173 Off Gaspé wc $20
175 Ute Trail, western spur of Spanish Peaks wc $65 S1-7
177 Holy Cross, Grand Manan wc $50 S1-50
1884 S1, Saint John
56 Fishing house wc $50
1885 202 Bar Harbour wc $45
221 Low tide wc $15
225 Off Bishop Rock wc $50
246 The Pool, White Mountains wc $50
261 A passing storm wc $20
263 The wreckers wc $50
264 Near Brockville, evening wc $40
265 Wood boats, Brockville wc $20

321 Peabody's River sketch wc $12
1886 Fla, London, Eng
1990, artist number
Lake Huron (J. Labatt, Esq, London, Ont)
Sheep (J. Labatt, Esq)
Cattle (A. Cleghorne, Esq London, Ont)
1888 46 Cucomonda Lierra, Madra Mountains wc $100
55 San Diego, Calfornia, wc $45
265 Wreck on the Pacific coast wc $100
280 On the Grand River, Doon wc $50
289 In San Antonio Canyon, Old Baldy the Snow Hunter wc $75

CREVECOEUR, JEANNE DE
Addr: 1910, 168 Mansfield St, Montreal; 1912-14, 168A Mansfield St, Montreal; 1915, 9 St Matthew St, Montreal
1910 44 Study in pastel
45 The red tuque pastel
1912 65 Mme C.E. Bonin pastel
1913 82 Automne
83 Mlle G, portrait pastel
84 Sketch pastel
85 Trottin pastel
1914 56a Femme à sa toilette
57 Marie pastel S5-68 illus
1915 60 Etude pastel

CRIPPS, W.H.
Addr: 1937, 153 Heriot St, Drummondville, Que
1937 311 The stoker linocut $50

CRISP, ARTHUR WATKINS American
26 Apr 1881, Hamilton flg 1961
B CWW61 F NGC TB2 WWA36
Addr: 1918N, 1947 Broadway, New York
1918N 35 The strollers

CRIST, LELA GURNEE
15 Dec 1895, Sheet Harbour, NS
Addr: 1933, 76 Morris St, Halifax
1933 41 Marcia min $100

CROCKART, JAMES BISSET
19 Jul 1885, Stirling, Scot
Addr: 1916-18, 314 Dorchester St W, Montreal
1916 284 Stirling from Millhall Siding etch
285 The Drip Bridge pencil drwg
1918A 212 The old bridge and Castle, Stirling etch

CROCKER, JAMES A. SYDNEY
d 1886 H
ARCA 1880 Painter
Addr: 1880-6, Toronto
1880 162 The Acaldi Santander, 1835 wc
1885 199 Announcement to the shepherds wc
279 Westminster Abbey wc

CROOKER, ISABELLE
1939 51 Miss Pamela Merrill nfs

CROOKSHANK
1880 319a Van Dyke painting one of King Charles' beauties (Thos. Reynolds)

CROSS, FREDERICK GEORGE
2 Sep 1881, Exeter, Devon, Eng 8 Sep 1941, Lethbridge, Alta M
ARCA 1937-9 Painter
Addr: 1931-5, Brooks, Alta; 1936-7, 1018 1st Ave, Lethbridge, Alta; 1938-9, Lethbridge, Alta
1931 52 Horses on the open range wc $50
53 The sketch wc $50
1932 36 Head of the herd wc $100
37 Bad Lands, Alberta wc $75
1933 42 L'église abondonnée wc $200
43 Main Street, Brooks wc $200 T34-18
1934 51 Good crop next year wc $125
52 Horses on Sand Creek wc $75 T35-19
1935 53 Horses, Circle Ranch, Alberta wc $150 T36-17
1936 55 Horses drinking wc illus $250 T37-21
56 Cameron Falls, Waterton wc $200
1937 52 Ox team wc $200 T38-12
53 Heading for the feed lot wc $100
1938 49 A mirage, Blood Indian Reserve wc $100
50 Sheep herders' camp wc $125
1939 52 Strip farming, Champion Alberta wc $150

1940 39 Fly-time on the range wc $100
40 Fording the river wc $75

CROUCH, PAUL R.
1971 12G Annual report, John Labatt Limited, 1970

CROUCH, ROBERT WEIR
b England d 1943, Lancaster, NH
H
1891 212 Wall paper design, and illumination
215 Etching in brass

CROWE, GEORGE KENNETH
b 1900
Addr: 1931, c/o F.G. Robb, 1178 Phillips Pl, Montreal
1931 349 Study for a parish church, for F.G. Robb, architect wc

CRUIKSHANK, WILLIAM
25 Dec 1848, Broughton Ferry, Scot
19 May 1922, Kansas City AGO EC H M NGC R2 TB1/3 W78
ARCA 1884 RCA 1895 Ret 1919 Council Painter
Addr: 1883, 146 King St W, Toronto; 1884-93, Toronto; 1894-8, Imperial Chambers, Adelaide St, Toronto; 1899-13, Yonge Steet Arcade, Toronto; 1914-19, Toronto; 1920-22 Kansas City
1883 46 Picking live down $140 Cruickshanks, mispr
304 Chase of a whiskey smuggler, North West Territory wc $60
1886 72 Mounted Police chasing a whiskey smuggler north west wc $50
115 Picking live down $100
197 Hauling the mast (J. Jardine) Selected for Fla, not in Fla catalogue
1892 10 On the field of Waterloo $100
1893 26 Drawing the mast F1-26
27 A free grant in Algoma
1894 26 Breaking a road 1896-28 1904-39 F4-19 S2-31 ◊NGC◊
1895 32 The sand wagon DW 1895 35 1/2 x 51 3/4 The gravel pit, mistitled
1896 29 Chicks
30 Study
1898 20 In the Eastern Townships
21 Ploughing 1900-15
1899 26 Ploughing, lower St Lawrence 1901-22 F2-16 F5-41 $500 ◊AGO◊
27 Sundown
1901 23 D. McNab, Esq
157 His capital wc F2-17 1902-192 1912-58
1902 39 Nymph and dolphin panel
40 Donald G. McNab
1904 40 and 41 Portrait
1905 53 A.E. Boultbee, Esq
1907 50 C. Douglas, Esq
51 Prof Jas. Mavor
1908 30 Principal Hutton
31 Miss Pattie Warren 1910-47
1909M 32 W.M. Boultbee, Esq
1909N 33 Dorothy ◊AGO◊
1910 46 William Boultbee, Esq 1912-57
1913 75 Alfred Boultbee, Esq
port: by A.C. Williamson, 1912-227

CRYDERMAN, MACKIE V. MACINTYRE (Mrs Clifford Cryderman)
c 1900, Dutton, Ont 19 Nov 1969, London, Ont WWA59
1938 51 Iris wc $45
1939 53 Mixed bouquet wc $50
54 Bridge prizes wc $50
1941 42 Sunshine after rain wc $50
43 Gladioli wc $50
1944 32 Jim nfs T45-9
33 A dahlia study wc $50
1945 51 Fall flowers wc $50

CSEREPY, MARY
1970 141 Book, Lost and found
142 Book, Bread, wine and salt
1971 13G Book, The mysterious naked man. Clarke, Irwin
14G Book, Short plays for reading and acting. Clarke, Irwin
15G Catalogue cover, Clarke Irwin 1970

CULLEN, MAURICE GALBRAITH
6 Jun 1866, St John's 28 Mar 1934, Chambly, Que AGO B CC2 CNS36 EC H M Mo12 NGC PMC R2 TB1/2/3 W78
ARCA 1899 RCA 1908 Council Painter
Addr: 1893, 562 Craig St, Montreal; 1897-8, Montreal; 1899-00, 96 St François Xavier St, Montreal; 1901-2, Montreal; 1903, c/o Scott & Sons,

Montreal; 1904, Montreal; 1905, P.O. Box 1159, Montreal; 1906-16, 3 Beaver Hall Sq, Montreal; 1918A, 363 Beaver Hall Sq, Montreal; 1919-25, 67 Ste Famille St, Montreal; 1927-8, c/o Watson Art Galleries, 679 St Catherine St W, Montreal; 1929, Chambly Canton, Que; 1930-1, Watson Art Galleries, Montreal; 1932, 3531 Ste Famille St, Montreal

1893 28 On the river at Grey $150 F1-27
29 A washhouse in Provence $100 F1-28
30 A study $40

1897 37 Winter, French Canadian
38 An old French house

1898 22 A yoke of oxen

1899 31 St James tower, Montreal, by moonlight
32 Craig Street at night
33 Study
34 Wood interior
35 Evening 1901-26

1900 13 A September day
14 Cap Tourmente

1901 24 Sunny September F2-18
25 Winter, Quebec

1903 34 Quai des Orfèvres, Paris
35 Moonlight, Venice
36 The wave
37 Dordrecht

1904 42 Wolfe's Cove F4-20 S2-32
43 Quebec from Levis F4-21 (J. Reid Wilson, Esq) S2-35 ◊MMFA◊
44 A March river F4-22 (A.A. Browne, Esq, MD)
45 The valley of the St Charles F4-23
46 The wharf, Levis
47 The ferry

1905 40 Work
41 After the storm
42 Shimmering light
43 On the Giudecca, Venice
44 On the lagune pastel
45 The hay barge pastel
46 On the St Charles pastel
47 The creek pastel

1906 60 Winter sunset, Covefields, Quebec
61 First snow F5-44 $75 F6-65 1908-23 ◊NGC◊
62 Winter, Brittany F6-63 $75
63 Petit Cap Lévis pastel
64 Early spring
65 Winter road F5-45 $150 F6-64 $150
66 March F5-42 $250

1906 F5, Halifax
43 Quebec $150
46 Early morning, Quebec $50

1907 52 A summer night DW 1908 29 1/2 x 39 1/4 1908-24 T51-12
53 The winter harvest F6-60 $300
54 Water carriers F6-61 $300 1909M-40 S2-33
55 St George's Church

1907 F6, Sherbrooke
62 Summer evening $300
63 Winter in Brittany $150

1908 25 Brittany washerwoman
26 The brook

1909M 37 After the storm 1909N-34
38 Forgotten
39 A winter stream pastel

1909N 35 Winter
36 Port Aven
37 A winter stream

1910 48 Misty afternoon, St John's, Newfoundland
49 St John's harbour ◊NGC◊
50 Newfoundland coast

1910 S2, Liverpool
34 Louise Basin, Quebec ◊NGC◊

1911 35 Misty day, St John's, Newfoundland ◊NGC◊
36 Old Montreal (Sir Thomas Shaughnessy)
37 Phillips Square, Montreal (C.B. Esdaile, Esq)
38 Dominion Square, Montreal
39 Evening, Quebec pastel

1912 59 Craig Street, Montreal
60 The bend in the river
61 The old homestead
62 Torbay, Newfoundland

1912 S3, Winnipeg
34 Old street, Montreal
35 Quebec, winter
36 Moonlight, St Eustache
37 A Montreal cab stand

1913 76 October moon
77 Lifting fog, St John's, Newfoundland S4-36 $350 nfs

1914 50 The ice harvest ◊NGC◊
51 Winter evening, Quebec ◊NGC◊

1914 S5, Patriotic Fund
51 Winter harvest illus

1915 51 Montreal harbour illus
52 Solitude pastel
53 The North River pastel

ØNGCØ
1916 45 Moonlight on the Cachée
46 Early spring
47 The dam
48 A northern brook illus
1918A 40 Early morning, Lac Tremblant illus
1919 31 Huy on the Meuse, Belgium (Canadian War Memorials)
1920 54 Spring illus
55 Harvest moon ØAGOØ
56 Winter
57 The September moon
1921 33 The St Lawrence illus
34 March ØNGCØ
35 The winter road
1922 42 Early spring
43 Commandant's Point S6-14 1923-31
44 The North River S6-15
45 Sun glow, Lac Tremblant pastel
1924 35 March afternoon illus
1925 44 A Laurentian valley, March illus
1927 39 March evening, Laurentians illus
1928 37 Chûtes aux Caron $2,500
1928 F8, London, Eng
118 Blizzard, Montreal $365
1929 35 The Saguenay $1,000
1930 32 Mount Rundle, Banff $700
33 Echo River, Banff illus $700
1931 54 The Echo River, near Banff pastel $850
1932 38 The Caché River $1,000
1954 14 Retro sec. Cap Diamant, Quebec, winter (Robert Pilot, RCA) ØAGHØ

CUMMINS, ETHEL M.
Addr: 1916, Pine Croft, Magog, Que
1916 40 Grove of young birch

CUNDY, PERCY M.
1945 52 Road to Bayeau, Normandy wc nfs

CUNNINGHAM, EVELYN M. (Mrs)
1939 55 La chaumière, Boucherville, Quebec $150

CUPIT, WILLIAM
b British Columbia
Addr: 1976, Vancouver
1976 S12, Montreal
175 Untitled/Sans titre hand-tinted photo/polychromie à la main 20 x 16 illus

CURL BROTHERS TEXTILES
Addr: 1938, Toronto
1938 S8, Toronto
78 Textiles, pylons of drapery fabrics 3 illus
79 Ivory lamp shade gauze
80 Multi-color lamp shade gauze

CURRY, ELIZABETH ELEANOR
1864, Russell, Ont 18 May 1941, Hamilton H
Addr: 1912, Ottawa Ladies College, Ottawa; 1924, 91 4th Ave, Ottawa
1912 63 In the valley
1924 36 Sand banks on Rideau River wc

CURRY, ERIC MACDONALD
13 Oct 1918, Halifax
1945 53 Down in Nova Scotia wc nfs

CURRY, PEGGY
21 Aug 1885, Gosforth, Northld, Eng
1947 37 Path of gold $100

CURRY, SAMUEL GEORGE
15 Jul 1854, Port Hope, Ont 10 Feb 1942 CWW36
ARCA 1885-97 Council Architect
Addr: 1883-95, Toronto; 1896, 70 Victoria St, Toronto; 1897, Toronto
1883 352 Suburban residence sketch
1896 269 Perspective, building for Philip Jamieson, Esq, corner of Yonge and Queen Streets, Toronto
see also Darling, Frank, 1883

CURTIN, WALTER ANTHONY
16 Aug 1911, Vienna
RCA(e) 1975 Council Photographer
Addr: 1976/79, Toronto
1976 S12, Montreal
176 Canadian musician, Glenn Gould photo 16 x 20 illus

CUTHBERTSON, GEORGE ADRIAN
b Toronto d 1969 M
1938 S8, Toronto
188 Book, Saguenay. G.A. Cuthbertson and others

CUTHBERTSON, GEORGE HARDING
3 June 1929, Brantford, Ont

RCA(e) 1974 Council Industrial designer
Addr: 1979, Oakville, Ont

CUTTS, GERTRUDE E. SPURR (Mrs William Malcolm Cutts)
1858, Scarborough, York, Eng 21 Jul 1941, Port Perry, Ont AGO H M NGC TB3
ARCA 1895 Sr 1937 Painter
Addr: 1893-00, 248 Gerrard St, Toronto: 1901, 95 Yonge St, Toronto; 1902, 15 Toronto St, Toronto; 1903, Gerrard St, Toronto; 1904, Toronto; 1905-09M, 248 Gerrard St E, Toronto; 1909N, 108 Yonge St, Toronto; 1910-11, St Ives, Eng; 1912, 79 Adelaide St E, Toronto; 1913-15, 304 Jarvis St, Toronto; 1916-41, Port Perry, Ont

1891 Spurr, to 1909M
51 Fruit
52 On the Llugwy, north Wales
91 Street in Clovelly, north Devon
99 Kingfisher

1893 137 Boston stump $45 F1-102
138 Grand River, Elora $40 F1-103
259 Upland Point, Port Levi wc $50 F1-189
260 By the lake shore, Mimico Creek wc $25 F1-190
261 Rapids above the falls wc $35 F1-191

1894 122 By the river, Mimico Creek
123 Drag Creek, Haliburton
124 A glimpse of Haliburton

1895 133 A corner of the orchard
134 A bright November day
135 In the beechwood

1896 159 Old Dutch farm in Ontario
160 Pool in the woods
161 Banks of blue iris, Grand River
162 Old willows, West Montrose
163 'Neath the beeches
164 On the GTR railroad to Galt

1897 145 Where the iris grow
48W Last days of autumn wc
49W Summer on the Humber wc

1898 103 Dead pheasant
104 A Surrey farm
105 Albury Heath, Surrey 1899-120

1899 199 Castle Rock, Lynton, north Devon

1900 106 Scarboro, old town
107 Betchworth, Surrey
108 Reigate Heath, Surrey 1901-108
109 Drag Creek, Haliburton
181 Touch of autumn wc

1901 107 Castle Rock, north Devon F2-65
109 Mending nets at Cape Cod
110 Firs, Cape Cod
209 Beeches wc

1902 151 On the Battenkill
152 Sunset, Taconic Mountains
153 A Welsh cottage 1903-117

1902 F3, Rochester
164 Princetown, Cape Cod $180

1903 115 The Fairy Glen, Bettws-y-coed, Wales F5-151 $125
116 Sunny land in a Welsh valley
118 Bridge on the Torrent Walk, Dolgelley, north Wales
119 Tyn-y-Cae, north Wales

1904 154 Pentre Ddu
155 Mount Dinas
156 The brook
157 Blue devils F4-77
158 The Delaware River

1905 173 Hay time, Beaupré
174 Marsh lands of the St Lawrence
175 A habitant's dwelling
176 A bit of old Quebec

1906 164 Through the fields
165 A Welsh mountain top
166 Crane's Mill, Surrey

1906 F5, Halifax
150 The Vale of Tintern illus (Ontario Government)

1907 180 Shades of evening, Vermont
181 The incoming tide, Château Richer
182 A blossomy weed corner
183 The spinner
184 Wayside, Château Richer
185 Harvest time

1907 F6, Sherbrooke
152 Incoming tide $90

1908 132 In a Larch farm kitchen wc 1909N-38
133 Autumn's golden fruits

1909M 127 Poor houses, Bruges
128 From the slate quarry
129 A peaceful moment

1909N 39 Habitant interior

1910 52 In old St Ives
1911 40 His only companion
1912 64 Night in old St Ives
1913 78 Low tide S4-37 $500 nfs (National Gallery)
1914 52 Mountain solitudes ≬AGO≬
1914 S5, Patriotic Fund
60 Evening, Mounts Bay illus
1918A 41 On the Grand River, Elora 1918N-36
1919 32 Garden treasures
1920 58 The favourites
1921 36 Cosmos
1922 46 A study of form and colour
1923 32 Peonies, old chintz and bric-à-brac 1924-37
1926 28 The artist's garden
1927 40 Zinnias
1929 36 A medley $250
37 The end of the game wc $200

CUTTS, WILLIAM MALCOLM
1857, Allahabad, India 29 Jan 1943, Port Perry, Ont CC1 H M NGC PMC TB3 W78
ARCA 1907 Sr 1937 Painter
Addr: 1895, 93 Langley Ave, Toronto; 1896-7, 43 Adelaide St E, Toronto; 1898-08, 45 Bleecker St, Toronto; 1909, 108 Yonge St, Toronto; 1910-11, 19 Bowling Green Terrace, St Ives, Eng; 1913-14, 304 Jarvis St, Toronto; 1915-43, Port Perry, Ont
1888 134 Portrait. M.Cutts, mispr
183 Toronto suburbs $100
196 and 218 Toronto suburbs $75 each A. Cutts, mispr
1891 233 Missed the way wc
1892 3 Morning hymn wc $300
1895 29 Portrait
30 A quiet evening on the Dorsetshire coast
1896 31 Seaton Beach, coast of Dorsetshire
32 The close of a wet day
33 Study of a village blacksmith
1897 41 Miss Orchard, portrait
1898 23 The Niagara Rapids above the Falls F3-43 $120
24 Winter, near Castle Frank
25 Night on the English coast
26 Catfish Pond, High Park
1903 29 The summer of life
160 Before the rain wc
1904 48 The evening glow
1905 48 Loughboro Lake
49 Evening
1906 F5, Halifax
48 Coming storm $75
1907 56 Fretted and whipped to a foam, like snow
1908 32 An autumn smile
33 An ocean graveyard
1909M 30 Night on the coast of Maine
31 The western glow
1909N 40 A summer's eve
41 Sunshine and shadow
42 When the leaves begin to turn
1910 51 The flowing tide
1911 41 On the Cornish coast
1913 79 Atlantic breakers
80 On the Dee, north Wales S4-38 $500
1914 53 The harbour mouth, Boscastle
54 On the Cornish coast
1914 S5, Patriotic Fund
5 A flowing tide illus
1915 54 The harbour mouth
55 Wind and wave
1916 50 The passing storm
51 Good night
52 Peace
1918A 42 Summer showers 1918N-37
43 The close of a stormy day illus
1919 33 The herring fleet 1920-59
34 The rocky valley
35 A Cornish barn yard
1921 37 In the fading light
38 A woodland stream
1923 33 The long roll of the Atlantic
1924 38 The silvery mist, Grand Manan wc
1926 29 The close of a breezy day 1927-41
1929 38 Night on the Cornish coast $850
1930 34 A ground swell temp illus $550
1931 55 Storm clouds, 1914 $250
1932 39 The squall $750
1934 53 Racing to the port $600
1935 54 Cornwall's rugged coast $150
55 Showery weather $100

CYOPIK, WILLIAM
17 Feb 1921, Welland, Ont IO M
1963 18 Balloon boy $350
1964J 16 Artist's children 48 x 36 $600

1964N 17 Grey and black 36 x 48 $450
1965 19 Tanganyika 48 x 36 $600
20 The enchanted mountain 60 x 60 $700
1968 16 Painting #2 48 x 60 $900
1970 15 Painting #2 36 x 48 illus $900
1971 7 Painting #2 36 x 48 $450

D

DABY and WILLIAMS
1882 305 Evening on the Thames (loan)

DAGLISH, PETER WILLIAM
1930, Gillingham, Kent, Eng M
Addr: 1976, London, Ont
1963 19 Storage $300
1976 S12, Montreal
140 Lady Lure (x) punch work, wool & canvas 43 x 30 illus
141 Lady Lure (x) II punch work, wool and canvas 43 x 30 illus

DAGYS, JACOB (b Jokubas Dags)
16 Dec 1905, Lithuania M WWA62
1964J 67 Go your own way bronze 16 x 14 x 6 $350
68 What a monster bronze 11 x 16 x 6 $400
1965 73 Would I had such power bronze 26h $400

DAIGNEAULT, ROBERT
1965 21 The school teacher 24 x 24 $175

DAIR, CARL
14 Feb 1912, Welland, Ont d 28 Sep 1967
RCA medal 1962
1970 143 Book, design with type
144 Brochure, Westvaco

DALE, MARIAN see SCOTT, MARIAN

DALLA-LANA, ALFRED BRUNO
6 Aug 1937, Trail, BC
RCA(e) 1978 Architect
Addr: 1979, Vancouver

DALLAIRE, MICHEL
15 Aug 1942, Paris
RCA(e) 1978 Industrial designer
Addr: 1979, Montreal

DALLEGRET, FRANCOIS
26 Sep 1937, Lyautey, Morocco
RCA(e) 1973 Council Industrial designer
Addr: 1976/79, Montreal
1976 S12, Montreal
64 Artbreakers solid brass plated with 22 karat gold and sterling silver/cuivre plaque or, 22 karat, et argent 2 x 4 x 1/4 each illus

DALTON, ERNEST ALFRED
1887, Brixton, Eng d 1963
Addr: 1924-36, 386 Annette St, Toronto
1924 39 Winter
1925 45 Swamp land
46 Buck Lake
1926 30 Afternoon
31 The north country
1927 43 A bit of Muskoka
1928 38 Sunlight $350
1929 39 The hill $300
40 In old Quebec $350 1930-36 illus
1929 S7, Calgary
35 Winter hill $300
36 The mill $45
1930 35 Lower Quebec, winter $350
1931 56 Ontario landscape $350
57 Sunday morning $200
1932 40 Shawn Fraser's $150
1933 44 The hills of Albion, Ont $600
1934 54 Buck Lake $200
1935 56 Burke's Falls $250 T36-18
57 Port Hope in winter $200
1936 57 Late afternoon, Quebec $200 T37-22
1941 44 Happy winter nfs

DALY, KATHLEEN FRANCES (Mrs George Douglas Pepper)
28 May 1898, Napanee, Ont AGO IO M WWA47
ARCA 1947 RCA 1965 Sr 1968 Painter
Addr: 1926-8, 441 Walmer Rd, Toronto; 1930-1, 16 Torrington Pl, Ottawa; 1932-5, 441 Walmer Rd, Toronto; 1936-7, 25 Severn St, Toronto; 1938-71/79, Toronto
1926 Daly to 1939; Pepper, 1941; Daly 1946-61
174 Ponte Vecchio aqua
175 Carcassonne dry pt

1928 39 St Urbain, Quebec $50
199 St Urbain, Quebec drwg $10
1930 37 March snow, Quebec $175
38 Indian boy $50
1931 58 Fishermen's house, Lake Superior $150
1932 41 Blue Rocks, Nova Scotia $65
42 Swordfisher $50
1935 58 Alphonse L'Abbé $250 T36-19
59 Madame L'Abbé $300
1936 58 Madame Gagnon $350
59 French Canadian girl $50 T37-23
1937 54 Habitant de l'Ile d'Orléans $200
1938 52 The Chief's mother $200
53 Indian girl $60
1939 56 Samuel $80
1941 149 Two-shoes with papoose illus $150 T42-43
1941 S9, Toronto
19 Cabbages $50
1946 26 Moraine Lake nfs
27 Lake O'Hara $60
1947 38 Stoney Indian boy illus $250 T48-10
1948 39 Mrs Moses Jimmy-John $50
191 Pensive boy chalk drwg $20
1949 21 Angela of Diamond Cross Ranch $500 T50-4
1950 31 Valley of the Ten Peaks 31 x 36 $350
32 David 24 x 25 $175
1951 23 Eskimo children, Labrador illus $350
1952 20 Eskimo children $350 T53-9 nfs
1955 27 Monassi Eskimo $600
94 Mexican market girl drwg $75
1959 22 An Arab gentleman 24 x 20 illus nfs
1960 23 Village, Andalusia 32 x 36 illus $400
1961 26 An Eskimo mother, Elisapie 30 x 25 illus $500 S10-22 illus nfs
DW 1965 An Eskimo mother 30 x 25

DALY, MARY MARGUERITE (RITA)
28 Apr 1892, Montreal
Addr: 1913-14, 39 Fort St, Montreal; 1915, 16 Maplewood Ave, Montreal: 1916-18, 399 Wilson Ave, Montreal; 1920-7, P O Box 241, Chicoutimi, Que; 1933-5, 67 Cartier St, Chicoutimi, Que

1913 81 Portrait
1914 55 Aunt Harriet
1915 56 Thinking
57 The canary
1916 53 The sleeping kitten
54 In Limerick lace
1918A 288 Prospect Park
289 Evelyn
288, 289, Trustees, National Gallery of Canada, Travelling scholarship competition
1918N 39 Prospect Park, New York
1920 60 A reflection
1921 39 An impression of a child
1922 47 A boy reading
1923 34 Autumn on the banks of the Saguenay
1925 47 The girl in gray
1927 293 Girl's head drwg
1933 45 Winter on the Rivière du Moulin $75
1935 60 In Quebec woods, autumn $50

DALY, THOMAS CULLEN (TOM)
25 Apr 1918, Toronto
RCA(e) 1978 Film maker
Addr: 1979, Montreal

DAMIANI, JAMES (JIMMIE)
1945 54 Giuseppe pastel $100
55 Cynthia pastel $60

DANBY, KENNETH EDISON
6 Mar 1940, Sault Ste Marie, Ont
CC2 IO M NGC WWA73
RCA(e) 1975 Painter
Addr: 1979, Guelph, Ont

DANIS, AIMEE
1971 KW plus film screened 7 Apr

DANKS, HILDA MARGARET (Mrs)
1893-1969
1952 21 Giant elm wc $75
22 Wintertime wc $75

DANSEREAU, MIREILLE
19 Dec 1943, Montreal WWA76
RCA(e) 1974 Film maker
Addr: 1979, Montreal
1971 Compromise film screened 21 Apr

DAOUST, SYLVIA MARIE EMILIENNE
24 May 1902, Montreal AGO CWW79
M NGC WWA47
ARCA 1943 RCA 1952 Sr 1971 Sculptor

Addr: 1933-7, 171 Beaubien St E, Montreal;1943-5, Montreal; 1946-59, Strathmore, Que; 1960-71, Dorval, Que; 1979, Chomedy, Laval, Que
1933 251 Miss L.H. bust
287 La Parthéon etch $10
1935 274 Lieut Gov de la Province de Québec médaille nfs
275 Arthur Labonté, guide de chasse sculp nfs
1937 273 Mlle R.M. Clarke sculp nfs
1943 124 Marie Auger plâtre patiné nfs
125 Fillet plâtre platiné illus nfs
1945 218 Tête d'enfant plaster $150
1946 130 Madone sculp acajou (Guy Corbeil)
131 Madone des Enfants sculp $10
1949 110 Madone sculp acajou $200
1951 113 Frère Marie Victorin, EC plaster, bronzed nfs
1952 104 Marie à Cana 'Vinum non habent' sculp illus nfs (AGO)
1954 102 Elizabeth, cousine de Marie sculp illus $20
1957 72 Mère et enfant sculp
1959 82 Madone mahogany 67h
1963 80 Figure sculp acajou $450
1964N 69 Femme debout sculp acajou 46h illus
DW 1953 Lucie plaster 10 1/4h

DARBY, ROBERT
b 1896
Addr: 1935, 428 Rideau St, Ottawa
1935 61 The bathers wc $75

D'ARCY, BARBARA M. CONYERS
Addr: 1927, 786 Dorchester St W, Montreal; 1928, 740 Sherbrooke St W, Montreal; 1929, 45 Esplanade Ave, Montreal; 1930-1, 30 St Louis St, Quebec; 1933, 1468 Peel St, Montreal
1927 294 Illustration, The knight errant
295 Illustration, The sleeping beauty
1928 200 Cinderella and the Fairy Godmother drwg $15
201 Cinderella and the Prince drwg $20
1929 41 Illustration, Tristan and Isolde, the love drink $20
42 The raising of the Cross by Jacques Cartier $25
1930 201 The burial of Montcalm drwg $50
1931 388 Payment of seignorial dues in old time Canada drwg $50
389 The seven dwarfs drwg $15
1933 46 Illustration, The haughty princess $20

DARLING, FRANK
17 Feb 1850, Scarborough, Ont 19 May 1923, Toronto Co Mo12 NGC R2 W78
ARCA 1880 RCA 1886-9 ARCA 1906 RCA 1908 Council Architect
Addr: 1880-9, Toronto; 1895, Mail Bldg, Toronto; 1906-23, Toronto
1881 186-8 Competitive designs for Parliament Buildings, Toronto
1883 Darling & Curry
353 Newmarket Church and parsonage
356 New Parliament Buildings, Toronto des
358 Newmarket Church, from southeast
369-70 New Parliament Buildings, Toronto. N S E and W elevations des
1895 20A St Mary Magdalene Church, Toronto des
21A St John the Evangelist Church, Berlin, Ont des
22A House des
Darling, Sproat & Pearson
53A St Andrew's Church, Belleville
1909M 145 Parliament Buildings, Toronto, competition des
DW 1909 Legislative Building, Toronto des drwg 30 5/8 x 49 3/8
port: by E.W. Grier, 1918A-225; H.H. Brown, 1919-15

DA ROZA, GUSTAVO see ROZA, GUSTAVO DA

DAUDELIN, CHARLES
1 Oct 1920, Granby, Que WWA47
ARCA 1972 Council Sculptor
Addr: 1976/79, Kirkland, Que
1976 S12, Montreal
65 Cube + ou- acier et plexi/steel & plexiglass 9 x 9 x 9 illus

DAVENPORT, SUMNER GODFREY
see MARANI, FERDINAND, 1939-273

DAVID, CHARLES
5 Apr 1890, Montreal 23 Nov 1962, Outremont, Que CWW61 PMC
ARCA 1948 Architect
Addr: 1948-62, Montreal

DAVID, JACQUES L.
11 Nov 1921, Montreal
ARCA 1967 Architect
Addr: 1968-70, Outremont, Que; 1971/79, Montreal

DAVIDSON, FLORENCE
Addr: 1920, 466 Guy St, Montreal
1920 61 Wind and shadow wc
62 Rocks and surf wc

DAVIDSON, HELEN L. (Mrs Frederic J. A. Davidson)
26 Sep 1878, Belleville, Ont
Addr: 1905, 22 Madison Ave, Toronto; 1923, Brockwood, Humber Bay, Ont; 1926, 1485 Queen St W, Toronto; 1927, 87 King St E, Toronto; 1928, 1483 Queen St W, Toronto; 1929, 87 King St E, Toronto; 1932, 1483 Queen St W, Toronto
1905 56 Joe
1923 35 Lotifa pastel
1926 32 Zenobia
33 José
1927 44 Ayssha
1928 40 Madame Butterfly pastel $300
41 Miss Hawaii pastel $300
1929 43 A Moroccan belle
1932 43 Juanita Mateu, Palma, Majorca, a portrait

DAVIDSON, IAN JOCELYN
21 Jul 1925, Toronto
ARCA 1971 Architect
Addr: 1979, West Vancouver

DAVIDSON, ROBERT CHARLES
4 Nov 1946, Hydaburg, Alaska
RCA(e) 1973 Sculptor
Addr: 1979, Queen Charlotte Islands, BC

DAVIES, GORDON ALBERT
23 Sep 1890, Toronto
Addr: 1911-14, 56 Wellesley St, Toronto; 1932-4, 59 Hillholm Rd, Toronto
1911 42 October sunset
43 Sketch
1914 56 Willows
1932 44 Doris
1934 55 Barbara
1942 31 Ettore Mazzoleni nfs

DAVIES, HAYDN LLEWELLYN
11 Nov 1921, Rhymney, Wales
RCA(e) 1978 Sculptor
Addr: 1979, Toronto

DAVIES, WILL
1924, Bellevue, Ont
RCA(e) 1974 Illustrator
Addr: 1979, Toronto

DAVIS, LAURA VAN VETCHEN
b 1911
1954 25 Blue jeans 30 x 24 $400
1955 28 Man in pink shirt $400

DAVIS, MARIE
1940 41 Violette $75
42 The beret $65 T41-12

DAWES, PRUDENCE ANN
b 1917
Addr: 1937, 3525 Ontario Ave, Montreal
1937 274 Margaret sculp $200 1938-233
275 Hector Prévost sculp $150
1938 234 Patricia sculp $150
1939 243 Speed sculp $35 1940-158 sculp oak $35

DAWSON, B. (Mrs)
Addr: 1935, 52 Rosemount Ave, Westmount, Que
1935 276 Naomi sculp nfs
277 Sally sculp nfs
1941 207 Bryony sculp nfs
208 A.D.M, study sculp nfs

DAWSON, F.A.
fl 1880-92 H
Addr: 1902, 38 Court St, Sherbrooke, Que
1902 41 Benedicite
42 Le gouter
43 Souvenirs

DAWSON-WATSON, DAWSON American
21 Jul 1864, London, Eng 3 Sep 1939, San Antonio, Tex B F H TB1/3 WWA36
Addr: 1902, Clarendon Hotel, Quebec

1902 44 Rainbow
45 Afternoon

DAY, FORSHAW
4 Nov 1837, London, Eng 22 Jul 1903, Kingston EC H M NGC W78 ARCA 1880 RCA 1881 Council Painter
Addr: 1880-2, Kingston; 1883, Royal Military College, Kingston; 1884-93, Kingston; 1894, Royal Military College, Kingston; 1895-7, Kingston; 1898, 25 Victoria Rd, Halifax; 1899, 184 Queen St, Kingston; 1900-03, Kingston
1880 78 Ravine, Wetterhorn, Switzerland
1881 238 On the Nouvelle River, Bay of Chaleur $150 DW 1881 21 1/4 x 39 1/2 1882-45 1883-77 T51-13
280 French soubrette costume, 100 years ago $80
308 Entrance to Hartfield Churchyard, Sussex $75
323 Moose hunting, Nova Scotia $25
1882 8 The brook $100
1883 74 A shady place $130
1884 25 View on the Escuminac, Bay of Chaleur $80
63 View on the Nouvelle River, near Le Clair $150
110 The Needles of Howth, Dublin Bay, looking south wc $120
148 Cottages three, Rock Mountain, Ireland wc $30 1885-237 Cottages, Three Rock Mountain, Ireland wc $30
162 The Needles, Howth, Ireland wc $75
1885 18 View near Kingston
41 View on the Musquodobit $130
91 Snow scene, Cedar Island $30
107 Junction of the Restigouche and Metapedia $100
112 Camping on the Tobique $40
223 Snowdon from Capel Curig wc $25
228 The Needles of Howth wc $120
275 Llanberis Pass, north Wales wc $35
285 Capel Curig looking north wc $25
1886 39 Cariboo hunting in Nova Scotia wc $75 Fla-1991
107 Old French lighthouse, Louisburg, Cape Breton $35
176 On the Nouvelle River, Quebec $500 Fla-1991
1887 39 In the forest, Nova Scotia, the moose $60
41 Cariboo hunting, New Brunswick $60
57 On the Nouvelle River, Nova Scotia $225 ≬NGC≬
99 American fishing vessels off Louisburg $175
114 On the coast, Cape Breton Island wc $40
1888 15 Mount Cheops, Selkirks wc $60
23 Hermit Glacier wc $45
32 A dark pool on a dull day wc $40
43 Mount Field from Kicking Horse Pass wc $100
48 Mountain, near Field station wc $25
52 Glacier Mountain, Selkirks wc $40
60 Rainy weather, Selkirk Range wc $60
141 Scene on the Bow River $50
153 Junction of the Bow and Spry Rivers, NWT $50 1889-89
251 Mount Ross Valley, Smoky Valley wc $40
256 Syndicate Peak wc $40
272 Bow River Falls, Banff wc $20
277 Lake at Laggan, NWT wc $120
298 Mount Deville Range, NWT wc $80
1889 1 Mount Lefroy, Laggan, NWT $50
9 Syndicate Range $100
22 Mount Cheops, Selkirks $250
73 Angling at the mouth of a run $35
111 Smoky day, Mount Ross Valley, Selkirks wc $40
113 Hermit Glacier, Selkirks wc $40
146 Glacier, Syndicate Peak wc $75
159 Glacier Mountain, Selkirks wc $40 1890-136 $30

1890 16 Angling at the mouth of a run $160
17 Mount Lefroy, NWT 4$0
18 The Bow Range $40
135 Smoky day, Ross Valley wc $40
137 Mount Cheops, Selkirks wc $40
1891 93 Angling at the mount of a run, New Brunswick
121 Cathedral Mountain wc
188 Syndicate Peak wc
225 Cathedral Mountain
1892 71 On the Musquodobit, Nova Scotia $53
136 Mount Deville, NWT wc $87
1893 31 Heart of the Selkirks $150 1895-33
32 Musquodobit Falls, Nova Scotia $60 F1-29
171 The Hermit Range wc $100 F1-128
172 Mount Stephen, from Kicking Horse Pass wc $60
173 The Glacier torrent wc $60 F1-129 1894-160 1895-19W
174 Bow River Falls wc $55
175 Cap Rouge, Quebec wc $65 F1-130 1894-162 1895-20W
176 The Hermit Range, from above Lake Marion wc $30 F1-131
177 Asulkan Glacier wc $35
1894 159 Falls, Bow River, Banff, NWT wc
161 The Hermit's Range, above Marion wc
163 Hermit Range, Selkirks wc
1895 34 Mount Cheops
17W The Hermit Range, Selkirks wc
18W The Hermit Range, above Lake Marion wc
1896 34 Banff, sketch
35 Mount Cheops, Selkirks
198 Cap Rouge, Quebec wc
199 Van Horne Range wc
1898 39 Bow River, Banff, oil sketch
154 Bow River, Banff wc
155 Cottage, Mount Bray, County Dublin
156 View at Gananoque
157 Bray Head, County Dublin
1899 36 On the Bow River, NWT
166 View on the Bow wc
167 Gananoque, Thosand Islands, Ontario wc
167a Bray Head, County Dublin, Ireland wc
1900 25 On the Bow River, NWT
133 On the Bow River, NWT wc
134 Near Gananoque, Ont wc
135 Bray Head, County Wicklow, Ireland wc
1901 37 On the Bow River, Banff, NWT
162 View north, Field, NWT wc
163 Mount Ross, Selkirks, BC wc
1903 161 The track of the avalanche, British Columbia wc

DEACON, PETER
1945, England
Addr: 1976, Calgary
1976 S12, Montreal
156 Deflexion I pencil on paper 22 x 32 illus

DEAN, THOMAS G.
1947, Ontario
1971 8 and 9 Untitled $600 each

DEANE, E. ELDON
Addr: 1915, 6 W 28th St, New York
1915 252 Old French house on Lachine Road, Montreal
253 Church of St Paul aux Récollets

DEANE, ELSIE
Addr: 1922, 305 Beaver Hall Hill, Montreal
1922 248 Cover des

DE ANGELIS, JOSEPH R.
b 1938
Addr: 1976, La Salle, Ont
1976 S12, Montreal
66 Pine piece laminated pine/contre-plaqué de pin 50 diameter x 49 illus

DE BELLE, CHARLES see BELLE, CHARLES DE

DE CONDE, KENT see CONDE, KENT

DEELEY, KENNETH EDWARD
b 1939
1964J 18 Thrust and counter etch 5 x 8 $35

DE FOREST, HENRY J.
5 Feb 1860, Rothesay, NB 23 Mar

1924, Calgary H
Addr: 1893, Saint John; 1899, 742 Craig St, Montreal; 1901-6, Vancouver
1893 33 Valley of the Wauganni River at evening, New Zealand $175 F1-30
1899 36a Still life
1901 50 Entrance to Yale Canyon, Fraser River
1906 F5, Halifax
49 Jervis Inlet $200

DE GRANDMAISON, NICKOLA see GRANDMAISON, NICKOLA DE

DEGUIRE, VINCENT
1971 16G Poster, Of many people
17G Poster, and folder, Week-end de cinema d'animation canadian, National Film Board

DE HEUSCH, LUCIO see HEUSCH, LUCIO

DE KERGOMMEAUX, DUNCAN see KERGOMMEAUX, DUNCAN CHASSIN DE

DE LALL, OSCAR DANIEL
12 Sep 1903, St Petersburgh 23 May 1971, Montreal CWW64 M NGC
ARCA 1946 RCA 1959 Council Painter
Addr: 1933, 1620 Sherbrooke St W, Montreal; 1935, 3805 Drolet St, Montreal; 1937, 2031 Union Ave, Montreal; 1946-57, Westmount, Que; 1958-71, Montreal
1933 49 Self portrait
288 Rabbi Mayer W. Cohen, portrait study charcl
1935 66 Miss Jacqueline de Rouen nfs
316 John Stadler, Esq charcl nfs
1937 57 Self portrait nfs T38-13
1938 57 Mrs Harry Thorp
249 Head of a man charcl $35
1939 57 Mrs J.McK. Wathen nfs
1940 43 Mr C.Hessey-White nfs
1941 45 Lt Col Charles Adams nfs
46 Hon T.D. Bouchard nfs
1943 23 Mr H.B. Bowen nfs
1945 56 S. Lupovich, Esq nfs
57 N. Brecher, Esq nfs
1946 28 Self portrait nfs
29 Soil toiler illus $600 T47-13
1947 39 E. Dyonnet, RCA nfs
40 The sweater woman $850
1948 41 Sandra nfs
42 Spring, Mont Tremblant $600
1949 22 Capt Beaufort S. Lewis nfs T50-5
1950 79 Mrs A. Sugden 34 x 26 nfs
1951 24 Miss P. Mason nfs
1952 23 Mr A. Bronfman nfs
1953 22 Mrs R. York Wilson illus nfs
1953 Travelling exhibit
17 Mr E. Cleghorn nfs
1954 26 Portrait in greys 30 x 36 illus $950
1955 29 Study in greys $900
1956 18 J. Meroz nfs
1957 21 Miss Susan Langston nfs
1958 25 Mrs T. Ballantyne nfs
1959 23 Mrs T. Walker 36 x 30 nfs
1960 24 Self portrait 24 x 32 nfs
1961 27 Habitant of Quebec 28 x 36 illus $850
1964N 18 Oil study 24 x 32 $500
DW 1960 Mrs G. Ballantyne 36 x 30
port: bust, by A. Zoltvany-Smith, 1937-298; by R. York Wilson, 1953-91

DELBOS, EDMUND
Addr: 1908, Upper Canada College, Toronto
1908 36 Solitude
37 An Ontario landscape

DELBUGUET, RENE
12 Sep 1930, France
RCA(e) 1979 Photographer
Addr: 1979, Montreal

DELFOSSE, MARIE JOSEPH GEORGES
8 Dec 1869, St Henri des Mascouche, Que 24 Dec 1939, Montreal CC2 CNS36 M Mo12 NGC PMC TB3
Addr: 1899, 1562 Ontario St, Montreal; 1910, 259 Sherbrooke St E, Montreal; 1913-20, 690 Sherbrooke St E, Montreal; 1925, 718 Sherbrooke St W, Montreal
1899 37 Still life
1910 53 Mon modele
1913 86 Au déclin
87 Etude
88 Vieilles tour du fort de la montagne, érigées par de Maisonneuve en 1677
1915 66 Peace, Canadian scenery

1916 57 Contemplation
1918N 42 Dollard des Ormeaux. La gloire sortant du combat
1920 67 Maison de Cavelier de La Salle ≬NGC≬
1925 52 The oldest house of Kingston, Ont, where the first Parliament of Canada was held in March 1841
1929 S7, Calgary
37 Spring $450
38 Old church at Nohant $400

DELORIMIER, GUILLENETTE
1950 87 Paris from my window 20 x 25 nfs

DE MERS, WALDYNE see MERS, WALDYNE

DEMSTER, ELIZABETH I.
Addr: 1905, Dovercourt Rd, Toronto
1905 55 Last of July

DENECHAUD, SIMONE
8 Oct 1905, Montreal 11 Sep 1974, Montreal WWA47
Addr: 1933, 5428 Hutchison Ave, Outremont, Que
1933 50 Nature morte $75
1943 24 F/L Guy H. Rainville, DFM RCAF nfs T44-10
25 Pivoines

DENNIS, CLAUDE W.
fl 1890-05 H
Addr: 1899-00, 68 Hypolite St, Montreal; 1902, Montreal; 1903, 104 Hypolite St, Montreal; 1904, Montreal; 1905, 229 1/4 St Urbain St, Montreal; 1907, Montreal; 1908, 229A St Urbain St, Montreal
1890 19 A shady nook $20
1899 165 Returning from pasture wc
1900 35 The dairy W.C. Dennis, mispr
1902 193 Fog wc
194 Pasture, Back River wc
1903 162 Evening in the harbour wc
163 Waiting for his master wc
164 The old oven wc
1904 215 The wharf, Cacouna
216 Mist, Cacouna
217 The convent, Back River
1905 57 Rev W. Barnes ivory min
58 Waiting for his master F6-67 $50
59 The old trading post, Lachine
60 Old oven
1907 57 Roadside pastoral, Lachine
58 Shades of evening
231 Early moonrise wc
1907 F6, Sherbrooke
66 Evening in the harbour $50
68 Low tide, Cacouna $35
69 Evening $35
1908 38 Roadside pastoral
39 Eventide

DENNISON, EMILY
H
1892 67 Melons $30

DENNISTOUN, MARY see KIRKPATRICK, MARY

DENOVAN, PARKER
1938 58 Half light $75
1939 58 Fishermen's houses $150
1940 44 Oakville stocks $150
1946 30 High water, Forest Mills $100 T47-13

DENTON, FRANCIS WILLIAM (FRANK)
b Toronto CWW36
1941 47 Richmond Hill nfs
1942 33 August nfs
1943 26 December morning, Burke's Falls nfs
1944 34 Shipyards, Toronto nfs
1945 58 Shipyard nfs T46-12
1946 31 Sea coast nfs T47-14
1948 40 Harbour scene nfs
1957 22 Phyllis nfs
1958 26 Portrait #1 nfs
1960 25 Portrait 20 x 24 nfs

DE PALMA, ARMAND see PALMA, ARMAND

DE PEDERY-HUNT, DORA see HUNT, DORA

DEROCHE, BESSIE BOGART (Mrs)
Addr: 1918-23, 318 Lyon St, Ottawa; 1925-35, 110 Cartier St, Ottawa
1918A 46 Parliament Hill, Ottawa
47 The Bay of Quinte 1922-52
1919 38 View from new Parliament Building, Ottawa
1920 68 Pasture fields
1921 44 161 York Street, Ottawa
1923 36 Daffodil study
1925 53 Across Cartier Square
1927 46 A grey day, looking toward Hull 1928-42 $150
1928 43 Still life $75
1929 S7, Calgary

39 Grey day, Hull, Quebec $100
40 Blue and gold $75
1930 42 Across the bay $75
1931 63 Connaught Place $150
1935 67 Green Point $50 T36-21

DERRETH, REINHARD
20 Feb 1928, Berlin
RCA(e) 1978 Graphic designer
Addr: 1979, Vancouver

DESAUTELS, AIME
10 Dec 1921, Montreal
ARCA 1970 Architect
Addr: 1971, Montreal; 1979, Laval des Rapides, Que

DESAUTELS, CHARLES EMILE
23 Jan 1912, St Hyacinthe, Que
1941 48 Couteau $75

DESBARATS, GUY
b Montreal
ARCA 1970 Ret 1973 Architect
Addr: 1970-1, Montreal

DESBIENS, GERARD
11 Feb 1925, Lévis, Que M WWA59
1954 103 L'Immaculée Conception sculp 41h $550

DES CLAYES, ALICE
22 Dec 1890, Aberdeen AGO CNS36 NGC
ARCA 1920 Non-res 1956 Painter
Addr: 1914-16, 6 Beaver Hall Sq, Montreal; 1918N-19, 360 Beaver Hall Sq, Montreal; 1920, 156 Holland Park Ave, London, Eng; 1921-5, 360 Beaver Hall Sq, Montreal; 1927-8, 1158 Beaver Hall Sq, Montreal; 1929, Chorley Wood, Eng; 1931-7, 1158 Beaver Hall Sq, Montreal; 1938-71, London, Eng
1914 58 Poor pastures
1915 61 Drawing water ≬NGC≬
62 Study of a polo pony
1916 58 Flooded land, Kirkfield, Ontario
59 A winter evening, Andreselles, France wc
1918N 43 After the day's work illus
44 Le retour wc
1919 39 Sand carts
1920 69 Toilers of the shore
70 A blue day illus ≬AGO≬
1921 45 A June evening
1922 53 Midi S6-17
54 A grey day in the dunes wc
55 Rough weather wc S6-18
56 Cutting clover wc
1923 37 The last furrow
38 Shoeing a grey horse wc
1925 54 Towing barges wc
55 Ploughing near Melbourne
1927 47 The roadmakers
1928 44 The harrow $200
1929 49 September in Hertfordshire wc $100
1931 64 Harvest time $75
65 Unharnessing wc $15
66 In the shade wc $15
1932 48 The old Berkeley Hunt at Shardeloes ivory min $40
49 Ploughing ivory min $30
1933 51 La Plage, Ambleteuse $175
52 Judging the farmers lots, Widecombe Fair $150
1935 68 Hunting on Dartmoor $250
69 Carting seaweed at Exmouth, Devon $250 T36-22
70 Ponies at Dartmoor $65
71 April sunshine $65
1937 58 The hay cutter $125 T38-14
1938 59 Carting seaweed $250
1939 59 The roller wc $35
60 Ploughing wc $35

DES CLAYES, BERTHE
1877, Aberdeen d 1968 AGO CNS36 NGC
Addr: 1912-16, 6 Beaver Hall Sq, Montreal; 1918A-25, 360 Beaver Hall Sq, Montreal; 1926, c/o Watson Gallery, 679 St Catherine St W, Montreal; 1927, 1158 Beaver Hall Sq, Montreal; 1929-30, Corley Wood, Eng; 1931-6, 1158 Beaver Hall Sq, Montreal
1912 66 Sur les dunes, Normandie
67 Sur la Seine, St Cloud, Paris
68 Sur la Seine, Paris
69 Paysage, Normandie
1912 S3, Winnipeg
38 Old Normandy cottage
39 In Normandy, France
1913 89 The shack in the bush, Barkmere, Que S4-41 $250 ≬NGC≬
90 Evening, Barkmere
91 The road through the woods
92 The willows
1914 59 Old cottages, Lachine, Que
60 On the canal, Lachine, Que
1914 S5, Patriotic Fund

79 Landscape illus
1915 63 The gateway
64 The road to the farm
1916 60 The goose girl
61 Homeward
1918A 48 The bridle path
49 The end of day
1918N 45 On the St Francis River, Melbourne, Quebec
46 The terrace
1919 40 A French farm
41 The covered bridge
1920 71 Souvenir de la guerre
72 French peasant woman
1921 46 Early spring in Picardy illus ◊AGO◊
47 In Gloucester harbour
1922 57 The harbour at Blue Rocks, Nova Scotia S6-19
1923 39 The valley road
40 October
1925 56 Gloucester harbour
57 Old man hoeing
1926 38 The canal at Rickmanceworth, Herts
1927 48 A Cornish land
1929 50 A little Nova Scotian $100
1930 43 Old habitant, Quebec $75
44 Bruges, the bridge $175
1931 67 Spring on a Hertfordshire farm $75
68 Children with sheep wc $75
1932 50 The woodsmen $350
1933 53 October $350 T34-19
54 Pentewen, Cornwall, England $225
1935 72 A March morning $350 T36-23
73 Crimson and gold, Melbourne, Quebec $325
1936 61 In a Quebec village $300
1938 60 The old corner store, St Andrews East, Quebec $500
61 Spring flowers $150
1939 61 Ploughing, Melbourne, Quebec $275
1939 F11, New York
18 Dominion Square, Montreal 32 x 25 (Blair Russell, Esq, Montreal)
1940 45 In a Quebec sugar bush $275
1941 49 Hauling logs $225
1941 S9, Toronto
21 In the pasture $150
1943 27 St Mary's Church, Como $200 T44-11
28 Autumn $275
1945 59 Going to the mill $450
T46-13
1947 41 Ploughing $350

DES CLAYES, GERTRUDE
1879, Aberdeen 23 Aug 1949, London, Eng B CNS36 NGC
ARCA 1914 Painter
Addr: 1912-16, 6 Beaver Hall Sq, Montreal; 1918A-25, 360 Beaver Hall Sq, Montreal; 1927-36, 1158 Beaver Hall Sq, Montreal; 1937-49, London, Eng
1912 70 Yvette
71 Lullaby
72 Un gentilhomme d'Espagne
73 Portrait of a man
1912 S3, Winnipeg
40 Autumn
41 Gentleman at the time of Elizabeth
1913 93 Miss Haswell S4-93 $1,000 nfs
94 Beatrice Mary Lyman, daughter of Mr and Mrs Walter Lyman
1914 61 Evelyn and baby, daughters of W.R. MacInnes, Esq 1916-62 illus
62 Mrs G.L. Ogilvie and her son
1914 S5, Patriotic Fund
76 Petite canadienne illus
1915 65 Mrs F. Beardmore illus 1919-42 illus, Mrs F.N. Beardmore
1916 63 Donald, son of F.C. Hanna, Esq pastel
1918A 50 George Beardmore, Esq, portrait sketch
51 Mrs Fisk illus Mrs. H.J. Fisk
1918N 47 Study of a child pastel illus
48 The grey barn pastel
49 The covered bridge, Upper Melbourne pastel
50 Vive la France
1920 73 F.N. Beardmore, Esq illus
74 Miss Betty Ogilvie
1923 41 Diana
42 Blue Rocks harbour, Nova Scotia
1925 58 Autumn pastel
1927 49 The drinking trough
1933 55 The pearly king $2,000 T34-20
56 Ranunculus pastel $150
1935 74 Paddy from Donaghadee

$250 1938-62
75 Avril $150
76 Rose on rose pastel $100
T36-24
1937 59 The Hindustani peacocks
$200 T38-15
1939 F11, New York
19 The blue bird 20 x 28
$1,000

DESGAGNE, LEONCE
1964N Desgagne & Côté
108-10 Eglise Notre Dame de Fatima. General view, exterior. Interior. Plan du rez du chaussée

DE SMEDT, JOSEPH
1945 60 Portrait study $225
61 Mount Assiniboine, Canadian Rockies $125

DESPARD, AMY CONSTANCE
b London, Ont
Addr: 1932, 10 Glen Rd, Toronto
1932 51 Sun on the rocks

DESROSIERS, ROGER PIERRE
1939 244 Confiance sculp $500

DEUTSCH, PETER ANDREW
31 Jul 1926, Truava, Czechoslovakia
WWA66
1967 16 Mainstream 72 x 36 illus
$650
1968 17 Quadratic 60 x 60 illus
$750
1970 16 Album 60 x 66 illus $900
17 Spell 72 x 48 $800
1971 10 Next time 72 x 72 illus
$1,000

DE VLETTER, FIONA see VLETTER, FIONA

DEVLIN, MURRAY JOHN
b 1924
1958 27 In the beginning $100

DEWAR, ANDREW
ARCA 1880-8 Architect
Addr: 1880-8, Halifax

DEWAR, P.
1970 99 Safety hat. Safety Supply Company

DIAMOND, ABEL JOSEPH
8 Nov 1932, Piet Retief, S Africa
WWA78
RCA(e) 1974 RCA 1976 Architect
Addr: 1979, Toronto
DW 1976 Architecture 40 col slides

DICK, DAVID BRASH
17 Jan 1846, Edinburgh 8 Sep 1925, Woking, Eng H NGC W78
ARCA 1880 RCA 1894 Ret 1906 Council Architect
Addr: 1880-2, Toronto; 1883, Toronto St, Toronto; 1884-94, Toronto; 1895, Canada Life, Toronto; 1896-04, Toronto; 1905-11, England; 1912-14, Winona, Horsell Rise, Woking, Eng; 1915-25, Woking, Eng
1880 263 Cabinet des H.B. Dick, mispr
368 Consumer's Gas Co, Toronto, office, with suggested extension
1883 351 Winona, residence at Norway
1885 328 Canadian Bank of Commerce, Guelph des
329 Gate lodge des
1894 198 Library building, Toronto University DW 1894 pen drwg 20 1/2 x 30 1895-24A
1895 23A University library, interior
25A University gymnasium Dick & Wickson
26A Store building, Yonge St, Toronto
27A Royal Canadian Yacht Club, Toronto, addition
1896 270 Chemical laboratory of Toronto University
271 Bank of Hamilton, at Wingham, Ont
272 Royal College of Dental Surgeons of Ontario
1899 243 Toronto University, gymnasium
244 Toronto University, library, interior of reading room
245 Gate lodge and gardener's house, views to park and road
1908 40 The harbour wall
1912 245 The Sphinx, Gizeh, Egypt
246 In San Remo, Italy
247 In the Piazzetta dei Leoni, St Mark's, Venice
1914 211 In the old town of Menton, France wc

212 A glimpse of the Italian frontier, from Menton, France wc

DICK, RONALD ALBERT
see MARANI, FERDINAND, 1966

DICKENSON, EDGAR A. (or DICKINSON)
fl 1871-00 H
Addr: 1900, Ottawa
1886 Dickenson
68 Street in Serrenugger, capital of Cashmere wc
96 Original sketch wc
1900 Dickinson
132 View near Bath, England wc

DICKSON, JENNIFER JOAN
17 Sep 1936, Piet Retief, Transvaal, S Africa WWA78
RCA(e) 1978 Print maker
Addr: 1979, Ottawa

DIERLANN, C.
H
1888 164 The old home $100

DIGNAM, MARY ELLA WILLIAMS (Mrs John Sifton Dignam)
13 Jan 1860, Port Burwell, Ont d 1938 CNS40 H Mo98/12 TB2
Addr: 1886, London, Ont; 1887, Yonge Street Arcade, Toronto; 1893-4, 509 Markham St, Toronto; 1896, 275 St George St, Toronto; 1900, 248 St George St, Toronto; 1916, 284 St George St, Toronto; 1924, 252 Poplar Plains Rd, Toronto
1883 70 A bright corner Dingnam, mispr
1885 60 Winter bouquet $75
150 Still life $100
177 Marigolds $30
1886 106 Roses $75
135 Peonies $150 F1a-1992
1887 13 Souvenirs $150
34 A bit of an old French garden $150
1888 80 Portrait
88 Study of a head $50
94 Leontine $250 Digman, mispr
184 Bit of Muskoka $75
204 Chrysanthemums $150
205 Nephotos roses $35
1889 29 Spring morning $100
52 Touched by the frost $200
104 Marigolds
164 A dream of roses wc
1890 20 Day dreams $200
21 An old man's garden $300
22 Pumpkin $200
23 Portrait nfs
1891 122 Peonies wc
218 Empty nest
224 Happy hours
234 Poppies
1892 27 Mid-day meal $150
29 Mamma wants me $35
84 Marigolds $25
1893 34 In the vineyard $200 F1-31
35 Still life, pumpkin $150 F1-32
1894 38 A poppy garden
1895 35 Roses
21W Roses wc
1896 36 The edge of the wood
37 Close of day
38 Roses, pot pourri
1900 24 Roses and bluebells
1901 35 Daily bread 1904-49
36 Roses
1907 60 Fishing boats, North Sea
61 Landscape, Holland
62 Goose girl, evening, France
1912 S3, Winnipeg
42 The dunes, Holland
43 Dutch interior
1916 64 Old water gate, canal, Venice
1924 43 Dunes, north shore

DILLE, LUTZ
29 Sep 1922, Leipzig
RCA(e) 1973 Photographer
Addr: 1979, Toronto

DIMAKOPOULAS, DIMITRI
14 Sep 1929, Athens
RCA(e) 1973 Architect
Addr: 1979, Montreal
see also Affleck, Raymond, 1964-1968

DIMITROV, ANTONIN
27 Feb 1928, Msecke, Zehrovice, Czechoslovakia
RCA(e) 1975 Stage designer
Addr: 1979, Mississauga, Ont

DIMITROV, OLGA
5 Jan 1933, Dvur, Kralove Nad, Labem, Czechoslovakia
RCA(e) 1975 Costume designer
Addr: 1979, Mississauga, Ont

DIMSON, THEO AENEAS
8 Apr 1930, London, Ont CWW79 WWA 73
ARCA 1971 RCA 1974 Graphic designer
Addr: 1979, Toronto
1970 145 Magazine (Abitibi) Impressions V2 #1 1969
146 Newspaper supplement cover, The human brain, Star Weekly, 29 Jan 1966
147 Annual report, Province of Ontario Council for the Arts, 5th report 1968-1969
148 Poster, Sevier
149 Poster, panda. Croydon Associates
DW 1974 3 posters, Richard Third, Time tango, Marilyn

DINGLE, JOHN ADRIAN DARLEY
4 Feb 1911, Barmouth, Wales 22 Dec 1974, Mississauga, Ont M WWA47
ARCA 1948 RCA 1968 Council Painter
Addr: 1934, 12 Palmer Ave, Oakville, Ont; 1937, 64 Grenville St, Toronto; 1948-51, Toronto; 1952-7, Cooksville, Ont; 1958-65, Erindale, Ont; 1966, Cooksville, Ont; 1967-8, Erindale, Ont; 1969-71, Mississauga, Ont
1934 56 A study in satins T35-20 nfs
1937 60 John Martin, Esq nfs
1938 63 Miss Hollis nfs
1939 62 Prelude to evening nfs
63 Merrily we go $150
1940 46 F/O S.H. Matheson nfs
47 On again, off again $200 T41-13
1941 50 Saturday morning $500
51 Scherzo $200 T42-12
1941 S9, Toronto
20 A frosty frolic $125
1942 34 Roses nfs
1944 35 Sylvan throne $150
1946 32 Old Tom's place $300 T47-15
33 Spring prelude $200 T47-16
1947 42 Ice storm $300
43 Caledon centenarian $450
1948 43 Morning, Eden Mills $400
44 Spring light $200
1949 23 Mary S. Edgar nfs 1950-33 40 x 30
24 Season's final hour $300 T50-6
1951 25 Este nfs
1952 24 Old ice house $400
1954 27 Take home pay 40 x 28 illus $600
28 Last of the snow 28 x 36 $550
1955 30 Monument to man $200
1956 18 Huttonville millrace $600 T56-18
1957 23 Scrapper II and friends $350
1958 28 The labour thereof $400
29 Maritime theme illus $500
1959 24 Fog shroud 20 x 37 illus $500
1960 26 Tomorrow and yesterday, Seville 48 x 25 illus $900 1961-29
27 Before the bullfight, Ronda 24 x 48 $900
1963 21 The Long Drop, east coast $1,000
1964N 19 Renaissence/63 28 x 48 nfs 1965-63 S10-23
1965 22 Accelerando 28 x 48 illus $1,100
1966 15 Concerto by Parris 38 x 48 illus $1,500 S11-15 acry polymer nfs
16 The village 38 x 24 $750
1967 17 Musical chairs 32 x 48 $1,200 S11-16 acry polymer nfs
1968 18 Principal flute 48 x 26 $1,100
19 Dingle Harbour, County Kerry, Eire 48 x 39 illus $1,550 DW 1969
1970 19 Timpani in black 48 x 39 illus $1,700

DINGLE, RUTH MARION (Mrs Peter Hugh Douet)
4 Dec 1908, Calgary
Addr: 1931-36, 582 Lansdowne Ave, Westmount, Que
1931 69 Vancouver, from False Creek $25
70 Mount Warren, Maligne Lake $25
1935 77 Summer flowers $100 T36-25
1936 62 Delphinium and gladioli $100
63 Tiger, tiger, burning bright $100
1939 64 Chinese whites $150
1941 52 Miriam $75 T42-13

DINGLE, THOMAS Jr English
fl 1879-07 DBA DVP RA
Addr: 1907, Plymouth, Eng
1907 233 Fishing village, River

Yealm, Devon wc

DIONNE, THERESE
1941 211 Mon père sculp nfs
1945 219 Leo Ayotte, peintre sculp nfs

DIX, WAKEFIELD G.
1888, Garden Island, Ont
Addr: 1936, 71 Lombard St, Toronto
1936 64 Tug wc
1938 64 Idle ships wc nfs

DODD SIMPSON PRESS
Addr: 1938, Montreal
1938 S8, Toronto
81-3 3 folders. Booklet with envelope. Folder. Charles Fainmel

DOERRIE, GERHARD
b Germany
RCA(e) 1973 Graphic designer
Addr: 1979, Oakville, Ont

DOGGETT, MEAVE O'BRYNE
Addr: 1912, Winnipeg
1912 S3, Winnipeg
261 Limoges enamel panels, in cabinet. The Lady Sinain. The sunbeam. The spirit of the rain cloud. baisse taille. Saint Columcille tryptyck

DOMINION OILCLOTH AND LINOLEUM CO, LIMITED
Addr: 1938, Montreal
1938 S8, Toronto
84 Square tile floor in bathroom
85 Black tile floor
86 Floor designs in East and Fudger Galleries

DOMINION TEXTILE CO, LIMITED
Addr: 1938, Montreal
1938 S8, Toronto
87 Textiles, pylons of dress fabrics 2 illus

DONAGHUE, JOHN
1882 287 Bas relief

DONAHUE, JAMES see DONOAHUE, JAMES

DONALD, ADELAIDE see WEBSTER, ADELAIDE

DONALDSON, JAMES MILLER
1968 Donaldson, Drummond & Sankey
98-02 Town of Mount Royal Library. A.View from bridge B.View towards bridge C. South courtyard, looking west, illus D.Adult library from reception desk

DONALDSON, M.
H
1880 253 Looking out of Hoosac Tunnel drwg

DONGES, LANGLEY THOMAS
17 Jan 1901, Toronto
1944 36 Erindale $250
1948 45 View from the studio $250
46 Snow storm $125
1951 26 Mud road $100
1952 25 Barn shadows $125

DONLY, EVA BROOK (Mrs Augustine William Donly)
30 Apr 1867, Simcoe, Ont d 1941
M Mo12 NGC TB3 WWA36
Addr: 1918-20, Simcoe, Ont; 1925, c/o Johnson Art Galleries, Montreal
1918A 52 Mountain ranges, Mexico City wc
1918N 51 Palm trees and huts, Mexico wc
52 Indian dooryard, Mexico wc
1919 43 Northland, Laurentians wc
44 Southland, Bermuda wc
1920 75 Marigolds
76 Zinnias
1925 59 Garden, Bermuda wc
60 Lane, Nantucket wc

DONNELL, JAMES M.
1884, Edinburgh d 1957
Addr: 1937, 1461 Bleury St, Montreal
1937 61 Donkey boy wc $35

DONOAHUE, JAMES THOMAS
15 Oct 1934, Walkerton, Ont
RCA(e) 1974 Graphic designer
Addr: 1979, Toronto
1970 150 Letterhead, Jim Donoahue
151 Letterhead, format
152 Christmas card, Jim, Judy, Zoe and Noah Donoahue
153 Symbol, Typographic Quebec

DORET, A.M. see CARTER, ALEXANDER, 1921, 1923

DORION, C.A.
H
1882 131 Village of Yamachiche wc $20

DORN, PETER KLAUS
30 Jun 1932, Berlin WWA76
RCA(e) 1974 Graphic designer
Addr: 1976/79, Kingston, Ont
1970 154 Catalogue, Royal Ontario Museum. Prized possessions from private homes
155 Book, Miraculous montages
156 Book, Reflections on love
157 Invitation, Yousuf Karsh reception
158 Title page, Aba Bayefsky portfolio 'Legends'
1971 18G Folder, Continuing education, Faculty of Dentistry
19G Booklet, Partners in development, Scarborough College
20G Book jacket, Neitzsche in England, University of Toronto Press
1976 S12, Montreal
116 Catalog, Tradition + 1

DOUGHTIE, WILLIAM
c 1846 Edinburgh 8 Jun 1882, Orlando, Fla H
ARCA 1880 Designer
Addr: 1880-2, Toronto
1880 280 and 282 Book cover
298 Wall paper. Prize award
299 Damask table cover des Governor General's bronze medal
299a Wall paper des
300 Centre design for damask table cover
301 Lace curtains, net des
1881 157 Calico print des $50
158 Oilcloth
160, 165 and 168 Book cover
161 and 166 Wall paper des
163 Damask table cover des
164 Lace curtains, net des $80
167 Damask table cover des $200
1882 212 and 215 Damask table cover
213 Net curtain lace des
214 and 215 Wall paper des
217-19 Book covers
220 Calico print des
221 Oilcloth des

DOUGLAS, BLOOMFIELD
1832-1906 H
Addr: 1896, 56 University St, Montreal
1896 Capt Douglas RNR
39 Wreck of the George Canway
40 The bay, southwest point, Anticosti
41 A heavy squall, Saint John harbour, NB

DOUGLAS, ELEANOR
fl 1894-00 H
Addr: 1898, 114 Yonge St, Toronto; 1900, Toronto
1898 37 Woodland
38 Beech trees
1900 32 Midsummer moon
33 By the river
34 The creek

DOUGLASS, LUCILLE
Addr: 1925, c/o Art Association of Montreal
1925 61 Wedding procession, Soochow pastel
286 Young sea pines, Monterey etch
287 Long Road Rest House, Soochow etch

DOWNES, LIONEL FIELDING
15 Apr 1900, Wigan, Lanc, Eng
d 1972
1945 62 Eda pastel nfs

DOWNING, ROBERT JAMES
1 Aug 1935, Hamilton, Ont
RCA(e) 1977 Sculptor
Addr: 1979, Toronto

DOWNS, BARRY VANCE
19 Jun 1930, Vancouver
ARCA 1970 Architect
Addr: 1971/76/79, Vancouver
1971 9A-12A Sedgewick Building, University of Victoria. Faculty office wing. President's office. Typical office, illus. Site plan
1976 S12, Montreal
Downs & Archambault
99 Residence, Hernando Island, BC 2 illus
see also Archambault, Richard, 1964N

DOWSLEY, E. (Mrs)
Addr: 1907, Montreal
1907 57 A bit of road, Covey Hill Corners

DRAHANCHUK, WALTER see DROHAN, WALTER

DRAKE, JOHN POAD English
20 Jul 1794, Stoke Damerel, Devon, Eng 26 Feb 1883, Fowey, Cornwall, Eng B Gr H TB
1881 335 Hon Chief Justice Blowers T.P. Drake, mispr

DRAKE, WILLIAM ALEXANDER
7 Nov 1891, Toronto 15 Sep 1946, Toronto AGO
Addr: 1916, c/o Ontario College of Art, St James Sq, Toronto; 1918, 37 Carlton St, Toronto; 1919, 157 West 59th St, New York; 1921, 108 West 103rd St, New York; 1928-9, 284 Glenholme Ave, Toronto
1916 65 Reflections and shadows
66 The shallow stream
1918A 53 A shallow stream, winter
54 A country mill, winter
1918N 53 A country cottage, winter
1919 45 War at home, forging 1920-77
1921 48 Rendez-vous
1928 202 Moulin Havigne, Veaux, Belgique etch $25
203 Journal Sauare Bridge under construction etch $20
1929 260 Three days out etch $25
261 A squatter's shanty etch $15

DREANY, EDWARD JOSEPH
1908, North Bay, Ont
Addr: 1934, 10 Gloucester St, Toronto; 1936-7, 534 Carlaw Ave, Toronto
1934 57 Corpus Christi Sunday $250
1936 65 The brick factory wc $35
1937 62 Sunshine camp wc $40
63 The timber cutters wc $40
1938 65 The brick kiln wc $50 T39-18
1939 66 Boat houses, Orillia $125
1943 29 Fishing village $125
30 Camp in the pines wc $40
1944 37 Nocturne wc $40
1945 63 Summer road wc $50

DREANY, FREDA see JOHNSON, FREDA

DRENTERS, ANDREAS
1937, Belgium
1966 74 Pilgrim sculp 80h $500
1968 55 The Ontario pioneer sculp $350

DRENTERS, YOSEF GERTRUDIS
25 Nov 1929, Poppel, Flanders, Belgium CC2 M
RCA(e) 1974 Sculptor
Addr: 1979, Rockwood, Ont
1963 81 Mother and child sculp 36h illus $500

DROHAN, WALTER (b Walter Drahanchuk)
27 Jul 1932, Calgary
RCA(e) 1976 Ceramist
Addr: 1979, Cochrane, Alta

DROPE, MCCLEARY HERBERT (c 1975 Swami Bodhi Anando)
31 Oct 1931, Detroit
1965 74 Hommage to Helios welded steel approx 60h $2,200

DROYE, NORMA
Addr: 1938, Toronto
1938 S8, Toronto
380 Wallpaper design. Hon mention. Canadian Wallpaper Manufacturers Limited

DRUMMOND, ARTHUR ALEXANDER
28 May 1891, Toronto WWA66
Addr: 1918-28, 63 Inglewood Dr, Toronto; 1934, Orono, Ont
1918A 55 Harvest
1918N 54 A forest glade 1919-46
55 Mount Sir Donald
1920 78 On the Conestogo River
1921 49 Incoming tide
1923 43 The copper shop
1925 62 In the Caledon Hills
1926 39 October woods, Muskoka
1928 45 Fishing boats, Rockport harbour $175
1934 58 Percé Rock wc $100

DRUMMOND, DEREK ARMOUR
see DONALDSON, JAMES MILLER, 1968

DRUMMOND, HARRIET O.
H
Addr: 1908, 36 Cecil St, Toronto
1908 41 Case of ivory miniatures

DRUMMOND, MOIRA ELIZABETH
1 Aug 1904, Montreal

Addr: 1934, 1455 Drummond St, Montreal; 1937, 18 Thornhill Ave, Westmount, Que
1934 59 Cowichan Indian dancers
60 Joe Smokisasett T35-21
1937 64 Sunflower $100

DRUMMOND, SOPHIE see PEMBERTON, SOPHIE

DRUTZ, JUNE
14 Feb 1920, Toronto IO WWA73
ARCA 1972 RCA 1974 Print maker
Addr: 1979, Toronto
1966 17 Gates of heaven sergph 35 1/4 x 46 $200
DW 1974 Renewal I. 1971 sergph 29 x 18 1/4

DUBE, LOUIS THEODORE
1861, St Roch des Aulnaies, Que
d 1925 B H
Addr: 1904, Paris; 1911, 16 ave de l'Alma, Paris
1904 50 Farm yard
311 Case of miniatures
1911 44 Room in the Louvre, Paris

DUBOIS, MACY
20 Dec 1929, Baltimore WWA76
ARCA 1971 Architect
Addr: 1979, Toronto
see also Fairfield, Robert, 1964N-68

DUCHARME, RAOUL
Addr: 1907, St Hilaire, Que; 1916, 150 Girouard St, St Hyacinthe, Que
1907 63 Beloeil by moonlight
1916 67 Morning charcl & wc
68 Evenine charcl & wc

DUCLOS, G. GILLELAN (Mrs)
Addr: 1931, 152 James St, Ottawa
1931 71 Florence H. McGillivray, ARCA pastel

DUDAS, KUYPERS, ADAMSON LIMITED
1970 100 Hockey helmet, CCM
1971 5I Electric kettle. Proctor-Lewyt division of SCM (Canada) Limited

DUDLEY, CAROL REID American
1 May 1908, Providence, RI DBA WWA36
Addr: 1937, 96 Perry St, New York
1937 65 Burning bush, Scotland wc $100
66 The peat gatherer wc $75

DUFF, ANN MACINTOSH
14 Jul 1925, Toronto AGO CWW79 IO M WWA76
RCA(e) 1973 RCA 1974 Council Painter
Addr: 1979, Toronto
1959 25 Northern landscape 20 1/2 x 28 1/2 $140
DW 1974 Evening view, North Channel. 1973 wc 21 x 29

DUFF, WALTER RAYMOND
3 May 1879, Hamilton 1 Sep 1967, Toronto
Addr: 1909N-11, Yonge Street Arcade, Toronto; 1913, 1 Breadalbane St, Toronto; 1915, 72 Isabella St, Toronto; 1922, 413 Dorchester St W, Montreal
1909N 43 Three miniatures
1911 45 Portrait of my father min
1913 355 Portrait of Madame X etch S4-148 $25 nfs
356 J.S.R. Wainwright etch S4-149 $25 nfs
1915 272 H.S. Osler, Esq, KC, Toronto etch
273 Miss Margaret Wainwright, Toronto etch
1922 249 The headlands soft ground etch

DUFFIN, HAROLD A.
1952 26 Wayside market wc $75

DUKES, CAROLYN
b Budapest
Addr: 1976, Winnipeg
1976 S12, Montreal
12 Landscape #3 acry 57 x 57 illus

DULUDE, CLAUDE
30 Mar 1931, Montreal
RCA(e) 1979 Painter
Addr: 1979, Montreal

DUMAS, ANTOINE
8 Dec 1932, Quebec
RCA(e) 1979, Painter
Addr: 1979, Sillery, Que

DUMOUCHEL, ALBERT
15 Apr 1916, Bellerive, n Valleyfield, Que 11 Jan 1971, St Antoine sur Richelieu, Que AGO B CCI

RCA medal 1978

DUNBAR, FREDERICK ALEXANDER TURNER
1849, Guelph, Ont d 1912
ARCA 1881-6 Sculptor
Addr: 1881-6, Toronto
1882 281 Bishop Fuller unfin bust
282 Jno. R. Robinson, Lieut Gov of Ontario unfin bust
283 Sir John A. Macdonald bust $10
284 Late Hon George Brown bust $10
377 N.G. Bigelow, Esq bust
378 Portrait bust
1886 122a Beatrice sculp L.A.T. Dunbar, mispr

DUNBAR, ULRIC STONEWALL JACKSON
31 Jan 1862, London, Ont 7 May 1927, Washington, DC AAA28 Mo12 TB1/3
1882 285 Priest of Vulcan medln $25
286 Portrait of Jack medln $25

DUNCAN, ALICE MCLAREN
1879, Colborne, Ont
Addr: 1919-23, Colborne, Ont
1919 47 A quaint old barn
1920 79 The old homestead
80 The harvest
1922 58 The willows
1923 44 Evening sunlight

DUNCAN, ALMA MARY
2 Oct 1917, Paris, Ont IO
1943 31 Army girl in warehouse $75 T44-12
1950 34 Tired nun 38 x 25 $150
1964J 19 Night coll 48 x 31 $300
1965 24 Nude crayon 25 x 23 nfs
1967 18 The family #2 24 x 40 $275
port: bust, by H.M. Miller, 1941-122

DUNCAN, DOUGLAS MOERDYKE
1902, Kalamazoo, Mich 26 Jul 1968, Toronto
RCA medal 1977
Addr: 1938, Toronto
1938 S8, Toronto
88 Book, Don Quixote. maroon morocco, gold tooling
89 Book, The wooden star. blue levant morocco, gold tooling
90 Book, Prayer book. red levant morocco, gold and blind tooling
91 Book, The note books of Samuel Butler. half brown levant morocco, gold and blind tooling
92 Book, Lambda. quarter black levant morocco, platinum tooling 5 illus
port: bust, by F. Gage, DW 1977

DUNCAN, E.
1880 329 Taken aback wc (Thos. Reynolds)

DUNCAN, JAMES D.
1806, Coleraine, Ireland 28 Sep 1881, Longueuil, Que H W78
ARCA 1880 Painter
Addr: 1880-1, Montreal
1881 40 Quebec from Montmorenci Road wc $60
53 View from the Priests', Montreal wc $100
73 Bay of St Paul, below Quebec wc $40
91 On the north coast of Ireland wc $75

DUNLOP, ALEXANDER FRANCIS
Aug 1842, Montreal 30 Apr 1923, Montreal H Mo98/12 NGC
ARCA 1883 RCA 1890 Council Architect
Addr: 1883-92, Montreal; 1893-06, Temple Bldg, Montreal; 1907-8, Montreal; 1909-10, Lindsay Bldg, Montreal; 1911, 518 St Catherine St W, Montreal; 1912-23, Montreal
1881 162 House in Montreal des
192 Proposed church at Côte St Antoine
199 Lachute Paper Mills
209 Mantel piece des
1882 15 Study of a dog's head
239 Prospective view of a dwelling des
1884 196 Snowshoer's arch, 1884
1886 186 Athletic Club House, Montreal
1887 187 St James's Methodist Church, Montreal des
1890 222 Temple Building, detail of entrance wc drwg DW 1890 16 1/4 x 12
223 Dunlop of Dunlop, Aryshire, Scotland drwg

1893 276 Queen's Hotel, perspective
1902 195 Murray Bay wc
241 The Carsley Co, new store
242 La Raquette Club House
243 Montreal Star Building
1903 203 Outremont Golf Club
1906 201 Lindsay Building, Montreal, interior
202 Commercial and Technical High School, Montreal
1909M 146 Business block, St Catherine St, Montreal
147 Molson's Bank, Revelstoke, BC
148 Sara Maxwell School, Montreal
1910 54 Lac St Antoine, Kaneron Club (painting)
209 A.E. Rae Ltd, department store, perspective
210 William Dawson School, Gilford St
1911 195 St James Methodist Church, St Catherine St, Montreal pen & ink perspective
196 Goodwin's store, University St, Montreal, interior sketch
1912 248 Country club house

DUNLOP, DANIEL TURNBULL
4 May 1920, Edinburgh
1970 Dunlop, Wardell, Matsui & Aitken
9A-17A Richview Public Library, Etobicoke. Children's library, story telling area. Children's library, with 100' skylight. View down east elevation. Detail of south elevation. General view from southwest. Plot, ground and 2nd floor, basement plans

DUPUIS-MAILLET, CORINNE (Mrs Maillet)
1947 44 Nature morte gouache $50

DURAND, CLOVIS
1971 Vroom film screened 14 Apr

DURAND, GEORGE F.
1850, London, Ont 20 Dec 1889, London, Ont
ARCA 1884 Architect
Addr: 1884-9, London, Ont

DURNFORD, ALEXANDER TILLOCH GALT
25 Jul 1898, Montreal 22 Mar 1973, Montreal CNS27 CWW64
ARCA 1950 RCA 1957 Sr 1968 Council Architect
Addr: 1951-71, Montreal
1952 Fetherstonhaugh, Durnford, Bolton & Chadwick, to 1954
99 Bank of Canada, Victoria Square, Montreal photo
1953 96 Jim Gray Power House, Chicoutimi, Quebec drwg
97 Residence, Westmount, Quebec drwg
1954 115 Bedford School, Montreal photo illus
1957 Durnford, Bolton, Chadwick & Ellwood, to 1963
98 Anglican House, adjacent to Christ Church Cathedral, Montreal DW 1958 15 3/8 x 19 1/2 photo
99 Residence, Town of Mount Royal, Quebec
1958 99 Bell Telephone Company of Canada, Dial C O Bldg, Ottawa
100 First Baptist Church, Hampstead, Quebec
1959 98 Air Terminal Building, Gander, Newfoundland
1960 97 Fraser-Hickson Library, Montreal photo
98 Standard Life Assurance Company, Montreal photo
1961 93 Central Heating Plant, Montreal International Airport
94 Men's residence and dining hall, McGill University
1963 111 Standard Life Building, Montreal
see also Fetherstonhaugh, Harold, 1937-1947; Bolton, Richard, 1966

DUROCHER, RENE FRANCOIS MARIE
11 Nov 1919, Fougere, France
1959 26 Sapins vert 20 x 24 $90
1961 30 Evocation marine 24 x 30 $120

DURR, PATRICIA BETH
18 Sep 1939, Kansas City IO
Addr: 1976, Ottawa
1976 S12, Montreal
157 Burning bush ink & gouache 26 x 20 6 frames illus

DYONNET, EDMOND
25 Jun 1859, Crest, France 8 Jul 1954, Montreal B CC2 CNS36 CWW49 EC H M NGC TB W78 WWA47
ARCA 1893 RCA 1903 Sr 1948 Council
Painter
Addr: 1893, 1002 Dorchester St, Montreal; 1894, Art Association of Montreal; 1896-11, 9 University St, Montreal; 1912-13, 283 University St, Montreal; 1914, 314 St Catherine St W, Montreal; 1916-23, 255 Bleury St, Montreal; 1924-54, Montreal

1893 36 Statuary (painting) $125 1-33
37 Montreal from the Island $75
38 Landscape $30
1894 39 Gordon Creek, BC
1896 42 Cariboo Road, BC
43 La plaine Anglaise, Forest of Fontainebleau
44 Harvest time at Sorgues, France
45 A street at Sorgues, France
1898 35 The modeller
36 The black cat
1899 39 Storm effect on the St Lawrence illus
40 A sunset in the Laurentians
1900 26 H.S. de Lotbinière Harwood, MP
27 A.J.H. St Dennis, Esq
28 Arthur Henshaw, Esq
29 Returning home
30 Landscape in France
31 The Laurentides
1901 38 Miss A. Lorin 1906-75
39 Portrait, in the studio F2-20
40 Mr Chas. Gill F2-22 F5-53
41 Landscape in France
42 Cattle returning home F2-23
1902 46 C.E.L. Porteous, Esq 1904-51 F4-24
47 The Outremont Road
48 Moonlight
49 The mountain road
50 A cloudy night
51 Full moon
1903 40 The mendicant DW 1903 29 1/4 x 23 1/2 T51-14 1954 Retro Sec 12
41 Moonlight
42 Sunrise
42a Head of a girl
1904 52 Paul T. Lafleur, Esq F4-25
53 The St Lawrence at Beaupré
1905 61 Rev Wm. Bond, Archbishop of Montreal
62 Man reading pastel
1906 73 Mr Alfred Burnet
74 Eugene Lafleur, KC, Batonnier Montreal Bar 1907-66
76 Lac Tremblant
77 Water fall at Lac Tremblant
1906 F5, Halifax
50 Boy playing a mandolin $150
51 Returning home $125
52 Cottage by moonlight $125
1907 64 The serenade F6-70 $250
65 An Italian girl
67 Rev T. Lafleur
68 Landscape at Beaupré
69 Landscape at Ste Adèle
1907 F7, Sherbrooke
71 Girl playing the tambourine $200
72 The reader $200
73 Beaupré, Quebec $60
1908 43 The guitar player
1909M 43 R. Pinkerton, Esq S2-37
44 The picture book 1909N-44 S3-47
1909N 45 Returning home
46 Storm on the St Lawrence
47 Giusseppina S3-45
1910 55 Lt Col J.H. Burland
56 Contadina
1910 S2, Liverpool
36 Prof J. Poivert
1911 46 Rosine
47 Girl reading 1912-75
48 A girl's head
1912 74 Mr Jules Poivert
76 A country road
77 Early morning, Berthier S3-44
1912 S3, Winnipeg
46 River Bayonne, Berthier
1913 95 T.J. Burgess, Esq, MD S4-43 $300 nfs
1914 S5, Patriotic Fund
53 Old sailor's leisure hour pastel illus
1916 69 Seargent P. Stearns, Esq illus
1923 45 In the garden
1928 F8, London
116 Charles Gill $420
1938 66 Portrait of the artist illus F11-20 18 x 24 $500

ǁMMFAǁ
1941 53 Rev Daniel J. Fraser, MA DD LLD Emeritus Principal Presbyterian College, Montreal illus nfs
port: by G.H. Russell, 1922-177; O. De Lall, 1947-39; F. Iacurto, 1948-84; bust, by G. Hill, 1932-211

DZENIS, EDUARD A.
18 Apr 1907, Latvia IO M
1954 94 Horse gr 20 x 14 illus $100
95 Horses gr 20 x 14 $100
1955 95 Horses gr $75
1958 30 Horses gr $100
1960 28 On the beach 28 x 40 $350
29 Red horses 28 x 40 illus $350
1961 31 Two horses 31 x 73 $400
32 Man with a horse dry pt 24 x 29 $200

E

EARLE, PAUL BERNARD
23 Sep 1872, Montreal d c 1955 Montreal M NGC PMC TB3 WWA47
ARCA 1926 Sr 1941 Painter
Addr: 1910, Thomson & Earle, Montreal; 1913, 530 Mount Pleasant Ave, Westmount, Que; 1914-19, 149 King Edward Ave, Montreal; 1920, 770 Côte St Antoine Rd, Montreal; 1921-32, 172 Edgehill Rd, Westmount, Que; 1933, 1475 St Catherine St W, Montreal; 1934, 172 Edgehill Rd, Westmount, Que; 1935-6, 1475 St Catherine St, Montreal; 1937, Coronation Bldg, Montreal; 1938-55, Westmount, Que
1910 57 The dam, Beaupré
58 Bend of the river
1913 96 Edge of the wood
97 Woodland path
98 Quebec farm house
1914 63 Windswept hillside
64 Quebec landscape
1915 67 Early evening
1916 70 In the park
71 Landscape, Notre Dame de Grâce
1918A 56 The silent pool
1918N 56 Before the storm
57 Awakening of spring
1919 48 The summer home
49 A northern river
1920 81 Early morning, St Joseph
82 Pastoral
1921 50 A peaceful valley
51 Early autumn
1922 59 Parish church, Limoilou
60 Road to old lumber camp S6-20
1923 46 Evening on the St Lawrence
1924 44 The lonely house
45 Crimson and gold
1925 63 Awaiting the tide
64 Clearing weather illus
1926 40 Dawn
1927 50 Winter evening
51 In the foothills
52 When summer ends
1928 46 Approaching storm $400
47 Morning sunlight $300
1929 51 Early morning, Baie St Paul $250 1930-45 $350 F10-131 $310
52 In the Laurentians $350
1929 S7, Calgary
41 Passing showers $350
42 Indian summer $350
43 Early spring $100
1930 46 Northern Quebec $450
47 The north country (price in catalog $ 00.00)
1931 72 Evening in the Laurentians $500
73 When summer ends $500
74 The last gleam $250
1932 52 The farm $450
53 Mid-day, Baie St Paul $450
1933 57 At sunrise $250
58 The squall $500 T34-21
59 Late summer $400
1934 61 Early evening $400
62 Autumn $350
63 Cloud shadow illus $400 T35-23
1935 78 The Gaspé coast $250
79 Clearing weather $450 T36-26 F11-21 40 x 30 $500
1936 66 Ste Famille, Ile d'Orléans $400
67 A northern lake $500 T37-24 1937-67
1937 68 Maple trees $350
69 The old farm $350 T38-16
1940 48 Wharf, Château Richer $200 T41-12

EASTCOTT, ROBERT WAYNE
20 Jul 1943, Trail, BC

RCA(e) 1976 Print maker
Addr: 1979, Vancouver
1970 19 Basilica, set C 36 x 24 $200

EASTLAKE, CHARLES HERBERT English fl 1889-1930 B DBA DBW DVP G TB WBA WWB29
Addr: 1907, London, Eng
1907 Mr and Mrs C.H. Eastlake
351 Brass tea box art metal & enamel
352 Brass cigarette box art metal & enamel
353 Bronze panel, with enamel
354 Silver panel, with enamel
355 Amethyst and enamel necklet
356 Mexican opal art metal & enamel
357 Opal and enamel
358 Brooch

EASTLAKE, MARY ALEXANDRA BELL (Mrs Charles Herbert Eastlake)
1864, Douglas, Ont 27 Jun 1951, Ottawa AGO B H M Mo98 NGC TB1/2/3 WWB27
ARCA 1893-7 Painter
Addr: 1887, Montreal; 1893, Almonte, Ont; 1894, c/o Mrs Fuller, Holly Wood, Duppas Hill, Croydon, Eng; 1895, Almonte, Ont; 1896, St Ives, Cornwall, Eng; 1900, c/o Scott & Co, Montreal; 1901, c/o John F. Stairs, Esq, 170 South St, Halifax; 1902, England, c/o J. Stairs, Halifax; 1904, London, Eng; 1906, 2 Cheyne Row, Chelsea, Longon, Eng; 1907, London, Eng; 1927, 731 Sherbrooke St W, Montreal
1887 Bell to 1900, Bell and Eastlake 1901, Eastlake, 1902-44
22 Study of a Hindoo $40
85 Repose $40
1890 2 Tranquil moments $125
3 The trivial round $50
4 La petite malade $250
1892 26 Child reading $40
40 Twilight reverie $250
56 A bit of moorland $25
1893 9 Portrait of a lady nfs F1-8
10 A September evening, Lake Huron $75 F1-9
11 Summer time $60 F1-10
1894 20 A nibble at last
21 Flower girl
1895 21 Moonrise
22 Treasure trove
23 Twilight on the beach
1896 11 A little sculptor
1900 11 When spring rides through the woods
1901 Bell, 15-18, Eastlake, 43
15 The Queen's Foresters
16 Mrs J. Stairs, Halifax
17 Treasure trove F2-11 F5-53a
18 Mother and child
43 Mrs John Stairs, Halifax
1902 52 Enchanted wood
1904 52 Dutch girl in church pastel
1906 F5, Halifax
53b The young sailors (Mrs J.F. Stairs, Halifax)
53c White hen and girl in pink pastel $35
53d and 53e Pastel $15 each
53f Collection of enamels
1907 234 Child feeding hen pastel
235 Girl with doll pastel
236 Dutch children pastel
351-8 see Charles Eastlake
1927 53 The old mill
54 Study
1941 54 Stormy day $100
1942 35 Dr Maude Abbot nfs
1943 32 Snow pattern $125
33 Flowers by the stream $100 T44-13
1944 38 Noonday rest

T. EATON COMPANY, LIMITED
Addr: 1938, Torontc
1938 S8, Toronto
93 Mahogany dining table and 4 chairs
94 Serving table
95 Sheraton settee
96 Miniature chest of drawers
97 Book case
98 Pair of chairs
99 Column table lamp
100 Bronze floor lamp

EAYRS, HUGH
1938 S8, Toronto
Macmillan Company
176 Book, Family portrait. Hugh Eayrs, G.E. Rogers
177 Book, Manitoba essays. Hugh Eayrs, G.E. Rogers
178 Book, Saucy again. Hugh Eayrs, G.E. Rogers
180 Book, Quebec. Hugh Eayrs,

Marius Barbeau
181 Book, Romancero du Canada. Hugh Eayrs, Marius Barbeau
182 Book, Speeches of Thomas D'Arcy McGee. Hugh Eayrs, G.E. Rogers

EBANA LASALLE INC
1971 13I Table, stool, chair

EBSEN, ALFRED KARL
29 Jul 1908, Berlin WWA76
RCA(e) 1974 RCA 1977 Calligrapher
Addr: 1979, Willowdale, Ont
DW 1977 20 slides

EDE, FREDERICK CHARLES VIPONT
22 Feb 1865, USA American
B H TB Y
Addr: 1893, Sorgues, near Paris; 1910, Toronto
1883 167 Guitar player wc $15
1884 S1, Saint John
1 Girls watching goats wc
67 Shepherdess wc $20
136 A summer day $30
1885 20 Saturday afternoon $35
289 A sharpshooter wc $25
1888 19 Divided wc $50
35 Peril on route wc $60 L.C.V. Ede mispr
51 High Park, Toronto wc $25
304 Cattle wc
1889 112 Dogs wc
126 On the road home, cattle wc $75
1891 54 and 60 Cattle
1893 39 Landscape with cattle, France $400 F1-34
40 Landscape with cattle, France $150 F1-35
41 Landscape with sheep, France $150 F1-36
42 At Sorgues, near Paris $125 F1-37
43 Landscape near Fontainebleau $100 F1-38
44 Barnyard with poultry $100 F1-39
1910 S1, Liverpool
38 Cattle drinking

EDELFELT, ALBERT GUSTAF ARISTIDES
21 Jul 1854, Helsinki Finnish
18 Aug 1905, Borga, Finland B TB
1882 303 Going to the Christening (loan)

EDSON, AARON ALLAN
18 Dec 1846, Stanbridge, Que 1 May 1888, Glen Sutton, Que AGO B EC H M NGC TB W78
RCA 1880 Council Painter
Addr: 1880-2, Montreal; 1883, Paris; 1884, Cernay la Ville, France; 1885-88, Montreal
1880 34 White Mountains
38 Old disused road in the forest
87 Trout stream in the forest 1881-262 DW 1882 23 1/2 x 18 1/4 T51-15
121 and 122 Painting, in oil on china
228 Summer time wc
229 Harvesters wc
1881 77 Evening at Glen Sutton wc $75
272 The river at Glen Sutton $100
1882 58 Cascades, Eastern Townships $350
103 Up the Seine $150
1883 3 Un jour de décembre, Cernay $175
4 Old willows at Cernay $150
1884 14 Shooting path in the park $125
45 Spring $100
120 Evening at Senlis wc $85
1886 F1a, London, Eng
1993 artist number
Landscape (J.R. Wilson, Esq, Montreal)
Mount Maurice at sunset, winter, with canoes (E. Atkinson, Esq, Rose Bank, Fowey, Cornwall)
The Ice Palace, Montreal
The river St Lawrence, winter
Landscape in the Eastern Townships (Her Majesty the Queen)
1887 6 Sunset on the Thames $50
70 The Star and Garter at Richmond, from Ham Park $40
90 Old stile at Ham, near Richmond $50
107 Early autumn, Glen Sutton $500
128c and 177 Autumn day wc $50 each
128d English lane near Windsor wc $50
156 Mount Orford, Eastern

Townships, evening wc $150
1916 The late Allan Edson
72 Lake Memphremagog

EDWARDS, ALLAN WHITCOMBE
15 Jan 1915, Edmonton WWA78
1939 67 Mrs Thomas C. Leighton nfs
1942 36 The black hat $1,000

EDWARDS, GORDON BUCHANAN
see BLAND, JOHN, 1964N
LE MOYNE, ROY, 1963, 1964N

EDWARDS, HENRIETTA MUIR (Mrs Q.C. Edwards)
1849, Montreal 1931 Macleod, Alta
H Mo12
1881 90 Tangle of roses $60
91 Lilacs $40
116 Bunch of roses $40
1892 75 Partridge
93 Sunset, flowers $75

EDWARDS, HOWARD S.
b 1886
1940 49 Self portrait nfs
50 Russell Reid, RCAF nfs
1941 55 Night portrait, self nfs
56 A prayer nfs T42-14
1942 37 Miss G. Germain nfs
1943 34 Study of self nfs
1944 39 Mrs H. Edwards nfs

EDWARDS, IDA
H
1892 9 Still life, my violin
72 Lemons $40

EDWARDS, O.E. (Mrs)
fl 1899-10 H
Addr: 1899-00, Montreal
1899 168 Case of miniatures wc
1900 136 Case of miniatures wc on ivory, and mineral paints on porcelain

EGAN, F. HUGH
Addr: 1904, Montreal
1904 54 Weeds

EGAN, J. HUGH
fl 1892-20 H
Addr: 1893, 310 Laval Ave, Montreal; 1907, Outremont, Que; 1920, 257 Durocher St, Outremont, Que; 1925, 730 Durocher St, Outremont, Que
1893 45 Maternity $40 F1-40
46 Scraps $35
1904 see F. Hugh Egan, may be mispr for J. Hugh Egan
1907 237 Sous le Cap wc
1920 83 Pasture
1925 65 The smile pastel

EHRICHT, HORST
dates not on file
RCA(e) 1978 Photographer
Addr: 1979, Kleinburg, Ont

EITEL, GEORGE EDWARD
25 Jan 1906, Preston, Ont 8 Nov 1961, Kitchener AGO M
1945 64 The courtyard wc nfs
1946 34 The typist wc $25
1948 47 Wood interior wc $35
1949 25 Antiques on a table wc $35
1951 27 Trees and rocks wc $50
1954 29 Shipwreck wc 15 x 21 nfs

ELIAS, ARTHUR EDWARD
1872, Llansadwrn, Wales
Addr: 1921-2, 158 Gilmour St, Ottawa; 1924, 486 Gilmour St, Ottawa
1921 52 Old London, Hal and Poins meet the town guard. 'Prince Henry' temp
53 Circe wc
196 The cloud pen & ink
1922 250 Decorative panel temp
251 Panel des
252 Drawing b&w
1924 46 Evening on the Mile
47 Reinforcements marching towards 'Suicide Corner' and St Julien, during the 2nd Battle of Ypres

ELLINGER, CARLTON D.
1938 S8, Toronto
Ryerson Press
265 Book, Selected poems of Sir Charles G.D. Roberts

ELLIOT, EMILY LOUISE ORR (Mrs John Ephraim Elliot)
22 Jul 1867, Montreal 28 Feb 1952, Toronto CWW49 H
Addr: 1898, 496 Church St, Toronto; 1905-10, 69 Bloor St E, Toronto
1898 158 Mammie, Millie wc
1901 164 Waiting wc
1905 63 Little Italina girl
64 Beryl
1908 46 The sick child
1909N 48 The cabbage patch 1910-59
1910 60 Sorting the flakes, St

John's, Newfoundland

ELLIOTT, VELMA
Addr: 1938, Toronto
1938 S8, Toronto
380 Wallpper design. Hon mention. Canadian Wallpaper Manufacturers Limited

ELLIS, JOHN
d 1888 H
ARCA 1884 Designer
Addr: 1884-8, Toronto

ELLIS, MARGARET B.
H
1891 220 Moonlight, bay shore

ELLISON, JOHN
24 Oct 1912, Hamilton d 1957 M
1944 40 Chinese fishermen, Vancouver $50 T45-10
41 Chinatown, Victoria wc $40
1945 WO John Ellison, RCNVR
65 Cooper's Mill, Conception Bay, Newfoundland wc $60
66 Lime Street, St John's, Newfoundland wc $60
1947 45 Old house at Thessalon wc $85
1948 48 Cod stages, Newfoundland nfs
49 Snow in the Rockies wc $85
1949 26 Gray morning, Newfoundland $175
1951 28 Water Street Way, St John's Newfoundland $200
29 Shipday at Whalehead, Labrador wc $150
1954 30 Up on the Gaff, Newfoundland 28 x 36 $300
1955 51 Kagawong $150

ELLWOOD, MICHAEL G.C.
see DURNFORD, Alexander, 1957-1961
BOLTON, RICHARD, 1964-1966

ELOUL, KOSSO
22 Jan 1920, Mourom, Russia IO WWA70
RCA(e) 1974 Sculptor
Addr: 1976/79, Toronto
1976 S12, Montreal
67 Kobar stainless steel 77 x 16 x 108 illus

ELPHICK, GERTRUDE JEAN see HANSON, GERTRUDE JEAN

ELPHICK, JOHN A.
1970 20 Circle of life 18 diam $200

ELTON, A. GRESLEY
see BROWN, MURRAY, 1957

ELWELL, FRANCIS EDWIN American
15 Jun 1858, Concord, Mass 23 Jan 1922, Darien, Conn AAA28 F
Addr: 1893, 114 W 18th St, New York
1893 182 Carl Ahrens bust

EMODI, ARNOLD IGNACE
15 Dec 1860, Tokay, Hungary H
Addr: 1920-1, 125 Simcoe St, Toronto
1920 84 In the Highlands Arnold J Emodi mispr
85 Red Lake
1921 54 North country

EMOND, PAUL
Addr: 1938, Montreal
1938 S8, Toronto
145 Original cover suggestions. Herald Press Co, Ltd

EMORI, EIKO
19 Mar 1938, Japan WWA78
RCA(e) 1975 Graphic designer
Addr: 1979, Ottawa

ENGEL, STAN
Addr: 1938, Montreal
1938 S8, Toronto
Ronalds Company
247 2 Normandie Roof folders, menu and book
248 Folders
249 Label bands

ENNS, MAUREEN
2 Apr 1943, Chilliwack, BC
Addr: 1976, Cochrane, Alta
1976 S12, Montreal
13 Nexus #2 acry 48 x 60 illus

ENSOR, ARTHUR JOHN
2 Jan 1905, Llanishen, Wales NGC
RCA(e) 1976 Industrial designer
Addr: 1979, Ottawa

ERICKSON, ARTHUR CHARLES
14 Jun 1924, Vancouver CWW79
ARCA 1966 RCA 1969 Council Architect
Addr: 1976/79, Vancouver
1964N 111-14 Danto residence,

Vancouver.Entrance approach. Entrance court from bedroom terrace. Living room, interior. General plan
1966 Erickson & Massey, to 1967
125-8 Simon Fraser University, Burnaby, BC. Entrance to University at Transportation Center. Steps of Central Mall, Library in background. Arcade. Central Mall. one illus
129-31 Graham residence, West Vancouver, BC, Entrance. View facing west. Exterior in setting
1967 116-22 Town houses, Point Grey Road, Vancouver. A. General view of project, illus B.Interior-exterior view C.Open court D.Exterior treatment E.Ground floor plan F.Main floor plan G.Top floor and roof plan
1976 S12, Montreal
100 Museum of Anthropology, University of British Columbia, Vancouver illus
101 Eppich house, West Vancouver, BC illus
DW 1969 Simon Fraser University, BC. Architectural model, 3 photos 20 x 30 each

ESKIND, WADDELL
Addr: 1976, Toronto
1976 S12, Montreal
117 Season's greetings greeting cards/cartes de souhaits illus

ESLER, JOHN KENNETH
11 Jan 1933, Pilot Mount, Man
AGO M WWA73
ARCA 1968 Print maker
Addr: 1970-71/79, Calgary
1968 20 Distant light, diary of a lost hunter 28 x 28 $95
1970 S11, Halifax
17 The winner. 1970 callograph 36 x 24 $90
18 Torso. 1970 callograph 36 x 26 $90

ESSEX, M. MARY (Mrs)
Addr: 1918N-20, 264 Beaver Hall Hill, Montreal
1918N 231 Illustration, Henry Birks & Sons charcl
232 Illustration, Episode of the Civil War charcl
1920 304-5 Illustration c/o Canadian Home Journal charcl

ETHERIDGE, CONSTANCE
Addr: 1907, London, Eng; 1908, Havergal College, Toronto
1907 238 The picnic wc
239 The daisy chain wc 1908-44
240 Summer days wc
1908 45 Loves me, loves me not

ETHRIDGE, H.A. English
fl 1882-3 DBA DVP H RSBA
1883 184 Flowers wc $12
233 A fair in Wales wc $20
240 A Welsh stream wc $15

ETIENNE, ERROL HERBERT RUSSELL
28 Apr 1941, Edinburgh
RCA(e) 1978 Designer
Addr: 1979, Vancouver

ETROG, SOREL
29 Aug 1933, Jassy, Roumania AGO CC1 CWW79 IO M WWA70
ARCA 1967 Council Sculptor
Addr: 1968-71/79, Toronto
1968 56 War remembrance 36 x 42 x 21 illus
1970 80 Prophet II 30h nfs

ETUNGAT, ABRAHAM
3 Mar 1911, Cape Dorset, NWT
RCA(e) 1978 Sculptor
Addr: 1979, Cape Dorset, NWT

EVANS, BLANCH B.
fl 1891-6 H
Addr: 1895, Bleury & Dorchester Sts, Montreal; 1896, 497 St Urbain St, Montreal
1895 36 La maison de Baptist
1896 46 The knot

EVANS, DENNIS J.
Addr: 1976, Calgary
1976 S12, Montreal
14 Untitled #1 ink/encre 7h illus

EVANS, OWEN NORTON
1864, Toronto d 1926 H
Addr: 1911-13, 31 Bishop St, Montreal

1911 49 Autumn carpet, Laurentians
1913 99 Sleet, Mount Royal S4-44 $75

EWART, J. ALBERT
20 Apr 1872, Ottawa 21 Apr 1964, Ottawa
Addr: 1903, 29 Carleton Chambers, Ottawa; 1909, Ottawa
1903 204-5 Ottawa Public Library. Front and side elevation, prize des
1909 149-50 Registry Office, Ottawa

EWART, MARY CLAY (Mrs Alan C. Ewart)
c 1861, Philadelphia flg 1945
Addr: 1912, Winnipeg; 1914, 12 Ruskin Row, Winnipeg
1912 245 The boy with the cape
1914 65 Alan C. Ewart, Esq
66 The gray cloak

EWART, PETER
1918, Kisbey, Sask
1947 46 Evening surf, British Columbia coast $250
47 Clearing weather $500
1950 35 Surf, British Columbia coast 30 x 40 $500

EWASIUK, TERRY
Addr: 1976, Vancouver
1976 S12, Montreal
68 Ascension of Ophelia polyester resin 5 x 10 x 6 illus

EWEN, WILLIAM PATERSON
7 Apr 1925, Montreal CC2 CWW79 IO M TB3 WWA78
RCA(e) 1975 Painter
Addr: 1979, Toronto

EYESACKERS, ANDRE
1928, The Hague, Netherlands
1964J 20 Untitled ink 24 x 22 $125

EYRE, IVAN KENNETH
15 Apr 1935, Tulleymet, Sask WWA76
RCA(e) 1974 Painter
Addr: 1979, St Norbert, Man

F

FABIEN, HENRI ZOTIQUE
4 Jul 1878, St Henri, Montreal 31 Dec 1935, Ottawa B CNS36 H M
Addr: 1899-02, 3169 Notre Dame St, Montreal; 1904, Montreal; 1909M, 16 Division St, Ottawa; 1912-14, 18 Division St, Ottawa; 1915-18, 188 Booth St, Ottawa; 1919-25, 340 Somerset St E, Ottawa; 1930-2, 590 Rideau St, Ottawa; 1933-5, 88 5th Ave, Ottawa
1899 46 Bric-a-brac, still life
47 Partridge
48 Study of fish
49 Study of duck
1902 53 Interieure d'une chaumière
54 Vieux Breton, Finistère
1904 55 Surf
56 Rough sea
57 Still life
1909M 45 Vallée de la Patie, Bretange, France
1912 78 Moonlight on the Gatineau
1913 357 Portrait of the artist pencil
358 D. Chéné, Esq pencil
1914 67 Gilmour Mill, Ottawa
1915 68 On the Ottawa River
1916 73 The park of the Château Laurier
1918A 57 Atlanta
58 The frozen fleet
213 Violet pencil
1919 50 Interior in Brittany, France
199 Sir Wilfrid Laurier, portrait after his death drwg
200 Jacqueline drwg
1920 264 Late Rt Hon Sir Wilfrid Laurier bust plaster
1922 61 Le perroquet d'émail
62 Pommes et raisins S6-21, Apples and grapes
1923 47 Dr R. Tait MacKenzie, the sculptor
1924 231 Youth sculp
232 Sir Wilfrid Laurier sculp
258 Portrait study pencil
1925 66 Narcissus, still life
67 Tanagra figure with white rose, still life
1929 S7, Calgary
44 Still life $200
1930 48 Attitude, Betty $350
49 Relevé, Evelyn $350
202 Pierrot, Lorne charcl $100
1931 75 Gwendolyn Osborne
76 R.V. Sinclair, Esq, KC

1932 54 Portrait of a ballerine, Betty $1,500 1933-60 T34-22
55 Portrait of a Spanish dancer, Ethel $1,500
1933 61 Dancer exercising nude $2,000
252 Bacchante sculp $500
1935 80 Avant de paraître nfs

FACEY, ARTHUR GEORGE
see CHAPMAN, ALFRED, 1946

FAED, THOMAS English
8 Jun 1826, Burley Hill, Scot 27 Aug 1900, London, Eng B H TB
1881 116-21 The soldier's return 6 drwgs (Jno. Esson, Esq)

FAINMEL, CHARLES
b 1904
Addr: 1928, 3531 Ste Famille St, Montreal; 1938, Montreal
1928 53 Portrait $250
237 Portrait sculp $250
1938 S8, Toronto
81-3 3 folders, booklet with envelope, folder. Dodd Simpson Press
101 Folder, Courtaulds
102 Booklet, Victor Globe Trotter
103 Folder, Birks
104 3 Beach folders
105 Advertisements, Courtaulds
106 Design for selling, Federated Press Limited
108 'Connor' manual, Federated Press Limited
245 4 folders. Ronalds Advertising Agency Limited

FAIRFIELD, ROBERT CALVIN
31 Jul 1918, St Catharines, Ont
CNS59 CWW79
1964J 101 Oxford University Press, Don Mills, Ont. Entrance
1964N Fairfield & Dubois, to 1968
115-19 Central Technical School Art Centre, Toronto. General view, exterior. Back, front views, exterior. View of art class. Cross section
1965 117-22 New College, University of Toronto. View from Spadina Ave, looking east, illus. Upper and lower Common Rooms. Dining hall, looking east. East elevation, looking south. 1st floor plan. Bedroom floor plan
1966 132-4 Dow Corning Silicones Limited. Main entrance. View of exterior treatment. Interior
1968 103-8 Ontario Government Pavilion, Expo 67. A.Roof plan B.Traffic plan C.Looking northeast from Restaurant D.Interior view at display E.Looking towards southwest of Pavilion F.Looking from platform at typical roof structure
see also Rounthwaite, Cyril, 1964J

FAIRLEY, BARKER
21 May 1887, Barnsley, Yorks, Eng
AGO Co CWW79 EC
RCA(e) 1979 Painter
Addr: 1979, Toronto
port: sculp by P. Redsell, 1958-93

FAIRMAN, OSCAR
Addr: 1928-30, 162 Medland St, Toronto
1928 48 Late October $200
1929 54 On Stoney Lake $100
1930 50 The old church $150

FAIRWEATHER, G.E.
ARCA 1880-4 Architect
Addr: 1880-4, Saint John

FALCONER, COLIN HARLEY
1941 57 Back yard $100

FALCONER, MARGARET
1964N 30 Night thoughts 25 x 23 $125

FALKENBERG, EDWARD GEORGE
30 Mar 1936, Edmonton IO
Addr: 1976, Claremont, Ont
1976 S12, Montreal
69 Reflection exchange stainless steel/acier inoxydable 76 x 36 x 60 illus

FANAIS, GEORGE SARRAS (b George Sarras Katsafanas)
25 Dec 1922, Windsor, Ont
1948 50 The white shawl nfs
1950 36 The law maker 20 x 16 $75

FANIEL, ALFRED JEAN JOSEPH
19 Apr 1879, Verviers, Belgium
d 1950
Addr: 1910, 1062 St André St, Montreal; 1915, 1262 Marie Anne St, Montreal
1910 61 The old walk
1915 69 L'entrée de petit béguinage, Bruges

FANSHAW, HUBERT VALENTINE
14 Feb 1878, Sheffield, Eng 11 Aug 1940, Winnipeg M NGC TB3
Addr: 1914, Winnipeg; 1922-31, 161 Lyle St, Winnipeg
1914 S4, Winnipeg
166 August evening
167 A Yorkshire valley
1922 63 Sunlit rocks wc
253 Pine clad shore col block
254 Prairie winter col block
1924 48 The shadowed hill wc
49 The Pacific coast wc
259 The Canadian Rockies col pr
260 Mount Shasta at sundown col pr
1925 68 A Manitoba harvest wc
69 La Canyada, California wc
1926 41 The Valley of Rock Lake, Manitoba wc
42 A threat to harvest, Manitoba wc ◊NGC◊
1927 55 Autumn in Manitoba wc
56 The doll
296 New Canadians at Gonner, Manitoba col block pr
1928 49 The wheat fields in October wc $200
1931 77 Beaver Trail, Clear Lake wc $50

FARINI, MAY L.
Addr: 1905, 50 Churchill Ave, Toronto
1905 218 Book illustration

FARLEY, LILIAS MARIANNE AR DE SOIF
2 May 1907, Ottawa M WWA59
Addr: 1936-7, 1443 Nelson St, Vancouver
1936 215 Head sculp $25
216 Carving mahogany $50
1937 276 Madonna sculp $60
277 Obeisance sculp $60
1939 245 Carved head $125
246 Dance pattern sculp $75
1945 220 Carving $125
1946 132 Leaf unfolding Liberian gum wd $150
1947 199 Fronds white mahogany $150
200 The Sister white mahogany $250

FARLOW, HARRY MACNAUGHTON American
11 Apr 1882, Chicago 1956, West Hartford, Conn B F TB2 WWA36
Addr: 1934, 31 Melrose Ave, Toronto; 1936-7, 96 Lawrence Cr, Toronto
1934 64 Jules $300
65 Blue and gold $200 T35-23
1936 68 Studio reflections $500
69 Nude $250
1937 70 Nude $400
71 Old gardener $300

FARNCOMB, CAROLINE
1858, or 1862, Newcastle, Ont
d 1951 H
Addr: 1899-00, 374 Central Ave, London, Ont; 1901-7, London, Ont; 1908, 52 Victoria Ave, Toronto
1899 41 Farm dog
42 Inmate of home for aged
1900 45 Landscape
46 Fruit piece
47 Letters
48 Some more, please
1901 46 Poor birdie
1902 55 Game piece
1903 53 Mother's girl
1907 70 Washing day
1908 51 Portrait, Mrs---

FARGUHARSON, JOSEPH English
1846, Edinburgh d 1935 B DBA G H TB
1882 323 Harvest time (loan)

FAUCHER, JEAN CHARLES
8 May 1907, Montreal B TB3 WWA47
1943 35 Ferme canadienne, St Laurent, Ile d'Orléans $250

FAULKNER, PHILIPPA MARY BURROWS
28 Feb 1917, Belleville, Ont IO
1953 23 Provincetown wc $80
1954 32 Autumn fiesta 30 x 20 $150
1958 31 Bottle sellers illus $300

FAUTEUX, HENRIETTE (Mrs Jules T. Massé)
30 Oct 1924, Coaticook, Que M
1945 67 Broken elm pastel $85

1949 27 Donald Newlands, Esq nfs

FAUTEUX, MARIE CLAIRE CHRISTINE
23 Sep 1890, Montreal CNS36
Addr: 1916, 284 Mackay St, Montreal; 1921-2, 100 Closse St, Montreal; 1929, Montreal
1916 74 and 75 Sketch pastel
1921 55 Decorative panel
56 Forest nymphs
1922 64 Composition S6-22
1929 S7, Calgary
45 Golden autumn $500
1947 48 Portrait, sisters nfs

FAUX, AL
1970 101 Series 2 drafting table, Norman Wade Co
102 G.2 stereo, Clairtone Sound Corp, Limited

FAVRO, MURRAY
24 Dec 1940, Huntsville, Ont IO WWA78
RCA(e) 1976 Sculptor
Addr: 1979, London, Ont

FAWCETT, GEORGE American
8 Apr 1877, London, Eng 4 Feb 1944, Miami, Fla F WWA38
Addr: 1914, Winnipeg; 1918A, Bell Block, Winnipeg
1914 S4, Winnipeg
175 Rochester Castle and Cathedral etch $12
176 Maldon etch $12
177 Fagin in Newgate wc $15
178 Portrait sketch
1918A 214 The Monks Bridge, St Norbert, Manitoba etch
215 A deserted Indian camp, Minaki, Ontario etch

FEATHERSTONE, GRACE L.
Addr: 1918N-22, 111 Bedford Rd, Toronto
1918N 58 The limekiln
1919 51 The pine tree dark and high 1920-86
1920 87 In the woods
1921 57 On the beach, Métis, Quebec 1922-65

FEDERATED PRESS LIMITED
Addr: 1938, Montreal
1938 S8, Toronto
107 Sports meeting souvenir booklet
108 'Connor manual'. Charles Fainmel

FEDIOW, PAULINE see REDSELL, PAULINE

FEDOR, JULIUS W.
1971 6I Display system, Julius Fedor, Trevor Giles. Fedor Incorporated

FEHELEY, MELVILLE F.
1948 51 Huntsville $200
52 Graveyard $200

FEIST, WARNER DAVID
3 Dec 1909, Augsburg, Germany WWA76
1971 21G Proposed symbol, Canadian Jewish Congress

FELLOWS, EVELYN see RIDOUT, EVELYN

FELSEN, PHYLLIS
Addr: 1937, 4142 Dorchester St W, Westmount, Que
1937 278 Self portrait nfs
279 Miss F. Lefell nfs

FEMAT CUSTOM FIBREGLAS MFG
1970 111 Kayak

FENN, HARRY American
14 Sep 1845, Richmond, Eng 21 Apr 1911, Montclair, NJ AAA28 B F H TB
Addr: 1898, Montclair, NJ
1882 244 The Sisters, Niagara monoc
1898 159 Corner of the studio wc

FENTIMAN, A.E.
1970 103 Triodetic structure. Triodectic Structures Ltd

FENWICK, KATHLEEN M.
17 Jun 1901, London, Eng 28 Sep 1973, Ottawa WWA47
Addr: 1929, 152 Argyle Ave, Ottawa
1929 262 Autumn etch

FENWICK, WILLIAM ROLAND (ROLY)
4 Feb 1932, Owen Sound, Ont IO
RCA(e) 1978 Painter
Addr: 1979, London, Ont
1964J 21 Figures in shadow 35 x 39 $600

FERGUSON, GRAEME
7 Oct 1929, Toronto

RCA(e) 1974 Film maker
Addr: 1979, Cambridge, Galt, Ont

FERRARO, ROBERT C.
Addr: 1976, Windsor, Ont
1976 S12, Montreal
15 Jav acry 75 x 60 illus

FERRIER, WALTER R.
Addr: 1935, 864 Bloomfield Ave, Outremont, Que
1935 81 Off the road wc $100

FERRON, MARCELLE
29 Jan 1924, Louiseville, Que
CC1 CWW79 M WWA78
RCA(e) 1974 Painter
Addr: 1976, St Lambert, Que; 1979, Outremont, Que
1963 22 Ombres palpées illus $1,200
1964J 22 Voyage à Spoléte $2,000
1976 S12, Montreal
16 Sans titre éléments hétérogènes/m med 35 x 29 illus
17 Sans titre éléments hétérogènes/m med 40 1/2 x 32 1/2 illus

FETHERSTONHAUGH, HAROLD LEA
31 Mar 1887, Montreal 3 Feb 1971, Ste Anne de Bellevue, Que NGC
ARCA 1936 RCA 1945 Sr 1957 Council Architect
Addr: 1937, 660 St Catherine St W, Montreal; 1938-71, Montreal
1937 Fetherstonhaugh & Durnford, to 1945
239 Residence at St Laurent
240 Interior detail, residence, Montreal
241-2 Douglas Hall, McGill University
1945 240 Brittany Row, apartment house for Aluminum Company of Canada, Arvida, Que photo
1947 Fetherstonhaugh, Durnford, Bolton & Chadwick, to 1954
190 Residence, Mr & Mrs J.G. Bourne photo
191 Stairway, office building, Aluminum Company of Canada photo
1952 99 Bank of Canada, Victoria Square, Montreal photo
1953 96 Jim Gray Power House, Chicoutimi, Que drwg
97 Residence, Westmount, Quebec, photo
1954 115 Bedford School, Montreal photo illus
DW 1949 Design for Winter Club, Quebeg drwg pastel 14 x 34 1/4

FIDOE, FRANK W.
fl 1927-71
Addr: 1927, 69 Gilmour St, Ottawa
1927 57 Portrait, artist's mother

FIELDING (Mrs)
d c 1883 H
1883 240 Monthly roses wc (Rev V. Clementi) Mrs Fielding, deceased

FIENNES-CLINTON, ELEANOR
1886, England flg 1976
Addr: 1931-4, 122 McNab St S, Hamilton
1931 78 The raffia hat $100
1934 66 The back of Augusta Street $100

FIGLIO
1880 120 Dead game and dog (Allan Gilmour)

FILION, ARMAND
10 Mar 1910, Montreal M
ARCA 1950 Council Sculptor
Addr: 1933, 560 Duquesne St, Montreal; 1950-7, Montreal; 1958-65, St Vincent de Paul, Que; 1966, Ville de Duvernay, Que; 1967-71/79, St Vincent de Paul, Que
1933 253 My mother's head sculp $125
254 Head of a young boy sculp $125
1948 161 Young girl at her toilet sculp $600
162 St Joseph and the Child sculp $100
1949 111 Jeune fille se coiffant sculp $500
112 Tête de faune sculp illus $250
1955 103 Standing women sculp $1,000
1957 73 Seated woman sculp $800
1966 75 Voie lactée sculp 18 x 22 $300

FILIPOVIC, AUGUSTIN
8 Jan 1931, Davor, Croatia, Yugo-

slavia AGO M WWA62
RCA(e) 1976 Sculptor
Addr: 1979, Niagara Falls, Ont
1960 86 Study #1 sculp $200
87 Study #2 sculp $200

FILLION, JOHN
1933, Little Current, Manitou Island, Ont B
RCA(e) 1976 Sculptor
Addr: 1979, Toronto

FINDLAY, F.R.
see FINDLAY, ROBERT

FINDLAY, ROBERT
1860, Inverness, Scot 5 Feb 1951, Montreal
Addr: 1937, 1188 Phillips Place, Montreal
1937 Robert & F.R. Findlay
243-4 Pavilion, Murray Park, Westmount. From southeast. From northwest

FINDLAYS LIMITED
Addr: 1938, Toronto
1938 S8, Toronto
109 Electric range, white with green trim illus
110 Gas range, ivory on black steel base, with black bakelite and chrome handles illus

FINKEL, HENRY
7 Nov 1910, London, Eng
RCA(e) 1978 Industrial designer
Addr: 1979, Westmount, Que

FINLAY, SAMUEL STEVENSON
19 May 1888, Lisburn, Ireland 26 Jan 1938, Toronto
Addr: 1936, 10 Balsam Ave, Toronto
1936 70 Summer day $60

FINLEY, FREDERICK JAMES
4 Jun 1894, Newcastle, Australia
14 May 1968, Toronto CWW55 NGC W78 WWA56
ARCA 1949 RCA 1955 Sr 1964 Council Painter
Addr: 1927, 26 Osborne Ave, Toronto; 1949-68, Toronto
1927 297 Salome etch
298 Uncharted ways etch
1944 42 Muskoka farmer $250 T45-11
43 Chinese group $130
1945 68 The J.B. Alexanders and their friends nfs T46-14
1946 35 Auction at Fox Lake $450 T47-17
36 Margot $150
1947 49 Judging the cattle $450
1948 53 Conversation in Cree illus $500
1949 28 Anglican Mission Church, at Lac La Rouge $500
1950 37 Cree dance, northern Saskatchewan 40 x 48 $500
1951 30 The lonely time illus $350 T53-10
1952 27 Birds and the sea $250
1953 24 Cree ceremonial illus $800 1954-31 48 x 60 illus
1956 20 Work in progress #1 illus $850
1957 24 Sea birds and sun illus $350
1958 32 Fishermen of Aran illus $450
1959 27 Johnny Morrow 40 x 30 illus
1960 30 Portrait 40 x 30 illus nfs
1961 34 Louis Riel at Batoche 30 x 30 $500
1965 25 Morning riders 24 x 30 illus $350 S10-25 illus
1966 18 Hunters in the Spinifex 30 x 40 $500
1966 S10, Charlottetown
24 Sun dance ending 48 x 60 $1,000
DW 1956 Young Métis at play 30 x 39 3/4

FINLEY, GERALD ERIC
17 Jul 1931, Munich WWA76
ARCA 1959 Painter
Addr: 1960-63, Toronto; 1964J-71/79, Kingston, Ont
1956 21 Causerie illus $175
22 Northern construction $200 T56-19
1957 25 Lamprey control, poisoning larvae in Lake Superior stream $200
1958 33 Temporary lamprey barrier, Dog River, Lake Superior #200
1959 28 English landscape, Kent 21 1/4 x 33 1/3 illus $300
1960 31 Red maple and pine, Georgian Bay 22 x 33 $225
1961 33 Red maple and pine, Georgian Bay 22 1/2 x 33 illus

$200 S10-26 illus $300
1966 S10, Charlottetown
27 Farm house in Kent, England
21 3/4 x 33 1/4 $225

FINLEY, SAMUEL ARNOLD
d 18 Jun 1933, Montreal
Addr: 1896, 2 Bishop St, Montreal; 1902-7, Temple Bldg, Montreal
1896 273 Sketch of an old house in the south of England
1902 Finley & Spence, to 1907
244-5 Liverpool & London & Globe Insurance Company, new building. Design. Floor plans
1904 269-70 Metropolitan Bank, Montreal, with preliminary study
271 McGill University, YMCA Building
272-3 Savings bank building, studies
274 Country house
1907 311 Design for office building
312 Molson's Bank, branch, Montreal
313-14 Design for a church

FISET, EDOUARD
7 Sep 1910, Rimouski, Que CWW79
ARCA 1957 RCA 1967 Council Architect
Addr: 1958-64, Quebec; 1965-71/79, Montreal
DW 1968 Université de Laval, Faculté des Sciences Humaines photo 29 7/8 x 40 1/8

FISHER, AGNES (Mrs)
c 1890
1939 247 Lucienne sculp nfs

FISHER, BRIAN RICHARD
10 Mar 1939, Uxbridge, Eng CC2
RCA(e) 1973 Ret 1980 Council Painter
Addr: 1979, Regina

FISHER, WILLIAM ROBERT
18 Apr 1823, Bainsville, Ont IO
1951 31 Peter $140

FITZGERALD, HELEN ROBERTA (Mrs John Steele) (Mrs Wilfred Bacon)
22 Jun 1919
1942 Steele, Mrs Helen
134 G.B. wc nfs T43-43
1944 44 Corps de ballet $75
45 Portrait $100

FITZGERALD, LIONEL LEMOINE
17 Mar 1890, Winnipeg 5 Aug 1956, Winnipeg CC1 EC M NGC TB2/3 W78 WWA47
Addr: 1912, Winnipeg; 1913, 108 Union Trust Bldg, Winnipeg; 1914, 18 Evanson St, Winnipeg; 1915, 305 Northern Crown Bank Bldg, Winnipeg; 1916-20, 18 Evanson St, Winnipeg; 1921, c/o Richardson Bros, Winnipeg; 1926, 160 Lyle St, Winnipeg
1912 S3, Winnipeg
246 Landscape
1913 100 The dying embers of autumn
1914 68 The poplars
69 The prairie
1914 S4, Winnipeg
168 Afternoon $20
168a Morning in the city $15
1915 70 Prairie trail
71 The concrete pier
1916 76 Near Birds' Hill
77 The bridge
1918A 290 Late fall, Manitoba ◊NGC◊
291 In the marsh
290-1, Trustees, National Gallery of Canada, Travelling Scholarship Competition
1918N 59 Autumn
1919 52 Summer afternoon
1920 88 The spirit of autumn
1921 58 Winter woods
1925 288 Bow River drwg

FLEMING, ALEXANDER M.
9 Sep 1878, Chatham, Ont 24 Jan 1929, Guelph, Ont
Addr: 1904-5, Chatham, Ont; 1909N-12, 361 Wellington St W, Chatham, Ont; 1918A, 69 1/2 King St, Chatham, Ont
1904 58 Fog lifting, north Wales
1905 69 A wet autumn near Chatham
1906 F5, Halifax
54 October in the Kent lowland illus $200
55 Low tide $200
1909N 49 A stormy day in heather time, West Highlands, Scotland
50 The old landing place, White Hills, Banffshire, Scotland
1910 62 Morning after rain, Cullin, Banffshire
1911 50 From green to gold in morning mist
1912 S3, Winnipeg

48 The moon and fading day
1918A 59 The melting snow

FLEMING, ALLAN ROBB
7 May 1929, Toronto 31 Dec 1977, Toronto WWA73
ARCA 1970 RCA medal 1965 Council
Graphic designer
Addr: 1971/76, Toronto
1970 159 Book, Canada: a year of the land
160 Book, Rural Ontario
161 Symbol, Ontario Hydro
162 Announcement, William Golden
163 Catalogue, Canada 101
164 Symbol, Design Centre
1971 22G Book, Goethe's Faust. University of Toronto Press
23G Cover, Scholarly Publishing. University of Toronto Press illus
1976 S12, Montreal
118 Book, Canada illus

FLEMING, ARCHIE G.
1948 54 Woods in winter wc $80
55 Harbour, Gloucester wc $80

FLEMING, ROBERT PERCIVAL
25 Apr 1914, Cooksville, Ont CWW79
see SMITH, JOHN ROXBURGH, 1953-1960

FLETCHER, FREDERICK ERNEST
18 Jan 1923, Toronto
RCA(e) 1976 Architect
Addr: 1979, Toronto
1964J 23 Northern town gouache 18 x 24 $100

FLEURY, WILLIAM E.
see ARTHUR, ERIC, 1957-96

FLEWWELLING, CHARLES H. (or FLEWELLING)
fl 1876-90 H
Addr: 1886, Saint John
1886 F1a, London, Eng
2029, artist number
Engraving on wood, with book of prints from the engravings
Engraved blocks

FLIESS, HENRY
see MURRAY, JAMES A, 1964N

FLINN, WESLEY ROBSON
b 1906
Addr: 1934, 184 1/2 Albany Ave, Toronto
1934 67 Maj Aleck Sinclair, VD

FLOOD, LOUISE BARBARA BLACK (Mrs Wilfrid John Flood)
5 Jul 1903, Sackville, NB
Addr: 1929, Sackville, NB
1929 17 Old man's head L. Barbara Black
1940 51 The snow shovelers $300 T41-15

FLOOD, WILFRID JOHN
17 Jan 1904, London, Eng 28 Mar 1946, Ottawa
Addr: 1935, 24 Kenora St, Ottawa; 1936-7, 401 Hamilton St, Ottawa
1935 82 Sandy MacDonald $75
83 Variety of tulips wc $25
1936 71 The prospector nfs
1937 72 Cloister $200
73 Approach to Hull $75
1938 67 Cleaning the caldrons, sugar bush wc $45 T39-19
68 Boiling the sap, sugar bush wc $45

FLOYD (Miss)
H
Addr: 1893, Owen Sound, Ont
1893 47 Still life

FOGT, MIMI
1941 58 Local news $75

FONTAINE, PIERRE
1970 165 Announcement, The Ernie game
166 New Year's card, dove
1971 24G Poster, Struggle for a border. National Film Board
25G Poster, Veritage. NFB
26G Promotion sheet, Finale de football. NFB

FOORD, GEORGE THOMAS
b 1908
Addr: 1933-4, 16 Fernwood Park Ave, Toronto
1933 62 Mount St Anne, Percé wc $45 T34-23
1934 68 Evening rain, Rice Lake wc $45

FORBES, DONALD R.
fl 1938-55
Addr: 1938, Montreal

1938 S8, Toronto
380 Wallpaper design. Hon mention, Canadian Wallpaper Manufacturers Limited

FORBES, FRANCES K.
Addr: 1936, 438 Quinpool Rd, Halifax
1936 72 Study $75

FORBES, JEAN MARY EDGELL (Mrs Kenneth Keith Forbes)
18 May 1897, Karachi, India M
ARCA 1944-59 Painter
Addr: 1932-6, 87 Alcina Ave, Toronto; 1944-59, Toronto
1932 56 Flowers wc $200
1934 69 The brook wc $150
1936 73 Flowers $250
1938 69 Flowers, decoration nfs
1940 52 Flowers $200 T41-16
1941 S9, Toronto
22 Spring flowers $75
1943 36 Flowers $250
37 The lobster $250 T44-14
1944 46 Magnolias $250 T45-12
47 Water lilies $200
1945 69 Gladioli wc $150
70 Spring flowers wc $150
71 Flowers nfs T46-15
1946 37 Rocky Mountains wc $75
1947 52 Peonies $300 T48-11
53 Pansies $150 T48-12
1948 56 Roses $150
57 Tulips nfs
58 Spring flowers $150
1951 32 The blue bird $300
33 Spring flowers nfs
1952 29 June flowers $400
port: by K.K. Forbes, 1925-71, 1927-59, 1932-58, 1935-85, 1940-53

FORBES, JOHN COLIN
23 Jan 1846, Toronto 28 Oct 1925, Toronto B EC H Mo98/12 NGC R2 TB1/3 W78
ARCA 1880 RCA 1882 Ret 1913 Council Painter
Addr: 1880-2, Toronto; 1883, Toronto St, Toronto; 1884-6, Toronto; 1887, Equity Chambers, Adelaide St, Toronto; 1888-92, Toronto; 1893, 14 Orde St, Toronto; 1894-00, New York; 1901, Ithica, NY; 1902, c/o Art Association of Montreal, Phillips Sq, Montreal; 1903, 998 Dorchester St, Montreal; 1904-24, London,Eng
1880 3 Sweet sixteen, portrait 1881-130 1882-97
93 Sunset
116 Hon Hector Langevin
118 D. Forbes
1881 254 Beware
1882 109 Beware! I know a maiden fair to see. Take care DW 1882 21 1/2 x 24 1/2 S1-118
1883 23 Love's lily unfin
135 The student
1884 67 Rocky Mountain canyon $600 S1-152 $500
1884 S1, Saint John
82 Shadow River, Muskoka $50
127 Fishing village, Lake Superior $50
158 Off Belle Isle $145
159 Mount of the Holy Cross $450
1885 16 Village forge $125
126 Daybreak $40
128 Peaches $75
130 Mount Stephen, CPR $400
150 Moonrise $15
176 Landscape $35
189 Bathing $25
1886 14 The village forge $150
15 Moonrise $20
16 Daybreak $35
40a Peaches $75
201 Mount of the Holy Cross, Colorado $300 F1a-1994
202 Rocky Mountain canyon $500
203 Mount Stephen $400
1886 F1a, London, Eng
1994, artist number
Rocky Mountain canyon
Mount Stephen
The village forge (Allan Gilmour, Esq, Ottawa)
1887 1 Rock slide at Glacier Mountain $50
8 Village forge $150
47 Old saw mill on the Ottawa $75
49 A Rocky Mountain ranch $125
54 Morning in British Columbia $75
62 Looking north from foot of glacier $100
68 Hermit Mountain from Rogers Pass $450
84 Glacier of the Selkirks $450
1888 85 Eveline

152 Dr Richardson
161 and 216 Portrait
171 Evening in the marsh $60
178 Pearl
1889 5 Mrs Church
7 Peaches $85
14 Dr Church
23 Evening in the marsh $85
25 Mayor McLeod Stewart
36 Pearl $300
1890 24 Hon Oliver Mowat nfs
25 Peaches $100
26 Grapes $100
27 Lily pond $100
28 October $40
29 Far west $75
30 Melons $100
31 Breezy morning $100
32 Sir John A. Macdonald, KCB $2,000 ◊NGC◊
1891 1 Coming storm
2 Willows, at Cushing's Island
3 Path through the willows
5 A.M. Cosby, Esq
7 After the shower
8 The storm
53 Samuel Nordheimer, Prussian Consul
1893 48 Chalk cliffs, near Dover $150 F1-41
49 Beach, near Dover $100
50 Coast of Maine $80 F1-42
51 Homeward bound $35
52 The old home $40 F1-43
53 Lily pond $75
1893 F1, Chicago
44 A Rocky Mountain canyon
1901 44 Master Norman Forbes
45 John Colin Forbes
1902 56 John Murphy, Esq
57 Miss Baumgarten
58 Piling clouds 1903-46
59 Lake Cayuga
60 Sheep
1903 45 Pasture land
47 Lily pond
48 Evening
1904 59 Rev James Barclay, DD

FORBES, KENNETH KEITH
4 Jul 1892, Toronto 25 Feb 1980, North York, Ont AGO CC2 CWW79 M NGC PMC TB2 WWA47
ARCA 1928 RCA 1933-59 Council
Painter
Addr: 1925, 246 Brunswick Ave, Toronto; 1926, 377 Mountain St, Montreal; 1927, 660 Sherbrooke St W, Montreal; 1928, 1374 Sherbrooke St W, Montreal; 1929-31, 64 Grenville St, Toronto; 1932-7, 87 Alcina Ave, Toronto; 1938-59, Toronto
1925 70 The red dress
71 My wife illus
1926 45 Mrs Clifford Sifton
1927 58 A.B. Cameron, Esq
59 Portrait of my wife 1929-55
1928 50 Arthur Hewitt, Esq 1929-56
1929 57 Miss Gweneth Wonham
58 Master Clifford Sifton
1930 51 W.G. Dean, Esq
52 Col Henry Brock
1931 79 Augustus Bridle, Esq
80 In the Rockies $1,000
81 The morning ride $1,000
1932 57 The polo player
58 Portrait of my wife 1933-64
1933 63 Capt Melville Millar T34-24
65 Sawback Range $700
1934 70 The catch illus
71 The Hon George Black, Speaker, House of Commons
1935 84 The Hon J.L. Bowman
85 Portrait of my wife $1,500
1936 74 Mrs Edward Gooderham nfs
75 The Eglinton Hunt $3,500
1937 74 Pres H.J. Cody, MA DD LLD, University of Toronto
75 The catch $2,000
1938 70 Rt Hon R.B. Bennett nfs
71 The orchid illus $5,000 1939-68 $3,000
72 Summer days nfs
1939 69 Maj D.S. Forbes, illus $1,500 T41-17
70 Silver sands of Morar $250
1939 F11, New York
22 Capt Melville Millar 42 x 34 1/2 $5,000
1940 53 My wife and Velasquez illus $5,000 1941-59
54 Silver and rose nfs
1941 60 My daughter June $1,500 T43-11
1941 S9, Toronto
23 Boy fishing $300
1942 38 Lt Col the Rev S.E. Lambert, OBE nfs
39 Prof J.C. Robertson nfs
1943 38 Hon J. Allison Glen, KC LLD nfs
39 Hon Thomas Vien, KC nfs
40 Sir Ernest MacMillan ill-

us nfs
1944 48 Prof E.J. Pratt illus nfs T45-13
49 Col Frederick Samuel Lampson Ford, CMG VD MD LMCC nfs
50 Col Elizabeth Smellie, CBE RRC LLD nfs
1945 72 T. Wade, Esq nfs
73 Silver and pink illus nfs
1946 38 Miss Mary Joyce Phelan nfs
39 John Rochfort Milner nfs
40 R.L. Crain, Esq nfs
1947 50 Hon Gaspard Fauteux, Speaker, House of Commons nfs
51 Sen J.H. King, Speaker, Senate, Ottawa nfs
1948 59 Rev Charles Carscallen, DD nfs
60 Col R.Y. Eaton nfs
1949 29 Jean illus $1,500
1950 38 George G. Thompson, Esq 42 x 34 nfs
39 Mrs Edward McCormack 24 x 20 nfs
1951 34 Miss Anna Por nfs
1952 28 Mrs Alan Hollinrake, Frank, Ruth, Kay and Ken nfs
DW 1933 Ironing 30 x 24 3/4 T51-16 1954 Retro sec 42

FORBES, MARY KATHLEEN see RIORDON, MARY KATHLEEN

FORD, HARRIET MARY
1859, Brockville, Ont 1939, England
AGO DBA H M NGC TB3
ARCA 1895-99 Painter
Addr: 1894-5, James Bldg, Room 42, Toronto; 1896, Confederation Life Bldg, Room 93, Toronto; 1897, Toronto; 1898, Newlyn, Eng; 1899, South Cottage, Fort Green, St Marlon, Bucks, Eng; 1902, Borringdon, Great Marlow, Eng; 1903, c/o McKenzie & Co, Toronto; 1904, Toronto; 1906, Great Marlow, Eng; 1911, Elms Court, Irvine Ave, Toronto; 1912, 102 St Vincent St, Toronto; 1914-16, 64 Prince Arthur Ave, Toronto; 1924, Marlow, Bucks, Eng
1894 41 The Annunciation 1895-39
42 A woman's story by a winter's fire
43 At the vintage S5-69 illus
44 Study of a piping boy
1895 40 My portrait
41 Decorative panel (Prof Mavor)
24W Girl in white pastel
1896 47 Portrait of a child
48 Portrait
49 By the studio fire
50 Study for mural decoration
1898 39a Santa Maria 1899-50 1904-60 F4-26
39b Head of a young girl 1899-51
1902 61 A standing pool
62 Sunshine
1903 51 Study of a head
52 Landscape
1904 61 Brittany peasant F4-27
1906 80 Miss Henrietta Vickers, a portrait study
1911 51 Portrait
52 Gardens in Versailles wc
53 A fountain in Versailles Gardens wc
1912 79 Boy and magpie
80 A fountain, Versailles wc
81 In the Gardens, Versailles wc
1912 S3, Winnipeg
49 Bruges
50 Au café
1914 226 Study for a portrait crayon
1915 72 La petite canadienne
1916 78 A winter landscape
79 St Marks, Venice
80 Entrance to British Museum wc
81 The market square, Segovia wc
1924 50 Snow

FOREST, LOUIS
Addr: 1938, St Vincent de Paul, Que
1938 S8, Toronto
111 Book, Péguy, cowhide binding with mosaic design
112 Book, Papineau, blue English morocco with metal plate
113 Book, Généalogie, maroon English morocco with mosaic design
114 Book, Tunis and Kaironan, sharkskin
115 Book, Epopée canadienne, red English morocco, wooden plaque, with mosaic design
116 Book, La paroisse, blue calfskin, leather design

FORGIE, GEORGE PATRICK
25 May 1932, Toronto IO

1967 19 Painting 20S 36 x 48 $400

FORGUES, MIMI
Addr: 1938, Montreal
1938 S8, Toronto
22 Book, Maria Chapdelaine. green levant morocco, mosaic des
1941 61 Miss Dénéchaud nfs

FORRESTALL, THOMAS DE VANEY
11 Mar 1936, Middleton, NS CC1 M WWA73
ARCA 1972 Painter
Addr: 1979, Dartmouth, NS

FORSTER, JOHN WYCLIFFE LOWES
31 Dec 1850, Norval, Ont 24 Apr 1938, Toronto AGO B CC1 CNS36 EC H M Mo98/12 NGC TB1/3 W78
ARCA 1884-05 Painter
Addr: 1883, 81 King St E, Toronto; 1884-96, Toronto; 1897-8, Manning Bldg, Toronto; 1899-00, 25 King St, Toronto; 1901, 24 King St W, Toronto; 1902, c/o McKenzie & Co, Toronto; 1903, Manning Arcade, Toronto; 1905-15, 24 King St W, Toronto; 1919-27, 27 Wellesley St, Toronto
1883 7 Gossips
15 Spring morning, Barbizon
45 The old, old story
81 Miss Libbie Jaffray
103 Mrs McMaster
120 Mrs Campbell
1884 41 Portrait
80 Reflections $375
1885 39 Study of a head $200
65 Capt W.F. McMaster
87 Portrait J.W.L. Foster, mispr
1886 112 The artist and the amateur
1887 17 Sisters
73 When you're happy don't forget your friends W.L. Foster, mispr
1888 133 By her ain fireside, a portrait
149 Mr Jacob Spence
1889 18 Portrait
1890 33 William Lee, Esq MMP nfs
1891 83 J.T. Fullerton, QC
1892 37 Portrait of my mother
63 Sandford Fleming, CMG
1893 54 The old story F1-45
55 Gossips F1-46
1894 40 Late Dr Nellis
1895 43 Rev Wm. Caven, DD, Principal of Knox College
44 Spring sunshine
1896 51 The ministry of love
1897 5 Late Hon John Beverley Robinson
1898 40 Theodore Harding Rand, DCL 1900-38
41 Sir William Meredith
1899 52 Portrait of a lady
53 Mrs McFarland
1900 37 A.A. McDonell, EA
1901 51 Rev John Wesley, MA
52 Mrs King
1901 F2, Buffalo
23 Hon G.W. Allan (Toronto Conservatory of Music)
1902 63 John Hoskins, KC LLD
64 John L. Blaikie, Esq
65 C'est bien philosophe tout de même
1902 F3, Rochester
61 The artist's mother $250 F5-56 nfs
1903 49 Rev G.M. Milligan, DD 1904-62 F4-28
50 FM Earl Roberts, GCB GCSI
1905 65 Ethel Kirkpatrick J.W.L. Foster, mispr
66 'Imam', Faith
1907 71 Rev Thos. Crosby
1907 F6, Sherbrooke
74 John Beverley Robinson $250
1908 47 Eventide J.W.L. Foster, mispr
48 John R. Booth, Edq
1911 54 Dr Goldwin Smith
1914 70 Lady Gibson
1915 73 Edward Gurney, Esq
1919 53 An incident, Toronto University Medical Corps
1924 51 The engagement ring, Macedonia
1926 44 Nyakawaya (Francis Nickawa)
1927 60 Rev James Henderson, DD

FORSYTH, W.
Addr: 1880, Quebec
1880 40 Pedestal, Quebec serpentine, for bronze bust of HE the Governor General

FORTIN, GILLES
1971 Amana film screened 2 Apr

FORTIN, MARC AURELE DE FOY
14 Mar 1888, Ste Rose, Que 2 Mar

1970, Montreal AGO B CC2 CWW61 EC M NGC TB2 W78 WWA47
ARCA 1942-55 Painter
Addr: 1910, 347 Durocher St, Montreal; 1915, 136 St Hubert St, Montreal; 1916-18, 210 Champ de Mars St, Montreal; 1925-9, 351 Notre Dame St E, Montreal; 1931, 449 Notre Dame St E, Montreal; 1933, 246 Blvd Ste Rose, Ste Rose, Que; 1935, 458 St Catherine St E, Montreal; 1942-55, Montreal
1910 63 A snow storm
64 Late spring, Alberta
1915 74 Effet de neige
1916 82 and 83 Paysage
1918N 60 A frosty morning
1925 72 The old elm tree
73 A Canadian landscape
1927 61 Passing storm, Montreal harbour wc
1929 59 Landscape at Hochelaga $125 (NGC)
1931 82 Landscape at Cartierville wc $125
83 Landscape at Hochelaga $150
1933 66 Landscape at Ste Rose $175 T34-25
1935 86 L'orme à St Martin wc $100 T36-27
1939 72 End of October $300
1939 F11, New York
23 Landscape at St Siméon 48 x 38 $800
1941 62 Landscape at St Siméon $400 T42-15
1942 40 Paysage de Gaspésie $600 T43-12
1943 41 Paysage de Gaspésie $500
42 Paysage de Gaspésie $350 T44-15
1944 51 Old mill at Ile d'Orléans $400 T45-14
52 St Laurent, Ile d'Orléans $400 T45-15
53 Paysage de Gaspésie $400
1945 74 Paysage de Gaspésie, Anse aux Gascone (Dr Oscar Mercier)
75 Rivière aux Renards $800
76 Hochelaga wc $150
1946 41 Anse aux Gascone, Gaspésie $450 T47-18
1947 55 Rivière aux Renard wc $200
56 Barge au quai $150
1949 30 Barques à Grande Baie casein $600

FORWARD, BERYL V.
Addr: 1925, 511 St Clarens Ave, Toronto; 1929, 1121 Bay St, Toronto; 1936, 764 Shaw St, Toronto
1925 254 Eleanor bust
255 Aphrodite statuette
1929 238 Miss Helen Halford sculp
1936 217 Supplication plaster $175
1948 163 Luigi sculp $150

FOSBERY, ERNEST GEORGE
29 Dec 1874, Ottawa 6 Feb 1960, Cowansville, Que AGO B CNS36 CWW55 EC M Mo12 NGC PMC TB2 W78 WWA47 WWB52
ARCA 1912 RCA 1931 Sr 1950 Council Painter
Addr: 1894, 479 Cooper St, Ottawa; 1895-6, c/o J. Wilson & Co, Sparks St, Ottawa; 1897-8, Ottawa; 1899-00, 479 Cooper St, Ottawa; 1911, 469 Albert St, Ottawa; 1912-13, 44 Central Chambers, Ottawa; 1914, 177 Sparks St, Ottawa; 1915-19, 138 Minto Place, Rockcliffe, Ottawa; 1920-4, 197 Sparks St, Room 39, Ottawa; 1925-6, Ottawa; 1927, 171 Manor Ave, Ottawa; 1928-33, 613 Banque Nationale Bldg, Rideau St, Ottawa; 1935-7, 571 Manor Rd, Ottawa; 1938-49, Ottawa; 1950-60, Montreal
1894 204 Parliament House, Ottawa sketch
1895 42 Cuttings
1896 52 Portrait of a lady
53 The art student
54 Landscape
55 Still life
1897 52 Sir James Grant, KCMG
53 Portrait of a lady
1899 54 Portrait of a young man
1900 41 Foggy day
42 A wind swept point
43 The pond
44 Bee hives
1911 55 George K. Staples, Esq, Buffalo, NY
56 Mrs George K. Staples
57 In the tracks of the sun
58 A.F. Neulands
1912 82 His Grace the Archbishop of Ottawa
83 The late G.B. Greene
84 In the track of the sun
85 Afternoon sunlight
1912 S3, Winnipeg

52 Lamplight S5-59 illus
1913 101 Thomas Ahearn, Esq S3-51
102 Playtime S4-45 $500
103 Interrupted
104 The tenderfoot S4-46 $350
105 Portrait of the artist
1914 71 Robert Gill, Esq
72 The Ven James John Bogert, Archdeacon of Ottawa 1915-76
73 Stella, daughter of Percy Todd, Esq 1915-77 illus
74 Scribbling
1915 75 Most Rev Charles Hamilton, MA DD DCL, lately Archbishop of Ottawa
78 The sheep pasture
1918A 60 Late T.C. Keefer, Esq illus (G.H. Keefer, Esq)
61 Thomas Ahearn, Esq (H.S. Southam, Esq)
62 Miss Connable (Ralph Connable, Esq)
216 The birth tree etch
217 St Andrew's Church spire, Ottawa etch
218 The storm mezz
219 The cafe mezz
1919 54 The bathers 1920-22
55 The red tam
56 Knitting
1920 89 William Southam, Esq
90 Mrs William Southam
91 Mrs W.J. Southam
1922 66 Mrs James Peck illus
67 G.E. Fauquier, Esq
68 Affy, daughter of the artist S6-23 ◊NGC◊
1924 52 Franklin Brownell, RCA
53 Catherine, daughter of C.B. Dougherty, Esq
54 Louie, daughter of F.A. Eddie, Esq
1927 62 Hon Hewitt Bostock, Speaker, Senate illus
299 Sen J.G. Turriff dry pt 1928-204 Turiff, mispr
300 Mr Alexander Ferguson dry pt
1928 51 Robert Stothers, BA
1929 60 Patricia, daughter of the artist $3,000 S7-46
61 Marcelled pastel $500
1929 S7, Calgary
47 The bathers $500
1930 53 James Wilson, Esq illus DW 1931 34 x 26 T51-17 1954 Retro Sec 29
1931 84 T.P. Foran, KC
1932 59 P.B. Rose, LLD
60 A.H. McDougall, LLD
1933 67 Hon P.E. Blondin, Speaker, Senate
68 Adm Sir Charles Kingsmill T34-26
69 Mrs Affy Joan Newson
1935 87 J.H. Putnam, Esq, BA DPAED nfs 1936-75 F11-24 35 x 40
1936 77 Miss Ruth Hughson nfs 1937-76 T38-17
1938 73 Hon Thomas Ahearn nfs
1939 73 W.W. Nichol, Esq, illus 1946-42 illus
1943 43 Dr Walter C. Murray (University of Saskatchewan)
1944 54 Sir Lyman P. Duff, PC illus nfs
1945 77 Evening, Cheticamp wc nfs
1946 43 Lieut Gen E.Q. Sansom, CB DSO
44 Cap Rouge, Cape Breton $500 T47-19
1947 54 Brig James L. Melville, CBE MC ED illus nfs
1949 61 Dr H.M. Tory illus nfs

FOSBERY, LIONEL GOOCH
12 Jan 1879, Ottawa 10 Feb 1956, Wakefield, Que M
Addr: 1912, Centennial Chambers, Ottawa; 1914, 144 2nd Ave, Ottawa; 1918A, 177 Spadina Ave, Ottawa
1912 234 Phyllis bust
235 Affy bust
1914 201 Memories bust
1918A 186 Master Thomas Henry Fosbery plaster
port: by D.K. Woodhead, 1947-186

FOSTER, BEN
H
1891 92 Landscape

FOSTER, HILDA VINCENT
24 Mar 1896, West Bridgeford, Notts, Eng M
Addr: 1936, 10072 91st Ave, Edmonton
1936 78 Fall flowers wc $50
1938 250 Illumination on vellum $20
1945 78 Decorative panel wc $50
79 Sparrow hawk wc $50

FOSTER, MURIEL AILEEN (MERLE)
11 Apr 1897, Toronto

Addr: 1921, 99 Beech Ave, Toronto; 1926, 2 Walton St, Toronto; 1928, 504 Church St, Toronto
1921 176 Elias Rogers sculp
1926 157 Dr Pyne sculp
1928 162 Portrait plaque sculp

FOUGERAT, EMMANUAL French
25 Dec 1869, Rennes, France 3 Sep 1953, Paris B TB1/2
Addr: 1924, 628 St Urbain St, Montreal
1924 55 Famille de l'artiste
56 Dos blond
261 Vieux Breton de Quimperlé drwg
262 Vielle Bretonne de Pont l'Abbé drwg

FOURDRINIER, EMILY LOUISE
7 Jul 1870, Waterloo Que 23 Aug 1896, Ottawa H
Addr: 1893, 12 Tupper St, Montreal
1893 56 Little rose madder $30
57 Tender memories recalled $85

FOWLER, DANIEL
10 Feb 1810, Down, Kent, Eng 14 Sep 1894, Amherst Island, Ont AGO B EC H M NGC R2 TB
RCA 1880 Council Painter
Addr: 1880-94, Emerald, Amherst Island, Ont
1880 206 Grapes and haws wc
207 The broken wing wc
208 Gloomy weather and gloomy man, a bad look out for fishing wc
209 Dead Canadian game 1881-45 Dead game, Canadian DW 1882 Canadian game 20 1/2 x 27 wc 1954 Retro sec 2
210 Gladiolus and China asters wc
211 Crimson roses and yellow briar wc
212 Desolation, Campagna of Rome, ruins of ancient aqueduct wc
213 Cologne on the Rhine, from a sketch made before work on the Cathedral was resumed wc
214 Mallard, a dead shot wc
215 Italian brigand wc
216 Canadian game wc (J. Spooner)
217 Grapes wc (J. Spooner)
218 Gladiolus wc (J. Spooner)
219 Black duck wc (J. Spooner)
220 Cottage wc (J. Spooner)
221 Canadian game wc (J. Spooner)
222 Phlox wc (J. Spooner)
223 A lonely road, evening wc (J. Spooner)
1881 14 Where the storm struck wc (R. Burgess)
19 Evening sketch wc $10
88 The fall and the fallen wc (Lucius R. O'Brien)
100 Shot but not got wc $100
1882 140 Past service wc $25
147 Mid-day wc $30
165 Dead game wc $125
170 Going home, last rays of September wc $125
180 Windsor Castle, from the forest wc $15
190 Near Rye harbour wc $10
194 Spring flowers wc $25
196 Kirkstall Abbey, Yorkshire wc $15
198 Valley of Desolation, Bolton Park wc $15
199 Old Folkstone, Kent wc $15
1883 148 Alpine solitude wc
157a Waterfall in Wales wc $30
159a Ironbound coast, south Italy, squally wc $35
160 Olevano, near Rome wc $30
170 Slowly home at eventide wc
176 Rough pasture wc $125
186 Street at Berncastle, on the Moselle wc (J. Spooner)
221 On the banks of the Moselle wc $50 S1-34
223 Interior of cottage, Sussex, Eng wc (J. Spooner)
229 Porta Nigra, Black Gate, Treves, Germany wc
267 Castle of Misocco, Pass of the Bernadine, Switzerland wc
281 Bridge in the Pass of St Gothard, Switzerland wc (J. Spooner)
1884 S1, Saint John
35 How is the mighty fallen wc
52 Bolton Abbey wc $50
55 Jacques and the wounded stag wc $35
1885 205 In Val d'Aosta wc
255 Pass of the Grimsel,

Switzerland wc
270 Dawlish, Devon, Eng wc
274 Island villa, Lago Maggiore wc
292 Mount Pilatus, Lake of Lucerne wc
299 Tivoli wc
320 Looking for father's boat wc $30

1886 101 Canadian dead game wc $150
102 Partridges wc
103 Canadian hare in winter coat wc $150 Fla-1995

1886 Fla, London, Eng
1995, artist number
lent by J. Spooner, Esq, Toronto
Canadian dead game (three)
Partridges
Evening
Gladioli
Grapes
Cactus
Sweet Williams

1887 112 At Cochem on the Moselle wc $35
113 A solitary pool, Amherst Island wc $50
116 A rubbish corner wc $50
122 Morrow's Bay, Amherst Island wc $50
127 A gleam in the woods wc $50
128 My boat house wc
163 Across the Limestone Ridge wc $125
168 At Zell, on the Moselle wc $35

1888 3 A storm beaten sandy shore wc $50
7 The last of a white birch wc $35
15 Mount Cheops, Selkirks wc $60
32 A dark pool on a dull day wc $40
40 Hickories in September wc $35
59 Toiling over the sand hills wc $50
66 Morrow Bay, Amherst Islet, October wc $60 (Marrow mispr)
249 Black oak in October wc $30
273 Snowy weather in the fall wc $35
309 On the lake shore wc

1889 128 Ruins of Vale Crucis Abbey, north Wales wc $35
136 Low water, Bay of Quinte wc $50
144 Heavy squall wc $35
152 A wanderer in the woodlands wc $60 ◊NGC◊
154 A very old olive tree at Tivoli wc $35

1890 138 Flower bed, studied from the object itself wc $125
139 Water mill near Bettws-y-coed, north Wales wc $75
140 A squall wc $60
141 What the wind did wc $50
142 Cool day in September wc $50
143 Warm afternoon in September wc $30
144 Dull weather wc $30
145 An Amherst Island road wc $35
146 Drooping elm in the fall wc $30

1891 163 Street at Merle, on the Moselle wc
164 Head of Amherst Island wc
165 Snowdon from Lynn Gwinnant wc
166 Sunshine and shadow wc

1892 99 Street scene wc $60
108 and 139 Merle on the Moselle wc $125 each
120 Water mills wc $30
127 Summer afternoon wc $60
131 Allington Castle, Kent, England wc $125
132 Mill stream on the Moselle, near Berncastle wc $60
145 Sunshine and shadow wc $60

1893 178 Shot but not got wc nfs F1-132
179 Group of Canadian dead game wc nfs F1-133
180 Peonies wc $75 F1-134
181 Gladiolus wc $60 F1-135
182 Group of gladiolus wc $60 F1-136
183 Rough pasture wc $125 F1-137
184 Summer afternoon wc $50 F1-138
185 Low water, Bay of Quinte wc $50 F1-139
186 Sunshine and shade wc $50 F1-140
187 Sand hills, Amherst Island wc $50 F1-141

188 Fisher boys of Hastings, England wc $40 F1-142 ◊NGC◊
189 Dark pool on a dull day wc nfs F1-143
190 Stork wc nfs F1-144
191 Duck wc nfs F1-145
1910 S2, Liverpool
the late Daniel Fowler
39 Dead game wc
40 Dead birds wc

FOWLER, GORDON LYLE MCLEAN
19 Apr 1909, Fillmore, Sask
ARCA 1960 RCA 1975 Architect
Addr: 1960-71, Toronto; 1979, Aurora, Ont
DW 1975 Department of Veterans Affairs, Ottawa, office building. 1948 pencil & charcl

FOX, GEORGE GREENFIELD
30 Jun 1870, Montreal 11 Nov 1933, Montreal
Addr: 1922-7, 761 Sherbrooke St W, Montreal; 1929-32, 1617 Sherbrooke St W, Montreal
1922 69 Boats, sketch
70 Rocks, sketch S6-21
1924 57 Fishing nets
1925 74 Lifting fog S7-48 $200
1926 45 A bit of the shore
1927 63 The harbour at low tide
1929 62 Surf $200
63 Marine $500
1929 S7, Calgary
49 Early winter $200
50 Morning mist $150
1930 54 Surf, Grand Manan, NB $500
55 Marine, Grand Manan, NB $500
1931 85 Coast, Grand Manan, NB $300
86 Lifting fog, Grand Manan, NB $300
1932 61 Full sea, Grand Manan, NB $400
62 Morning light, Grand Manan, NB $400

FOX, JOHN RICHARD
26 Jul 1927, Montreal B CC1 M NGC WWA73
ARCA 1959-61 Painter
Addr: 1959-61, Montreal

FOX, MIRIAM H.
b Toronto
Addr: 1936, 119 Glen Rd, Toronto
1936 79 Old French home, Baie St Paul, Quebec wc $50
80 Early spring, Ontario wc $50 T37-26

FOX, ROBERT ATKINSON
1860, Toronto H
1885 125 Music hath charms $50
149 Sketch $25
167 Skinner's Cove, Labrador $50
174 Landscape $50
198 The gourmet $150

FRAME, MARGARET JOSEPHINE GERALDINE FULTON (Mrs H.S. Beatty)
2 Jun 1903, Oxford, NS M
Addr: 1922, 2159 Osler St, Regina
1922 71 Old Austrian woman

FRAME, STATIRA ELIZABETH WELLS (Mrs William Frame)
15 Sep 1870, Waterloo, Que 29 Nov 1935, Vancouver
Addr: 1926, 1999 Beach Ave, Vancouver
1926 46 The pilot's house

FRANCE, EURILDA LOOMIS (Mrs)
fl 1898-01 H
Addr: 1899, 102 St Matthew St, Montreal
1899 57 Old fashioned garden
169 Summer wc

FRANCE, J.L.
Addr: 1899, 102 St Matthew St, Montreal
1899 55 Foggy day, Brittany
56 The road to Berthier
170 Twilight in Holland wc

FRANCHERE, JOSEPH CHARLES
4 Mar 1866, Montreal 12 May 1921, Montreal CC2 H NGC TB3 W78
ARCA 1902-19 Painter
Addr: 1893, 1644 Notre Dame St, Montreal; 1896-00, 376 Lagauchetiere St, Montreal; 1901-2, 169 Peel St, Montreal; 1903-18, 60 St Denis St, Montreal; 1919-20, 67 Ste Famille St, Montreal
1893 58 Fantaisie japonaise $100 F1-47
59 Still life $40 F1-48
1896 56 and 57 Study of a cast
200 On Lake Champlain wc
1899 43 Mr J. Rivet

44 Etude fantaisie
45 Head of a girl
1900 39 Thinking
40 Study of a head
1901 47 Canadian Japanese
48 Country life scene
49 The little epicure F2-24
1902 66 Hon Judge Mathieu
67 Hon Senator Dandurand
68 La modèle
1903 43 Pensive
44 The first pipe
1904 63 American beauties
1904 F4, St Louis
29 Country people, province of Quebec
1905 67 After the bath F5-59 $90 F6-75
68 The fortune teller
1906 78 Lake Muskoka
1906 F5, Halifax
57 Country people $150
58 A girl in Japanese costume $150
1907 72 P.B. Mignault, KC
73 At the Hôtel Dieu
293 Drawing charcl
1907 F6, Sherbrooke
76 Country work $125
77 Jacques Cartier Square market $60
1908 49 Indiscretions
50 Winter scene
1909M 44a Country girl
1909N 51 Fortune teller
1910 65 Hon Judge H. Archambault
66 Solitude
1910 S2, Liverpool
41 After the ball
1911 59 Lassitude S3-53 S5-54 illus
1912 86 Winter
1913 106 Dr E.P. Lachapelle
107 Sir Alexandre Lacoste
108 Le bon vieux temps
1914 75 Old French Canadian
76 Winter scene
1914 S4, Winnipeg
47 Old French Canadian habitant $125
1915 79 Fantaisie
80 La cigarette
81 Ostende pastel
1916 84 Sylphide (NGC)
85 La grand'mère illus
86 Hiver
87 Fascination pastel
1918A 63 Golden youth
64 Winter
1918N 61 Mr Charles Chaput illus
62 Le camp
63 Surprise
1919 57 Old Montreal
58 The two friends
1920 93 Mr G.N. Ducharme
94 Mlle Odette Masson
95 Le verglas
96 Le Pic de l'Aurore, Percé

FRANCIS, JAMES BLAKE
15 May 1916, Toronto
1955 32 Sisters illus $350

FRANCIS, VINCENT
23 Dec 1912, London, Eng
1948 62 Central Park at 87th $50
1949 31 Studio still life #2 $50

FRANCK, ALBERT JACQUES
2 Apr 1889, Middleburg, Netherlands
28 Feb 1973, Toronto AGO M WWA56
ARCA 1961-70 Sr 1969 Painter
Addr: 1961-70, Toronto
1948 63 Bendale Church $200
1949 32 Wagon sheds $200
33 Old house, McCaul Street $200
1950 40 Herrings 16 x 20 $150
1951 35 Walton Street $300
1952 30 House on Bleeker Street $300
1963 23 House on Isabella Street 30 x 24 illus $475 S10-28 nfs
24 Sumach Street, near Bloor Street East $500

FRANCK, FLORENCE see VALE, FLORENCE

FRANKLIN, HANNAH
20 Jun 1937, Poland
1971 3S Soft mufti form 60 x 36 x 24 $300
4S Soft 3 red forms #1 72 x 72 x 24 $300

FRASER, CAROL LUCILLE HOORN (Mrs John Fraser)
5 Sep 1930, Superior, Wisc CC2 WWA78
RCA(e) 1976 Painter
Addr: 1979, Halifax

FRASER, DONALD GORDON
11 Jun 1921, Charlton, Ont
1950 41 Demolition 23 x 28 1/2 $75

FRASER, FREDERICK ALEXANDER

17 Jun 1897, Toronto
Addr: 1926-30, 23 Albany Ave, Toronto
1926 47 October snow, Alton, 1925
1930 56 Yellow October, Forks of the Credit wc $85
57 A Norwegian tramp, Montreal dry docks wc $200

FRASER, JOHN ARTHUR
1838, London, Eng 1 Jan 1898, New York AGO B EC H M Mo98 NGC TB W78
RCA 1880 Hon Non-res 1887 Council
Painter
Addr: 1880-2, Toronto; 1883, 39 King St E, Toronto; 1884-5, Toronto; 1886-8, Ottawa; 1889-92, New York; 1893, 114 W 18th St, New York; 1894, 157 W 47th St, New York; 1895-8, New York
1880 50 Day break, low tide, Restigouche
53 At a lobster fishery, Bay of Chaleur
56 Laurentian splendour 1881-311 DW 1883 19 1/4 x 37 1/2 S1-85
57 In breezy October, Bay of Chaleur
59 A grey morning, dropping tide
62 Study for a large picture (in possession of Lady Howland)
92 A last ray in the White Mountains
175 A rocky beach wc
176 Autumn study wc
178 Squally morning in October, mouth of the Restigouche wc
179 Early morning, Dalhousie, NB wc
180 A frowning cape wc (James Smith)
1881 11 Sketch at Percé wc
39 Nature arches wc
41 Acadian pastoral wc
63 On the shingly shore wc
81 In golden autumn wc $50
84 Twilight wc (J. Spooner)
105 The Bird Rock wc
255 Breezy October
297 On the beach at Percé $600
325 Low tide, Bay of Chaleur (Ontario Society of Artists)
1883 94 artist's name, title blank
1886 43 Showery day in the Passe des Monts de St Urbain wc $150
55 At Percé, French Canada, Bonaventure County wc $400
64 A salmon pool on the Restigouche wc $80
1886 Fla, London, Eng
1996, artist number
A showery day in the Passe des Montes de St Urbain
At Percé, Quebec Province
A salmon pool on the Restigouche
Seaside idyll (O. Howlands, Esq, Toronto)
Breezing October (Geo. Haig, Esq, Montreal)
Landscape (R.B. Angus, Esq, Montreal)
Mount Stephen, summit of the Rocky Mountains, near Sencloile, Canadian Pacific Railway, 12,000 feet above tide, 8,500 feet above railway track (Sir George Stephen, Bart)
Mount Hermit, summit of the Selkirk Range, British Columbia. Main peak 5,500 feet above railway track. Glaciers from 500 to 800 feet deep (Sir George Stephen, Bart)
Summit Lake, Rocky Mountains, Canadian Pacific Railway (Sir George Stephen, Bart)
1890 147 Midst meadow, moor and mountain wc S2-41
148 In the mists and rain at Appin wc $175
149 In scented summer wc $125
150 In the kitchen garden of the castle wc $225
151 On a fresh June morning wc $225
152 A grey afternoon on the farm wc $225
153 Midst rustling leaves and fountains murmuring wc $200
154 Where a Highland river meets the sea. The mouth of the Awe, coming storm wc $200
155 At Brodick, Arran, NB wc $80
156 A pretty nook wc $80
157 Deserted wc nfs
158 Through the hay wc nfs

1891 88 In the Pass of Buander
89 Angling in the Highlands, November morning
90 'Neath threatening skies in springtime
1893 60 A Highland November morning $750 F1-49
192 A bit of Ightan mote house wc $125 F1-146
193 On a blowy morn in June wc $250 F1-147
194 At the solemn hour wc $250 F1-148
195 In the wild Highlands wc $175 F1-149
196 November twilight, Perthshire wc $175 F1-150
197 The haunt of the muskrat wc $200 F1-151
198 By the meadow stream wc $200 F1-152
199 The weird house in the moat wc $250 F1-153
200 On the Loch Etive side wc $100 F1-154
201 The sunset flush wc $200 F1-155
202 'Twixt Achray and Katrine wc $350 F1-156 nfs
203 Percé wc nfs F1-157
1894 164 On the Lintire Loch, from Appin wc
165 On a Scotch river wc
166 At Gorrie, Arran wc
167 A bye path wc
168 Grey morning on the Thames wc
169 River side wc
1910 S2, Liverpool
42 Meadow, moor and mountain wc late John Fraser
43 In the mists wc

FRASER, WILLIAM
1908 167a Council Hall, Dunoon, Scotland

FRAYN, CONSTANCE E.
Addr: 1916, 36 St Matthew St, Montreal
1916 88 Still life wc

FRECHETTE, ACHILLE
13 Oct 1847, Lévis, Que 15 Nov 1927, San Diego, Cal H
Addr: 1887, Ottawa
1886 11 Portrait
99 Alphonse Lusignan wc
100 Sir A.P. Caron b&w
101a Portrait wc
1887 7 Le livre d'hier soir $20
189 Madame B crayon

FRECHETTE, MARIE MARGUERITE
Apr 1878, Ottawa F H
Addr: 1906, 177 Sparks St, Ottawa; 1920, 67 Somerset St, Ottawa; 1922, 1050 Jervis St, Vancouver
1906 81 The child who pouts
1920 97 Le petit Laurent
98 Lamplight
1922 72 Lady Anne Cavendish min

FREIFIELD, ERIC
13 Mar 1919, Saratov, Russia IO M
WWA62
ARCA 1963 Council Painter
Addr: 1964-71/79, Toronto
1952 31 Ichabod wc nfs
1957 26 Back door nfs
1959 29 Gomorrah 22 x 30 nfs
1966 19 Alfred's room 23 x 29 nfs
1970 21 Self portrait 20 x 15 3/8 illus nfs
22 Tutt's barn 20 x 27 nfs
1971 11 The Macneil place 22 3/4 x 30 3/4 illus nfs

FRENCH, BETTY see MCCAUGHEY, BETTY

FRENCH, MAIDA see PARLOW, MAIDA

FRENCH, REGINALD E.
1947 57 The old flume, Ogilvie Flour Mills, Montreal wc $150
58 Round house, Turcot wc $75

FRESCHI, BRUNO BASILIO
18 Apr 1937, Trail, BC
RCA(e) 1973 Council Architect
Addr: 1979, Vancouver

FREYVOGEL, CHARLOTTE R.
Addr: 1938, Montreal
1938 S8, Toronto
390 Wallpaper design. Hon mention. Canadian Wallpaper Manufacturers Limited

FRIEND, WASHINGTON English
c 1820, Washington, DC B H
Addr: 1886, Fitzalan House, Littlehampton, Sussex, Eng
1886 F1a, London, Eng
1997, artist number

The Falls of Niagara, summer
Sherbrooke, Eastern Townships
Lake Memphremagog
The Straits of Belle Isle
Shawinigan, near Quebec (Shewanagan , mispr)
Shooting the rapids

FRIESEN, VICTOR
11 Apr 1911, Lesnoy, Ukraine
1941 63 Coal dock wc $60

FRIPP, JOHN
1901 165 Sunset, Hatzic Lake, BC wc

FRIPP, ROBERT MACKAY
Addr: 1901, Vancouver
1901 242 Anglican Church, Auckland, NZ
243 Public school, Auckland, NZ
244 Suburban cottage, Auckland, NZ

FRIPP, THOMAS WILLIAM
23 Mar 1864, London, Eng 30 May 1931, Vancouver CC2 H NGC TB3
Addr: 1922, 342 Pender St W, (Vancouver; 1930, 1323 Harwood St, Vancouver
1922 73 Evening, D'Arcy, BC wc
1930 203 Eiffel Mountain from Paradise Valley charcl $25

FRY, BEATRICE ADELAIDE (BESSIE) (Mrs Symons)
1884, Berkshire, Eng 26 Jan 1976, Victoria
Addr: 1930-3, Columbia College, New Westminster, BC
1930 58 Flowering north
1932 63 The dogwood tree wc $25
1933 70 Western slopes wc $100
71 Lakeside, October wc $75

FRYER, BRYANT WILKINS
1897, Galt, Ont Oct 1963, Toronto
Addr: 1928, 43 Cheritan Ave, Toronto
1928 52 Hilltops $400

FRYER, STANLEY THOMAS JOHN
2 May 1885, Sawston, Cambs, Eng
Addr: 1913, 207 Clyde Bldg, Hamilton, Ont; 1930, 82 South Drive, Toronto
1913 336 Entrance to Court of Justice S4-140 $30 nfs
1930 168 A cathedral of commerce $30

FUGLER, GRACE (Mrs Leonard Hutchinson)
22 Jun 1915, Hamilton AGO
Addr: 1935-7, 12 Hamilton Ave, Hamilton, Ont
1935 317 Bricks wd cut $7.50
318 The hitching post wd cut $7.50 ◊AGO◊
1936 237 Mill bridge block pr $10
1937 312 7 o'clock block pr $7.50

FULFORD, PATRICIA PARSONS
21 Mar 1935, Toronto B M
RCA(e) 1978 Sculptor
Addr: 1979, Ganges, BC
1963 82 Dreamer plaster $450
1970 81 Black and white #11 48 x 36 x 30 $850

FULLER, THOMAS
14 Mar 1822, Bath, Eng 28 Sep 1898, Ottawa Co H Mo98 NGC
RCA 1882 Council Architect
Addr: 1882-98, Ottawa
1882 235 New Capitol at Albany, NY
1883 338 Church, sketch
342 Assembly Chamber, New York State
Fuller & Jones
337 Parliament Buildings, Ottawa des
DW 1883 Parliament Building, Ottawa pen & wc drwg 22 x 36

FURBY, G.E.
H
1889 37 Bananas, a study $25

FYLES, FAITH
b Cowansville, Que
Addr: 1918N-20, 368 Frank St, Ottawa; 1924-5, 51 James St, Ottawa; 1927-9, 340 McLaren St, Ottawa; 1933-7, 96 Maple Lane, Ottawa
1918N 64 The last leaves
65 Hawthorns in fruit
1920 99 Melting snows, Gatineau
100 A lonely road
1924 58 Menton pencil
1925 75 Morning light pastel
1927 64 Windy day, Bermuda pastel
65 Elba Beach, Bermuda pastel
1929 64 Larkspur $250
65 Lilac time at Lake Massa-

wippi $500
1929 S7, Calgary
51 Mount Edith Cavell, Jasper Park pastel $125
1933 72 Home in the hills, Jamaica $150
1937 77 Lilies and clematis wc $35
1939 74 Forsythia $150

G

GABOURY, ETIENNE JOSEPH
24 Apr 1930, Swan Lake, Man
ARCA 1966 Architect
Addr: 1967-71, St Boniface, Man; 1979, Winnipeg
1964N 120-2 Architect's studio, St Boniface, Manitoba. Exterior views 1 and 2. Interior
1970 18A-22A Residence of Mr and Mrs E.J. Gaboury. Interior. Front view. Side view. Main plan. Basement plan

GADBOIS, MARIE MARGUERITE LOUISE LANDRY (Mrs Emilien Gadbois)
27 Nov 1896, Montreal M NGC WWA47
1950 42 Les danseurs 40 x 30 $600

GAGE, FRANCES MARIE
22 Aug 1924, Windsor, Ont M WWA62
RCA(e) 1973 RCA 1977 Sculptor
Addr: 1976, Toronto; 1979, St Clements, Ont
1952 105 Spring wd rel $50
1960 77 Portrait of a person sculp nfs
1976 S12, Montreal
70 Wave form bronze 12 1/2 x 16 illus
DW 1977 Douglas Duncan. 1957 bronze 18h

GAGE, ROBERT
1841, Ireland
ARCA 1880-92 Architect
Addr: 1880-92, Kingston, Ont

GAGEN, CAROLINE S.
fl 1879-85 H
1883 238 Study of flowers wc $15
241 Lilac wc $15
1885 253 Flowers wc $15
311 Cineraria wc $15

GAGEN, ROBERT FORD
10 May 1847, London, Eng 2 Mar 1926, Toronto AGO B CCI EC H M NGC RI TB1/3 W78
ARCA 1880 RCA 1914 Council Painter
Addr: 1880-2, Toronto; 1883, 79 King St W, Toronto; 1884-98, Toronto; 1899-03, 90 Yonge St, Toronto; 1904, Toronto; 1905-6, Medical Council Bldg, Toronto; 1907, Toronto; 1908-9, Mail Bldg, Toronto; 1910-15, 28 College St, Toronto; 1916-20, 707 Yonge St, Toronto; 1921-6, 143 Elm St, Toronto
1881 103 Camelias wc (Ontario Society of Artists)
1883 69 The ocean, sketch $40
141 A fisherman's daughter wc $20
1884 S1, Saint John
49 Double hollyhock wc $80
57 The Ovens, Mount Desert wc $35
1885 23 Apple gathering $35
25 The locks, Bobcaygeon $65
45 The end of day, Mount Desert, southwest harbour $50
256 Old mill, evening wc $50
258 Old farm house wc $20
273 A rural ferry wc $20
1886 46 A rural ferry wc $45
95 In the conservatory wc $40
199 Cockscombs wc. Selected for Fla, not in Fla catalogue
1890 159 Bugler, 1st West Indian Regiment, Nassau, Bahamas wc $35
160 Near the Queen's Stairs, Nassau, Bahamas wc $40
161 Petticoat Lane, Nassau $40 Peticoat, mispr
162 View from my window, Nassau $40
163 Road near Government House, Nassau wc $30
164 Interior of a West Indian kitchen, Nassau wc $30
165 Peonies wc $35
1891 117 Old street, Nassau, NP, Bahamas wc
186 Spongus, NP, Nassau wc
1892 94 Somme's Sound, Mount Desert wc $35
142 Dirty weather, Peak's Island wc $35
1893 204 Rhododendrons wc $30
205 A clear morning, Frenchman's Bay, Maine wc $30
206 Ebb tide, West Goldes-

borough, Maine wc $50
1894 47 Under the birches gouache
170 Lilacs wc
1895 31W A road to the sea, Ammuguan, Mass wc
32W Early morning, Mount Elephantus, Quebec wc
33W Owl's Head, Lake Memphremagog wc
1897 14W A New England stream wc
15W Sunrise, Mount Elephantus wc
1898 160 The fringe of the lake wc
161 New England wc
162 The afternoon of a hot summer day wc
163 Near Georgeville, Lake Memphremagog wc
164 A silent summer noon wc
165 Two ivory miniatures
1899 58 A calm summer afternoon
171 Just above high tide wc illus, Left at high tide
172 At Rocky Neck, Gloucester, Mass wc
1900 137 When the flowing tide comes in wc
138 A lobster catcher wc
139 A sheltered cove wc
140 A New England fisherman's home wc
141 Sunset Rock, Eastern Point, Gloucester, Mass wc
142 A colour study, Gloucester harbour wc
143 A cloudy summer day wc
144 The willow road wc
1901 166 The end of day wc
167 Evening glow, Selkirks wc F2-25 1902-198
168 A storm in the Selkirks wc F2-26 1902-196
1902 197 Deep-sea fishers wc
199 The Hermit Range, Selkirks wc
200 Out of a job, Gloucester, Mass wc
201 A summer afternoon, Cape Ann wc
1902 F3, Rochester
63 Evening in the valley of the Great Glacier, near Glacier BC wc $120 1903-169
1903 165 The end of day, Selkirks wc
166 The beginning of day, Selkirks wc
167 Wind and rain, the Persians, Gloucester, Mass wc
168 Getting ready for work, morning wc
1904 219 Evening, Grand Manan wc F4-101
220 Dulce gathering, Grand Manan wc
221 Herring fishers wc
222 Great Glacier, Selkirks wc
223 In the Rockies wc
1904 F4, St Louis
100 Dark Harbour, Grand Manan wc
1905 76 The sun's good night, Selkirks
77 Riding on the Cod Banks
78 Dulce gathering, Grand Manan Island, NB
79 Returning from their nets, New Brunswick
1906 83 The fog bell F5-60
84 Crossing the bar
85 Manana F5-61
86 On Monhegan's cliffs
1907 241 Calm before storm wc
242 Off for Boulogne wc
(#243 not in catalog)
244 In the Grampians wc
245 North Devon cliffs wc
1907 F6, Sherbrooke
78 Wind and rain at the Great Glacier, Selkirks $250
79 Lilacs $200
1908 52 Rain storm on the Great Glacier
53 On the cliffs of Monhegan, Maine
1909M 49 On the Cod Banks of the Atlantic
50 Purple gloom of evening, Selkirks
51 Morning near the Great Glacier, Selkirks
1909N 52 Wind and rain, Selkirks, BC
53 Fog clearing, hauling a trawl, New Brunswick
1910 67 Fog coming in with the tide, Monhegan Island
68 White Head, Monhegan Island
1910 S2, Liverpool
44 A valley of the Rockies, rain
45 Evening in a New Brunswick harbour
1911 60 Hills of the Saguenay
61 St Lawrence near Tadousac
62 Sunlit peaks

1912 87 Plastered Rocks
88 Nearly high tide
1912 S3, Winnipeg
54 The restless sea
55 Evening, valley of the Selkirks wc
1913 109 Ledges
110 Sunlit rocks
111 Gloucester rocks wc
112 At low water wc
113 A foot of the cliffs wc
114 Ledges wc
1914 77 The seaworn coast of Monhegan
78 Temples of commerce
79 Part of the Hermits, Selkirks, BC wc
80 White Head, Monhegan Island, Maine wc
1914 S4, Winnipeg
48 Sunlit rocks $500
49 Gloucester rocks wc $75
50 Ledges wc $75
1914 S5, Patriotic Fund
15 Nearly low tide illus
1915 82 A rugged coast
83 Fishermen's property
84 The seventh wave
85 Part of the Hermit Range wc
1916 89 White Head illus
90 Cod Bankers ◊AGO◊
91 Mananna wc
92 Sea fog wc
1918A 65 Anchored for the night illus 1918N-66 illus
66 In the haven
67 How the sea comes in wc
68 Surf wc
1918N 67 In the haven, Monhegan
68 Study of incoming tide wc
69 The seventh wave wc
1919 59 Trawlers riding at anchor illus
60 Morning fog, clearing up
1920 101 Fountains of the deep
102 Lobster Cove
103 Reefs
1921 59 The blue boat
60 Plastered Rocks, Monhegan, Maine 1922-77 S6-27
1922 74 The end of the storm S6-25
75 A chasm in the cliffs
76 Hazy day, Monhegan Island illus S6-26
1923 48 At the mouth of the ravine
49 Late afternoon ◊NGC◊
1924 59 Fog burning out
60 Sunshine and shadow
61 Summer time by the sea illus
1925 76 Mount Marpole, Rockys
77 A cove in the cliffs illus
78 Shadow of the cliffs, afternoon
79 Clearing after a blow
DW 1915 The Pulpit Rock 26 3/4 x 35 3/4 T51-18

GAGNON, CHARLES
23 May 1934, Montreal B CC2 M
ARCA 1970 Council Painter
Addr: 1971/79, Montreal
1971 Le 8ième jour film screened 31 Mar

GAGNON, CLARENCE ALPHONSE
8 Nov 1881, Montreal 5 Jan 1942, Montreal AGO B CC1 EC M Mo12 NGC TB1/2 W78
ARCA 1909 RCA 1922 Council Painter
Addr: 1902, 25 Melbourne Ave, Westmount, Que; 1904, Paris; 1905, Montreal; 1906-8, c/o Henry Morgan & Co, Montreal; 1909M, King's Hall, 591 St Catherine St, Montreal; 1909N-12, 9 rue Falguière, Paris; 1914-15, c/o Art Association of Montreal; 1916, c/o Art Club, 51 Victoria St, Montreal; 1918A-19, 9 rue Falguière, Paris; 1920-22, c/o Art Association of Montreal; 1923-4, Baie St Paul, Que; 1925-7, 9 rue Falguière, Paris; 1928-37, Paris; 1938-42, Montreal
1902 69 The willows
70 Road through the woods
71 Still life
1904 64 Oxen ploughing F4-30 ◊MMFA◊
65 Weaving rag carpets F4-31
66 Winter
67 The old barn F4-32
1905 72 Twilight, Luxembourg Gardens
73 Outside walls of Tangiers
74 Interior
75 Old woman reading ◊MMFA◊
1906 90 Autumn morning
91 Autumn, Pont de l'Arche ◊MMFA◊
92 Old trees
93 A frugal meal F5-63 $300 F6-81 ◊NGC◊
1906 F5, Halifax
62 Early morning $200

64 Evening $500
1907 74 Spanish dancer
75 Moonlight across the valley
76 Criqueboeuf, on the Seine
77 Freheuse, on the Seine
1907 F6, Sherbrooke
80 Spanish dancing girl $100
82 Early morning, Normandy $500
83 Evening, Normandy $500
84 Six etchings, $10 each
1908 56 A Japanese fantasy
57 Street scene
1909M 54 Two plages, Parame et St Malo ◊BAG◊ (Two 'flags' mispr)
55 Early winter, moonrise S2-46
1909N 54 Early morning, autumn Moret
55 Château Gaillard, Les Andelys
1910 69 Laurentians, twilight
70 Street scene, moonlight
71 Winter, Baie St Paul
72 Grey day, Baie St Paul
73-76 Nine etchings
1910 S2, Liverpool
47 A mountain stream
1911 63 Moonlight, St Eustache
64 Autumn evening, Baie St Paul
65 Autumn afternoon, La Selle-sur-Seine
66 Early morning mist, Pont de l'Arche
202 Group of six etchings
1912 89 The Campo, Siena
90 Late winter afternoon in the Alps
91 Early morning mist, Château Gaillard
92 St Malo from the cliffs of St Briac
93 Late summer afternoon, Les Andelys
1912 S3, Winnipeg
56 Les deux plages, Parame et St Malo
57 Autumn scene, Baie St Paul
58 The Seine, at St Mammes
59 Twilight in the Laurentians
174-5 Eleven etchings
176 Old windmill, St Briac etch
177 Isola San Burano, Venice etch
178 La Salute, Venice etch
179 Courtyard of San Gregorio, Venice etch
180 Une rue à Nemours etch
181 Old windmill, Picardy etch ◊AGO◊
1914 81 Old houses, winter ◊NGC◊
82 Village street, morning, winter
83 Early Canadian winter scene
84 Twilight in the Laurentians, winter
1914 S5, Patriotic Fund
7 Early morning sun illus
1915 86 Late afternoon sun, winter 1916-93
87 Lake of Geneva
1916 94 Early October moonrise
95 The wayside Cross, autumn illus ◊NGC◊
96 Village street, winter
1918A 69 Late evening sun, Venice illus
70 Early morning in the Laurentians
71 The train, winter scene
1918N 70 Evening, Siena
71 A stream in the Laurentians
72 Mountain landscape
1919 61 March in the birch woods ◊AGO◊
62 Winter evening in the Laurentians
63 Laurentian homestead, winter 1925-80 ◊NGC◊
201 In the northern woods wd cut col
1920 104 New moon, winter night in the Laurentians
105 October landscape
106 The farm on the hillside, winter afternoon
107 Peasants crossing on ice bridge, Quebec
1921 61 A silent stream of the north
62 Winter afternoon sun illus
63 The pond in October DW 1923 27 x 37 T51-19 The pond, October
1922 78 Indian summer S6-28
79 Early morning in March
1923 50 Early spring morning in the Laurentian wilds
51 A lonely village of the north shore ◊AGO◊
1924 62 Evening on the north shore illus ◊NGC◊

63 Schooner in the ice pack
64 Winter in the Laurentian highlands
1927 66 Quebec village, winter illus (NGC)
67 Horse races in winter, Quebec (AGO)
68 Grey day, Laurentian village street
69 Cloud shadows, winter landscape
1939 75 The ice harvest, Quebec $900
1939 F11, New York
24 La maison rose 27 x 19 nfs
1954 22 Retro Sec. Lonely village on the St Lawrence (AGO)

GAGNON, WILLFORD A.
Addr: 1933, 2039 Mansfield St, Montreal
1933 73 Palais Ugoccioni, Place de la Seigneurie, Florence sketch wc

GALAND, LEON LAURENT French
18 Apr 1872, Montpellier, France
14 Nov 1960, Clichy la Garenne, France B TB1/2
Addr: 1918N, Paris
1918N 73 Les vedettes illus

GALBRAITH, ELIZABETH ROBERTA (BETTY) (Mrs Cornell)
15 Jan 1916, Montreal M
1961 25 Fin d'hiver 22 x 34 $200

GALE, WILLIAM English
1823, London, Eng d 1909 B DBA H TB
Addr: 1895, c/o R. Gagen, King St, Lakefield, Ont
1895 45 The pasha's wife
46 My prisoner or my guest? Caged

GALLAGHER, SEARS American
30 Apr 1869, Boston 1930, Boston AAA29 B F TB
Addr: 1918A, 486 Bolton St, Boston
1918A 220 Ship yard, Camden, Mass etch
221 T wharf, Boston, Mass etch

GALLOP, JOHN
1970 167 Poster, Klaus Nienhamper Limited
168 Menus, service brochures, The Sherway Inn
169 Mailer, A is for Aardvark
1971 27G Poster, Interiors International Limited

GANGNON, PATRICIA (Mrs Grimanis)
b 1937
Addr: 1976, Toronto
1970 170 Booklet, Brock University Calendar, 1969-1970
1976 S12, Montreal
120 La Superfrancofête book/livre illus Grimanis

GARDINER, FRANK G.
see THORNTON, PETER, 1953-1965

GARDINER, J.W. RAWSON
H
Addr: 1896-99, Molson Bank Chambers, Montreal; 1902, Temple Bldg, Montreal; 1907, Montreal; 1910, Quebec Bank Bldg, Montreal
1896 274 Residence, Dorchester St, Montreal
1899 251 Office building, Montreal des
1902 246 College buildings, Grande Ligne des
247 Electric light fixtures des
1907 315 Residence, J. Gardner Thompson, Esq, Côte des Neiges Rd
316 Summer cottage, Dr Stirling, Lake St Louis
1910 211 Carmichael Memorial Church

GARDINER, PERCIVAL MACDONALD
1950 43 Mill wheel 16 x 20 $100

GARDNER, EDWIN ALEXANDER
14 Jul 1902, Pembroke, Ont
ARCA 1955 Sr 1968 Architect
Addr: 1956-71/79, Ottawa
1963 112 Commonwealth Airforce Memorial

GARNER, ALEC JOHN
c 1900, Southampton, Eng M
1939 76 Looking back from Morine Lake wc $50
77 The Ten Peaks, Morine Lake wc $50

GARRETT, ROBERT MICHAEL

19 Sep 1931, Winchester, Eng
RCA(e) 1978 Architect
Addr: 1979, Vancouver

GARSIDE, THOMAS HILTON
16 Jan 1906, Duckinfield, Ches, Eng
18 Jan 1980 M
ARCA 1945 Painter
Addr: 1937, 1682 Le Caron St, Montreal; 1945-62, Montreal; 1963-71/79, Westmount, Que
1937 78 Portrait of a lady $150
1938 74 Barns in afternoon sunlight, Ville Lasalle $150
75 Barn interior $100
1939 78 The green glass $50
79 Late summer near Georgeville $150
1940 55 Sunlit hills, St Jean de Matha, Que $150
1942 41 Sanguinet Street from my window $150
1943 44 Spring break-up $300 T44-16
45 March afternoon $250
1944 55 Reflection, Rouge River $500 T45-16
1945 80 Winter's end, Rouge River illus $750
81 The ice cutters $750 T46-16
1946 45 Laurentian village nfs
1947 59 Autumn $500
60 River bend, Mont Tremblant $500
1948 64 The Devil's River, Mont Tremblant, Quebec nfs
65 The wharf, Bic, Quebec $750
1950 44 Panorama of Bic, Quebec 30 x 28 nfs
1953 25 Still life nfs

GARWOOD, AUDREY ELAINE (Mrs H.R. Hosie)
7 Jul 1927, Toronto WWA73
ARCA 1972 Print maker
Addr: 1979, Berkeley, Cal
1954 33 The diggers 36 x 28 $300
34 Train 38 x 24 illus $300
1955 33 Game illus $150
34 Identity $200
1958 32 Red in a tree claw growing $150
1960 32 The actress 60 x 48 $500

GAS, JOHN
Addr: 1976, Aylmer, Que
1976 S12, Montreal
119 Canada book, Expo '70 English and Japanese versions illus

GASCON, GILLES
1971 Québec en silence film screened 31 Mar

GASS, MARJORIE EARLE
1889, Saint John 1928, Montreal
M NGC
Addr: 1916, 4339 Westmount Ave, Westmount, Que; 1921, 50 Chesterfield Ave, Westmount, Que; 1922-6, 414 Mackay St, Montreal
1916 97 Landscape
98 Impression
1921 64 Little wayside cottage
1922 80 Landscape, Georgeville, Quebec S6-29
81 On the hillside
1923 52 The hillside ◊NGC◊
53 Summer landscape
1925 81 Old house, west of Saint John, NB
1926 48 The harbour, Saint John
49 Fishing nets

GATHE, ASBJORN R.
see THORNTON, PETER, 1960-1965

GAUCHER, YVES
3 Jan 1934, Montreal AGO B CC2 M WWA78
ARCA 1970 Council Painter
Addr: 1971/79, Montreal
1971 12 IX 1970. 48 x 114 nfs

GAUTHIER, JEANNETTE
1943 46 Nature morte $100
47 Intérieur canadien $75
1945 82 Légumes frais $150 T46-17
83 Cyclamen $75

GAUTHIER, JOACHIM GEORGE
20 Aug 1897, North Bay, Ont CNS40 M WWA47
ARCA 1946 RCA 1974 Sr 1968 Painter
Addr: 1932-6, 184 Ranleigh Ave, Toronto; 1938/1947-71/79, Toronto
1932 64 March wc $150
1936 81 In the garden illus $300 T37-27
1938 76 Winter's mantle $350
1938 S8, Toronto
Sampson, Matthews Limited
290 McCormick's, Krackers carton

296-7 Shirriff's jam jar labels
1939 F11, New York
26 Stormy day 30 x 36 $300
1940 56 Northern lake shore $150 T41-18
1942 42 Nellie Lake $200 T43-13
1946 45 Northern autumn $500 T47-20
1947 61 Conflagration $200
1948 66 Snow-bound road $350
1949 34 Pin rouille $250
1950 45 Rusted pines 30 x 36 $250
1951 37 Palmer Rapids, Madawaska River wc $175
1952 32 Palmer Rapids wc $150
33 Fast waters $350
1953 26 Stormy sky, Yantha Lake $350
1955 35 Yantha Valley $500
1959 30 Stormy sky, Barry's Bay 30 x 36 $350
DW 1974 Tamaracks in autumn

GDANSKI, R.C.
1970 104 Coin sorter, Nadex Industries

GEDDES, FRANCES MILDRED (Mrs)
b 1888, England
Addr: 1918A, 62 Laing St, Toronto; 1918N-19, 10 1/2 King St W, Toronto
1918A 72 Dolce far niente
1918N 74 Chinese fantasy
75 Aileen
1919 64 The letter

GEESON, JEAN EARLE
Addr: 1904, Toronto
1904 224 Double peonies wc

GELDART, MARY E.
H
1898 43 Study of grapes
44 Study of plums and brass pot

GEMMELL, JOHN
1851, Ayrshire, Scot 28 Mar 1915, Toronto
ARCA 1880-13 Architect
Addr: 1880-13, Toronto
see also Smith, James Avon, 1881

GENDRON MANUFACTURING CO, LIMITED
Addr: 1938, Toronto
1938 S8, Toronto
117-21 Perambulator. Child's wagon. Carrier. Kiddy car. Rocking horse illus

GENDRON, PIERRE
3 Jul 1934, Montreal CC1 M TB3
1963 25 Percaline $275
26 Les baladins illus $125

GENERAL STEEL WARES LIMITED
Addr: 1938, Toronto
1938 S8, Toronto
#122-38 Stainless enamelled kitchen ware
122-5 Ivory and blue: milk or rice boiler, colander, oval roll-rim dish pan, covered sauce pan
126-30 Ivory and black: seamless tea kettle, shallow sauce pan, seamless coffee percolator, with stainless steel cover, oval roaster
131-4 Ivory and green: seamless mixing bowl, English style tea pot, London kettle, lipped sauce pan
135-8 Ivory and red: seamless tea kettle, potato pot, seamless coffee percolator, sink strainer
one illus

GENEREUX, MARIE ARLINE
6 Feb 1897, Quebec
Addr: 1931, 16 Saunders St, Quebec
1931 87 Portrait of my sister pastel

GENEST, PIERRE M.A.
1844, St Joseph de Lévis, Que
1901, Quebec H
Addr: 1886, Quebec
1886 F1a, London, Eng
2025, artist number
Miss F plaster bust
Panel, 4 medallion studies and portraits ter cot
Finland artist, portrait ter cot

GENTLEMAN, WALLY
1970 0-0 film screened 12 Feb
1971 This virbant land film screened 21 Apr

GENUSH, LUBA (Mrs Gloor)
9 Sep 1924, Odessa M TB3
Addr: 1976, Montreal

1971 13 White abstraction 51 x 36 $300
1976 S12, Montreal
158 Dwellings photo & styro-foam 36 x 72 illus

GERIN-LAJOIE, GUY
6 May 1928, Montreal WWA76
ARCA 1970 Council Architect
Addr: 1971/79, Montreal
see also Papineau, L.J, 1976

GERMAN, JOHN
1970 171 Portfolio, 5 woodcuts of Chateauguay
1971 28G Symbol for transportation, A & F Bailliargeon Express Inc

GERSON, WOLFGANG
18 Mar 1916, Hamburg
RCA(e) 1975 Architect
Addr: 1979, Vancouver

GERSOVITZ, SARAH VALERIE GAMER (Mrs Ben Gersovitz)
5 Sep 1920, Montreal M WWA73
ARCA 1971 RCA 1976 Print maker
Addr: 1971/79, Montreal
1961 35 Young woman with long hair dry pt 21 1/2 x 13 illus $30
36 Antedeluvians col linocut 15 1/2 x 15 1/2 $35
1963 27 Council etch & aqua $35
1964J 24 The idol etch 13 x 8 illus $45
25 Le temps perdu etch 13 x 11 $55
1964N 21 The game etch 20 x 12 1/2 $50
1965 26 Inmate etch 21 x 10 1/2 $50
1967 20 Sidewalk artists etch 14 x 15 1/2 $75
1968 21 Yellow waters, yellow skies 20 x 28 $125
1970 23 A coming to terms 22 x 15 1/2 $175
DW 1976 Silk and wood I print

GERVAIS, JACK
1948 67 Autumn woodlands, Lachute, Quebec wc $40

GERVAIS, LISE
2 Sep 1933, St Césaire, Rouville Co, Que CC1 M
1964N 22 Les plaines infinies 60 x 72 illus $900

GESNE, A. DE French
1882 321 Hunting at Fontainebleau (loan)

GIANOVETTI, PAUL
Addr: 1976, Toronto
1976 S12, Montreal
177 Shadow of self photo cyanotype 14 x 11 illus

GIBB, DAVID ALEXANDER
b 1884 24 Mar 1971, Galt, Ont M W78
Addr: 1908-9, Galt, Ont; 1912-13, 44 Park Ave, Galt, Ont
1908 54 September pastoral
55 Morning in the woods
1909M 46 The new sown field
1912 94 The open fields 1913-116
95 The hickory tree, November
1913 115 The way through the woods
117 The line fence, October S4-51 $30

GIBSON, WILLIAM ALLAN
9 Sep 1925, Detroit
see HELMER, D'ARCY, 1971

GIFFORD, WILLIAM BRENT
27 Sep 1940, New Westminster, BC
1967 21 Activity on red $500

GIGNAC, GILBERT L.
Addr: 1976, Ottawa
1976 S12, Montreal
18 Portrait de la famille Séguin 48 x 96 oval illus

GIGUERE, E. LOUISE DE MONTIGNY (Mrs Giguère)
28 Apr 1878, La Prairie, Que
Addr: 1920, 67 Ste Famille St, Montreal; 1922, 717 Shuter St, Apt 14, Montreal; 1924, 64 Jeanne Mance St, Montreal; 1925, 15 Durocher St, Montreal; 1929-31, 8248 St Denis St, Montreal; 1933, 7944 St Denis St, Montreal; 1935, 8137 de Gaspé St, Montreal
1920 108 A Vermont girl
265 Madame V. Roberge plaster
1922 214 Florence Davidson plaster bust
1924 233 L'épave plaster
1925 256 Le pas de trois bronze

257 Colons plâtre
1929 239 La balançoire clay
1930 185 Hon Carine Mackay Wilson. First woman appointed to Senate of Canada sculp $300
1931 310 Jean et Aline plâtre $150
311 L'adolescent et la chimère plaster $500
1933 255 Rev Sister St Joseph de la Nativité sculp $150
256 Etude d'enfant sculp $100
1935 278 Madame R, portrait plaster $150
279 Etude de jeune homme plaster $150

GILBERT, JOHN MARTIN
7 May 1926, New York
1971 29G Safety poster, Workmen's Compensation Board of BC

GILBERT, WILLIAM HERBERT
19 Dec 1926, Regina CC2 M TB3
1967 22 Galaxie 24 x 48 $150

GILES, TREVOR P.H.
1971 6I Display systems, Fedor Incorporated. T.P.H. Giles, Julius Fedor

GILHOOLY, DAVID JAMES
15 Apr 1943, Auburn, Cal IO WWA73
RCA(e) 1979 Sculptor
Addr: 1979, Calgary

GILL, CHARLES IGNACE ADELARD
21 Oct 1871, Sorel, Que 16 Oct 1918, Montreal CC1 EC M W78
Addr: 1899, 12 Place d'Armes, Montreal; 1902-7, Montreal; 1914, 1263 de Lorimier Ave, Montreal
1890 34 Red onions $15
35 Dead birds, study nfs
1899 59 Miss R.G.
60 The lake
1902 72 Honeymoon
73, 74, 75 Nenuphar (three, same title)
1904 68 Portrait
1904 F4, St Louis
33 Portrait
1906 87 The problem
1907 78 L'anse St Jean
79 Time and beauty
1914 S5, Patriotic Fund
66 An old artist illus

GILL, MINNIE (or MAY)
fl 1897-05 H
Addr: 1899, Lennoxville, Que
1899 60a Tor in the Laurentians

GILL, WILLIAM
fl 1881-90 H
Addr: 1881-6, Halifax
1881 8 Moonlight, Boston harbour wc $12
58 Wind blowing, waters flowing wc $12
83 A March picture wc $12
1886 Fla, London, Eng
1998 artist number
Edge of dyke lands, Grand Pré
Entrance to the village of Grand Pré
Uncultivated corner of Grand Pré

GILLESPIE, WALTER
Addr: 1938, Montreal
1938 S8, Toronto
139 Original drawing for Holt Renfrew
140 Newspaper advertisement from the above

GILMOUR (Mrs)
H
1885 216 Cottage near Hartlebury wc $12

GILMOUR, H.M.
Addr: 1933, 465 Argyle Ave, Westmount, Que
1933 74 Mr H.de M. Molson

GILMOUR, M.
Addr: 1932, 3480 Côte des Neiges Rd, Montreal
1932 65 Breton girl $300

GILVERSON, QUEENIE VIOLA (Mrs C.H. Sorley)
1890, Toronto
Addr: 1915-16, 21 Roxborough Dr, Toronto; 1918, Dominion Bank Chambers, Bloor & Sherbourne, Toronto; 1919-20, 21 Roxborough Dr, Toronto; 1922, 10 Garfield Ave, Toronto; 1923, 240 Dupont St, Toronto
1915 88 The story
1916 99 The spinner
1918A 292 Fairy tales
293 Winter scene
292-3, Trustees, National

Gallery of Canada, Travelling Scholarship Competition
1918N 76 Sunshine and butterflies
77 In old Salem
1919 65 The little blue bird 1920-110
66 The old mill stream
1920 109 Afterglow
1922 Mrs Queenie Sorley, to 1923
191 The intruders
1923 159 Winter

GIOVANELLI, P.
Addr: 1916, 428 Bleury St, Montreal
1916 244 Neptune's daughters marble

GIRARD, CLAUDE
30 Nov 1938, Chicoutimi, Que
RCA(e) 1979 Painter
Addr: 1979, Montreal

GIRARD, MARCEL
8 Jun 1936, Montreal
RCA(e) 1973 Industrial designer
Addr: 1979, Town of Mount Royal, Que

GIRVIN, GEORGE
Addr: 1920, 3359 Bloor St W, Toronto
1920 111 Woodland
112 Birches

GISSING, ROLAND
14 May 1895, Broadway, Eng 29 Sep 1967, Okotoks, Alta M W78
Addr: 1934, Ghest River, Alta; 1935, P O Box 165, Cochrane, Alta
1934 72 Summer clouds $60
1935 88 October morning $150

GIUNTA, JOSEPH
2 Oct 1911, Montreal
Addr: 1937, 7112 Drolet St, Montreal
1937 79 Flowers $125
1945 84 Fishing boats, Rockport, Mass $300
1946 47 Fishing schooners, Gloucester, Mass $400
1947 62 Cold winter day $500
1948 68 Winter in port, Gloucester, Mass $700
1967 23 Composition #2 drwg 36 x 48 $300
port: sculp, by U. Bruni, 1939-242

GLADSTONE, GERALD
7 Jan 1929, Toronto AGO B CC2 IO M TB3
RCA(e) 1974 Council Sculptor
Addr: 1979, Toronto
1963 83 Optical orbital metal $900
84 Time space metal $1,700
1964N 91 Small galaxy welded steel
92 Novae welded steel

GLAZEBROOK, HUGH DE TWENEBROKES
Mar 1855, London, Eng English
6 May 1937, London, Eng B DBA G H RA TB2/3 WBA
1888 174 Portrait Hugh de J. Glazebrook mispr

GLEICHEN-RUSSWURM, HEINRICH LUDWIG VON (Baron) German
25 Oct 1836, Greifenstein, Bonnland
9 Jul 1901, Weimar B TB
1882 304 Evening landscape (loan)

GLEN, EDWARD RANDOLPH
1887, London, Ont 4 Feb 1963, London, Ont AGO
Addr: 1912, 252 1/2 Dundas St, London, Ont; 1913-30, 718 Colborne St, London, Ont
1912 96 Le Pont Neuf
97 The Paris girl
98 The gay musician
99 Costume study
1913 118 French flower market, Paris
1914 85 Sunny afternoon, Beaupré, Quebec S5-46 illus
86 Knitting
1915 89 Canadians at St Julien retaking the trenches
90 Study
1916 100 The absent one
101 October afternoon, Quebec
1918N 78 November twilight
1921 65 Fish girl, Etaples, France
1922 82 Le déjeuner S6-30
1923 54 November on the Thames
55 Normandy twilight
1925 82 A suburb of Florence, Italy
1929 66 The blind musician, Algeria $250
67 Une jeune mauresque, Biskra $100
1930 59 Portrait

GLYDE, HENRY GEORGE
18 Jun 1906, Luton, Bedfs, Eng
AGO CC2 CWW79 M NGC WWA47

ARCA 1942 RCA 1949 Painter
Addr: 1942-5, Calgary; 1946-65, Edmonton; 1966, Port Washington, B.C: 1967-71, Edmonton; 1979, Port Washington, BC
1940 57 Self portrait $200
1941 64 Crucifixion illus $700 T42-16
65 Hilda $200
1942 43 Moving in illus $200 T43-14
44 Portrait
1943 48 Edmonton, 1943 nfs
1944 56 Yukon River, Whitehorse $200 T45-17
57 Manoeuvres, Calgary illus $200 T45-18
1945 85 Yukon $200
86 Alaska Highway, northern British Columbia $200 T46-18
1946 48 Saskatchewan River illus $250 T47-21
1948 69 Vegreville, Albèrta $250
1951 38 Road below Rundle, Canmore temp $400
1951 Travelling exhibit
20 Miners' cottages, Canmore, Alberta DW 1950 temp & oil 30 x 33 3/4 1954 Retro Sec 51
1952 34 Aftermath $500
1955 36 Bankhead $650
1957 27 End of the prairies $300
1958 35 Nude $400

GNASS, PETER ERNST
20 Mar 1936, Rostock, Germany
RCA(e) 1976 Sculptor
Addr: 1979, Montreal

GODFREY, WILLIAM FREDERICK GEORGE
12 Jun 1884, London, Eng 2 Mar 1971, Toronto AGO CWW64 M
Addr: 1923-4, 40 Wood St, Toronto; 1925-8, 186 Fern Ave, Toronto; 1932, 3362A Yonge St, Toronto; 1935, 131 Lawrence Ave W, Toronto; 1937, 108 Moore Ave, Toronto
1923 205 Dusk, Scarboro Bluffs drwg
1924 65 Low tide, Victoria, BC pastel
66 The hilltop oak wc
1925 83 The Old Curiosity Shop
289 The freighter pencil
290 The waterfront, Toronto pencil
1926 50 St Maurice Street, Montreal, winter wc
1927 70 Old Toronto, Adelaide Street, wc
301 Maison de Montcalm, Québec dry pt
302 Hay Market, Montreal dry pt
1928 205 St Maurice Street, Montreal, winter block pr $8
1932 66 Downtown, Montreal wc $200
1935 319 The deserted lime kiln wd cut $10
320 Rustic bridge, Mount Hamilton, Ont wd cut $10
1937 313 Where field and forest meet wd cut $15
314 Summer sunshine wd cut $12

GODWIN, EDWARD WILLIAM (TED)
13 Aug 1933, Calgary AGO CC1 M
RCA(e) 1974 Painter
Addr: 1979, Regina

GOETZ, PETER HENRY
8 Sep 1917, Slavgorod, Siberia
CWW79 IO M WWA56
1958 37 Saint John, NB $150
1959 31 Halifax harbour 22 x 30 nfs
32 Red masts of New London 22 x 30 $150
1961 37 Petty Harbour, Newfoundland wc 22 x 30 $175
38 Château Frontenac wc 22 x 30 $175
1963 31 On the hill $200
1965 27 Florenze wc 26 x 40 $350

GOLD, ALAN
13 Aug 1930, Ottawa
1963 32 Margaret 24 x 36 illus $500

GOLDBERG, REGINA see SEIDEN, REGINA

GOLDHAMER, CHARLES
21 Aug 1903, Philadelphia AGO CNS40 CWW79 IO M TB2 WWA47
Addr: 1926, 183 Roncesvalles Ave, Toronto; 1930-6, 1 Starr Ave, Toronto
1926 176 Shipping etch
177 Masquerade programme des
1930 60 Wash day, Manitoulin Island wc illus $100
204 Fisherman's shack pen drwg $20
1931 390 Waterfall, northern Ontario drwg $35
391 Brook, Manitoulin Island drwg $35

1932 235 Meadowvale drwg $25
236 Trees drwg $25
1933 289 Farm house, Meadowvale drwg $25
290 Vacant house, Meadowvale drwg $25
291 Ontario village litho $10
292 Fishing sheds, Georgian Bay litho $10
1935 89 Village of St Urbain, Quebec wc $75 T36-28
90 Interior of work shop, St Urbain, Quebec wc $75
1936 82 M Arthur Côte, La Rémie, Québec wc $75
83 M Cliff Simard, La Rémie, Québec wc $75 T37-28
1940 58 Baie St Paul, Québec wc $75
1941 S9, Toronto
24 Meadowvale, Ontario $45

GOLDIE, CHARLES A. English
fl 1901-12 DBA RA
Addr: 1907, St Servan, France
1907 246 Berceuse du rouet
247 La vielle Nanon
248 Vieux puits, Morbihan
249 Ancien manoir

GOLDSMITH, SIDNEY CHARLES JOSEPH
29 Jan 1922, Toronto M TB3
1952 115 Pièta monot $35
1953 27 Man in a boat illus $150 ◊NGC◊
1954 35 Horse and rider 43 x 26 1/2 $200
1957 28 Rescue $150
1958 36 Man and boat $200
1959 33 Table with grapes 36 x 36 $175
1964N 23 Triumphant figure 48 x 30 $300
1965 28 Configuration with circles 48 x 36 $300

GONTARD, LUDWIG VON
19 Oct 1922, Berlin
1954 36 Midnight sun 26 x 12 1/2 $90

COOD, CATHY
Addr: 1976, Toronto
1976 S12, Montreal
71 Flexible sculpture foam rubber & chicken wire/caoutchouc mousse et treillis 84 x 48 x 48 illus

GOODALL, JOHN
1947 63 Mountain road, Baie St Paul wc $100

GOODIER, MARINA (Mrs Norman Goodier)
11 Feb 1906, St Petersburg
Addr: 1932, 51 Howland Ave, Toronto
1932 67 Still life $40

GOODSTONE, ALBERT J.
1939 80 Souvenir de Moscou $200

GOODWIN, BETTY ROODISH (Mrs Martin Goodwin)
19 Mar 1923, Montreal M
1964N 24 Falling figures 36 x 42 $395
1965 29 Edge of night 40 x 50 $400
1971 14 Vest #2 22 x 28 illus $110

GORANSON, PAUL ALEXANDER
27 Apr 1911, Vancouver M WWA47
1940 170 Purse seiners dry pt $10
1941 234 The artist's father dry pt $15

GORDANEER, JAMES EDWARD
14 Apr 1933, Toronto M
ARCA 1972 Painter
Addr: 1979, Victoria
1955 37 Elora $100
1958 38 Autumn growth $250
1959 34 Olive grove, Ibiza 23 1/2 x 36 $150
1960 33 And where no gold is 47 1/2 x 58 $300
1964J 26 Warrior's retreat 40 x 36 $300
1965 30 Black and green 48 x 48 $350

GORDON, FREDERICK CHARLES S.
30 Jun 1856, Cobourg, Ont 20 Mar 1924, Westfield, NJ AAA24 B F H TB
ARCA 1887-92 Painter
Addr: 1884-92, Brockville, Ont
1884 9 Study
58 Portrait group
74 Portrait
1885 64 Among the water lilies $150
99 Washing $50
108 Apples $20
160 The hammock $100 1886-141
1886 149 The painter, from a mirror 1887-77

150 Washing day $50 Fla-1999
196 May $150 Selected for Fla not in Fla catalogue
1887 38 Reverie 1888-195 $35
59 Among the water lilies nfs
93 Sporting news $125

GORDON, HENRY BAULD
30 Sep 1854, Toronto 4 Mar 1951, Toronto CWW10 Mo98/12
ARCA 1880-96 Architect
Addr: 1880-94, Toronto; 1895, 26 King St E, Toronto; 1896, Toronto
1880 356 Fraser Institute, Montreal
361 Western Insurance Company, Toronto office
367 Queen's College, Kingston. Perspective view
1883 Gordon & Helliwell, to 1895
360 Parliament Building des
1891 203 Residence, W. Goulding, Esq
207 Residence, J.K. Fisken, Esq
1895 31A Church of Messiah, Toronto
32A Town Hall, Orillia
33A Queen's College, Kingston
34A Library building, Milwaukee des
35A Rectory, Church of Messiah, Toronto
36A, House, Queen's Park, Toronto
37A House, Rosedale Road
38A House, Rusholme Road
39A Summer cottage, Kingston Heights

GORDON, HORTENSE CROMPTON MATTICE
(Mrs John Sloan Gordon)
24 Nov 1887, Hamilton, Ont 6 Nov 1961, Hamilton, Ont AGO CC2 CWW58 M W78
ARCA 1930 Sr 1958 Painter
Addr: 1909N, Hamilton, Ont; 1923-37, 101 Spadina Ave, Hamilton, Ont; 1938-61, Hamilton, Ont
1909N 97 Early morning in the cornfield Mattice
1923 56 Study of tulips
1924 67 Overlooking the harbour, Gloucester
1925 84 The float, Gloucester
85 Landscape, Dogtown Hills, Massachusetts
1926 51 From the float, Gloucester
1927 71 La cour
303 Textile des
304 Wallpaper des
1928 53 Market place, Etaples, France $200
1929 68 Early morning $200
263 Printed textile des $75
1930 61 Garden flowers $150
62 Jean Brown's wharf $150
205 Printed textile des $75
1931 88 St Brelades Church and Fishermen's Chapel, Jersey $150
89 Old buildings, Folkstone, England $100
1932 68 Mount Orgueil Castle, Jersey $150 Orgueuil mispr
69 Mist rolling in, St Aubine, Jersey $150
1933 75 Early morning, Gorey Castle, C.I. (Dr Wm. Carrick) T34-27
1934 73 L'Tacq, Jersey, Channel Islands $150 T35-24
1935 91 From Devil's Elbow, overlooking the Alleghanny Valley, Pa $125
92 Barges loading sugar, Barbadoes $150
93 Old Norman mill, Jersey wc $150 T36-29
1937 80 Early thaw, near Hamilton $100 T38-18
1938 77 The mill settlement, Burk's Falls $150
1939 81 Point à Pitre, Guadeloupe $100
1941 S9, Toronto
25 The market place, Etaples, France $150
1946 49 Light housekeeping wc illus $150 (AGO)
1947 64 Space, form and tension $200
65 Ontario peaches $100
1948 70 Abstract forms, studio interior $500
1949 35 The Japanese print $200
1950 46 Vertical arrangement 30 x 22 $200
1951 39 Studio accoutrements $300
1953 28 Study in space $100 1954-37 26 x 20 illus
1954 38 Studio impressions 30 x 22 $150
1955 38 Abstraction $100
1957 29 Ribbon building

1958 39 Wharf
1959 25 The wharf, abstraction 30 x 25 $200

GORDON, JOHN SLOAN
6 Jul 1868, Bratford, Ont 1940, Hamilton, Ont CWW36 M NGC TB3
ARCA 1923-39 Sr 1938 Painter
Addr: 1906-15, 28 King St W, Hamilton; 1923-37, 101 Spadina Ave, Hamilton; 1938-9, Hamilton
1906 F5, Halifax
65 Early snow $50 F.S. Gordon mispr
1909N 57 Old Kirby mill, Brantford ◊NGC◊
58 Gloaming
1910 S2, Liverpool
48 First snow ◊AGH◊
1914 87 A Venetian night S5-38 illus
1915 91 In Padua
92 Pines
1923 57 Dundurn Castle, Hamilton, time of Sir Allan McNab
58 Interior of St Etienne du Mont, Paris wc
1924 68 Nocturne vert
69 Study wc
1931 90 The coast of Maine at Friendship wc $125
91 On the Maine coast wc (Dr D. McGregor)
1932 70 Near Dundas wc 1933-76 $200 T34-28
1933 293 Study of rocks, Maine chalk $25
1934 74 The gateway at Longpont, France $150
1935 94 Idyll, illustration wc $50
95 The Barbican, Sandwich, Kent, England $300
1936 84 Green night wc $25
1937 81 Mont Orgueil Castle, Jersey, CI wc nfs Orgeuil mispr
1938 78 Figure in sunlight $200
port: bust, by J. Sloan, 1924-44

GORDON, M.C. (Miss)
H
1891 56 Apple blossoms

GORE, MILLICENT (Mrs P.H. Anderson)
fl 1893-09 DBA
Addr: 1905, 278 Grand Allée, Quebec; 1909M, c/o James Wilson Co, Ottawa
1905 83 The cares of a family 1909M-47
84 On strike
85 Thames barges
1909M 48 From the Ramparts, Quebec

GORESKO, J.
1945 87 Still life $150

GORESKO, W.J.
1946 50 Pleasure of youth $500 T47-22

GORMAN, RICHARD BORTHWICK
20 Dec 1935, Ottawa AGO M
RCA(e) 1976 Painter
Addr: 1976/79, Ottawa
1960 34 Core 72 x 60 $400
1964J 27 North east 69 x 94 $800
1976 S12, Montreal
19 Jacks V oil & lucite 96 x 76 illus

GORMLEY, ANNA
fl 1894-07 H
Addr: 1907, Toronto
1907 80 Old house, Dordrecht, Holland

GOTTHANS, MANFRED
28 Feb 1922, Mannheim, Germany
RCA(e) 1978 Graphic designer
Addr: 1979, Toronto

GOTTSCHALK, FRITZ
30 Dec 1937, Zurich WWA78
RCA(e) 1973 Council Graphic designer
Addr: 1979, Zurich
1970 172 Cover, ICSID Canada Congress
173 Symbol and application, Broome Transit

GOUINLOCK, GEORGE ROPER
5 Nov 1896, Toronto 10 Aug 1979, Toronto
see ALLWARD, HUGH, 1949-1963

GOUINLOCK, GEORGE WALLACE
1 Aug 1861, Paris, Ont 13 Feb 1932, Toronto Mo12
Addr: 1895, 53 King St E, Toronto
1895 30A Sketch design, Sheppard Publishing Company's proposed building, Toronto

GOULD, JOHN HOWARD
14 Aug 1929, Toronto IO M WWA73

ARCA 1963-8 RCA(e) 1973 Painter
Addr: 1964N-8, Toronto; 1976/79, Wabaushene, Ont
1963 28 The matador illus $300 ≬LAG≬
1964J 28 Ancestors 30 x 40 illus $30
1964N 25 Seeding plant #2 30 x 40
1976 S12, Montreal
168 Waubaushene faces 16mm b&w 6 min

GOULET, CLAUDE
5 Jun 1925, Montreal WWA78
RCA(e) 1976 Painter
Addr: 1979, Longueuil, Que

GOUPIL, JULES ADOLPHE French
7 May 1839, Paris d 28 Apr 1883
B TB
1882 309 Une inconnue. Pupil of Ary Scheffer, école française (loan)

GOVE, H.G.
1940 59 Zinnias pastel $20

GRAEB, MARGARET
M
1966 76 Triad sculp 34 x 12 $350

GRAHAM, JAMES LILLIE
2 Aug 1873, Belleville, Ont AGO
H M NGC TB3
ARCA 1894 Sr 1942 Painter
Addr: 1893, 125 Bleury St, Montreal; 1894, 128 Marie Anne St, Montreal; 1896, 709 Dorchester St, Montreal; 1901, c/o Scott & Son, Montreal; 1902, c/o Art Association of Montreal; 1904, England; 1906 c/o Johnson & Copping, Montreal; 1907-9, Montreal; 1910-19, 195 Dunn Ave, Toronto; 1920, 146 Carling Ave, Ottawa; 1922-3, 255 Bleury St, Montreal; 1924, 1207 Bleury St, Montreal; 1925, 146 Carling Ave, Ottawa; 1926-8, Montreal; 1929, 3465 Jeanne Mance St, Montreal; 1930, 84 Monkland Ave, Montreal; 1931-5, Montreal; 1936, 1096 Beaver Hall Hill, Montreal; 1937-71, Montreal
1893 61 Pastures green $200 F1-50
62 Study of a cow $15 F1-51 nfs
1894 48 Across the lea ≬NGC≬
1895 46a Horses drinking
1896 58 Tillers of the soil
59 Going for water
60 A pasture
61 In a corner of the cow shed
201 Study of a tigress pastel
1901 55 Dinner time in a stable F2-29
56 Ploughing, near London F2-30
57 Carting sand F2-31 F5-66 $75
1902 76 Dinner time in the stable F6-87 $80
77 Ploughing in Essex
78 Carting to the village F6-88 $80
1904 69 The farm
70 Twilight
71 The stable F4-34
72 The cart F4-35
1906 F5, Halifax
67 Milking time $50 F6-89
1907 F6, Sherbrooke
90 In the fields pastel $50
1909M 53 Landscape
1910 77 Afternoon, Epping Forest
78 On the edge of the Lea Marshes, England
79 Horses in pasture
80 Indian summer, afternoon
1910 S2, Liverpool
49 The prodigal son 1911-102 ≬AGO≬
50 A stable interior
1911 67 Girl and cow
1912 100 By the birch grove
101 Tillers of the soil
103 Brookside pasture
1912 S3, Winnipeg
60 Interior of a cattle stall
61 Returning from pasture
62 Afternoon in Epping Forest
63 In the pasture at twilight
1915 93 Nightfall in the barnyard
1918N Pte J.L. Graham, somewhere in France
79 Farm yard, evening illus
1919 67 Approaching storm 1920-113 illus
68 Morning light on the pasture
69 Toward evening
70 On the road
1920 114 On Rotten Row
115 Sunlight in the dusk
116 Interior of a cow stable in Belgium

1922 83 Château Ramezay pastel S6-31
84 Miss MacNab pastel
85 Spring evening, Mount Royal Park pastel S6-32
86 Flemish stable interior 1923-61 S6-33
215 Circe sculp
1923 59 Place d'Armes, Montreal 1924-71 illus
60 Study of a tiger pastel
62 Autumn in the woods pastel
1924 70 Approaching storm
72 Au Marché Bonsecours, Montréal
73 A Flemsh pastoral scene
1925 86 Cattle under a shade tree
87 Winter scene along the riverfront, Montreal
88 By the strawstack pastel
89 Sketch pastel
1926 52 A sheltered corner of the pasture
53 When driving home the cows
54 Winter scene along by Christ Church Cathedral, Montreal
55 Beach at Laguna, California wc
1929 69 September morning by the Scheldt $300
70 Ploughing toward evening $100
71 Eveningtime by the Bay of Bic $150
72 Potato planting in Flemish country $75
1929 S7, Calgary
52 Summertime pastorale $700
53 Inside the stable door $350
54 Deer in the forest $360
1930 63 Summertime in the pasture $800
64 End of day by the docks at Antwerp $580
1930 F10, London, Eng
170 Summer pastoral $825
1936 84a Winter morning, Bonsecours Market, Montreal $500
1943 49 Wintertime along the riverfront, Montreal $350 T44-17
50 Turkey cocks fighting $650 T44-18
1945 88 In a Flemish stable at milking time $285 T46-19
89 Along the Seine at Paris $285

GRAHAM, KATHLEEN MARGARET HOWITT
(Mrs Wallace Graham)
9 Sep 1913, Hamilton, Ont IO WWA76
RCA(e) 1974 Painter
Addr: 1979, Toronto

GRAHAM, MONICA (Mrs)
1939 82 Sea scout min nfs

GRANDMAISON, NICKOLA DE (NICOLAS)
24 Feb 1892, Moscow 23 Mar 1978, Banff, Alta M WWA47
ARCA 1942 Sr 1962 Painter
Addr: 1929-35, 332 Main St, Winnipeg: 1942-71, Banff, Alta
1929 48 Ruthenian type in Manitoba $150
1935 64 Timmy, portrait of Master Donald F. Cameron pastel nfs
65 Lassie, portrait of daughter of A. McNeil, Esq pastel nfs
1942 32 Indian child pastel $275
1943 22 Sketch of Sarcee Indian from Alberta $450 T44-9

GRANT, BEATRICE LIECHENSTEIN
14 Nov 1909, Halifax M
Addr: 1933, Bellevue Quarters, Halifax
1933 77 Fish stores $50

GRANT, D.L.
ARCA 1881-2 Painter
Addr: 1881, Montreal

GRANT, DUNCAN EDMUND
16 Mar 1846, Roseneath, Scot flg 1924 H
Addr: 1893, 14 Amble St, Quebec
1893 207 Chill October nfs

GRANT, LEWIS JOHN MASON English
1881, Bhagulpur, Bengal, India d 1909 DBA DVP
Addr: 1905, 236 Bloor St E, Toronto; 1906, 28 Toronto St, Toronto; 1909N, Mackenzie Ave, Toronto
1905 81 On the dunes near Bromers, Kotkje, Holland Louis J.M. Grant mispr
82 Crooked hawthorne
1906 94 Tea time, an English cottage interior
95 On Maldon Drive, Downs, Essex, England
96 Near Highbridge, England
1906 F5, Halifax

68 Tea time $200
1909N 59 Don Valley, Todmorden

GRANT, MARY
1875, Huntington, Que d 1957
Addr: 1923-4, 131 Stanley St, Montreal; 1926-30, 2055 Mansfield St, Montreal; 1931, 5530 Queen Mary Rd, Montreal
1923 63 Norton's Reef, Monhegan
1924 74 Fishing boats, Grand Manan, New Brunswick
75 Incoming tide 1926-56
1927 72 Fundy fishing boats S7-56 $225
1929 73 In the harbour $225 1930-65
74 Sea and rocks $200 1930-66
1929 S7, Calgary
55 The bathing beach, Grand Manan $100
57 Monhegan harbour $30
58 Windy day, Nova Scotia coast $30
1931 92 Clearing $250

GRATTON, AUBRY ARMAND
26 Sep 1935, North Bay, Ont
RCA(e) 1977 Industrial designer
Addr: 1979, Mierlo, Netherlands

GRAUER, GAY SHERRARD (SHERRY) (Mrs John William Keith-King)
20 Feb 1939, Toronto M
RCA(e) 1978 Sculptor
Addr: 1979, Vancouver

GRAVEL, RAYMONDE
18 Jun 1913, Montreal M
Addr: 1936, 1803 Ottawa St, Windsor, Ont; 1937, 1509 Ottawa St, Windsor, Ont
1936 85 Engineering vs nature $250 T37-29
1937 82 Abraham's sacrifice $60
1944 58 Man eating his soup $100 T45-19 nfs
1945 90 Fruits of the earth, still life $150

GRAY, CLAUDE W. English
c 1880 d 1940 DBA G
Addr: 1912-14, Winnipeg
1912 S3, Winnipeg
247 The axe grinder wc
248 Landscape wc
1914 S4, Winnipeg
C.W. Gray, ARCA, London
169 Lancashire girl wc $100
170 Portrait study $50
171 Sketch $25
172 Bridge, Little Stony Mountain $25

GRAY, JOHN
1884 S1, Saint John
205 and 206 On the Saint John River (R.P. Starr, both)

GRAY, JOHN WARREN
1824, England 24 Feb 1912, Maisonneuve, Que H
Addr: 1887, Montreal
1880 184 A sketch on the English coast wc
254 Study of sheep drwg
1882 14 Sunset on the Essex coast
37 Evening among the islands, Ottawa River
112 View from Mount Royal, looking towards St Lambert
117 Under the maples
1887 24 Path through the woods
66 On Marble River, Chateaugay $40
96 Passing shower, Owl's Head, Memphremagog

GRAY, KATHERINE E.
Addr: 1927, 621 Sherbrooke St W, Montreal; 1928-33, 3449 Peel St, Montreal
1927 73 Interior
74 Roofs of Montreal wc
305 Adoration engr
306 Second hand books engr
1928 206 La veillée wd engr $10
207 The washerwoman wd engr $10
1929 75 Bonsecours Market, Montreal wc $50
264 The Séminaire, Notre Dame Street b&w $12.50
265 The sandman b&w $10
1930 206 French Canadian dancer wd engr $15
1933 294 The shrine wd engr $15
295 The reapers wd engr $15

GREENAWAY, ROY
c 1891, Toronto 18 Nov 1972, Toronto M
1942 45 The net menders, Percé nfs
1943 51 Winter twilight nfs
52 Building minesweeper,

Toronto, nfs
1944 59 Third Avenue elevated, New York nfs
1945 91 Late winter afternoon, Portland Street, Toronto nfs T46-20

GREENE, EVAN LOREN ROBERT
8 Oct 1910, Edmonton M
1938 79 Mary $300 Evan S.R. Greene mispr

GREENE, MARIE ZOE (Mrs)
31 Mar 1911, Madison, Wis M
1945 221 Head of a young woman sculp $55
222 Young logger, Gatineau River, Quebec sculp $45

GREENE, THOMAS GARLAND
12 Sep 1875, Toronto 22 Nov 1955, Orillia, Ont AGO CNS36 M NGC
Addr: 1912, Toronto; 1914-18, 70 Lombard St, Toronto; 1922, 14 Elm St, Toronto; 1923, Willowdale, Ont; 1928, 14 Elm St, Toronto; 1930-2, 24 Grenville St, Toronto
1912 S3, Winnipeg
64 Barn raising
182-4 Illustrations, 3, b&w
1914 88 Sunset glow
1914 S5, Patriotic Fund
62 Crossing the portage illus
1915 94 The express stand
1918A 73 Maple sap
222 Roadside etch
223 Team #2 etch
224 Cabine de l'habitant etch
1922 87 Lingering snow
1923 238 Grand Council at Sault Ste Marie, 1671. Mural decorative paintings competition
1928 54 Passing storm $225
1930 67 Lorne Pierce, MA PhD LLD
68 The interlude $500
207 Reginald Stewart, Esq charcl
1931 93 J. Lewis Milligan
1932 71 La belle canadienne $1,000
72 Reverie

GREENHAM, ELVINA K.
Addr: 1906, 374A Greene Ave, Westmount, Que; 1907, Westmount, Que
1906 F5, Halifax
69 A soldier $45
1907 81 Miss Margaret MacKenzie

GREENSTONE, MARION (Mrs)
1925, New York M TB3
1959 36 Composition with brown #2 36 x 59 $450
1960 35 Composition #131 48 x 58 illus $500
1963 29 Composition 167a illus $450
30 Composition 176 $675
1964J 29 Composition 141 50 x 62 $675

GREENWOOD, CHARLES JAMES
12 Sep 1893, Bradford, Yorks, Eng
Addr: 1934, 213 Glencoe Ave, Montreal
1934 75 Lake on the Hanging Glacier $175

GREENWOOD, CHARLOTTE
fl 1895-7 H
Addr: 1895, Whitby, Ont
1895 49 A study in pottery

GREENWOOD, DOROTHY (Mrs)
Addr: 1913, 180 Mansfield St, Montreal
1913 359 Easter lilies pastel S4-150 $125

GREER, WILLIAM NEWTON
21 Feb 1925, Kingston, Ont
ARCA 1971 Architect
Addr: 1979, Toronto

GREGG, ERICA DEICHMAN (Mrs Kjeld Deichman) (Mrs Milton Fowler Gregg)
c 1914, Denmark M
RCA(e) 1978 Ceramist
Addr: 1979, Fredericton, NB

GREGOR, HELEN FRANCES LORENZ (Mrs Tibor P. Gregor)
28 Jun 1921, Prague CWW79 IO WWA73
ARCA 1971 RCA 1974 Council Designer
Addr: 1976/79, Toronto
1967 24 Landscape tap 22 x 26 $450
1970 24 Op horizon #2 45 x 96 1/2 $900
1976 S12, Montreal
142 The wave #2, earth series tap 84 x 85 x 8 illus
DW 1974 Op horizon. 1969 triptich tapestry 120 x 60

GREGORY, A.T. (or T.A.)
fl 1877-90 H
1880 291 and 295 Paper hanging,

four des
1888 286 Sonning Church, near Reading, England wc

GERGORY, MARY see PATTULO, MARY

GRESHAM, ARTHUR
1891, Sheffield, Eng
Addr: 1923-30, 49 1/2 Helena Ave, Toronto; 1933-5, 46 Joicey Blvd, Toronto
1923 64 Vanity wc
65 Bobette wc
1928 55 My wife wc
1929 76 Autumn wc $40
77 Among the islands, Georgian Bay wc $40
1930 69 The Japanese parisol $250
1933 78 Wm. Gray Mitchell, Esq
1934 76 Gordon Dagger, Esq
77 Ice on Lake Simcoe wc $50
1935 96 Estuary of the Severn, Georgian Bay $75
1953 29 Sandra nfs

GREY, JERRY
25 Feb 1940, Vancouver IO
Addr: 1976, Toronto
1976 S12, Montreal
20 Four by four acry 62 x 62 illus

GRIER, EDMUND GEOFFREY
22 Nov 1899, Toronto 9 Sep 1965, Ottawa M WWA47
ARCA 1943 Painter
Addr: 1924, 711 Yonge St, Toronto; 1943-6, Montreal; 1947, Ste Anne de Bellevue, Que; 1948-65, Montreal
1924 76 The temptation
77 In the Pennsylvania Hills
1941 66 Rosemary nfs T42-17
67 Treble nfs
1942 46 The green suit $500
1943 53 Subaltern illus $750 T44-19
54 Ship's cook $500
1944 60 On the bridge $750
1950 47 Ted 30 x 36 nfs

GRIER, EDMUND WYLY (Sir) DCL
26 Nov 1862, Melbourne, Australia
7 Dec 1957, Toronto AGO B CC2 CNS36 CWW55 EC H M NGC TB1/2/3 W78
ARCA 1893 RCA 1895 Sr 1941 Council Painter
Addr: 1883, Toronto; 1893-4, Canada Life Bldg, Room 37, Toronto; 1895-19, Imperial Bank Chambers, Toronto; 1920, 21 Bloor St W, Toronto; 1921-8 771 Yonge St, Toronto; 1929-37, 6 Crescent Rd, Toronto; 1938-57, Toronto
1883 21 In the studio $150
68 Portrait
320 At work drwg on wood $20
1892 12 The Golden Lion, St Ives, Cornwall $100
81 Portrait of a physician 1893-64 F1-53 nfs
87 The Fates, a rehearsal $500
92 The rising moon $50
1893 63 Miss Mabel Cawthra F1-52
1894 45 Bereft 1895-47
46 Mrs Eber Ward 1904-75
1895 48 Fifty years ago (Diploma picture, error)
1896 62 Jessie, daughter of E.F.B. Johnston, QC
63 A pastoral symphony
1897 54 Mrs Edward Blake
55 Mrs. E.F.B. Johnston
56 Mrs E. Wyle Grier
1898 42 Hon G.W. Allan, Chancellor, Trinity University
1900 49 E.F.B. Johnston, QC 1903-54 1904-73 F4-36
1901 53 Mrs J.K. Kerr F2-27
54 Frederick Wyld, Esq F2-28
1903 55 N.W. Hoyle, KC
1904 74 Rev Prof Clark, DCL F4-37
1904 F4, St Louis
38 Mrs R. Matthews
1905 70 John T. Ryan, Esq
71 Daughter of the Empire
1906 89 An old miner
1906 F5, Halifax
70 Mrs Parkyn Murray
71 Little patriot $200
1908 58 The dreamer S2-52 1954-26 Retro Sec (E. Geoffrey Grier)
59 The late Hon Chief Justice Sir George Burton
60 James Smith, Secretary,RCA
61 A meadow at Blair
1909M 52 Noel Marshall, Esq, Toronto
1909N 60 Mrs J.Y. Ormsby
61 Mr Justice Riddell
1910 81 The blue scarf 1912-66 S5-39 illus
82 Girl in red S2-53 S3-67
83 Geo. S. Lyon, Esq
1910 S2, Liverpool
51 Mrs Agar Adamson
1911 69 Mrs Chester Glass
1912 104 Dr R. Wilkie, Esq

105 The confidante
106 A Canadian explorer
1912 S3, Winnipeg
65 Portrait of my father
1913 119 The Master of Northcote ◊NGC◊
120 W.R. Gregg, Esq S4-52 $300 nfs
1914 89 His Hon Judge Benson ◊CAG◊
90 L.A. Hamilton, Esq
91 Sylvia
1915 95 Col James Land Milligan illus
96 Noon ◊NGC◊
97 R.E. Kingsford, Esq
1916 102 Principal Gordon, Queen's University illus
103 Basil Morgan, Esq
1918A 74 W.S. Jackson, Esq illus
75 The late F/L Ford Strathy, RN
225 Frank Darling, Esq, RCA charcl ◊AGO◊
1918N 80 Maj Gen S.C. Mewburn, Minister of Militia
81 Dr D. Jamieson, Speaker, Ontario Legislature illus
1919 71 Hon G.H. Murray, Premier, Nova Scotia illus
72 D. Macgillivray, Esq
73 Hon Robert E. Harris, Chief Justice of Nova Scotia
1920 117 Lieut Col K.R. Marshall, CMG DSO illus
1921 66 Dr Chas. E. Moyse, Dean, Faculty of Arts, VP Emeritus, McGill University illus
67 Portrait of a young girl
68 Augustus Bridle
1922 88 Sir Edmund Walker, CVO illus 1923-56 S6-28 ◊AGO◊
89 John Northway, Esq
1923 66 Rev Canon A.J. Fidler, MA
67 S.J. Moore, Esq
68 Col Alexander Fraser
1924 78 Bertram Forsthy, as Prospero
79 Col W.R. Land illus
1925 90 Henry W. Darling, Esq, former Pres Canadian Bank of Commerce illus
1926 57 Miss Margaret Cockshutt
58 H.C. Fox, Esq
59 Portrait of a lawyer illus
1927 75 Peleg Howland, Esq
76 A. Monro Grier, Esq, KC illus
1927 F7, London, Eng
163 W.H. Harris, MD nfs
1928 56 Dr Abraham Groves
57 Prof Geo. M. Wrong, MA LLD
58 W. Martyn Sibbald, Esq
208 Arthur J. Hughes, Esq charcl
1929 78 F.A. Merrick, Esq
79 Summer afternoon $1,000
1929 S7, Calgary
59 The cameo $200
1930 70 Sir Joseph Flavelle, Bart
71 Hon Newton W. Rowell, KC
72 Miss H. Walsh, late Prin, Bishop Strachan School
1931 94 Emeritus Prof Irving H. Cameron, MB FRCS LLD
95 R.A. Gray, Esq, BA
1932 73 Mrs Wm. Mowbray
74 Lt Col Wm. C. Michell illus
75 Prof N.C. James
1933 79 G.H. Duggan, Esq, LLD
80 W. Perkins Bull, Esq, KC $1,500 T34-29 $750
81 La poudreuse
1934 78 Edward Johnson, Esq, Mus Doc
79 G.A. Morrow, Esq illus
80 Wm. Mowbray, Esq, MA
81 Davidson Harman, Esq ◊AGH◊
1935 97 Mrs A. Monro Grier nfs
98 Henry A. Stone, Esq, Pres Vancouver Art Gallery nfs ◊VAG◊
99 Dr W.B. Hendry
1936 86 John A. Pearson, Esq, DA RCA nfs 1937-84
87 Miss Jean I. Gunn, OBE nfs
88 Magnolias $75 T37-30
1937 83 Dr James Douglas (McGill University)
85 Miss Jessie K. Wilson nfs
1938 80 Hon H.E. Rose, Chief Justice of the High Court nfs
81 His Hon Judge F.M. Morson nfs 1939-85
82 Arthur B. Wood, Esq, FIA FAS illus nfs
83 John J. Gibson, Esq, LLD nfs
1939 83 J.F. Weston, Esq illus nfs
84 M. Ross Gooderham, Esq nfs
86 A.B. Wiswell, Esq, nfs
1939 F11, New York
27 John W. Brookfield, Esq 32 x 27 nfs
1940 61 Lieut Col Sidney C.

Coland, Hon ADC nfs
62 Mrs H.S. Morton nfs
1941 70 Rt Hon Lennox Williams, DD, former Lord Bishop of Quebec illus nfs
1941 S9, Toronto
26 The top of the morning $100
1941 Travelling exhibit
40 Uncle Dave $500
1942 47 Rev Frank G. Vial, BD DCL nfs
1947 66 R.P. Jellett, Esq nfs T48-13
DW 1897 A summer idyll 49 1/2 x 59 1/2
port: by S. Grier, 1944-61

GRIER, STELLA EVELYN (Mrs A.E. Gould)
6 Jan 1898, Toronto M TB2
ARCA 1931 Sr 1968 Painter
Addr: 1921, 711 Yonge St, Toronto; 1928, 891 Bay St, Toronto; 1929, 43 Dewson St, Toronto; 1930-32, 6 Crescent Rd, Toronto; 1933, 248 Brunswick Ave, Toronto; 1934, 6 Crescent Rd, Toronto; 1935-45, Toronto; 1946-51, Uxbridge, Ont; 1952, Peterborough, Ont; 1953, Preston, Ont; 1954, Peterborough, Ont; 1955, Preston, Ont; 1956-63, Toronto; 1964, Hamilton; 1965-71/79, Toronto
1921 69 Eve
1928 59 Mother and child 1929-80 $500 F9-187 nfs
60 Joan $100 S7-60 nfs
1929 81 J. Geale Dickson, Esq
1929 S7, Calgary
61 The engineer $100
1930 73 Miss Eleanor Barton illus
74 George Erskine Oxley, Esq
1931 96 Early Victorian $500
97 Sylvia and Sootie
1932 77 Flowers in an old English vase temp $50
1933 82 One of them $300 T34-30
1934 82 The late Dr J. Fleming Goodchild
1940 60 J.B. O'Brien, Esq nfs 1941-68 $500 T41-19 nfs
1941 69 Study nfs
1944 61 Sir Wyly Grier, RCA DCL $300
1945 92 S/L Wm. Wood nfs
1960 36 Judith 38 x 27 nfs

GRIERSON, WILLIAM G.
see BANZ, GEORGE, 1966

GRIFFIN, CONSTANCE M.
Addr: 1931, 4930 Côte des Neiges Rd, Montreal
1931 98 A Chinese girl pastel $35
99 Portrait study pastel

GRIFFIN, GEORGE HENRY
Mar 1898, Uckfield, Sussex, Eng
Addr: 1925-8, 18 Redpath Ave, Toronto; 1930-2, 1874 Bloor St W, Toronto
1925 91 Children by a brook 1926-60
1926 61 Bringing home the cows
1928 61 Frosty morning $300 1929-82
1930 75 An autumn morning $300
1931 100 The launching $300
1932 78 Matapedia Valley wc $200

GRIFFITH, JULIUS EDWARD LINDSAY
21 Apr 1912, Vancouver AGO IO M WWA59
RCA(e) 1974 RCA 1976 Painter
Addr: 1979, Toronto
1947 67 St John's Nurse reading $150
DW 1976 White road near Arthur. 1975 wc 29 x 21

GRIFFITHS, JAMES
1814, or 1825, Newcastle, Staffs, Eng 10 Aug 1896, London, Ont EC H M NGC W78
RCA 1880 Council Painter
Addr: 1880-2, London, Ont; 1883, Court House, London, Ont; 1884-92, London, Ont; 1893-6, Bleak House, South London, Ont
1880 28 Peonies DW 1880 oil on wood 21 1/4 x 15 1/2 1881-289
32 Hollyhocks
186 Group of flowers wc
187 Grapes wc
188 Hollyhocks wc
190 Flowers and fruit wc
191 Group of fruit wc
192 English roses wc
193 Branch of peaches wc 1881-46 $35
1881 15 White grapes wc $35
16 Hollyhocks wc $35
47 Dahlias wc $40
61 Peonies wc $40
70 Roses wc $40
71 Fruit wc nfs
89 Grapes and peaches wc $25
99 Roses and lilacs wc $40

263 Vase of flowers, enamel on china $75
282 Fruit $50
1882 118 and 211 Flowers wc $25 each
164 Phlox and balsam wc $35
169 Vase of flowers wc $40
183 Red and yellow roses wc $15
210 Fruit wc $25
1883 190 Flowers wc $10
197 A variety of roses wc $20
198 Morning glories wc $35
231 Vase of flowers wc $20
244 Flowers and fruit wc $45
268 Roses wc $15
280 Phlox wc $25
295 Hollyhock wc $10
313 Fruit wc $40
1884 119 White grapes wc $30
123 Flowers wc $20
124 Phlox and balsams wc $30
142 Roses wc $20
1884 S1, Saint John
3 Phlox and balsams wc $15
13 Flowers wc $20
19 and 73 Flowers wc $15 each
72 Roses wc $20
1885 204 Flowers wc $15
254 Flowers and fruit wc $35
315 Vase of roses wc $25
1886 17 Jacqueminot roses $20
44 Grapes and peaches wc $15
66 Hollyhocks wc $30
84 Princess Charlotte roses wc $25
89 Roses and phlox wc $25
1886 F1a, London, Eng
2000, artist number
Roses and phlox
1887 119 Peony, roses and tulips wc $35
134 Fruit and flowers wc $50
150 Petunias wc $15
157 A vase of flowers wc $40
164 Roses wc $30
1888 8 Roses and hollyhock wc $35
70 Vase of flowers $40
182 Flowers $40
252 Roses wc $10
262 Petunias wc $10
294 Fruit wc $40
1889 105 Roses wc $30
122 Basket of flowers wc $25
151 Fruit wc $30
162 Morning glories wc $30
1890 166 Vase of flowers wc $35
167 White grapes wc $30
168 White roses wc $30
1892 95 and 161 English roses wc $40 each
135 Flowers and fruit wc $50
1893 208 English roses wc $50 F1-161
209 Peonies wc $40 F1-162
210 Flowers wc $40
211 Canadian roses wc $20 F1-163
212 Flowers enamel on china $75
1895 25W Peonies wc
26W Vase of roses wc
27W Double petunias wc
28W White grapes wc
29W English roses wc
30W Canadian roses wc
1896 202 Vegetables wc
203 Tulip and roses wc
204 Roses wc

GRIGNARD, ALBERT
H
1880 312 Specimens of lithography
313a Specimens of fossils drawn from nature

GRIMANIS, PATRICIA see GANGNON, PATRICIA

GRIMSHAW, FRANK
Addr: 1929, 11 St Patrick St, Magog, Que; 1930-1, 5 Merry St, Magog, Que; 1932, P O Box 329, Magog, Que
1929 83 Still life wc $30
1930 208 and 209 Design for printed silk $10 each
1931 392 and 393 Design for printed silk $20 each
1932 237 Design for drapery, printed cotton $80

GROSSMAN, IRVING
7 Dec 1926, Toronto CWW79
RCA(e) 1973 Architect
Addr: 1979, Toronto

GROULX, PIERRE
Addr: 1976, Montreal
1976 S12, Montreal
178 Briques -3- photo 16 x 20 illus

GROVES, NAOMI see JACKSON, NAOMI

GRYMONPRE, JEAN
Addr: 1927, 53 Isabel St, Winnipeg

1927 77 Study

GUARD, MARIE CECILIA (Mrs J. Kenneth Phillips)
8 Oct 1908, Toronto M
Addr: 1930, c/o Mrs Kenneth Phillips, Etobicoke, Ont; 1934, 43 Charles St E, Toronto
1930 76 From an August garden wc $75
1934 83 Idyl $200
83 Once upon a time $150 T35-25

GUAY, MIMI
Addr: 1937, 120 Sherbrooke St W, Montreal
1937 315 Dr Gérard de Montigny charcl nfs

GUDE, HANS FREDERICK Norwegian
13 Mar 1825, Christiana 17 Aug 1903, Berlin B H TB
1882 320 The harbour at Christiana, foggy weather (loan)

GUERIN, THOMAS
Addr: 1920, 4 Edgehill Ave, Montreal
1920 266 Tête de viele habitant bronze

GUEST, MARIE OLIVIA see HEWSON, MARIE OLIVIA

GUILD, KEN
1963 85 Sculpture $250
86 Sculpture $225

GUILLON, JACQUES SILAS
27 Jul 1922, Paris
RCA(e) 1973 Industrial designer
Addr: 1976/79, Montreal
1976 S12, Montreal
134 LRS. Train à haute vitesse/high speed train Jacques Guillon Designers Inc illus

GUITE, SUZANNE (Mrs Alberto Tomni)
10 Dec 1927, Percé, Que M WWA62
RCA(e) 1975 Sculptor
Addr: 1979, Percé, Que

GUNN, EMILY M.
fl 1893-7 H
Addr: 1893, Toronto
1893 65 Still life

GUNN, PATRICIA (PADDY) see O'BRIEN, PATRICIA GUNN

GUSH, WILLIAM English
fl 1833-74 B G H TB
1881 333 Gen Sir John Inglis (loan)
338 Gen Sir Frederick William of Kars (loan)

H

HAANEL, FLORENCE EUGENIE
c 1867, Leslie Ridge, Mich May 1950, Ottawa H
Addr: 1929, Ottawa
1929 S7, Calgary
62 Woman knitting $75
63 Zinnias $50

HADDOCK, WILLIAM RICHARD
2 Mar 1909, Birmingham, Eng M
Addr: 1935, 648 Sherbrooke St W, Montreal; 1937, 1506 Mackay St, Montreal
1935 100 Buildings and shadows wc $40
101 Waterfront, sketch wc $25
1937 86 Summer time wc $30

HAGAN, ROBERT FREDERICK
21 May 1918, Toronto M WWA47
1939 88 Funeral $100
1944 62 Locker room $250
1949 127 Circus clowns col litho $15 unfrmd
1953 127 All day suckers col litho $21
1958 40 Sand box print $35
1959 37 Sunbather on the stone litho 24 x 18 $110
1960 37 Baby asleep 17 x 13 $50
1961 39 A door is for swinging litho 24 x 18 $110
1966 20 Lives of Muskoka desiring 47 x 64 illus

HAGARTY, BEATRICE (Mrs Percy Robertson)
1879, Toronto
Addr: 1907, Toronto; 1908, 21 Walmer Rd, Toronto; 1910, Imperial Bank Chambers, Toronto; 1911, 21 Walmer Rd, Toronto; 1928-37, 2 Oaklands Ave, Toronto
1907 Hagarty, to 1911
83 The curtsey 1908-80

84 George F. Hagarty, Esq
1908 79 Head of an old woman
1910 84 Little German girl
85 Sleeping child
1911 71 The late Rev Canon Cayley
1928 Robertson
132 A lady of the old school $100
1929 190 Mrs Edward Sullivan
1930 147 Phlox $50
1931 249 Trilliums $60
250 Phlox and old china $60
1932 163 August noon $65
1933 199 The Chinese figure $200
1934 166 Petunias $75 T35-61
1935 226 Petunias in blue bowl $75
1937 192 Syringa $75
193 Gold and grey $65
1938 185 Lucy Jane $300
1939 198 White roses $75
1941 S9, Toronto
52 Early spring $80

HAGARTY, CLARA SOPHIA
28 June 1871, Toronto 18 Jan 1958, Toronto AGO CNS36 CWW55 M Mo12 PMC ARCA 1903 Sr 1940 Painter
Addr: 1894, 233 Simcoe St, Toronto; 1895, Prince Arthur Ave, Toronto; 1896-8, 233 Simcoe St, Toronto; 1899-00, York Chambers, Toronto; 1901, 233 Simcoe St, Toronto; 1902, 13 Spadina Rd, Toronto; 1903, York Chambers, Toronto; 1904, Toronto; 1905, 13 Spadina Rd, Toronto; 1906, 36 Toronto St, Toronto; 1907, Toronto; 1908-12, 13 Spadina Rd, Toronto; 1913-27, 6 Chestnut Park, Toronto; 1928-31, 18 Grenville St, Toronto: 1932, 261 Poplar Plains Rd, Toronto; 1933-37, 29 St Mary St, Toronto; 1938-58, Toronto
1894 58 Peconic Bay
59 Indian reservation, Long Island
1895 62 A tangled corner Haggarty, mispr
63 First touch of autumn
64 The inlet
36W Study of a head pastel
1896 64 Oat field at Shinnecock
65 Vegetable garden
66 Pier at Canoe Place
67 On the beach
1897 68 Gertie in the garden
69 Blakeney harbour, Norfolk
70 High Street, Cley, at sunset (cat #60 mispr)
71 Roofs of the Cley village
72 Study
1898 55 Tidal channel, Norfolk
56 Spinning, Dutch interior
57 Pete, Dutch interior
58 Waiting, Dutch interior
1899 61 Portrait of my sister
62 Repost
1900 62 In old Madrid
63 Field flowers, Norfolk, England
64 Interior, Lower Canada
1901 58 and 59 Dutch interior F2-32 and 33
1902 79 An old peasant
80 Fountain in Paris
1903 60 Alice, portrait
61 On the quai, France
62 Village street
1904 76 Dutch interior
77 In the sunshine
78 Washing day F4-39 F5-72
79 Return of the fishers
80 Old peasant woman
1905 94 The brass kettle
95 The lady in black
96 Cleaning lamps, France
1906 97 Miss S. Hagarty
98 The grey kimono
1907 85 Tête à tête
86 A lonely meal
1907 F6, Sherbrooke
91 Tea time $40
92 The old housewife $50 1908-75
1908 73 Alice
74 Reflections
1909M 60 Col Biscoe
61 In the window
1910 86 Playing by the surf
87 The marsh, late afternoon
88 Afternoon on the beach
89 Picking flowers
1911 72 A windy day, Holland
73 A canal, Holland
74 Luxembourg Gardens, Paris
1912 107 Carmen, portrait study
108 Sunny morning, Holland
1913 121 Fish market, Etaples ≬LAG≬
122 Farm children, Brittany S4-53 $100
123 Convent garden, Brittany S4-54 $100
1914 92 Girl with the blue scarf
1914 S5, Patriotic Fund
70 Dutch interior illus
1915 98 Brittany children
1916 104 Dahlias

1920 118 In a Brittany garden
119 La petite soeur
1922 90 The blue lacquer bowl S6-35
1923 69 Iris 1924-80
70 Study in flame colour
1924 81 Morning on the sands
1925 92 Morning on the beach
93 Peonies
1926 63 Anemonies
1927 79 White peonies 1928-64 $100 F8-123 $75
80 Zinnias
1928 65 Iceland poppies $60
1929 85 Mauve and silver $75
86 An arrangement
1929 S7, Calgary
64 Chrysanthemums $100
65 Iceland poppies $60 1930-79 $75
1930 78 A July bunch $125
1931 101 A bunch of flowers $125
102 A Chinese figure $75
103 Calendulas $45
1932 79 White blossoms $75
80 The convex mirror $150
1933 83 The geranium $125
84 Roses $125 T34-31
85 White roses $150
1934 85 Pale peonies $100
86 Peonies $100 T35-26
87 Trilliums $50 1935-105
1935 102 The white jug $175
103 The green jug T36-30
104 Phlox $150
1936 89 June $200
90 July $150
1937 87 Johanna Hill roses $125
88 Peonies T38-19
1938 86 The white hydrangea $150 1939-89 F11-28 26 x 22
87 Peonies in window $150
1939 90 July flowers $150
91 The twisted jar $100
1940 63 Late summer $75 T41-21
1941 71 White and green $200 ◊LAG◊
72 Garden flowers $100 T42-18
1941 S9, Toronto
27 Flowers $100
1942 48 Garden flowers $100

HAGELL, EDWARD FREDERICK (TEDDY)
1895, Lethbridge, Alta d 1964, Alberta M
Addr: 1935, 5829 Hudson St, Vancouver
1935 321 On the iron-bound roof of the world ink $100

HAGUE, LAWRENCE
1880 286 Book cover, cloth and gold des

HAGUE, MARY ELIZABETH (LIBBY)
20 Aug 1950, St Thomas, Ont IO
1971 15 Fried eggs #3 50 x 52 $600

HAHN, EMANUEL OTTO
30 May 1881, Reutlingen, Germany
14 Feb 1957, Toronto AGO CC1 CWW55 EC M NGC W78 WWA47
ARCA 1927 RCA 1931 Sr 1951 Council
Sculptor
Addr: 1908-13, 433 Indian Rd, Toronto; 1914, 272 Poplar Plains Rd, Toronto; 1915-18, 289 College St, Toronto; 1922-37, 32 Adelaide St E, Toronto; 1938-57, Toronto
1908 170 Figure of a young boy sculp
1913 219 Blackfoot Chief Thundercloud sculp
1914 202 Head plaster
203 Sketch model for a memorial sculp
1915 299 War's toll tinted plaster
1916 245 The Indian scout tinted plaster ◊bronze, NGC◊
1918A 187 Head plaster
1922 216 Fate bronze DW 1932 24h S6-106
217 St Lambert's Soldiers' Monument, figure photo
1924 234 Late Sir William Mackenzie bust tinted plaster
1926 158 Sketch model for a cenotaph plaster illus
159 Edward Hanlan Memorial photo
1927 258 John Galbraith, University of Toronto plaster
259 Head of an Indian girl plaster
1929 240 Beethoven tinted plaster cast in iron $1,600
1930 186 Sir Adam Beck Memorial, Toronto sketch model
187 Commemorative tablet model
1931 312 Wilhjalmur Stefansson bronze $1,000 ◊NGC◊
313 Canadian deer bronze $350
314 Elizabeth Mitchell, portrait sculp
1932 209 Madame X in mood Y marble $650 1933-257
1935 280 Equestrian fragment

plaster bronze $2,000
1937 280 Canadian silver dollar working model
281 New Canadian coinage, 10¢ and 25¢ pieces working model
282 Canadian National Exhibition medal 1937, working model
1938 235 Engineering Alumni, University of Toronto medal obverse & reverse, working models
1939 249 1940 silver dollar reverse, working model
250 Commemmorative medal reverse, working model
1940 159 Dr Daniel David Palmer sculp nfs
1941 212 Elizabeth Malcolm plaster
1941 S9, Toronto
28 Samuel Lount and Peter Matthews, Patriots of 1837 rel heads, tinted plaster $25 each
1942 162 Negress plaster $650
1944 146 Model of Crucifix, to be cast in bronze for Society of St John the Evangelist, Bracebridge, Ont nfs
1945 223 Crucifix for altar, Society of St John the Evangelist, Bracebridge, Ont plaster model nfs
1947 201 Stephen Leacock Memorial Medal working model nfs
1948 164 Henry Girdlestone Acres Medal, University of Toronto working models
165 Ontario College of Art Medal working models
1951 115 Chemical Institute of Canada Medal obverse & reverse models & impressions nfs
port: bust, by E.B. Holbrook, 1947-203 1952-107 1959-85

HAHN, GUSTAV
27 Jul 1866, Reutlingen, Germany
1 Dec 1962, Toronto B CC1 CWW58
M NGC TB W78 WWA47
ARCA 1901 RCA 1906 Sr 1936 Council
Designer
Addr: 1899, 21 Marlboro Ave, Toronto; 1901, 79 King St W, Toronto; 1904, Toronto; 1905-8, 96 Boustead Ave, Toronto; 1909N, 79 King St W, Toronto; 1910, 29 King St W, Toronto; 1911-14, Wychwood Park, Toronto; 1915-17, Toronto; 1918A, 52 Duggan Ave, Toronto; 1919-62, Toronto
1899 247 Panel des
248 Decoration of a hall des
249 Decorative panel
1901 226 and 228 Decoration
227 Panel for screen
1904 275 Dining room frieze, W.H. Elliott 3 sections
276 Decoration F4-102 wc
277 Decorative panel, drawing room, Mr. A.G. Gooderham
278 Drawing room frieze, Dr Scadding
279 Drawing room frieze, Fred Nichols F4-103 wc
280 Decorative panel
1905 219 Die drei Nornen panel over mantel gesso & inlay
220 Bank of Montreal, Toronto panel col sketch
221 Central Methodist Church, Toronto panel sketch
1906 102 Hail Dominion! dec panel DW 1906 79 x 53
103-5 Study 3 pastels
1906 F5, Halifax
73 Easter lilies $50 F6-97
1907 319 Harmony dec panel pastel 1908-76
320 Dawn dispelling the shades of night ceiling, morning room, Hon Mr Jones, Toronto dec panel pastel
1907 F6, Sherbrooke
96 Blowing bubbles $100
98 Decoration for ceiling $100
1908 77 The Three Fates panel for over mantel
1909M 175 Harmony protecting the melodies from discord sketch for ceiling & wall, music room, Mrs Massey Treble, Toronto
1909N 62 Council Chamber, City Hall, Toronto, Truth dec panel
63 Council Chamber, City Hall, Toronto, Justice dec panel
64 Frieze Comedy and Tragedy, Chester Massey, Esq, Toronto
1910 212-13 Lunette, billiard and palm rooms, E.R. Wood, Esq
1911 212 Panel des
1912 263 Decorative panel
1914 93 Prometheus dec panel pastel
94-5 Decorative panel pastel

1914 S5, Patriotic Fund
72 Blowing soap bubbles illus
1918A 226 Sketch for decoration
227 Charity sketch
228 and 229 Panel sketch
port: by S. Hahn, 1947-68

HAHN, SYLVIA
2 May 1911, Toronto M WWA47
1947 68 Gustav Hahn, RCA nfs
69 Mrs Gustav Hahn nfs

HAINES, FREDERICK STANLEY
29 Mar 1879, Meaford, Ont 21 Nov 1960, Thornhill, Ont AGO CC2 CWW49 EC M NGC PMC TB2 W78 WWA47
ARCA 1919 RCA 1933 Sr 1950 Council
Painter
Addr: 1905-12, Meadowvale, Ont; 1914, Studio Bldg, Toronto: 1918A-24, Thornhill, Ont; 1925, Colborne St, Thornhill, Ont; 1926-8, Thornhill, Ont; 1929, Grange Park, Toronto; 1930-2, Toronto; 1933-7, Ontario College of Art; 1938-49, Toronto; 1950-60, Thornhill, Ont
1905 97 Meditation
1906 110 The shepherds
111 An intruder F5-74 illus $100
112 Greyhounds F6-95 $25
1907 87 At play
88 Dorcas of Gloster
89 Possession
90 Calves
1907 F6, Sherbrooke
93 The only one left $75
94 Barn interior with calves $50
1908 62 Sheep in a wood
1909M 62 The siesta
63 Symphony
1910 90 Forgotten
91 Stolen sweets S3-71 S5-63 illus
1912 S3, Winnipeg
70 Dinner time
1914 96 Who goes there?
1918A 76 The pride of the farm 1918N-82
77 Fly time illus 1918N-83
78 Between lights
230 Fall evening etch 1918N-233
231 Spring etch 1918N-234
232 Elms etch 1919-203
233 Edge of the woods etch
1919 74 Homeward 1920-120
75 Pasture illus ◊AGO◊
202 Evening etch
1920 121 The gravel pit
122 The last gleam ◊NGC◊
123 Mare and colt
306 The dead tree col aqua
307 Dawn col aqua
308 A York County bridge col aqua
309 Aquatine
1921 70 Turtle Lake
1923 206 Pastorale aqua
207 Twilight in the woods aqua
1924 82 Evening
83 Summer pasture
1925 94 The two year old illus
95 The birch
1926 64 The beech tree
178 The dead tree aqua
1927 F7, London, Eng
35 Bass Bay, Ontario aqua $50
1929 87 Wayside elms
88 Shady pasture
1929 S7, Calgary
66 Bewdley poplars $400
1932 81 Winter, Mary Lake illus $600 1933-89 $500
82 Autumn, Mountain Lake $600
1933 86 October, Haliburton $500
87 June, Eppingham $500
88 May sunlight, Niagara $500 T34-32
1934 88 Trillium time illus $600 T35-27 1935-107 $500
89 Market gardener $600
90 June landscape $400
1935 106 Birches, Haliburton $500 T36-31
1936 91 Jack pine $350 T37-31
92 Rocks and trees $450
1937 89 Cranberry Lake $500 T38-20 ◊LAG◊
90 Zero weather $500
1938 88 Morning, Froud Lake $500 F11-29 42 x 48
89 Grace Lake $400 T39-20 1940-64 illus T41-22
90 Morning, Haliburton $400
1938 S8, Toronto
141 The hunters
142 Landscape dec panel
143 Flowers dec panel
1939 92 Apple blossoms $600
93 Haliburton beeches illus $400
94 Blue water $400
1940 65 Island, Grace Lake $250

66 Red pines $250
1941 73 Haliburton maples $400
74 The dead Jack pines $350 T42-19
75 Northern landscape $600
1941 S9, Toronto
29 Road to Willisville $150
1942 49 Beech, spring temp $350 T43-15
50 Autumn lilies temp $150
51 Winter landscape temp $200
52 Begonia temp $200
1943 55 Bridge on Whitefish River $400 T44-20
1946 51 Beech woods, spring $300 T47-23
1947 70 Main channel, Pointe au Baril $500 T48-14
1948 71 Passing shower $400
1949 36 Beech woods in winter $500 T50-7
37 Passing shower, Whanipiti Bay $600
1950 48 Three pines, Whanipiti Bay 40 x 48 $500
1951 Travelling exhibit
21 A Muskoka farm DW 1934 28 x 34 1954 Retro Sec 30
1953 30 Spring in the wood lot illus $250
1954 39 Late fall 30 x 40 $350
1955 39 March evening $250
1960 38 Six beeches 24 x 32 $350
port: by J.S. Hallam, 1943-56

HALDENBY, ERIC WILSON CBE MC VD
5 Jun 1893, Toronto CWW52
see MATHERS, ALVAN, 1955/57/59

HALHED, HARRIET English
b Australia fl 1890-11 B DVP G TB
Addr: 1911, 5 Trebovir Rd, London, Eng
1911 75 The late M Louis Deschamps
76 Mrs Harrod, Frances Forbes-Robertson

HALIBURTON, ROBERT GRANT
3 Jun 1831, Windsor, NS 7 Mar 1901, Pass Christian, Miss H Mo98 W78
1880 271a Sketches (two) R.G. Haliburton

HALL, HARRY
see TAYLOR, ANDREW, 1884

HALL, JOHN ALEXANDER
10 Oct 1914, Toronto AGO CWW79 IO M WWA47
1946 52 The elm trees $300 T47-24
53 The yellow farm $300
1950 49 Congo 28 x 24 $300
50 The black fish 24 x 28 $300

HALL, JOHN SCOTT
17 Jan 1943, Edmonton WWA78
RCA(e) 1975 Painter
Addr: 1976/79, Calgary
1971 17 Runner 65 x 96 $1,000
18 Pepsi 65 x 96 $850
1976 S12, Montreal
21 Blackjack acry 84 x 65 illus

HALL, JOICE M. (Mrs John Scott Hall)
b 1943, Edmonton
1971 18 White flowers growing 65 x 65 $500

HALL, PHILIP
1942 53 Rosine $125 T43-16
54 Tolpt's farm $115

HALL, SYDNEY PRIOR English
18 Oct 1842, Newmarket, Eng 15 Dec 1922, London, Eng B DBA DVP G H RA TB WBA
1880 45 Marriage of Marquis of Lorne and Princess Louise (Marquis of Lorne)

HALL, THOMAS H.
6 Mar 1886, Ackworth, Yorks, Eng d 1972
Addr: 1913, 303 St James St, Montreal; 1938, Montreal
1913 124 Scarborough Bay, England wc $125
125 Old English cottage
126 On the Rivière des Mille Isles S4-55 $25 nfs
1938 S8, Toronto
144 Two posters, Canadian Pacific Railways

HALLAM, JOSEPH SYDNEY
19 Jul 1899, Manchester 26 Nov 1953, Toronto AGO CWW49 M NGC WWA47
ARCA 1943 RCA 1950 Painter
Addr: 1928-36, 35 Fairlawn Ave, Toronto; 1943-53, Toronto
1928 66 Rock Lake, Algonquin Park $200

1932 83 October $75
1936 93 Marsh's Falls, Oxtongue River $200
1938 91 Haliburton morning $150
1938 S8, Toronto
Sampson Matthews Ltd
333 Goodyear Tire, card
1939 F11, New York
30 Threshing bee 37 x 45 $300
1941 S9, Toronto
30 Ontario farm $50
1942 55 Nancy $100
1943 56 F.S. Haines, Esq illus nfs
57 Piano practice wc
1944 63 North of Manitoulin illus $300
64 Local freight $300 T45-20
1945 93 The white church $150
94 Spring morning $250 T46-21
1946 54 Penthouse $180 T47-25
55 Weekend rest $300 1947-71 T48-15
1948 72 Golden wedding illus $400
1949 38 Horse shoes $400 1950-51 30 x 40
1951 40 Greenhouse illus $400
1951 Travelling exhibit
22 Wayside market DW 1950 board 30 x 40 1954 Retro sec 25 Roadside market mispr
1952 35 Mixed doubles illus $400 T53-11
1953 31 Lanterns illus $400 S10-29 30 x 40 $600

HALLFORD, DONALD GORDON
26 Feb 1927, Toronto
1964N 123-5 Esquesing Municipal Office. General exterior view. Exterior. 1st floor plan

HALLIDAY, FRANCIS ROBERT
11 Jun 1884, Toronto flg 1975
Addr: 1914, 79 Spadina Ave, Toronto
1914 227 The Tower Bridge, London, England
228 Aquatint

HALLIDAY, RICHARD STUART
17 May 1939, Vancouver M
Addr: 1976, Montreal
1976 S12, Montreal
22 Expulsion acry 67 x 67 illus

HAMEL, JOSEPH ARTHUR EUGENE
14 Oct 1845, Quebec 20 Jul 1932, Quebec EC H M NGC TB3
RCA 1880 Ret 1885 Council Painter
Addr: 1880-5, Quebec
1880 55 Tableau de fruits d'aprês nature
95 Giovannina, paysanne romaine, portrait d'aprês nature
113 Portrait d'un militaire Belge, d'aprês nature DW 1880 25 1/2 x 20 Portrait d'un officier Belge 1881-279 Portrait 1954 Retro Sec 6 A Belgian officer
231 Ruins of the tomb of St Gobert wc
252 Zacharie Vincent, le dernier des Hurons de Lorette, pres de Québec, portrait au crayon de mine de plomb

HAMER, JACK
20 Aug 1914, Brighouse, Eng IO M
1943 58 Mississauga dam wc $25
59 Town creek wc $25
1944 65 Scott's Mills, Buckhorn, Ontario wc $35
66 Jackson's Creek, Peterboro $35 T45-21
1945 95 Sunday morning wc $35
96 Late March wc $25
1947 72 Bell Telephone trucks, Peterboro wc $55
73 Winter coal yard wc $35
1948 73 Snow water wc $75
1951 41 Bruce Parker's horses wc $50
42 Quiet Bay, Eels Lake $75
1952 36 Thaw weather $150

HAMILTON, HAMILTON American
1 Apr 1847, Oxford, Eng 4 Jan 1928, Norwalk, Conn AAA28 B F H TB1/2
1882 161 Old fashioned flowers wc $275

HAMILTON, IDA GERTRUDE
1887, St Mary's, Ont
Addr: 1925-6, 276 Charlton Ave W, Hamilton, Ont; 1929, 21 Avenue Rd, Toronto; 1931, 99 East Ave S, Hamilton, Ont; 1932-3, 94 Longwood Ave S, Hamilton, Ont
1925 96 Ledge Lane, East Gloucester, Mass
97 Dahlias, still life
1926 65 A group of houses, Glou-

cester, Mass
1929 89 Sunlight and shadow $250
1931 104 A Summer landscape $250
1932 84 Still life $175
1933 90 The green bowl $175
91 Winter, St George Street, Toronto $150

HAMILTON, PETER WILLIAMSON
15 Jul 1941, Toronto
RCA(e) 1978 Architect
Addr: 1979, Toronto

HAMILTON, THOMAS F.
Addr: 1976, Medicine Hat, Alta
1976 S12, Montreal
23 Untitled #1 oil on paper 22 1/4 x 30 illus

HAMME, J.H.
1880 15 By the fountain, Ariccia, Italy, after sunset (Allan Gilmour, Esq)

HAMMOND, JOHN A.
11 Apr 1843, Montreal 10 Aug 1939, Sackville, NB B G H M Mo98 NGC TB3
ARCA 1890 RCA 1893 Ret 1933 Council
Painter
Addr: 1890-2, Saint John; 1893, Owens Art Gallery, Saint John; 1894, Mount Allison College, Sackville, NB; 1895-01, Art Association of Montreal; 1902-24, Sackville, NB; 1925-5, Salem St, Sackville, NB; 1927-39, Sackville, NB
1884 S1, Saint John
203 Salmon pool (R.P. Starr)
204 Wharf in Carleton (R.P. Starr)
1891 18 Normandy roadway
23 Misty morning
32 In the village of Valmoidois
62 Misty morning, Saint John harbour
1892 5 Sunlight and fog $150
24 Evening $150
48 Harbour of Saint John, NB $500
1893 66 Herring fishing, Bay of Fundy F1-54 nfs DW 1894 31 1/2 x 41 1/2 1894-50
67 The Great Illecillewaet Glacier, Selkirks $350 F1-55
68 The Fraser River, Yale $350 F1-56
1894 49 The dulce gatherers
1895 67 The Willows, Sackville, NB
68 Blackfoot encampment, Calgary, Alberta
69 Bruges, Belgium
70 In the Saint John's harbour
1896 68 Sand dunes, Holland
69 Tantramar Marsh, NB
70 Summer
71 Early morning, Bay of Fundy
72 Evening, Bay of Fundy
1897 58 Saint John's harbour
1898 54 Gaspereaux fishing 1902-84 1903-69
1899 71 Outward bound
72 Windmill, Holland illus 1902-82
73 Gaspereaux fishery
1901 66 Herring fishing, Bay of Fundy nfs F2-38 (Sir William Van Horne)
1902 81 Sunrise, Bay of Fundy
83 Evening, Bruges
1903 68 Evening, Holland
1904 81 Fuji, Japan
82 Sunset, Saint John harbour F4-40
83 Summer in New Brunswick F4-41 1905-89
84 Fishing boats, Bay of Fundy F4-42
85 Rising moon F4-43
86 Misty morning F4-44
1905 90 Sandy Cove, Bay of Fundy
91 Inward bound
92 Sunrise
93 Outward bound
1906 106 Low tide, Saint John, NB
107 Belfry of Bruges F5-75 $200
108 Barges F5-76 $200
109 Sheep ranch
1906 F5, Halifax
77 Sheep ranch, Calgary, Alberta $65
1907 91 On the seashore F6-100 $250
92 Summer F6-99 $225
93 Dutch farm
94 Sand dunes, Holland
95 Dulce gathering F6-102 $60
1907 F6, Sherbrooke
101 Girl with sheep $250
1908 64 Evening
65 Battymith Channel
1909M 63b Willow Creek, Sackville
63c Market slip, Saint John
1910 92 Summer 1911-78
93 Mill pond
94 Landscape

95 Summerland 1911-77
1910 S2, Liverpool
54 Knocke, Belgium 1912-109
1912 110 Courtney Bay, Saint John
111 Landscape with sheep
112 Among the alders
113 Saint John harbour
114 On the Tantramar
1912 S3, Winnipeg
72 Harbour of Saint John, NB
73 Summer, Sackville
74 Return of the flock
75 Misty morning
76 The Willows
77 Dutch scene
1913 127 September ◊NGC◊
128 Bruges
129 Summer time S4-56 $75
130 Autumn F4-57 $75
1914 97 Bruges, Belgium
98 Barbizon, France
99 On the Oise, France 1916-105
1914 S5, Patriotic Fund
8 Herring fishing, Bay of Fundy illus
1915 99 Evening illus
100 Cattle drinking
101 Landscape, Belgium
1916 106 Birch Dale, NB
107 Under the willows, NB
1918A 79 Tantramar Marsh
1925 98 Knocke, Belgium
1926 66 Old mill at Knocke, Belgium
1927 81 Low tide, Bay of Fundy
1928 67 On the Marne $600
1929 90 Birch trees, Sackville, NB $250
1931 105 Canton, from the West River, China $1,500
1932 85 New York harbour $400
1933 92 Bay of Fundy, NB $500
1935 108 Fish weirs, Saint John, NB $500
port: by R. Harris, 1898-49

HAMMOND, KATHARINE
Addr: 1931, Sackville, NB
1931 106 Portrait study

HAMMOND, RODY see COURTICE, RODY

HANCOCK, HENRIETTA see BRITTON, HENRIETTA

HANCOCK, HERBERT
b 1830 d Dec 1880
ARCA 1880 Architect
Addr: 1880, Toronto
1880 345 Trinity Church, Belleville
350 Hamilton Court House
354 House erected for Henry Wickson
355 Equity Chambers
37- County art school museum library (in cat between 373 and 373a)

HANES, URSULA ANN
18 Jan 1932, Toronto CWW79 M WWA59
ARCA 1961 Sculptor
Addr: 1961-70, Toronto; 1971, Africa; 1979, Toronto
1955 104 Donald Davis sculp illus $300
1957 74 Clemence Dane, novelist bust $600
1959 83 Pan, fountain figure, Welland County General Hospital, Welland, Ont bronze 21 1/2 x 18 x 15
1960 78 Evan McGowan sculp nfs
1963 87 Dr Sidney Smith, late Pres University of Toronto sculp nfs
1965 78 Simon bronze 14h $1,200

HANKEY, ROLAND ALERS
Addr: 1931, 3459 McTavish St, Montreal
1931 394 and 395 Monogram bookplate des

HANNAFORD, CHARLES E. English
b 1863 21 Oct, 1955, England DBA DVP TB3 WBA WWB29
Addr: 1907, London, Eng
1907 250 Evening mists, Dartmoor wc

HANNAFORD, MICHAEL
1832, Stoke Gabriel, Devon, Eng
7 May 1891, Toronto H W78
ARCA 1880-8 Painter
Addr: 1880-2, Toronto; 1883, Metcalfe St, Toronto; 1884-6, Toronto; 1887, Saint John; 1888, Toronto
1880 74 The Chat Falls, Ottawa River
101 Gorham Gorge, White Mountains, NH
1881 17 Scene in Devon wc $30
306 Mountain range, New Zealand $20
1882 29 In Rosedale, Toronto $60
77 Source of the Otira,

Westland, New Zealand $300
1883 27 Autumn $35
57 Early summer, Rosedale $40
137 The Don Valley, a part of the proposed Toronto park scheme $150
1884 S1, Saint John
89 Scarboro' Cliffs $50
139 Megantic Range, from Spider Lake $30
1885 82 and 90 Berry Pomeroy Castle, Devon $20 each
119 Evening $20
120 The Lovers Leap, on the Dart, Devon $20
140 Near the Glen House, White Mountains $20
296 Rosedale $30
1887 88 Early autumn, Rosedale, Toronto $100
140 On Spider River, Eastern Townships wc $25
1888 95 Toronto from Scarboro' Heights $100
102 Rosedale $50
119 Devonshire coast $40
157 Toronto, from Norway $700
176 Berlin Falls, Androsogon River $100
189 Rosedale, Toronto $50
208 Rosedale Creek $35
227 On the Credit River $15
1891 181 On the Dart, Devonshire wc

HANNIBAL, ERIC
Addr: 1933, 1229 Mountain St Montreal
1933 258 Portrait head plaster

HANSON, GERTRUDE JEAN (Mrs John A. Elphick)
27 Sep 1933, Toronto CWW79 M WWA56
1963 33 Legendary land $200

HARCOMBE, RENEE (Mrs)
1939 95 Moonlight in Florida wc $75

HARDER, ROLF PETER
10 Jul 1929, Hamburg
RCA(e) 1974 Graphic designer
Addr: 1976/79, Montreal
1970 174 3 packages, pharmaceutical sample boxes. Herder mispr
175 Invitation, Montreal Symphony Orchestra
176 Advertisement, Noludar 300, pharmaceutical product
177 Advertisement, Librium, pharmaceutical product
178 Advertisement, for the graphic design magazine Format
179 Poster, Les matinées symphoniques
180 Symbol, Northern Venetian Blinds
181 Symbol, Canadian Association for Retarded Children
1971 30G Annual report, Royfund Ltd
31G Pharmaceutical sample, Hoffman-LaRoche Limited
32G Cover, type catalogue, Fonderia Tipografica Co-operative project
33G Symbol, IMASCO Limited, Rolf Harder, Ernst Roch
1976 S12, Montreal
121 Excel Modular Wall Systems, symbol illus
122 Queenswear (Canada) Annual Report 1973 illus

HARDIE, ISOBEL
Addr: 1929-30, 71 Russell Ave, Ottawa
1929 91 Yellow rose pastel $75
92 Iris pastel $50
1930 80 Yellow roses pastel $60

HARDING, EDITH NEILSON (EDYTHA)
Addr: 1932-7, 3783 Hampton Ave, Montreal
1932 86 The barn yard $75
1934 91 Laurentian village $75
92 Mount Rolland $75
1935 Edytha N. Harding
109 Solitude $75
110 Autumn $75
1937 91 Farm house in the Laurentians $100 T38-21

HARLANDER, SUSAN MICHEL (SUZANNE) (Mrs Théodore Harlander)
28 Nov 1920, Stuttgart IO M
1965 76 Encounter cement fondu 78 x 36 $2,600
77 Tree ter cot 16 x 16 $250

HARLANDER, THEODORE
1920, Germany M
1965 75 Joy cement fondu 94 x 69 photo $1,900
1966 77 First steps sculp illus $275

1967 75 Embrace cement fondu 48h $750

HARMAN, JACK KENNETH
31 Jul 1927, Vancouver M WWA73
ARCA 1971 Sculptor
Addr: 1979, North Vancouver

HAROLD, ELIZABETH M.
Addr: 1931, 339 Victoria Ave, Westmount, Que
1931 107 Young girl pastel $100

HARPER, JOHN RUSSELL
15 Apr 1914, Caledonia, Ont CWW79 WWA78
1941 76 Harvest morn $100

HARRINGTON, A.L. (Mrs)
H
1882 130 Martyrs to bush fire wc
208 Boule Rock, Little Métis wc

HARRINGTON, REBECCA CHRISTINA
21 Apr 1869, Toronto d 1930
Addr: 1928-9, 55 Elm Ave, Rosedale, Toronto
1928 68 Violets wc $400
69 Cinerarias wc $300
1929 93 Spring wc $500

HARRINGTON, RUTH M.
Addr: 1907, Montreal
1907 251 Evening pastel

HARRIS, ALFRED PETER
4 Apr 1932, Toronto M WWA73
1963 34 Figure in interior summer 62 #1 $400
1964N 26 Voyage 40 x 36 $300

HARRIS, BESS LARKIN (Mrs Frederick Broughton Housser) (Mrs Lawren Stewart Harris)
18 Nov 1890, Brandon, Man 28 Sep 1969, Vancouver M
1950 52 Summer shore 30 x 36 $200

HARRIS, J.T.
1938 S8, Toronto
Pringle & Booth, Limited
209 Photomontage decoration
210 Group of photographs
209-10 J.T. Harris, Bruce Milne

HARRIS, LAWREN PHILLIPS
10 Oct 1910, Toronto AGO B CC1 CWW66 M NGC TB3 WWA47
ARCA 1943 RCA 1966 Council Painter
Addr: 1936-7, 25 Severn St, Toronto; 1943-6, Toronto; 1947-71/76, Sackville, NB; 1979, Ottawa
1936 94 Septuagenerian $250
95 Chinese $250 T37-32
1937 92 Elfreda $75
1939 96 Decorative nude $200
1939 F11, New York
31 Amos 36 x 44 $250
1941 S9, Toronto
31 Figure $12
31a Ballerina $15
1945 Capt L.P. Harris
97 Battle ground before Ortona, Italy (Chief of General Staff, Lieut Gen Charles Foulkes, CB CBE DSO)
1950 55 Night forms 28 x 36 $300
1953 32 Monument $400
1964J 30 Derailment 21 x 42 illus $600 S10-30 illus
1966 21 Night garden 45 x 42 $850
1966 S10, Charlottetown
31 Alternating sequence 49 1/2 x 36 $850
1970 31 Planes in space 46 x 78 $1,000
1971 19 Theme and variation #2 75 x 40 $1,200
1976 S12, Montreal
24 Parallels $3 acry & latex 40 x 78 illus
DW 1967 Spring garden oil on board 32 x 36

HARRIS, LAWREN STEWART LLD
23 Oct 1885, Brantford, Ont 29 Jan 1970, Vancouver AGO CC2 CWW66 EC M NGC TB2 W78 WWA47
RCA medal 1969, Group of Seven
Addr: 1912, 2 Bloor St W, Toronto; 1913, 18 Clarendon Ave, Toronto; 1914-27, Studio Bldg, 25 Severn St, Toronto
1912 115 The corner store 1913-132 S4-59 $500 nfs S5-75 illus
116 Houses in the Ward
117 The Eaton Mfg Building
1912 S3, Winnipeg
78 Deserted barn
79 Row of houses, Wellington Street, Toronto
185-90 Pencil sketches
1913 131 Sunrise through rime S4-58 $500 nfs

1914 100 Winter morning ◊NGC◊
1919 76 Snow VII
1922 91 Beaver swamp S6-36 ◊AGO◊
92 Elevator Court, Halifax ◊AGO◊
1923 71 Pines, Kempenfelt Bay
72 Above Lake Superior ◊AGO◊
1927 82 Mountain form S7-68 nfs
83 Ontario hill town illus
1929 S7, Calgary
67 Lake Superior nfs
1950 53 Formative 40 x 51 nfs
54 South Peak, Mount Victoria 51 x 36 $750
Tribute to Lawren Harris, by R.Y. Wilson, 1971-46

HARRIS, ROBERT CMG
18 Sep 1849, Tyn-y-Groes, Wales
27 Feb 1919, Montreal AGO B CC1 CWW10 EC H M Mo98/12 NGC R1 TB1/3 W78
RCA 1880 Council Painter
Addr: 1880-1, Toronto; 1882, Paris; 1883, Montreal; 1884, 40 St John St, Montreal; 1885-6, Montreal; 1887, Bolton Studio, Radcliffe Rd, Fulham Rd, S Kensington, London; 1881-92, Montreal; 1893, YMCA Bldg, Montreal; 1894-11, c/o Art Association of Montreal, 23 Phillips Sq, Montreal; 1912-19, 11 Durocher St, Montreal
1880 36 The chorister DW 1880 29 1/4 x 24 1/4 1881-314
52 Boy's head, study
54 Alice Mitchell, Micmac Indian of Prince Edward Island
64 The exile, study
70 The news boy (Ontario Society of Artists) 1881-259 ◊AGO◊
111 The rejected suitor
112 The unruly guest; portraits of children of G. Stethem, Esq
1881 218 Enoch Arden (Jas. Jardine, Barrie, Ont)
227 Toronto Arabs playing jack knife (W.H. Howland)
258 Anxious moments $20
281 Landing the lobster catch (H. Suckling)
324 Miles Standish, the Puritan Captain $75
1882 23 An Arab on the lookout $60
53 A hearer of St Paul ◊MMFA◊
70 The flute player
84 For all his days are sorrow
1883 13 Chaff $250
30 'And marked the conquered patriot's brow, when Caesar's triumph thronged the streets of Rome' $100
35 'And whosoe'er the fight's event, he keeps his honest soldier's name' $115
39 Ante-room of the Atelier Bonnat, Paris $75
42 Romany girl $75
67 Girl's head $15
82 Charcoal dealer's yard in a French village $90
86 Finishing touches $40 S1-141
102 A Roman model $40
109 Cut out $50
1884 7 Canadian fiddler $200
13 and 86 Portrait
17 Tobogganning up the gully to park slide $55
24 Meeting of the delegates of British North America to settle terms of Confederation, Quebec, October 1864
32 Boy from the Campagna, Rome $75
35 All, all are gone, the old familiar faces $175
65 '...and son from sire, through passing generations, learns the fate of all' $200 S1-138 $150
71 A glass too much $65 S1-104
76 At it again $65
90 The colour sergeant hard-pressed $200 S1-81
93 A waif $75
115 Boss of the shanty wc $50
181 Burd Hellen wc $50
1884 S1, Saint John
4 Master of the situation wc $35
39 Birds of a feather wc $65
48 An old man wc $40
106 Somebody's grandfather $75
113 An ecclesiastic $150
1885 9 Waiting to confess $110
28 An old soldier $175
37 Comrades $250
48 From the Campagna $70
101 A Roman model $90
1886 125 By the shores of Gaspé $1,000
152 The castaway sold
156 Meeting of the trustees

of a back settlement school, Canada, the teacher talking them over $1,000 ◊NGC◊ Fla-2001
174 Indian squaw and papoose $300 Fla-2001
177 Prairie Indian, N W of Canada $300 Fla-2001
1886 Fla, London, Eng
2011, artist number
By the shores of Gaspé
1887 48 Sunday afternoon $40
51 A village maiden $25
100 A lady fair $16
102 The old batchelor and the old maid $140
1888 107 Composing his serenade $250 Fl-59
112 Little gossips $100
120 Taking his top note, the tenor of Spruce Creek School District $800
150 Portrait $100
154 A Chelsea Pensioner $60
172 Friends $60
175 Harmony $100 1893-75 $140 Fl-64 nfs ◊NGC◊
215 Autumn $60
1889 26 The local stars, Pine Creek School District $800 ◊CON◊
31 Bad dog $60
53 Hon G.W. Allan, Speaker, Senate 1891-65
64 In a studio $55
102 Near Sturgeon Point $50
116 Two of a kind wc $60
1890 36 Sir Joseph Hickson nfs ◊NGC◊
37 and 38 Portrait of a lady
39 In a convent of the 16th century $550
40 A tough subject $60
41 At a wharf, Charlottetown $30
42 The lark's death $175
43 An ancient Briton $110
1891 46 In the woods
55 Near Sandy Hook, Sturgeon Lake
59 On the cottage steps
63 The dead bird
64 Going wrong 1892-49 $500
66 An old friar
67 The cow pen
68 Portrait of a lady
69 Prelude
1892 34 Portrait $220
42 With thoughts not on her work $40
47 Near Brachley Point, PEI $40
85 Portrait of a lady
128 Portrait
1893 69 Sir John Allen nfs
70 Portrait of a lady nfs
71 O.R. Jacobi, RCA nfs ◊NGC◊
72 Miss Peterson nfs Fl-60
73 Master Lionel Lindsay nfs
74 The homely house that harbours quiet rest $550 Fl-61
76 In July, Métis $55
1893 Fl, Chicago
57 Gilman Cheney, Esq nfs
58 Mrs Ross nfs
1894 60 A.F. Gault
61 Canadian backwoodsman
62 Youth and age
63 Study of a head
1895 58 P.A. Peterson, Esq
59 Selim
60 On the Maine coast
61 Head
1896 73 Francis J. Shepherd, MD
74 Mrs P.A. Peterson
75 Coming in, Gulf shore fishing boat
76 Percé Rock, summer's day
77 North Bay, Percé
78 Early morning, Percé
79 Hauling the flat
80 Melodia 1897-62
1897 59 Peter Redpath, Esq (#60 not in cat)
61 The summer moon, fishing village, Percé
63 Near Cap à l'Aigle
64 Spruce trees, North Shore
1898 46 Summer, Phillips Square, Montreal
47 The nihilist
48 Robert Lindsay, Esq
49 John Hammond, RCA
50 Come, if you dare
51 Looking at the miniature
1899 63 Mrs C.E.L. Porteus and children
64 The late Robert Hamilton, Esq, Quebec
65 Study of a head
66 The vision of Père Breboeuf, martyred in the Jesuits Huron Mission, 1649 illus
1900 50 Hon W.H. Tuck, Chief Justice, New Brunswick
51 Young Canada

52 The love letter
53 Portrait study
1901 61 Mrs A.F. Riddel F2-34
62 Mrs R.H. F2-35 1906-100 F5-78 Mrs Robert Harris $750 S2-56 Mrs Robert Harris
63 Banjo boy F2-36 F6-103 $700
1902 85 Mrs W.W. Watson
86 Mrs G.W. Stephens
87 Mother and daughter
88 G.M. Kinghorn, Esq
89 Evening
90 Oriental dealer
1902 F3, Rochester
72 Before the song illus $280 1903-58 1905-101 1908-68
1903 56 HE the Countess of Minto. Commissioned by Art Association of Montreal F4-45 S2-55 [MMFA]
57 Sir Louis H. Davies. Presented by friends in Prince Edward Island on his elevation to the Bench, Supreme Court of Canada
1904 87 Dr William Osler, Baltimore F4-46
88 John Hope, Esq
89 Mrs Roswell Fisher
90 Mrs Charles Martin
91 Mrs F. Mathewson
92 Mrs J.B. Porter
93 Mrs Eugene Lafleur
1904 F4, St Louis
47 Portrait
1905 99 Mrs E.F.B. Johnston
100 Mrs W.R. Riddell
102 Man's head, a study
1906 99 Hugh Graham, Esq, Montreal
101 'A thought ungentle canna be the thought of Mary Morrison' F5-79 $500 1908-96
1907 96 Robertson Macaulay, Esq. Commissioned by Directors of Sun Life Assurance Company
97 Judge Doherty. Presented by a number of his confreres on his retirement from the Bench
98 Abner Kingham, Esq
99 In wonderland
100 Leezie Lindsay. 'She's off wi' Lord Ronald Macdonald, his bride and his darling to be.'
1907 F6, Sherbrooke
104 Head of a girl $450
1908 67 Mrs J.K.L. Ross and children
1909M 63a Highland lassie
1909N 65 Miss Canada
66 Man's head, study
1910 96 Time and tide will wait for no man
97 Mrs D.A. Gurd
98 The student
99 An old man
1910 S2, Liverpool
57 Lost in the forest
1911 79 Old fisherman, Normandy
80 From a Normandy fishing village
81 Man's head, study
1912 118 The happy task
119 Cinderella
120 Man's head, study
121 The post office, Etaples
1912 S3, Winnipeg
80 The banjo player
81 Adversity
1913 133 John Cox, MA LLD. First Professor of Experimental Physics, McGill University
134 The reader S4-60 $600
1914 101 Man's head, study
102 Summer moon
1914 S5, Patriotic Fund
4 Steady and unafraid illus
1915 102 The old hulk, Etaples
103 Mariuccio
104 Sir Thomas Roddick, LLD illus
1916 108 Portrait illus [Self portrait MMFA]
109 Percé Rock
110 Man's head, study
1918N 84 Late David Stewart, Esq

HARRIS, WILLIAM CRITCHLOW
30 Apr 1854, Bootle, Eng 16 Jul 1913, Halifax
ARCA 1881 Architect
Addr: 1881, Charlottetown; 1882-92, Winnipeg; 1893-10, Charlottetown; 1911-13, Halifax
1881 202-7 Church des
1886 189 Holy Trinity Church, Winnipeg competitive des
190 Municipal Buildings, Winnipeg competitive des
191-2 Holy Trinity Church. Front. Interior, col. competitive des
193 Minerve des
1895 43A St Dunstan's Cathedral, Charlottetown, PEI
44A St Dunstan's interior

45A St Paul's Church, Charlottetown, PEI
1900 192 Presbyterian Church, Windsor, NS
193 Residence, Wm. Carter, Esq, Charlottetown
194 Academy at Pictou, NS des
195 Memorial Library, Auburn, NY des
196 Holy Trinity Church, Winnipeg des
197 St Dunstan's Cathedral, Charlottetown des

HARRISON, ALLAN see HARRISON, WILLIAM ALLAN

HARRISON, EDITH ELIZABETH (Mrs)
6 Apr 1907, London, Ont M
1941 77 Winter harvest $75 T42-20

HARRISON, LOVELL BIRGE American
28 Oct 1854, Philadelphia 12 May 1929, Woodstock, NY AAA29 B F H TB
Addr: 1904, Quebec
1904 94 The woodsmen
95 Logging in winter

HARRISON, WILLIAM ALLAN
27 Dec 1911, Montreal M
RCA(e) 1979 Painter
Addr: 1979, Montreal
1970 182 Book jacket, The Quebec revolution

HARROD, STANLEY
fl 1910-38
Addr: 1918, 83 MacPherson Ave, Toronto; 1937, 231 Garden Ave, Toronto
1918A 234 Book plates etch
235 Book plates print
1937 316 Illum address to HE Lord Tweedsmuir
317 Decorative heraldry nfs
1938 251 Illum address to His Honour Albert Matthews, LLD, Lieut Gov of Ontario
252 Illum text nfs

HART, PERCIVAL see TUDOR-HART, PERCIVAL

HARTLEY, MURIEL see COTTINGHAM, MURIEL

HARVEY, A.F.
1939 267 and 268 Interior perspective wc $50 and $30

HARVEY, DESMOND VACHELL (signs Desmond Vachell)
Addr: 1929, 24 Summerhill Ave, Montreal
1929 210 Portrait of a boy pastel

HARVEY, DONALD
14 Jun 1930, Walthamstow, Eng M
WWA76
ARCA 1970 Painter
Addr: 1971/76/79, Victoria
1966 22 Moonlighter 56 1/4 x 70 $700
1970 26 Trailing window landscape 60 x 60 $1,000
1976 S12, Montreal
25 Inside and out oil & lucite 60 x 66 illus

HARVEY, GEORGE H.
1846, Torquay, Devon, Eng 1910, England H
ARCA 1882-01 Painter
Addr: 1881-2, Halifax; 1883, 43 Victoria Rd, Halifax; 1884-92, Halifax; 1893, People's Bank Bldg, Halifax; 1894-01, Halifax
1881 109 Sketch wc
115 Sketch in harvest wc
296 The labourer's rest $75
303 Sunshine after storm $35
315 By the weir, on the Thames $45
316 A Welsh farmyard $60
321 Leafless $150
1882 41 A sunny corner $200
1883 100 Early morning $300 1884-59
1884 70 Winter toil $75
1886 13 In the Annapolis Valley $250 Fla-2002
1893 77 Afterglow, Annapolis Valley, NS $400

HARVEY, (Mrs) GEORGE H. see HARVEY, PRISCILLA

HARVEY, HESTER (Mrs)
Addr: 1916, Government House, Sackville, NB
1916 246 Cypress bronze
247 Mélisande bronze

HARVEY, PHYLLIS NELSON (Mrs Cecil Richards)
17 Nov 1906, Montreal
Addr: 1932, Studio Bldg, 25 Severn St, Toronto
1932 87 Glads $25

HARVEY, PRISCILLA (Mrs George H. Harvey)
fl 1883-6 H
Addr: 1883, 43 Victoria Rd, Halifax
1883 117 Portrait nfs
1886 116 Near Point Pleasant

HARVEY, SYDENHAM PARKER
2 Jan 1914, Cobden, Ont M
Addr: 1934-7, 57 Palmer Ave, Toronto
1934 202 Mallards bronze
1935 281 Striped skunk bronze $125
282 Young fox bronze $125
1936 218 Racoon sculp $150
1937 283 Racoon sculp Sitka spruce $125

HARVOR, STIG
1 Feb 1929, Helsinki
1971 Schoeler, Heaton, Harvor & Menendez
13A-15A Office building, PSAC Holdings, Ltd, Ottawa. View of building from Gilmour St. Panel, end view of building, floor plans, building section. Panel, carved door in Conference Centre, sculptor James Boyd. Detail, carved doors, building facade, view of Conference Centre Hall, and ground floor exterior

HASPEL, TUTZI (Mrs Seguin)
14 Oct 1911, Romania IO WWA47
1938 Seguin
194 Roumanian landscape $100 T39-49
1951 Haspel-Seguin, to 1952
133 Cape Cod drwg nfs
1952 37 Flowers $150
1953 Seguin, to 1961
77 Cape Cod wc $100
1955 98 Saguaros $75
1961 73 Girl with bird 18 x 35 $150

HASSELL, HILTON MACDONALD
14 Mar 1910, Lachine, Que 2 May 1980 IO M
RCA(e) 1973 RCA 1976 Painter
Addr: 1936, Port Credit, Ont; 1979, Picton, Ont
1936 96 Ex-MP Samuel Charters nfs
1938 92 Trixie nfs
93 Rev Archd C. Saddington nfs
1938 S8, Toronto
E.W. Reynolds & Co, Limited
217 6 scratchboard drwgs, advertisements for Magazine Publishers Association
218 Cylinder carton, Simms lather brush. H.M. Hassell, J.M. Bowman
1958 41 Ship shapes $350
1959 38 Quarry facets 38 x 24 $350
39 Cove shapes 28 x 36 $400
1960 39 Dock and dory 28 x 42 $750
1961 40 Harbour rides, Looe, Cornwall 36 x 24 $500
41 Little market, Cadaques, Spain 24 x 40 $600
1965 31 One morning in Ireland 20 x 48 $750
1966 23 Pause 28 x 40 $700
DW 1976 Axel Heiberg, Eureka Sound, eastern Arctic acry on masonite 36 x 48

HAWKSETT, SAMUEL C.
1827, London, Eng d 1903, Montreal H
1880 67 Fruit piece

HAWKSLEY, J. FREDERICK (or Hawkesley) H
Addr: 1886, London, Eng
1882 87 Portrait of a horse
1886 Fla, London, Eng
2003, artist number
Bend of a river in the Eastern Townships, autumn

HAWLEY, WILHELMINA D.
fl 1898-05 H
Addr: 1899, 16 Rusholms Rd, Toronto
1899 173 The cold bath wc
174 Cleaning brass wc
175 Le bien Aimée wc
176 La bataille du fleurs wc

HAWORTH, BOBS see HAWORTH, ZEMA

HAWORTH, PETER
28 Feb 1889, Oswald Twistle, Lincs, Eng AGO CC2 CWW79 EC IO M NGC TB2/3 WWA47
ARCA 1946 RCA 1954 Sr 1962 Council Painter
Addr: 1923, 100 Pricefield Rd, Toronto; 1930-6, 100A Pricefield Rd, Toronto; 1937, 111 Cluny Dr, Toronto; 1946-71/79, Toronto
1923 73 The red cap
208 Stained glass window col cart
1930 81 Trees wc $75

82 Water colour $75
1931 108 Outhouses wc $100 ◊NGC◊
109 Tree wc $75
396 Bunyan Memorial window, Hamilton, Ont. st gl des
397 Templeton Memorial window st gl des
1932 88 Bleak farm wc $100
89 Flour mill wc $100
1933 94 Black Rock, Nova Scotia wc $75
95 Back street wc $75 T34-34
1934 94 Harbour beach, Grand Etang, Cape Breton $100 T35-29
1935 112 Blue derrick wc $50
113 Riding stables wc $75 T36-33
1936 98 Bic, Quebec wc $75
99 Range light, Fox River, Quebec wc $75 T37-33 ◊NGC◊
1937 94 South shore, St Lawrence wc $75
95 The Saguenay wc $75
1938 95 White Fish Falls, Ontario wc $75 T39-21
96 Pines wc $75
1939 98 Old apple orchard wc $75
99 Incoming tide wc $50
1940 69 Nauset Light wc $75
1941 S9, Toronto
33 Sand hills, Cape Cod $75
1942 57 King County, November wc $80 T43-18
1944 69 Fishing village with nets drying, Cape Breton wc illus $75
70 Pool wc $75
1946 56 A Laurentian valley wc $100
57 Lobster buoys, Cape Breton $100
1947 76 Tarring nets wc $50
77 Old water wheel $150 T48-17
1948 75 Sand dunes wc $65
76 Laurentian village wc $70
77 Harbour wc $85
1949 40 Fishermen at work wc $100
41 Caulking wc $90
1951 45 North country lake wc $125
46 Haliburton wc $125
1952 39 Swamp bonnets, arum lilies wc $125
1953 33 Driftwood wc illus $125 DW 1956 19 1/2 x 25 1/4
1954 41 The saucy Jane wc 21 x 26 illus ◊LAG◊
42 Flowers of the field wc 21 x 26 $150
1955 42 Mist on the lake illus $150
43 Village by the sea $150
1956 23 Ice on the lake $175 T56-20 1958-55 illus $200
1957 32 Scarecrows on the fish racks $200
33 Fishing fleet illus $200
1958 43 Late autumn $175
1959 42 Barachois bridge 20 x 25 illus $200
43 Ontario village 20 x 25 $250
1960 41 Herring weir 21 x 25 $250
42 Estuary 22 x 30 illus $300
1961 43 Hill town 30 x 22 $350
44 Floating dock 20 x 25 $250
1963 35 Dark lake tangle $350
1964J 31 Mine shaft m med 25 x 20 $225
1964N 27 Woodland 30 x 32 illus $350
1965 33 Frozen river 22 x 30 $350 S10-34
34 Lake fringe 22 x 30 illus $350 S10-35 illus
1966 25 Track of the beaver 22 x 30 $350
26 Sea-swept trees 22 x 30 $350
1967 25 Ice-break 22 x 30 $350
26 Storm swept 22 x 30 $350
1968 23 Pebbles on the beach 20 1/2 x 25 $275
24 Reeds in the lake 22 x 30 illus $350

HAWORTH, ZEMA BARBARA COGILL (BOBS)
(Mrs Peter Haworth)
20 Jan 1904, Queenstown, S Africa
AGO CWW79 IO M NGC TB3 WWA47
ARCA 1948 RCA 1963 Painter
Addr: 1923, 100 Pricefield Rd, Toronto; 1930-6, 100A Pricefield Rd, Toronto; 1937-71/79, Toronto
1923 74 The bathers wc
75 Derelicts wc
1930 83 and 84 Water colour $75 each
1931 110 Bridge wc $100
111 Shore road wc $75
1932 31 Reflections wc $100
1933 93 Riding stables wc $75 T34-33
1934 93 Closed season, Grand Etang, Cape Breton $100 T35-28
1935 111 Nunzio T36-32
1936 97 Burnt stump, Cap des Rosiers, Quebec wc $75
1937 93 Apple trees and barn, Ontario wc $60

1938 94 King Ridge, Ontario, summer temp $75
1939 97 King Ridge wc $75
1940 67 Kelligs and claw temp $75
68 Beach, Petit de Grat, CBI temp $75
1941 S9, Toronto
32 The estuary, Cape Cod $60
1942 56 Swordfish boat, Cape Breton Island $400 T43-17
1944 67 Farmer Jones, his family and his farm $150 T45-22
68 Coastal schooner, St Lawrence gouache $75
1946 58 Barns, St Agnes, Quebec gouache $85
1947 74 Fisherman's paraphernalia, CBI gouache $125 T48-16
75 Low tide, north shore, Quebec gouache $125
1948 74 Dear departed gouache $100
1949 39 The old order m tech $250 T50-8
1950 56 Our town on the beach 26 x 31 $300
57 A summer pattern 26 x 21 $150
1951 43 The old root fence, Ontario $350 1952-38 T53-12
44 Estuary gouache $100
1953 34 Pale autumn $350
35 Boats black and white and Percé Rock gouache illus $150
1954 40 Way north wc 21 x 26 illus $150
1955 40 Grebe family $350
41 Harbour, boats and fish and things illus $150
1957 30 Boscastle harbour, Cornwall $325
31 Blue bridge $175
1958 42 Scarecrows, for fishing flakes illus $200
1959 40 Ontario village 28 x 40 illus $400
41 Bridgeside, wharfside 22 x 30 $300
1960 40 Afterglow 30 x 22 $300
1961 42 Tangled Island 40 x 54 illus $600
1964J 32 Beach m med 22 x 31 $300
1965 32 Gros Thorn 46 x 60 $700
1966 24 Promontory 57 x 43 illus $700
1966 S10, Charlottetown
32 Autumn and the lake $600
33 Gros Morn 46 x 60 $700
1967 27 Blue tulip 54 x 40 $650
28 Chrysalis emerging 45 x 55 $700
1968 22 Spring thaw 45 x 55 illus $700
1970 27 Red tulip 42 x 54 illus $600
DW 1963 Village, Percé gouache varnished 30 x 22

HAWTHORN, HENRY GILBERT
11 Jan 1939, Honolulu
RCA(e) 1974 Architect
Addr: 1979, Vancouver

HAWTHORNE, MARION MCLURE
14 Mar 1897, Montreal CNS36
Addr: 1934-6, 4505 Cumberland Ave, Montreal
1934 95 Sunflowers $50 T35-30
1935 114 Church, Ste Adèle $100
1936 100 Marigolds $45 T37-34
1941 78 Ranunculi nfs T42-21

HAY, JOHN
Addr: 1931, 100 Flora St, Toronto
1931 112 Passé pastel $35
398 Portrait of a gentleman steel engr $25

HAY, NORMAN KYLE
1883, Ottawa
Addr: 1935, 2 York Apts, South St, Halifax
1935 115 A bit of coast, Prospect, Nova Scotia $50

HAYDEN, MICHAEL
15 Jan 1943, Vancouver IO M
RCA(e) 1975 Sculptor
Addr: 1979, Agoura, Cal

HAYES, G. BALY (Mrs)
Addr: 1922, 602 Devon Court, Broadway, Winnipeg
1922 93 Madame Neduzak
94 Brownie pastel

HAYMAN, STANLEY
30 Nov 1910, Toronto M
1952 106 Frame of medals. R Adm Lord Mountbatten; Gov Gen Viscount Alexander; P M Louis St Laurent; Secy of Defence, USA, General Marshall; Gov Gen Rt Hon Vincent Massey; P M of GB Rt Hon Winston Churchill; Prometheus; Peterborough Cen-

tennial

HAYNES, DOUGLAS HECTOR
1 Jan 1936, Regina M WWA73
ARCA 1970 Painter
Addr: 1971/79, Edmonton
1971 20 #3 August 1970 40 x 66 $1,000

HAYWARD, ALFRED FREDERICK WILLIAM
1856, Ravenscourt, n Port Hope, Ont
14 Mar 1939, Hemingford, Hunts, Eng
B DVP H RA TB
Addr: 1895, Troyford, Winchester,Eng
1888 83 Narcissus
97 Flowers $25
181 Yellow roses F. Hayward mispr
199 Feeding the hens $80 F.A.C. Hayward mispr
1895 50 Rose, Anna Oliver
51 Christmas roses
52 Fruit
53 Oranges and grapes

HAYWARD, GERALD SINCLAIR
22 Jan 1845, Port Hope, Ont 1 Apr 1926, New York. H M Mo12
Addr: 1915, 684 Sherbrooke St W, Montreal
1915 274 Case of miniatures wc on ivory

HAYWARD, JAMES
dates not on file
RCA(e) 1978 Industrial designer
Addr: 1979, Scarborough, Ont

HAZELGROVE, ALBERT JAMES
10 Jun 1884, London, Eng 19 May 1958, Ottawa CWW55
Addr: 1930, 63 Sparks St, Ottawa
1930 169 Christ Church Cathedral, Ottawa, the new Chancel

HAZELL, EILEEN LONG (Mrs Stanley G. Hazell)
7 Mar 1903, Richmond, Surrey, Eng
M
1963 88 Alert cer $100

HEAD, GEORGE BRUCE
14 Feb 1931, St Boniface, Man CCI M WWA73
ARCA 1970 Painter
Addr: 1971/76/79, Winnipeg
1965 35 Section one, 65 61 x 45 $600
1976 S12, Montreal
26 Redhead acry 50 x 58 illus

HEALEY, MARY
5 Jan 1885, Bradford, Yorks, Eng
12 Jan 1923, London, Ont
Addr: 1920, 143 Sydenham St, London, Ont
1920 124 Portrait of a girl
125 Near London, Ontario wc

HEASLEY, DONALD J.
Addr: 1925, 116 Jeanne Mance St, Montreal
1925 258 Portrait bust

HEATHCOTE, ERIC T.
Addr: 1930, 107 Wanless Ave, Toronto
1930 85 Beauport, Quebec wc $40

HEATON, ALEX M.
see HARVOR, STIG, 1971
SCHOELER, JEAN, 1976

HEAVEN, ETHEL R.
fl 1897-02 H
Addr: 1900, York Chambers, Toronto; 1901, 46 Gerrard St E, Toronto; 1902, McKenzie & Co, Toronto
1900 58 Study of an Indian pastel
59 Evangeline
60 Portrait study
61 Kathleen Mavournine
1901 64 Fisherman's wife
1902 202 Twilight in Holland wc

HEBERT, ADRIEN
12 Apr 1890, Paris 7 Jun 1967, Montreal B CC2 CNS36 CWW61 M NGC TB2 W78 WWA47
ARCA 1932 RCA 1942 Sr 1959 Council Painter
Addr: 1910, 217 Berri St, Montreal; 1915, 182 St Catherine St E, Montreal; 1916-18, 34 Labelle St, Montreal; 1920-5, 7 Ste Julie St, Montreal; 1931, 7 Place Christin, Montreal; 1932-7, 341 Place Christin, Montreal; 1938-67, Montreal
1910 100 Sunrise
1915 105 Clair de lune
1916 111 Dans un parc
112 Sunrise
1918A 294 Une nuit, un faune appelait
295 Paysage
294-5, Trustees, National Gallery of Canada, Travel-

ling Scholarship competition
1918N 85 Le train de banlieu
86 Le grain
1920 126 Le danse
127 Bacchanale
1924 84 La Place St Henri, Montreal
1925 101 Paysage de Provence
292 Le port drwg
293 Portrait drwg
1931 113 Hangars et élévateur $200
1932 90 Château Ramezay $200 1933-96 $175
238 and 239 Landscape charcl $75 each
1933 97 Vue de Montréal $175 T34-35
296 Duchess of Richmond charcl $75
1934 96 Winter sports $350 T35-31
1935 116 La Place Jacques Cartier $500 T36-34
1937 96 La Côte Lamontagne, Québec $225 T38-22 F11-32 25 x 30
97 Vue de Québec $350
318 La pluie, Québec drwg $50
1939 100 In the harbour, Montreal illus $300
1939 Travelling exhibit
22 Québec $250
1940 70 Parc Montmorency, Québec $350 T41-23
1941 79 Le port $600
80 Le petite école $250 T42-22
1942 58 L'Archevêché à Québec $350 DW 1942 32 3/4 x 32
59 Vue de Québec $300 T43-19
1943 60 Matin au port illus $400 T44-21
61 Dans l'atelier appartient à Roger Maillet nfs
1944 71 Landscape, Quebec $325 T45-23
72 Harbour, Montreal $300
1945 98 La rue $400
99 L'église Saint Pierre $150
1946 59 The harbour $500
60 The rain $200 T47-26
1947 78 Place Jacques Cartier illus $750 T48-18
79 Le port $300 T48-19
1949 42 Coin d'atelier illus $300 T50-9
1950 58 Street scene 30 x 40 $500
59 Harbour, Montreal 34 x 36 $500
1951 47 On the waterfront $500
1952 40 Le port illus $500
41 Intérieur $500 T53-13
1953 36 SS Empress of Canada $500
1954 41 Retro Sec. Market, Place Jacques Cartier (MMFA)
1960 43 Colonne Nelson 24 x 30 $400
port: by T.R. MacDonald, 1947-110

HEBERT, HENRI
3 Apr 1884, Montreal 11 May 1950, Montreal AGO B CC2 CNS36 CWW48 M NGC TB2 WWA47
ARCA 1912 RCA 1922 Council Sculptor
Addr: 1910-25, 34 Labelle St, Montreal; 1926-37, 1238 Labelle St, Montreal; 1938-50, Montreal
1910 200 M Lassalle bust plaster
201 Le grain de beaute bronze
1911 186 Study plaster
1912 236 Le vie est parsemée de roses et d'épines plaster 1913-320 1914-204 bronze
237 Pauline plaster
238 L'Abbé Mélançon plaster
1913 321 Study bronze
1914 205 Silence plaster S5-82 illus
1915 230 King Edward VII sketch model
231 Sir William Edmund Logan sculp
232 Bicot plaster
1916 248 G. Horne Russell, Esq plaster 1919-178 Mr G.H.R.
249 Le masque plaster
250 Study of a head plaster
251 Mlle Madeleine de L. plaster
1918A 188 Fatum plaster 1919-177
1918N 210 Dr D.M. sculp
1919 175 Evangeline sculp 1921-177 bronze (NGC)
176 1914 plaster 1922-219 illus bronze DW 1923 14 1/2h S6-107
1920 267 Mr J.B. Learmont plaster
268 Le faune plaster
269 Life is full of thorns bronze
270 Mr G.D. plaster
1921 178 Portrait sculp
179 Habitant plaster
1922 218 Yarmouth boy plaster
220 Sir Rodolphe Forget plaster
1923 76 Mlle Cécile P. pastel
185 Outremont War Memorial plaster
1925 259 L'avenir. Ecole Ste

Julienne Falconieri plâtre
260 Jean Bourgoin, portrait plâtre
261 Sir Alexandre Lacoste plâtre
262 Symbole de St Mathieu, église St Ambroise plâtre
1926 160 Alphonse Jongers bronze illus S7-162 nfs F7-186 plaster $55 ◊bronze AGO NGC MQ◊
161 Etude plaster
162 Outremont War Memorial. Base in collaboration with J. Roxburgh Smith photo
1927 260 Sir Andrew Macphail plaster illus
261 The flapper plaster 1928-165 bronze $150
1928 163 Mr J.A.E. Dubuc plaster
164 The charleston bronze $150 S7-161
166 Hon L.O. David plaster
1930 188 Gui Couture, Esq KC $400 bronze or marble
1931 315 John Murray Gibbon, Esq plaster
316 Dean Moyse bronze $200
1933 259 St Christophe sculp
1934 203 St Christophe sculp 1ère étude
1935 283 Mme F.R. plaster nfs 1936-219
1937 284 Rt Hon R.B. Bennett bronze nfs
285 Mr J.B. Rolland plaster nfs
1939 248 Kateri Tokakwita plaster
1940 160 Danseuse d'Oslo bronze limited to 3 copies $1,500
1943 127 Armand Dupuis, Prés, Maison Dupuis Frères nfs 1944-147
128 Louis Francoeur, journaliste nfs
129 Dr Montgomery nfs 1945-224 plaster
1945 225 Charles Fitzgerald plaster nfs
1947 202 Ezechiel Hartt, MPP, 1807-1808 plaster nfs
1949 113 Frère Marie Victorin, EC plaster nfs
114 Medaille Agfas gilded silver nfs

HEBERT, JULIEN
19 Aug 1917, Rigaud, Que M TB3 WWA59
ARCA 1970 Industrial designer
Addr: 1970-1/79, Montreal

HEBERT, LOUIS PHILIPPE CMG LH(Fr)
27 Jan 1850, Ste Sophie d'Halifax, Que 13 Jun 1917, Westmount, Que
B CC1 EC M Mo98/12 NGC R1 TB1/3 W78
ARCA 1880 RCA 1886-9 ARCA 1905 RCA 1906 Council Sculptor
Addr: 1880-9/1904-5, Montreal; 1906-15, 34 Labelle St, Montreal; 1916-17, Montreal
1880 128 The Passover wd carv
131 The Last Supper wd carv
143 Adoration of the shepherds and magi sculp
145a Crucifix sculp
1881 211 Medallion
1886 122b Lucien sculp
122c Blanche sculp
122d Sir H. Lafontaine statuette
122e Msgr Déziel sculp
1886 Fla, London, Eng
2026, artist number
Sir Herbert Langevin, KCMG, Minister of Public Works statue
1904 297 Sans merci, group bronze
298 Kironyare statuette S2-115
299 Le rêve du fumeur statuette
300 Mirror frame carv wd
1906 191 L'Inspiration, group bronze F5-80 $100 DW 1907 22 1/2h
1910 202 Maritine messier, groupe sculp
203 Fugitive, épisode du massacre de Lachine en 1689
1910 S2, Liverpool
114 A chance for freedom sculp
116 Mlle de Verchères sculp
1915 233 A la claire fontaine sculp
1918A the late L.P. Hébert
189 Kironyare bronze
190 Coeur qui chante bronze port: by J. Saint Charles, 1904-38

HECHT, ESTELLE
b Montreal 1971, Montreal M
1961 45 The city in a dream etch 10 x 14 $25

HECHT, ETHEL
Addr: 1929, 401 Marcil Ave, Montreal; 1930-3, 3797 Marcil Ave, Montreal
1929 266 Snap dragons temp $15
267 Bowl of flowers temp $15
1930 86 Garden flowers temp $15
87 Nasturtiums temp $15
1931 114 Flower study I temp $15
115 Flower study II temp $15
1933 98 and 99 Flower study temp $15 each

HEDRICK, ROBERT
1 May 1930, Windsor, Ont AGO IO M
RCA(e) 1973 Painter
Addr: 1979, Toronto
1963 36 Island passage $1,000
1964J 33 In transit 70 x 70 illus $900
34 Over blue 84 x 60 illus $900

HEGEMANN, HEINER
1970 183 Book cover, Emile Zola: The naturalist novel
184 Book cover, Dorothy Henderson: The heart of Newfoundland

HEIMLICH, HERMAN
18 Jun 1904, Setoraljaujhely, Hungary
Addr: 1935, 223 Mount Royal Ave W, Montreal
1935 117 Girl in bathing suit pastel $60
1939 101 Quebec landscape $75
1961 46 Composition with bottle 25 x 53 $100

HEINRICH, F.W.
Addr: 1909M, Ottawa
1909M 58 Girl watering

HELLAND, EARL
1971 7I Storage units, Cameron-McIndoo Limited

HELLER, MARY IDA CLAIR
15 Feb 1909, Toronto
Addr: 1932, Toronto
1932 210 Head of a man plaster

HELLIWELL, GRANT
3 Nov 1855, Todmorden, Ont 26 Dec 1953, Toronto H
see GORDON, HENRY BAULD, 1883-1895

HELME, J. BURN
Addr: 1931, Smith Falls, Ont
1931 116 French village wc $80

HELMER, D'ARCY GRAHAM
28 Apr 1923, Newington, Ont
1971 Helmer & Gibson
16A-19A Sparks Street Mall, Ottawa. Provincial rock garden, 'Contemplative'. Looking east from Bank Street, a citizens forum and meeting place. Looking west from Elgin Street, the planters provide additional seats. Complete plan from Elgin through Bank Streets

HEMING, ARTHUR HENRY HOWARD
17 Jan 1870, Paris, Ont 31 Oct 1940, Hamilton, Ont B CC2 CWW10 M Mo98 NGC TB W78 WWA40
ARCA 1934 Sr 1939 Illustrator
Addr: 1912-29, Toronto; 1930-2, 64 Grenville St, Toronto; 1933-6, 57 Bloor St W, Toronto; 1937-40, Toronto
1912 S3, Winnipeg
191 The fur trapper
192 The fur trader
193 The fur trader's daughter
194 Royal North West Mounted Policeman
195 Study of an antelope
1929 S7, Calgary
69 Wolves attacking a wolverine $300
70 The forest fire $300
71 Mother bear caught in a snare $300
1930 88 Canadian white-water men $1,000
1931 117 Where the Red Gods live $1,000
118 Voyagers crossing the Rockies $650
1932 91 In Canadian wilds illus $1,200
1933 100 Canadian jam crackers (Frank P. O'Conner, Esq) T34-36
101 Canadian timber cruisers $550
1935 118 Northern morning (Charles Watson, Esq)
119 On the Alaska border $500 T36-35
120 Voyageurs, 'Spelling one

smoke' $1.000
1936 101 The Abitibi fur brigade $1,000
1938 S8, Toronto
MacLaren Advertising Co, Ltd
175 Booklet, Canada, your friendly neighbour invites you. Arthur Heming & others
1939 102 In the white man's country $1,000
1939 F11, New York
33 The caribou hunter 30 x 40 nfs

HEMINGWAY, PETER
6 Sep 1929, Minster, Sheerness, Eng
RCA(e) 1975 Architect
Addr: 1976/79, Edmonton
1976 S12, Montreal
102 Muttart Conservatory, Edmonton 2 illus

HEMMING, EDITH
fl 1896-03 H
Addr: 1901-2, 582 Church St, Toronto
1901 169 Case of miniatures wc
1902 262 Ivory miniatures
263 Two portraits min

HEMSTED, MARGARET J. (Mrs)
b England d before 1924 H
Addr: 1898, 415 Shaw St, Toronto
1898 168 A glance of sunshine wc
169 In the country places wc

HENDERSON, JAMES
21 Aug 1871, Glasgow 5 Jul 1951, Regina M NGC W78
Addr: 1935, Fort Qu'appelle, Sask
1935 121 October in the valley nfs
122 The creek in winter nfs

HENDERSON, W.R.
1898 166 Evening landscape wc
167 Moonrise wc

HENEKER, EVE
Addr: 1927-9, 1533 Mackay St, Montreal
1927 84 Still life
1929 94 Sketch $125
268 The hill town drwg

HENEY, F.E.
1939 103 March afternoon nfs

HENNESSEY, FRANK CHARLES
12 Jan 1894, Ottawa 7 Nov 1941, Ottawa AGO CCI M NGC W78
ARCA 1934 RCA 1941 Painter
Addr: 1921, 400 Cumberland St, Ottawa; 1924, 239 Chapel St, Ottawa; 1927-30, 91 Rideau St, Ottawa; 1931, 401 Albert St, Ottawa; 1932-3, 95 Rideau St, Ottawa; 1934-6, 135 Nepean St, Ottawa; 1937, 176 1/2 Nepean St, Ottawa; 1938-41, Ottawa
1921 71 Crows
1924 85 Tiger resting
86 Winter hare
1927 85 Northland twilight
1928 70 Gulls resting $200
1929 95 Grey day in March, Quebec $150
96 Houses in the hills, Quebec $150
1930 89 The hunter illus $300 1931-120
1931 119 The home in the hills $300
1932 92 Fin de la visite $500
1933 102 The ice sawyer pastel $300 T34-37
103 The winter road pastel $300
1934 97 Morning sun illus $500 T35-32 ≬AGO≬
98 Hibou River pastel $300
1935 123 The forest pool $400
124 Autumn day $400
125 Summer evening pastel $150 T36-36
126 Jobber's camp pastel $75
1936 102 Mont Louis, Gaspé pastel $200 T37-35
103 At Rivière â la Martre, Gaspé pastel $150
1937 98 Winter in the Gatineau $300 T39-23
99 Ice cutting on the Pickanock $300
100 Winter road $300
101 Gatineau home pastel $100
1938 98 In the forest $500
99 Poplars in spring $300 T39-23
100 Road in winter $300
101 Gatineau River pastel illus $200
1939 104 Fall River $700
105 Gatineau road $300
106 The trout fisherman $300 1940-72
107 Gatineau Lake $300
1939 F11, New York
34 Winter landscape 34 x 40 $700

1940 71 Morning after the snowfall $500 T41-24
73 November day pastel $100
74 Bridge at Farrelton pastel $100
1941 81 Winter landscape $700
82 The setting sun $700
83 Laurentian landscape $700 ◊NGC◊
84 Edge of the forest $300
1954 24 Retro Sec. Sugar bush DW 1945 34 x 40. Presented by Mrs George Elliott, Trenton Ont, in place of DW

HENNING, JACOBSEN
1971 O Canada film screened 31 Mar

HENRIQUEZ, RICHARD GEORGE
5 Feb 1941, Annotta Bay, Jaimaca
RCA(e) 1978 Architect
Addr: 1979, Vancouver

HENRY, FREDERICK
8 Aug 1865, London, Ont 7 Feb 1929
Addr: 1895, London, Ont
1895 40 Residence, J.S. Smallman, Esq, London
41 Residence, R.C. Struthers, Esq, London
42 Episcopal Church, Glencoe

HENSHAW, ARTHUR N.
fl 1885-01 H
1885 51 Hot house grapes A.M. Henshaw, mispr
172 Flowers

HERALD PRESS CO, LIMITED
Addr: 1938, Montreal
1938 S8, Toronto
145 Original cover suggestions Paul Emond

HERBERT, WILLIAM BEVERLEY PEY
1916, Medicine Hat, Alta M
1947 80 Mount Assiniboine $200

HERDER, ROLF see HARDER, ROLF

HERDMAN, ROBERT Scottish
17 Sep 1829, Rattray, Scot 10 Jan 1888, Edinburgh B DBA DVP H TB
1881 30 Rose Bradwardine and Waverley wc (Miss J. McHinch)
34 Flora McIvor wc (Miss J. McHinch)

HERIOT, J.C.A.
see MACVICAR, DONALD, 1902-25

HERKOMER, HUBERT VON (Sir) English
26 May 1849, Waal, Bavaria 31 Mar 1914, Budleigh Salterton, Devon, Eng B DBA G RA TB
1881 147 Portrait etch (Lady Macdougall)

HERTZBERG, PHYLLIS see ARMOUR, PHYLLIS

HERZOG, SAUL
see SECORD, JAMES EDWIN, 1964N

HETMANN, DALE
Addr: 1976, Richmond, BC
1976 S12, Montreal
143 Stuffed post fabric 12 x 12 illus Hetman, mispr

HEUSCH, LUCIO DE
5 Jun 1946, Sherbrooke, Que
Addr: 1976, Montreal
1976 S12, Montreal
11 Peinture #10 acry 72 x 72 illus

HEWARD, EFA PRUDENCE
2 Jul 1896, Montreal 19 Mar 1947, Los Angeles AGO CC1 EC M NGC W78 WWA47
Addr: 1924-7, 390 Sherbrooke St W, Montreal; 1928-9, 904 Sherbrooke St W, Montreal; 1936, 3467 Peel St, Montreal
1924 87 Eleanor
88 Portrait study
1926 67 Florence, Italy
1927 86 Anna illus ◊NGC◊
87 Gwyneth
1928 71 Girl on a hill $600 ◊NGC◊
1929 97 At the theatre $600
1936 104 Rosaire $1,000

HEWETT, FRANK English
fl 1903-13 DBA RA
Addr: 1913, West Buckland, Eng
1913 135 In a Devonshire valley wc S4-61 $52.50
136 The road to the village, Buckland, south Devon wc

HEWSON, MARIE OLIVIA (Mrs Benson Guest)
21 Aug 1880, Oxford, NS d 1965 M
Addr: 1912, Amherst, NS; 1914-18

10 Rupert St, Amherst, NS; 1926-30, 109 Lenore St, Winnipeg
1912 122 Early autumn
1914 103 A clearing-up shower, Provincetown, Mass
104 The Butter Hall, Bruges wc
1918N 87 Gateway, Provincetown
88 Hollyhocks
1926 Guest, to 1939
62 Gateway, Provincetown
1927 78 Polish women in fields of Manitoba
1928 62 A Ukrainian girl $300
63 Morning in the Winnipeg market pastel $75
1929 84 Market gossip pastel $40
1930 77 Afterglow $150
1938 84 Mike Garega's place $85
85 The Assiniboine in winter $85
1939 87 Riding the storm $150

HEWTON, RANDOLPH STANLEY
12 Jun 1888, Maple Grove, Megantic, Que 17 Mar 1960, Belleville, Ont
AGO CC1 CWW58 M NGC PMC TB2 WWA47
ARCA 1921 RCA 1934 Sr 1955 Council
Painter
Addr: 1907, Montreal; 1910-12, 26 rue des Fleurus, Paris; 1914-15, 74 44th Ave, Lachine, Que; 1920-4, 258 Bishop St. Montreal; 1925-6, Montreal; 1927, 805 Keefer Bldg, St Catherine St W, Montreal; 1928-32, 1850 Lincoln Ave, Montreal; 1933-4, Glen Miller, Ont; 1935, Box 860, Trenton, Ont; 1936-60, Trenton, Ont
1907 102 Winter
1910 101 Street scene, Venice
102 Atlantic combers
1911 82 Jardin du Luxembourg, winter
83 Jardin du Luxembourg, autumn
84 A wet day
85 Venetian canal
1912 123 Moonlight, Camaret-sur-Mer
124 Camaret-sur-Mer, twilight
125 Mrs C. Arnold Slade
1914 105 Portrait
106 Landscape
1915 106 April
107 May
1920 128 Miss Sybil Robertson illus 1921-72 illus
1922 95 Portrait
96 Carmencita
97 Dulcinia
98 Fishing quarter S6-38
1923 77 and 78 Portrait
1923 S6, Hamilton
37 Portrait
1924 89 Miss B. Warner (NGC)
90 Portrait
91 Murray Bay church
263 Conté drawing
1927 88 Miss Audrey Buller illus
1928 72 Miss Ethel Williams 1932-96 DW 1935 'Portrait of a young lady' 50 x 48 T51-23
1929 98 Sleeping woman (NGC)
1931 121 Benedicta $1,000 1932-93 illus $3,000
122 Decoration $700
123 Standing figure $300
124 The village of Bic
1932 94 Nude $500
95 Landscape $1,000
1933 104 T.A, portrait T34-38 nfs
1934 99 Marie $600 T35-33 1935-127 nfs
1935 128 Betty nfs
1937 102 Miss Benedicta Caverhill nfs
103 Portrait in sunshine nfs
1939 108 Mon homme nfs
109 Les Eboulements en haut nfs
110 Winter in the province nfs
1942 60 Nancy nfs T43-20
1945 100 Freda nfs 1946-61
101 Jim Green's cottage nfs T46-22
1946 62 Vanishing snow $125 T47-27
63 Winter sketch nfs T47-28
1948 78 Miss Janet Saylor nfs
79 Autumn trees $200
80 The Murray River, Quebec $125
81 Hills, Port au Persil, Quebec $125
1954 40 Retro Sec. The bathers (Arts Club of Montreal)

HEYMANN, GUNTER
1 Jan 1908, Berlin d 1960
1947 81 Stable interior wc $75

HEYWOOD, JOHN CARL
6 Jun 1941, Toronto IO M WWA76
RCA(e) 1973 Print maker
Addr: 1976/79, Kingston
1971 21 Disparates 26 x 31 illus $125

1976 S12, Montreal
159 Beware the past screen pr/sérigraphie 29 x 43 illus

HICKLING, WALTER ROBERT
1 Mar 1924, Delhi, Ont M WWA56
1949 45 The clown band $250 Hicklin, mispr
1966 27 Prophecy 58 x 36 nfs
28 Boatman III 48 x 54 $385
1968 25 Osiris 40 x 48 $375

HICKS, RICHARD PERCIVAL DANIEL (Rev)
1903, Sussex, Eng 18 Jan 1973, London, Ont M
1968 26 March the 25th 21 1/2 x 29 1/2 $250

HIESTER, MARY see REID, MARY

HILDEBRAND
1880 49 Double effect (Major De Winton)

HILL, DONALD RICHINGS
12 Jun 1900, Buffalo, NY 1939, Toronto M
Addr: 1920-7, 361 Kensington Ave, Westmount, Que
1920 129 Self portrait
1922 99 A young Spaniard S6-39
100 Mr Thomas Harding min
101 Miss Alice Lighthall min
1923 79 Peggy
1925 102 Claire, daughter of W.R. Watson, Esq min
1927 89 Mr David S. Walker

HILL, GEORGE WILLIAM
6 May 1862, Shipton, Que 17 Jul 1934, Montreal CC2 M NGC PMC TB2 W78
ARCA 1908 RCA 1917 Council Sculptor
Addr: 1896, YMCA, Montreal; 1907-14, Montreal; 1915-18, 255 Bleury St, Montreal; 1919-30, Montreal; 1931-2, 1207 Bleury St, Montreal; 1933-4, Montreal
1896 281 Proposed monument, Samuel de Champlain, at Quebec sketch model
282 Panel, symbolizing wealth sculp
1907 F6, Sherbrooke
171 Rt Hon Lord Strathcona and Mount Royal, GCMG bust $500
172 Fred Ully bust bronze $700 1908-183, Fred Ulley
1915 234 Late Hon T. Berthiaume funeral monument model
235 Strathcona Horse photo
236 Cartier Monument fragment photo
237 Monument model photo
1916 252 Late Hon T. Berthiaume bust bronze
1918A 191 Wm. Brymner, Esq, CMG RCA bust bronze DW 1918 19h 1918N-212 illus
1918N 211 Motherhood. Tribute to the hero of the Battle of the Long Sault sculp
1931 317-20 James Mitchell Memorial Fountain, Sherbrooke, Quebec. Spring, summer, autumn, winter
1932 211 Edmund Dyonnet, RCA plaster illus 1933-260

HILL, JAMES THOMAS
30 Dec 1930, Hamilton, Ont M
RCA(e) 1973 Illustrator
Addr: 1979, Toronto

HILL, KATE FOSS
1846, Halifax 1936, Windsor, NS H
Addr: 1906, Rockingham, NS
1906 F5, Halifax
81 Duncan's Cave $25
82 Old canal, France $35
83 Nasturtium $10
84 Daffodils $10
85 Pelargoniums $9
86 Canal, Crecy en Brie $15
87 Rose garden $15
88 Willow pond $15

HILLENBRAND, JOSEPH
Addr: 1933, 4643 Sherbrooke St W, Westmount, Que
1933 297 Soft night wd engr $10

HILLYARD, CAROLINE LEAROYD (CARRIE)
b St Mary's, Ont H
Addr: 1895-04, 79 Czar St, Toronto; 1905-8, 9 Sultan St, Toronto
1895 56 Alicia, portrait Hilliard, mispr
57 Study of daffodils
1898 52 Portrait study
53 Portrait
1901 60 One of the students
1904 96 The young sculptor
97 The morning glory F4-48
1905 87 Summer time

88 Lights and shadows
1906 F5, Halifax
80 The choristers $200
1907 104 The winter girl F6-107 $125
1907 F6, Sherbrooke
108 Mrs Wm. Roberts, Granby, Que $75 nfs
109 Marguerite $75
110 Harvesting in western Ontario $30
1908 70 Guiseppe Donato, sculptor

HILTS, ALVIN
2 Apr 1908, New Market, Ont IO M WWA59
1954 104 Dancer sculp 36h nfs
1955 105 Fifteen sculp $400
1956 48 Figure sculp $300
1959 84 Junior executive sculp 20 x 20 $450
1961 80 Torso #18 sculp 30h $250

HINE, CICERO
1880 270 Cabinet des prize award

HINGSTON, LILLIAN ISABEL PETERSON
(Mrs Donald Alexander Hingston)
Aug 1881, Montreal 29 May 1967, Montreal Mo12
Addr: 1929-35, 1000 Sherbrooke St W, Montreal
1929 99 Poppies $75
100 Hydrangea $75
1931 125 Dahlias $110
126 A March windowsill $60
1935 129 Nasturtiums $100
1939 111 December dusk $50

HIRSCHBERG, MARTIN
3 Dec 1937, Toronto IO M
1966 29 Luve 48 x 72 $600

HITCH, JOHN
1971 81 Lighting fixture, Galaxi Lighting Limited

HODGSON, THOMAS SHERLOCK
5 Jun 1924, Toronto AGO CC2 M NGC ARCA 1961 RCA 1970 Council Painter
Addr: 1961-71/79, Toronto
1952 42 Yellow circle wc $65
1953 37 Clam shell scoop wc illus $100
38 Derelict $400
1954 43 Blue beach 24 x 36 illus $120
1955 44 Non objective, greenish illus $180
1961 47 Shirt 51 x 34 illus $350
1963 37 Two faces of Sophia 82 x 61 illus $900 S10-37
1966 S10, Charlottetown
36 Midriff $900
DW 1970 Handy's ceramic sculptures ink & wash on paper 39 3/8 x 29 5/8

HOGAN, THOMAS
H
1882 256 Islands in Georgian Bay monoc

HOGG, CECILY
1951 48 Pearl McCarthy Sabiston nfs

HOIT, ALBERT GALLATIN American
13 Dec 1809, Sandwich, NJ 18 or 19 Dec 1856, West Roxbury, Mass Gr H
1881 331 Judge Haliburton Hoyt
332 T.C. Haliburton, Sam Slick

HOLBROOK, ELIZABETH MARY BRADFORD
(Mrs John G. Holbrook)
7 Nov 1913, Hamilton, Ont M WWA73 ARCA 1972 RCA 1975 Sculptor
Addr: 1979, Hamilton, Ont
1947 203 Emanuel Hahn, RCA SSC bust plaster nfs
1948 166 Perce Tacon, MA BPAED plaster for stone nfs
1949 115 The young David plaster nfs
1951 116 Reginald Godden, pianist, Principal, Hamilton Conservatory of Music plaster for bronze nfs
1952 107 Emanuel Hahn, RCA SSC, portrait head #2 sculp 1953-115 illus
1955 85 Harry Somers, Canadian composer sculp nfs
1959 85 Late Emanuel Hahn, RCA SSC sculp $2,000
86 Federal Building, Hamilton, stone carv. Husband & Wallace architects
1963 89 Hon Ellen Fairclough, Post Master General, Canada bronze $2,000 1964J-71 1965-81
1968 57 Rev James H. Robinson life size head and neck sculp illus nfs
DW 1975 Charles Fraser

Comfort, 1973 bronze 1 1/4 life size bust, on granite base

HOLDEN, SARAH B. (SARA)(Mrs Hunter)
b Belleville, Ont H
ARCA 1895-04 Painter
Addr: 1893-7, 49 Belmont Park, Montreal; 1898-01, Montreal; 1902-4, USA
1887 108 A corner of my studio
1890 44 Maidenhood nfs
45 The loving gaze $25
169 Only a rose wc $5
1893 78 Portrait nfs F1-63
79 A Brittany interior nfs F1-64
80 A son goût $200 F1-65
81 Study of a head $25
1894 51 Widowed but not forsaken
52 A grey day at Lachine
53 La rue Petit Champlain
1896 81 'I was an hungered' Matt. 25:35
82 The hour of service, Holland
83 The poppyfield, Holland
1897 66 Portrait
67 Paint me, Auntie

HOLDER, EDWARD HENRY English
1864, Scarborough, Eng 1917, Eng
B DBA DVP G RA TB
Addr: 1902, Redhill, Surrey, Eng
1902 93 Surrey trout pool E.R. Holder, mispr

HOLGATE, EDWIN HEADLEY
19 Aug 1892, Allandale, Ont 21 May 1977, Montreal AGO CC1 CNS36 M NGC TB2 WWA47
ARCA 1934 RCA 1937-45 RCA 1954 Sr 1962 Council Painter
Addr: 1915-19, 44 Rosemount Ave, Westmount, Que; 1920, 305 Beaver Hall Hill, Montreal; 1922-6, 67 Ste Famille St, Montreal; 1927-8, 364 Dorchester St W, Montreal; 1929-30, 648 Dorchester St W, Montreal; 1931, 65 Rosemount Cr, Westmount, Que; 1934-6, 3535 Lorne Ave, Montreal; 1937-45, Montreal; 1954-71, Morin Heights, Que
1915 108 Yokohama
1916 113 A study
114 Noonday
1919 77 Amiens station, March 29th 1918
78 Dugout in Chalk, near Blangy
1920 130 Jamaican shore
131 Late afternoon, Jamaica
1922 102 Suzy ◊NGC◊
102 Young woman in red
255 Young woman sewing charcl
256 Portrait study sanguine illus S6-118
1923 80 Study
209 Drawing chalk
1924 92 Two friends
93 The lumber jack 1927-90
264 The log driver wd block
265 Laurentian landscape wd block
1926 68 Quebec village
179 Tsimshian chief drwg
180 Tsimshian Indian drwg
1927 91 Portrait illus
1928 73 Portrait sketch
74 Laurentian lake $250
1929 101 Gitseguklas $400 ◊NGC◊
102 Paul, trapper $300
1930 90 Ludivine $350
1931 127 Laurentian snow $350
399 Drawing $50
400 Winter litho $10
1934 100 By the lake illus $400 T35-34
1935 130 Ski tracks $100
131 Portrait, Constance $80
132 Quebec coast line $100 T36-37
133 Portrait nfs
1936 105 The skier illus nfs T37-36
238 Pencil drawing $40
1938 102 Early autumn nfs DW 1939 28 1/2 x 29 1/2 T51-24 1954 Retro Sec 43
1939 112 Azalea nfs
1939 F11, New York
35 The bathers 32 x 32 (Art Association of Montreal)
1941 85 At an eastern port, March '41 $200
1950 60 Laurentian cemetry 20 x 24 $200
1955 45 Little girl $225
port: by L. Newton, 1934-221

HOLLAND, MIRIAM RAMSAY
19 Aug 1904, Montreal 13 Apr 1953, Montreal
Addr: 1932-5, 1477 Fort St, Montreal; 1936-7, 1471 Closse St, Montreal
1932 92 Blue Rocks, harbour, Nova

Scotia $150
1935 134 Landscape, Laurentian Mountains $150 T36-38 1938-104
1936 106 Village street, St Hippolyte $150
1937 104 Winter in the alley $85 1938-103 $100
1940 75 Farm houses $125
76 Sunlight and shadows $85
1941 86 Rock formation, New Brunswick $60
1951 49 Geranium on window sill

HOLLINGSWORTH, FREDERICK THORNTON
8 Jan 1917, Goldborne, Lancs, Eng
RCA(e) 1974 Architect
Addr: 1979, Vancouver
1964N 126-9 Berkeley Private Hospital, White Rock, BC. Exterior view 1 and 2. Interior view of canopy. Ground floor plan

HOLMAN, DONALD R.
20 May 1946, Kansas City
RCA(e) 1978 Print maker
Addr: 1979, Toronto

HOLMAN, JAMES HENRY
1821, London, Eng d 1891 H
Addr: 1884, Saint John
1884 182 Portrait (Mr Johnston)
183 Kathleen and Saint Kevin (T. Furlong)
191 Portrait (Mr Parks)

HOLMDEN, KENNETH HENSLEY
23 Feb 1893, Montreal 8 May 1963, Montreal
Addr: 1929, 1134 Beaver Hall Hill, Montreal; 1932, 1483 Closse St, Montreal; 1935, 388 Olivier Ave, Westmount, Que; 1937, 4081 Dorchester St W, Westmount, Que
1929 103 A holiday visit dec panel $500
1932 240 The phoenix dec panel in metal & oils $150
1935 135 Catfish panel, metal cols $100
1937 105 The breakfast $100
1939 113 The glazen earthenware horse $75
114 The red lacquer cabinet $125
1941 235 Map of Quebec, capital of New France $175
1947 82 The old sand pit $300 T48-20

HOLMES, EYRE
Addr: 1920, 338 Somerset St E, Ottawa
1920 132 Along the Ottawa

HOLMES, REGINALD
4 Nov 1934, Calgary IO M WWA59
RCA(e) 1974 Painter
Addr: 1979, Toronto

HOLMES, ROBERT H.
25 Jun 1861, Cannington, Ont 14 May 1930, Toronto AGO CC2 M NGC R1 TB2 W78
ARCA 1909 RCA 1921 Council Designer
Addr: 1908-1909M, Graphic Arts Club, 70 Victoria St, Toronto; 1909N, Graphic Arts, Yonge St Arcade, Toronto; 1911-13, 140 Bond St, Toronto; 1914-28, 24 Isabella St, Toronto; 1929-30, Toronto
1908 71 Gentians
1909M 173 A heraldic battle des textile hanging
174 Illuminated address Homes mispr
1909N 67 Morning
68 Evening
69 The showy orchid
1911 213 Pitcher plants des
1912 264 Fireweed wc
265 Epipactis wc
266 Pyrolas wc
267 Coral root wc
268 Hepaticas wc
269 Columbine wc
1913 360 In the sphagnum swamp wc S4-151 $300
1914 S5, Patriotic Fund
80 Trilliums illus
1916 115 Fireweed wc
116 Sunflowers wc
117 Milkweed wc
1918A 80 Yellow water lillies wc
81 Mocassin flowers wc (NGC)
82 Pink lady's slipper wc 1920-311
1920 310 Cardinals wc
1921 73 Autumn fluff dec panel DW 1922 26 x 39 1/2
1922 104 Pipsissewa wc
105 Canada anemone wc S6-40
106 Coral root #2 wc
1923 210 Pink lady's slipper wc 1925-103

211 Tulips dec panel wc
1924 94 Jack-in-pulpit wc
95 Coral root wc 1925-106
96 Evening primrose wc
97 Purple loosestrife wc 1925-104 F7-30 $500
266 Tulip tree dec panel 1925-294
267 Illustration 'Rambles of a Canadian naturalist'
1925 105 Jewel weed wc
1926 69 Gerardia wc
1928 75 Turk's caps wc $300
1929 S7, Calgary
72 Yellow gerardia wc $500
73 Showy orchids wc $300
74 Great lobelia wc $300

HOLMFELD, EYVINO H. DE DIRKINCK VON (Baron)
b Denmark fl 1893-05 H
Addr: 1902, Monument National, Montreal
1902 158 Fall evening, Lake Washington

HOLMSTED, MARIE H. (Mrs)
1857, Toronto 1911, Moose Jaw, Sask H
Addr: 1895-9, Dundas, Ont; 1901, 124 University Ave, Toronto; 1907, Toronto; 1908, 166 Wright Ave, Toronto
1895 34W On the Mountain, Dundas wc Holmested,mispr
35W Study, blue bird wc
1897 16W Game wc
17W Marsh hawk wc
1898 170 The Horseshoe Falls from the west wc Hemsted, mispr
171 Owl and blackbirds wc
172 Roses wc
1899 177 Cotton-tail rabbit wc 1901-171
178 An evening effect, Niagara Falls wc
179 Green winged teal wc 1901-170
1907 253 Some mallards wc
1908 78 Waterfall in Algonquin Park

HOLT, EDWIN ALBERT
23 May 1921, Toronto
1940 77 The artist's mother nfs
1941 87 George E. Victor, Esq nfs
1944 Lieut E.A. Holt
73 Nancy $500 T45-24

HOLT, GEORGE ALBERT COCHRANE
10 Oct 1902, Montreal
Addr: 1931, 85 Church Hill Ave, Westmount, Que
1931 128 Landscape wc $35
129 St Paul du Ver wc $30

HOO, SING (HOO SING YUEN)
c May 1909, Canton CWW79 M WWA47
ARCA 1948 RCA 1966 Sculptor
Addr: 1948-71/79, Toronto
1938 236 Toiler sculp $800
1939 251 Astonishment sculp $800
252 Mr Sidney Chong sculp $500
1941 213 Toiler sculp $500
1942 163 Helen sculp $500
164 Prayer sculp $800
1943 120 Meditation sculp $800
1944 148 Youth sculp $300 1945-227 $500
1945 226 Old age sculp $500
1946 133 Beverley sculp $500 1947-204
134 Dreaming sculp $500 1947-205
1948 167 The child sculp illus $200 1949-116 $350
168 The thought sculp $500
1949 117 Catherine sculp $500
1951 117 Catherine sculp $600
1953 116 Child sculp nfs
1954 105 Elizabeth sculp 12 x 14 illus nfs
1955 107 Catherine sculp nfs
1956 49 Catherine sculp $800
1957 75 Meditation sculp $500
1958 87 Thinking sculp nfs
1959 87 Catherine sculp 21 x 8 nfs
1960 79 Cecelia sculp nfs
1964J 73 Catherine sculp 20h $1,000
1964N 72 Child sculp 9 x 11 nfs
1965 79 Bear sculp 7 x 11 nfs
80 Child sculp 11 x 9 illus nfs
1968 58 Spring sculp 9 x 15 $1,200
DW The sculptor's wife, Noral Chambers bronze 16h

HOOD, HARRY
7 Feb 1876, Cupar Scot 10 Jul 1956, Vancouver
Addr: 1935, 1103 Robson St, Vancouver
1935 136 English Bay, Vancouver wc $40 T36-39
1938 105 The back steps $40
1939 115 Industrial interlude $75

HOOKER, MARION see NELSON, MARION

HOOLE, KATE see SMITH, KATE

HOOVER, DOROTHY HAINES (Mrs G.L.J. Hoover)
10 Mar 1904, Toronto
Addr: 1933-7, 11 York St, Apt 3, St Catharines, Ont
1933 105 Turner's house, Bear Island wc $25
1934 101 Low tide, Dorail wc $25
102 Bishop's boats wc $25 T35-35
1935 137 Coal siding wc $35
138 Mme Gagnon's wc $35 T36-40
1937 106 Charlton Rock $300
107 Alligator Point $150

HOPE, WILLIAM R.
May 1863, Montreal 5 Feb 1931, Montreal H M Mo12 NGC W78
ARCA 1895 RCA 1902 Council Painter
Addr: 1893-7, 1226 Dorchester St, Montreal; 1898-01, 291 Mountain St, Montreal; 1902, Fraser Institute, Montreal; 1903, 1737 Notre Dame St, Montreal; 1904-7, Montreal; 1908-24, 994 Dorchester St W, Montreal; 1925-31, Ritz Carlton Hotel, Montreal
1890 46 March day $60
47 Study of snow nfs
1893 82 Table du Roi, Forest of Fontainebleau $175 F1-66
1895 65 Moonlight on the Loing, France
66 Moorlands, near Fontainebleau
1897 73 Landscape, departing day
1898 45 Salmon fishing in Gaspé
1899 67 Approaching storm, St Andrews, New Brunswick illus
68 Moonrise, Bord à Plouffe
69 Burning rubbish, Bord à Plouffe
70 Evening after rain
1901 65 York Beach, Maine F2-37
1902 94 Eastport, Maine
95 Clearing land
96 Stumping
97 Approaching thunder storm
1903 63 Summer day
64 Woodland road
65 St Andrews, New Brunswick DW 1903 21 1/2 x 47 1/4
1904 98 Early summer F4-49
99 Early moonrise F4-50
1906 F5, Halifax
90 Evening $500
1907 105 The flying Dutchman
1907 F6, Sherbrooke
105 Landscape (James Ross, Esq) $1,000 nfs
1908 63 Evening landscape (James Ross)
1910 103 Marine
1911 86 The hurricane, St Andrews, NB, July 1911
87 In the woods, autumn
1912 126 Landscape
1912 S3, Winnipeg
84 Woodland
1914 107 The sand bar ◊NGC◊
1914 S5, Patriotic Fund
47 Summer evening illus
1919 79 The track of the column
1923 81 St Andrews, New Brunswick
1924 98 Mons from Havre
99 Night in the Rockies
100 Woodland scene
1925 107 Bath Abbey illus
108 Chamcook harbour
1927 92 Birches and alders

HOPKINS, JOHN WILLIAM
19 Sep 1825, Liverpool 11 Dec 1905, Montreal NGC
RCA 1880 Council Architect
Addr: 1880-05, Montreal
1880 373a Merchants Bank of Canada, Montreal
373b Bank of Montreal, Ottawa
373c Royal Insurance Company Building. Late Merchants Bank, Montreal DW 1880 wc drwg 23 x 17 (Royal Institute, error) 1881-185

HOPKINS, WILLIAM
H
1880 324 Sketch of canoes (Thos. Reynolds)

HOPKINSON, WILLIAM JOHN
25 Nov 1887, London, Eng 21 Feb 1970, Aurora, Ont
1945 101a Breezy day, September $100

HOPPER, HENRIETTA M. (Mrs)
1938 106 David pastel nfs

HOPPNER
1881 214 Dr Hoffman (Miss Hoffman)

HORNE, ARTHUR EDWARD CLEEVE
9 Jan 1912, Jamaica CC1 CWW79 M
NGC TB3 WWA47 WWB56
ARCA 1947 RCA 1951 Sr 1967 Council
Sculptor
Addr: 1928-37, 54 Scarborough Rd, Toronto; 1947-71/79, Toronto
1928 167 The reader sculp
1929 241 Margot sculp
242 Dr Fletcher McPhedren sculp
1932 212 Maj A.C. Horne plaster
1934 204 Boris Hambourg, cellist port head sculp
1935 139 Maj A.C.W. Horne oil nfs 1948-83 1949-44
140 Wood interior oil $250
1936 220 Mark Hambourg sculp illus $200
221 Charles McCrea sculp $200
1938 107 Mrs Winnett Thompson oil nfs
1942 61 Lt Col K.M. Holloway, GSOI MD.2 oil nfs
165 VAdm P.M. Nelles, Chief, Naval Staff, RCN plaster nfs
1946 64 Dr A.P. Steckel, Youngstown, Ohio oil nfs
1947 83 Dr W.E. Gallie, surgeon oil nfs
84 Dr Robert I. Harris, surgeon oil illus nfs
1948 82 R.S. Waldie, Esq oil nfs
104 Alexander Graham Bell Memorial. Bell Telephone Co of Canada, Brantford, Ont. Light green patinated bronze Marani & Morris, architects photo
1950 61 Chief Justice J.C. McRuer oil 62 x 44 nfs
62 James S. Duncan, Esq oil 46 x 39 nfs
1951 50 C.L. Burton, Esq oil illus
119 War Memorial, 1939-1945, Law Society of Upper Canada. sculp Marani & Morris architects photo
1952 43 Howard Dunnington Grubb, Esq oil nfs S10-38 S11-19
108 Memorial to H.M. Hart, Sr. White Motor Company Limited port head bronze nfs
1953 39 James A. Gairdner oil illus nfs
117 James A. Duncan sculp nfs
1954 44 Hon J.W. Pickup, Chief Justice of Ontario oil 52 x 39 illus nfs 1955-46 illus
108 Crown Life Insurance Co. 2 rel Indiana stone 72 x 72 Marani & Morris, architects
1956 24 Sir Ernest MacMillan oil illus nfs
1957 34 D.W. Ambridge, Esq oil illus nfs
1958 45 W. Earl Smith, Esq, QC Sec Law Society of Upper Canada oil illus nfs S10-39
85 Bank of Canada, Toronto 2 granite plaques 21ft Marani & Morris, architects
1959 44 Hon Dana Porter, Chief Justice of Ontario oil 55 x 37 illus nfs
1960 44 Dr Charles R. Knowlton, KCSG, Chief of Staff, St Joseph's Hospital oil 48 x 33 illus nfs
DW 1953 Shakespeare bronze 21 1/2h
RCA medal, sculp by Horne, des S. Watson 1963 p2 illus
Studio of artist, G.S. Adamson, architect 1949-01

HORNE, JEAN MILDRED HARRIS (Mrs Arthur Edward Cleeve Horne)
19 Sep 1914, Toronto
ARCA 1954-7 Sculptor
Addr: 1955-7, Toronto
1951 118 Reclining figure plaster $350
1952 109 Study for garden sculpture stone 28h $1,500
1953 118 Figure study sculp $300
1954 106 Beggar of Fez sculp 17 1/2h illus $250
107 Mexican mother and child sculp $250

HORNE, MERCEDES
23 May 1925, Birmingham, Eng M
RCA(e) 1976 Council Painter
Addr: 1979, Oakville, Ont

HORNE, S.M.K.
1970 113 Telephone set, Northern Electric Co Limited. S.M.K. Horne and J.F. Tyson

HORNING, BENJAMIN
H
Addr: 1899, Turkish Baths Hotel, Montreal
1899 180 Clearing garden wc

181 Old meadow hayricks wc
182 The homeward road wc

HORNYANSKY, NICHOLAS
11 Aug 1896, Budapest 25 May 1965, Toronto AGO CWW61 M TB3 W78 WWA47
ARCA 1943 Engraver
Addr: 1932-3, 16 McMaster Ave, Toronto; 1935, 228 Cottingham St, Toronto; 1944-65, Toronto
1932 98 Street scene $700
1933 106 Evening call $1,000 T35-39
1935 323 St Martin Street, Courtrai col aqua $10
324 First solitude, from 'A life' col aqua $12
1939 293 Moses etch $15
1940 78 Wooden world illus $500
1941 236 The market, IV from 'A life' col aqua $15
237 Noah etch $15 1943-140 $20
1942 176 Bygone days, Holland col aqua $18
1943 141 Filtering light col aqua $20
1944 157 Gray clouds over the Maritimes col aqua $24
1945 102 Niagara boat $600 T46-23
243 Old briggs at rest col aqua $25
1946 159 Grace Church on the Hill, Toronto col aqua nfs
160 Rideau mill col aqua $30
1947 223 Moses etch $25
224 Landing on the Nottawasa River softground $25
225 Closing time col aqua $27.50
1948 194 St Jean, Quebec col aqua $35
1949 128 The Anglican Cathedral, St John's, Newfoundland col aqua $27.50
1950 63 The cove 35 x 40 $600
1951 51 Solemn hour $350
52 Turtle Cove $175
1952 44 The cove $800 T53-14
116 Indian poachers aqua $24
1953 40 Visage d'autrefois $600 1954-45 28 x 35 $300
128 November snow aqua $22
1957 35 Foreboding dawn $250
1958 46 Budgies $450
1959 45 Boreas etch 20 x 24 $52
1960 45 Old net poles 25 x 30 $250
46 Space superimposition 25 x 28 illus $52
1961 48 Old net poles 24 x 30 $300
49 Grace and grotesque etch 20 x 24 $52

HORSBURGH, VICTOR DANIEL
9 Dec 1866, Edinburgh 12 Sep 1947, Victoria
Addr: 1932, 25 King St W, Toronto
1932 202 The Canadian Bank of Commerce, St Catherine & Metcalfe Streets, Montreal

HORSFALL, ARTHUR
13 Jul 1915, Winnipeg
RCA(e) 1976 Painter
Addr: 1979, Winnipeg

HORWOOD, EDGAR LEWIS
27 Jul 1868, Caerleon, Monms, Eng
8 Sep 1950, Ottawa CWW36 Mo12
ARCA 1911 Sr 1938 Architect
Addr: 1910, 130 Sparks St, Ottawa; 1925, Fraser Bldg, Ottawa; 1935, 53 Queen St, Ottawa; 1936-50, Ottawa
1910 214 Office building
215 Public library
1925 237 Tower des pen & ink
1935 265 Residence, Col R.H. Stewart pencil
see also Burke, Edmund, 1895

HOSIE, AUDREY
1959 46 Passing landscape and after image 36 x 38 $250

HOSKINSON, CATHARINE ANN
14 Sep 1949, Montreal
1971 22 Lake 15 x 19 $60

HOUGH, MICHAEL
5 Aug 1928, Nice, France
RCA(e) 1976 Landscape architect
Addr: 1979, Toronto

HOUGHTON, FRANK
fl 1887-1925 H
1887 131 Sketch from nature wc

HOUGHTON, MARGARET (Mrs Jules Brunn)
23 Sep 1865, Montreal flg 1922
B H Mo12 TB
ARCA 1897-02 Painter
Addr: 1893, 44 Lorne Ave, Montreal; 1894, Montreal; 1895, c/o Scott & Son, Montreal; 1896-7, 35 Tupper St, Montreal; 1898-9, Montreal;

1900-3, Scott & Son, Montreal; 1904, Dol de Bretagne; 1907, Paris; 1909N, Johnston & Copping, Montreal

1893 83 Wishing on the moon $200 F1-67
84 Sea urchins $75
85 Old fishing stage, Louisbourg $35 F1-68
1894 54 A cloudy morning
55 A sunny morning in Margaree
56 A foggy morning over the bar
57 A sunny day, Fontainebleau
1895 54 A bleak pasture
55 Salt to the sheep
1896 84 Landscape
85 Le repas du midi
86 French Canadian cottage, Ste Anne de Bellevue
87 A grey day
1897 65 The family shoemaker
1900 54 Last rays, a study of sunlight
55 In a Capri garden
56 Spring in Capri
57 Frost effect in Brittany
1903 66 The shining way
67 The wind blows inward from Eternity
1904 100-3 Concarneau 4 oil prints
1907 106 The morning prayer
107 Sketch of boats
1909N 71 The hour of prayer
1910 S2, Liverpool
58 The prayer

HOUSSER, BESS see HARRIS, BESS

HOUSSER, MURIEL YVONNE MCKAGUE (Mrs Frederick Broughton Housser)
4 Aug 1898, Toronto AGO CC2 CWW64 M NGC TB2 WWA47
ARCA 1942 RCA 1951 Sr 1968 Painter
Addr: 1923, 18 Tyndall Ave, Toronto; 1925-6, 96 Albany Ave, Toronto; 1928-34, 18 Grenville St, Toronto; 1936, 158 Madison Ave, Toronto; 1942-6, Toronto; 1947, Todmarten, Ont; 1948-9, Toronto; 1950-61, Markham, Ont; 1963-71/79, Toronto

1923 McKague, to 1936
119 A study
1925 157 On the beach
1926 98 Miner's shack, Cobalt
1928 110 The Tower of Babel, Moraine Lake $300
1929 149 Tower of Babel, Rocky Mountains $300
1934 135 Portrait study $300 T35-48
1936 144 Whitefish Falls $150
1938 108 The corn crop $200 T39-24
1939 116 Cornwall $300
117 Mexican village $50
1940 79 Thanksgiving day $300
80 Sumac in winter $75 T41-25
1941 S9, Toronto
34 Thanksgiving day $35
1942 62 Datura $100
63 Sun-soaked valley, Quebec $200 T43-21
1944 74 The black stove $75 T45-25
75 Mrs Buckshot $65 1945-26
1949 45 Little girl, Jamaica $200
46 Tropic rain, Jamaica $150 T50-10
1950 64 The sleep walker 32 x 24 $200
65 Old garden gate, Jamaica 44 x 36 $350
66 Jamaica 24 x 18 $100
1951 53 Edge of the field $200
1952 45 Funeral in December $200
46 This green world $200
1953 41 Sugar bush, October illus $300
42 Beach, Provincetown $75
1954 47 Retro Sec. The little clearing DW 1952 The little clearing, Georgian Bay board 23 3/4 x 32
1955 47 Spring pattern illus $500
1957 36 Hill town, Mexico illus $200 (AGO)
1959 47 The sisters, Tobago 38 x 24 $400
1960 47 Rock patterns 30 x 36 $400
1961 52 End of October 27 x 36 illus $400
53 Reflections in my window 40 x 32 $400
1964J 35 November liquitex 28 x 36 $450
1964N 28 June evening 48 x 26 $600
1965 36 Summer time 36 x 24 $350 S10-40
37 Windows of the night 32 x 24 $400 S10-41
1966 30 August 28 x 34 illus $450
1967 29 Mexican family 48 x 40 $600
30 Shattered glass 48 x 24 $500

HOUSTON, ALISON see NEWTON, ALISON

HOUSTON, GEORGE Scottish
20 Feb 1869, Dalry, Scot 5 Oct 1947, Scotland B DBA DVP TB1/3 WBA
Addr: 1907, Montreal
1907 108 An Ayrshire burn in November
109 Spring in a Scottish glen

HOUSTOUN, DONALD MACKAY
27 Nov 1916, Stevensville, Ont AGO IO M
ARCA 1960 RCA 1966 Council Painter
Addr: 1960-71, Toronto; 1979, Elora, Ont
1950 67 Mood 30 x 34 $200
1954 46 Steam roller 48 x 40 $350
1955 48 Dry dock, Gloucester $300
1956 25 Still life with lemons illus $250 T56-21
1958 47 Landscape illus $450
1961 50 Composition red theme #3 84 x 36 $750
51 Spring flood 40 x 50 $600
1963 38 Evolution 72 x 60 illus $1,000 S10-43 $900
1965 38 Painting, evolution series 60 x 50 illus $850 S10-42
1966 27 Molecular assemblage 60 x 50 illus $1,000 1970-28
1970 29 Predominating red 60 x 48 illus $1,000
DW 1967 Life force #2 48 x 36

HOVADIK, JAROSLAV
8 May 1935, Zlin, Czechoslovakia
1970 30 Poem II 4/50 9 1/2 x 14 illus $135

HOVERMANN, H.
1947 85 Still life with beer mug nfs

HOVERMANN, W.
1945 103 Waterfall $150
104 Old power house $150

HOWARD SMITH PAPER MILLS see SMITH, HOWARD

HOWARD, ALFRED HAROLD
12 Jul 1854, Liverpool 17 Feb 1916, Toronto AGO M NGC W78
ARCA 1881 RCA 1883 Council Designer
Addr: 1881-2, Toronto; 1883, Rolph Smith & Co, Wellington St, Toronto; 1884-00, Toronto; 1901-9, Temple Bldg, Toronto; 1910-11, Toronto; 1912-16, 1107 Temple Bldg, Toronto
1880 288 Wall paper des Alfred A Howard, mispr
1881 156 Ornamentation studies des $25
210 Wall paper competitive des
1882 222 Wall paper des
224 RCAA, Academician's diploma des
1883 329 Wall paper des
330 Piano forte desk fretwork des
331 Address
332 Lord's prayer
1885 331 Coil screen, diaper des
333 Frieze des
1890 224 Some original initials nfs
225 and 226 Frieze des nfs A.S. Howard, mispr
1891 209 Conservatory of Music diploma des
1901 229 Eventide des
230 Late summer des
231 On the Welland des
232 Old Simon the cellerar des 1902-283
233 Happiness of a country fireside des 1902-285
234 First chapter of St John's Gospel des 1902-286
235 Book cover des
236 The Vicar of Bray des 1902-284
1902 F5, Halifax
92 Pages of a book, poppies and violets des
1906 203, 204, 206 Book page des
205 Fragment of a book des
207 Subscription page sketch des
208 Title page sketch des
209 Dundonald coat of arms 1908-175
210 Stained glass des
1908 176 Wickham coat of arms
177 Fragment of book des
178 Page for book des
1909M 169a, 170, 171 Frontispiece sketch
172 Book page sketch
1909N 72 Address to Princess of Wales, frontispiece sketch
73 Page of address, sketch
74 Book page, sketch
1912 270 Achievement of arms
271 Decorated poem
1914 229 Decorated poem

1915 275-6 The garden gate. china vase decoration. Elevation. Projection
277 The Red Cross Knight. decorated poem
DW 1886 Page of illuminated capitals pen, ink & col 13 x 16

HOWARD, HELEN BARBARA (Mrs Richard Daley Outram)
10 Mar 1926, Long Branch, Ont AGO M
RCA(e) 1975 RCA 1979 Council Painter
Addr: 1979, Toronto
DW 1979 Sand and water

HOWARD, JOHN GEORGE (b Corby, John. c 1832, Howard, John George)
27 Jul 1803, n London, Eng 3 Feb 1890, Toronto Co H W78
ARCA 1880 RCA 1881 Ret 1882 Architect
Addr: 1880-90, Toronto
1880 360 Government House, Toronto, 1834, estimated cost 50,000 pounds. J.W. Howard, mispr
DW not recorded

HOWARTH, GLENN EDWARD
1 Sep 1946, Vegreville, Alta
RCA(e) 1978 Painter
Addr: 1979, Victoria

HOWARTH, T.
see ADAMSON, GORDON, 1965-107

HOWELL, ALFRED
16 Jul 1889, Oldburg, Eng M NGC
Addr: 1918A, 62 Howland Ave, Toronto; 1923, 208 Kingswood Rd, Toronto
1918A 192 Our joy sculp
193 The soul's anguish sculp
1923 186 Memorial at Sault Ste Marie sculp sketch model
187 Memorial at Saint John, NB sculp sketch model photo

HOWLAND, HENRY STARK (Jr)
1855, Kleinberg, Ont AGO DBA H
1885 10 A path in the woods $35

HOWLIN, JOHN
16 Apr 1941, London, Eng IO
Addr: 1976, Toronto
1976 S12, Montreal
27 Amida/Arc #2BW acry 90 x 70 illus

HOWSON, JULIET H.
fl 1891-3 H
1891 85 Still life

HOYT, ALBERT see HOIT, ALBERT

HUBEL, VELLO
12 Dec 1927, Tallinn, Estonia
RCA(e) 1973 Council Industrial designer
Addr: 1979, Toronto
1971 9I Rib seating, Protective Plastics Limited

HUDDELL, IDA M.
b Montreal
Addr: 1929-31, 471 St James St, Ville St Pierre, Que
1929 104 Still life $45
1931 130 Still life $35

HUDSPETH, R.A.
Addr: 1897, Adelaide St, Toronto address listed, but no entry of work exhibited

HUDSPETH, ROBERT NORMAN
2 Jul 1862, Caledonia (Seneca) Ont 1943, Concord, Mass H TB WWA36
Addr: 1906-7, Lennoxville, Que
1906 F5, Halifax
91 Case of miniatures
1907 F6, Sherbrooke
105a Landscape
105b Play

HUFFMAN, ISOBEL MARY KNOX (Mrs Percival Huffman)
18 Jan 1895, Toronto WWB29
Addr: 1933, 27 Rosedale Rd, Toronto
1933 107 Mrs Hugh Eayers and the children on ivory

HUGGARD, LEONARD ROY
14 Aug 1920, Norton, NB M
1950 68 Men with hope 25 1/2 x 20 $65

HUGGINS, W.H.
Addr: 1916, 447 Somerset Ave, Ottawa
1916 118 Winter at Quebec wc
119 Fog on the Nova Scotia coast wc

HUGHES, ANDREW ROSS
b 1904
Addr: 1929, 68 Grenville St, Toronto

105 Mr H.J.H. Shorse, organist
106 Caledon Mountail, Peel County

HUGHES, EDWARD JOHN
17 Feb 1913, North Vancouver AGO CC1 CWW79 M NGC WWA47
ARCA 1966 RCA 1969 Painter
Addr: 1967-71, Vancouver Island; 1979, Duncan, BC
1950 69 Logs, Lady Smith harbour 30 x 40 illus $275
70 Entrance to Howe Sound 32 x 36 $275
1968 28 Freighter at the wharf, Cowichan Bay 30 x 40 illus $2,500
1970 31 Finlayson Arm 38 x 51 illus, Finlayson Arm, looking north $3,500
DW 1969 Kaslo on Kootenay Lake

HUGHES, H. GORDON
Addr: 1931, 4784 Victoria Ave, Westmount, Que; 1933, Pinehurst, Almonte, Ont
1931 401 Smile, darn you, smile lino block $10
402 Old mill, Quebec lino block $10
1933 108 The red boat wc $35

HUIBERS, JAN DERK Dutch
1829-1919
1882 310 Une prise de tabac Modern Dutch school (loan)

HULBERT, RICHARD ELLIOT
5 Dec 1945, St Louis, Mo
RCA(e) 1978 Architect
Addr: 1979, West Vancouver

HULL, J.M. (Mrs)
Addr: 1927, 295 Charlton Ave W, Hamilton, Ont
1927 93 Still life

HUMME, JOSEPH JULIUS
1825, Prussia 1889, Point Ideal, Lake of Bays, Ont H
1885 195 The wind $40

HUMPHREY, JACK WELDON
12 Jan 1901, Saint John 23 Mar 1967, Saint John AGO CC2 CWW64 M NGC TB3 W78 WWA47
1950 71 Association of outdoor objects 28 x 36 $400
72 Girl with red hair 20 x 24 $250

HUMPHRIES, JOHN
6 May 1882, Blockley, Glos, Eng 15 Dec 1958, Lachine, Que CNS36 M
Addr: 1935-7, 2230 Harvard Ave, Montreal
1935 141 The trail of the North River wc $75 T36-41
142 The village of Kamouraska, Quebec wc $40
1937 108 A north river valley wc $100
1938 109 A lower St Lawrence village wc $150 T39-25
1939 118 On Nicholson's farm, Ville La Salle, Que wc $100
1945 105 Mid-winter, Craig Street and Champ de Mars, Montreal wc $200
106 A valley of the Laurentians wc $175

HUNG, CHUNG (ALLAN)
8 Feb 1946, Canton
RCA(e) 1978 Sculptor
Addr: 1979, Vancouver

HUNT, DORA DE PEDERY (Mrs Albert M. Hunt)
16 Nov 1913, Budapest AGO CC1 CWW79 IO M NGC TB3 WWA56
ARCA 1956 RCA 1967 Sculptor
Addr: 1957-71/79, Toronto
1948 de Pedery, to 1951
160 African elephant bronze
1951 114 Stations of the Cross sculp nfs
1955 108 Peasant life sculp $750
1956 47 Artist sculp illus $1,000
1957 76 Dreamer sculp $1,500
1963 59 White and grey oil $150
90 Portrait of Chizuka Shimano bronze $450 1964N-70 6 x 8
91 Suzanne and the Elders bronze $120
1964J 73 The Minotaur medal bronze 4h $65
74 Christ bronze 7h $180
1964N 71 Owl bronze 4h $75
1965 82-3 Dante medal bronze obverse & reverse $150
1966 78 Eric, Robert, Nos Rose medals nfs
DW 1968 4 bronze medallions

Christ 2 5/8 Dante 3 3/8
Dante and Beatrice 3 7/8
Mater Dolorosa 2 3/4 x 2 5/8

HUNT, HERBERT GARVIN
1888, London, Eng
Addr: 1935, 333 18th Ave W, Calgary
1935 143 Autumn, Morley wc $45

HUNT, JOHN POWELL
14 Dec 1854, St Mary's, Ont 1932, London, Ont H
Addr: 1913, 423 Dundas St, London
1882 92 Taking a rest $100
1913 137 Autumn woods

HUNTER, DAVID
1970 185 Presentation, for the Secretary of State
186 Package, Man's World toiletries

HUNTER, GEORGE
11 May 1921, Regina
RCA(e) 1977 Photographer
Addr: 1979, Toronto

HUNTER, I.A.W. (Mrs)
Addr: 1927, 11 Killarney Gardens, Point Claire, Que
1927 94 A study of flowers wc

HUNTER, J.D.
1971 34G Book, Aprons off. Fuller Brush Co
35G Corporate idendity programme, Dominion Glass Co

HUNTER, SARAH see HOLDEN, SARAH

HUNTER, WILHELMINA BLEWETT ELLIOTT (Mrs Hunter)
11 Mar 1893, Hamilton, Ont
Addr: 1930, 860 Palmerston Ave, Toronto; 1934, 19 Penrose Rd, Toronto
1930 91 Still life $75
103 Garden flowers $55

HUNTLEY, WALTER EDWIN
1887, Newark, N.J. 1 Feb 1931, Toronto M
Addr: 1922, 197 Wellesley St, Toronto; 1923-5, 246 Heath St W, Toronto; 1927, 73 Richmond St W, Toronto; 1928, 160 Richmond St W, Toronto; 1929, 333 Walmer Rd, Toronto
1922 107 Afternoon glow, Muskoka S6-41
1923 82 Sunny fields
1924 101 Spring mood, Manitoba
102 A bit of Muskoka
1925 109 Lake Louise
110 November
1927 95 By the Athabaska, Algonquin Park
96 North lake country
307 Portrait study drwg
1928 76 On the Madawaska, Algonquin Park $375
77 On Lake Mazinaw, Ont $500
1929 107 October, Haliburton, Ontario $375
1929 S7, Calgary
75 On Gull Lake $375

HUOT, CHARLES EDWARD MASSON
26 Mar 1855, Quebec 27 Jan 1930, Sillery, Que CC1 H M NGC PMC W78
Addr: 1902, 19 1/2 St Ursule St, Quebec; 1903, St Ann St, Quebec; 1908, 24 Stanilas St, Quebec; 1925, Maguire Ave, Bergerville, Que
1902 98 Mr J.E. Prince
99 Winter ferry at Quebec
100 and 101 Study
1903 59 Portrait
1908 72 Through grief and sorrow
1925 111 Le Sanctus à la maison
112 Intérieur de l'église de Saint Malo, France pastel

HURTUBISE, JACQUES
28 Feb 1939, Montreal AGO CC2 M WWA73
ARCA 1971 Painter
Addr: 1976/79, Terrebonne, Que
1968 29 Artemise 80 x 80 illus $1,900
1970 32 Juanita 80 x 120 $3,200
33 Jasmine 80 x 80 $2,100
1971 23 Marie Jeanne 3 panels 66 x 100 each illus $5,000
1976 S12, Montreal
28 Sirose acry 48 x 96 illus
29 Sapoline acry 36 x 72 illus

HUSHLAK, GERALD
15 Feb 1944, Edmonton WWA78
Addr: 1976, Calgary
1976 S12, Montreal
30 Untitled, Calgary series acry & oil 78 x 78 illus

HUTCHINSON, GRACE see FULGER, GRACE

HUTCHINSON, LEONARD
8 Apr 1896, Manchester 9 May 1980
IO M
ARCA 1936 Engraver 1953 Designer
RCA 1966 Designer Sr 1966
Addr: 1924, 111 E 24th St, Mount Hamilton, Ont; 1932-7, 109 E 19th St, Mount Hamilton, Ont; 1938-45, Hamilton, Ont; 1946, Toronto; 1947-9, Hamilton, Ont; 1951-62, Langstaff, Ont; 1963-71, Richmond Hill, Ont; 1979, Thornhill, Ont
1924 103 City lights
1932 241 Quiet waters col pr $12.50 Hutchison mispr
242 Twilight col pr $12.50
1933 208 Van Wagner's beach col pr $12.50
209 On the Goshen road col pr $12.50
1934 218 Windy morning col block pr $15
219 Northern landscape col block pr $20 T35-36
1935 325 The road to Niagara col block pr $12.50
326 Mount Albion col block pr $12.50
1936 239 Ontario landscape col pr $20
240 Grist mill engr $12.50
1937 109 The grist mill wc $45
319 Fred Fisher, Lake o' Bays engr $10
320 Back water engr $10
1938 253 Recessional engr $10.50
254 Inland waters engr $10.50
1939 119 The rusted plough $150
294 Homes and gardens engr $10
295 Rolling logs, Lake of Bays engr $10
DW 1967 Fisherman, Lake of Bays wd cut 11 x 11 1/4

HUTCHISON, ALEXANDER COWPER
2 Apr 1838, Montreal 1 Jan 1922, Montreal EC H Mo12 NGC W78
RCA 1882 Ret 1920 Council Architect
Addr: 1882-3, Montreal; 1884, 181 St James St, Montreal; 1885-96, Montreal; 1897, 151 St James St, Montreal; 1898-14, Montreal; 1915, 240 Kensington Ave, Westmount, Que; 1916-20, Montreal
1883 339 New building, McGill University, Montreal des
DW 1882 drwg 24 7/8 x 59
1884 Hutchison & Steele
190 Hon J.J.C. Abott residence, perspective pen & ink drwg
191 R. Lindsay, Esq, residence perspective pen & ink drwg
192 Canada Paper Co warehouse perspective pen & ink drwg
1897 67A Melville Church, Westmount des
68A YMCA Building, perspective pen & ink drwg
1899 Hutchison & Wood, to 1907
246 La Press Building, Montreal des
1907 317 Canadian Express Co, bldg, McGill Street perspective
318 Macdonald College, Ste Anne de Bellevue. Main bldg, perspective
1915 254-6 Church, sketch des. Front, side elevations. Longtitudinal section

HUTCHISON, FREDERICK WILLIAM
13 Mar 1871, Montreal 1 May 1953, Hudson Heights, Que AGO CWW49 M NGC WWA47
RCA Hon Non-res 1937 RCA 1941 Sr 1948 Painter
Addr: 1902, Fraser Institute, Montreal; 1910, 4404 St Catherine St W, Montreal; 1912-15, 45 E 59th St, New York; 1929-33, 36 W 12th St, New York; 1935-9, 29 W 9th St, New York; 1940-1, New York; 1942-53, Hudson Heights, Que
1902 102 Brittany woman
103 Marine
104 Moonrise
105 March landscape
1907 F6, Sherbrooke
106 Old Peter, the fisherman $150
1910 104 Landscape
105 Road through the woods
1912 127 The hillside
1913 138 The melting snow S4-62 $300 S5-78 illus
139 The waterfall S4-63 $350
1914 108 Village street
1915 109 The village store
1929 108 St Urbain $1,000
109 Avallon, spring time $700
1930 92 Saint Siméon $1,000
1931 131 Village street $1,000
1933 109 Landscape nfs T34-40

1935 144 The road to Tadousac $750
1937 110 The melting snow $400 F11-36 30 x 25 (MMFA)
111 Marsh haying T38-24 DW 1942 25 x 30 1954 Retro Sec 18
1940 81 Ripening grain $750 T41-26
1942 64 Early spring $500
1946 65 Les Eboulements, Charlevoix County $750 T47-29
1946 66 Afternoon of life $2,500
1947 86 Old house, Baie St Paul $800
87 Sherbrooke Street $800 T48-21
88 Moulin Larouche, Baie St Paul $600
1948 84 Mr E. Dyonnet, RCA illus nfs
1950 73 Farmer at Charlesbourg 30 x 24 $1,500
1951 54 Reminiscent $1,200
1952 47 Fogeron du village nfs T53-15 $2,000
1957 37 Old gondolier $1,500

HUTCHISON, J. CAMERON
Addr: 1902, 234 Guy St, Montreal; 1904, Montreal
1902 287 Arms of Kirkpatrick
288 Heraldic emblazoning
1904 281 Private greeting card des
282 Achievement of Monmouth
283 Heraldic emblazoning

HUTCHISON, LILLIE I.
Addr: 1910, 227 Milton St, Montreal
1910 106 Princess Street, Edinburgh

HYDE, GEORGE TAYLOR
see NOBBS, PERCY, 1919, 1925, 1933, 1937, 1939

HYMAS, JANE ALISON
19 Jan 1932, Calgary
RCA(e) 1978 Interior designer
Addr: 1979, Toronto

HYNDMAN, ROBERT STEWART
28 Jun 1915, Edmonton M WWA47
1960 80 Torso sculp $150

HYNES, M.J.
1885 334 Lawrence Coffee, Esq sculp

I

IACURTO, FRANCESCO
1 Sep 1908, Montreal M WWA73
ARCA 1945 Painter
Addr: 1946, Quebec; 1947-8, Montreal; 1949-51, Quebec; 1952-5, Montreal; 1956-71/79, Quebec
1943 62 Miss Janet $400
63 Philip wc $100
1944 76 War worker, Arvida, Quebec nfs
77 Mechanic, Joliette, Quebec illus nfs
1945 107 Veteran, World War I $500 T46-24

IANZELO, TONY (b Frank Anthony Ianuzielo)
13 Jun 1935, Toronto
RCA(e) 1979 Film maker
Addr: 1979, Town of Mount Royal, Que

IDE, KATHARINE T.
Addr: 1937, 447 Riverdale Ave, Ottawa
1937 112 In the garden pastel nfs
1938 110 Girl knitting $50

ILAN, ELI
1928, Winnipeg
Addr: 1976, Old Jaffa, Israel
1976 S12, Montreal
72 Floating anchor bronze 49 x 31 x 27 illus

ILES, TERRANCE
1970 187 Advertisement, Canadian Association for Retarded Children

IMLACH, AGNES C. Scottish
fl 1880-01 DBA H
1880 43 Bedroom of Mary Queen of Scots, Holyrood (HRH Princess Louise) Imlac mispr

IMPERIAL RATTAN CO, LIMITED
Addr: 1938, Toronto
1938 S8, Toronto
347 6 piece bedroom suite in white maple, for Robert Simpson Co, Limited

IMREDY, ELEK
13 Apr 1912, Budapest
1961 96 Sculpture, Holy Redeemer College, Edmonton. Peter Thornton, architect illus

INGLE, BERTHA MAYLAW
1878, Nassagaweya, Ont 20 Oct
1962, n Guelph, Ont
Addr: 1909N, 160 Robert St, Toronto; 1910, 230 Robert St, Toronto
1909N 75 Did you lay that?
1910 107 When the world is glad and gay

INNES, ALICE AMELIA
1890, Brooksdale, Ont 30 Dec 1970, Woodstock, Ont M
ARCA 1936 Sr 1959 Painter
Addr: 1930-7, Studio Bldg, 25 Severn St, Toronto; 1938-45, Toronto; 1946-8, Barrie, Ont; 1949, Vancouver; 1950-5, Oakville, Ont; 1956-7, Willowdale, Ont; 1958-70; Woodstock, Ont
1930 93 Birch woods $150
1931 132 Autumn, Beaver Lake $300
133 Water soaked elm $400
1932 99 Autumn, Doe Lake, Ont $350
100 Winter sunshine $250
1933 110 Spring freshet $350 T34-41
1934 104 Woodland interior $350
105 Winter, Kearney, Ont $300 T35-37
1935 145 The mountain, Burke Falls $300 T36-42
146 Easter time, Parry Sound district $450
1936 107 Early spring, northern Ontario $500
108 May, Parry Sound district $250 T37-37
1937 113 Open water, Parry Sound district $300
114 Easter time, Willisville $350
115 March, Willisville $350 T38-25
1938 111 Easter time, northern Ontario $250 T39-26 1939-120
112 Morrison Lake illus $250 F11-37 30 x 36
113 Early autumn, Parry Sound district $300
1939 121 Road to Frood Lake $300
1940 82 Spring, northern Ontario $500 1941-88
83 Winter sunshine $300
84 Easter, Parry Sound district $175 T41-27
1941 S9, Toronto
35 Ice house, Frood Lake $125
1942 65 December $350
66 Late afternoon, northern Ontario $350 T43-22
1943 64 Hear Burleigh Falls $300 T44-22
1945 108 Burleigh Falls $150
109 Edge of the city $175 T46-25
110 Snow squall $150
1947 89 Stirling Falls $100
90 September $300

INNES, JOHN
17 Mar 1863, London, Ont 13 Jan 1941, Vancouver CC1 H M Mo12 W78
Addr: 1899-03, Mail Bldg, Toronto; 1904, Toronto
1899 74 Strangers, hello!
75 The blizzard
76 Pursued
1903 70 The outlaw, a Canadian cattle ranch scene
1904 104 When days are short F4-51
105 Storm birds

INUKPUK, JOHNNY (JOHNNIE) E9-904
summer 1911, n Inouchjouac, Richmond Gulf, Que AGO ED
RCA(e) 1973 Sculptor
Addr: 1979, Port Harrison, Que

IOLA E7-923
1936, Lake Harbour, NWT ED
Addr: 1976, Lake Harbour, NWT
1976 S12, Montreal
73 Mother and child soapstone/saponite 11 1/2 x 7 x 9 1/2 illus

IRVING, DAPHNE BUTLER (Mrs Ronald Ian Irving)
6 Nov 1931, Elizabeth, NJ
RCA(e) 1978 Painter
Addr: 1979, Cornwall, PEI

IRVING, VERA ISABEL MATTHEWS (Mrs Irving)
1 Sep 1913, Toronto
1948 85 Sunday concert $350
1949 47 Victoria Day $175 T50-11
1950 74 Laurentian vespers 20 x 24 $200
1966 32 Low tide 36 x 46 $850

IRVING, WILLIAM
1830, Edinburgh 11 Jun 1883, Toronto
ARCA 1880 Architect
Addr: 1880-3, Toronto

IRWIN, DE LA CHEROIS THOMAS (Lieut Col)
31 Mar 1843, Co Armagh, Ireland
d 1928 H Mo12
Addr: 1881, Quebec
1881 106 Strasbourg, and Lake of Brientz 2 sketches wc
134 and 135 Sketches wc
143 Lake Lucerne, from Alpacht 2 sketches wc

IRWIN, ELEANOR M.
fl 1898-09 H
Addr: 1904, Montreal; 1909M, Place Viger Hotel, Montreal
1904 225 Windsor Street
226 Last glimpse
1909M 65a The Euse at les Damps

IRWIN, J.D.
Addr: 1900, 170 Cooper St, Ottawa
1900 65 Rostrevor, old bridge, Ireland

IRWIN, STEPHEN VAN EYMOND
10 Mar 1939, Toronto
RCA(e) 1977 Architect
Addr: 1979, Toronto

ISABEY, LOUIS GABRIEL EUGENE French
22 Jul 1803, Paris 27 Apr 1886, Paris B DBA TB
1880 8 Marine sketch (Quetton St George, Esq)
11 Dutch fishing scene attr to Isabey (Thos. C. Keefer)

ISKOWITZ, GERSHON
24 Nov 1921, Kielce, Poland AGO IO M WWA59
RCA(e) 1974 Painter
Addr: 1979, Toronto

IVENS, DOROTHY
Addr: 1933, 182 Pearson Ave, Toronto
1933 300 Nora charcl

IVES, ANTOINETTE
fl 1882-9 H
1882 168 Eunice, a study wc
175 The waif wc

IZARD, ELEANOR (Mrs Edward Whitaker Izard)
Addr: 1935-7, 980 Arundel Dr, Victoria
1935 147 Miss Prudence Verburgh min nfs
148 Miss Margaret Izard min nfs
1937 116 The blue dress min nfs

IZUMI, KIYOSHI
24 Mar 1921, Vancouver WWA76
RCA(e) 1973 Architect
Addr: 1979, Waterloo, Ont

JACK, MARION ELIZABETH
b Saint John fl 1898-14 DBA
Addr: 1908-14, Saint John
1908 83 Decorative panel
84 French woodland scene
1914 109 The Lecture Pine, Green Acre, Maine

JACK, PATTIE (Mrs)
fl 1881-00 DBA
Addr: 1900, 206 O'Connor St, Ottawa
1900 65 Highland interior
66 Tinker's tents on a Fife moor
67 The old basket maker
145 Bass Rock from Elies, Fife, Scotland wc
146 A Canadian study wc

JACK, RICHARD
15 Feb 1866, Sunderland, Eng 30 Jun 1952, Montreal B DBA DVP G H M RA TB1/2/3 WBA WWB29
RCA Hon 1940 Painter
Addr: 1931, 563 Victoria Ave, Westmount, Que; 1940-52, Montreal
1931 134 The house of Sir Christopher Wren, Hampton Court $1,500 Richard Jack, RA
1940 85 Interior $1,500 T41-28
86 Still life $750
1941 89 The scarf $650
90 Still life, the dolphin illus $650
91 Interior $650 T42-23
92 Still life $650
1941 S9, Toronto
36 Winter in the Laurentians $300
1942 67 Edward, son of Brig G.V. Whitehead nfs
68 Hugh G. Jones, RCA nfs
69 and 70 Still life one illus $500 each T43-23 one
1943 65 Walter A. Merrill, KC, Mayor of Westmount nfs

66 and 67 Still life $500 each T44-23 and 24
68 Still life $400
1944 78 F/L Cheng illus nfs
79 Peonies $500
80 Still life, dolphin $650
81 Still life $650
1945 111 Special Convocation McGill University, to confer degrees on President Roosevelt, and Rt Hon Winston Churchill, Quebec, Sep 14th 1944 nfs
112 Peonies $600
113 Gardenias illus $400
1946 67 HE Baron de Cartier de Marchienne, Belgian Ambassador, Court of St James nfs 1947-91
1947 92 Still life $650
93 Gladioli $500
1948 86 Rt Rev John Dixon, Lord Bishop of Montreal DD DCL nfs
87 Still life $650
1949 48 The Italian room, 1475 Pine Avenue $2,000
port: bust, by M. Winslow, 1947-222

JACKSON
1881 29 Sunset wc (Lady MacDougall)

JACKSON, ALEXANDER YOUNG CMG LLD
3 Oct 1882, Montreal 5 Apr 1974, Kleinberg, Ont AGO B CC2 CWW64 EC M NGC TB1/2 W78 WWA47
ARCA 1914 RCA 1919-32 RCA 1954 Sr 1954 RCA medal 1969, Group of Seven Council Painter
Addr: 1904, Montreal; 1907, Westmount, Que; 1910-12, 69 Hallowell St, Westmount, Que; 1914-15, Studio Bldg, Toronto; 1916, 69 Hallowell St, Westmount, Que; 1919-32, Studio Bldg, Toronto; 1954-5, Toronto; 1956-61, Manotick, Ont; 1963-7, Ottawa; 1968-71, Kleinberg, Ont
1904 227 The sluice wc
1907 110 Summer haze
1910 108 Edge of the maple wood S2-59 Corner of maple wood, mistitled [NGC]
109 The Georgian Bay
1910 S2, Liverpool
60 Early spring
1911 88 September skies
89 The quay, Dordrecht
90 Dawn, Georgian Bay
1912 128 Pont de la Tournelle, Paris
129 Au bord de la Somme
130 The Valley of the Hyères, Brittany
131 The marshes
1912 S3, Winnipeg
85 The red mill
86 A Picardy village
1914 110 Red maple [NGC]
111 Evening, Mount Robson
1914 S5, Patriotic Fund
9 In the north country illus
1915 110 Birches, Quebec
111 The brook
112 Maples, early spring illus
1916 Pte A.Y. Jackson
120 Factories at Leeds, England
121 The cedar swamp [AGO]
1918N Lieut A.Y. Jackson
89 The north country
90 The last snow
91 The lake shore
92 Burnt country
1919 80 The Olympic in Halifax harbour illus (Canadian War Memorials collection)
81 Ships entering Halifax harbour
82 Cité de Bois de Liéven
1920 133 Storm over a frozen lake
134 A Nova Scotia village
135 Winter, Georgian Bay
1921 74 A lake in the hills
75 The winter road 1922-109 S6-43
1922 108 Entrance to Halifax harbour S6-42
110 March snow illus S6-44
1923 83 Tamarac
84 A village
85 November [NGC]
86 Early spring, Quebec 1925-115 [NGC]
1924 104 Algoma in October
105 Hills, Lake Superior
106 Georgian Bay, November illus
1925 113 Moose country
114 Winter night illus
295 Wild geese pen drwg
296 The artist's stamp pen drwg
1926 70 Barns illus 1927-98 (Art Gallery of Toronto)
1927 97 October in Algoma (National Gallery)
99 A Quebec village

100 Winter, Quebec
1928 78 Winter morning $300
79 Winter, Baie St Paul $300
80 Indian village $300
1928 F8, London, Eng
117 Indian home, BC nfs
1929 110 Laurentian hills $600
111 November, Georgian Bay
112 Grey day, St Urbain
1929 S7, Calgary
76 Lake Superior country $500
77 Baffin Bay $400
78 A street in Baie St Paul $40
1930 94 Labrador coast illus $800
95 The St Lawrence in winter $350
1930 F10, London, Eng
174 Kane Basin $300
1931 135 Autumn, French River $375
136 Les Eboulements, early spring $200 (MMFA)
137 The road to St Fidèle $350
1932 101 Grey day, Laurentians $275 (MMFA)
102 Eskimos of Pangnirtung $250
1940 87 The road to St Simon $350
1941 93 Village in the Laurentians illus nfs
94 Gem Lake $350
1941 S9, Toronto
37 Grey day, October $50
1942 71 Grey day, L'Islet $200
1949 49 Alberta rhythm $650
1950 75 Early snow, Alberta 32 x 46 nfs
76 Quebec village 25 x 32 illus nfs
1951 Travelling exhibit
25 The convoy 1954 Retro Sec
34 Camouflaged ships, mistitled DW 1921 24 1/2 x 36
1954 47 North shore, Great Bear Lake 25 x 32 $350
1955 49 Hills at Hunter Bay, NWT illus nfs
1957 38 Gaspé shoreline nfs
port: head, by L. Mol, 1964J-77

JACKSON, ERNA NOOK
30 Nov 1886, Petrolia, Ont
Addr: 1936, 19 Oaklands Ave, Toronto
1936 109 From the Malahat Drive, Vancouver Island $150
1942 72 Lush August $125
1944 82 July on the farm $100

JACKSON, HENRY ALEXANDER CAMERON
1877, Montreal d 1961 M
Addr: 1902, Montreal
1902 203 Tugs in harbour wc

JACKSON, NAOMI CATHERINE (Mrs J. Walton Groves)
1910, Montreal M WWA56
Addr: 1934, 35 Campbell Ave, Montreal West
1934 106 Fields near Murray Bay, Quebec $100

JACOBI, OTTO REINHOLD
27 Feb 1812, Konisberg, Prussia 20 Feb 1901, Ardoch, ND AGO B EC H M Mo98 NGC R2 TB W78
ARCA 1880 RCA 1883 Council Painter
Addr: 1880-2, Toronto; 1883-5, Manvel, Dakota; 1886, Perth, Ont; 1887-91, Montreal; 1892-3, Toronto; 1894-5, 80 Summerhill Ave, Toronto; 1896-01, Toronto
1881 275 Landscape (J.H. Mason)
1883 36 Landscape DW 1883 21 1/2 x 35 1/2 T51-26 1954 Retro Sec 3
181 An autumn idyl wc (Dr Baldwin)
193 An approaching storm wc (Dr Baldwin)
1884 24 A young pioneer $300 S1-116 $100
114 and 128 Landscape wc $35 each
165 Landscape wc $36
1885 17 Cradle of Montmorency $50
32 St Louis River $80
53 Adirondack Mountains $125
109 Near Cross Lake $50
129 Evening $25
147 Morning $25
1887 120 Woodland sunset wc $80
1888 4 Sunset, Georgian Bay wc $40
9 Georgian Bay wc $86
16 Under the old trees wc $84
26 Burning bush wc $50
58 Upper Montmorency wc $50
168 Pines in the backwoods $84
187 Evening $40
1889 115 Fall at Rat Portage near Winnipeg wc $40
155 Sunset in the backwoods wc $120
1890 48 Coaticook, near Lennoxville, Quebec $50

170 Evening, Chaudiere River wc $100
1891 70 Idleness, a figure
71 Old saw mill on Rivière du Loup
1892 6 Old mill in the Hartz Mountains $50
7 On the Mississippi, Ontario $75
22 A forest stream $50
30 Fall on the Mississippi, Ontario $150
57 Raspberrying $30
1893 F1, Chicago
69 Landscape with gipsies nfs
70 and 71 Landscape
1894 64 Near Fort William
65 Madoc Falls, St Maurice River
66 Sunset
1895 71 Old saw mill on the Coaticook River, Lennoxville
37W St Louis River, near Duluth wc
38W Scene near Port Arthur wc
39W Young people in the country wc
40W A game wc
1896 88 and 89 Near Fort William
90 Falls of Rivière du Loup, Cacouna
91 School children
92 Country sweethearts
208 Evening wc
1897 75 Near Fort William
76 The old mill
1898 61 Afternoon on the Humber
62 Boating on the Humber
1910 S2, Liverpool
Late O.R. Jacobi
61 Mohawk Falls
61 Morning ǂAGOǂ
port: by R. Harris, 1893-71

JACOBS, MICHEL
10 Sep 1877, Montreal B CWW61
Addr: 1913, 6 Beaver Hall Sq, Montreal
1913 140 The crystal gazer
141 In the arbour
142 Israel Zangwill

JAMIESON, MARTHA GREENING
22 Jan 1918, Calgary M
1941 95 Portrait nfs

JANES, PHYLLIS HIPWELL (Mrs Henry F. Janes)
15 Feb 1905, Alliston, Ont M WWA59
1960 48 Little girl and brother 44 x 23 $350
1965 39 Back and forth 48 x 36 illus $700

JANIS, RICHARD
1970 188 Symbol, Ontario Provincial Dailies Association
1971 36G Symbol, York Gymnastic Club, Toronto

JANOWSKY, BELA
12 Apr 1900, Budapest
Addr: 1923, 1058 Ossington Ave, Toronto
1923 188 Portrait of a blind man low rel

JACQUE, LOUIS (b Beaulieu, Louis Jacques)
1 May 1919, Montreal M WWA76
RCA(e) 1978 Painter
Addr: 1979, Outremont, Que

JARRY, ANDRE
27 Aug 1926, Montreal
RCA(e) 1979 Industrial designer
Addr: 1979, Montreal

JARVIS, DONALD ALVIN
24 Apr 1923, Vancouver CC1 M NGC TB3 WWA78
ARCA 1962 RCA 1967 Painter
Addr: 1963-71/79, West Vancouver
1964J 36 Red landscape 50 x 36 $400
1964N 29 Red core #2 58 x 47 $500
1967 31 Eclipse 59 1/2 x 47 $500
32 Interior 34 x 25 illus $200
1970 34 Equinox 49 x 59 1/2 $600
35 Summer crossing 48 x 37 illus $450
1970 S11, Halifax
20 Autumn core. 1965 48 x 48 $600
21 Journey to the mountain. 1968 47 x 40 1/4 $500
DW 1968 Red core #3 47 1/4 x 35 1/2

JARVIS, EDGAR BEAUMONT
7 Jul 1864, Toronto 2 Jun 1948, Toronto
Addr: 1895, Traders Bank, Yonge St, Toronto
1895 28A Hotel for Centre Island
29A I O F Building

JARVIS, KENNETH
1948 49 Michael Head sculp nfs

JARVIS, LUCY MARY HOPE
27 Jul 1896, Toronto flg 1975 M
Addr: 1930, 829 George St, Fredericton, NB; 1931, Fredericton, NB
1930 96 Mr Thomas Holden
210 Mr Hamilton Hartwic charcl
1931 138 Miss Madeleine Chapman

JAWORSKA, TAMARA HANS (Mrs, m Tadeusz Jaworski)
20 Jul 1928, Archangel CWW79 IO WWA78
RCA(e) 1975 Textile designer
Addr: 1979, Willowdale, Ont

JAWORSKI, TADEUSZ
20 Feb 1926, Poland
RCA(e) 1978 Film maker
Addr: 1979, Willowdale, Ont

JEAN-LOUIS, DONALD CHARLES
17 May 1937, Ottawa AGO M
RCA(e) 1978 Sculptor
Addr: 1979, Toronto

JECTKEY, D.
Addr: 1920, 3167 St Denis St, Montreal
1920 312 D. Jectkey, drwg by himself
313 Bernatte drwg

JEFFERIES, GLORIA
23 Apr 1923, Toronto M
1946 135 May sculp $500
136 Mother and foal sculp $350

JEFFERYS, BARBARA ALICE WEST
1916, York Mills, Ont
Addr: 1936, York Mills, Ont; 1937, 4111 Yonge St, York Mills, Ont
1936 241 Old apple trees drwg $35
1937 117 Brooks and roses wc $75
312 Apple trees drwg $35

JEFFERYS, CHARLES WILLIAM LLD
25 Aug 1869, Rochester, Kent, Eng
8 Oct 1951, York Mills, Ont AGO CC2 CWW49 EC M Mo12 NGC PMC TB2 W78 WWA47
ARCA 1912 RCA 1927 Sr 1940 Council Painter
Addr: 1894, 402 Wellesley St, Toronto; 1895, c/o Matthews Bros & Co, Toronto; 1896-7, Toronto; 1901, New York; 1905, The Star, Toronto; 1907, Toronto; 1908, 108 Pembroke St, Toronto; 1909, 216 Garden Ave, Toronto; 1910, Toronto; 1911-51, York Mills, Ont
1894 171 A day in June wc
1895 37 Autumn in the Catskills
38 In October
22W A hillside in spring wc
23W A June morning wc
1896 209 Northern hills wc
210 A spring afternoon wc
211 Poplar Hill in summer wc
1897 74 The pines
1901 67 March on the hill top F2-39 F5-93 $50
172 Autumn oak and beech wc
1904 F4, St Louis
104 The pine woods wc (Ontario Government)
1907 111 The stump fence
112 Field of oats, Manitoba
1907 F6, Sherbrooke
111 Hollow Lake, Haliburton $30
112 The St Lawrence at Sorel $30
113 Aster and golden rod $30
1908 81 Sundown in the pine wood
82 A prairie stream
1909M 64 Church at Chateauguay, Que
65 The Battle of Lundy's Lane
1909N 76 Prairie flowers
1910 110 The prairies pen & ink
111 All Saints Day, Quebec village
1910 S2, Liverpool
63 Linemen in New Ontario wc
1911 91 Western sunlight, Last Mountain Lake ‖NGC‖
92 Approaching storm, Qu'appelle Valley
1912 132 The valley, Saskatchewan
133 Grey day in the autumn woods
134 A prairie trail 1954-17 Retro Sec (Art Gallery of Toronto)
1912 S3, Winnipeg
87 Storm on the prairie
88 Qu'appelle Valley wc
89 Flight of ducks, Saskatchewan wc
196 The round-up, Alberta pen
197 After mass in a Quebec

village pen & ink F7-9 nfs
1913 143 The plains of Saskatchewan S4-64 $200
144 Bright day in Qu'appelle
1914 112 Autumn's garland
1914 S5, Patriotic Fund
24 Snowshoers illus
1915 113 Verendrye discovering the Rocky Mountains wc
114 Simon Fraser on the Fraser River wc
115 Champlain's 'Ordre de bon temps', Port Royal 1606 wc
116 Jacques Cartier at Hochelaga wc
1916 122 Willow Creek, February wc
123 Willow Creek, May wc
1918A 83 Rocks of Georgian Bay wc ◊NGC◊
263 Keewaydin litho
1921 76 Woodland interior wc ◊AGO◊
77 Time wc ◊NGC◊
197 Jesuit preaching to the Hurons
198 Champlain's first sight of Georgian Bay
199 Alexander Mackenzie arriving at the Pacific coast
200 A pioneer settler sowing grain in his clearing
#197-200 pen & ink illus for Ontario Public School 'History of Canada'
1922 111 Highlands of Ontario wc S6-45
1923 87 Polish army soldiers bathing at Niagara wc
212 Recording a will in the reign of Justinian
213 An ecclesiastical Court of Probate in the Middle Ages
214 A court of law in the Tudor period
215 Making a will in the time of Charles II
#212-15 pen & ink, National Trust Company
1925 116 A prairie town
117 Breezy autumn
118 Champlain's first sight of Georgian Bay wc & crayon
297 Pioneer settler of 1784 pen & ink
298 Wolfe leading the attack at Quebec, 1759 pen & ink
299 Mackenzie reaches the Arctic Ocean pen & ink
300 Courcelles' expedition meets the English envoys wash drwg
1926 71 The founding of Halifax, 1749 wc illus 1927-102 ◊AGO◊
72 Jacques Cartier at Gaspé, 1535 wc
181 Maisonneuve carrying the Cross to the summit of Mount Royal pen & ink
182 Meeting of Marie Jacquelin and La Tour pen & ink
183 The Battle of Stoney Creek pen & ink
184 Sam Slick, the clockmaker pen & ink
1927 101 The brothers La Verendrye in sight of the western mountains wc ◊AGO◊
103 The pioneer wc
104 Willow Creek in May wc
1928 81 Loyalists drawing lots for the lands wc 1929-113 F9-91 nfs
209 Champlain leaving Quebec, a prisoner pen & ink
210 Presbyterian open air communion pen & ink
211 The Queen's Rangers cutting out the line of Yonge Street pen & ink
212 Champlain using the astrolabe on the Ottawa pen & ink
1929 S7, Calgary
79 Prairie town $800
80 The brothers La Verendrye wc nfs
81 Beech and maple wc $250
1931 139 January in St Anne's Bay wc $150
140 Cocoanut palms and sea, Jamaica wc $150
141 Mountains at Constant Springs wc $350
142 Woodland pasture and hill, Monteague, Jamaica wc $350
1932 104 Wolfe viewing the departure of troops from Louisburg, for the capture of Quebec (Canadian Bank of Commerce)
1933 111 Gull Lake, autumn wc $300
112 Rackety Creek, October wc $400
113 Hills of Monteague, Jamaica wc $150
114 Indians paying hommage to the Chaudière manitou

sketch for mural, Chateau Laurier, Ottawa $250
1935 149 It's a cold world $350
T36-43
150 The dark hunstman wc $300
327 Brûle at the mouth of the Humber, 1615 pen & ink $150
1936 242 Militia training day, Upper Canada, about 1805 drwg $200
1937 118 Cymbal fantasia wc $350
1938 255 The grist mill, 1830 pen drwg nfs
256 The circuit rider pen drwg nfs
257 The Royal Mail pen drwg nfs
258 Doorway of old house at Bath, Ont. pen drwg nfs
1938 S8, Toronto
274 Book, Canada's past in pictures. Ryerson Press
1939 F11, New York
38 A prairie town 28 x 40 $750
1941 S9, Toronto
38 Rocky pasture, Muskoka $150
1951 Travelling exhibit
27 Willow Creek, May DW 1928 wc 19 x 25 3/4
1956 Memorial section, photo of artist, notes by William Colgate, and biog.
All works selected from the Imperial Oil, C.W. Jefferys collection, acquired 1952
1 Etienne Brûle at the mouth of the Humber, 1615 13 x 16
2 John Cabot sighting the New Found Land, 1497 11 1/4 x 15 1/4
3 Cadillac landing at Detroit 13 x 17
4 Cartier erecting a Cross at Gaspé, 1534 22 x 28
5 Cartier meets the Indians of the St Lawrence, 1535 12 x 15
6 Champlain taking an observation with the astrolabe, on the Ottawa, 1613 13 x 14
7 Champlain leaving Quebec, a prisoner on Kirk's ship, 1629 11 1/4 x 15
8 Champlain superintending the buildings of the Habitation of Port Royal, the first permanent settlement in North America 8 x 10
9 Captain Cook at Nootka, 1778 16 x 13
10 Samuel Hearne on his journey to the Coppermine, 1770 10 x 15
11 LaSalle on the Toronto carrying-place, August 1681, on his way to the Mississippi 12 x 13 1/4
12 The brothers LaVerendrye in sight of the western mountains, New Year's Day, 1743 13 1/4 x 10 1/2
13 Mackenzie at the Arctic, 1789 10 x 8
14 Marquette and Joliet on the Mississippi, 1673 11 1/2 x 11 1/2
15 Radisson meets the Indians in a winter camp 6 x 9
16 St Lusson taking possession of the west, at Sault Ste Marie, 1671 11 x 15
17 David Thompson in the Athabaska Pass, 1810 16 x 13 1/2
18 Rev John Black preaching at Stoney Mountain during the Red River flood 10 1/2 x 12
19 Rev James Evans teaching Indians his system of Cree syllabic writing 13 1/2 x 11
20 Father Lacombe persuades Chief Crowfoot and the Blackfoot to allow the railway to be built across their reserve 13 x 11 1/2
21 Mother Marie de l'Incarnation teaching Indian children 13 x 15
22 The Rev John McDougall among the Crees 13 1/2 x 11 1/2
23 Rev Silas T. Rand taking notes in a Micmac Indian camp 12 1/4 x 13 1/4
24 Battle of Batoche, 1885 15 x 12
25 Champlain's fight with the Iroquois, 1609 17 x 14 illus
26 D'Iberville's defeat of the English ships in Hudson Bay, 1697 12 x 14
27 Battle of Lake Erie, 1813 13 x 10
28 Mme La Tour defending Fort St Jean 13 1/2 x 10 1/2
29 Maisonneuve's fight with the Indians 13 1/2 x 14 1/4

30 Montcalm at Ticonderoga 13 1/4 x 10 1/4
31 Battle of Ste Foye, April 28 1760 13 x 10 1/4
32 De Salaberry at Chateauguay, 1813 12 1/2 x 10 1/2
33 The relief of Fort Vercheres 16 x 11
34 Wolfe leading the line at the Battle of the Plains, September 13 1759 11 x 9
35 Frontenac on the way to Cataraqui, 1673 14 x 10
36 Frontenac joins in the war dance 11 1/2 x 10
37 Queen's Rangers under Lieut Gov Simcoe cutting out Yonge Street, 1795 12 3/4 x 13 1/2
38 The Simcoe family at York, 1793 17 1/2 x 15
39 Talon inspecting shipbuilding at Quebec 13 x 13
40 Embarkation of the Acadians, Quebec, 1755 12 1/2 x 10
41 Joseph Brant and Mohawks at Grand River 12 1/4 x 14
42 Brock landing at Detroit 12 x 9 1/2
43 Meeting of Brock and Tecumseh, 1812 11 x 13
44 Judge Haliburton listening to conversation in a Nova Scotia inn 13 1/2 x 10 1/4
45 John Jewitt, captive of Chief Maquina at Nootka, 1802 13 x 15
46 Meeting of Françoise Marie Jacquelin and Charles de la Tour 13 1/2 x 10 1/4
47 A political meeting at 'The Corners', 1837 11 x 14
48 Pontiac's meeting with Gladwyn at Detroit, 1673 16 1/2 x 13
49 Laura Secord tells her story to Fitzgibbon, at De Cou's house, 1813 15 x 13
50 Wolfe chooses his battleground and landing place 14 x 11
51 Indians breaking into a beaver house 13 1/2 x 10 1/2
52 Hunting bison 16 1/4 x 12
53 Indian trading furs, 1785 9 1/2 x 14
54 Stone-headed clubs, shield, arrow and spear heads, quiver, bows 10 1/2 x 7 1/2
55 Costume of central Eskimo 10 x 7 1/4
56 Sled with sail 10 x 7 1/2
57 Doorways of houses, Upper Canada 10 x 15
58 Early building construction A.Palisade construction B.En colombage construction C.Corner construction 11 x 8 1/2
59 Cathedral, Quebec, after seige of 1759, showing ruins 5 3/4 x 4
60 York boats 16 x 10 1/2
61 Carioles and sleighs 8 1/2 x 12
62 Red River cart 13 x 18
63 Country dance, Upper Canada 1840 12 1/2 x 15
64 Horses racing outside walls of Fort Garry, Manitoba, on 24th of May 11 x 14
65 Furniture, French, early 17th century 12 x 10
66 Furniture, French, late 17th century 12 x 9
67 Spinning wheel 10 x 11 3/4
68 Fashions, 1869 9 1/4 x 13
69 Clearing land, about 1830 14 1/2 x 9 1/2
70 Emigrants, on ship 9 x 11
71 Métis hunting the buffalo 10 x 14 1/2
72 Loyalists camping 9 1/4 x 12
73 Prayer meeting, Presbyterian 16 x 18
74 First raft on the Ottawa, 1806 illus
port: by M. Long, 1945-30

JEROME, JEAN PAUL
19 Feb 1928, Montreal M TB3
RCA(e) 1978 Painter
Addr: 1979, Montreal

JEWISON, NORMAN F.
21 Jul 1926, Toronto CWW79
RCA(e) 1975 Film maker
Addr: 1979, Malibou, Cal

JOHNSON, BRADLEY ROBERT
9 Oct 1936, Toronto
RCA(e) 1975 Architect
Addr: 1979, Toronto

JOHNSON, BRUCE HENDERSON
18 Mar 1926, Toronto M
1959 48 Champion 36 x 36 $500

49 Girl swimming in the nude
20 x 54 $450
1961 54 Politician 40 x 40 $400

JOHNSON, CLAUDE EDWARD
7 May 1886, Drummondsville, Ont 18 Dec 1958, Ottawa
Addr: 1925, 87 Cameron St, Ottawa
1925 301 Study of a head crayon

JOHNSON, DAVID American
10 May 1827, New York 30 Jan 1908, Walden, NY AAA28 H
1882 300 On the Unadilla at New Berlin, NY

JOHNSON, DOROTHY
Addr: 1930, 146 Dunn Ave, Toronto
1930 97 Late afternoon $175

JOHNSON, ELAINE
1945 114 Lois nfs

JOHNSON, HELEN G.
fl 1893-4 H
Addr: 1893, 897 Dorchester St, Montreal
1893 86 Study of ducks nfs
87 Red roses $40
88 Pink roses $20

JOHNSON, KATHLEEN BEATRICE
4 Jul 1917, n Toronto IO M
1968 30 Light matter 40 x 40 $500
31 Calculating centre 24 x 24 $250

JOHNSON, PAULINE F. (Mrs)
Addr: 1935-7, 4 Chelsea Pl, Montreal
1935 284 Chinese sketch sculp nfs
1936 222 Sketch plaster $50
1937 286 Jane sculp nfs 1938-237 $50
1941 214 Gyde sculp nfs
port: bust, by O. Wheeler, 1948-79

JOHNSTON, ALEXANDER
H
1881 221 Phyllis (H.F. George Twining)

JOHNSTON, D.J.
1939 114 Self portrait nfs

JOHNSTON, FRANCES ANNE (Mrs George Franklin Arbuckle)
9 Oct 1910, Toronto CWW79 IO M
ARCA 1948 RCA 1963 Painter
Addr: 1932, 1104 Bay St, Toronto; 1933, 78 Avenue Rd, Toronto; 1936, 64 Grenville St, Toronto; 1948-57, Montreal; 1958-71/79, Toronto
1932 105 Autumn hillside $200
1933 115 The shadowed pool $250
Johnson, mispr
1936 110 Zuleika $100 T37-38
111 Woodland pool $200
1940 88 South window $300 T41-29
1946 68 Still life $350
1947 94 Still life monot $50
1948 88 Victorian sitting room nfs
89 Victorian dining room nfs 1949-51
1949 50 October $350 1950-77 27 x 20
1952 48 Victuals $450
49 South window $450
1953 43 Flowers and fruit $450
1953 Travelling exhibit
16 Pink chair $400
1954 48 Fruits and wine 30 x 36 illus $450 1955-51 illus
49 Apples and jugs 20 x 37 $400 1955-50
1957 39 Pochette $300
1959 50 Winter window 26 x 20 illus $300
51 September 22 x 30 $400
1960 49 Sun and gourds 28 x 34 illus $400
50 Arrangements in grey 19 x 39 1/2 $350
1961 55 Homage to Juan Gris 36 x 30 $450
56 Still life 28 x 40 illus $400
1963 41 Still life $650
1964J 37 Still life 30 x 48 illus $650
1964N 30 Still life with fruit 32 x 40 $650
1965 40 Etude 32 x 40 illus $650
41 Garden arabesque 22 x 30 $400
1966 33 Chez moi #3 36 x 42 illus $900 1967-34
1966 S10, Charlottetown
44 Victorian sitting room $300
45 Sun and gourds $550
1967 33 Peripatetic geranium 22 x 30 $400
DW 1964 Still life oil on board 30 1/8 x 48 1/8

JOHNSTON, FRANCIS HANS (FRANZ)
19 Jun 1888, Toronto 9 Jul 1949, Toronto AGO CC1 CWW48 EC M NGC PMC TB2/3
ARCA 1919-39 RCA medal 1969, Group of Seven Painter
Addr: 1918A, 96 Keewatin Ave, Toronto; 1922, 198 Walnut St, Toronto; 1923-4, Winnipeg; 1925, Centre St, Thornhill, Ont; 1926, 2474 Yonge St, Toronto; 1927, 224 Bloor St W, Toronto; 1928-30, 14 Elm St, Toronto; 1931, 122 Roxborough St W, Toronto; 1932-5, 78 Avenue Rd, Toronto; 1936-9, Toronto
1918A Francis H. Johnston, to 1919
84 The silver silence temp
85 Forest fancy temp
86 Guardian of the gorge gouache illus ◊NGC◊
237 Such dreams as stuff are made of. decoration
238 The dog train. decoration
239 The fairy ring. decoration
240 The magic pool. decoration ◊NGC◊
1918N 93 The dagabo of dreams temp
94 The ladies of the lake temp
1919 83 The beckoning
204 Reflections, Agawa Canyon temp
205 Fantasy dec drwg
1920 Frank H. Johnston, to 1925
136 Beaver haunts
137 Wild cherry and live forever temp
138 Agawa Canyon temp
139 Sentinels, Algoma temp
1922 112 Air castles, Lake of the Woods
1925 119 Silver heights
120 Illecillewaet Falls
1926 Franz Johnston, to 1941
73 Moon ring illus
74 Field, BC temp
1927 105 The rapids, northern Quebec
106 The dark wood, northern Quebec
107 Drenched, northern Quebec
1928 82 Hunting lodge, northern Quebec $700
83 Autumn tapestry, northern Quebec $700
84 The flaming maple, Algoma temp $300
85 The portage, Mongoose Lake temp $300
1928 F8, London, Eng
121 On such a night temp $100
1929 114 Belle River, Quebec $700
115 Gleam of gold temp $350
1929 S7, Calgary
82 Northern haze $350
83 Agawa Rapids $125
1930 98 The decorative north $1,000
1931 143 Timberline $800
144 Midsummer sun, Georgian Bay $350
1932 106 Beauty, mantled deep $2,800
1934 107 House on the hill $200
108 Glowing snow $250
1935 151 Morning in the Abitibi $400
1938 S8, Toronto
183 Book, The Beauport Road
187 Book, The flying canoe
1940 89 Wildcat Cafe, Yellowknife, NWT $180
1941 S9, Toronto
39 Winter's cathedral $200
port: bust, by C. Adamson, 1928-60

JOHNSTON, FREDA (Mrs Edward Joseph Dreany)
Addr: 1937, 107 High Park Ave, Toronto
1937 119 Peggy wc $35
1939 65 Afternoon on the farm nfs Dreany

JOHNSTON, LUCY
Addr: 1938, Toronto
1938 S8, Toronto
380 Wallpaper design. Hon mention. Canadian Wallpaper Manufacturers Limited

JOHNSTON, PAUL see RODRIK, PAUL

JOHNSTON, RANDOLPH WARDELL
23 Feb 1904, Toronto CWW79
Addr: 1925, 9 Silver Birch Ave, Toronto; 1930, 23 West Island Dr, Hanlan's Point, Toronto
1925 263 Lorne Pierce bust
264 Football player, study sculp
1930 99 The fireworks, Canadian National Exhibition $75
189 Fountain, sketch model white metal

190 Head of artist's daughter ter cot $60
211 Study of a nude drwg $20

JOHNSTON, ROBERT EDWIN
14 Sep 1885, Toronto 1933, Leonia, NJ B M TB2
Addr: 1909N, 184 Lansdowne Ave, Toronto; 1918A, c/o Saturday Night, Toronto
1909N 77 The Lansdowne subway, Toronto
1918A 241 Illustration, poem 'In Flander's fields' charcl
242 Whither? cart charcl

JOHNSTONE, JOHN YOUNG
12 Nov 1887, Montreal 13 Feb 1930, Havanna M NGC TB3 W78
ARCA 1920-7 Painter
Addr: 1915-20, 223 Ontario St W, Montreal; 1923, 781 University St, Montreal
1915 117 Côte de Beaupré
118 A dog
1916 124 Rue de Venise, Paris
125 Pont Aven, Bretagne
286 The Béguinage of Bruges pencil
287 Bonsecours Market col drwg
1918N 95 The road to Château Richer
96 The old abbey, Paris
225 Sketch col drwg
1919 84 View from the Rigi, Switzerland
85 Sunny day
1920 140 Ile aux Coudres, Quebec
141 Old barn, Beaupré, Quebec
1923 88 The road, St Joachim, Quebec ◊NGC◊
89 Bonsecours Market, Montreal wc

JOHNSTONE, MAY
H
1889 60 A study table $100

JOHNSTONE, WILLIAM
1868, Edinburgh
Addr: 1920, 313 Tegler Bldg, Toronto
1920 314 St Andrew's Castle etch
315 Knitting by the Zuyder Zee etch, after painting by R.G. Hutchison

JONES, CHILION
10 Oct 1835, Brockville, Ont 1 Apr 1912, Bermuda Co PMC W78
see FULLER, THOMAS, 1883

JONES, FRANCES M. (Mrs Hamlet Bannerman)
1855, Halifax, NS 1940, England
DBA DVP H
ARCA 1882-8 Painter
Addr: 1882-8, Halifax
1881 253 An Italian girl $50
290 The young mountaineer $50 E.M. Jones, mispr
1882 3 Breton peasant spinning $150
6 Spring $100
1883 25 A good gossip $60
48 The Presbytère $100
55 Autumn sunbeams $50
56 Sonata pathetique $60
61 Pot au feu $60

JONES, HARRY ERNEST
31 Aug 1892, Bracknell, Berks, Eng
M
1939 122 Sketch, Yellowknife, NWT $100
123 Sketch, cabins, Yellowknife, NWT $100

JONES, HENRY WANTON
11 May 1925, Waterloo, Que
1964J 38 Women 43 x 59 illus $650
1964N 76 Victim of Ticonderoga wld steel & copper 25h $400

JONES, HUGH GRIFFITH
3 Dec 1872, Randolph, Wis 16 Feb 1947, Montreal CWW48 NGC PMC
ARCA 1925 RCA 1927 Council Architect
Addr: 1913-22, King Edward Apts, 10 Oldfield Ave, Montreal; 1923, Drummond Bldg, Montreal; 1924, 511 St Catherine St W, Montreal; 1925-6, 276 Pine Ave, Montreal; 1927, 1411 Stanley St, Montreal; 1931-7, 1227 Sherbrooke St W, Montreal; 1938-47, Montreal
1913 145 West Virginia hills
1916 126 An early autumn
127 Near New London, Conn
1918M 97 Evening, Château Richer
98 Afternoon, Sault à la Puce
1920 142 Garden, Quebec
143 Gardens, Hampton Court
1922 113 Afternoon, Paris
1923 179 CPR Station, Moose Jaw, Sask photo
180 Toronto Union Station photo
1924 107 Evening, St Martins

Churchyard, Canterbury
108 Late afternoon, Château Richer 1925-122
221 Section of railway station facade study
1925 121 Evening, Manchester, Vt
238 Dominion-Douglas Church, perspective
1926 150 Church interior study
1927 108 Château Gaillard, Normandy wc
109 Evening, Canterbury wc
110 Grey day, Bratton, England wc
111 The castle, evening wc
236 Dominion-Douglas Church, Westmount, photo
237 Dominion-Douglas Church, chancel furniture photo
238 Pavilion tower, Harbour Bridge charcl
1931 145 Evening, St Lawrence River
146 Late afternoon, Taormina, Sicily
1932 107 Cliffs at Sorrento wc
108 Sunrise, Venice wc
1933 116 At the Dogana, Venice wc
117 The terrace, Bathing Club, L.I. wc
118 Late afternoon, Lake Macdonald, Que wc T34-42
1935 152 Background
1936 112 A relic of ancient Rome wc nfs T37-39
113 Rome, evening, constitutional wc illus nfs
114 Venice, morning wc nfs
1937 120 Evening at St Angelo Bridge, Rome nfs
1943 69 Callaro Bay, Dalmatia nfs
1944 83 On the Ombla, Dalmatia nfs
84 Civic Centre, Ragusa nfs
1945 115 Late afternoon, Quebec nfs T46-26
116 An English cottage, near Bath wc nfs
1946 69 Evening, ancient Ragusa harbour nfs
DW 1928 Pavilion tower, Harbour Bridge wc drwg 41 1/2 x 21
port: by R. Jack, 1942-68

JONES, J.L.
1850, London, Eng H
Addr: 1886, Toronto
1886 Fla, London, Eng
2030, artist number
Wood engraved blocks, wood engr and des

JONES, JACOBINE see JONES, PHYLLIS

JONES, MARVIN HAROLD
19 May 1940, Flora, Ill
1971 24 Making radish roses 17 x 22 $500

JONES, PHYLLIS JACOBINE
4 Apr 1898, London, Eng 13 Sep 1976, Niagara-on-the-Lake, Ont M
NGC TB3 WWA47
ARCA 1943 RCA 1951 Sr 1967 Sculptor
Addr: 1932, 27 Grenville St, Toronto; 1935, Highland Cr, York Mills, Ont; 1943-55, York Mills, Ont; 1956-9, Toronto; 1960-5, Milton, Ont; 1966, Niagara-on-the-Lake, Ont; 1967-71, Milton, Ont
1932 213 Kitty, portrait of cart mare sculp
1935 285 Black cavalry black marble $2,000 1940-161 $5,000
1942 166 Mother and child plaster $250
167 Fox Belgian marble $300 1943-131 $350
1943 132 The refugees stone group sketch model $25
1944 149 Torso direct carv, Indiana limestone $150 1945-228
1946 137 Horse direct carv, red sandstone $350 1947-206
1947 207 Our Lady of Mercy and the three generations of man photo
208 York County Registry Bldg, Richmond St, Toronto, figure photo
1948 170 Bank of Montreal, Toronto, model panel 'British Columbia' plaster for stone Marani & Morris, architects
1949 118 The frog prince plaster for bronze
1952 110 St George. War Memorial, Manufacturers Life Assoc, Toronto des Marani & Morris, architects
111 Bank of Nova Scotia, Toronto, panel Mathers & Haldenby, architects illus
1954 109 Mouse alabaster 3h nfs
1955 109 Confederation Life Bldg, low rel over main entrance

Marani & Morris, architects
1956 50 Vulture sculp illus $1,500
1957 77 Hon George S. Henry sculp nfs
78 Protective form. Greenacres Home for the Aged. sculp H. Chapman, architect illus
1960 81 St Joseph. Mother House of St Joseph. sculp Marani & Morris, architects photo
1961 81 United Empire Loyalists, Chrysler Park, head of memorial figure sculp nfs
82 Central Services, General Hospital, Toronto panels sculp. Mathers & Haldenby, architects photo
1964N 73 Mr Hamadryas sculp stone $500
1965 84 Mens sana in corpore sano sculp photo nfs
85 Percheron foal bronze 6 1/2 x 8 x 3 illus $800
DW 1954 Equestrian figure bronze 11h

JONGERS, ALPHONSE
17 Nov 1872, Mézières, France 2 Oct 1945, Montreal B CC1 M NGC TB
ARCA 1937 RCA 1940 Sr 1942 Painter
Addr: 1924-37, Ritz Carlton Hotel, Montreal; 1938-45, Montreal
1924 109 Dr J.F. Shepherd illus
1925 123 Sir Vincent Meredith, Bart illus
124 Jules Hamel, Esq
1927 112 Robert Howard, Esq
1929 117 Hon Athanase David
1931 147 Capt T.T. McG, stoker
1933 119 Hon Chief Justice Greenshields 1938-115 illus nfs F11-39 28 x 36
120 Portrait of Meg
1935 153 HE Lord Bessborough, Gov Gen of Canada nfs
1937 121 Marquis de Simone nfs
122 Sir James Dunn, Bart nfs
1938 116 F.N. Southam, Esq nfs
117 AirM W.A. Bishop nfs
1939 124 Ross McMaster, Esq nfs
125 Samuel Bronfman, Esq nfs
1940 90 Col George S Cantlie nfs
91 Mrs Ronald Graham nfs
92 Self portrait illus nfs
DW 1940 28 1/2 x 22 T41-30
1954 Retro Sec 19
1941 96 HRH Prince of Luxembourg nfs
1942 73 HE Baron Silvercruys nfs
74 Trallero nfs
75 Sub Lieut Edmond J. de Lotbinière nfs
1943 70 Mrs F.R. Peverley illus nfs
71 George S. McIntosh, Esq nfs
1944 85 Mrs Wallace T. Orr nfs
86 Capt James Calder nfs
port: bust, by H.Hébert, 1926-160

JONGMAN, HENK
1970 189 Cover, University of Toronto, Graduate Study and Research, Dept of Chemistry

JOPLING (Miss)
H
1885 332 Design for wd engr

JOPLING, FREDERIC WAISTELL
23 Apr 1859 or 1860, Kensington, London, Eng Apr 1945, Toronto
AGO H M
Addr: 1918A-19, 125 Collier St, Toronto
1883 196 Norwegian peasant wc $45
296 Mischievous marauder wc $35
1885 175 Study of a fish $30
231 An old New England orchard wc $25
1918A 243 Increasing tonnage dry pt etch
1919 86 Launching a Canadian built war ship wc
206 A lady in fur dry pt etch

JORGENSEN, FLEMMING
29 May 1936, Aalborg, Denmark M WWA76
RCA(e) 1973 Painter
Addr: 1976/79, Victoria
1970 36 Triumph 72 x 72 $800
37 Triple landscape 48 x 65 $600
1976 S12, Montreal
31 White Island #2 acry 42 x 54 1/4 illus

JOSLIN, MAURICE
1968 32 Medallion cross 58 x 58 $800

JOST, JOSEF German
6 Aug 1875, Heckendalheim B TB1/2
Addr: 1913, Travancore, Cedar Ave, Montreal

1913 322 Tiger kampfbereit sculp
323 Bear with boy sculp
324 Awakening sculp
325 Evening prayer marble

JOST, OTTILIE see PALM, OTTILIE

JUDAH, DORIS MINETTE TROTTER (Mrs E. Lionel Judah)
7 Mar 1887, Montreal CNS40 M
Addr: 1931, 3638 Durocher St, Montreal
1931 321 Late Dean H.M. Mackay plaster $250 bronze $500
322 Youth plaster $100 bronze $250

JUDSON, WILLIAM LEE American
1 Apr 1842, Manchester, Eng 1928, Los Angeles B F H
Addr: 1881-3, London, Ont; 1884, Paris; 1887, c/o G. Pell, Montreal
1880 110 Caught in the act
1881 236 Poor relations $60
1882 31 Bed time $45
204 Blue and gold wc $40
W.J. Judson, mispr
1883 17 Shy $90
132 An odalisque $80
283 Hyacinth wc $40
1884 31 Beach at St Malo $50 S1-130
1884 S1, Saint John
94 Washing $25
99 Harvest in Brittany $50
1885 24 Cabbage $80
93 Valley of the Seine $300
131 Going to market $125
1886 4 Golden rod in bloom
6 Chrysanthemums Fla-2004
9 Fruit Fla-2004
207 Aboriginal hunter $50
210 Indians of the Saskatchewan $200
207-210 Selected for Fla, not in Fla catalog
1887 89 Chrysanthemums dec panel $100
94 Two hundred years ago $150
1888 203 Head of an old man $40

JULE, WALTER
1940, Seattle, Wash
RCA(e) 1979 Painter
Addr: 1976/79, Edmonton
1976 S12, Montreal
123 Poster, Jazz Society, 1973 season schedule col illus

JULIEN, OCTAVE HENRI
14 May 1852, St Roch, Que 17 Sep 1908, Montreal CC2 H M R2 W78
Addr: 1899, 675 St Denis St, Montreal; 1907, Montreal
1899 77 Le retour
1907 113 La chasse galerie

JUNEAU, DENIS
30 Sep 1925, Montreal B M TB3
RCA(e) 1973 Painter
Addr: 1979, Montreal
1967 35 Entre le bleu et le rouge 58 x 58 $550

K

KAHANE, ANNE (Mrs Robert Langstadt)
1 Mar 1924, Vienna AGO CC1 M NGC TB3 WWA59 WWB54
ARCA 1961-71 Council Sculptor
Addr: 1961-71/76, Montreal
1964J 75 Wayfarers sculp 42 x 14 x 17 $1,200
1966 79 Victim 21 x 46 x 13 illus $750
1967 76 Kite man 78 x 51 x 9 $800
1970 82 Group 64 x 38 x 19 illus $2,000
1976 S12, Montreal
74 Couple 2 wood/bois 64 x 13 x 14 illus

KAISER, ROBERT J.
16 Mar 1925, Detroit
RCA(e) 1974 Council Industrial designer
Addr: 1979, Toronto
1971 101 Chair, Concept Furniture International Limited

KAKINUMA, THOMAS
4 Oct 1908, Tochigi-Ken, Japan M
1953 44 The interior $300
1955 110 Sculpture $350

KALLMEYER, MINNIE
1882, Detroit 22 Mar 1947, Toronto M NGC TB2
Addr: 1911-36, 94 South Dr, Toronto
1911 93 Clodgy Point, Cornwall
1918A 87 September in the Catskill Mountains
88 October in the Catskill Mountains
1918N 99 September day
1919 87 Summer morning

1920 144 A mountain home
1921 78 The fruit shop, Boothbay Harbour, Maine
79 The cove
1922 114 The hillside
115 The cliffs
1923 90 Pigeon Cove, Mass
91 At dock, Gloucester, Mass 1924-110
1926 75 Bend of the river
1927 113 Baie St Paul, Quebec
1928 86 Drying the nets at Lunenburg, Nova Scotia $600
1929 118 Drying the sails, Lunenburg, Nova Scotia $600
119 Fishing boats at St Ives $300
1929 S7, Calgary
84 Spruce Point $200
1930 100 Fishing boats at anchor $500
101 Along the Nova Scotia coast $250
1931 148 Along the cliffs $600
149 At Lunenburg, Nova Scotia $400
1932 109 Blue Rock, harbour, Nova Scotia $80
1933 121 Blue Rock, Nova Scotia $400 T34-43
1934 109 Grand Etang, Cape Breton $100
1935 154 Peggy's Cove, Nova Scotia $600 1936-115 $500 T37-40

KALVAC, HELEN W2-428
1901, Holman Island, NWT ED M
RCA(e) 1974 Graphic designer
Addr: 1979, Holman Island, NWT

KANANGINAK E7-1168
c 1935, Cape Dorset, NWT ED M
RCA(e) 1979 Print maker
Addr: 1979, Cape Dorset, NWT

KANGIRUAQ
Addr: 1976, Baker Lake, NWT
1976 S12, Montreal
160 Woman haunted by birds. Kangiruaq and Kukiyaut stencil/dessin du pochoir 22 1/8 x 29 3/4 illus

KARMAN, ROBERT
17 Feb 1933, Montreal M
1958 48 Spit $100
1959 52 Decomposition 20 x 34 $100

KARSH, YOUSUF
23 Dec 1908, Mardin, Armenia
CWW79 EC WWA66
RCA(e) 1975 RCA medal 1964 Photographer
Addr: 1979, Ottawa

KASYN, JOHN
21 Jan 1926, Winnipeg IO
1959 53 Snow covered field 20 x 25 1/4 $175
1960 51 Rock formation 29 1/4 x 39 1/4 $300
1961 57 Sun and rock 30 x 40 $400
58 The red farm house wc 20 x 26 $100

KAYE, DAVID HAIGH
1947, Kingston, Ont IO WWA78
Addr: 1976, Guelph, Ont
1976 S12, Montreal
144 Linen & jute #3 woven tapestry 48 x 72 illus

KEAGEY, JAMES WILLIAM
29 Apr 1878, Dundas, Ont
Addr: 1918A, Dundas, Ont
1918A 244 Old Muski, Cairo etch

KEARNS, CELIA BRUCE
fl 1890-23 H
Addr: 1922, 650 McDermot Ave, Winnipeg; 1923, 12A Guelph Apts, McMillan St, Winnipeg
1890 49 Greek slave $95
1922 116 Landscape
117 Children in the park wc S6-46
1923 92 A summer afternoon wc
93 Children wading wc

KEATING, HARRIETTE
1898, Seattle, Wash
Addr: 1933, 22 The Chateau, Regina
1933 122 Barbara Barber T34-44
123 Emily Delay $300

KEEFER, EMAIME (Mrs)
1939 126 Flowers nfs Emaime Keefer
127 Destiny pastel $35
1941 97 Trailer home, Timmins nfs Emaine Keefer

KEEFER, SAMUEL
20 Jan 1811, Thorold, Ont 7 Jan 1890, Brockville, Ont W78
1880 371 Clifton Suspension Bridge

KEENE, CALEB
b c 1866 flg 1940, Oakville, Ont M
Addr: 1915, 14 Oldfield Ave, Montreal
1915 119 and 120 Near Lac Supérieur, Quebec

KEENE, LOUIS
21 Sep 1888, London, Eng M
Addr: 1913, 4585 Sherbrooke St W, Westmount, Que; 1914, 1 Abbotsford Apts, Oldfield Ave, Montreal; 1915-16, 14 Oldfield Ave, Montreal; 1918N, 5 Bloor St W, Toronto; 1919, 731 Yonge St, Toronto; 1921, Oakville, Ont
1913 148 Laden with the treasure of the east S4-65 $450
149 Early morning, clearing mist
1914 113 A summer storm
1914 S5, Patriotic Fund
36 Battle of the Whip and Broom illus
1915 Lieut Keene
121 'At 2.30 the infantry will attack.' Brigade order illus
278 Ypres on the ninth of August b&w
1916 Capt Keene
128 To fill the gap
288 Maj Gen Wilson study in charcl
289 Recruiting poster des
1918N 100 How we came back
1919 88 The 20th Machine Gun Company, CEF's on parade in front of their barracks at Gornastai, Siberia, 1919 temp
89 Fighter and trader too wc
1921 80 The frozen sea wc

KEER, J.
H
Addr: 1881, Toronto
1881 67 Rustic bridge, near Toronto wc $25

KEITH-KING, JOHN WILLIAM
21 Jun 1939, Ancaster, Ont
RCA(e) 1978 Architect
Addr: 1979, Vancouver

KELLAND, GEORGE W.
1880 265 Cabinet, Grecian des
268 Medieval sideboard des
271 Cabinet, Jacobean des
279 Book covers des
303 Canadian plants, leaves and flowers des

KELLETT, ARTHUR
Addr: 1922, 2172 Queen St E, Toronto
1922 118 The Thames at Wapping wc S6-47
119 In the Chiltern Hills, Buckinghamshire wc

KELLY, GILES TALBOT see TALBOT KELLY, GILES

KELLY, HANNAH RUSK (Mrs Samuel L.P. Kelly)
1860, Elderslie, or Elmslie, Ont H
Addr: 1923, 4 Hampton Court, 18 East Ave N, Hamilton; 1926-8, 244 1/2 James St S, Hamilton
1923 94 Miniatures A. Constance Webster B. Rosalind
1926 76 Miniatures on ivory
1928 87 The Spanish shawl $250

KELLY, JOHN DAVID
15 Oct 1862, Gore's Landing, Ont
27 Dec 1958, Toronto AGO H M W78
Addr: 1895, 30 Sussex Ave, Toronto; 1901, 17 Classic Ave, Toronto; 1912, Toronto
1895 42W Fishing boat in a squall off Bermuda wc
43W A glimpse of the Atlantic, Bermuda wc
44W The farmer's daughter wc nfs
45W After ducks, early morning wc
1901 173 First ship on Lake Erie, LaSalle, 1679 wc F2-40
174 A nor'wester wc
1912 S3, Winnipeg
198 Storm on Lake Nipissing crayon
199 The woodsman b&w

KELSEY, CHARLES WILLIAM
19 Apr 1877, London, Eng 27 Jan 1975, Montreal PMC
Addr: 1922, 155 Mance St, Montreal; 1923-4, 196 Staynor Ave, Apt 1, Montreal; 1925-7, 278 West Hill Ave, Montreal; 1928-37, 4148 Dorchester St W, Westmount, Que
1922 120 And his banner over me was love

257 Stained glass window des
1923 95 Spring as youth, with attendant spirit
96 Summer as womanhood, with attendant knight
216 Stained glass window des
1924 111 Mural painting, sketch wc
112 Winter panel
268 Stained glass window des
1925 125 A Red Cross Knight's vision of the Seven Gifts of the Holy Spirit: Sapientia, Intellectus, Consilium, Fortitude, Scientia, Pietas, Timor
1926 185 Wilcocks Memorial, Richmond, Que st gl des
1927 114 Helen, daughter of Maj Sham, MC
115 On Scarborough Bluffs
1928 213 Stained glass window des
1929 120 Woman, where are those, thine accusers? $200
269 The sleeping beauty st gl des, for Mrs Sidney Levitt
1929 S7, Calgary
85 Jean and Sebastian Cabot sight coast of North America $200
86 My heart is like a bird $200
1930 102 King Arthur and his knights wc $200
1931 150 Andrea del Sarto, from Browning's poem wc $500
403 Stained glass panel des, for C.H. Linton, Esq
1933 124 Preparing for the bath wc $100
125 Winter, Montreal $30
301 Loyola College, The first Canadian martyrs st gl sketch
1939 128 Rock garden, Edgehill, Westmount wc $150
296 Westmount Park Webster Memorial United Church st gl window des
1947 226 Sedberg School, 4 panels st gl des

KELSEY, DORA see WOODHEAD, DORA

KELSEY, LEONARD EDGAR
12 Dec 1883, London, Eng 3 Jul 1975, Vancouver
Addr: 1913, 2155 Esplanade Ave, Montreal; 1933-5, 322 Ballantyne Ave N, Montreal West
1913 361 Skyward pen & ink
1933 126 Log cabin, Lac Tremblant wc $40
1935 155 Flower study wc $30
1945 117 Summertime wc $45
118 Rawdon wc $45

KEMBLE, ROGER IAN
4 Jul 1929, Hull, Eng
ARCA 1971 RCA 1975 Council Architect
Addr: 1971/79, Vancouver
1970 23A-27A Dominion Astrophysical Observatory, Victoria, 16" telescope housing. Interior, showing telescope. Exterior, from sw and se. Longtitudinal section and side elevation. Floor plan
DW 1975 Architectural works, 1960-75 100 slides

KEMP, ANTHONY LESLIE
9 Jul 1936, Kingston, Eng
RCA(e) 1979 Architect
Addr: 1979, Toronto

KEMP, JAMES ALEXANDER
6 Oct 1914, Toronto CWW79 IO M
1952 50 Two nudes $1,500
1953 45 Uncertainty $250
46 Girl with mirror $60
1954 50 Cottage interior 32 x 24 illus $150
51 Figure 20 x 16 $75
1955 52 Musician $150
53 Two figures illus $200
1956 26 Two figures $300 T56-22
27 Musician illus $300
1956 Travelling exhibit
23 Museum $300
1957 40 Two figures $350
1958 49 Two figures illus $300
1959 54 Figure 32 x 24 $175
1960 52 Figure 36 x 26 illus $250
1964N 31 Figure in landscape 24 x 32 illus $250

KENDALL, NICHOLAS
Addr: 1976, Kingston, Ont
1976 S12, Montreal
169 Bill and John film 16mm col 13 min
170 Surface film 16mm col 8 min

KENDERDINE, AUGUSTUS FREDERICK LAFOSSE (GUS)

31 Mar 1870, n Blackpool, Eng 1 Aug 1947, Saskatoon CC2 M NGC TB2 WWA47
Addr: 1931, University of Saskatchewan, Saskatoon; 1936, Regina College, Regina
1931 151 Autumn $500
152 The taxidermist (University of Saskatchewan)
1936 116 Reflections $250 T37-41

KENNEDY, FREDERICK DAWSON
11 Jan 1906, Peterborough, Ont M
1953 47 Haven wc $150

KENNEDY, JAMES
Addr: 1913-14, 792 Shuter St, Montreal
1913 150 The stake wc
151 The foundry wc
1914 114 Montreal harbour wc

KENNEDY, JOHN DE NAVARRE
31 May 1888, London, Eng CNS36 CWW79 M
Addr: 1930, 14 Summerhill Gardens, Toronto; 1932-3, 10 Montclair Ave, Toronto
1930 103 Birch trees wc $50 T. de N. Kennedy, mispr
1932 110 Tim Casey's barn yard wc $50 T. de N. Kennedy, mispr
1933 127 Barn yard, Ontario wc $75

KENNEDY, RALPH
1963 42 Composition #2 $500

KENNEDY, SYBIL
13 Aug 1899, Quebec CWW79 M TB3
ARCA 1953 Sr 1969 RCA 1975 Sculptor
Addr: 1953-71/79, New York
1953 119 Cellist sculp nfs
1954 110 Conversation sculp 13 x 11 illus $254
1958 89 Descent from the Cross sculp $225
1959 88 Reading monk bronze 10 x 12 illus $300
1960 82 Young mother sculp $300
1963 92 Guitarist bronze $400
DW 1975 Sculpture bronze 12 x 7

KENOJUAK E7-1035 (Mrs Johnniebo)
1927, Baffin Island, NWT CC1 ED M WWA78
RCA(e) 1974 Print maker
Addr: 1979, Cape Dorset, Baffin Island, NWT

KEPPEL, C.W.
Addr: 1886, 187 St James St, Montreal
1886 Fla, London, Eng
2031, artist number
Wood engraving

KERGOMMEAUX, DUNCAN ROBERT CHASSIN DE
15 Jul 1927, Premier, BC CC1 IO M NGC TB3 WWA76
RCA(e) 1975 Painter
Addr: 1979, London, Ont

KERR, ESTELLE MURIEL
16 Apr 1879, Toronto d 1971 M Mo12
Addr: 1907, Toronto; 1911, 14 Madison Ave, Toronto; 1912, 76 Yonge St Arcade, Toronto; 1913, 14 Madison Ave, Toronto; 1914-32, 80 Spadina Rd, Toronto; 1934-6, 78 Spadina Rd, Toronto
1907 114 Fisher folk of Volendam
115 Lamp light
1911 94 Berneval Beach
95 Seine fishermen
96 Normandy farmyard
97 Low tide
1912 135 Market day, Dieppe
1912 S3, Winnipeg
200 Volendam fisherman b&w
1913 152 Canal in Bruges
1914 115 The panier frock
1915 122 The picnic
1916 129 Reflections illus
1918A 89 The vigil
1920 145 Margaret
1923 217 Pearl dec mural des
1923 S6, Hamilton
48 Midsummer
1924 113 The bamboo curtain
1925 126 Mrs Gordon Hellmuth, portrait sketch
1926 77 The red screen
1928 88 Madonna of the maples
1930 212 Peonies des $100
1932 111 October bouquet $150
1934 110 Mexican girls $100 T35-38
1935 156 Nassau market woman $200
1936 117 Bunny Lang nfs
118 Fall flowers $60
1938 118 The balcony $50 T39-27
1941 S9, Toronto
40 October $50
1950 78 Mexican boys 22 x 28 $150

KERR, GERTRUDE
Addr: 1910, Newlyn, Cornwall, Eng

1910 112 Across the valley
113 The farm, Steading, Cornwall

KERR, ILLINGWORTH HOLEY
20 Aug 1905, Lumsden, Sask CC1
CWW79 M NGC TB2/3
RCA(e) 1975 Painter
Addr: 1934, Lumsden, Sask; 1979, Calgary
1934 111 A western theatre $100

KERR, J.B.
H
Addr: 1895, Franklin, Man
1895 77 A corner in home, sweet home

KERR, K.E. ROBERT
1971 McCarter, Nairne & Partners
20A-22A Moore Business Forms Ltd. View from main entrance. View from Bute St, showing stairs to pedestrian space. Ariel view

KERR, RONALD
Addr: 1922, 24 Mercille Ave, St Lambert, Que; 1923, 104 Birch Ave, St Lambert, Que; 1925-6, 1056 Durocher St, Montreal; 1927-9, 820 Troie Ave, Montreal; 1932-7, 6554 Durocher Ave, Outremont, Que
1922 all works in pastels
121 The harbour S6-49
1923 97 Whiteface
98 November
1925 127 Path of the sun
128 Cool woods
1926 78 Pleasant shade
1927 116 Reflections
1929 121 The motor boat garage
1932 112 The river rocks $15
1933 128 Gleam of autumn $18
129 The old barn $15
1937 123 September sun and cloud $25
124 When the lake is still $25
1938 119 The manor house $25
120 The river in October $25
1941 98 October sunlight $25
99 Chateauguay $25
1942 76 Boats $25
1945 119 The smiling river $25
120 The dam $25

KERR-LAWSON, JAMES see LAWSON, JAMES KERR

KERWIN, CLAIRE (Mrs George Kerwin)
Chatelet, Belgium IO
RCA(e) 1976 Print maker
Addr: 1979, Toronto

KEWELL, JOHN J. (b Kugel, John J. c 1940, Kewell)
Addr: 1937, 1472 Mackay St, Montreal
1937 John J. Kugel
245 Willowcourt Apartment building, Outremont
246 The Barbizon, residential hotel, Montreal

KEYL, FRIEDRICH WILHELM English
17 Aug 1823, Frankfurt-on-Main 5 Dec 1871, London, Eng B DVP G TB
1880 325 Roe deer chalk sketch (HRH Princess Louise) Keyle, mispr

KIDD, JOSEPH M.
b Athlone, Ont fl 1892-05 H
Addr: 1893, 68 Pembroke St, Toronto; 1894, 215 W 57th St, New York; 1895-6, 68 Pembroke St, Toronto
1893 89 Reflection $100
90 Roses $35 F1-72
1894 70 September noon day at Wiarton
71 Wheat sheaves, near Athlone
1895 74 The beech trees in November
75 In the daisy fields of Connecticut
76 Roses
41W A rising storm at sunset wc
1896 93 The drover

KIERAN, PHILIP PETER
1898, Dublin
Addr: 1924, 151 Craig St, Montreal; 1925, 190 Mercille Ave, St Lambert, Que; 1927, St Louis Ave, Beaurepaire, Que
1924 269 Brome Lake, Knowlton, Quebec etch 1925-303
270 Book plates
1925 302 Le moulin, Verchères dry pt & mezz
304 Bookplates etch & engr
1927 308 Portrait of an old man dry pt

KILBOURN, ROSEMARY ELIZABETH
3 Apr 1931, Toronto IO M
RCA(e) 1977 Print maker

Addr: 1979, Caledon East, Ont

KILGOUR, ANDREW WILKIE
1868, Kirkcaldy, Scot 28 May 1930, Strathmore, Que M NGC TB3
Addr: 1911-20, 176 Fairmount Ave W, Montreal; 1921-4, 84 St François Xavier St, Montreal; 1925, 1070 Bleury St, Montreal; 1927, 907 Hartland Ave, Outremont, Que; 1928, 963 Hartland Ave, Outremont, Que; 1929, 1070 Bleury St, Montreal

1911 98 October afternoon, Mount Royal
99 Dawn, a summer idyl
100 Sun breaking thro' fog bank, on Thames
101 The girl from Victoria, BC
1912 136 Early morning in the Laurentians
137 Morning, the mill at Sixteen Island
138 The mill at Sixteen Island
1913 153 September in the wilds S4-66 $70
154 Five Finger Point
1914 116 Portrait of a curler
117 Flecked by the morning sun ◊NGC◊
1915 123 Portrait
124 On the river at St Eustache
1916 130 Indian summer
1918A 90 Jeune fille pensive 1918N-101
91 L'été
1918N 102 Nellie
1919 90 Spring's carpet
1920 146 Morning, Rouge River, St Andrews East
147 October, the fringe of the St Lawrence
1921 81 The graduation play princess
82 March in the Laurentians
1923 99 October's misty veil, Val Morin
1924 114 October's misty veil
1925 129 Early winter
1927 117 A winter idyll
118 Shedding winter's garb
1928 89 The spring break-up $250
90 March evening on Black Creek $150
1929 122 Hurrying down to the Lowlands $250
123 Winter closing in $150
1929 S7, Calgary
87 Wet snow in Quebec $100
88 Winter's hold is waning $150

KILLAM, EDITH HUMPHREY (Mrs Lawrence Killam)
1882, Hampton, NB d 1962
Addr: 1924, 523 Argyle Ave, Westmount, Que; 1925, 40 Vernon St, Halifax

1924 115 Clouds, St John's River
1925 130 An old farm house

KILPIN, LEGH MULHALL
5 Nov 1853, Ryde, Isle of Wight
3 Nov 1919, Montreal H M NGC
Addr: 1907, Westmount, Que; 1910, 147A Stanley St, Montreal; 1911, 2 Mackay Apts, Montreal; 1912, 3 Beaver Hall Sq, Montreal; 1913, 203 Esplanade Ave, Montreal; 1914-16, 4152 Sherbrooke St W, Westmount, Que; 1918N, 4472 Sherbrooke St W, Westmount, Que

1907 116 Miss McAllister as Hetty Sorel
117 Dr R. Campbell, DD
1910 114 The Gates of the Infinite wc 1911-102 1912-139
115 The western path
1911 103 To the west wc
1912 140 Path to the west wc
1913 155 A habitant of to-day wc
156 Point â Pic, Murray Bay wc
1914 118 Lambeth, foggy morning pastel S5-14 illus
1915 125 Portrait
1916 131 Your fare, my friend, fare well wc
290 A bit of old Antwerp etch
291 Conway Castle etch
1918N 236 Ste Anne de Beaupré monot
237 The smithy, Wales monot
1920 Late L.M. Kilpin, Mrs L.M. Kilpin, 174 Hampton Ave, Montreal
148 Loading wood wc
149 The old Hull monot
316 Poplars, Les Eboulements etch
317 Evening, the return to the fold aqua

KIMBER, HETTY DONNE
fl 1891-1913 H

Addr; 1896-02, Willow Cottage, Sydney, Cape Breton, NS; 1906, Cape Breton, NS; 1907-13, Sydney, Cape Breton, NS
1896 212 Splendid isolation, in Cape Breton wc
213 The old Fairbanks house, 1664, Dedham, Mass wc
214 Brookdale, Cape Breton wc
1899 183 Evening, Louisburg wc
184 In the spring of the year, Montreal wc
185 Looking southwest from the old town of Louisburg wc
1902 204 A Louisburg moor in autumn wc
205 Early spring, Montreal wc
206 A February evening, Montreal wc
1906 F5, Halifax
94 Golf links, Adirondacks $20
95 A goldenrod marsh $20
96 Mira, Cape Breton $15
97 Mira Valley, Cape Breton $15
98 Big Ridge, Mira, Cape Breton $12
99 Sydney $10
100 Black Rock, Louisburg $10
101 Evening $10
1907 254 The valley of the Mira, Cape Breton wc
1913 157 Across the moor wc
158 Near Sydney, Cape Breton wc
159 Big Ridge, Mira, Cape Breton wc
160 Delphiniums wc

KING, ALLAN WINTON
6 Feb 1930, Vancouver CC2 CWW79
RCA(e) 1975 Film maker
Addr: 1979, Toronto

KING, ETHEL M.
Addr: 1902, 17 Melbourne Ave, Westmount, Que; 1910-13, 2 Belvedere Rd, Westmount, Que
1902 207 Scene in Montreal Harbour wc
1910 116 Above the city
117 A cloudy day
1913 161 A quiet pathway wc

KINGAN, EDWARD NATHAN (TED)
12 Oct 1927, Lytham St Annes, Lancs, Eng M
RCA(e) 1976 Painter
Addr: 1979, North Vancouver

KINGSFORD, WINNIFRED
1880, Toronto 4 Feb 1947, Toronto
M
Addr: 1914, Toronto; 1918A, 600 Sherbourne Ave, Toronto
1914 207 Portrait of a young girl sculp
208 A woman seated statuette
1918A 194 Architectural head plaster
195 Portrait of an actor plaster

KINNEAR, JOHN H.
b England M
1966 34 Red land 40 x 48 $750

KINOSHITA, GENE
18 Jan 1935, Vancouver WWA76
RCA(e) 1973 Council Architect
Addr: 1979, Toronto
1967 Moffat, Moffat & Kinoshita
129 Toronto residence, alterations and additions
see also Moffat, Donald, 1976

KINTON, JERRINE WELLS (Mrs)
b 1892
1938 121 South coast, Bermuda $400
1939 129 The pool in the rock $200
1942 77 Come on in, the water is fine $50

KIPLING, BARBARA ANN (Mrs Leonard Epp)
26 Feb 1934, Victoria M
RCA(e) 1978 Painter
Addr: 1979, Falkland, BC

KIRKPATRICK, MARY LYDIA DENNISTOUN (Lady, m Gen Sir George Macaulay Kirkpatrick)
1940 93 Poppies in a June border wc nfs

KIRSHNER, SAMUEL S.
Addr: 1925, 628 St Catherine St W, Montreal
1925 265 Jacobin Rosmarin, pianist sculp

KISS, ZOLTAN SANDOR
12 Jan 1924, Gyor, Hungary
RCA(e) 1974 Architect
Addr: 1979, Vancouver

KIYOOKA, HARRY MITSUO
18 Feb 1928, Calgary CC2 M
RCA(e) 1978 Painter

Addr: 1976/79, Calgary
1965 42 Red contiguous 44 x 56 $900
1966 35 Skein of time 70 x 70 $1,800
1976 S12, Montreal
22 The Aegean #3 acry 92 x 92 illus

KIYOOKA, ROY KENZIE
18 Jan 1926, Moose Jaw, Sask AGO CC1 M NGC TB3
ARCA 1965 Painter
Addr: 1965-8, Montreal; 1969-71/79, Vancouver
1952 51 The white buildings $200
1964J 39 Saggital 96 x 72 $1,000
1966 S10, Charlottetown
46 Untitled $1,000

KLEEFELD, HANS
1970 190 Symbol and application, Air Jamaica
191 Symbol, Bank of Montreal
192 Symbol, Stancor Furniture Manufacturing Limited
193 Magazine (Abitibi) Impressions Vol 1 #2
1971 37G Corporate stationery, Fairfield & Dubois
38G Corporate stationery, Vickers & Benson
39G Corporate design, Walbner KG/Germany

KLEIN, JACK
28 Sep 1927, Hamilton
RCA(e) 1973 Architect
Addr: 1979, Toronto

KLITGUARD, C.B.
Addr: 1903, Salisbury Flats, Guy St, Montreal
1903 76 Lamplight
217 Head of a lady min
218 Head of a gentleman min

KLUNDER, HAROLD
1943, Netherlands
1971 40G Poster, Self promotion
41G Book, Benson & Hedges
42G Book illustration, Cape & Company

KNELLER, GODFREY (Kniller, Gottfried) Sir English
8 Aug 1646, Lubeck, Germany 7 Nov 1723, London, Eng B TB
1881 328 HM George II
330 HM Queen Caroline
328, 330 Sir Geoffrey Rueller, error; mistitles for George I, Queen Sophia

KNOPF, ERNESTINE
b Toronto M
Addr: 1929, 1041 Decarie Blvd, Montreal
1929 124 A gitana $40

KNOWLES, ELIZABETH ANNIE BEACH (Mrs Farquhar McGillivray Strachan Stewart Knowles)
8 Jan 1866, Ottawa 4 Oct 1928, Riverton, NH AGO H M NGC R2 W78
ARCA 1908 Painter
Addr: 1902, Confederation Life Bldg, Toronto; 1906-11, 340 Bloor St W, Toronto; 1912-14, 278 Bloor St W, Toronto; 1915-16, Toronto; 1918A, 800 Riverside Dr, New York; 1919, c/o Roberts Gallery, Toronto; 1920-1, 100 Smith St, Peekskill, NY; 1922, c/o K.E. Hillary, 6 Hayden Ave, Toronto; 1924, 729 Yonge St, Toronto; 1925-6, New York; 1927, 340 W 57th St, New York
1902 106 An August evening
1903 72 A sun dried pasture
73 October twilight
1905 105 A July evening
106 Moonrise 1906-117
107 Dawn
1906 115 Spring time
116 A weedy pasture
1906 F5, Halifax
102 In August's glow illus $175
103 The farmyard pump $25
1907 118 Autumn
119 Misty morning
120 Old pines
1907 F6, Sherbrooke
114 Birches $100
1908 89 Nocturne ◊NGC◊
90 The corn is in the stock S2-65
1909M 72 In the dew drenched stilly night 1909N-79 S2-64
73 Fall of the year 1909N-78
75 In durance vile (#74 not in cat)
75a Evening
1909N 80 Lady Disdain
81 Corner of an old barn
1910 118 Evening glow
1911 105 October afternoon

106 Case of miniatures
1912 141 Peace 1913-162 1914-119
142 Lowlands
143 On guard
1912 S3, Winnipeg
92 The dreamer
93 Evening
94 A meadow
1913 163 Case of miniatures
164 Autumn in the birch woods
165 Life in the barn yard S4-68 $150
1914 120 Spring
121 Beech wood in autumn
122 October sunlight
1914 S4, Winnipeg
67 Case of miniatures $200
1918A 92 A hillside orchard wc on ivory
93 The sentinel wc on ivory
94 Drink to me only with thine eyes
95 Sweethearts 1918N-103
1919 91 The orphan 1920-150
1920 151 Phlox at twilight
1921 83 A visit to father
84 A confab
1922 122 The bully S6-50
1924 116 An exciting moment 1925-131 ◊AGO◊
1927 119 The toilet 1928-92 $400
1928 Late Mrs E.McG. Knowles
91 Call to dinner $300
93 Spring time $500 ◊AGO◊

KNOWLES, FARQUHAR MCGILLIVRAY STRACHAN STEWART
22 May 1859, Syracuse, NY 9 Apr 1932, Toronto AAA32 AGO B H M Mo12 NGC R2 TB1/2 W78
ARCA 1890 RCA 1898 Ret 1930 Council
Painter
Addr: 1884, York Chambers, Toronto; 1890-2, Toronto; 1893, 162 Jarvis St, Toronto; 1894, c/o W.G. Beach, 162 Jarvis St, Toronto; 1895, 1 rue Crevante, Paris; 1896, 162 Jarvis St, Toronto; 1897-8, Yonge St, Toronto; 1899, Confederation Life Bldg, Toronto; 1900-1, 144 Yonge, Toronto; 1902-5, Confederation Life Bldg, Toronto; 1906-11, 340 Bloor St W, Toronto; 1912-14, 278 Bloor St W, Toronto; 1915-16, Toronto; 1918A, 800 Riverside Dr, New York; 1919 c/o Roberts Gallery, Toronto; 1920-1, 100 Smith St, Peekskill, NY; 1922, c/o K.E. Hillary, 6 Hayden St, Toronto; 1923-4, 729 Yonge St, Toronto; 1925-7, New York; 1928-30, 29 Grenville St, Toronto; 1931, 262 Jarvis St, Toronto
1883 66 On the Credit River $35
1884 28 Under Cape Diamont, Quebec $25
146 Rustic home, Beaufort valley wc $25
154 Low tide, River St Lawrence wc $25
179 Sunset, Bridgewater Cove, Quebec wc $10
183 The brook wc $15
1885 42 Catherine Bay, St Lawrence River $100
247 Saguenay River wc $35
1888 74 River St Lawrence and Point Levis, from Quebec $40
101 River, Point Levis $40
109 Sunset, near Quebec $25
114 Our camp, Lake Joseph $25
140 Sunrise, Bridgewater Cove, Quebec $40
145 On the St Lawrence $25
1890 171 Morning after rain wc $100
172 Evening, coast of Maine wc $75
173 Old piers, Camden, NJ wc $100
174 Daybreak, Philadelphia harbour wc $125
1891 120, 177 and 193 Study wc
123 Are you ready, lads? wc
152 North Bay, Percé wc
153 At low tide wc
154 Noon wc
184 Early morning
1892 130 Wolfe's Cove, Quebec wc $300
1893 213 When lengthening shadows chase the evening glow wc $75
214 Gathering kelp, Porthgwarra Cove, Land's End, Cornwall wc $100
215 Crab fishing off the coast of Cornwall on a foggy morning wc $75
216 Cleaning fish, Percé wc $300
1893 F1, Chicago
164 Percé fishermen, Gulf of St Lawrence wc
1894 67 St Levan's Church, Cornwall ◊NGC◊
68 A Yorkshire lane

69 The Tower of London
172 Farm lane wc
1895 72 Early morning
73 Return of the fisher girl sketch
1896 94 and 95 Portrait
96 Pool of London
97 Westminster DW 1899 29 x 35 1/2 T51-28
98 Moonlight on the Thames
99 Lake Neuchâtel, Switzerland
100 Notre Dame, Paris
101 English country type
102 Bit at Whitby, England
103 Harvesting, Brittany
1897 77 Silken threads
78 Brittany spinner
79 Cancale Bay, Brittany
80 Surf, coast of France
81 Orchard, Tregony, Cornwall
82 O.F. Rice, Esq
83 Mrs Eaton
84 Portrait of a lady
85 Study of a girl's head
1898 63 Hero finding the body of Leander 1899-79 1901-68 1904-107
64 Inspiration
65 Study, Falmouth Bay, Cornwall
1899 78 Psyche illus
80 The last of the harvest 1902-109
81 Gathering kelp
82 Percé milk maid
83 Bit on the Thames
1900 147 Return of the fishers, Cancale wc
148 By the river side wc
149 St Paul's, from Fleet Street, London wc
150 Newlyn, Cornwall wc
1901 69 Limehouse Reach, River Thames F2-41
1901 F2, Buffalo
43 The Pool, River Thames
1902 107 Sunlight and shadow
108 The last load F2-42
110 Below London Bridge
208 The fountain, St Sulpice, Paris wc
209 Cancale peasants wc
1902 F3, Rochester
94 August evening, Whitby, Yorkshire $180
1903 74 Landing the catch (loan) 1904-106 F4-52
75 Edge of the wood
171 Boat, Quebec wc (loan)
172 Evening, Percé Bay wc (loan)
1905 103 After the rain
104 Incoming tide, Cornish coast
1906 113 On the River Thames
114 Below Tower Bridge, London
1906 F5, Halifax
104 Incoming tide $100
105 Evening on the Thames illus $250
106 On the beach, Percé $100
107 Study, the carnation $100
1907 121 Street in Whitby, Yorkshire
255 The end of the day wc
1908 85 An old street in Whitby, Yorkshire
86 The wayside Cross ◊NGC◊
87 August moonrise
88 Head of a young girl nfs
1909M 68 Departure of the 'Indomitable' from Quebec, 1908. 1909N-82 S2-64
69 La Grande Rivière, Beaupré, Québec 1909N-83 S2-66 S3-95
70 Queen of the night 1909N-84 S2-67 1911-108
71 Moonrise
1909N 85 Moonrise, Quebec
1910 119 Timber days, Quebec
120 The 'Indomitable' leaving Quebec
1911 107 Evening glow 1912-145
109 On the beach, Cancale
110 August weather
1912 144 In the gloaming
146 Moonrise on the river
1912 S3, Winnipeg
96 An August evening
97 Harvest time
1913 166 Rosy evening, Beaupré
167 Showery day on the coast
168 An autumn evening S4-69 $150
169 A windy sky S4-70 $75
1914 123 On the beach, Percé, Que
124 Wood gatherers, Quebec
125 Coming storm
1918A 96 Shimmering afternoon illus 1918N-104 illus
1919 92 The thunder cloud illus 1920-152
93 Fishing boats, Penzance wc
1920 153 Windswept S6-51 1924-118
1921 85 The shades of evening,

coast of Quebec
86 A road near Beaupré, Que
1922 123 Past and present
124 Off the fishing grounds illus S6-52
1923 100 Moonlight, Percé Rock
1924 117 A midsummer night illus 1925-132
1928 94 Moon witchery $450
95 Coast of Maine $500 F9-186
1930 104 Midsummer night $400
105 Laurentian Mountains $150
106 On the beach, Percé $150
1931 153 Percé Rock in moonlight $300

KNOWLES, LILA CAROLINE TAYLOR (Mrs Farquhar McGillivray Strachan Stewart Knowles)
10 Sep 1886, Granton, Ont flg 1963 M
Addr: 1924, Granton, Ont; 1931, 262 Jarvis St, Toronto
1924 Taylor
195 The homestead
1931 154 Rocks and splash

KNOWLES, MAIDA see PARLOW, MAIDA

KNUDSEN, NIELS CHRISTIAN
3 Jun 1945, Vorup, Denmark
1971 25 Time, Lake Athabasca, Alberta, 1970 30 x 30 $300
26 Time, Montreal, 1970 30 x 30 $300

KOBERWEIN English
1880 46 The Princess. 1871 (HRH Princess Louise) Coberwein, mispr

KOKS, ENDEL
b Estonia
1967 36 Calceolaria 55 x 43 $800
1968 33 Letter to Joy #2 36 x 28 illus $500
34 Letter to Joy #6 36 x 28 $500
1970 38 Espaceonata 56 x 44 $900

KOLISNYK, PETER HENRY
30 Nov 1934, Toronto CWW79 M
RCA(e) 1976 Sculptor
Addr: 1979, Cobourg, Ont
1963 43 Plant matter $160
44 Echo $160
1964N 32 Margin released 57 x 57 $500

1965 43 Eclipse 65 x 65 $550

KOOCHIN, WILLIAM
15 Dec 1927, Brilliant, BC M WWA76
RCA(e) 1974 Sculptor
Addr: 1979, West Vancouver

KOPMANIS, AUGUST ARNOLD
17 Mar 1910, Riga 27 May 1976, Genoa CWW64 M WWA59
RCA(e) 1974 RCA 1977, posth Sculptor
1957 79 Lad sculp $500
1958 90 Brothers sculp $500
1960 83 Standing figure high rel photo nfs
1961 83 Draped figure bronze 9 1/2h $110
1963 93 Mother and child bronze $250
1964N 75 Memorial, Happy Valley Camp, Utopia 72h photo nfs
76 Prophylactic bronze 30h $550
1965 86 Memorial for Julija Jegers sculp photo nfs
1966 80 Upright figure sculp $330
1967 77 Rain god 54h $500
DW 1977 Man at work granite 26h 4h base

KORNER, JOHN MICHAEL ANTHONY
29 Sep 1913, Novy Jicin, Czechoslovakia AGO CC2 M NGC TB3 WWA66
ARCA 1960-6 Painter
Addr: 1961-6, Vancouver
1965 44 Red flowers I 48 x 39 $700

KOST, FREDERICK W. American
15 May 1865, New York 28 Feb 1923, Brookhaven, NY AAA28 B TB
1882 88 Summer day on Morris Canal, New Jersey $125

KOSTYNIUK, RONALD PETER
8 Jul 1941, Wakaw, Sask M WWA78
RCA(e) 1975 Sculptor
Addr: 1979, Calgary

KOTCHEFF, WILLIAM THEODORE (TED)
7 Apr 1931, Toronto
RCA(e) 1975 Film maker
Addr: 1979, Beverly Hills, Cal

KRAMER, BURTON
25 Jun 1932, New York WWA76
RCA(e) 1974 Council Graphic designer
Addr: 1976/79, Toronto
1970 194 Poster, New Year 1968

195 Catalog cover, Royal Ontario Museum, Craft dimensions Canada
196 Invitation, ROM, The arts of forgotten people
197 Invitation, ROM, Gallery of minerology
198 Booklet, Ontario Dept of Education, Remembrance Day
199 Cover, Report of the Committee on French language schools in Ontario/Rapport du Comité sur les écoles de langue française de l'Ontario
1971 43G Symbol and guide, Ontario Educational Communications Authority
44G Symbol, Hamilton-Hastings Limited
45G Magazine cover, Orbit, Ontario Institute for Studies in Education
46G Symbol and journal, Interchange, Ontario Institute for Studies in Education
47G Poster, ROM
1976 S12, Montreal
124 CBC cymbol/Emblème de Radio Canada illus
125 Reed symbol/Emblème Reed illus

KRAMOLC, THEODORE MARIA (TED)
27 Mar 1922, Ljubljana, Yugoslavia AGO IO WWA59
1954 96 Tower of Babylon 16 x 11 $35
1955 54 Yonge street, early morning $200

KRAVIS, JANIS
20 Oct 1935, Riga CWW79 WWA78
RCA(e) 1975 Interior designer
Addr: 1979, Toronto
1970 105 Waste basket #2618, Karelia International Limited

KRIEGHOFF, CORNELIUS DAVID
19 Jun 1815, Amsterdam 8 Mar 1872, Chicago AGO B DCB EC H M NGC TB
1882 312-14 loans
312 The breaking up of the merrymaking, Montmorenci
313 Old French fort, Chambly
314 Split Cape, Bay of Fundy
1886 F1a, London, Eng
2005, artist number
Death (Thos. Cross, Esq)
On the look-out (Thos. Cross, Esq, Ottawa)
French Canadian habitant (James Baine, Esq, Dept of Railways & Canals, Ottawa)

KUBOTA, NOBUO
27 Jun 1932, Vancouver M
RCA(e) 1976 Sculptor
Addr: 1979, Toronto

KUEHNER, MARTHA
b 1937
Addr: 1976, London, Ont
1976 S12, Montreal
179 Window reflections photo 14 x 20 illus

KUGEL, JOHN J. see KEWELL, JOHN J.

KUKIYAUT
see KANGIRUAQ

KULMALA, GEORGE ARTHUR
19 Jan 1896, Pori, Finland 21 Feb 1940, Toronto AGO M
Addr: 1924-5, 3022A Dundas St W, Toronto; 1926-7, 248 Lauder Ave, Toronto
1924 121 Summer day
122 Our back yard
1925 133 At Beaver Lake
134 Mill, Algonquin Park
1926 79 Hillside, winter
80 The mill
1927 120 Canoe Lake, Algonquin Park
121 The north country S7-89 $350
1929 S7, Calgary
90 Winter $250
1939 F11, New York
58 Saw mill, northern Ontario 40 x 45 $350

KURELEK, WILLIAM (WASYL)
3 Mar 1927, n Whitford, Alta 3 Nov 1977, Toronto AGO CC1 M WWA73
RCA(e) 1973 Ret 1975 Painter

KUSHNER, PATRICIA ANNE
28 Aug 1939, Vancouver
Addr: 1976, Coquitlam, BC
1976 S12, Montreal
75 Portrait of a woman trapped in unhappiness by fears and responsibilities m med 48 x 24 illus

KUYPERS, JAN
13 Feb 1925, Nymegen, Netherlands
RCA(e) 1973 Council Industrial designer
Addr: 1979, Toronto

KYLE, GWENDOLEN
Addr: 1918, 421 Mount Stephen Ave, Westmount, Que
1918A 97 Miniature sketches
1918N 105 Rough seas, Ogunquit
106 After the storm, Ogunquit

L

LABELLE, HENRI SICOTTE
15 Jan 1896, Montreal CNS44
Addr: 1925, 511 St Catherine St W, Montreal
1925 239 Garde meubles. J. Baillargeon Express Lté photo
240 Magasin à rayons, Dupuis Frères Lté photo
see also Venne, Joseph, 1913

LABERGE, PAUL
1945, Cap de la Madelein, Qué
1971 28 Un morceau d'ciel, s'ou plaît #1-2-3-4 72 x 70 $2,000

LACHAPELLE, C.W.
1958 50 Night scene nfs

LACOSTE, JACQUES
1971 48G Folder, The top ten NFB
49G Promotion sheet, Hiroko Ikoko NFB
50G Promotion sheet, Maboule National Film Board

LACROIX, JOSEPH SAMUEL RICHARD
14 Jul 1939, Montreal AGO B CC1 CWW79 M WWA73
1963 45 Cascades $55

LAFFIN, W.M.
H
1882 all works in monochrome
242 A coming squall
259 Evening, East Rockaway
261 The Monastery Hill, Cincinnati
262 Lake Roukoukoma
266 East River docks, New York
272 Long Island marshes
274 Long Island landscape
275 On the East River
276 On the Hudson

LAFONTAINE, MARGUERITE DE MONTIGNY (Mrs Georges Lafontaine)
21 Aug 1890, Montreal CNS36
Addr: 1929-35, 5739 11th Ave, Rosemount, Que
1929 243 Mlle Corinne Rocheleau, femme de lettres sculp $150
1931 323 Mlle Fabiola Poirier plaster $50 marble $1,000
324 Etude d'anatomie sculp $100
1932 214 Rodolphe Plamondon, tenor plaster $50 marble $500
1933 261 Mon père, O.P. de Montigny sculp
1935 286 Etude, vieux philosophe plaster nfs

LAGACE, MICHEL
1950, Rivière du Loup, Qué
Addr: 1976, Montreal
1976 S12, Montreal
33 8 espaces crayon 36 x 36 each illus

LAGET, JULES
Addr: 1928, 100 Lake Shore Blvd, Toronto
1928 96 Still life
97 Jean

LAING, MARION
1849, Quebec Mar 1932, Montreal H
Addr: 1893, 123 Mackay St, Montreal; 1897, Montreal
1893 91 Clover $15
1897 87 A corner of the Flower Market, Paris
88 Violets

LAING, WILLIAM JOHN HOUSTON (BILL)
2 Jun 1944, Glasgow
Addr: 1976, Vancouver
1976 S12, Montreal
161 Near sunset & western #2 litho 20 x 25 illus

LALANDE, E. see PATTERSON, EDITH

LALIBERTE, ALFRED
18 May 1878, Ste Elizabeth, Que
13 Jan 1953, Montreal B CC2 CNS36 CWW49 EC M NGC PMC TB1/2/3 WWA47
ARCA 1912 RCA 1922-50 Sr 1948
Council Sculptor

Addr: 1908, 296 rue St Laurent, Montréal; 1909M, Monument Nationale, Montreal; 1911-16, 296 St Lawrence St, Montreal; 1918N-26, 67 Ste Famille St, Montreal; 1927-35, 3531 Ste Famille St, Montreal; 1936-50, Montreal

1908 168 M Payette, Maire de Montréal buste
169 M de Montigny, écrivant half bust
1909M 166 The kiss plaster group
1910 S2, Liverpool
117 The mendicant sculp
118 Woman carrying water sculp
1911 187 La rivière blanche marbre
188 Le sourire marbre
189 Le rêve brisé marble S5-81 illus
190 Le bucheron bronze
1912 239 Sir G.E. Cartier plâtre bust
240 Sir H. Lafontaine plaster bust
241 Col Labelle bronze
242 E. Nelligan, le vaisseau d'or bronze
1913 326 Alex Carli plâtre patiné
327 Balboni plâtre patiné
328 Le vaisseau d'or, encrier bronze
329 Le défricheur plâtre 1915-238
330 Le lieur plâtre
1915 239 Le mal de vivre plâtre
1916 253 Le ber groupe plâtre
254 Les martyrs Brébeuf et Lalement haute rel plâtre
255 Mon père buste plâtre
256 Jeune fille mystique marbre
1918N 213 Bella matribus destestata plâtre illus 1919-182 illus
214 Portrait de l'artiste plâtre
1919 179 Vicomte de Manneville plâtre
180 Mon potrait plâtre
181 Aram Pothier, ex-Gouv de l'Etat du Rhode Island plâtre
1920 271 Baldwin statue plâtre
272 Le rêveur statue plâtre illus
273 Juge Choquette buste plâtre
1922 221 Scientia plâtre
222 Sén Belcourt bronze S6-109
223 Buste de l'artiste bronze illus S6-108 DW 1923 18 1/2h
224 Recorder Dupuis bronze
1923 189 Les ailes brisées sculp
1924 235 Canada plâtre illus F10-199 bronze $310
236 Nos mères canadiennes plâtre
1925 266 Le semeur plâtre
267 Le Fardeau plâtre illus
268 Le peine plâtre
269 L'orgie. Surtout de table 1928-168 bronze $450
1927 262 La poésie marbre
263 L'âme du marbre marbre
264 Le cultivateur plâtre illus
265 Le notaire plâtre
1928 169 Terre mourante marbre $350
1929 244 Les fumeurs bronze $250
245 La drave bronze $200
246 Notre mère bronze $200
247 L'equarrissage bronze $200
1929 S7, Calgary
163 The water carrier bronze
164 The sower bronze $150
1931 325 Les maquignons bronze $350
326 Le vieux pécheur bronze $300
327 Gagné bronze $300
328 Le javeleur bronze $300
1935 287 Angoisse plâtre $300
1941 215 Hon Sén Raoul Dandurand sculp nfs
216 L'homme de demain sculp
1943 133 La Croix Rouge sculp nfs
port: by A.S.Scott, 1934-170

LALONDE, JEAN LOUIS
17 Jun 1923, Montreal CWW79
ARCA 1965 Council Architect
Addr: 1965-71/79 Montreal

LAMARCHE, ULRIC
1867, Oakland, Cal 1921, Montreal
H M
Addr: 1907, Montreal; 1910, 618 Mentana St, Montreal
1907 122 Early spring
123 April
1910 121 Sous les pommiers
122 Paysage

LAMB, CHARLES COWAN
b 1904
1938 122 Winter, Toronto Bay $100 T39-28

LAMB, MOLLY see BOBAK, MOLLY

LAMBART, EVELYN
23 Jul 1914, Ottawa
RCA(e) 1979 Film maker
Addr: 1979, RR4, Sutton, Que

LAMBE, LAURENCE M.
fl 1882-92 H
Addr: 1887, Montreal
1882 150 Under the pines, Mount Royal Park sketch wc
1887 129 Sketch at Percé wc nfs
1889 109 Percé, Baie de Chaleurs wc
142 Cliffs at Murray Bay wc
1892 114 On the Ottawa wc $30
Lawrence Lambe, mispr

LAMBE, SARAH M.
H
Addr: 1887, Montreal
1887 3a Study of hollyhocks $100

LAMBE, WILLIAM BUSBY
1862, Montreal H
Addr: 1887, London, Ont
1882 179 Autumn foliage wc $25
268 Old Government House, Montreal monoc $25
1887 132 Maple woods, autumn, Mount Royal wc
135 Le petit ruission, Murray Bay wc
149 Old Quebec wc

LAMBERT, PAUL E.
see BLOUIN, ANDRE, 1968

LAMBERT, PHYLLIS BRONFMAN (Mrs Lambert)
24 Jan 1927, Montreal WWA78
RCA(e) 1977 Architect
Addr: 1979, Montreal
1941 Bronfman, to 1945
206 Study of a head sculp nfs
1942 160 Study of a head sculp nfs
161 Helen MacDonald sculp nfs
1943 123 My mother sculp nfs
1944 145 Lindy Lou sculp illus nfs
1945 216 Study sculp pine nfs
port: bust, by H.M. Miller, 1944-151

LAMBERT, RICHARD TULLIE
12 May 1923, London, Eng M
1945 121 Lo $80
1953 120 Awakening sculp $75
121 The embrace sculp $100

LAMBERT, RONALD M.
26 Aug 1927, Oshawa, Ont
1946 70 March hills, near Port Hope

LAMONT, THOMAS REYNOLDS Scottish
b 1826 1898, Greenock, Scot B DBA DBW G TB
1880 327 Scene from 'School for scandal' wc (loan)
335 The artist monk wc (loan)

LAMPERT, EMMA ESTHER (Mrs Colin Campbell Cooper) American
Nunda, NY 30 Jul 1920, Pittsfield, NY AAA28 B F H TB1/3 Y
Addr: 1897, Toronto
1897 86 A souvenir

LANDSLEY, PATRICK ALFRED
13 Aug 1926, Winnipeg CC2 M
1964N 33 Landscape through a window 33 x 45 $600
1967 39 Crucifixion 72 x 60 illus $1,500
1970 39 Northern landscape 33 x 39 illus $600
1971 27 Silent winter 66 x 54 illus $1,000

LANE, LEONARD CHARLES
b Bristol, Eng
1948 90 August moon rise, Bermuda $175

LANG, BYLLEE FAY
4 Dec 1908, Didsbury, Alta 10 Dec 1966, Bermuda M W78
Addr: 1937, 322 Main St, Winnipeg
1937 287 Ramona Sinclair sculp $250
1938 238 Baboushka plaster $150
1939 253 Nude plaster $125
1941 217 Manitoban plaster $125
1942 168 Sitting woman plaster $75

LANGHAM, E. (Hon Mrs) English
fl 1879-82 DBA DVP H
1880 41, 42, 44a and 47 Landscape sketch

LANGLEY, HENRY
26 Nov 1836, Toronto 9 Jan 1907, Toronto Co NGC
RCA 1880 Ret 1905 Council Architect
Addr: 1880-07, Toronto
1880 366 Metropolitan Methodist Church, Toronto DW 1880 des

pen & bistre drwg 32 x 24 3/4
1881-180

LANGLEY-DONGES, THOMAS see DONGES, LANGLEY THOMAS

LANGLOIS, JEAN
17 Jan 1916, Montreal M
Addr: 1937, 7423 Blvd St Laurent, Montreal
1937 125 Paysage, Rigaud $25
126 Le petit cirque $30
1939 132 Le village $75
1940 94 Quiet day, Rigaud, Que $125
95 The thaw $125
1941 100 Rural Quebec, recruiting $125 T42-24
101 Interior $75
1942 78 Crossing the bridge $75 T43-24
79 Market in winter $100
1943 72 Intérieur $150
1944 87 Market in March $100
88 Circus $75
1945 122 Old house $50
1947 95 Oka $200
96 Fisherman from St Pierre Miquelon nfs
1948 91 Circus $150
1950 80 Landscape, Oka, Quebec 24 x 36 $200
1953 48 Quebec pastoral

LANGLOIS, MARIE
30 Apr 1929, Montreal
1971 29 Marginal 36 x 36 $250

LANGSTADT, ANNE see KAHANE, ANNE

LANGSTON, HENRY THOMAS
1 Oct 1913, Sidney, Australia
1939 130 The logging shed, Bark Lake $75

LANGTON, WILLIAM ALEXANDER
8 Jun 1854, Peterborough, Ont 3 Apr 1933, Toronto W78
Addr: 1895, Canada Life Bldg, Toronto
1895 46A House, O.F. Burton, Toronto
47A Sketch for St Hilda's College, Toronto

LANSDOWNE, JAMES FENWICK
8 Aug 1937, Hong Kong M WWA76
RCA(e) 1974 Painter
Addr: 1979, Victoria

LA PALME, ROBERT
14 Apr 1908, Montreal M TB3
RCA(e) 1979 Caricaturist
Addr: 1979, Montreal

LA PIERRE, THOMAS
28 Dec 1930, Toronto IO M WWA73
ARCA 1971 Painter
Addr: 1979, Mississauga, Ont
1966 36 Grandparents in the play-pen 30 x 36 $2,000
1967 37 House of mirrors copper engr 16 x 12 $60
1970 40 Loving roses 18 x 18 $800

LAPINE, ANDREAS CHRISTIAN GOTTFRIED (ANDRE) (b Andrejs Lapins)
27 Oct 1866, Skujene, Riga, Russia
27 Feb 1952, Minden, Ont AGO CC1 CWW49 H M NGC TB3
ARCA 1919 Sr 1938 Painter
Addr: 1908-9, Yonge Street Arcade, Toronto; 1910, 92 Bay St, Toronto; 1914-26, c/o Brigden Ltd, 160 Richmond St W, Toronto; 1927-9, Mossom Rd near Old Mill Tea Gardens, Toronto: 1931, 101 King St W, Toronto; 1932-4, 60 Front St W, Toronto; 1935, 586 Shaw St, Toronto; 1936-7, 430 Parliament St, Toronto; 1938-52, Toronto
1908 93 Rest
94 The excavation
1909N 86 At the warehouse
87 Tommy
1910 123 The woodcutter
124 At the stone quarry
1914 S5, Patriotic Fund
11 Sawmill illus
1915 126 A gray day
127 The team ◊NGC◊
1916 132 A misty morning
133 At the river
294 Lulu col chalk
295 Bia col chalk
1918A 98 Wagon shed
99 La Noni wc 1918N-107 illus
247 The windmill etch 1918N-238
1918N 108 Sketch wc
239 The book drwg
1919 94 At the warehouse wc 1920-155
95 Noon hour
1920 154 Noon hour at the water front wc illus
318 The first reading drwg
319 Recollections drwg

1921 87 Grading wc
88 Long house by the lake wc
89 Woman's head
201, 202 and 203 Man's head drwg
1922 125 Trucking at the bay 1923-123 S6-53
126 A gray day S6-54
258 At the gravel pit etch
259 Noon hour dry pt
260 The etcher dry pt
261 Man's head etch S6-119
262 and 263 Man's head drwg
1924 124 Early morning wc
125 The stream
126 At the river
271 Homeward bound etch
272 Noon hour etch
273 Resting etch
274 Spinning, Latvia drwg
275 Market day, Latvia drwg
276 Peasant house, Latvia drwg
1925 135 Le rendez-vous wc illus
136 The gravel pit wc
137 Spring wc
1926 81 Dans la carriére illus
82 Attelage
83 Vieux serviteur wc
186 La lecture drwg
1927 122 Over the hill
1928 98 The round-up $600
1929 125 Through the woods $800
1929 S7, Calgary
91 In the sand pit $400
92 Noon hour wc $150
1931 155 When the day's work is done $600
1932 113 Homeward $600
1934 112 The departure $600 T35-40
1935 157 Hillside wc $80
158 The old barn wc $60
159 Stacking oats wc $80
160 Storm cloud wc $80 T36-44
1936 119 The advance $150
120 Grading $250 T37-42
1937 127 The exodus $600 T38-26
128 Mist and smoke $300
1938 123 The alarm $300 S9-41 $150
124 The white horse $300 T39-29
1939 131 Silence of the twilight $200
297 Farm house in Latvia drwg $40
1939 F11, New York
41 The departure 24 x 30 $450
1940 96 After the day's labour $250 T41-31
1941 102 Gray day $150 T42-25
1942 80 Late afternoon $300
81 Cloudy evening $400

LAPOINTE, FRANK
11 May 1942, Port Rexton, Nfld
WWA78
1970 41 Labrador barrens #2 21 1/4 x 29 $200

LARIVIERE, ROGER
b Ottawa M
1954 53 Still life with negro statuette 24 x 36 $125
1955 55 The iron chair $125

LARKIN, RYAN
1970 Walking film screened 10 Feb

LARKING, PATRICK LAMBERT
15 Apr 1907, Rudgwick, Sussex, Eng
DBA TB3 WBA WWB56
Addr: 1930, 129 Shuter St, Toronto; 1933, 1195 Scollard St, Toronto; 1934, 51 Water St, Toronto; 1936, Toronto; 1937, 24 Selby St, Toronto
1930 107 John
1933 130 Marjorie, daughter of Mr and Mrs Henry Latter
1934 113 Miss Margaret Newburn
1936 121 Portrait of a young lady nfs
1937 129 Maj Cecil Kerr nfs
130 Betty nfs

LAROSE, LUDGER
1 May 1868, Montreal 1915, Montreal
CC2 M
Addr: 1896, 4121 St Catherine St, Montreal; 1907, Montreal
1896 104 Christmas eve
1907 124 Mountain in winter

LARSON, EDWARD (TED)
b Vancouver
1970 203 Advertisement, Imperial Tobacco
204 Poster, Teatro Stabile de Genova
1971 51G Invitation, Penthouse
52G Illustration, Avis-Case Associates

LATCHOLASSIE E7-1055
1919, Cape Dorset, NWT ED
Addr: 1976, Cape Dorset, NWT
1976 S12, Montreal

76 Two owls soapstone/saponite 8 x 12 x 6 illus

LATOUR, CLAIRE
Addr: 1976, Montreal
1976 S12, Montreal
145 Femme douceur et force batik sur sois/batik on silk 37 x 44 illus

LATOUR, GEORGE
Addr: 1918N, 1719 Mance St, Montreal
1918N 109 Abbotsford Mounts

LAUFER, MURRAY BERNARD
26 Oct 1929, Toronto
RCA(e) 1973 Set Designer
Addr: 1979, Toronto

LAUTERMAN, DINAH
6 Aug, 1889, Montreal 14 Jun 1945, Montreal
Addr: 1929, 2014 Peel St, Montreal; 1931-3, 33 Côte St Antoine Rd, Westmount, Que
1929 248 Le silence du tombeau sculp
1931 329 Head of an Indian Chief of Caughnawaga sculp
330 Garden fountain, baby on a sea-horse sculp
1933 262 Prof H.T.B. bust
263 Mrs M.B.L. bust

LAVALEE, ANDRE
b c 1835
1967 40 Formation du solide #2 53 x 35 $300
41 Rencontre 36 x 57 $300

LAVERGNE, RENAUD
Addr: 1925, Arthabaska, Que
1925 270 Tête de Christ plâtre
271 Mme R.L. portrait ter cot

LAVERTY, SAMUEL GEORGE EDWARD
19 Dec 1922, Watford, Herts, Eng
1963 46 Niagara $800

LAVUT, MARTIN
1970 At home film screened 10 Feb

LAW, CHARLES ANTHONY FRANCIS
15 Oct 1916, London, Eng M WWA47
1938 125 Contrast, Rivière du Loup, Quebec $200 T39-30
1947 97 Destruction of old Chelsea Church by V2, London, England $175
1970 42 Winter, Terrance Bay, NS 30 x 40 nfs
1971 50 Arctic spring, Brevoort Island, NWT 40 x 36 $800

LAW, FREDERICK CHARLES (Comdr RN)
27 Mar 1841, Somms, Eng d 1922 H Mo12
Addr: 1895, 504 Sherbroune St, Toronto
1895 48W The British Fleet, headed by Lord Nelson, in the Victory, bearing down upon the enemy, off Cape Trafalgar, Oct 21st 1805 wc
49W HMS Royal Alfred, 18 guns, running before a heavy gale, in the north Atlantic, Dec 1873 wc

LAWDER, JAMES T.
fl 1873-80 H
1880 276 Medieval sideboard des
285 Book cover des
290a Wall paper des
304 Stained glass window des

LAWRENCE, HENRY WYNDHAM
19 Oct 1924, Swansea, Wales
RCA(e) 1973 Sculptor
Addr: 1979, Toronto

LAWRENCE, WILLIAM
ARCA 1881-2 Painter
Addr: 1881-2, Montreal

LAWRENSON
1883 Lawrenson (Rome)
33 Muzio Clementi, composer (Rev V. Clementi)

LAWSON, ARTHUR WENDELL PHILLIPS
25 Sep 1898, Toronto 10 Jun 1952, Columbus, Ohio M
Addr: 1928, Leaside, Ont; 1932, Eglington Ave E, Leaside, Ont
1928 99 The Roman Bridge, Ronda, Spain wc $100
1932 114 The church wc $50

LAWSON, EDITH see COOMBS, EDITH

LAWSON, ERNEST American
22 Mar 1873, Halifax, NS 18 Dec 1939, Miami, Fla AGO CC2 H M NGC TB1/2
Addr: 1913, 23 MacDougal Alley, New York

1913 170 Summer, boys bathing S4-71 $400
171 Willows in winter
172 Evening, St John's Cathedral S4-72 $400
173 Garden

LAWSON, JAMES IRVING
d 18 Jan 1964, Ottawa WWC30
see MARANI, FERDINAND, 1937-1939

LAWSON, JAMES KERR
28 Oct 1862, Anstruther, Scot 1 May 1939, London, Eng B CC1 DBA DVP H TB1/2 WBA
ARCA 1885-92 Painter
Addr: 1883, c/o J.E. Lawson, Hamilton, Ont; 1885-92, Toronto
1882 12 Twilight in Italy $100
61 An old Roman building $58
65 Study in Rome $50
85 Bay of Naples $50
1883 8 The cactus bower $100
14 Capri landscape $100
92 Winnowing $100
1885 31 Village green, Runswick, England $75
35 Piping Pan $75
73 Twilight 1886-1 $50
76 After the carnival $75 1886-181
1886 42 Sketch wc J.A. Lawson mispr
130 'Music when soft voices die, vibrates in the memory' Shelley
136 Orphans $150
171 A colloquay $100
185 James Smith, Treasurer RCA $185
1889 2 and 3 Market scene, Tangier, Morocco $25 each
4 Street scene, Tangier, Morocco $25
12 Hazy day on the Mediterranean $25
13 Mediterranean coast, Morocco $25
17 Summer landscape, southern France $40
34 Moorish landscape $30
78 Moorish court $25
82 At Brollco, Fontainebleau

LAWSON, ROBERT ANDREW
24 Nov 1926, Toronto
RCA(e) 1977 Set Designer
Addr: 1979, Toronto

LAWSON, WENDELL see LAWSON, ARTHUR

LAYNG, JOHN ARTHUR
19 Mar 1912, Smith Falls, Ont 8 Sep 1974, Oshawa, Ont
1955 87 Residence, R. York Wilson, Esq, Toronto
88 Owen Sound Collegiate and Vocational Institute. South wing

LEACH, BEVERLY
1970 248 Poster, War theatre by Beverly Leach and Robert R. Reid

LEADER, BENJAMIN WILLIAMS (b Benjamin Williams) English
12 Mar 1831, Reading, Eng 22 Mar 1923, Surrey, Eng B DBA DVP G H TB WBA
1882 318 On the Conway, Wales (loan)

LEAF, CAROLINE
12 Aug 1946, Seattle, Wash
RCA(e) 1979 Film maker
Addr: 1979, Montreal

LEATHERS, WINSTON LYLE
29 Dec 1932, Miami, Man M WWA78
RCA(e) 1975 Council Print maker
Addr: 1979, Winnipeg
1965 45 Nubular #9 etch 19 x 26 $125
1966 37 In search of spring pr 26 x 18 $125
1967 42 Almost too small for deaths because to find sergph 18 x 24 $100
1971 31 Temperate zone 15 x 21 $125

LEAYCROFT, IDA
Addr: 1904, Montreal
1904 228 In the gloaming wc

LEBEL, MAURICE
1898, Montreal Jun 1963, Montreal CNS36 M
1945 123 Fishing boats, Chaleur Bay, Quebec $150 T46-27
1947 98 Rain storm, near Rimouski, Quebec nfs T48-22
99 Bic's Islands, Bic, Quebec nfs

LEBENSOLD, FRED DAVID
1917, Warsaw
RCA(e) 1975 Architect
Addr: 1979, Montreal
1970 Affleck, Desbarats, Dimakopoulos, Lebensold & Sise
28A-36A National Arts Centre, Ottawa. View over Rideau Canal, illus. Interior, with Micheline Beauchemin tapestry. Interior, with William Ronald mural. Interior, with Jordi Bonet doors. Interior, experimental theatre. Interior, opera house. Plot, and 2 plans
see also Affleck, Raymond, 1964-1968

LE BLANC, JEANNE
1939 133 Paspébiac $75

LE BLANC, MICHEL
see PAPINEAU, LOUIS JOSEPH, 1976

LE BOUTILLIER, RUBY VIVIAN
b Montreal
Addr: 1931-3, 486 Argyle Ave, Westmount, Que
1931 156 Columbine wc $15
350 A colonial living room des
351 A child's playroom des
1933 131 Peonies wc $100

LE DAIN, BRUCE
1928, Montreal M
1966 38 Quiet dissolution 28 x 48 $500

LEDSON, SIDNEY ALBERT JAMES
16 Apr 1925, London, Eng
1951 55 Study of a young man $400
1952 52 Study of James Rowan nfs

LEDUC, OZIAS
8 Oct 1864, St Hilaire, Que 15 Jun 1955, St Hyacinthe, Que B CC1 CWW 48 H M NGC PMC TB3 WWA47
ARCA 1916 Sr 1937 Painter
Addr: 1893-55, St Hilaire, Que
1893 92 Nature morte, oignons $60 F1-73
93 Nature morte, étude à la lumière d'une chandelle $90 F1-74
1894 73 Still life, open book
1895 89 Books and skull
1899 84 Portrait of a woman
1900 69 Still life
1912 147 Guy Delahaye
1913 174 Fin de jour S4-73 $90
1914 126 Le cumulus bleu
1914 S5, Patriotic Fund
37 Effet gris, neige illus
1915 128 The concrete bridge
1916 134 Neige dorée ǁNGCǁ
296 Mme Josie La Roque de Roquebrune charcl
1920 320 Head of Christ study charcl
321 The Good Shepherd charcl
322 The elm, night effect crayon
323 Nuit d'été crayon

LEE, FREDERICK WALTER
1863, London, Eng 1941, BC H
Addr: 1899, 2303 St Catherine St, Montreal; 1900, Montreal
1899 186 Case of miniatures
187 Confessor's tomb, Westminster Abbey wc
188 Wingfield Castle wc
189 A bit of picturesque London wc
1900 151 A sunny silence, Qu'appelle Lakes wc

LEE-SMITH, MARIANNE
1872, Sutton-on Hull, Eng
Addr: 1924, 414 Huron St, Toronto; 1929, 19 Oaklands Ave, Toronto; 1931, 262 Jarvis St, Toronto; 1932, 82 Millwood Rd, Toronto; 1933, 44 Farnham Ave, Toronto
1924 Smith, Marianne Lee
187 Still life, green and gold
1929 Lee-Smith, Marianne, to 1933
126 Mountain country, New Hampshire $125
1931 157 Still life group $85
1932 115 Still life $70
1933 132 Blue, silver and gold $80

LEFEBVRE, JEAN PIERRE
1970 Don't let it kill you/Il ne faut pas mourir pour ça film screened 12 Feb

LEFORT, MARIE AGNES
5 Jan 1891, St Remi, Nappierville, Que 9 Feb 1973, Montreal M WWA47
Addr: 1931, 2058 Maplewood Ave, Montreal; 1935-6, 1414 Drummond St, Montreal

1931 158 Still life $75
159 Miss Kathleen Murphy
1935 161 Nude $300
1936 122 Mrs G.W. portrait
123 After the storm $75 T37-43
1938 126 La Madone des Iles $400
1939 134 The ice breaker $100
135 Winter morning, Montreal $60
1941 103 Gaspésienne, nude $75

LEGAULT, GUY ROBERT
16 Jan 1932, Montreal
ARCA 1972 Architect
Addr: 1979, Montreal

LEGENDRE, IRENE
19 Nov 1904, Fall River, Mass M
1950 81 Les enfants des barraques 39 x 51 $500

LEGER, J.A.
Addr: 1915, 681 Ontario St E, Montreal
1915 240 Amour maternal plaster
279 Miss B.L. col pen & ink

LEGER, ONESIME ANDRE
b 1881 24 Mar 1924, Quebec
Addr: 1919, L'Epiphanie, Que
1919 96 Les ronces

LEIGHTON, ALFRED CROCKER
27 Oct 1901, Hastings, Eng 6 May 1965, Calgary CC2 M NGC W78 WWA47
ARCA 1935-46 Painter
Addr: 1931, Booth Art Shop, Calgary; 1932, Technical Institute, Calgary; 1933-4, Booth Art Shop, Calgary; 1935, c/o Calgary Draughting, Calgary; 1937, P O Box 134, Calgary; 1938-46, Calgary
1931 160 Floe Lake $400
161 Lake of the Hanging Glacier wc $150
1932 116 The footpath wc $150
117 Brixton, Devon wc $130
1933 133 Trail riders, Goodoir Plateau wc $100
134 Evening, Vancouver wc $100 T34-45
1934 114 Old Edmonton wc $100
115 Lake Louise wc $100 T35-41
1935 162 Skoki, Canadian Rockies $350 T36-45
163 Kokosila, Indian village, Duncan, BC $350
1937 131 On the Simpson, Canadian Rockies $150 T38-27 F11-42 30 x 24 $450
132 Aberford Mill, Yorks $85
133 Richmond, Yorks $100
1938 127 On the Simpson Plateau $400
128 Top of the world illus $400

LEIGHTON, FREDERICK (Lord Leighton of Stretton) English
3 Dec 1830, Scarborough, Eng 25 Jan 1896, London B DBA DBW DVP G TB
1883 40 Sansone, study from life. Presented to the RCAA by Lord Leighton, Pres Royal Academy, London

LEIGHTON, THOMAS CHARLES
1909, Toronto M
1938 129 Peonies and lillies pastel $250
1939 136 Still life $500
137 James F. Flynn, Esq nfs
1940 97 Utility $200
1941 104 Sergt-Pilot Jack Haisle, RCAF pastel nfs
1942 82 Mixed bouquet pastel $300
1948 Capt T.C. Leighton
92 Zilba nfs

LEITERMAN, RICHARD
7 Apr 1935, South Porcupine, Ont
RCA(e) 1974 Film maker
Addr: 1979, Toronto

LEITHEAD, WILLIAM GRIER
16 Oct 1920, North Allerton, Yorks Eng CWW79
ARCA 1965 Architect
Addr: 1965-71/79, West Vancouver

LEMASNIE, GAMBLE SHERIDAN
fl 1905-33
Addr: 1930-3, 2051 Dorchester St W, Montreal
1930 213 Sandunes charcl
1931 162 The blue pot wc $100
404 Sussex barn crayon $50
405 Sand, Provincetown charcl $75
1932 243 Sand and wind charcl $75
1933 302 The river charcl $35

LEMIEUX, EMILE
30 Apr 1889, Montreal M

Addr: 1913, 1105 St Denis St, Montreal; 1916, 1099 St Denis St, Montreal; 1918N-20, 1839 St Urbain St, Montreal; 1933, 5403 Durocher St, Montreal
1913 362 Ile d'Orléans crayon S4-152 $30
363 Vieille grange crayon
364 Notre Dame de Bonsecours crayon S4-153 $20
1916 135 Peupliers, Ile d'Orléans
136 La maison blanche
297 Grenier, Ile d'Orléans pencil
298 Vieille maison, Ile d'Orléans pencil
1918N 110 and 111 Paysage
240 Les terres, Ile d'Orléans pencil
241 Vieille grange, Ile d'Orléans pencil
1919 97 Beaupré
98 A D 1714
1920 324 Goélettes au quai de St François drwg
325 Granges canadiennes, Ile d'Orléans drwg
1922 264 Chemin du Roi pastel
1933 135 Hiver, Val Morin $250 T34-46
136 Première neige $100
1942 83 August reflexions $300
1943 73 Bouteilles vertes $75
1945 124 Fin d'après-midi nfs
125 Grange du Terroir wc $150
1947 100 Ferme dans la Beauce $300
1948 93 Isle of Orleans, Quebec $450
94 Reflections, study $450
1949 52 Etude, nature morte $350

LEMIEUX, JEAN PAUL (Marie Joseph Jean Paul Lemieux)
18 Nov 1904, Quebec AGO B CC1 M NGC TB2/3 WWA47
ARCA 1951 RCA 1966 Painter
Addr: 1934, 3610 Durocher St, Montreal; 1952-71/79, Sillery, Que
1934 116 Les Laurentides à St Hilarion $125 T35-42
1942 84 L'an quarante $200
1950 52 Bélanger rural 25 x 21 $150
1951 56 Marine $150
1952 53 Paysage à St Siméon $250
1953 49 Orage sur Québec $700
1966 97 Mural, Confederation Centre, Charlottetown. Concourse corridor. R.T. Affleck architect
1966 S10, Charlottetown
47 La Pointe d'Islet nfs
48 Rayon de soleil nfs
1967 38 Madeleine 24 x 51 1/2 illus nfs
1970 43 Le rapide 39 x 80 illus nfs
DW 1967 Claude Ives, portrait 24 x 19

LEMIEUX, LUDGER
Addr: 1931, 1260 University St, Montreal
1931 Ludger & Paul M. Lemieux
352 Marché du nord
353-4 Bain St Henri. By day. At night time

LEMIEUX, MARGUERITE
11 Mar 1899, Montreal CNS36 M
Addr: 1929-31, 1260 University St, Montreal; 1933, 5319 ave Notre Dame de Grâce, Montréal
1929 127 Portrait pastel $100
128 Rue de la Montagne, Ste Geneviève wc
1931 163 Pont Neuf wc $50
164 Parc de Westmount wc $50
1933 137 Le Trocadéro wc $35

LEMIEUX, PAUL M.
Addr: 1931, 1260 University St, Montreal
1931 355-6 Project d'un club de tennis. Plan. Elévation
357-9 Project d'une gare d'honneur. Plan. Elévation. Petit plan
see also Lemieux, Ludger

LEMOINE, EDMOND
1877, Quebec d 1922 M
Addr: 1907, Quebec
1907 125 The statuette
126 Paysage

LE MOYNE, ROY EMILE
1963 Bland, LeMoyne & Edwards
113-14 Northern Electric Research & Development Laboratories, Ottawa photo
1964N LeMoyne, Edwards, Shine & Trudeau
130-2 McGill University Lab-

oratories and Dormitories, St Hilaire, Que. Exterior view 1 and 2. General plan. see also Bland, John, 1964N-102-4

LENNARD, JOHN BARRY
3 Nov 1937, Barrie, Ont M
1968 35 Scape 45 x 48 illus $500

LENNIE, EDITH BEATRICE CATHARINE
16 Jun 1906, Nelson, BC M WWA59
Addr: 1932, 1737 Matthews Ave, Vancouver
1932 244 Marionette design for The firebird $10
1938 239 Portrait mask of Moira sculp $125
1951 120 Vancouver Labor Temple, mural sculp photo
121 Academy of Medicine Bldg, Vancouver. Hippocrates sculp photo
1953 122 Ryerson Memorial Centre, 'Suffer little children' sculp photo

LENNOX, EDWARD JAMES
1855, Toronto 16 Apr 1933, Toronto
Co Mo98
Addr: 1895, King & Yonge Sts, Toronto
1895 48A Design for hotel, Toronto
49A Beard's office and hotel building, Toronto
50A Toronto Athletic Club Building, Toronto

LEONARD, JOHN C.
5 May 1944, Oxted, Surrey, Eng
RCA(e) 1976 Painter
Addr: 1979, Toronto

LEPAGE, T.J.
ARCA 1880-1 Architect
Addr: 1880-1, Quebec

LE ROY, HUGH ALEXANDER
9 Oct 1939, Montreal B M
RCA(e) 1974 Sculptor
Addr: 1979, Westmount, Que

LESSORE, FREDERICK English
19 Feb 1879, Brighton, Eng 14 Nov 1951, London, Eng CWW49 DBA TB2 WBA WWB27
Addr: 1919, c/o Canadian Bank of Commerce, St Catherine & Crescent Sts, Montreal; 1920-1, 79 Adelaide St E, Toronto
1919 183 Adam Dollard des Ormeaux, proposed memorial, competitive scale model
184 On guard bronze
1920 274 Hon William Hamilton Merritt, builder of the first Welland Canal bust
1921 90 R.H. Hathaway, Esq pastel
91 Henry Sproatt, Esq pastel
204 Campbell McInnes, Esq charcl
205 Baby charcl

LETENDRE, RITA (Mrs Eloul Kosso)
1 Nov 1928, Drummondville, Que AGO B CC2 IO M TB3 WWA76
ARCA 1971 Council Painter
Addr: 1979, Toronto
1964J 40 Terra feconde 60 x 68 $900
1964N 34 Staccato 59 1/2 x 67 $900
1967 43 Univers clos 40 x 48 $600
1970 44 Influx 60 x 80 $1,800

LEVESQUE, A.
fl 1880-10
ARCA 1880-2 Architect
Addr: 1880-2, Montreal

LEVY, TSIPORA (Mrs)
1934, Israel
Addr: 1976, Montreal
1976 S12, Montreal
146 Formation mixed fibres/fibres diverses 90 x 36 illus

LEWIS, HERBERT
Addr: 1886, Winnipeg
1886 F1a, London, Eng
2027, artist number
20 sketches of Rocky Mountain scenery

LEWIS, IVOR RHYS
c 1882, Wales 25 Nov 1958, Toronto
Addr: 1912, Toronto; 1918A, 29 Winchester St, Toronto
1912 S3, Winnipeg
201 and 202 Monotype
1918A 248 Up the Don dry pt
249 Study of a girl dry pt

LIBLING, GERALD A.
1964N Libling, Michener & Associates, to 1966
133-7 Faculty of Education

Bldg, University of Manitoba
Exterior view. Entry steps.
Interior stairway court.
Front elevation. Plans 1 & 2
1966 135 Public Safety Building, Winnipeg. General view.
see also Michener, Mel, 1964J

LICENSE, R.J.
d 1896 H
1891 19 Study of a rabbit

LICUSHINE, DIMITRY SEMENOFF
24 Oct 1896, Rostoffon, Russia M
Addr: 1933, 3521 Ste Famille St, Montreal; 1936-7, 3427 St Lawrence Blvd, Montreal
1933 138 Still life $50
1936 124 Still life, samovar $100 T37-44
1937 134 Légumes verte, étude $50 T38-28
1938 130 Coin de Montréal $100

LIM, BEN
1970 205 Symbol and letterhead, Burnaby Aquarium of Ecology
206 Letterhead, Paste-Up Services Limited
207 Symbol and letterhead, Capital Management Limited
208 New Year mailer, Sanpan Oriental Shop

LINDENFIELD, MARIANNE
1939 138 Still life wc $20

LINDGREN, CHARLOTTE (Mrs Edward Lindgren)
1 Feb 1931, Toronto
ARCA 1972 Textile designer
Addr: 1979, Halifax

LINDNER, ERNEST
1 May 1897, Vienna AGO CC1 CWW79 M WWA66
RCA(e) 1977 Painter
Addr: 1979, Saskatoon
1939 139 Silent audience wc $150
1945 126 Muskeg wc $130

LINDOE, CARROLL see MOPPETT, CARROLL

LINDOE, LUKE ORTON
8 Mar 1913, Bashaw, Alta M
1944 89 Erosion forms $100
90 The little fox temp $100
1945 127 Shepherd at Ravenscrag nfs

LINDSAY, FANNY LORD
Collingwood, Ont fl 1895-36 CNS36
1901 70 Fruit
71 Violets

LINDSAY, IAN GRAHAM
Addr: 1935-7, 456 Pine Ave, Montreal
1935 328 The Arab drwg
329 Chinese laundry shop drwg $17
1936 243 The derelict, Quebec City charcl $20
244 Coaling, Montreal harbour brush drwg $15
1937 322 Illustrations, Book of Genesis des nfs
1938 259 The yellow boat reed pen & wc $20
1938 S8, Toronto
380 Wallpaper design. Hon mention, Canadian Wallpaper Manufacturers Limited

LINDSAY, ROBERT HENRY
23 Apr 1868, Prescott, Ont Mar 1938, Brockville, Ont H M
Addr: 1901-18, Brockville, Ont; 1920-34, 38 King St W, Brockville
1891 226 Winter
1901 175 Winter wc
1911 111 Autumn woods
112 Scarlet and gold
1912 148 Morning
149 The corn field
1913 175 The pool S4-74 $25
176 Clearing weather S4-75 $40
177 Autumn
178 Grant's Creek, Brockville
1914 127 The coast of Antrim
1916 137 A quiet pool
138 Early snow
1918A 100 The silent woods $100
101 A French window
1918N 112 Twilight
1920 156 Cape Neddick, Maine
1922 127 On the upper St Lawrence S6-55
1929 129 Fish house, Blue Rocks, NS $50
1931 165 Autumn morning $35
1934 117 Harvest $75

LIPARI, FRANCOIS AMEDEO ANGELI (FRANK)
21 May 1927, Montreal M

RCA(e) 1978, Graphic designer
Addr: 1979, Montreal

LISMER, ARTHUR LLD
27 Jun 1885, Sheffield, Eng 23 Mar 1969, Montreal AGO B CC2 CWW64 EC M NGC PMC TB2 WWA47
ARCA 1919 RCA 1947 Sr 1956 RCA medal 1969 Group of Seven Council Painter
Addr: 1912, Toronto; 1914-15, 25 Severn St, Studio Bldg, Toronto; 1916-18, Bedford, NS; 1919-21, Studio Bldg, Toronto; 1922-37, 69 Bedford Park Ave, Toronto; 1938-9, Toronto; 1940, Ottawa; 1941-69, Montreal

1912 S3, Winnipeg
98 The quarry
99 An Ontario landscape
203 Portrait study b&w
204 Cathedral door, St Jacques, Antwerp b&w
205 Cathedral door etch

1914 128 Spring on the old logging road
129 The guide's home, Algonquin 1915-129 ◊NGC◊

1914 S5, Patriotic Fund
25 Breezy weather, Georgian Bay illus

1916 139 Winter afternoon
140 A westerly gale, Georgian Bay ◊NGC◊

1918A 102 The harbour, Halifax, NS, time of war illus
103 Winter camouflage ◊NGC◊
104 The transport convoy 1918N-114
250 The transport, Halifax, NS litho 1918N-242

1918N 113 Halifax harbour, NS, time of war

1919 99 Home again, troopship's arrival in Canada
100 The hillside, Nova Scotia

1920 157 Rock and water
158 Logging, Nova Scotia

1921 93 Poplars

1922 128 Islands of Spruce, Algoma S6-56 1924-127
129 September gale, Georgian Bay ◊NGC◊

1923 102 A northern town, Mattawa
103 Ontario village

1926 187 A Quebec village drwg
188 An old barn, Ile aux Coudres, Quebec drwg
189 Old mill, Quebec drwg
190 Rock and pine, Georgian Bay drwg

1927 123 The happy isles
124 Pines, Georgian Bay
309 The weaver of homespun pencil
310 The fiddler, Quebec habitant pencil
311 Cod splitters shacks, Gaspé reed pen drwg 1929-271 $45

1928 100 Cathedral Mountain $750 1929-130

1928 F8, London, Eng
110 The old mill, French Canada $500

1929 270 Barachois, Gaspé reed pen $45
272 Pine woods chalk $50

1929 S7, Calgary
93 Evening silhouette, Georgian Bay $600
94 The little green boat $250
95 Boats, Percé $75

1930 102 Fishing village, Nova Scotia illus $700 ◊NGC◊

1931 166 Sunlight in a wood $600 ◊AGO◊
406 Wood interior brush & ink $45
407 Pine tops brush & ink $40
408 Tree roots chalk $40

1932 118 The brink of the falls, Georgian Bay $350

1933 139 Nova Scotia fishing village $650
140 Little Haven, Nova Scotia $500 1934-47 ◊MMFA◊
141 September sunlight, Georgian Bay $500
303 Pine trees, Georgian Bay ink & brush $40
304 Rocky landscape, Georgian Bay ink & brush $45
305 Jack pines, Georgian Bay ink & brush $40

1934 118 Impression of Basutoland $150

1935 164 Rocky Channel, McGregor Bay, Ontario $250
165 Habitant home, Quebec $250
166 Basutoland, South Africa $150 T36-46
167 Rock juniper wc $75

1937 135 Native dancers, South Africa wc $200
136 South African coast wc

$200 T38-29
1939 140 Bright land $750
1941 105 Derelict pier $300 T42-26
106 The survivor $300
238 Fishing shacks b&w $60
239 Tubs and tackle b&w $60
1945 128 The blue boat, Cape Breton $350
244 Ingonish, Cape Breton reed pen $75
245 Drift wood in the harbour reed pen $75
1947 101 Summer gale, Georgian Bay illus $400 T48-23
227 Sumac reed pen drwg $60
228 Rock pool reed pen drwg $60
229 African melody reed pen drwg $100
1948 95 Fisherman's gear, with pail, Cape Breton Island $350
96 Small islands, Georgian Bay $225
192 Georgian Bay island brush & ink drwg $100
1949 53 Bush altar, Georgian Bay $200 1950-83 16 x 20 $250
54 Torbay, Newfoundland $250 1950-84 16 x 30 $250
1950 85 Pine rhythm, Georgian Bay 21 x 26 $350
1951 57 Timber, BC $375
58 Forest and shore, Vancouver Island, BC $375
1951 Travelling exhibit
29 Pine wrack DW 1948 36 1/2 x 42 1954 Retro Sec 35
1952 54 In the forest, Vancouver Island, BC $375
1953 Travelling exhibit
18 Open water, Georgian Bay $250
1954 53 Morning in the forest, British Columbia 28 x 20 $400
1960 53 Growth and undergrowth, forest, BC 24 x 30 $600
1961 59 Big tree, British Columbia forest 24 x 20 $550

LITTLE, HAROLD B.
see PERRY, ALFRED, 1937, 1939

LITTLE, JOHN GEOFFREY CARUTHERS
28 Feb 1928, Montreal M NGC TB3
ARCA 1961 Painter
Addr: 1961-71, Montreal; 1979, Town of Mount Royal, Que
1952 55 Mulberry Street, New York City $200
1966 S10, Charlottetown
49 Summer night, Belmont Park $750

LIVING, MARION A.
H
Addr: 1894-8, 160 Lyon St, Ottawa
1894 173 Study of roses wc
1895 78 A working woman
46W Roses wc
1897 18W Yellow roses wc address listing, Mary Living, mispr
19W A hint of Japan wc
1898 173 Une serviteure wc

LIVINGSTON, ALICE
fl 1891-7 H
Addr: 1896, 1018 Sherbrooke St, Montreal
1896 105 Lilacs
215 Low tide, l'Ile d'Orléans wc
216 Wolfe's Headquarters, l'Ile d'Orléans wc

LOATES, MARTIN GLEN
3 May 1945, Toronto M
RCA(e) 1974 Painter
Addr: 1979, Scarborough, Ont

LOCHHEAD, KENNETH CAMPBELL
22 May 1926, Ottawa AGO CC1 M NGC TB3 WWA53
1964J 41 Blue extension illus $800

LOCKERBY, MABEL IRENE
1887, Montreal 1 May 1976, Montreal
AGO M NGC TB2
Addr: 1915-26, 408 Mackay St, Montreal; 1927-9, 1444 Mackay St, Montreal
1915 130 The black cat
1920 159 In the garden
1922 130 Summer
131 Cat and butterflies S6-57
1923 104 Decoration
105 The turkey 1924-124
1925 138 March ◊NGC◊
1926 84 In the farmyard
1927 125 In Montreal
126 Early winter
1928 101 Marie et Minou $200 ◊NGC◊
1929 131 Feeding turkeys $150

LOEMANS, ALEXANDER FRANCIS
fl 1882-94 H

1882 28 Salmon River Mountains $150
278 Minnesota scene monoc $6
279 Coast of Maine monoc $25

LOGAN, CLIFFORD
Addr: 1938, Montreal
1938 S8, Toronto
380 Wallpaper design. Hon mention, Canadian Wallpaper Manufacturers Limited

LOGAN, MARTHA ALEXANDER
27 Jul 1863, Hartford, Conn c 13 Aug 1937, Toronto H M
Addr: 1907, Quebec
1907 127 In days of yore

LOGGIE, JOHN MILLAR
4 Jun 1896, Langside, Scot CNS36
Addr: 1933-35, Chateau Apts, 1321 Sherbrooke St W, Montreal
1933 142 Sunrise, Edith Cavell, from Shovel Pass $700 T34-48
1935 168 Morning on the Saguenay $275
1938 S8, Toronto
Loggie & Partners, Montreal
154 Box, Petal Tone face powder
155 Lipstick, rouge compact, tooth paste tubes, Huguette de Jito
156 Tooth paste tube, Mintys
157 Typographical series, 'Paper on Parade'
158 Newspaper advertisements

LOHSE, WALTER
Addr: 1931, 6014 Park Ave, Montreal
1931 167 Science temp $90

LOMAX, GABRIELLE
Addr: 1938, Hamilton
1938 S8, Toronto
380 Wallpaper design. Hon mention, Canadian Wallpaper Manufacturers Limited

LOMER, LORNA GERTRUDE (Mrs Robert R. Macaulay)
18 Jul 1881, Montreal M
Addr: 1904, Montreal; 1905-6, 9 University St, Montreal; 1906, 45 St Sacrement St, Montreal; 1907, Paris; 1931-6, 1 Elmwood Ave, Senneville, Que; 1938, Gardenvale, Que
1904 Lorna Lomer, to 1907
108 Head of an old man Laura Lomer, mispr F4-53
1905 109 Portrait
110 Study of a head
111 Sweet sixteen F5-109 $50
112 Little Dutch girl
1906 118 Mother and child
1906 F5, Halifax
108 Portrait $150
1907 256 From my window in Paris pastel
1931 Macaulay, to 1947
172 Near Ste Geneviève pastel $50
409 Mary Joy charcl
1932 245 Sketch
1936 127 Hester Spriggs pastel $100
1938 S8, Toronto
380 Wallpaper design. Hon mention, Canadian Wallpaper Manufacturers Limited
1944 93 Girl in green $250
1945 133 Paul McKenzie, Esq pastel nfs
134 Toronto crepuscule wc $200
1947 105 Robert R. Macaulay, Esq pastel

LONG, MARION
19 Sep 1882, Toronto 19 Aug 1970, Toronto AGO CWW64 M NGC TB2/3 W78 WWA47
ARCA 1922 RCA 1933 Sr 1952 Painter
Addr: 1905, 9 Toronto St, Toronto; 1908, 29 Cecil St, Toronto; 1909N, 261 Poplar Plains Rd, Toronto; 1912-14, 468 Yonge St, Room 7, Toronto; 1915-26, Studio Bldg, Toronto; 1927, 261 Poplar Plains Rd, Toronto; 1928-37, 18 Grenville St, Toronto; 1938-70, Toronto
1905 108 Mother and child pastel 1908-92
1908 91 Connie
1909N 88 Satisfaction
1912 150 Mother and baby
151 Woman in black
1912 S3, Winnipeg
206 An impression, King and Yonge Streets, Toronto b&w
1913 365 Gossip crayon S4-154 $20 nfs
366 The Italian fruit store crayon S4-155 $20 nfs
367 New CPR Building, Toronto, on a foggy day crayon
1914 130 The Japanese kimono
1915 131 Sisters

132 Portrait of a lady
1916 141 The black fan
142 The gold fish bowl
299 Killed in action crayon
300 The altar charcl
1918A 105 The woman in black 1918N-116 illus
106 Japanese parasol 1918N-115
107 A child
108 The yellow cushions
251 Girl's head charcl
252 Good-bye crayon
253 Sketch crayon
1919 101 Woman with heads
102 Fortunes
207 The black fan crayon
1920 160 Waiting
1921 94 Lantern light 1922-133
95 Mrs Arthur W. Dyas
1922 132 The furnace man illus S6-58
1923 106 The golden age
1924 129 The old pipe illus
130 The Japanese parasol
131 The dreamer pastel
1925 139 Mother and baby
140 Poppies
305 A Scotsman charcl
1926 85 Girl with fruit
1927 127 Worship
128 Portrait
1928 102 Dr W.D. Cowan (Saskatoon Dental Society)
1929 132 The green jar $400 S7-96
133 Shadows $300 S7-97 F10-156 $350 DW 1934 30 x 25 1/2 1954 Retro Sec 33
1930 109 Mme Nina de Gedeonoff, in Russian costume
1931 168 Eighty years $500
169 Sunshine and flowers $350
1932 119 Miss Constance Burns nfs 1933-143 T34-49
1933 144 The Mexican dancer $500 1934-120 T35-43
1934 119 Evan Macdonald, OSA illus 1935-169 F11-43 42 x 36 $500 ØLAGØ
1935 170 White and green $150 T36-47
1936 125 Miss Constance Pole nfs
126 Miss Mabel Cartwright, BA LLD nfs
1937 137 Florence H. McGillivray, ARCA OSA nfs
1938 131 Jean in green nfs T39-32 1939-142 $500
132 Easter lilies $150
133 George A. Reid, RCA nfs
1939 141 The white collar $500
143 Bill $150
1940 98 The moving finger writes $600 T41-32
99 Miss Gloria Riddell nfs
1941 107 The green cape $500
108 Jobless $250 T42-27
1941 S9, Toronto
42 An arrangement $100
1942 85 Maj Gen C.F. Constantine DSO nfs 1943-76
86 A Norwegian veteran pilot nfs
1943 74 Lieut Comm Taylor WRCNS illus nfs
75 The enlegened Norwegian boy nfs
1944 91 An officer of the Royal Norwegian Air Force nfs
92 The young stoker $200 T45-27
1945 129 From the Ark Royal $350
130 Charles W. Jefferys, RCA LLD nfs
1946 71 Mrs Christopher Dobson nfs 1947-102
72 Wounded veteran of the Italian campaign $300 T47-30
1948 97 The briefing nfs
98 From eastern lands $300
1949 55 The maroon coat $800
1950 86 Zilba Georgieva 42 x 36 $750
1951 59 Miss Ada MacKenzie (Ladies' Golf and Tennis Club, Toronto)
1952 56 Miss Portia White nfs
1956 28 Black and gold
1957 41 The student illus $500
1958 51 Girl with a fan illus $900

LOOMIS, CLARENCE AINSLIE
9 Jun 1917, Toronto M
1948 99 Early spring, Ontario $250

LORCINI, GINO
7 Jul 1923, Plymouth, Eng B IO M WWA73
ARCA 1968 Council Sculptor
Addr: 1970-1/79, London, Ont
1964N 77 Beta VI structural rel $250
1965 87 Alpha XIII sculp 21 x 45 $400
1966 81 Beta trio major sculp 34 x 48 $900
1967 78 Primus duet 2/5 sculp 10 x 6 x 4 illus $480
1970 83 Quadrille 3/5 sculp 21 x 48 $800

84 Atem prismus 2/5 sculp 14h $750
1971 5S Theta magna sculp 46 x 78 $2,200

LORING, FRANCES NORMA LLD
14 Oct 1887, Wardner, Idaho 5 Feb 1968, Newmarket, Ont AGO CC2 CWW64 EC M NGC W78 WWA47
ARCA 1920 RCA 1948 Sr 1957 Council Sculptor
Addr: 1908, 36 1/2 King St W, Toronto; 1915-19, 114 1/2 Church St, Toronto; 1921-37, 110 Glen Rose Ave, Toronto; 1938-68, Toronto
1908 174 Bust
1915 241 Lamia bronze
242 Book ends bronze
1918A 196 La misère du siecle plaster
1919 185 The hound of heaven plaster
1921 180 The derelicts sculp
1922 225 Marion bas rel plaster S6-110
226 Mrs E. plaster
1928 170 The cloud plaster Bedford stone $1,200 marble $1,500
171 Osgoode Hall War Memorial sculp photo
1932 215 Figure for a fountain stone $500 cement $300
1933 264 Turkey plaster stone $500
265 Girl with fish plaster stone $500
1934 205 Sir Frederick Banting bronze $2,500 1935-288 ◊NGC◊
1937 388 The miner stone or wood $750
1941 218 Margot nfs
219 Kim nfs
1942 169 Eskimo mother and child bronze $6,000 ◊EAG◊
1943 134 Soldier plaster nfs
1946 138 Mother and child plaster stone $2,500
1947 209 Dr C.H. Best plaster nfs
210 Mother and child plaster stone $1,500
1948 171 Carvers, working model, plaster for stone, Bank of Montreal, Toronto, Marani & Morris, architects
1949 119 Head butternut DW 1949 27 3/4h
1951 122 Woman mahogany illus $250
1952 112 Rooster wood $375
port: 'The artist' sculp head, by D.P. Hunt, 1956-47; bust, by L. Mol, 1960-84

LOUDON, ISABEL MARY
8 Nov 1884, Toronto M
Addr: 1924-5, 230 Chapel St, Ottawa
1924 132 Fishing schooners, Quebec
277 Foulard dress silk des
278 Lining silk des
1925 306 Cretonne des
307 Post card des

LOUGHEED, ROBERT ELMER
27 May 1910, Massey, Ont M WWA66
1945 131 Last day of fall $900
1947 103 Below St Janvier $650
1948 100 The purebred mare $645
1952 57 Sunday afternoon, north of Ste Rose, Quebec $850

LOUISE CAROLINE ALBERTA (d Queen Victoria, m John Douglas Sutherland Campbell, Marquis of Lorne, Duke of Argyle)
18 Mar 1848, Windsor Castle 3 Dec 1939, Kensington Palace, London
Addr: 1880-3, Rideau Hall, Ottawa; 1886, Kensington Palace, London
1880 314 Lady Elizabeth Campbell pencil
315 Haunted house in Kent wc
316 Wild cherry blossoms, study from nature wc
317 Datura, study from nature
318 Mrs S.L. Motley, author of 'The rise of the Dutch Republic' pencil
319 Study of figures wc
1881 1 Near Salzburg, Austria oil sketch
2 Near Salzburg wc sketch
3 Cherry blossoms wc
4 Col de Winton (Marquis of Lorne) 1882-326
5 Lily wc
6 Pencil sketch
7 Col McNeill, VC photo of portrait
1883 89 Loch Tyne, Inverary
90 Richard Duthie, boatman on the Cascapedia River
91 River scene
150 Mount Baker, Washington Territory, Vancouver Island wc
151 and 156 View from Government House, Vancouver Island wc

152 On the Arno, Florence wc
153 Santa Barbara, California 3 wc sketches
154 View near Monterey, California wc
155 Near Ogden wc
157 Hamilton harbour, Bermuda wc
321 Austrian peasant drwg
1886 Fla, London, Eng
1984, artist number
Niagara Falls, Canadian side

LOUVIN see VINEBERG, LOUISE

LOVERING, IDA R. English
fl 1881-15 DBA DBW DVP
Addr: 1909, 24 Yeoman's Row, Brompton Rd, London, Eng; 1910, 36 Toronto St, Toronto
1909 76 Fine feathers make fine birds
77 A Blue Coat School boy
1910 125 J. Knight, Esq
126 Harold, son of M.O. Hammond, Esq

LOVEROFF, FRED NICHOLAS (b Frederick Nicholas Postnikoff)
c 8 Jun 1894, Terpania, Russia 12 Aug 1959, Redwood City, Cal AGO CC2 M NGC PMC TB2
ARCA 1920-33 Painter
Addr: 1915, 14 Dundonald St, Toronto; 1916, YMCA, Toronto; 1918A-28, 13 Ottawa St, Toronto; 1929-31, 272 Manor Rd, Toronto; 1932-3, Toronto
1915 133 The barnyard
134 The old cart
1916 143 The apple tree
144 An old mill
1918A 296 The beech tree
297 The sky
#296-7, Trustees, National Gallery of Canada, Travelling Scholarship competition
1918N 117 Spring in the woods
118 Village landscape illus
1919 103 October day
104 Wet snow
1920 161 Bloor Street Bridge, winter
162 Yachts
1921 96 White cottage illus
97 Winter evening
1922 134 Snow on the hillside illus S6-59
135 Wood interior, winter S6-60
1923 107 Autumn afternoon
108 Winter landscape
1924 133 Don Valley
134 Ontario farm landscape illus
135 York Mills
1925 141 Golden glow S7-98 $600
142 Wet snow
143 Lumbering in Canada
1926 86 The red barn
1927 129 Northern Canada
130 Winter in Ontario
1927 F7, London, Eng
154 York Mills in March $600
1929 134 Pine trees, winter $1,200
1929 S7, Calgary
99 Canadian farm landscape $800
1930 110 The steel age $600
1931 170 Northern lake $500

LOW, COLIN ARCHIBALD
24 Jul 1926, Cardston, Alta CC2 M
RCA(e) 1973 Film maker
Addr: 1979, Montreal

LOW, THOMAS
24 Nov 1875, Glasgow M
Addr: 1934, 17 Keele St, Toronto
1934 121 Edge of the wood wc $50

LUCOW, MARION
10 Jun 1918, Winnipeg M
1964J 43 Nude with blue 50 x 40 $200

LUKACHKO, ANDREAS LEONARD (ANDREW)
17 Mar 1927, Czechoslovakia M
1946 73 Hilltop wc $50
1953 50 Windswept beach wc $75
1955 56 North country $100

LUKE, ALEXANDRA see LUKE, MARGARET

LUKE, JANE CORBUS (Mrs E.B. Luke)
25 Sep 1881, Chicago M
Addr: 1927-34, 41 Brock Ave N, Montreal West
1927 131 A bit of Provincetown
1929 135 Still life
1931 171 Venetian accordian player $350
1933 145 Dogwood and redbud $100
1934-122 $125
1941 109 Wisteria $150
110 Peonies $100 T42-28
1945 132 Capo di Monte parrots and summer flowers $350

LUKE, MARGARET ALEXANDRA (Mrs Marcus Everett Smith) (Mrs Clarence Ewart McLaughlin)
14 May 1901, Montreal 2 Jun 1967, Oshawa, Ont M TB3 WWA56
1953 55 Full blown $550
1954 54 Exanimo 32 x 48 $300
1959 55 Prophesy 60 x 48 $850
1964J 44 Sound vibrations 32 x 40 illus $300 ◊LAG◊

LUKE, MORLEY C.
see PERRY, ALFRED, 1929-1939

LUKEMAN, EDWARD ARTHUR
24 May 1924, Toronto M NGC
1946 74 Duke Street School wc nfs

LUMBERS, CAROL
Addr: 1976, Toronto
1976 S12, Montreal
34 Untitled acry & polyurethane 66 x 90 illus

LUND, CARL C.
1874, Newcastle-on-Tyne, Eng M
Addr: 1918N, Ottawa
1918N 119 In the woods

LUNDGREN, EGRON SELLIF Swedish
18 Dec 1815, Stockholm 16 Dec 1875, Stockholm B DBW DVP TB
1881 21 Spanish gipsies wc (Lady MacDougall)

LUPPEN, FRANCOIS VAN Belgian
11 Dec 1838, Antwerp 18 Nov 1899, St Josse-ten Noode, Belgium B TB
RCA 1880-4 Council Sculptor
Addr: 1880-4, Montreal
1880 127 The snowshoer statuette
129 A cricket player statue
130 A lacross player statuette DW 1880 (no record of deposit at National Gallery)
132 Sun dial. Life size statue des. Commissioned by Marquis of Lorne

LUSCOMBE, ROY
1948 101 Springtime $175

LUZ, VIRGINIA ERSKINE (Mrs Edgar Luz)
15 Oct 1911, Toronto M WWA56
RCA(e) 1977 RCA 1978 Painter
Addr: 1979, Toronto
1952 58 Hirsau, Germany gouache $65 ◊LAG◊
1958 52 Village of the sea $150 DW 1978 R P R #2 acry

LYALL, LAURA see MUNTZ, LAURA

LYLE, JOHN MACINTOSH
13 Nov 1872, Belfast 20 Dec 1945, Toronto Co NGC TB3
ARCA 1925 RCA 1927 Sr 1942 Council Architect
Addr: 1924-33, 230 Bloor St W, Toronto; 1934-45, Toronto
1924 222 Memorial Arch, Royal Military College, Kingston photo
1925 241 Bank of Nova Scotia, Ottawa. 1927-241 DW 1928 wc drwg 21 3/4 x 22 3/4
242 Residence, F.F. Dalley, Esq, Ancaster, Ont preliminary sketch drwg 1926-151
1926 152 Gage Memorial Fountain, Hamilton, Ont preliminary sketch drwg
153 National Commemorative War Monument, Ottawa, competition drwg
1927 239 Residence, Mrs R.J. Christie, Toronto sketch drwg
240 Proposed golf and country club
1928 180 Proposed casino and golf club
1929 222 Runnymede Branch, Toronto Public Library
223 Gage Memorial Fountain, Gage Park, Hamilton, Ont
224 Dominion Bank, Bleury & St Catherine Sts, Montreal. Main entrance
1930 170 Residence, F.F. Dalley, Esq, Ancaster, Ont
171 Residence, W.R. Johnston, Esq, Orillia, Ont
172 Runnymede Branch, Toronto Public Library. Detail of entrance
173 Dominion Bank Bldg, Yonge & Marlboro Sts, Toronto
1931 360-3 Bank of Nova Scotia, Halifax. Main entrance, detail. Main banking room, windows. Side elevation Spandril panels, the silver fox, the turkey
1932 203-4 Bank of Nova Scotia, Halifax. Bronze and monel metal transom grille. Ceiling motif main banking room

1933 241-2 Bank of Nova Scotia, Halifax. Key stone over main banking room windows, male head, marine life, female head, field life
1939 269-72 Garden, Col R.S. McLaughlin, Oshawa, Ont. View of garden looking towards tea house, urn in foreground. General view of garden from terrace. View of central motif to terrace. Close-up view of tea house

LYMAN, GORDON
Addr: 1920, 74 McTavish St, Montreal
1920 279 Place des Voges, Paris
280 Durham

LYMAN, IDE
Addr: 1935, 2049 Aylmer St, Montreal
1935 289 Caroline plaster $50

LYMAN, JOHN GOODWIN
29 Sep 1886, Biddeford, Me 26 May 1967, Barbados B CWW64 M NGC TB2 WWA47
Addr: 1927, 21 Peronne Ave, Outremont, Que; 1934, 1524 Bishop St, Montreal
1927 133 The Arab philosopher
134 The stocking
1934 123 Girl in gray

LYNCH, AGNES
1943 77 The victory tree $125 T44-25

LYNCH, ELSIE
Addr: 1934, 204 Cottingham St, Toronto
1934 124 Adoration wc $40 T35-44

LYNCH, JAMES O'CONNOR
8 Oct 1908, Sydney, NS WWA59
1945 246 The merchant seaman drwg nfs

LYON, N.T.
fl 1880-90 H
1880 233 Mrs Delaney's cottage, Penetanguishene, Ont
305 Staircase window des
309 Vestibule light des
351 Memorial window des

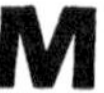

MCARTHUR, BETTY MARIE
4 May 1923 IO
1961 60 Winter scene 17 x 42 $225

MCARTHUR, L.C. (Mrs)
H
Addr: 1893, Winnipeg
1893 94 Gateway, old Fort Garry, Winnipeg $500 F1.75
95 Runswick Bay, Yorkshire $100

MACAULAY, JOHN PHILIP RANKIN
26 Jun 1926, Montreal M
1947 104 October $50

MACAULAY, LORNA see LOMER, LORNA

MCAVOY, O. HAROLD
c 1891 26 Nov 1977, Toronto
1940 110 A floating wharf, Gloucester $175 T41-36

MACBEAN, CLARA SOPHIA
1841, Cobourg, Ont H M Mo12
Addr: 1910, 22 Colonial Ave, Montreal
1910 127 Played out

MCCALL, ANN
1941, Toronto
Addr: 1976, Montreal
1976 S12, Montreal
162 Mountains #3 silkscreen 37 x 26 illus

MCCARTER, JOHN YOUNG
see KERR, K.E. ROBERT, 1971

MACCARTHY, COEUR DE LION
1881, London, Eng 22 Jan 1979, Montreal M
Addr: 1900, 177 Sparks St, Ottawa; 1903, Stafford House, Ottawa; 1907, Ottawa; 1910, 524 St Catherine St W, Montreal; 1913, 21 Wurtele St, Maisonneuve, Que
1900 200 Sir Wilfrid Laurier sculp
201 Gen Wolfe sculp
1903 214 Hamilton Plantagenet MacCarthy, RCA sculp
1907 363 Sir Wilfrid Laurier cabinet bust
1910 204 Lt Col A.A. Stevenson

bronze bust
1913 331 John Horne, Esq plaster bust
332 Sporting trophy scale model, plaster

MCCARTHY, DORIS JEAN
7 Jul 1910, Calgary AGO CWW79 IO M WWA47
ARCA 1951 RCA 1974 Painter
Addr: 1934-36, 134 Balsam Ave, Toronto; 1951-71, Toronto; 1979, Scarborough, Ont
1934 134 Fishing fleet, Barachois, Gaspé $120 T35-47
1936 138 The blue slippers $150
1944 96 The harbour at Barachois nfs
97 Stage Head at Barachois $100 T45-30
1946 80 Low tide, Barachois $150 T47-36
81 Horses seen from a train $150
1949 61 Sunday, Mal Bay $200
1950 93 Flotsom and netsom 24 x 27 $150
94 Bulrushes, Haliburton 24 x 30 $175
1951 64 Square in St Tropez wc $100
65 Sou'easter in the harbour wc $75
1952 64 Yorkshire roundabout $200
65 Corner of the beach, Gaspé $200 T53-21
1953 51 Borley churchyard $300
52 Point St Peter illus $250
1954 55 Dee's boat 24 x 27 $300
56 Barachois village 24 x 27 illus $300
1955 57 The old dyke at Barachois $250
1957 44 Barachois beach with tar barrel $125
1958 58 Five boats at Barachois illus $300
1959 58 Whitby Abbey 30 x 22 illus $150
1960 56 Incarnatus est mosaic triptych 36 x 48 illus $1,200
1965 51 Keyhole Harbour 24 x 30 $400 S10-53
1966 43 Blue chevrons 48 x 72 illus $450
1967 45 Wavement #1 36 x 48 $500
1970 47 Banner #1 48 x 60 $600
DW 1976 Iceberg fantasy, before Bylot. 1974 30 x 48 oil over acry

MACCARTHY, HAMILTON THOMAS CARLETON PLANTAGENET
28 Jul 1846, London, Eng 24 Oct 1939, Ottawa B DBA EC G M Mo98/12 NGC PMC TB1/3 W78
ARCA 1886 RCA 1892 Ret 1923 Council Sculptor
Addr: 1887, Yonge Street Arcade, Toronto; 1888-92, Toronto; 1893, 204 McCaul St, Toronto; 1894, Toronto; 1895-98, 28 Toronto St, Toronto; 1899-00, 177 Sparks St, Ottawa; 1901-2, Ottawa; 1903, Stafford House, Ottawa: 1904-8, Ottawa; 1909M-18, 377 O'Connor St, Ottawa; 1919-23, Ottawa; 1924, 79 Main St, Ottawa; 1925-39, Ottawa
1886 122f Late Sir George Colley. Killed at Majuba Hill sculp 1888-324b
122g Russell Gurney, Recorder of London sculp 1888-324a
1887 181 Col Gzowski sculp copy $50 1888-323, ADC to Her Majesty
182 Dr Daniel Wilson, Pres University College, Toronto bust copy $30 1888-324d (loan) 1889-188
183 Robert Barnes, Esq, MD, London, Eng copy $50
1888 321 HE the Most Hon Marquis of Lansdowne to be executed in marble
322 Prof Goldwin Smith, LLD to be executed in marble
324 Late Rev D. Ryerson sketch model for colossal statue, to be executed in bronze and erected in Toronto 1889-185
324c Parting of Paul and Virginia statuette 1889-186 copies $25
324e Sunbeams statuette
1889 187 Late Col Williams, sketch model for heroic statue, to be erected in bronze, Port Hope, Ont
1890 231 Hon Edward Blake bust 1892-172
1891 1S L.R. O'Brien, Esq ter cot bust 1892-171 DW 1892 24 1/4 h
2S Lady, 'It is Isis, Goddess of Grace' ter cot bust

3S Herbert Spencer, Esq bust ter cot
4S Prof Huxley bust ter cot
1892 173 A.T. Todd, Esq bust ter cot, to be executed in bronze for the Toronto Club
174 Sir John A. Macdonald, GCB bust ter cot
1893 281 Rev Dr Williamson bust, to be erected in Queen's University
282 Hon G.A. Kirkpatrick, Lieut Gov of Ontario bust
283 Equestrian group, Herne the hunter, from Ainsworth's 'Windsor Castle' bronze 1895-74S
284 Miss Lily Fraser, Port Hope sculp
1895 75S Sir John A. Macdonald, proposed memorial for Montreal, competition model
76S Marble bust unfin
1896 283 Rev J. Geo. Hodgins, LLD, ex-Deputy Minister of Eductkion, Ontario bust
284 Rev Henry Scadding, DD port medln 1897-74S ter cot
1898 242 Kivas Tully, CE bust
1899 259 Late William Kingsford, LLD, Hamilton bust
1900 198 HE the Earl of Minto sculp
199 Countess of Aberdeen sculp 1901-247 F2-83
1901 246 Lord Strathcona and Mount Royal sculp F2-82
248 The messenger of love sculp
1903 215 Late Maj Harold Borden bust, heroic size to be executed in bronze, to surmount memorial at Canning, NS
216 Late Lieut Woodburn Osborne, killed at Spion Kop, South Africa. medln, part of large bronze panel to be erected at Brantford, Ont
1904 301 Sir Galahad statuette
1907 362 Bust plaster
1909M 167 Bronze portrait bust from life
168 Sir Sandford Fleming, KCMG sculp
169 Late Mayor Samual Bingham, bronze bust, for City Hall Ottawa 1910-205 (Corporation of Ottawa)
1909N 80 Sir Isaac Brock statue des
1912 243 Maj Gen Sir Isaac Brock, KCB statuette, des for statue
244 Late Queen Victoria sculp
1915 243 Marchioness of Aberdeen bust ter cot
1916 257 Edith Cavell Memorial bust
1920 275 Late Maj E.C. Noseworthy, killed at Langemarck, April 22nd 1915 bust
1924 237 Sir Sandford Fleming, CE KCMG sculp
port: bust, by C.L. MacCarthy 1903-214

MCCAUGHEY, BETTY M. FRENCH (Mrs Lloyd O. McCaughey)
1921, London, Ont M
1960 57 Interior 22 x 30 $70

MCCAUSLAND, JOSEPH
1829, Co Armagh, Ire d 1886 H
1883 McCausland & Son
336 and 376 Stained glass window des
see also McCausland, Robert

MCCAUSLAND, ROBERT
1856, Toronto c 21 Jul 1923, Toronto H M Mo12
ARCA 1882-92 Designer
Addr: 1880, Toronto; 1883, King St W, Toronto; 1884, 76 King St, Toronto; 1885-92, Toronto
1880 306 Spring des
307 Glass panels des
308 Stair case windows des
308a Door panels des
308b Stained glass window screen des
#306-308b, prize awarded
310 Winter des
351a Memorial window des
351b North transept window des
351c Church window with figures des
1883 327 Morning and night, dec heads for glass
334 Dorcas, memorial st gl des
335 Frog and owl, grotesque sketch for glass & tile
336, 366-8 and 376 Stained glass window des
343 St John the Baptist st gl memorial des
345 Spring and winter, dec

heads for glass
346 Morning and night, dec figures for glass
347 Storks, grotesque sketch for glass
372 and 374 Cartoon stained glass window
373 Where are you going, my pretty maid?
375 Cleopatra cartoon for window st gl
1884 203 Household stained glass des
204 Episcopal Church, Bobcaygen, Ont memorial window des
1884 S1, Saint John
160 North transept window, R C church, Sarnia des
161 Stair case window des
1885 44 Twixt day and night

MCCLAIN, HELEN CHARLETON L.
1884, or 25 May 1887, Toronto d 1960 M WWA36
Addr: 1936-7, 30 College St, Toronto
1936 139 Flowers from the garden $150
140 The red sweater $400 T37-47
1937 149 White peonies $300 T38-34
1938 153 Zinnias $300
1948 113 White peonies $300
1950 95 Zinnias with silver 28 x 30 $200

MCCLELLAND & STEWART LIMITED
Addr: 1938, Toronto
1938 S8, Toronto
183 Book, The Beauport road. Franz Johnston
184 Book, Legends of Vancouver. J.E.H. MacDonald
185 The book of Ultima Thule. Thoreau MacDonald
186 Book, Stories of the land of Evangeline. J.E.H. MacDonald
187 Book, The flying canoe. Franz Johnston
188 Book, Saguenay. Thoreau MacDonald, G.A. Cuthbertson, Paul Caron
189 Book, Indian nights. Thoreau MacDonald

MCCLUNIN, F.A.
Addr: 1924, 634 St Catherine St W, Montreal
1924 143 The harbour

MCCONNELL, M. CARY (Miss)
Blyth, Huron Co, Ont fl 1890-39 H
Addr: 1895, 106 Queen St, Toronto; 1897, Queen & Victoria Sts, Toronto
1890 50 Preparing for dinner $50
51 Hen's nest $20
52 Apples $15
1891 230 Portrait
1892 88 Meadow stream $25
1895 79 Mrs E. Matthews
1897 37W The spinner wc

MCCONNELL, ROSS
see CHETWYND, ARTHUR

McCORKINDALE, JAMES
c 1886, Glasgow 6 Aug 1956, Montreal
1939 160 Misty morning, Gloucester $150 Jos McCorkindale mispr
161 The Cove, Laneville $150
1945 144 Gloucester harbor $250 T46-31
1947 117 The old wharf $200
118 Pidgeon Cove

MCCREA, HAROLD WELLINGTON
13 Jan 1887, Peterborough, Ont Feb 1969, Toronto AGO M TB2
1938 S8, Toronto
MacLaren Advertising Co
175 Booklet, Canada - your friendly neighbour invites you. Harold McCrea & others

MCCULLOCH, ELIZABETH (Mrs)
Addr: 1936, 28 Grenville St, Toronto
1936 141 Mother and child wc $40

MACDERMOT, AUDREY M.
1948 102 Old coffee pot $50

MACDONALD, ALBERT ANGUS
22 Jul 1909, Bristol, Eng CWW79 M ARCA 1944-55 Painter
Addr: 1932, 600 Lonsdale Rd, Toronto; 1936, 26 Grenville St, Toronto; 1944-55, York Mills, Ont
1932 120 Autumn tree $100
1936 128 Oval in silver $65
129 Design in yellow wc $25
1938 134 Over on the third $100
1939 144 The birch woods nfs
1940 100 Chinese vase $75

101 Red poppy $45
1942 87 The lighthouse at Wicked Point illus $500
88 Punt in the willows $700
1943 78 Design for solitude illus $300
1944 94 Kamparkurkarkas $750 T45-28
95 Shadowed arch $200 T45-29
1945 135 Clear day, Unionville $500
136 Spring at the Red Indian Station $400
137 V E Day on a sideroad $400 T46-28
138 The slip on a rainy day temp $300
1946 75 Bradford egg temp $350 T47-31
1947 106 Le bateau de M Arpin $250
1948 103 Raining in Hamilton $150
1949 105 Doors, for Aluminium Company photo

MACDONALD, ERROL DAVID
25 Sep 1924, Halifax
1949 56 The dance platform, country fair wc $100
1954 58 Landscape, York Mills Road 20 x 30 $50

MACDONALD, EVAN WEEKES
9 Jun 1905, Guelph, Ont c 24 Jan 1972, Guelph, Ont CNS36 M
ARCA 1947 Painter
Addr: 1932, 68 Grenville St, Toronto; 1934, 27 Grenville St, Toronto; 1947-71, Guelph, Ont
1932 121 J.E. McAllister, Esq
1934 125 Mrs K.D.M. Spence
126 Noranda Mine, Rouyn
1945 139 Herbie Lawson nfs T46-29
1946 76 Portrait of my wife nfs T47-32
77 Boys playing, Cobalt, Ont temp illus $400 T47-33
1947 107 Mr William Krug nfs
108 John Rockwood nfs
1948 104 The old mill race $400
105 Sunday morning, RR #6 nfs
1951 60 Old houses, Elora $300
1957 42 Boys in an old mill $400
1958 53 White Fish Falls $450
1959 56 Dr R.M. Manske 24 x 20 nfs
port: by M. Long, 1934-119

MACDONALD, GRANT KENNETH
27 Jun 1909, Montreal AGO CC1 CWW79 EC IO M TB2 WWA53
ARCA 1954 RCA 1966 Painter
Addr: 1954-71/79, Kingston, Ont
1949 57 Heads, peace on earth $300 T50-12
1951 61 Woman in white $300
1952 59 Three women and a bird illus $500 T53-19
1953 53 Two young people $600
1954 57 Seated figure 20 x 16 illus $300
1955 58 Listeners $500
1963 47 Eclipse on a red landscape $950
48 Embarkation 24 x 53 illus $800
1965 46 The late cousin Charles 44 x 38 $900
47 Under four moons 30 x 40 $800 S10-51
1966 39 Encounter 40 x 35 illus $825
1970 45 Time piece 40 x 50 illus $1,500
DW 1967 Man in an eclipse 50 7/8 x 25

MACDONALD, JAMES EDWARD HERVEY
12 May 1873, Durham, Eng 26 Nov 1932, Toronto AGO CC2 EC M NGC R2 TB2 W78
ARCA 1912 RCA 1932 RCA medal 1969, Group of Seven Painter
Addr: 1909N-10, 105 Quebec St, Toronto; 1912, 32 Adelaide St E, Toronto; 1913, Thornhill, Ont; 1914-32, Studio Bldg, 25 Severn St, Toronto
1909N 90 The pine, moonlight
91 Book covers
1910 128 By the lake, October afternoon S3-101
129 Grey winter
1910 S2, Liverpool
68 Snowshoers, moonlight
69 A grey day, winter
70 October on Howard Lake
1912 152 The snow cloud
153 Spring breeze, High Park, Toronto ◊NGC◊
154 A passing gleam
1912 S3, Winnipeg
100 Tracks and traffic, winter morning ◊AGO◊
102 Summer clouds
1913 179 Fine weather, Georgian Bay
180 The lonely north S4-77 $350 S5-40 illus

181 Northland, spring moonlight
182 The shining river, early spring ≬NGC≬
183 The homeseekers
184 Twilight
1914 131 March evening, northland ≬NGC≬
132 A Laurentian hillside, October
133 The edge of the town, winter sunset
1914 S4, Winnipeg
76 Fine weather, Georgian Bay $500
1915 135 March evening, northland
136 Fields, early spring illus
137 Logs on the Gatineau
138 Sleeping fields
1916 147 The tangled garden ≬NGC≬
148 A Laurentian village, October
301 Illustration, Belgium 1914
302 Illustration, War matters
1918A 111 Cattle by the creek illus ≬NGC≬
112 October, Laurentians gouache
1918N 120 Wild ducks illus
121 In November
122 October hillside, Laurentians wc
1919 106 Beaver dam illus ≬AGO≬
107 Leaves in the brook 1920-165
1920 163 The river valley ≬AGO≬
164 Harvest evening illus
1921 99 A northland hilltop
1922 136 October, shower gleam S6-61 S7-103 $500
137 Mist fantasy, northland ≬AGO≬
138 Young Canada
1923 239 A friendly meeting. Mural decorative painting competition
1924 136 Gleams on the hills illus 1927-136 F10-114 nfs ≬NGC≬
137 Design. Mural decorative painting competition
1925 145 Mountain chaos ≬MMFA≬
146 Lake McArthur, Rocky Mountains
1927 135 The solemn land ≬NGC≬
137 Near Mount Goodsir, Canadian Rockies illus
1928 F8, London, Eng
98 The little fall $500
1929 136 The hilly farm $350
137 Rain in the mountains $700
1929 S7, Calgary
102 The fall of the leaf $700 ≬NGC≬
1931 173 Autumn in Algoma $700
174 Dark autumn, Rocky Mountains $175 ≬NGC≬
1932 122 Lichened rocks, mountain morning $175
123 Goat Range, Rockies illus $175
124 Mountain solitude $175
1938 S8, Toronto
McClelland & Stewart Limited
184 Book, The legends of Vancouver
186 Book, Stories of the land of Evangeline
Rous & Mann Limited
257 Book, J.E.H. MacDonald Canadian artists series illus
Ryerson Press
267 West by east and other poems, by J.E.H. MacDonald drwgs by Thoreau MacDonald illus
1954 20 Retro Sec. Falls, Montreal River. 1920 (Art Gallery of Toronto)
DW not presented

MACDONALD, JAMES WILLIAMSON GALLOWAY (JOCK)
31 May 1897, Thurso, Scot 3 Dec 1960, Toronto AGO CC2 CWW58 M NGC TB2 W78 WWA53
ARCA 1959 Painter
Addr: 1930-1, 3615 1st Ave, Vancouver; 1932, 2417 Point Grey Rd, Vancouver; 1933, 2456 Point Grey Rd, Vancouver; 1959-60, Toronto
1930 111 Lytton Church, BC $450 ≬NGC≬
1931 175 Sailors Sand Bar, Fraser Canyon, BC $450
1932 125 The Black Tusk, Garibaldi Park, BC $450
126 The white forest $425
246 The cove pen drwg $25
247 Indian salmon rack lino cut $18
1933 146 6,000 feet up $275 T34-50
306 Still grasping pen drwg
1938 135 Glacier Caves, Garibaldi Park, BC $425 T39-33
136 Meadow trees, Garibaldi

Park, BC $50
1938 S8, Toronto
Ryerson Press Limited
273 Book, The neighing north
1939 145 Drying herring roe $425
146 Tantalus Range, from Garibaldi Park $350
1941 113 Mount Hungabee, Lake O'Hara, BC $225 T42-29
1942 89 8,000 feet up nfs
1959 57 Maquinna 48 x 59 1/2 illus $900
1960 54 Elemental fury 47 1/2 x 54 illus $800

MACDONALD, JOHN BLAIR
22 May 1931, Calgary
RCA(e) 1973 Architect
Addr: 1979, Vancouver
see ARCHAMBAULT, RICHARD, 1964N

MACDONALD, MALCOLM PHILIP
1 Mar 1879, Stornaway, Isle of Lewis Mar 1965, Toronto AGO
Addr: 1923-5, 200 Highbourne Rd, Toronto
1923 112 The Grand Banks
1924 138 The squall wc
1925 148 The open sea

MACDONALD, MANLY EDWARD
15 Aug 1889, Point Anne, Ont 10 Apr 1971, Toronto AGO CC2 CWW64 M NGC TB2 WWA47
ARCA 1919 RCA 1948 Sr 1959 Painter
Addr: 1915-20, Point Ann, Ont; 1921, c/o Ontario Society of Artists, 14 Elm St, Toronto; 1923-5, Studio Bldg, Toronto; 1926, 143 Roxborough St E, Toronto; 1928-37, 56 Grenville St, Toronto; 1938-71, Toronto
1915 139 The white calf
140 In the shade
1916 149 Harvest time
150 Full summer
1918A 298 In the shack
299 Haying
298-299, Trustees, National Gallery of Canada, Travelling Scholarship competition
1919 108 Dressing fish
109 Mill on Salmon River
1920 166 Fishermen, Lake Ontario illus ≬NGC≬
167 The soap maker
168 Coal schooners
1921 100 Spanish market
101 Venetian fishing boats illus
206 and 207 French peasant col drwg
208 French peasant drwg
209 Peasant etch
1923 111 Old saw mill, Canifton
1925 147 Gordon Payne, Esq
1926 89 Mme Gaskins illus
1928 104 Miss Edna Fraser
1929 186 The hilly farm $350
187 Rain in the mountains $700
1929 S7, Calgary
104 Portrait of a girl $500
105 Fisherman, Lake Ontario $500
1932 127 The checked shirt $500
1933 147 The ravine, winter $350 T34-51
1934 127 S.H. Armstrong, Esq
128 Autumn, Bay of Quinte $250
1935 171 Sally nfs
172 Duncan nfs
173 The mill, Green River $400 T36-48
1936 130 The sugar bush $400 T37-45
1937 138 Forest mills $400
139 Boy fishing $400 T38-30
140 The model plane $400
1938 137 Shannonville mill $400
138 Mill on the Salmon River $500 T39-34
139 Fishing boats $250
1939 147 The mill, Salmon River $500
148 Mill at Lonsdale $300 1954 Retro Sec 39
149 The Salmon valley $300
1939 F11, New York
44 Lonsdale mill 28 x 36 $400
1940 102 Mill on the Moira River illus T41-33 $400
1941 111 River Moira, Belleville $400 T42-30
112 Lost Channel, Moira River $300
1941 S9, Toronto
43 The stream, winter $200
1942 90 Early spring, Bedford Mills nfs T43-25
1943 79 Farm buildings, Bay of Quinte $400 T44-26
1946 78 The stream, York Mills $500 T47-34
1947 109 Lonsdale Valley $500 T48-24
1948 106 Mill on the Moira River

$500 DW 1949, Chisholm's mill, Moira River 28 x 36
107 Boys fishing $500
108 On the Don $350
109 Summer evening $350
1949 58 The stone mill, Odessa $500
1950 88 Fishing village 28 x 36 $500

MACDONALD, MURRAY MALCOLM
15 Apr 1947, Cape Breton
Addr: 1976, Vancouver
1976 S12, Montreal
79 Untitled stone/pierre 17.2" x 19.2" x 15.4" illus

MACDONALD, ROBERT HARRIS
1875, Melbourne, Australia 18 Dec 1942, Montreal Co PMC
see ROSS, GEORGE, 1920

MACDONALD, THOMAS REID DDL
28 Jun 1908, Montreal 15 Oct 1978, Paris CC1 CWW64 IO M NGC TB3
ARCA 1947 RCA 1960 Council Painter
Addr: 1931, 3531 Ste Famille St, Montreal; 1933-5, 1104 Beaver Hall Hill, Montreal; 1937, 3531 Ste Famille St, Montreal; 1947-51, Hamilton, Ont
1931 176 Portrait
177 Still life $50
1933 140 The poet Leo Kennedy
1935 174 John in the studio $100
1937 141 Night club $100 T38-31
142 Nude $75
1939 F11, New York
46 Portrait 22 x 27 nfs
1947 110 Adrien Hébert, RCA nfs T48-25
111 Man at a table illus $150 T48-26
1948 110 Man in black coat $250
1949 59 Dancer resting illus $150
1953 54 Night portrait $200
1956 29 Camp chair $200
1957 43 Raw morning $150
1958 54 Study illus $250
1961 61 Sheila 48 x 36 illus $300 S10-50 illus
1965 48 Miss V. 60 x 35 illus $500
1966 40 Victoria 60 x 35 $500
1968 36 Sandra in the mirror 48 x 36 illus $600
1970 S11, Halifax
22 Yoritomo. 1960 32 x 32 $400
23 Miss T. 1964 28 3/4 x 21 1/4 $300
DW 1961 Nude in mirror 18 x 24

MACDONALD, THOREAU
21 Apr 1901, n Toronto AGO M NGC TB2 WWA47
1938 140 Redtail hawk $65
141 Great horned owl $75
1938 S8, Toronto
168 Book, Some tools of the pioneers
169 Book, A landmark lost
170 Book, A few of the old gates at Thornhill and some nearby farms illus
171 Book, Village and field
172 Book, My high horse
173 Book, Some proverbs from Russia
174 Book, A year on the farm
McClelland & Stewart Limited
185 The book of Ultima Thule illus
188 Book, Saguenay, Thoreau MacDonald, and others
189 Book, Indian nights
Ryerson Press Limited
267 Book, West by east, and other poems by J.E.H. MacDonald illus
268 Book, Poems by Francis Sherman
1939 F11, New York
45 Hawk study 23 x 24 $85

MCDONIC, HENRY REED (HARRY)
24 Oct 1904, West Hartlepool, Eng
ARCA 1964 Architect
Addr: 1936, 111 Hazelton Ave, Toronto; 1964-71/79, Toronto
1936 142 Snow forms wc $100
143 Lower Quebec wc $100
1938 154 Early morning wc $150
155 The silent sentinels wc $150
1939 162 Winter steam wc $150
1940 111 Old school house, West Hill wc $100
112 Winter fishing wc $100
1941 126 Grain elevator wc $150
1942 92 Fishing boats wc $100 T43-26
1943 82 Frozen river wc $150
1944 98 Brick kilns wc $100
1945 145 Old houses, winter wc $150

146 Back yard, Colonial wc $100
1946 82 Old mill wc $200
1947 119 Forest Hills wc $200
120 Brick kilns wc $150
1948 114 Drying sheds, evening wc $150
115 Derelict wc $150

MACDONNELL, HARRIET J.
Addr: 1893, Victoria School of Art, Montreal; 1895-02, 91 Aylmer St, Montreal; 1907, Montreal
1882 132 Study of a staircase and hall wc
1893 217 On the North River, Quebec wc $25
218 Old saw mill, St Andrews, Quebec wc $20 F1-165
1895 70W Stormy evening, Cape Breton wc
1896 217 Sous le Cap Street, Quebec wc
218 Little Champlain Street, Quebec wc
219 Shirley poppies wc
220 Quebec, from l'Ile d' Orléans wc
1899 207 Murray Bay from Cap à l'Aigle wc
208 Sous le Cap, Quebec wc
209 Entrance to Sous le Cap wc
1902 210 Village street, Murray Bay wc
211 Murray Bay, from Drumtarlie wc
1907 261 Knight's Chamber and Abbot's Gate, Peterborough wc

MACDOUGALL, (Lady, m Sir Patrick Leonard MacDougall) English H
Addr: 1881, Halifax
1881 22 Lugano wc
24 Niagara wc
25 Study of trees, Canada wc
31 Gate at Cairo wc
94 Chievenna Como wc

MCDOUGALL, JAMES CECIL
4 Jul 1886, Three Rivers, Que 20 Apr 1959, Montreal CWW55 PMC
Addr: 1931, 1221 Osborne St, Montreal
1931 368-9 Montreal General Hospital, Private Pavilion
370-2 Jewish General Hospital, Montreal
see also, Smith, John Roxburgh, 1953

MCDOWELL, MADELEINE
1970 85 Penumbra I sculp 15 x 10 x 61 illus $1,200

MCEACHERN, JOHN
1970 225 Calendar, Herzig Somerville Limited
226 Letterhead, Film design, Vladimir Goetzelman Limited
227 Letterhead, Donald Watt

MCELCHERAN, WILLIAM HADD
17 Sep 1927, Hamilton, Ont M WWA73
ARCA 1971 RCA 1974 Sculptor
Addr: 1979, Toronto
1953 123 Sad song sculp $250
1954 116 Sanctuary furniture, St Michael's Church, Edmonton photo
117 Architectural sculpture, St Anthony's Church, Hamilton photo
1966 82 Jacob and the Angel rel 42 x 18 $800
1970 86 On the board walk sculp 28h illus $800
DW 1974 Time wise sculp

MCEVOY, HENRY NESBITT (HARRY)
1828, Birmingham, Eng 21 Apr 1914, Detroit Gr H
Addr: 1886, London, Ont
1886 F1a, London, Eng
2006, artist number
Eugene Falls

MCEWEN, JEAN ALBERT
14 Dec 1923, Montreal AGO B CC1 CWW79 M TB3 WWA62
ARCA 1964 RCA 1968 Council Painter
Addr: 1965-71/79, Montreal
1963 50 Monogram du Roi Blanc $1,400
51 En remontant les jaunes $1,300
1964J 45 Cyclades #2 50 x 50 $950
1964N 36 Le drapeau inconnu 72 x 66 illus The unknown flag $2,000 S10-52
1967 44 Blue à ma jolie 68 x 78 $2,100
1968 38 Le feu des signes 78 x 68 illus nfs DW 1969

1970 48 Ocre travessant le feu des signes 72 x 72 illus $2,000
1970 S11, Halifax
24 and 25 Flowers for hippies, part 1 and 2 of diptych. 1970 polymer 72 x 72 each $2,800 each
1971 34 Aquarelle de l'Ile du Prince Edouard #1 12 x 16 illus $200

MACFARLANE, DAVID HURON
1875, Montreal 1 Feb 1950
ARCA 1923 Sr 1944 Architect
Addr: 1914-18, New Birks Bldg, Montreal; 1922-3, 611 Sydenham Ave, Westmount, Que; 1924-5, Westmount, Que; 1926-34, St Hilaire, Que; 1935, c/o Scott & Sons, Drummond St, Montreal; 1936-50, St Hilaire, Que
1914 213-14 High school building, Westmount, Que. Detail of main entrance. View from west 2 photos
1918N 221 House at St Hilaire, Que
1922 236 A country house
1923 181 A country house at Hudson Heights, Que
182 A suburban church
1926 90 On the Island of Orleans wc
154 Proposed country house
1929 225 Additions to house at St Hilaire
1933 149 Cap des Rosiers, Gaspé, sketch wc $40
1935 175 Afterglow, winter wc $50 T36-49
176 Lac Tremblant wc nfs
1941 114 Winter, Béloeil wc $50

MCGILL, DAVID
Addr: 1933-5, 602 Grosvenor Ave, Westmount, Que
1933 156 Valley of the Gouffre $35
1935 182 Late summer, Lake Champlain $125 T36-53

MCGILLIVRAY, FLORENCE HELENA
1864, Whitby, Ont 7 May 1938, Ottawa AGO B H M NGC TB2
ARCA 1925 Painter
Addr: 1914, 292 Frank St, Ottawa; 1915-16, Whitby, Ont; 1918-31, 292 Frank St, Ottawa; 1933-5, 20 Wellesley St, Toronto; 1936-7, Toronto
1914 139 Afterglow ◊NGC◊
140 Tidewater
1915 143 Rocky Skye
144 Cheville, Paris wc
1916 151 A rocky stream, Skye
152 A Scottish hillside
1918A 121 A corner of the Grove, Whitby 1918N-131 illus
122 Canal, Venice
123 Midwinter, Dunbarton, Ontario wc ◊NGC◊
1918N 132 Buckle factory in winter, Whitby
1919 117 Ice in the Bight, St Anthony pastel
1920 179 On the edge of the Grove, Whitby
1921 108 Ice about, Twillingate, Newfoundland illus ◊NGC◊
109 Sea shore, La Folla, California
1922 145 Off the Labrador coast pastel
146 Labrador fishing stage temp S6-63
1923 118 San Giogio, Venice
1924 144 La Chûte, Gatineau
145 Murphy's Fleet, Ottawa
1925 155 On the sea wall, Georgetown, Demarara
156 Sea craft, Venice
1926 95 The edge of the Grove, Whitby
96 Murphy's Blue Fleet
97 Bridge Market, Bridgetown, Barbados
1927 150 Coconut grove, Trinidad
151 Midwinter in the city S7-109 $150
1929 145 Anchored fishing boats, Venice $250
146 Uncertain weather on the Savannah $175
147 Emerald Lake, BC $175
148 Autumn, Gatineau River $150
1929 S7, Calgary
108 Factory buildings, Whitby $150
110 Fishing stage, Labrador $200
1931 190 Newly fallen snow, up in the Gatineau $200
191 Dandelion time, near Toronto $150
1933 157 Busy days, Percé, Quebec $75
158 Palms, Jamaica $75
159 Pier Street, St Ives, England wc $100

160 Midmarch, Pickanock, Quebec wc $75
1935 183 Lost Cascades, Gatineau River, Quebec $500
184 Covered bridge, Val Desbois, Quebec $500
port: by G.G. Duclos, 1931-71; M. Long, 1937-137

MCGIVERN, HAROLD MACKINTOSH
28 Jun 1900, Ottawa M
Addr: 1924, c/o Bank of Nova Scotia, Victoria
1924 145 August breeze

MACGREGOR, CHARLES
4 Nov 1893, Edinburgh AGO M
ARCA 1939-43 Painter
Addr: 1928, 3 Carlton St, Toronto; 1929, 760 Spadina Ave, Toronto; 1932-4, 122 Glen Rd, Toronto; 1936, 18 Grenville St, Toronto; 1939-43, Toronto
1928 105 Mother F9-178 nfs
106 Miss Marion Wood, Prin, Havergal College
1929 138 Charles G.D. Roberts $750
1932 128 Mrs E. Hawkins F11-47 24 x 20 nfs ◊AGO◊
1934 129 Margaret 1938-142 nfs
1936 131 Brother Rogatian nfs T37-46
132 H. Griffen, Esq nfs
1938 143 T. Kennedy, MA nfs
1939 150 W.C. Noble, Esq nfs
1941 S9, Toronto
44 Snapdragons $150

MACGREGOR, JAMES G.
1898, Glasgow M
Addr: 1933, 822 Banning St, Winnipeg
1933 150 The coming squall wc $30
1939 151 Wrought iron derelict $100
1940 103 Still Water Valley $100 T41-34
1941 115 This year begins $150 T42-31
1943 80 The home front $110 T44-27

MACGREGOR, WILLIAM FIRTH
1896, Edinburgh
1945 140 D.I. McLeod nfs

MACINNIS, GARFIELD ALLISTER
8 Mar 1936, Barrie, Ont
RCA(e) 1976 Architect
Addr: 1979, Toronto

1968 Gordon S. Adamson & Assoc
109-14 Northern Electric Co, Ltd, Toronto, branch laboratory. A.Plan, 1st floor B. South elevation C.North elevation. D,E.Southeast, east elevations. F.Main entrance

MCINTOSH, LAWRIE GANDIER
24 Jun 1924, Clinton, Ont
RCA(e) 1974 Industrial design
Addr: 1979, Etobicoke, Ont

MACK, MARY AGNES
12 Jun 1899, Cornwall, Ont M
Addr: 1926, Cornwall, Ont; 1927, Goodhall House, Cornwall, Ont; 1930-7, 223 2nd St E, Cornwall, Ont
1926 91 Moonlight, Paris
1927 138 Old houses wc
1930 112 Village, lower St Lawrence wc $50
1933 151 Among the hills wc $35 T34-52
1934 130 Paysage Temiscouata County wc $40 T35-45
1937 143 View of golf club, Cacouna wc $50

MCKAGUE, MURIEL YVONNE see HOUSSER, MURIEL YVONNE

MACKAY, ABIGAIL (Mrs)
1964J 37 Hilltop town 23 x 19 1/2 $50

MACKAY, DONALD CAMERON
30 Mar 1906, Fredericton M WWA54 WWB52
Addr: 1930, 107 Spring Garden Rd, Halifax; 1931-2, 58 Rosehill Ave, Toronto
1930 214 Shipyard, Lunenburg, NS etch $7
1931 178 Bear River wc $18
410 Boat landing, Saint John River etch $12
1932 248 Swapping horses dry pt $8
249 Saturday morning etch $8

MACKEAN, J.T.C.
ARCA 1880-8 Architect
Addr: 1880-8, Saint John

MACKENZIE, ALICE BEIRNE SAWTELLE
(Mrs Hugh Mackenzie)
7 Mar 1898, Fort Riley, Kans
1950 89 The concert 24 x 50 $75

MACKENZIE, HUGH SEAFORTH
19 Jun 1928, Toronto M WWA73
ARCA 1972 Painter
Addr: 1979, Toronto

MACKENZIE, PHILIP HAMILTON
26 May 1920, Montreal
1950 90 Late autumn afternoon 24 x 30 nfs

MCKENZIE, ROBERT TAIT
26 May 1867, Almonte, Ont 28 Apr 1938, Philadelphia AGO B H M Mo12 NGC TB2 W78
RCA Hon Non-res 1928 Sculptor
Addr: 1900, 56 Metcalfe St, Montreal; 1901-3, 913 Dorchester St, Montreal; 1906, 121 S 18th St, Philadelphia; 1910, Philadelphia; 1929-31, 2014 Pine St, Philadelphia; 1932-8, Philadelphia
1900 Tait McKenzie, MD
159 An old willow, early spring wc
160 Apple blossom wc
161 Craig Street, November wc
1901 256 The skater bas rel plaster (E.R. Peacock, Upper Canada College) F2-89
1901 F2, Buffalo
44 Study of willows
1902 290 The sprinter sculp F3-99
1903 212 The athlete sculp (AGO)
1906 123S Statuette plaster
1910 206 Late Dr A.A. Browne bronze medln
1914 206 The joy of effort bronze medln
1929 249 Gen Wolfe study of head for statue in Greenwich Royal Park, London
1931 331 E.W. Beatty, Esq, KC sculp
port: by H. Fabien, 1923-47

MACKIE, STELLA (Mrs)
b England
1947 112 First Communion pastel $250

MCKIEL, CHRISTIAN (Mrs)
27 Sep 1889, Pictou, NS
Addr: 1920-31, Sackville, NB; 1932-5, Salem St, Sackville, NB; 1937, Mount Allison University, Sackville, NB
1920 327 An old model drwg
1931 413 Portrait drwg
1932 135 A man in a blue shirt pastel $15
1935 185 Mary Laura pastel nfs
1937 150 Phlox $100
1938 156 Portrait of a little girl nfs
1944 99 Peonies $85
1945 147 Sylvia $50
1946 83 Portrait study $50

MCKIM, IRENE
b Kingston, Ont M
1970 49 Oligoclace 72 x 48 $600

McKINLEY, RUTH GOWDY (Mrs Donald Lloyd McKinley)
14 Jun 1931, Brooklyn, NY WWA78
RCA(e) 1976 Designer
Addr: 1979, Mississauga, Ont

MCKINNON, JOHN CHARLES
27 Jan 1953, Brantford, Ont IO
Addr: 1976, Toronto
1976 S12, Montreal
80 Calling my own #3 stick construction 84 x 65 illus
81 Calling my own #5 stick construction 59 x 29 illus

MACLAREN ADVERTISING CO LIMITED
Addr: 1938, Toronto
1938 S8, Toronto
175 Booklet, Canada - your friendly neighbour invites you. Arthur Heming, Harold W. McCrea, Jack Bush. Bomas Engravers

MCLAREN & MCCAUL LIMITED
Addr: 1938, Toronto
1938 S8, Toronto
Clair Stewart
190 2 menu covers, T. Eaton Co Limited
191 Mailing folder, Buntin Reid Co Limited, Toronto
192 2 mailing folders 'Boats' Buntin Reid Co Limited
193 Spring and summer announcement folder, Cook Clothing Co Limited
195 3 newspaper advertisements, National Trust
196 China booklet, Birks-Ellis-Ryrie Limited
197 Gift book 'Caravanserai', Birks-Ellis-Ryrie Limited

198 Deluxe jewellery book, 1936, Birks-Ellis-Ryrie
200 House organ booklet, Canadian Ink Co
202 Business forms, letterhead, 2nd sheet, envelope, invoice statement, address label, package label, sticker McLaren & McCaul Limited
J.W. McLaren
194 Picnic service folder, Toronto Transportation Commission
199 Deluxe jewellery book, 1937, Henry Birks & Sons, Limited, Montreal
201 Display card, 'Hockey', Canada Cycle & Motor Co Ltd

MCLAREN, DORA
1947 121 Muriel $50

MCLAREN, JOHN WILSON (JACK)
11 Aug 1896, Edinburgh AGO M
Addr: 1926, 348 Windemere, Toronto
1926 99 The Dumbell illus
1938 S8, Toronto
McLaren & McCaul Limited
194 Picnic service folder, Toronto Transportation Commission
199 Deluxe jewellery book, 1937, Henry Birks & Sons, Limited, Montreal
201 Display card, 'Hockey', Canada Cycle & Motor Co Ltd
Ryerson Press
271 Book, Our great ones
1942 93 John Smith's Bay $500
94 Belmont Manor $500 T43-27

MCLAREN, NORMAN
11 Apr 1914, Stirling, Scot CCl Co CWW79 M WWA73
ARCA 1971 RCA 1973 RCA medal 1962 Council Film Maker
Addr: 1971/79, Montreal
1970 Pas de deux film screened 19 Feb
DW 1974 Blinkity blank. 1954 16mm col 5 min 15 sec

MCLAREN, THOMAS
see PEDEN, FRANK, 1974

MCLAUGHLIN, ISABEL GRACE
10 Oct 1903, Oshawa, Ont AGO CWW79 M NGC TB3
1950 96 Bermudiana 25 x 26 $250
97 Spring fantasy 24 x 32 $300

MCLEAN, R.G., LIMITED
Addr: 1938, Toronto
1938 S8, Toronto
H.L. Pinkerton
203 6 pieces, Goodyear truck tire campaign
204 10 pieces, Goodyear automobile tire campaign

MACLEAN, SARAH JEAN MUNRO (Mrs Lachlan A. Maclean)
9 Dec 1873, Pictou, NS 21 Feb 1952, Montreal CNS36 M NGC TB3
Addr: 1927, 154 McKenna Ave, Montreal; 1931, 5306 McKenna Ave, Montreal
1927 139 The Chinese vase wc
140 Day dreams wc
1931 179 The flame coloured dress

MCLEAN, THOMAS WESLEY
17 Nov 1881, Kendall, Ont 8 Dec 1951, Toronto AGO M
Addr: 1912, Toronto; 1928, 101 Erskine Ave, Toronto; 1932, 90 Erskine Ave, Toronto
1912 S3, Winnipeg
105 The voyagers
209, 210 and 211 North country study b&w
1928 111 Fishing village $150
1932 136 Rest $500

MACLEAY, ROSANNA MACLEAY STEWART (Mrs Stewart MacLeay)
26 Sep 1887, Wakarusa, Kans
1945 141 Run, boy, run $60 T46-30
142 Asbestos, from Richmond road $60

MCLEISH, MINNIE
Addr: 1912, 68 St Stephen's Rd, Hounslow, London, Eng
1912 272 Strand on the green pastel
273 Dance of the mannikins pastel

MACLELLAN, JOHN BORLAND
25 Dec 1913, Stevenstons, Ayres, Scot M
1940 104 The red blouse $250
1941 116 Rundle Range, Canmore, Alberta wc $45

240 Stephania drwg $40
1943 81 The Seven Pillars of Wisdom $300 T44-28

MACLENNAN, IAN ROY
9 Apr 1919, Regina
ARCA 1967 Council Architect
Addr: 1968-71, Ottawa; 1979, White Rock, BC

MCLENNAN, K.
Addr: 1925, Petersfield, Sydney, NS
1925 158 The old telephone pole

MCLENNAN, LOUISE RUGGLES BRADLEY
(Mrs John S. McLennan)
Aug 1860, Chicago 1912, Sydney, Cape Breton, NS H
Addr: 1887, Montreal
1887 145 Evening wc
169 Black Rock, Louisbourg wc

MCLENNAN, S.B.
H
1882 54 Rover
162 Bachelor's quarters wc $275

MACLEOD, ALEX
1970 209 Poster, Facad
210 Poster, Blue S.A.
211 Magazine cover, Stimulus Oct-Nov 1968
212 Advertisement, T D F Film Productions Limited
213 Magazine cover, (Abitibi) Impressions Vol 2 #3 1969
214 Poster, The fantastic 4
215 Poster, A complete visual communications service
1971 53G Poster, The global village
54G Advertisement, T D F Artists Limited

MACLEOD, DONALD IVAN
20 Sep 1886, Owen Sound, Ont d 1967
CWW36 M WWC40
Addr: 1933, 43 Glen Ayr Rd, Toronto; 1936, Metropolitan Bldg, Toronto
1933 161 Silver glen
1936 145 Gloucester Mass nfs T37-48
1939 163 Winter spruce nfs
1941 127 Autumn, Muskoka nfs
128 Gray harbour day nfs T42-34 1942-95
1945 148 Low tide nfs T46-32
1947 122 The sword fisherman nfs
123 Old fishing boats nfs
port: by W.F. McGregor, 1945-140

MCLEOD, ELIZABETH A.
1875, Pointe du Bute, NB 14 Nov 1963, Sackville, NB
Addr: 1915, Point Du Bute, NB; 1918N, Sackville, NB; 1931, Mount Allison University, Sackville, NB
1915 145 Peonies
1918N 133 Zinnias
1931 192 Tulips
193 Zinnias

MCLEOD, JEAN
1938 S8, Toronto
167 Sanctuary window des by OCA students assisted by Rowley Murphy

MACLEOD, PEGI NICOL see NICOL, PEGI

MCLOUGHLIN, BERNARD
12 Jul 1925, Fort William, Ont M
1953 56 Fiesta fireworks $500

MCLOUGHLIN, MICHELE
18 Jan 1944, Calgary
RCA(e) 1975 Council Interior designer
Addr: 1979, Vancouver

MACLURE, SAMUEL
1860, New Westminster, BC 8 Aug 1929, Victoria
Addr: 1906, Victoria
1906 192 Bungalow, Seymour St. Dining room, bungalow, Seymour St, Victoria. Bungalow, Pemberton Rd, Victoria
193 Residences: G. Michaelis, Esq, Elliot St, Victoria; Capt J.W. Troup, Esquimalt Rd, Victoria; B. Wilson, Esq, Rockland Ave, Victoria
194 Residences: Dr J.H. Sterling, Rockland Ave, Victoria; G.A. Campbell, Pemberton Rd, Victoria A. Maclure mispr

MACMILLAN COMPANY OF CANADA LIMITED
Addr: 1938, Toronto
1938 S8, Toronto
Hugh Eayrs, G.E. Rogers

176 Book, Family portrait
177 Book, Manitoba essay
178 Book, Saucy again
182 Book, Speeches of Thomas D'Arcy McGee
Bertram Brooker
179 Yearbook of the arts in Canada
Hugh Eayrs, Marius Barbeau
180 Book, Quebec
181 Book, Romancero du Canada

MACMILLAN, DUNCAN PARK
Jul 1873, Cornwall, Ont d 16 Apr 1908 H
Addr: 1893, 807 Dorchester St, Montreal; 1896-7, 9 Hanover St, Montreal; 1904, Montreal; 1905, 2 Brunswick St, Montreal; 1906, 2256 St Catherine St, Montreal; 1907, Montreal; 1908, 9 Hanover St, Montreal
1890 53 A study $10
1893 96 Dismal hollow $100 F1-76
97 June morning, Outremont $25
98 Under the starlight $175
1896 106 Mother!
107 Study of a head
108 Eulalie
1897 97 Isabel
98 The old green boat, Gananoque
1904 109 The mantilla
1905 129 What's the use W. Park MacMillan mispr
130 Percita
1906 124 Il penseroso
1906 F5, Halifax
110 La penserosa $200
1907 128 Greta, portrait of a child F6-115 $500
1908 102 The Chinese lantern

MCMURRICH, NORMAN HAY
2 Jun 1920, Toronto CWW79
see SOMERVILLE, WILLIAM, 1964N

MCNALLY, LORNE WILLIAM
30 Apr 1942, Port Colborne, Ont M
1967 46 Scan coll 20 x 16 $110

MCNAUGHTON, ETHEL P.
1950 98 Ski house, St Sauveur, Quebec 21 1/4 x 17 1/2 $50

MACNAUGHTON, JOHN H.
fl 1867-99 H
Addr: 1896, 27 Rosemount Ave, Westmount, Que
1890 54 Canadian sport $150
55 Still life in the camp $25
56 Steamer Druid at Quebec $25
1896 221 A market day, Jacques Cartier Square, Montreal wc
222 A Fraser Highlander at Quebec, 1759 wc
223 Fraser's Highlander wc
224 Old market man, Quebec

MCNICHOL, ROBERT
ARCA 1883-8 Architect
Addr: 1883-8, Winnipeg
1883 361 Terrace, Kennedy St, Winnipeg des
362 Residence, J.B. McKilligan, Esq, Winnipeg
McNicol/McNicoll mispr
see also Chesterton, Walter, 1883-357

MCNICOLL, HELEN GALLOWAY
14 Dec 1879, Toronto 27 Jun 1915, Swanage, Eng CC1 M NGC TB3 W78
ARCA 1914 Painter
Addr: 1906, 3 Côte St Antoine Rd, Westmount, Que; 1907, Westmount, Que; 1908-14, Braleigh, 2 Forden Ave, Westmount, Que
1906 130 The brown hat F6-117 $100
131 Old street, St Ives
132 In the sun
133 In an orchard
1906 F5, Halifax
121 Old English court $90
122 Girl in the sun $50
1907 135 Watching her chickens
136 Street in Montreal F6-119 $75
137 Near Outremont
138 The little worker F6-118 $100
1908 105 September evening
106 A farm yard
1909M 92a Washerwoman on the Loing
92b The gleaner
1910 130 Among the flowers
131 On the sands
1910 S2, Liverpool
73 In a Surrey orchard
74 In the farm yard
1911 113 The bathers
114 Sketch
115 The little busybody
116 The old barn
1912 155 The bean harvest
156 Market place, Montreal

1912 S3, Winnipeg
106 The artist
107 Picking flowers
108 Feeding chickens
1913 185 The baby S4-78 $150
186 Venetian boats
1914 141 The white umbrella
142 Sunny September
1914 S5, Patriotic Fund
30 The farm yard illus

MACNUTT, H.R. (Miss)
fl 1890-02 H
1890 57 A yard of roses $35

MACPHERSON, ANNIE H.
fl 1887-96 H
Addr: 1887-96, Montreal
1887 111 Portrait
1896 225 The beach at St Patrick, Rivière du Loup wc

MACPHERSON, DUNCAN IAN
20 Sep 1924, Toronto AGO CWW79 M RCA(e) 1973 RCA medal 1966 Illustrator/cartoonist
Addr: 1979, Toronto

MACPHERSON, KENNETH ROSE
19 Feb 1861, Montreal 26 Apr 1916, Montreal H
Addr: 1896, 211 Stanley St, Montreal; 1899, 119 Shuter St, Montreal; 1906, 229 Stanley St, Montreal; 1907-10, Montreal; 1913-15, 229 Stanley St, Montreal
1896 109 Bad weather, Cap à l' Aigle
110 Winter, from an upper window
111 Over the roofs
112 The new village, Murray Bay
1899 92 On the links
93 A conference of the powers
1906 F5, Halifax
111 On the lower St Lawrence $75
112 The old trout pond $75
113 The seventh hole $50
114 The red farm $125 F6-116
1907 129 A summer shower
130 A shady spot
1910 S2, Liverpool
71 The farm by the river 1911-117 S3-103
72 The edge of the wood 1911-118 S3-104
1913 187 Cloud and sea
188 Old willow
189 The vegetable garden
190 Woodland and hill
1914 S4, Winnipeg
79 The bar, St Ann's Bay, NS $200
80 Old cottage, Métis $150
1914 S5, Patriotic Fund
29 Farm on the river illus
1915 141 The lighthouse, Métis, Quebec
142 Moonlight, August, Métis

MACQUARRIE, DONALD
7 Dec 1872, Greenock, Scot
Addr: 1912, Winnipeg; 1913, Museum of Fine Arts, Winnipeg
1912 S3, Winnipeg
251 Evening on the canal
252 Spring pastoral
253 Golden afternoon, Fraser's Cove
254 Wooded landscape wc
1913 191 September morn S4-81 $75
192 Moonlight on the Red River S4-82 $40
193 Before the gloaming S4-83 $30
194 The Nixies wood wc

MACVICAR, DONALD NORMAN
17 Aug 1869, Montreal 29 Mar 1929, Montreal PMC
ARCA 1903 Architect
Addr: 1902, 36 Canada Life Bldg, Montreal; 1903-9, Montreal; 1910-15, 104 Union Ave, Montreal; 1916-17, Montreal; 1918N-25, 628 Union Ave, Montreal; 1926-9, Montreal
1902 MacVicar & Heriot
248 Public school, Vankleek Hill
249 Dining room, interior
250 New premises, St Catherine Street
251 Store interior, St Catherine Street
1903 208 Residence, Westmount
209 Sketch in Rheims, Bruges
210 Tower of St Leu, Amiens
211 New public school, Chesterville, Ont
1907 MacVicar & Heriot
321 Apartment house, University Street
322 Armory, Prince of Wales Fusileers

323 Cottage, Bois Briand
D.N. MacVicar
324 Piazza, Genoa
325 Campanile, Siena Cathedral
326 Leaning tower, Ravenna
1909M 151 Residence, John Fair, Esq, Montreal
152 School, Verdun, Quebec
153 Grand Trunk Railway Building, Seattle Exposition
1910 MacVicar & Heriot, to 1925
216 Residence, C.J. McCuaig, Esq
217 Residence, Herbert B. Walker Esq
218 Caron Building, concrete facade
1913 337 Strathcona Academy, Outremont, Quebec
338 Grenadier Guards Armory, Montreal S4-141 $50 nfs
339 Institutional Church, Rosemount, Quebec
1915 257 Residence, St Andrews, Que
258 Residence, Windsor Mills, Quebec
259 Episcopal Church, Ahuntsic, Quebec
260 Florence, Italy D.N. MacVicar
1918N 123 Ogunquit Beach, Maine wc Norman MacVicar
222-3 Outbuildings at Cartierville, Lord Atholstan photo
1925 243 Building, Cassity Limited, Toronto
244 Guy Drummond School, Outremont, Quebec
245 Parke Davis Building, Montreal
246 Caron Building, Montreal

MACVICAR, ELIZABETH M.
Addr: 1922-3, 293 Yale Ave, Winnipeg; 1925, 2 River Apts, Winnipeg; 1927, 3426 McTavish St, Montreal; 1931, 1545 Mackay St, Montreal
1922 139 Miniatures:
Late John Moss, KC, Toronto 1923-113
Late Mrs E.L. Drewry, Winnipeg
Late Mrs C.A. Richardson, Winnipeg
Miss Nora Page Richardson, Montreal
Lieut Leo Nicholson, Winnipeg
Miss Ruth Taylor, Winnipeg 1923-113
1923 113 Miniatures on ivory:
John Gooderham, Winnipeg
Late Mrs Clark
Mrs Murray Hendrie, Hamilton
Patricia Murphy, Winnipeg
1925 149 Miniatures:
Mrs Stuart MacTier
Miss Helen McKim
Miss Edwina Higging
Master Guy Drummond
Master Thornley Stokes
1927 141 Miniatures on ivory:
Miss Mary Grace Pitfield
Miss Brenda Sutherland
Master Teddy MacTier
Capt K.L. Duggan
1931 Miniatures on ivory
180 Norma, daughter of Mr and Hon Cairine Wilson
181 Child's head sketch

MCWHIRTER, JOHN English
27 Mar 1839, Inglis Green, n Edinburgh 28 Jan 1911, London, Eng
B DBA DVP G H TB WBA
1881 229 Cloisters at Fièsole (Frank West)

MCWILLIAMS, ALLAN
1944, Vancouver
Addr: 1976, Surrey, BC
1976 S12, Montreal
82 The passing of Kekui sculp m med 7 3/8 x 13 3/8 x 9 1/2 illus

MCWILLIAMS, LUCY
Addr: 1925, 26 Maynard Ave, Toronto
1925 272 The prodigal's return sculp

MADDEN, ORVAL CLINTON
2 Feb 1892, Napanee, Ont 15 Dec 1971, Toronto M
Addr: 1932-5, 179 Delaware Ave, Toronto
1932 129 Stacking $225
1934 131 Harvesting $225
1935 144 Cement plant $130
1938 144 Northern waterfall $225
145 Sawmill $225
1939 152 The crusher $200
153 Charcoal kilns $125
1941 117 Early spring $250

MAGGS, ARNAUD
b 1927

1970 216 Poster, Antiques and things
217 Poster, Graphics
218 Rolland Paper 1969 vacation schedule
219 Magazine cover, Imperial Oil Review, Aug 1964
220 Self mailer, 'Big eater' Associated Illustrators and Photographers Limited
221 Mailer, Associated Illustrators and Photographers

MAHER, PETER
1970 222 Book, Lawren Harris

MAHON, CHARLES
Addr: 1913-20, 1215 Greene Ave, Westmount, Que; 1931, 1614 St Catherine St W, Montreal
1913 195 Portraits on ivory
1920 169 Portraits on ivory
1931 182 Portraits on ivory

MAILLARD, CHARLES
8 Feb 1887, Tiaret, Algeria flg 1971, Montreal M
Addr: 1913-16, 149 Bureau Ave, Montreal; 1920, 1158 St Denis St, Montreal
1913 196 Mme Lallemand
1916 Sergt Maillard, somewhere in France
153 Poilu, portrait de l' auteur
154 Notre Dame de Paris, intérieur
1920 170 Mme B, portrait
171 Minou

MAINWARING, G.B.
Addr: 1923-4, 4 Ashland Court, Winnipeg
1923 114 The emigrants wc
1924 139 Early autumn wc

MAJOR, GERALDINE (Mrs Wrangel)
Addr: 1927, 7 Chelsea Place, Montreal
1927 142a A medieval shop, Menton wc
1943 Wrangel, to 1945
118 The shack $75
1945 210 Old houses, Craig Street, Montreal wc $25

MAJOR, RICHARD WALTER
20 Nov 1899, Toronto flg 1978 M
Addr: 1932, 18 Grenville St, Toronto; 1937, 7782 Champagneur St, Outremont, Que
1932 130 Nancy $400
1937 144 Mine head at Creighton, Ontario $175
1939 154 The prodigal son $350
155 Mrs E.H. Major nfs
1940 105 Doreen $100

MAKSOLLY, MAXIMILLIAN
Addr: 1937, 1500 Bishop St, Montreal
1937 145 Gladioli $250

MALAMUD, ISRAEL
b 1904
1941 118 Old trees wc $75
119 The approach of autumn wc $35

MALCHI, BEZALEL
26 Nov 1902, Simno, Lithuania CNS36 M
1947 211 The mulatto plaster $175

MALDARELLI, FEDERICO Italian
2 Oct 1826, Naples 7 Dec 1893, Naples B G TB
1880 14 Ladies at the bath, Pompeii (Allan Gilmour)
16 At the bath, Pompeii (Allan Gilmour)

MALLOCH, STIRLING
Addr: 1901, 961 Dorchester St, Montreal
1901 80 Maple leaves
81 Riddling potatoes
82 Jack, son of Alex Walker, Esq, Montreal

MANGOLD, CARL
1901, Trimback, Switzerland M
1938 S8, Toronto
63 Booklet, ABC of CIL, C. Mangold, A. Cloutier Saturday Night Press
337 Book, Canadian Industries Limited, C. Mangold, R. Purves
343 Letterhead, CIL

MANIAS, GRACE
15 Feb 1942, Milan, Italy IO
Addr: 1976, Windsor, Ont
1976 S12, Montreal
77 Toy piece alum & acry

10 x 10 x 4 illus

MANLY, CHARLES MACDONALD
Sep 1855, Englefield Green, Surrey, Eng 3 Apr 1924, Toronto AGO CC2 EC H M NGC TB3 W78
ARCA 1890 Painter
Addr: 1890-2, Toronto; 1893-8, 75 Adelaide St E, Toronto; 1899, York Chambers, Toronto; 1900, Toronto; 1901, Yonge St Arcade, Toronto; 1902, 8 Yonge St, Toronto; 1903-12, Yonge Street Arcade, Toronto; 1913-19, 34 North St, Toronto; 1921-2, 36 North St, Toronto; 1923-4, Toronto

1888 28 Summer is queen wc $100
33 At the sign of the Rest and be Thankful wc $45
234 Spring is here and summer is coming wc $85
244 June days wc $30
1889 133 Midsummer day wc $45
150 Cold Creek, Bolton, Ont wc $120
172 The sparkling Teign, Dartmoor, Eng wc $120
173 A Canadian Sleepy Hollow wc $100
1890 175 Storm clouds wc $25
176 November's bareness everywhere wc $50
177 In old Quebec wc $100
1891 125 Hidden stream wc
126 A wide, wide moor wc
132 Clearness after rain wc
133 Last of the leaves wc
134 In the heart of the hills wc
1892 14 Between the showers sweet sunlight gleams $350
45 O'er the hills and far away $350
119 Spring stirred and broke wc $75
125 A street in Point Levis, Quebec wc $100
138 Leafy June a'summering comes wc $100
1893 219 Midsummer days wc $200 F1-166
220 The creeping sea came in wc $200
221 Shimmering heat wc $65
222 Autumn scatters the leaves again wc $65
223 The house among the poplars wc $50
224 Heather land wc $100 F1-167
225 Land of the peach and vine wc $200 F1-168
1894 74 Under the greenwood tree
174 The coming of the leaves wc 1895-53W
175 The winds of spring are out at play wc
176 In old Champlain, Que wc
1895 79 Upland
50W A sunlight stream wc
51W Flowers of the field wc
52W After rain wc
1896 226 The Wiltshire Avon wc
227 The Avon at Christchurch wc
228 October at Yeo, Devon wc
229 Studland Sands wc
230 Meadows at Salisbury wc
1897 90 A Canadian homestead
27W Britford Vale, Wiltshire wc
28W The heart of the hills wc
29W A Wiltshire haying wc
30W Daylight dies wc
31W Spring stirred and broke wc
32W Hampshire hedges wc
33W Batworthy Water, Dartmoor wc
1898 77 A sinking sun shall shine
78 Moorland drovers
188 Robe of gold wc
189 The summer prime wc
190 Batworthy Water wc
1899 195 In the Pass of the Glencar wc
196 A world of heather wc
197 Mowat house at Britford wc
198 A watergate at Fladbury wc
1900 80 The river road
153 A heavy rain wc
154 St David's Pool wc
155 Sunlit meads, Wiltshire wc
156 The hills of Glencar wc
157 A moorland cleeve wc
1901 72 Nightfall 1902-111
198 Summer breezes wc
199 The day is done wc F2-45 1902-214
200 Woodland waters wc
1902 112 Golden pathway of the sun
212 Pear blossom wc
213 Above the sea wc
215 A river begins wc
1902 F3, Rochester
103 Gold of eventide $170

1904-229 F4-105
1903 175 Last gleam wc
176 Stream that flows through Richby wc
177 Eventide wc
178 Evening in the Lowlands wc
179 Glory of the year wc
1905 116 The burning golden rose of the day
117 New Brunswick
118 The creaming shore
1906 119 Beaver River, Nova Scotia
120 Before the gloaming
121 Lift of the fog
122 Spring stirred and broke
1906 F5, Halifax
115 A hill town in Nova Scotia $75
116 Pine clad hill, St Martin's, NB $60
1907 139 The sea comes in F6-121 $500 1908-95
140 The thresh of the sea
141 In the fields, Nova Scotia
262 The trail of the sunset red pastel S2-75
263 Above the valley wc
1909M 86 Evening on the Conestogo
87 Noon
88 Afternoon sun 1909N-93
89 Glory of the year 1909N-92
1910 132 A mood of Dartmoor
133 Veiling mists, Dartmoor
1911 119 Rain and flood, Dartmoor
120 On the Gatineau, Quebec wc 1912-158
1912 157 The little flowers of spring wc
159 A Dartmoor stream wc
1912 S3, Winnipeg
109 Autumn on the Conestogo wc
110 Dartmoor weather wc
111 Smother of waters wc
207 Harvesting, Eastern Townships b&w
208 A city's waterfront b&w
1913 197 At the back of beyond
198 The Irish shore wc S4-85 $25
199 October on the Conestogo wc S4-86 $100 S5-6 illus
200 Tile kilns, moonlight wc S4-87 $40
1914 134 Valley of the West Ockment wc
1915 146 Moonlight, tile kilns, Conestogo wc
147 The little fires of spring wc
1916 155 A little side door at Clonrath wc
156 Early September wc
1918A 113 Cape Cove, Baie des Chaleurs
114 Top of the stack 1918N-124
115 In the air, winter pastel 1918N-126
254 Lithograph
1918N 125 The barn door wc 1919-111
243 Charcoal drwg
244 Lévis, Québec charcl
1919 110 Waters meet, Conestogo wc
112 Sunlit meads wc
208 Chemin de fer, Lévis, Québec charcl
1921 102 Lower town, Quebec wc
103 Mid-September wc
1922 265 A noon-tide flutter pen & ink
266 The little grocer shop dry pt
267 Trouble with the old clay mixer pen & ink

MANNING, JOANNE ELIZABETH (Mrs Rothfels)
11 Dec 1923, Sidney, BC WWA73
RCA(e) 1978 Print maker
Addr: 1979, Toronto

MANSARAM, PANCHAL
4 Mar 1934, Mount Abu, Rajasthan, India WWA76
1970 58 Rear view mirror #1 50 x 50 $300 Panchal, Mansaram

MARANI, FERDINAND HERBERT OBE
8 Aug 1893, Vancouver 18 Jul 1971, Toronto CNS40 CWW36 PMC
ARCA 1936 RCA 1947 Sr 1963 Architect
Addr: 1937, 46 Bloor St W, Toronto; 1938-71, Toronto
1937 Marani, Lawson & Morris, to 1939
247-50 Gore District Mutual Fire Insurance Company, Head Office Building, Galt, Ont. View from west. View from southwest. Rear entrance doorway. Rotunda
1939 273-4 Bank of Canada, Head

Office Building, Ottawa. View from Wellington Street. Sparks Street entrance. With S.G. Davenport Assoc
275 Mercy Hospital, Toronto drwg
276 Ridley College, St Catharines, Ont. Gymnasium and swimming pool building drwg

1946 154 Ridley College, St Catharines, Ont. Memorial Hall

1947 Marani & Morris, to 1957
192 Bell Telephone Company of Canada, Central Office Building, Brantford, Ont. Perspective rendering 1948-183
193 Ridley College, St Catharines,Ont. Gymnasium and swimming pool building photo 1948-184
194 New grand stand, Canadian National Exhibition, Toronto model

1948 182 Stratford General Hospital, Stratford, Ont rendering
185 Stadium, Canadian National Exhibition, Toronto photo

1949 106 Manufacturers Life Insurance Company, Toronto, extension model
107 Bell Telephone Company, Office and exchange, Brantford, Ont. Entrance, main portico and statue of Alexander Graham Bell, by Cleeve Horne photo

1951 107-10 Ridley College, St Catharines, Ont. Great Hall and Memorial from quadrangle. War Memorial cloisters. Great Hall interior. Great Hall east side and Infirmary photo

1952 100-1 Canada, Dept of Health and Welfare, Ottawa, Food and Drug Laboratory. Virus laboratory model
102 Crown Life Insurance Company, Toronto, new head office building, Toronto model

1953 98 Manufacturers Life Insurance Company. Lobby corridor photo
99 Confederation Life Association, new head office model
100-3 Manufacturers Life Insurance Company. Directors dining room. Typical general office space. Garden elevation. Board room, ante room. 4 photos
104 Canadian Embassy, Washington, DC. Military component preliminary sketch
105 Manufacturers Life Insurance Company. Additions and alterations model

1954 118 Confederation Life Assurance, Toronto, head office building and staff house model illus
119 Continental Casualty Co, Toronto, head office building model
120-1 Manufacturers Life Insurance Co, additions and alterations. Garden elevation. Lobby corridor, looking east photo illus

1955 89 Crown Life Insurance Co, head office building, Bloor St E, Toronto 2 photos
90 Traders Finance Corporation Limited, and Associated Companies, head office building, Church & Charles Streets, Toronto model

1957 100 An institution in eastern Canada

1959 Marani, Morris & Allan, to 1964
99 Shell Building, University Ave, Toronto photo illus
100 St Joseph's Mother House, Willowdale, Ont. General view. Chapel

1960 99 Shell Oil Company of Canada Limited, head office photo
100 Great West Life Assurance Company photo illus

1963 115-16 St Joseph's Mother House, Morrow Park, Toronto. Interior (2)
117 Bell Telephone Company of Canada. Replacement of 76 Adelaide St W, Toronto model

1964J 107-8 Canadian National Exhibition, Better Living Centre model plan

1966 Marani, Rounthwaite & Dick
136 London Life Insurance Co Limited, London, Ont.

Addition to head office building. General view
137 Royal Bank of Canada Building, Toronto. View looking east
1967 Marani & Rounthwaite
123-5 Metropolitan Toronto Court House. A.The library, and York County Law Association B.The Mall C.Plot plan
DW 1948 H.M. Hughson house, Ottawa des pencil 16 x 21 1/4
see also Chapman, A.H., 1946

MARCH, SYDNEY English
1876, Hull, Eng B G TB3
1941 120 Mrs C.R. Turner nfs
121 Last of the snow $60

MARCHAND, JEAN OMER
28 Dec 1872, Montreal 11 Jun 1936, Montreal NGC
ARCA 1925 RCA 1928 Architect
Addr: 1927, 190 St James St, Montreal; 1928, 486 Wood Ave, Westmount, Que; 1929-36, Montreal
1927 242 Hunting lodge for Lord Strathcona
1928 181 Study for a library DW 1929 pencil 45 1/2 x 27 3/4

MARCHESCHI, HARRY A. (HARRY A. MARCHE)
1941 Marcheschi
220 Impulse stone
1946 Marche, to 1947
139 Western bronco sculp nfs
1947 212 Orlando plaster nfs

MARCKE DE LUMMEN, EMILE VAN French
20 Aug 1827, Sevres, France 24 Dec 1890, Hyèrès, France B TB
1882 316 Returning from pasture (loan)
317 Homeward bound (loan)
324 Milking time (loan)

MARIS, JACQUES (JACOB HENRICUS MARIS) Dutch
25 Aug 1837, The Hague 7 Aug 1899, Carlsbad B TB
1882 311 Landscape. Modern Dutch school

MARKELL, JACK HAROLD
14 May 1919, Winnipeg 12 Apr 1979, North Vancouver M WWA56
1953 57 Lady with a guitar $325
1955 59 Two figures illus $200
1956 30 The bull illus nfs

MARKSON, JEROME
21 Mar 1929, Toronto CWW79
ARCA 1972 Architect
Addr: 1979, Toronto
1964J 109-12 International Woodworkers of America, office building. Interior (2). 1st floor plan. Section
1966 138-41 Group Health Centre, Sault Ste Marie. General view. View from mezzanine. Main stairway. General plan

MARKSON, MAYTA
24 Mar 1931, Winnipeg
RCA(e) 1976 RCA 1978 Designer
Addr: 1979, Toronto
DW Greek village porcelain sphere 8"

MAROIS, A.
fl 1882-6 H
1882 250 Study from the antique monoc A. Morois
255 Study from the antique monoc

MARQUETTE, HILDA see RUSTON, HILDA

MARQUIS, M.
Addr: 1920, 347 Garnier St, Montreal
1920 326 La tristesse dessin à la plume

MARSH, WINIFRED FLORENCE PETCHEY (Mrs Donald Marsh)
31 Mar 1905, London, Eng
1938 Life of the Padlemuit Eskimos, 1938, 1939, 1942, 1943-93, 1947
146 Fall wc nfs T39-35
147 Early spring encampment wc nfs
1939 157 Drum dance wc nfs
158 Arctic fisherman wc nfs
1940 106 Fall migration wc nfs
Petchey, to 1947
1941 153 Tents on dull day wc nfs
1942 109 The widow wc $75
110 At school wc $50
1943 93 Igloo entrance wc $50
94 The icebound shores of Hudson Bay wc $50
1947 138 The moss carriers wc nfs

MARSTON, J.B. American
1807, Boston B F Gr H TB
1885 161 Ducks $17
163 That pigeon $17

MARTIN, ANNIE D.
fl 1885-94 H
1885 26 Apple blossoms $25
43 Grape vine $25

MARTIN, BERNICE FENWICK (Mrs Langton Martin)
7 Jul 1912, Shelburne, Ont WWA56
1945 143 Down on the farm $150
1947 113 Spring sunshine $150
114 Repairs $100

MARTIN, EMMA MAY
3 Jan 1865, Toronto d 1956 CNS36 H M
Addr: 1887, Rosedale, Toronto; 1893, North Dr, Rosedale, Toronto; 1895, 28 Toronto St, Toronto; 1897-00, Toronto; 1910-13, 225 Cottingham St, Toronto
1887 101 Bananas and oranges $25
101a Canadian wild flowers $25
1888 96 Apple blossoms $10
230 In the woods wc $10
246 Spring flowers wc $7
255 By the lakeside wc $15
274 Among the birches wc $25
1889 163 The meadow path wc $30
1891 169 In Markham Township wc
183 By the lake, Muskoka wc
1892 97 Trading Lake wc $20
156 Late twilight wc $75 1893-228 F1-170
1895 54W Rosedale Creek wc
1897 20W Farm lane, Eglington wc
1898 177a Macdonald Falls wc
1900 158 A quiet nook wc
1910 134 Hudson Heights
1912 160 In the woods wc
1913 201 A mossy log wc

MARTIN, HENRY (HY)
c 1832, Painswick, Glos, Eng 20 May 1902, Toronto H
ARCA 1880 Painter
Addr: 1880-9, Hamilton; 1890-2, Toronto; 1893, 608 Church St, Toronto; 1894, Church & Isabella Sts, Toronto; 1896-00, 56 Gloucester St, Toronto; 1901-2, Toronto
1880 182 Ruins of Castle Connell, Ireland wc
200 Kilkenny Castle, Ireland wc
201 Glimpse of the cloisters, Muckross Abbey wc
224 Muckross Abbey, Ireland wc
1883 65 Bluebells, Fontainebleau $16
92 Moonlight peep at the Market Place, Verona $40
149 St Erasmus Chapel, Westminster Abbey wc $35
159 North ambulatory and chantry, Westminster Abbey wc $125
203 North cloister door, Westminster Abbey wc $35
213 Fontainebleau beeches wc $25
1884 83 Corner of a Highland field $75
140 Cottages at Barbizon, Forest of Fontainebleau wc $75
143 Bridge at the Moness River, Aberfeldy wc $75
1885 288 Tay Bridge, Aberfeldy wc
301 Burnham Common wc
314 Melrose Abbey wc
1887 136 On the Cornish coast wc $35
176 Otter Creek, Vermont wc $30
1888 2 Ready for a walk wc
69 Keene's Valley, Adirondacks wc $40
191 Cloisters, Chester Cathedral $60
219 Westminster Abbey, interior, south cloister door $100
242 A nook in the Adirondacks wc $30
296 Benmore, from River Dochart, Scotland wc $35
298 Niagara River, morning wc $20
1891 84 Grapes
124 Peonies wc
179 Prouts Neck, Maine wc
182 Cottage at Barbizon wc
1893 226 Lilies, New York Central Park wc $50
227 Westminster wc F1-169
1894 177 Killin Moor, near Loch Tay, Scotland wc
178 Toronto shipping wc
1895 55W Falls near Loch Tay wc 1896-234
56W Look across Arganout Club wc

57W The oriole wc
58W River Neckar, from Heidelberg Castle wc
1896 231 Shipping at East Boston wc
232 Boston harbour, from a port-hole of the Wabash wc
233 Freshwater Bay, Gloucester wc
235 Fish wharf, Gloucester wc
236 In Gloucester harbour wc
1898 176 Country bridge wc
177 Summer in Rosedale wc
1899 210 Dieppe Cathedral and market place wc
211 Market place, Como wc
212 Roman arches at Verona wc
213 Market place, Bologna wc
1900 172 A bit of the Maine coast wc
1901 178 Chester Cathedral from the choir wc
179 St Paul's Cathedral, from the Strand wc

MARTIN, IAN
1964N Ian Martin Associated Limited 138-9 Cantlie House Apartment Hotel, Montreal. Exterior view from northwest. Exterior entry view, Peel Street

MARTIN, JOHN
1 Aug 1904, Nuneaton, Eng 6 Nov 1965, Ayr, Ont CWW61 M WWA47
ARCA 1951 RCA 1965 Painter
Addr: 1952-3, Toronto; 1954, Sheffield, Ont; 1955-65, Ayr, Ont
1938 148 The boat yard, winter $250
149 October morn $200 T39-36
1940 107 A spring dawn $400
1941 122 March morning $150 T42-32
123 Millon's barn $150
1941 S9, Toronto
45 Homestead $100
1944 158 The hills beyond dry pt $10
1946 79 Zion $100 T47-35
1947 115 Willow $150
1948 111 Desolate temp $150
1950 91 Composition, 'Bass' 20 x 27 $150
1951 62 St George the Martyr $300
63 Xochimilco $200
1952 60 Royalty wc $200 1954-59 20 x 25
61 Greek things wc $200
1958 55 Bottle and pestle nfs
1959 59 Sleeping village 22 x 30 $300
1960 55 White cock at dawn 20 x 24 $200
1963 49 Grecian collage $400
1964N 35 Ancestor worship 26 x 30 $200 DW 1967 m med
1965 49 Equilibrium 20 x 24 illus $200
50 Grave of kings 20 x 24 $200

MARTIN, THOMAS MOWER
5 Oct 1838, Inner Temple, London
15 Mar 1934, Toronto AGO CC1 EC H M Mo98/12 NGC TB3 W78
RCA 1880 Ret 1918 Council Painter
Addr: 1880-2, Toronto; 1883, 28 Toronto St, Toronto; 1884-6, Toronto; 1887, Equity Chambers, Toronto; 1888-92, Toronto; 1893, North Dr, Rosedale, Toronto; 1894, Quebec Bank Bldg, Toronto; 1895, 28 Toronto St, Toronto; 1896-8, North Dr, Rosedale, Toronto; 1899-00, 110 Crescent Rd, Toronto; 1901, Park Rd, Toronto; 1902, Toronto; 1903, Victoria; 1904, Toronto; 1905-6, 225 Cottingham St, Toronto; 1907, London, Eng; 1908-18, 225 Cottingham St, Toronto; 1919-24, 115 Erskine Ave, Toronto; 1925-34, 135 Erskine Ave, Toronto
1880 4 Summer time 1881-237 Summer afternoon mistitle DW 1882 61 1/2 x 53
19 Cattle
40 Portrait of an artist
146 Lilac wc
147 Peonies wc
148 Ducks wc (W.S. Robinson)
149 Petunias and white peony wc
153 Muskoka Lake, near the mouth of the river wc
163 Cactus wc
168 Wharf, Ch.S, Toronto wc
194 Clay cliffs Lake Ontario wc
196 Castle Cliff, north shore, Lake Ontario wc
198 Bed of a stream wc
227 Toronto Water Works, evening wc
232 Scarborough Cliffs, north shore, Lake Ontario wc
1881 104 A tributary of Lake

Superior wc
112 Union Station, Toronto wc
138 Norton's Falls, Muskoka, Ontario wc
140 On Cushing's Island, Maine wc
141 Norton's Falls, upper chute wc
225 Duck on-board $35
241 Autumn on Hollow Lake, Muskoka $225
256 November day in Ontario $100
269 Pike $35
278 Looking for snipe $30
288 The gossips $60
302 The untrodden wilds $300
317 On the Sydenham River, Owen Sound, Ontario $30

1882 19 First touch of frost $30
52 Flat lands on the Restigouche River $100
66 The portage $300
72 The mouth of the Current River, Thunder Bay $175
75 On the coast of Nova Scotia
104 Shot on the run $400
114 Ripe and ready $50
160 On Beaver House Creek wc $100
172 The Wolf's Throat, Wilson's Falls, Muskoka wc $100

1883 11 Port Credit $40
12 Where the lilies grow $40
16 Margin of Muskoka River $75
19 Near Todmorden $50
22 When the snow has gone $50
41 Near Meaford $40
50 Among the water lilies $65
51 Muskoka harvest $200
53 Wet day in Muskoka $75
62 Shadow Pool, Muskoka River $50
80 Logging
85 Cattle $75 (the artist)
121 Morning in Muskoka $300
124 Sunset shadows $250
177 Gleams of sunshine wc $40
188 Rocks, Niagara wc $40
205 Afternoon in the meadow wc $75
245 Noon under the elms wc $100
254 Rapids, Niagara wc $75
259 A Muskoka road wc $75
266 A bit of Niagara wc $35

1884 18 In dry summer time $30
39 On Muskoka River $40 1885-38 $50
46 Late for school $25
49 Canoe Lake, Muskoka $75
66 Morning on the prairie $200 S1-153 $125
72 In the Laurentian Range $500
73 Not caught yet $100
75 In the back country $75
77 Waiting for the weather $25

1884 S1, Saint John
15 Elms near Toronto wc $55
63 Elms wc $75
80 The toilet $25
83 A quiet pool $15
86 Bound to have him $50
110 Misty morning $25
122 Beside the still waters $35
137 Misty morning, Georgian Bay $40
144 Muskoka River $40
145 Falls at Water Down $20
148 Staff of life $35
149 Massa home $15
150 A barn yard $100
162 Bridge near Ancaster etch $2.50
163 Elms etch $2.50
164 Muskoka River etch $2.50

1885 3 After the winter $20
5 In the stable $50
29 Redhead ducks $40 1886-34
34 When the summer is over $350
58 On the hillside $15
96 Homeward bound $25
98 An April day $150
113 A showery day $250
143 After the winter $20
169 On the coast of Long Island $25
171 By the Restigouche $65
206 Before the summer comes wc $100
219 Fairy Falls, Muskoka River wc $75
242 Central Park, New York wc $12
245 Near Halifax, NS wc $45
266 A spring study wc $15
269 Old bridge, Todmorden wc $40

1886 52 Old house at Ancaster wc $35

58 Back country road wc $40
74 Afterglow, Georgian Bay wc $40
1886 F1a, London, Eng
2019, artist number
Laughing eyes
Fog clearing off at low tide
Last rays
Bay of Fundy (L.R. O'Brien)
Rainy day, Saint John River
1887 9 On Muskoka River, below Bayville $40
12 Sunset on the marsh $40
43 Old house at Ancaster, Ont $30
76 Far from the haunts of men $300
110 The end of the farm $250
128a On the north shore, Cape Breton wc $100
128b Ring-tailed grouse wc $50
128e The last snarl wc $200
142 Entrance to the village of Ancaster wc $75
175 In Wentworth County wc $75
1888 5 Mount St Dennis, Summit Lake, Rocky Mountains wc $150
36 Martin's Peak, Kicking Horse Pass wc
111 Anthracite Mountain, from Banff $250
138 In the wild woods of Algoma $300
142 Castle Mountain, from the Bow River $250
177 Moonrise on the prairie, the old bull on guard $175
188 Any port in a storm $80
197 Indian summer near Huron Bay, Lake Superior $250
201 In the clearing $300
214 The scare $500
220 First flowers of spring $30
250 The last shard wc $150
271 Wild swan wc $75
292 Sunset on Muskoka Lake wc $50
307 Pigeons wc $50
1889 33 Summer afternoon $125
35 Waiting for spring
95 After the snow has gone $40
124 Canadian woodlands wc $125
160 At the back of the farm wc $40
176 Twilight etch $10
177 Untrodden forest etch $15
178 Settler's home, Muskoka etch $10
1890 58 Ah! There! $150 1893-102 $200 F1-79
59 Twilight in Rosedale $125
60 With the wind $150
61 Fruit $50
178 Cascade Mountain wc $150
179 Good for one meal wc $35
1891 101 On the shore, Lake Superior
104 Mount Field, from Kicking Horse Lake
105 Portage in Muskoka
106 Harvest time
109 Twilight
110 Within the city limits, 1890
112 At the end of winter
176 Sunset, Lake Simcoe wc
217 The wayside meal
1892 5a Putting out the dogs $150
24a Waiting $150
28 Disturbed $150
83 In charge $1,000
102 Evening in the Rocky Mountains wc $40
106 Smoky weather in the Rockies wc $40
1893 99 Summer $75
100 Evening after winter $150 F1-77
101 Ducks $50 F1-78
103 On guard $500 F1-80
1894 79 The flock at rest
80 Planning for the new barn
81 Toronto Bay and old stone wharf
82 The end of the clearing
83 Waiting for another shot
84 The wary woodcock
85 The path through the woods
86 A neglected corner
1895 83 In the beech woods 1897-92
84 Early morning in spring
85 A pack of cowards
86 The last of the winter
87 Harvest time
88 Road through the woods
59W A gray day in the fall wc
60W Sunlight wc
1896 113 The return of the raid
114 The taxidermist's workshop 1897-91

115 On the lookout
116 A blue bill duck
1897 93 A day in November
94 A pair of mallards 1899-100
21W In the back woods wc
1898 67 After a day's sport
68 Mallard and redhead ducks
174 Road through the woods, Rosedale wc
175 A pair of mallards wc
1899 98 Early morning, BC, pheasants feeding
99 English Bay at low tide illus
101 A pair of blue grouse
102 Shore of Stanley Park
1900 75 The Asulkan Glacier
76 Clouds resting on Burrard Inlet, Vancouver
77 Mount Baker, Victoria, BC
166 Early spring at Springfield on the Credit wc
167 Mountains at Laggan wc
168 Bala, the portage wc
1901 73 Mount Sir Donald
74 Among the beeches
75 Mallards
76 Canvas back ducks
180 Mallards wc F2-46
181 Blue-bill ducks wc F6-126 $40
1902 113 Indian life, Vancouver Island
114 Blackfoot Indian crossing glacial stream
1902 F3, Rochester
104 Court of Vancouver Island, near Victoria, BC $300
1903 84 Mount Temple and Pipestone River
180 Trees in Beacon Hill Park, BC wc
1904 239 On Georgian Bay wc
240 Near Sudbury wc F4-107
241 On British Columbia coast wc
1905 114 Home of the Canadian goose
1906 125 Coast, 20 miles north of Vancouver
1906 F5, Halifax
118 November $250
119 On a Scotch moor $100
1907 142 British Columbia coast
143 Mount Sir Donald
264 Sheep shed, south Devon wc
265 Sunset, Dartmoor wc
1907 F6, Sherbrooke
122 Rockies in BC $250
#123-4 not in catalog
125 Golden eagle $150
1908 103 The afternoon of a hot day
103a Winter in BC
1909M 83 Buffalo shedding their summer coat
84 Indian village, coast of British Columbia
85 A pair of mallards
1910 135 Still life
136 Wild hyacinths, Kew Gardens
1910 S2, Liverpool
76 Muskoka River
1911 121 The rest by the way
1912 161 Sunrise, early morning mist, Lake Louise wc
162 A red headed diver wc
1913 202 Early morning on the farm
203 Back from the farm S4-8 $150
204 On a northern river wc
205 A Canadian back country road wc
1914 135 Near Lake Simcoe wc
136 A road in the backwoods wc
1914 S5, Patriotic Fund
48 Waiting at the bais illus 'bais' mispr of bars 1920-173 1929-139 $125
1915 148 River in Eastern Townships
149 The ford
1916 157 A disappointed man
158 Near Ste Marguerite, Laurentians
1918A 116 September in the moose country wc
1919 113 Canadian grouse
114 A backwoods road wc
1920 172 October's restful tones
1921 104 North fork of the Kicking Horse River wc
1922 140 A bit of south Devon
1923 115 In Algonquin Park
1924 140 The wild garden at Kew
1925 150 Ruffed grouse at home
1927 143 A Canadian trout stream wc
144 Beautiful in their still repose wc
145 Sunset after rain wc
1928 107 From a Toronto garden $60
1929 140 Peonies $100
1930 113 Coast of British Columbia $100
114 Burnham beeches $125

1931 183 The last portage of the season $250
1932 131 Where the Fraser River comes from $275
1933 152 The spectators $200

MARTYN, CAROL E.
1916, Stratford, Ont
1966 41 Auto-analysis #1 56 x 40 $300
1968 37 Contravision series #4 72 x 72 $500
1970 46 Warp #1 60 x 84 $500

MARX, MAY (Mrs Karl Marx)
16 Jan 1928, Toronto IO M
1964N 78 Temple dancer sculp 34 x 16 x 10 illus $800
79 Torso sculp 15 x 16 1/2 x 16 $600

MASON, DENNIS R.
1970 223 Brochure cover, Rehabilitation Foundation for the Disabled: Report to the people of Ontario, 1967-68
224 Letterhead, Toronto Business Ministry

MASON, WILLIAM CLIFFORD
21 Apr 1929, Winnipeg WWA76
RCA(e) 1974 Film maker
Addr: 1979, Old Chelsea, Que

MASOURE, LEON E.
22 Dec 1918, Odessa, Russia
1938 S8, Toronto
167 Sanctuary window des, by OCA students, assisted by Rowley Murphy
1942 91 Russian icon wc nfs

MASSARI, SIDNEY
1947 213 Jeune canadien sculp nfs

MASSE, GEORGES SEVERE
10 Aug 1918, Montreal WWA56
1948 112 Twilight at Mount Levis, Quebec $250
1958 56 Boats & boathouses $200

MASSEY, GEOFFREY
29 Oct 1924, London, Eng
RCA(e) 1973 Architect
Addr: 1979, Vancouver
see also Erickson, Arthur, 1966, 1967

MASSEY, HART
30 Mar 1918, Toronto
ARCA 1967 RCA 1970 Council Architect
Addr: 1934, 87 Forest Hill Rd, Toronto; 1968-71, Ottawa; 1979, Port Hope, Ont
1934 149 Corn against white barn $10 T35-55 signed Clayton Norfield
1964N 140-4 House in Rockcliffe, Ont. Exterior view. Interior view. Facade detail. Floor plan 1 and 2
DW 1973 Sir John Carling Bldg, Central Experimental Farm, Ottawa photos in portfolio 17 x 56

MASSEY, PIXIE MUDGE
30 Apr 1944, Toronto
1965 88 Ballerina bronze 28h $300

MASSON, HENRI LEOPOLD
10 Jan 1907, Namur, Belgium AGO B CC2 M NGC TB2 WWA47
Addr: 1935-7, 351 Slater St, Ottawa
1935 178 Hull, Quebec $125 T36-50
1936 133 Hockey $75
134 Melting snow $125
1937 146 Ice harvest $75 T38-32
147 Log drivers $75
1938 150 Threshing $150 T39-37
1939 159 Snow clearing $150
1939 F11, New York
48 The ice house 26 x 30 $150
1940 108 Small town $85

MASTERS, NOREEN
1938 151 Cacti wc $50 T39-38

MATHER, JEAN
fl 1914-44
Addr: 1925, 85 Westgate, Winnipeg
1925 151 Lone pine wc

MATHERS, ALVAN SHERLOCK
16 Jul 1895, Aberfoyle, Ont 27 Jun 1965, York Mills, Ont CNS36 CWW63 NGC TB3
ARCA 1928 RCA 1937 Council Architect
Addr: 1929, Toronto; 1930-2, 96 Bloor St W, Toronto; 1933-65, Toronto
1930 174 Botany Building, University of Toronto. Perspective sketch
175 University Club of Toronto photo

1931 364 Entrance to a house photo
365 Battlewood house photo
1955 Mathers & Haldenby, to 1959
91 Bell Telephone Company, University Avenue, Toronto, office building model
92 National Library and Archives, Ottawa model illus
1957 101 Imperial Oil Building, Toronto illus
102 Sir Daniel Wilson Residence, University College, Toronto
1959 101 #10 St Mary Street, Toronto
DW 1938 Globe & Mail Building, Toronto wc drwg 17 x 24

MATHEWS, RICHARD GEORGE
16 Jul 1870, Montreal Mo12 TB2 WWB34
Addr: 1902, 25 Sussex Ave, Montreal; 1904-7, Montreal
1902 275 Mr Craigie pastel
276 Mr George Arliss pastel
277 Mrs Patrick Campbell, as the 'Notorious Mrs Ebbsmith' pastel
278 Mr George Arliss making up as the duke
1904 233 Mrs Langtry pastel
234 Mrs Forbes Robertson pastel
1907 144 Sardine fishing, St Andrews
294 Mr. J. Forbes Robertson pastel
295 Mr H.B. Irving pastel
1907 F6, Sherbrooke
120 Sardine fishers $125

MATHUR, FLORENCE
b 1934
Addr: 1976, Ancaster, Ont
1976 S12, Montreal
136 Institutional furniture/ Meubles pour instutions 2 illus

MATSUI, I. ROY
see DUNLOP, DANIEL, 1970

MATTAR, JOHN SOLOMON
22 Sep 1935, Haifa, Israel IO M
1966 42 Two figures 32 x 50 $200

MATTHEWS, MARMADUKE
29 Aug 1837, Barcheston, Eng 24 Sep 1913, Toronto AGO CC2 EC H M Mo98/12 NGC R2 TB3 W78
ARCA 1880 RCA 1883 Council Painter
Addr: 1880-2, Toronto;1883, 14 King St W, Toronto; 1884-92, Toronto; 1893-8, Bracondale, Ont; 1899-00, Toronto; 1902, c/o McKenzie & Co, Toronto; 1903-8, Bracondale, Ont; 1909-10, Wychwood Park, Toronto; 1911, 782 Davenport Rd, Toronto; 1912-13, Toronto
1880 159 The mountains, North Conway wc
170 Study in the Notch, shewing Mt Willard, NH wc
171 The cemetry dell wc
172 Study on the old Portland Road, NH wc
189 St Albans, Vermont wc 1881-18 $20
197 Pulpit Rocks, Crawford Notch, NH wc
202 Morning in the Crawford Notch, NH wc
203 The Crawford Notch, White Mountains, NH wc
204 Noon in the Crawford Notch, NH wc 1882-167 $100
1881 9 Sketch wc $15
20 Still life, sketch wc $15
68 Evening on the Summits, NH wc $75
74 Crawford Notch, NH wc $75
76 Summer day near North Conway, NH wc $20
96 In the Crawford Notch, NH wc $30
1882 171 Mount Washington, from the Ammonoosuc, near sundown, Fabyans wc $125
207 Crawford Notch, NH, sunset wc $75
1883 158 Mount Jefferson, NH wc $150 1884-104 S1-36
187 A wet day in the White Mountains, looking across Tuckerman's Ravine wc $200
DW 1883 26 1/2 x 49 View from Mount Washington mistitle
297 Happy days wc $15
1884 48 Mountain gloom, New Hampshire $100
126 On the Peabody, NH $110
127 Under the walls, Quebec wc $50
132 A land of streams wc $30
1884 S1, Saint John

42 Morning, looking towards Gorham wc $50
68 The Citadel, Quebec wc $20
77 On the White Mountains
1885 243 A study wc
322 Landscape wc $15
1887 37 Mount Washington from the Glen $200
64 Mount Carter $50
71 Dull day for a picnic $100
118 August afternoon wc $75
124 Failing pastures wc $75
151 Neglected corner wc $50
1888 12 Mounts Lefroy and Louise wc $50
16a Path to the glacier wc $50
17 Mount Sir Donald and glacier wc $100
25 National Park, Banff wc $50 F3-105 National Park Bank $40 'Bank' mispr
27 Mount Cheops from the glacier wc $100
31 Cascades, near summit, Rogers Pass wc $100
64 Mount Cheops wc $40
93 Earl's Peak $100
105 Mount Stephen, Kicking Horse Pass $30
126 Mount Louise $250
128 Mount Sir Dondald, in the Selkirks, early morning $500
200 The Blue Cut, in Kicking Horse Pass wc $250
233 Head waters, Kicking Horse Pass wc $50
264 Head waters of the Kicking Horse River wc $50
283 Sunrise on Hermit Range wc $200 (AGO)
291 Emerald Lake, near Laggan wc $65
1889 119 Evening on the Pipestone River, Rocky Mountains, near Laggan wc $50
137 A neglected corner in my garden wc $35
149 Apples and grapes wc $35 1891-131
161 Source of the Kicking Horse, near Hector, BC wc $35
1890 62 The Rundle Peaks, Banff $30
63 The Bow River from the bridge $40
180 Musing in the wood wc nfs
181 Rocks and ice contending, edge of glacier of the Selkirks wc $40
182 The glacial stream of the Illecillewaet wc $30
183 Looking down the Goat Pass from the foot of the glacier wc $150
184 The shadowed valley, from the glacier wc $50
185 Mount Sir Donald and part of the glacier wc $100
186 Path of the avalanche wc $30
187 Great tree, Stanley Park wc $30
1891 127 Rest at evening wc
128 Mount Macdonald wc
129 Old willow bed wc
130 Oaks in Wychwova Park
156 The crest of Canada wc
180 The Hermit Glacier wc
197 A Vancouver Island stream wc
1892 104 Old house at home wc $60
105 Old board fence wc $30
110 Asulkan Glacier wc $100
113 Kamloops, BC, in 1887 wc $150
129 Lake Louise, the gem of the Rockies wc $250
148 Cottage by the brook wc $50
153 Mount Stephen and Kicking Horse Lake wc $200
154 Bruin's Castle wc $75
160 Pleasant it was when woods were green wc $400
1893 104 Rogers Pass, Selkirk Mountains, from the Asulkan Glacier $500
105 Spuzzum Creek on the Fraser River $100
229 Indian salmon catch on the Fraser River wc $250
230 Lifting mists in the Kicking Horse Canyon wc $125
231 Mount Begbie at Revelstoke, BC wc $100
232 The Selkirks Glacier from the CPR wc $50
233 Rainy day at Field station, CPR wc $50
234 An Indian fishing trail, Fraser River $50
1894 78 The way home in the afternoon
1895 61W A saucy truant wc
62W A Muskoka rendezvous wc
63W Mount Washington from

the Glen wc
64W Under the oaks wc
65W Old saw pits in Oxfordshire wc
66W An old homestead at Dundas wc
67W Overlooking Marion Lake and Rogers Pass wc
1896 237 Evening in the gorge wc
238 Fishing path, bank of the Fraser wc
239 Looking down the road wc
1897 22W Rainy River, Fraser Canyon wc
23W Wychwood woodlands wc
24W Through the Otter Tails on the CPR wc
25W Head of the Illecillewaet, from Mount Abbott wc
26W Hector on the Kicking Horse Lake wc
1898 180 Forest glade wc
181 Mount Sir Donald wc
182 Going into the Otter Tail wc
183 Beeches wc
184 A group of maples wc
1899 214 A sunny Sunday
1901 184 In sunny summer time wc F2-47
185 Wychwood Pond wc
186 North branch Kicking Horse River wc F2-48
187 Part of the Otter Tail Range wc
188 Twilight at home wc
189 Mount Macdonald wc
190 A peaceful hour wc
1902 216 A cove in shadow wc
217 Looking over Parkdale wc
218 Overlooking the Fraser at Spuzzum wc
219 Just before the fall wc
220 Hazy in the canyon wc
1903 181 Near sundown in the Selkirks wc (#182 not in cat)
183 In the Bow River country wc
184 An early climb, Banff wc
1904 230 The rendezvous wc
231 Risky rapids wc
232 Out camp on the Pipestone wc F4-106
232a Canadian prairie after rain wc
1905 124 The land where it was always afternoon
125 Away down the stream
126 On the upper Don
127 Ross Park, Selkirks
128 Rapids on upper Kicking Horse
1906 F5, Halifax
120 Gorge in the Rockies $125 illus
1907 266 View from my window wc
1908 104 Evening light on the Asulkan Glacier
1909M 93 Cayuga limestone
94 Clouds on the plains
95 The last tunnel westward
1909N 95 The Pipestone River, smoky effect
96 A gleam in the forest
1910 137 Evening, Burleigh Falls
1911 122 A hazy pastoral
1912 S3, Winnipeg
112 Rogers Pass, Selkirks wc
113 Woodland wc
#112-13 entry Edmund Morris, mispr

MATTICE, HORTENSE see GORDON, HORTENSE

MATTICE, MARION EVE
b 1878 d 1956
Addr: 1905, Commercial C Building, Hamilton; 1908-9, Hamilton
1905 113 Sunlight and shadow
1908 96 In port
97 Sunshine and shadow
1909N 107 Bit of old Quebec
108 Quebec

MAW, KATHERINE BEATRICE (BETTY)
1910, Hull, Eng
Addr: 1931-6, 148 Glencairn Ave, Toronto
1931 411 Decorative panel temp $35
1932 132 The north road $75
1933 155 Gaspé fisherman $50
307 The chase mural dec $175
1936 135 Swedish peasant harvesting $75
136 Flower girls $75

MAW, SAMUEL HERBERT
12 Sep 1881, Needham Market, Eng
19 Aug 1952, Toronto AGO M PMC
Addr: 1918A, 200 Fairmount Ave, Ottawa; 1925-7, 274 Beaver Hall Hill, Montreal; 1931-5, 148 Glencairn Ave, Toronto
1918A 255 Sienna Cathedral, interior etch

256 New Sun Life Building, Montreal etch
257 Sirens etch
258 The Lagoon, Venice etch
1925 308 Bank of Montreal, Montreal etch
309 The dome of St James Cathedral etch
1926 191 Sherbrooke Street, Montreal etch
192 Rio del Carmine, Venice etch
1927 243 Rendering of the Royal Bank of Canada, Head Office, Montreal
312 Memorial Tower, Ottawa. For the Queen's doll house etch
313 The Royal Bank Building etch
1931 412 The Rock, Percé etch $15
1935 330 An Ontario farm etch $12.50
1941 241 A Canadian farm etch $12.50
242 The old grist mill etch $15
see also Turner, Philip, 1930

MAX, JOHN
23 Sep 1936, Montreal
RCA(e) 1974 Photographer
Addr: 1979, Montreal

MAXFIELD, JAMES E. American
1848, Detroit flg 1909 B H TB Y
Addr: 1883, Munich
1883 63 Early sorrow (T. Mower Martin)
1889 88 All about the 'lection $15
97 Juliet $30

MAXWELL, EDWARD
31 Dec 1867, Montreal 1923, Montreal Co Mo12 NGC
ARCA 1903 RCA 1908 Council Architect
Addr: 1902-7, Montreal; 1908-17, 6 Beaver Hall Sq, Montreal; 1918-20, 360 Beaver Hall Sq, Montreal; 1921-3, Montreal
1902 252 Country residence
1908 153 Saskatchewan Legislative and Executive Buildings, Regina 1909M-154 DW 1911 wc & temp drwg 19 1/2 x 29 1/2
154-5 Proposed Justice Building, Ottawa. Elevation, and perspective
1920 174 The moose country wc
see also Maxwell, Edward and William

MAXWELL, EDWARD and WILLIAM
1904 248 CPR Hotel and Station, Winnipeg
1907 327 Post office, stores, etc, Antilla, Cuba
328 Hotel at Antilla, Cuba
329 Residence, D. McNicoll, Esq, Westmount
330 Outbuilding, Hon L.J. Forget, Senneville
331 Interior, Church of the Messiah, Montreal
332 Residence, Mr David Walker, Montreal
333 Entrance gateway, Royal Victoria Hospital, Montreal
1910 219 Dominion Express Company, Montreal
220 New art gallery, Sherbrooke Street. Perspective. Plans
221 Parliament Building, Regina, main pediment des
1911 197 CPR Hotel, Calgary. W.S. Maxwell drwg
198 Office building des
1912 249 CPR Hotel, Calgary
1913 340 Montreal General Hospital
341 Cartier Memorial, Montreal S4-142 $200 nfs
1914 215 Justice and Departmental Buildings, Ottawa
216 Maxwelton Apartments, Montreal
1915 261 Departmental and court buildings, Ottawa des
262 Mr R.B. Angus, conservatory photos
263 Mr H. Vincent Meredith, residence photos
264 Mr W.S. Maxwell, residence photos
1916 262-3 Oratory in a Montreal residence, and detail photos 1918A-204-5
1918A 202 Altar candelabra, J.T. Davis, Esq, residence
203 Unitarian Church, Montreal, bronze memorial tablet
1918N 224 Altar candelabra photo
225 Palliser Hotel, CPR, Calgary photo

1920 281 New Chateau Frontenac, Quebec

MAXWELL, WILLIAM SUTHERLAND
11 Nov 1874, Montreal 25 Mar 1952, Montreal CNS36 Co CWW49 Mo12 NGC PMC TB3
ARCA 1909 RCA 1914 Sr 1943 Council Architect
Addr: 1907-13, Montreal; 1915-16, 6 Beaver Hall Sq, Montreal; 1917-26, Montreal; 1927-37, 1158 Beaver Hall Sq, Montreal; 1938-52, Montreal
1916 264 Chair des photo
1927 Maxwell & Pitts, to 1937
244-6 St Matthew Presbyterian Church, Wellington & Bourgeois Streets. Interior, 3 views photos
247 Conservatory, W.W. Skinner residence
1928 182 House, Robert Dodd, St Andrews, NB 1929-226
183 St Matthew Presbyterian Church, Montreal
184 Sun room, Dr W.W. Chipman, residence 1932-207
185 Drawing room, P.P. Cowan, Esq, residence
1929 227 Mashrak-El-Kazar, to be erected in Chicago des
228 and 229 Canadian Battlefields Memorial des
230-1 Residence, and dining-room, Sir Thomas Tait, St Andrews, NB photos
1930 176-7 Sir Thomas Tait, residence, St Andrews photos
178-9 Kanawaki Golf Club. Women's wing. Entrance posts photos
1931 366 Bedroom fireplace, showing modern treatment of gas grate photo
367 Bedroom photo
1932 205 Chimney piece in Montreal residence photo
206 Chimney piece with gas burning grate photo
1933 243-4 Sir Thomas Tait, estate, St Andrews. Residence, Group of farm buildings photos
245 Two family farm dwelling wc
1936 209 Ephraim Scott Memorial Church, Montreal
1937 251 A Canadian provençal house
1938 247 Maison canadienne-provençale, Laurentides
1938 S8, Toronto
19-20 Pair of fire dogs, and basket des by W.S. Maxwell, Paul Beau craftsman
1907 267 Beaupré wharf wc
268 Beaupré at ebb tide wc
1915 150 Beaupré wharf
1916 159 Street scene, Dinan, Brittany pastel
1931 184 The old shipyard, St Jean, Island of Orleans temp
185 The church at St Jean, Island of Orleans temp
186 Water Lot Inn, Bermuda temp
187 Little ship yard, Hamilton, Bermuda temp
1933 153 Harbour scene, Seal Cove, Grand Manan, NS wc $40 T34-53
154 Old courtyard, Seal Cove, Grand Manan, NS wc $30
DW 1915 Justice and Departmental Buildings, Ottawa des pen drwg 23 x 33 1/2 1914-215, Maxwell, E & W
see also Maxwell, Edward and William

MAY, HENRIETTA MABEL
1884, Westmount, Que 8 Oct 1971, Vancouver AGO CC1 M NGC TB2/3 WWA47
ARCA 1915 Sr 1954 Painter
Addr: 1910-35/37, 434 Elm Ave, Westmount, Que; 1936, c/o National Gallery of Canada; 1938-48, Westmount, Que; 1949-71, Vancouver
1910 138 Composition, sketch
139 Sketch
1913 206 Winter, Montreal S4-89 $75
207 Fishing boats
208 The market under the trees S4-90 $150 nfs purchased by National Gallery
209 Cloud effects S4-91 $150
1914 137 Watching the regatta ◊NGC◊
138 Street scene, Montreal ◊NGC◊
1914 S5, Patriotic Fund
33 Canal scene, Venice illus
1915 151 Knitting
152 Waiting for the picnic boat illus

1916 160 Low tide illus
161 Boats on the St Lawrence ≬NGC≬
162 After the bath
163 Winter 1918A-120
1918A 117 The ferry
118 In the bay
119 The canal
1918N 127 Windy day
128 Station scene illus
129 Harbour de Grâce
130 Sketch
1919 115 Snowy day illus
116 Landing, Peak's Island
1920 175 The pink balloon illus
176 Resting
177 The wharf
178 Landscape
1921 105 Early spring
106 In the Laurentians illus ≬NGC≬
107 Canal bank, late afternoon
1922 141 The sunlit valley S6-62
142 Train shunting
143 The winter glow
144 The creek
1923 116 Landscape
117 Early autumn wc
240 Early settlers on the banks of the St Lawrence. Mural decorative painting competition
1924 141 The road to the lake
142 Sunny September
1925 152 Ripening fields
153 The village ≬NGC≬
154 Early spring
1926 92 Winter landscape illus
93 Sail boats
94 Maples, autumn
1927 146 Melting snow 1928-108 $500
147 Autumn trees
148 The village, winter illus
149 The bridge
1928 109 Snow flakes $300 F9-144
1929 141 The bay $450
142 Autumn, Laurentian Mountains $450
143 Winter landscape $450
144 Summer $300
1929 S7, Calgary
106 Old house, Ile Perrot $350
107 Autumn $350
1931 188 Wenonah $300
189 The farm $350
189a Barns, winter $350
1932 133 The hillside farm $300
134 Ile Perrot, Quebec $350
1933 132 A Laurentian village $400 T35-46
133 Happy valley $350
1935 179 A village street $350 T36-51
180 The river road $250
1936 137 Winter sunshine $300
1937 148 The lake $300 T38-33
1938 152 Birch trees $300
1939 F11, New York
49 Old house by the road side 27 x 22 $200
1940 109 Mountain slope $300
1941 Travelling exhibit
35 Mountain side $300
1947 116 The farm $250 T48-27
1949 60 The blue cape $250 1950-92 27 x 22
1952 62 Head of a young girl $150 T53-20
63 Ripening fields $250

MAY, ISABEL
1913 #206-9 H. Mabel May. No entry Isabel. Addr list, Isabel, 434 Elm Ave, Westmount, H. Mabel May not listed

MAY, PERCY MORELAND
4 Apr 1886, Birkenhead, Eng CNS36
Addr: 1935, 5031 Grosvenor Ave, Montreal
1935 181 Mountain farm nfs T36-52
1941 124 Near St Hilarion $100 T42-33

MAY, WALTER WILLIAM English
1831-96, England B DBA DBW DVP G H TB
1881 37 A summer midnight Arctic scene wc (Sir Leopold McClintock)
55 The Franklin search, sledging over the ice, fair wind wc (Sir Leopold McClintock)

MAYEROVITCH, HARRY
16 Apr 1910, Montreal M
RCA(e) 1975 Architect
Addr: 1936, 1060 Bernard Ave, Outremont, Que; 1937, 2040 Union Ave, Montreal; 1979, Westmount, Que
1936 331 Phillips Square, Montreal etch $10
1937 323 Mr Maurice Frigon drwg nfs

1939 156 Mexican child duco $40
1941 125 Caricature of Fridolin $40
1954 97 Robbie 18 x 24 drwg nfs
1958 57 Robbie with yo-yo 40 x 40 nfs

MAYERS, ARLENE MARCY
Addr: 1976, Toronto
1976 S12, Montreal
147 Apricot ice is hot to wear woven dress/robe tissée illus

MAYHEW, ELZA EDITH LOVITT (Mrs C. Alan Mayhew)
19 Jan 1916, Victoria M WWA76
RCA(e) 1974 Council Sculptor
Addr: 1976/79, Victoria
1963 94 Cerebus sculp $500
1964J 76 Prisoners sculp 48h $850
1976 S12, Montreal
78 Old gate bronze 10 1/2 x 9 1/2 x 4 1/2 illus

MAYOR, ROBIN
9 Oct 1937, Louth, Lincs, Eng
RCA(e) 1978 Painter
Addr: 1979, Vancouver

MEADOWCROFT, JAMES CURZEY
29 Nov 1890, Montreal d Sep 1969 TB3
ARCA 1951 Sr 1964 Architect
Addr: 1952-69, Westmount, Que
1949 108-108a Shipshaw Power House. Exterior. Interior

MEADOWS, JAMES EDWIN English
1828-88, England B DBA G H TB
1881 228 Marine view (His Lordship, Bishop of Nova Scotia)

MEAGHER, GEORGE ALFRED
6 Dec 1867, Kingston, Ont H
Addr: 1900, c/o Montreal Art Gallery
1900 70 Gananoque by moonlight Meagre, mispr

MEARES, HERMINA (INA)
12 Oct 1921, Grays, Essex, Eng M
1959 60 The heart of the city 30 x 36 $150
1967 47 Ulysses 57 1/2 x 47 1/2 $600

MEISTER, PAUL ALFRED see ALFRED, PAUL

MELBYE, VILHELM Danish
14 May 1824, Helsingor, Denmark
6 Oct 1882, Roskilde, Denmark B G TB
1880 126 Off Gibraltar (Allan Gilmour)

MELCHIOR, NORMAN
M
1971 55G Booklet, En route, Air Canada

MELDRUM, AILEEN
1938 S8, Toronto
167 Sanctuary window des, by OCA students, assisted by Rowley Murphy

MELOIN, HATTIE see MELVIN, HATTIE G.

MELVIN, GRACE WILSON
c 1896, Glasgow 3 Mar 1977, Vancouver M TB2 WWA59 WWB34
Addr: 1932, 2925 W 43rd Ave, Vancouver
1932 250 The year illum on vellum $250
251 Adoration of the Magi, altar piece illum on vellum $250

MELVIN, HATTIE G.
H
1887 3 Study of shells $100
Meloin, mispr

MENDELL, CHARLES M.
Addr: 1913-15, 1131 St Urbain St, Montreal; 1918A, 60 Park Lafontaine, Montreal
1913 210 Le petit Hélène de Longpré S4-92 $175 Mendel mispr
211 Evening in Japan S4-93 $75
212 The old house by the brook
1915 153 and 154 Portrait, Mendel mispr
1918A 124 Portrait of the artist
1939 164 The gardener $150
1941 129 A farmer $500 T42-35

MENENDEZ, C. JAMES
see HARVOR, STIG, 1971
SCHOELER, JEAN, 1976

MENKES, RENE
see WEBB, PETER, 1964N

MENSES, JAN
28 Apr 1933, Rotterdam M WWA73
ARCA 1966 Council Painter
Addr: 1967-71/76/79, Montreal
1967 48 Kaddish series #24 32 x 24 illus $550
49 Kaddish series #18 32 x 24 $550
1970 50 Klippoth series #12-6 30 x 22 illus $900
51 Klippoth series #12-8 30 x 22 $900
1971 32 Klippoth series #6-12 30 x 22 $1,200
33 Klippoth series #6-18 30 x 22 $1,200
1976 S12, Montreal
36 Klippoth series cycle 6, #12 temp 30 x 22 illus
37 Klippoth series cycle 6, #6 temp 30 x 22 illus

MEREDITH, JOHN (b John Meredith Smith)
24 Jul 1933, Fergus, Ont AGO B CC2 IO M WWA73
RCA(e) 1974 Painter
Addr: 1979, Toronto

MEROLA, MARIO VIRGILIO
31 Mar 1931, Montreal CC1 M TB3
RCA(e) 1976 Designer
Addr: 1979, Ahuntsic, Que

MEROZ, JEAN
5 May 1911, Montreal M
1939 254 Beethoven buste bronze $1,200
255 St Jean Baptiste tête bronze $650
1946 140 Beethoven bronze illus $800

MERRICK, PAUL MCCARLEY
20 Nov 1938, North Vancouver
RCA(e) 1978 Architect
Addr: 1979, Vancouver

MERRILL, GRACE
1910, Toronto
Addr: 1928-32, 25 Wroxeter Ave, Toronto
1928 214 and 215 Illustration Merril, mispr
1932 137 Unfinished portrait

MERS, WALDYNE DE
1941 209 Portrait bust
1943 126 Victor E. de Mers sculp

METCALFE, E. BELLE
fl 1897-02 H
Addr: 1902, 153 Rupert St, Toronto
1902 115 Reverie

MEUX, GWENDOLYN American
WWA36
Addr: 1923, c/o Rev Peter Bruce, 2 Highview Cr, Toronto
1923 120 Red mounds, Oklahoma
121 Rancho de los Burros, Cantadores, NM

MICHAELSON, HUGH
1970 229 Cover, Probings
230 Book, Shadbolt: In search of form
231 Advertisements, Toronto Star
1971 56G Book, Horizons, Dept of University Affairs, Ontario Government
57G Invitation, Page & Steele

MICHALESKI, BERNARD R.J.
1970 232 Poster, Man of La Mancha
233 Poster, Galileo

MICHAUD, JEAN
see AFFLECK, RAYMOND, 1964J-1968

MICHENER, MEL P.
1964J Libling, Michener & Assoc
103-6 Grosvenor House Apartments. Entrance. Exterior. Site plan. Floor plan

MICKLE, ALFRED ERNEST
26 Feb 1869, Guelph, Ont Sep 1967, St Catharines, Ont CWW49 M NGC TB3
ARCA 1918 Sr 1938 Painter
Addr: 1905-6, 8 Rosedale Rd, Toronto; 1907, Toronto; 1908-9M, Torrance, n Glasgow; 1909N, Wareham, Dorset, Eng; 1910-12, 32 Adelaide St E, Toronto; 1913-15, 48 Heath St E, Toronto; 1916-25, 32 Adelaide St E, Toronto; 1927-36, 121 Walker St, Toronto; 1937-8, Toronto; 1939-45, Ottawa; 1946-67, St Catharines, Ont
1905 115 The moonbeam, misty rays
1906 134 A field of asters and goldenrod
135 A sweep of the river
1907 145 Far from town
1908 98 In old Dorsetshire

1909M 92 Harvest in England
1909N 98 The old church, Berkshire
99 Cottage, Bullington, Hampshire
1910 140 Bluebells, Dorset
1911 123 A field of poppies S4-94 $300 1913-213
1912 163 Old tower and mill, Swanage, Dorset
164 Near Grand Pré, NS
1913 214 In September, Hampshire
1914 143 Iris meadow, New Brunswick
144 Harvest, dyke lands of Grand Pré
1915 155 The meadows of Minas
156 Dyke lands of Grand Pré ◊NGC◊
1916 164 Meadow flowers
165 Sunflowers
1918A 125 Flowers, land of Evangeline
126 White flowers, White Cliffs, England
1918N 134 White flowers, White Cliffs, Dorset
1919 118 Flowers
1920 180 A riot of flowers, Rowencroft Gardens
181 Passing storm, dyke lands of Grand Pré
1921 110 Old stone crusher on the St Lawrence
111 Devil's paint brush, near Sherbrooke
1922 147 Flowery meadows S6-65
1923 122 Early autumn, Compton, Quebec
123 Church at Valcartier, Quebec
1924 147 A July day, Sutton, Quebec 1925-159
1925 160 Autumn, Eastern Townships, Quebec
1927 152 The village of Rock Island, Quebec 1928-112 $500
153 The mill, St Gabriel de Brandon, Quebec
1929 150 Fishermen's houses, Percé $300
151 Near the Green Mountains, Quebec $150
1930 115 Prospect Hill $500 1931-194
116 Harvest in the Eastern Townships $150
1931 195 The village of St Siméon, Quebec $500
1932 138 Devil's paint brush flowers, West Shefford $225
1933 162 Fishing boats, Bay des Chaleurs $500 T34-54
1935 186 Laurentian trout stream $500
1936 146 At Les Eboulements $500
1938 157 Dalhousie, NB, from the south $500

MIDDLETON, BERNARD
1 Oct 1909, Derbyshire, Eng M
Addr: 1937, 609 1st St W, Calgary
1937 151 Water front, Nanaimo nfs T38-35
1938 158 From the Banff School window $100 T39-39
159 The Sheep River Valley, Okotoks $125
1940 113 Evening, Banff-Jasper Highway wc nfs
1942 96 Gray day, Chilliwack valley illus $125 T43-28
1943 83 Rooming house, Edmonton wc $50
84 Alberta farm land wc $50

MIDDLETON, MARGARET
Addr: 1929-30, 56 Grenville St, Toronto
1929 152 Lobelia cardinalis wc $50
153 Hops wc $50
1930 117 Jack-in-the-pulpit berries wc $75

MIKUSKA, FRANK PETER
4 Oct 1930, Winnipeg M
1963 52 Autumn remnants $150

MILBURN, MARILYN
1930, Ottawa
Addr: 1976, Westmount, Que
1976 S12, Montreal
37 Sunset #10 ink on paper 24 x 36 illus

MILES, FREDERICK H.C.
1863-1918, Saint John H
Addr: 1884-95, Saint John
1884 S1, Saint John
84 Hay boats on the Saint John $15
134 Foggy morning off the Boar's Head $20 sold to Jas. Smith, RCA
140 River road $20 sold to F.M. Bell-Smith, ARCA
1885 12 Taking a tug off the

Beacon Light $20
56 Moonlight $20
1895 68W Bay shore wc
69W Moonlight, Saint John harbour wc

MILES, JOHN CHRISTOPHER
17 Mar 1837, Saint John 2 Dec 1911, Saint John EC H M Mo12 W78
ARCA 1880 Painter
Addr: 1880-94, Saint John; 1895, 68 Prince William St, Saint John; 1906-11, Saint John
1880 1 Study of pears (G. Ludlow Robinson)
2 Study of partridge (Mrs J. Farmer Lloyd)
75 View of Spoon Island, River Saint John, NB (John W. Nicholson)
81 Study of teal (Mrs J. Farmer Lloyd)
100 View of the Restigouche River
183 Indian camp, Metapedia River wc
1881 136 Coast view of Grand Manan wc $15
139 Split Rock, Bay of Fundy wc $25
144 Bay Shore, New Brunswick wc $15
234 Partridge $50
244 Malaga grapes $50
251 Ducks and partridges $100
277 Study of pears $50
298 A misty morning $100
1882 21 Quebec, sunset $350
100 Morning effect, River Saint John $75
106 Musquash marshes, NB $75
110 Swallow Light, Grand Manan $120
1883 79 Sport of the waves $100
1884 12 On the sands, Courtney Bay $100
88 Bay of Fundy cliffs, NB $350
1884 S1, Saint John
93 A brown study (W.P. Dole Esq)
117 Partridge Island, from the new pier $50
126 Bay of Fundy cliffs $250 (G.L. Robinson)
170 Pears (G.L. Robinson)
171 Pears (Mr Murphy)
173 Spirit of the times (S. L.T. Frost)
178 View of Saint John harbour (J.M. Grant)
185 Oysters (G.L. Robinson)
186 Landscape (R.P. Starr)
188 Afterglow (Mrs Peters)
208 On the English coast (L. Millidge)
1885 11 New Brunswick pasture $50
46 Bay of Fundy, Rodger's Head $75
68 Clearing off, Bay Shore, NB $75
89 A sketch of Gagetown $50
135 On the Bay shore, Saint John $75
188 Willow Brook $40
1886 40 Below the old fort, Jemseg River, Saint John $50
117 New Brunswick landscape $500
1886 Fla, London, Eng
2007, artist number
A New Brunswick landscape, Jemseg River, Saint John
Trout
Cherries
Partridges
1887 81 Afternoon, Saint John River $75
83 Dulse gatherers, Saint John harbour, NB $75
1890 64 A glimpse of the river $250
211 Megones, Baie Française pastel $35
212 The derelict pastel $40
213 Valley of the Kennebecasis pastel $45
1891 159 Hay boats, River Saint John wc
1892 1 The Beacon Light, Saint John harbour $75
1894 77 Light house, Saint John harbour
1895 81 Old French dykes, NS
82 Old French bridge, NS
1897 90 Landscape, a summer afternoon, New England
1903 85 A shady retreat 1907-146
174 Hay stack on the marsh, Gagetown, NB wc
1907 147 Coast view, Bay of Fundy
147a Tokay grapes

MILES, JOHN H.C.
Addr: 1887, Saint John
1887 98 Winter twilight $35

1891 50 Meadow Brook, NB
58 A misty morning
61 After the shower

MILLAIS, JOHN EVERETT (Sir) English
8 Jun 1829, Southampton, Eng 13 Aug 1896, London B DBA DBW DVP TB
1886 8 Rt Hon Marquis of Lorne, founder of the Academy, presented to the RCA by the artist. Presented by late Sir Jas. E. Millais, RA, error

MILLAR, ALEXANDER SAMUEL
30 Aug 1921, Toronto IO M NGC TB3
1953 58 The young girl $200
1954 60 Caminante de Mavab 24 x 36 $150
1957 45 Tamarack swamp illus $200
1959 62 Northern swamp 24 x 36 $200
1963 53 The thorn tree of Jonas 96 x 42 illus $1,000
1965 52 The wild goat 36 x 48 $400
1966 44 Evening, Newfoundland 72 x 48 illus $1,200

MILLAR, CHARLES BLAKEWAY
1 May 1935, Vancouver
ARCA 1972 Council Architect
Addr: 1976/79, Toronto
1970 37A-44A House, F.S. Eaton, Esq, Georgian Bay, Ont. Interior, living room. View from Bay, from west at water level. Exterior gallery. View from south. View from west. Interior, spiral stair. 2nd floor plan. Ground floor plan one illus
1976 S12, Montreal
103 Georgian Bay house, Georgian Bay, Ont 2 illus
104 Noodles Restaurant, Toronto col illus

MILLAR, CLARA LOUISE NEADS (Mrs T. Bonne Millar)
c 1888, Bowmanville, Ont M
Addr: 1934, 1506 W 13th Ave, Vancouver
1934 136 Flowers wc $25 T35-49

MILLARD, CHARLES STUART
22 Jun 1837, n Weston, Ont 1917, Cheltenham, Eng B H M NGC
RCA Hon Non-res 1881 Ret 1913
Painter
Addr: 1881-17, Cheltenham, Eng
1881 43 Stroan, Scotland wc $50 1882-142 $40
44 The Mumble's lighthouse wc 1882-136 $75
48 Loch Ken, Scotland wc
49 Oystermouth Castle, south Wales wc
66 Dolgelly Castle, north Wales wc 1882-151 $50
78 The Dochart, Scotland wc 1882-156 $20
79 La Cloche Mountains wc 1882-197 $20
90 Ben Nevis, Scotland wc 1882-133 $75
1882 188 A Welsh cornfield wc $75
1885 278 Among the hills, north Wales wc. Artist's gift to National Gallery. 1970 cat listed, in error, as DW 1880, Landscape wc 10 1/2 x 18 1/2
1886 Fla, London, Eng
2008, artist number
Waterfall, Dunkeld, Scotland (Princess Louise)
1888 21 Walna Scar wc $30
44 Cottage near Llanberis, north Wales wc $60
308 Coniston Falls, Cumberland wc $30
1913 215 Harlech Castle, Wales wc 1914-146 S4-95 $70
216 Hangman's Hill, England wc 1914-145 S4-96 $70
217 On the skirt of the forrest wc S4-97 $12
1914 147 On the Snowdon moor wc
148 Barnmouth Sands wc

MILLER (Miss)
1880 386 Pansies
1882 82 Water lily

MILLER, E. CHESEBRO
Addr: 1903, c/o McKenzie & Co, Toronto; 1904, Toronto
1903 78 An alien
79 Study of an old man 1904-111 F4-54

MILLER, HERBERT MCRAE
3 Nov 1895, Montreal CWW79 M NGC TB3 WWA47
ARCA 1943 RCA 1955 Sr 1966 Sculptor
Addr: 1931-2, 2048 McGill College Ave, Montreal; 1933, 3668 Durocher St, Montreal; 1944-60, Montreal;

1961-71/79, Ste Agathe des Monts, Que
1931 332 Elizabeth O'Toole sculp
333 Dr W.S. Phelps sculp
1932 216 M.S. Threlfall bust
217 Carmencita sculp
1933 266 Torso plaster $75
267 Head of a negress plaster $75
1939 256 Trilby sculp $65
257 Jeanne, portrait bust nfs
1940 162 Miss Margaret Yuen sculp nfs
1941 221 Carlotta sculp nfs
222 Miss Alma Duncan sculp 1942-171
1942 170 Peggy in the rain sculp $250 1943-135 $500
1944 150 Lieutenant sculp $500
151 Miss Phyllis Bronfman sculp nfs 1945-229
1945 230 Louise sculp illus $200
1946 141 Malinche sculp $300
142 Figure for fireplace niche sculp nfs
1947 214 Figure for wall niche sculp nfs
215 Juliette sculp $300
1948 172 Dulcie Henderson sculp nfs
1949 120 The shawl plaster $150
1951 123 Rossetti sculp $150
1955 111 Pacific Plante, Esq plaster $500 bronze $1,000
1957 80 Lumberjack plaster $500 bronze $800 1961-84 plaster 22 x 10 nfs
1959 89 Lieutenant sculp 18 x 18 nfs
DW 1956 October light bronze 19h

MILLER, JOHN MELVILLE
15 Jun 1875, Montreal 17 Sep 1948, Montreal M NGC PMC
ARCA 1911 RCA 1927 Sr 1944 Architect
Addr: 1911-14, Royal Insurance Bldg, Montreal; 1915-18, 2 Place d'Armes, Montreal; 1919-27, 364 Dorchester St W, Montreal; 1928-34, Montreal; 1935, 611 St James St, Montreal; 1936, 4749 Roslyn Ave, Montreal; 1937-48, Montreal
1911 199 Residence, Westmount
200 Commercial building, St Catherine St, Montreal
1914 217 Residence, Westmount, Que wc
218-19 Temple Emanu-el, Montreal. Exterior. Interior 2 photos
220 Entrance, residence, Montreal photo
1915 265 Residence, suburbs, Montreal
266 Landscape
1918N 226 Mechanics Institute Bldg
227 Country residence, Hudson Heights
1919 191 Residence, Montreal
192 Commercial building
1924 223 Shriners Hospital for Crippled Children, Montreal col crayon
224 Ark-Shaar Hashomayim Synagogue, Westmount photo
1926 155 Amusement centre
156 Apartment house
1927 248 Residence, Knowlton, Que
DW 1928 des wc drwg 17 1/2 x 25
1935 266 Gatehouse building oil nfs
267 Office building wc nfs
1936 210 Residence
211 Country residence
1939 277 and 268 Residence, Town of Mount Royal wc

MILLER, MAXWELL
28 Jul 1925, Tasmania
1967 126-8 Simpson-Sears premises, Kitchener, Ont. Bird's eye view of building. Exterior view. Exterior treatment

MILLET, FRANCIS DAVIS American
3 Nov 1846, Mattapoisett, Mass
15 Apr 1912, SS Titanic AAA28 B
DBA F TB Y
Addr: 1883, New York
1883 44 Turkish café $200

MILLET, JEAN FRANCOIS French
4 Oct 1814, Gruchy, n Greville, France 20 Jan 1875, Barbizon, France B TB
1882 322 A shepherdess, twilight (loan)

MILLS, GRAY HOYE
23 Feb 1929, Cleveland M
ARCA 1963-4 RCA(e) 1973 Sculptor
Addr: 1964, Mono Mills, Ont; 1979, Caledon East, Ont
1956 31 Floes illus $100 T56-24
1957 46 Big dead thing $200
1958 59 March '58 illus $200

1959 61 Mackinaw Bay 35 x 50 $300
1961 63 Huron shore 23 1/2 x 48 illus $200
1963 54 Composition black and gray $300
55 "X" 28 x 28 illus $300
1964J 46 Form in space stone, wood, oil 60 x 48 $500
1964N 38 Ascending form 60 x 48 $700
1970 87 Small green monument to Crazy Whitey sculp 24 x 48 x 48 $700

MILNE, BRUCE LANE
20 Jun 1910, Toronto M
1938 S8, Toronto
Pringle & Booth Limited
Bruce Milne, J.T. Harris
209 Photomontage decoration
210 Group of photographs
1940 114 Aunt Florrie nfs
1941 130 The book nfs
1942 97 Dorothy, Grace and Pet nfs
1944 100 George Hebden Corsan, man of nature $300
1947 124 Sitabai Dhundale nfs

MILNE, ROSE ELEANOR
14 May 1925, Saint John CWW79 M
1955 112 Christ with little children sculp $300
1956 51 Christ stilling the waters sculp $500
1961 85 Head of Christ bronze 30h (Col H.M. Dallaire, Montreal)

MILTON, NICK
1970 234 Symbol and application, Ontario Government participation Expo 70, Osaka
235 Book spreads, Canada at war
236 Poster, The National Ballet of Canada

MITCHELL & RAINE
1908 167b Baronial mansion

MITCHELL, HUTTON
1872-1939
Addr: 1929, Montreal
1929 S7, Calgary
111 St Jovite, Quebec $300
112 Fall in the Laurentians $125

MITCHELL, JAMES
Addr: 1907, Montreal
1907 269 York Minster, England wc

MITCHELL, JANET
24 Nov 1912, Medicine Hat, Alta
CC2 M NGC
RCA(e) 1977 Painter
Addr: 1979, Calgary

MITCHELL, MICHAEL EDWARD
3 Jan 1921, Toronto AGO
1950 100 Low tide 28 x 24 $400

MITCHELL, THOMAS WILBERFORCE
14 May 1879, Clarksburg, Ont 18 Dec 1958, Barrie, Ont CWW55 M NGC TB2/3 WWA47
ARCA 1926 Sr 1950 Painter
Addr: 1913-18A, 825 Gladstone Ave, Toronto; 1918N-21, 44 Stibbard Ave, Toronto; 1925-35, 192 Glencairn Ave, Toronto; 1936-41, Toronto; 1942-58, Barrie, Ont
1913 218 In the Beaver Valley S4-98 $25
1914 149 Nearly noon
1914 S5, Patriotic Fund
77 Mowing illus
1915 157 The hill country
1916 166 After a shower
167 The lumber yard
1918A 127 The kiln 1918N-135
1918N 136 The back yard, autumn
1921 112 A wet day wc
1925 161 The clay bank
162 Against the current
1926 100 Haney Lake
101 Hudson's Bay Point, Mattawa illus
1927 154 Road building in Haliburton
155 Astoria Pass
1929 154 Notre Dame du Lac $500
155 By the St Lawrence $400
1929 S7, Calgary
113 Jack Pine Portage $400
1930 118 Gray and gold $500
1931 196 Climbing $500
1932 139 Blossom time $160
140 Old orchard $160
1933 163 Portal Valley $600 T34-55
1935 187 The ironwood tree $400

MITCHELL, WINIFRED LAURA (Mrs George Mitchell)
1917, Fernie, BC M
1961 62 Carnival 16 x 20 $75

MOFFAT, DONALD ORMOND
11 Nov 1933, Hamilton

RCA(e) 1978 Architect
Addr: 1976/79 Toronto
1976 S12, Montreal
Moffat, Moffat & Kinoshita
105 Brock University, Physical Education and Recreation Centre, St Catharines, Ont 2 illus
see also Kinoshita, Gene, 1967

MOFFAT, ORMOND GEORGE
7 Apr 1903, Seaforth, Ont 19 May 1974, Hamilton
see MOFFAT, DONALD, 1976

MOFFAT, ROBERT REID
see SHORE, LEONARD 1958-1959, 1961-1971

MOFFATS LIMITED
Addr: 1938, Weston, Ont
1938 S8, Toronto
159 Electric range, table top model
160 Electric range, cabinet style
161 Electric refrigerator, porcelain enamel finish

MOIR, LILY MAITLAND
fl 1897-04 H
Addr: 1897, Ottawa; 1898-02, 479 Albert St, Ottawa; 1904, Ottawa
1897 95 Morning after the fire, Western Block
96 Roses
1898 70 Study of a head
71 Lilacs
1899 85 Roses
1902 116 Study of a head
1904 112 Study of a man's head

MOL, LEO (b Leonid Molodoshanin)
15 Jan 1915, Ukraine AGO M WWA73
ARCA 1966 Sculptor
Addr: 1967-71/79, Winnipeg
1955 113 Frederic Chopin sculp $50
114 Negro girl sculp $50
1957 81 Torso sculp $400
1958 91 Nude sculp illus $115
1959 90 Standing ter cot $125 1961-187 illus
91 Blessed Virgin with Christ sculp photo nfs
1960 84 Miss Frances Loring sculp $600
1961 86 V. Sifton sculp nfs
98 St John's College Chapel, University of Manitoba. Gable end sculp, H. Moody, architect illus
1963 95 Frederick Varley bronze $900
96 Lawrence Green, B.Arch FRAIC bronze $800
1964J 77 A.Y. Jackson bronze illus $900 ◊AGH LAG◊
78 Torso bronze $245
1964N 80 Dr Ferdinand Eckhardt sculp $900
81 Monument to T. Sherchenko, Washington, DC photo
1965 89 B.B. Dubienski, QC bronze illus $900
1966 83 A. Eastman bronze $1,200
84 Dreams bronze illus $425
1967 79 Mr Marius Barbeau sculp $1,000
1968 59 Helen sculp $1,200
60 Balance sculp $585
1970 88 Gisele sculp 19h $630

MOLINA, VALENTINO
Addr: 1915, Lennoxville, Que
1915 158 Children of the sun
159 Morning

MOLINARI, GUIDO
12 Oct 1933, Montreal AGO B CC2 M WWA70
ARCA 1964 RCA 1969 Council Painter
Addr: 1965-5, St Laurent, Que; 1967-71/79, Montreal
1964N 39 Rouge asymétrique 47 1/2 x 57 1/2 $900
1966 45 Mutation athématique rouge-vert 69 x 51 $1,500
1966 S10, Charlottetown
54 Mutation athématique vert-ochre $1,500
1970 52 Structure #1 91 x 115 $6,000
53 Structure #2 91 x 115 $6,000
1970 S11, Halifax
26 Seriel ocre-bleu. 1968 acry 78 x 90 $4,500
27 Seriel brun-vert. 1968 acry 45 x 68 $2,100
1971 35 Dyptique triangulaire 91 x 115 $14,000
DW 1969 Hommage à Borduas, 1963 50 x 40

MONETTE, G.A.
fl 1893-40
Addr: 1902, 97 St James St, Montreal
1902 253 St Leon's Church, Westmount. Front elevation

MONGRAIN, HENRI
1934, Trois Rivières, Que M
1964J 47 Apothéose pastel 31 1/2 x 36 $300

MONK, BENEDICTA
Addr: 1926, 48 The Boulevard, Montreal
1926 102 Gloucester, Mass wc

MONTALBA (Miss) English
1880 40c HE the Governor General bronze bust
320 Sketch of St George's Chapel, marriage of Duke of Connaught and Princess Louise Margaret of Prussia (loan)

MONTCASTLE, CLARA see MOUNTCASTLE, CLARA

MONTEFIORE, NANCY SEBAG (Mrs Montefiore)
1 Jul 1920, Montreal
1950 101 Driftwood 28 x 28 $100

MONTGOMERY, GLADYS ELEANOR
b Jarvis, Ont M
Addr: 1934, 17 Maynard Ave, Toronto
1934 137 Old house $100 T35-50

MONTIGNY, MARGUERITE see LAFONTAINE, MARGUERITE

MONTIZAMBERT, BEATRICE B.
24 Feb 1874, Quebec B M TB
Addr: 1931, 3680 St Urbain St, Montreal
1931 197 Harry, son of F.W. Ross, Esq, Quebec

MONTREAL ELECTROTYPERS & ENGRAVERS LIMITED
Addr: 1938, Montreal
1938 S8, Toronto
162 2 newspaper advertisements for Canadian Refactories Limited

MOODIE, CAMPBELLINE
Addr: 1934, 7 Clarey Ave, Ottawa
1934 138 Still life wc

MOODY, HERBERT HENRY GATENBY
12 Mar 1903, Winnipeg CWW64
ARCA 1958 RCA 1961 Architect
Addr: 1958-71, Winnipeg; 1979, Mahone Bay, NS
1961 Moody, Moore & Partners, to 1965
97-8 St John's College Chapel, University of Manitoba. Gable end sculpture, Leo Mol illus
1963 118 Hudson's Bay Company, retail store, Saskatoon. DW 1961 photo 12 1/2 x 16 1/4
1965 127-8 University College, University of Manitoba. Main entrance. General view
129-32 Athabaska Hall, University of Saskatchewan. Entrance. Model. Exterior. 1st floor plan

MOORE, ERNEST DARBY
1884, Oakville
Addr: 1912, Toronto
1912 S3, Winnipeg
212 Illustration b&w
213 Illustration col
214 Girl and geese poster col
215 Decorative illustration b&w

MOORE, ROBERT E.
8 Dec 1909, Winnipeg CWW58
see MOODY, HERBERT, 1961-1965

MOOREHEAD, CLAYTON
1971 111 Office scale. Student entry, 1971 Cominco design competition

MOPPETT, CARROLL MAY LINDOE (Mrs Ronald Benjamin Moppett)
b 1948 M
Addr: 1976, Calgary
1976 S12, Montreal
83 Placement m med 36 x 46 x 53 illus

MOPPETT, RONALD BENJAMIN
31 Dec 1945, Woking, Surrey, Eng M
1971 36 Landscape composition #8 63 x 60 3/4 $750

MORAN, J. THOMAS American
12 Jan 1837, Bolton, Lancs, Eng
26 Aug 1926, Santa Barbara, Cal B F Gr H TB
1886 F1a, London, Eng

2028, artist number
b&w drawings:
2 views, upper Kootenay Valley
Kootenay Lake
Kootenay Valley
Ranch on lower Kootenay River
Hunting camp in the upper Kootenay Valley

MORENCY, ANDRE
10 Sep 1910, Montreal CNS36 M
Addr: 1933-5, 1425 St Hubert St, Montreal; 1937, 3739 St Hubert St, Montreal
1933 164 Château de Ramezay $100
1935 188 Rivière du Nord, Mont Rolland $125
189 Rue Sous le Cap, Quebec wc $40
1937 152 Rocher Percé $250
153 Cap à l'Aigle, La Malbaie $150

MOREY, CHARLES T.
1927, Cummington, Mass M
1965 63 Canadian landscape, rocks 18 x 21 $75

MORGAN, MARY VERNON (Mrs Walter Jenks Morgan) English
fl 1880-30 DBA DVP G H WBA
Addr: 1881, Athol, NS
1881 273 Dead game $250
286 Water lilies $150

MORIN, JEAN
1970 237 Symbol and application, Loomloft Designs Limited
238 Symbol, Queen Elizabeth
239 Symbol and application, Architecture Concept
240 Symbol and application, Asbestos Eastern

MORIYAMA, RAYMOND
11 Oct 1929, Vancouver Co CWW79
ARCA 1970 Architect
Addr: 1971/79, Toronto

MORLAND, M. NORRIS
1938 S8, Toronto
Roden Bros Limited
237 Silver deposit water pitcher
238 Silver deposit vase
240 Silver deposit jug

MORRELL, CHARLOTTE see SCHREIBER, CHARLOTTE

MORRICE, JAMES WILSON
10 Aug 1865, Montreal 23 Jan 1924, Tunis AGO B CC2 EC H M Mo12 NGC R1 TB W78
RCA Hon Non-Res 1913 Painter
Addr: 1893-00, Montreal; 1901, c/o Scott & Son, Montreal; 1906-10, Paris; 1912, Paris, c/o Scott & Son, Montreal; 1914, 45 Quai des Grands Augustins, Paris; 1915-23, Paris
1888 226 Evening W.G. Morrice, mispr
306 On the Atlantic coast J.W. Morice mispr
1893 106 Entrance to Dieppe $125 F1-81
107 Early morning effect on the Conway, Wales $150 F1-82
1900 74 At Charenter, France, washing day
1901 87 The beach of St Malo F2-50
1906 F5, Halifax
123 The public gardens, Venice (E.B. Greenshields, Esq)
1907 149 Le Place Chateaubriand, St Malo
1910 141 Havre
142 Chrysanthemums
1912 165 Palazzo Doria, Venice
166 Venice, night ◊NGC◊
167 Dieppe
168 Mountain Hill, Quebec
1914 S5, Patriotic Fund
35 Dieppe illus
1953 Memorial section, biog by Robert W. Pilot, photo of artist
listed by lender
David R. Morrice
1 Moroccan landscape 29 x 21
2 Beach, West Indies 23 x 17
4 Fruit market, North Africa 23 x 19
8 Street scene, southern France 10 x 7
13 Card players, Spain 10 x 7
14 Riviera shore 13 x 9
Drawings, pencil
David R, and F. Eleanor Morrice
Sketches, 39, oil
Miss F. Eleanor Morrice
3 The blue umbrella 21 x 18
5 Autumn, Quai des Grands Augustins 18 x 15

9 Bois de Boulogne, Paris
10 x 7
10 Port at Dieppe 10 x 7
12 Grand Canal, Venice 10 x 7
15 Plage, St Malo 10 x 7
16 Doge's Palace, Venice
10 x 7
17 Beach, Parame 10 x 7
Mrs A.A. Morrice
6 Quebec Citadel by moonlight
21 x 15
7 Citadel, Quebec 25 x 19
11 Rialto Bridge, Venice
10 x 7
Mr. Bennett
18 Gibraltar 24 x 32
Mr Norman Dawes
19 Winter, Beauport, Quebec
Mr Sidney Dawes
20 The little wine shop, Quebec 19 x 23
21 Pallazzo Darrio, Venice
28 x 23
Mrs Allan Law
22 View towards Levis from Quebec 24 x 33
23 Waiting for the boat, Tangiers 23 1/2 x 29
Mr Lawrence Hart
24 Port of Algiers 22 x 28
25 From a window, Tangiers
18 x 24
26 Shipping, Algiers 22 x 28
27 Port of Algiers, study
12 x 17
28 Trinidad 15 x 18
29 Landscape, Algiers wc
10 x 12
Mr Murray Vaughan
30 Sail boats 15 x 18
31 Jamaica 21 x 28
32 The black goat 16 x 20
Mrs Howard Pillow
33 Plage
34 Bungalow in Trinidad
35 Concarneau
36 Morocco
37 Book stall on Seine
38 Nude
39 Moroccan girl
40 Turkish dancing girl
Robert W. Pilot
41 Horses, winter, Quebec
7 x 10
Montreal Museum of Fine Arts
42 Village street, West Indies 26 x 32
43 Quebec farm 32 x 24
44 Ste Anne de Beaupré
18 x 26
45 Circus at Santiago, Cuba
1954 13 Retro Sec. Market place, Concarneau (AGO)

MORRIS, CAROLYN L.
Addr: 1924-9, 514 Cooper St, Ottawa; 1931, 337 Somerset St W, Ottawa
1924 148 At even, when the sun was set wc
149 Softly the twilight steals o'er land and sea wc
1929 156 Bittersweet $40
1931 198 After the storm $40

MORRIS, EDMUND MONTAGUE
18 Dec 1871, Perth, Ont 21 Aug 1913, Portneuf, Que AGO CC1 M Mo12 NGC TB3 W78
ARCA 1898 Painter
Addr: 1897-8, 471 Jarvis St, Toronto; 1899-00, 32 Adelaide St E, Toronto; 1901, Yonge St Arcade, Toronto; 1902-6, 9 Toronto St, Toronto; 1907, Toronto; 1908-12, 43 Victoria St, Toronto
1897 99 Girl in a poppy field
(AGO same 1901-85)
100 Man in black
101 Dutch interior
1898 72 French Canadian interior
73 Woman and child
198 Children wc
199 Interior wc
1899 86 Landscape, Côte de Beaupré illus
87 At the docks, low tide
88 Evening, St Andrews
89 The edge of the downs, Holland
190 Evening, Holland wc
191 Evening, Ronan wc
192 Place du Carrousel, Paris wc
193 Street scene, York, England wc 1900-170
194 Sketch, Dutch interior wc
1900 78 Landscape, County Montmorency
79 A habitant home
169 St Fereol Falls, Que wc
171 Landscape, near Alknaar, Holland wc
1901 83 Between the showers
84 Autumn F3-131 $60
85 Poppy fields (B.E. Walker, Esq) F2-49 (AGO Gathering

poppies, Holland◊
1902 117 Côte de Beaupré
118 An old mill, France
119 A harvest field
120 Spring
221 The Seine, Paris wc
222 St Joachim wc 1903-186
1903 86 Scotch valley (Frederick Nicholls, Esq) 1905-120
87 Old Scottish mills
88 Côte de Beaupré (E.R. Wood)
89 Wheat field
1904 113 Cape Tourmente F4-55 ◊NGC◊
114 A Quebec landscape F4-56
115 The coast
116 The Laurentians F4-57
117 The old fort, Toronto
1905 119 Coast scene, lower St Lawrence
121 The Grand Battery, Quebec
122 Evening, Cap Tourmente
1906 126 Old British earth works, Quebec, storm effect
127 Wolfe's Cove, Quebec (O. R. Wilkie, Esq)
128 A rancher
129 Young sailors aboard the Snow Queen
129a Gaspé sailors
1906 F5, Halifax
124 Quebec $200
1907 148 The Pic River, Thunder Bay district
1907 F6, Sherbrooke
127 Citadel, Quebec $200 1908-100 1909N-102
128 French Canadian bateaux $30
129 A lone widow $30
1908 99 Cap Tourmente
101 A northern river
1909N 100 Cove fields, Quebec S2-78 S3-114
101 Evening, Beaupré
103 Landscape, Beauport, Que
1910 143 An old Cree Indian
144 A Salteaux, Thunder Bay
1910 S2, Liverpool
77 Little Shield, a Blackfoot Indian S3-116
79 Old Piegan Indian
1911 124 A faraway voice, Blackfoot Indian pastel
125 Chief of the Bloods pastel
126 A Blood Indian pastel (Ontario Government)
1912 169 Saskatchewan landscape
170 St Monace, Fifeshire
171 Cap Tourmente, Quebec
172 Railway camp, northern Ontario pastel
173 Galicians on strike, railway camp pastel
1912 S3, Winnipeg
115 Cree lodges, in the File Hills #114-16 M. Matthews, mispr

MORRIS, JENNY
1938 S8, Toronto
167 Sanctuary window des, by OCA students, assisted by Rowley Murphy

MORRIS, KATHLEEN MOIR
2 Dec 1893, Montreal CC2 CNS36 CWW79 M NGC TB2 WWA47
ARCA 1929 Sr 1963 Painter
Addr: 1916, 31 Lorne Ave, Montreal; 1918N, 778 Shuter St, Montreal; 1920-1, 35 Hampton Court Apts, Montreal; 1922, 15 Parkside Place, Côte des Neiges Rd, Montreal; 1923-8, 172 O'Connor St, Ottawa; 1929, 57 Athletic Ave, Montreal; 1930, 57 Mountain Slope Ave, Montreal; 1931, 3745 Mountain Slope Ave, Montreal; 1932-7, 3745 ave de l'Oratoire, Montreal; 1938-71/79, Montreal
1916 168 The barnyard
1918N 137 The clearing
1920 182 A snowy day
1921 113 Market day, Berthier
114 Old kitchen, Berthier
1922 148 A barn at Berthier, Que
149 Market scene, Berthier S6-65
1923 124 Market day, Ottawa
125 The fruit stall
1924 150 The market, Berthier
151 At the Hay Market, Ottawa
1925 163 Point Levis, Quebec ◊NGC◊
164 St Roch's Market, Quebec
1926 103 Nuns, Quebec
104 The fruit shop, Ottawa
1927 156 A village street
157 After grand Mass
1928 113 The fish market, Quebec $150
1929 157 St Stanislas Street, Quebec $140
158 Notre Dame des Victoires, Quebec $175
1930 119 Maison Montcalm, Quebec

$200 F11-50 30 x 24
120 St Joseph's Oratory, Montreal $150
1931 199 St Sauveur, Quebec $150 1932-141
200 A winter road $150
201 Street scene $150
1932 142 Sunday morning illus $150
143 Market square $150
144 Guy Street and Côtes des Neiges, Montreal $100
1933 165 A bit of old Quebec $90 T34-56
1934 139 Peanut man $50
1935 190 Quebec $150 T36-54 1936-148
191 An old timer $150
1936 147 House on the hill $100
1937 154 St Sauveur, Quebec $150
155 Belmont Street, Montreal $150
156 Window view, Beaver Hall Hill $150 T38-36
1938 160 St Sauveur $150
161 St James Cathedral $150
1939 165 Hôtel Dieu, Montreal $75
1940 115 Old Montreal $100 T41-37
1941 131 Old buildings, Quebec City $150 T42-36
132 Shawbridge, Quebec $150
1942 98 Old Buildings, Quebec City $125 T43-29
1943 85 A morning chat $100
1946 84 Morin Heights, Quebec $150 T47-37
1949 63 Mountain Hil, Quebec $175 T50-13
1950 102 Old house, Côte des Neiges 20 x 24 $150
1951 66 Old house, Berthierville, Quebec $100
1952 66 Recreation hour $75
1953 Travelling exhibit
22 Near Bordeaux, Que $150
1957 47 Old Hurtubise house, Westmount, Quebec $175
1958 60 Thrashing $150

MORRIS, LINCOLN GODFREY
10 Dec 1887, Newport, Monms, Eng M
Addr: 1922, 274 Union Ave, Montreal; 1938, Montreal
1922 268 Boat at anchor, Murray Bay pencil Lincoln E, mispr
1938 S8, Toronto
163 Fire dogs handwrought iron
164 Candle scone with repousé iron work, surrounding a 15th century Persian book cover
165 Fire screen, iron & brass with Chinese motif
166 Repousé copper panel, designed to use as model for casting. Used in making of electrical fixtures, Royal Bank of Canada, Vancouver
1944 149 Mountain path wc $75
150 Laurentian landscape wc $100
1947 125 Laurentian landscape $100

MORRIS, ROBERT SCHOFIELD
14 Nov 1898, Hamilton 5 Jun 1964, Ottawa CNS40 CWW61
ARCA 1954 RCA 1960 Architect
Addr: 1955-64, Toronto
DW 1961 Shell Building, Toronto photo 18 1/8 x 15 5/8
see also Marani, Ferdinand, 1937-1964

MORRISEY, DARRELL
fl 1916-28
Addr: 1922, 85 Church Hill Ave, Westmount, Que; 1923, 102 Chomedy St, Montreal; 1925, 581 Sherbrooke St W, Montreal; 1927, 872 Sherbrooke St W, Montreal
1922 150 A canal in Venice 1923-126
1925 165 Fishing boats at St Ives
1927 158 Children by the river
159 Street in Paris
314 Gondola stand, Venice drwg
315 Regie Poste, Venice drwg

MORRISON, ALAN S.
1941 133 Laurentian sunlight wc $100

MORRISON, IRENE ELAINE (Mrs Donald M. Morrison)
23 Feb 1906, Jefferson, Okla M
1964N 40 September 40 x 50 $250

MORRISON, OLIVIA (Mrs)
1949 121 Contemplation cer sculp $300

MORRISSEAU, NORVAL (COPPER THUNDERBIRD) CM
14 Mar 1931, Fort William, Ont AGO M
RCA(e) 1973 Painter
Addr: 1979, Beardmore, Ont

MORSE, SUSAN MARY (Mrs Charles Morse)
1862, Saint John d 1939 H M
Addr: 1913-22, 44 McLeod St, Ottawa
1913 219 Old cottage, Liverpool, NS
220 Low tide, Métis
221 On the beach, Métis S4-99 $25
1916 169 Blueweed
170 Cottage, Meach Lake, Que
1920 183 Chelsea Valley, Gatineau, Quebec
1922 151 Down in the flaming valley ways
152 Flowers

MORTIMER, ALEXANDER English
fl 1880-8 DBA H
1880 313 Lithography, specimens

MORTIMER, FLORENCE MAUD (Mrs Percival Barling Mortimer)
1 Dec 1879, Wakkerstroom, S Africa
8 Oct 1959, Edmonton M
Addr: 1937, 10011 103rd St, Edmonton
1937 157 David min nfs
1939 166 Grandfather wc nfs
167 Lesley Anne wc nfs

MORTON, DOUGLAS GIBB
26 Nov 1926, Winnipeg CWW79 IO M
ARCA 1968 Painter
Addr: 1969-70, Regina; 1971/79, Toronto

MORTON, EDITH see POWER, EDITH

MOSS, CHARLES EUGENE
10 Nov 1860, Pawnee City, Neb 25 Jan 1901, Ottawa H M NGC W78
ARCA 1897 RCA 1898 Council Painter
Addr: 1884, Ottawa; 1894, c/o Scott & Sons, Montreal; 1896, 19 Webster Pl, Orange, NJ; 1897-8, Ottawa; 1899-01, 445 Daly Ave, Ottawa
1884 36 Portrait
1884 S1, Saint John
78 Polly, the housemaid $20
1886 5 Portrait of a lady
20 Brigham's Creek $30
38 Cut Knife (Frank Newby)
174 Before you folks were born $450
179 Dawn of a truth (Achille Fréchette)
1887 28 The morning prayer $125
78 Gilmore's wharf, Ottawa River $30
1889 68 Spring $15
85 An old salt $50
100 The haymaker $15
1892 123 On the banks of the river wc $20
133 High and dry wc $20
155 The brook wc $15
1894 75 At Quebec
76 Bonsecours Market
179 At Lachine wc
1896 117 Jeannette 1897-102
240 Fireside reverie wc 1897-34W 1898-179 1901-193 F2-52
241 Hillside barn at St Remi wc
242 In profile wc
1897 103 Noontide
35W The sheep flock wc
1898 74 The goose girl DW 1898 The gooseherd mistitle 33 1/2 x 43 T51-30
75 Melodies of the forest 1901-86 F2-51
76 Wm. Kingsford, LLD FRS
178 Vieux habitant wc
1899 91 An auld licht illus 1900-72
199 At Banff, NWT wc
200 A habitant wc
201 In the music room wc
203 Brunette wc #202 not in cat
1900 71 With the flag
73 Sir Sandford Fleming, Chancellor, Queen's University
162 Montreal harbour wc 1902-121
163 Mending the net wc
164 Unloading a schooner at low tide wc
165 A veteran wc
1901 deceased. J. Wilson & Co, 123 Sparks St, Ottawa
191 Sunshine and shadow wc
192 Jeanette wc
194 Chelsea Brook wc
195 Harvest field wc
196 English highway wc
197 English homestead, by lily pond wc
1902 Moss estate, 445 Daly Ave, Ottawa
223 The lily pond wc
224 Street in Chester wc
225 Evening wc
1903 deceased
90 Return of the fishers

MOULDING, PETER
1970 241 Book jacket, A.W. Purdy: Wild grape vine

MOUNT, RITA
7 Feb 1885, or 1888, Montreal 22 Jan 1967, Montreal CWW64 M NGC TB3 WWA47
ARCA 1939 Sr 1955 Painter
Addr: 1910-27, 416 Dorchester St E, Montreal; 1928-37, 832 Dorchester St E, Montreal; 1938-67, Montreal
1910 145 Le petit hameau
1913 222 Autumn
1915 160 Le métier
161 Mademoiselle Marie
1916 171 On the mountain
172 The red barn
1918N 138 A street in Banff
139 Lake Louise
1919 119 Gray day, Carleton
1920 184 Cartelin, Baie des Chaleurs
1922 153 Murray Bay River S6-66
1925 166 September, Les Eboulements
167 Salt meadows, Les Eboulements
1926 105 Just arriving
106 The hay cart
1927 160 Sunny day, Port Daniel
161 Le Pont Rouge, Port Daniel
1928 114 Evening calm, Gaspé coast $400
1929 159 Fishing boats, Gaspé coast $300
160 In the harbour, Gaspé coast $125
1929 S7, Calgary
114 Splitting codfish $125
115 Village, Port Daniel $150
1930 121 Sunset at Newport, Gaspé $125
1931 202 Anchored, Gaspé $225
1933 166 Cap Bon Ami, Gaspé $250 1934-57
167 North wind, Petit Cap, Gaspé $150
1934 140 Petite Rivière aux Renards $350 T35-51
1935 192 Late afternoon, Barachois $125
193 Fishing boats, Anse à Beaufils $250 T36-55
1936 149 Late afternoon, Glace Bay $200 T37-49
1937 158 Lake Louise $150
159 Fishing boats, Glace Bay, Cape Breton $300 T38-37
1938 162 Splitting codfish, Gaspé $200 T39-40
163 Sister ships $150
1939 168 Late afternoon, Percé $300
169 Grey day, Gaspé coast $150
1939 F11, New York
51 Village scene, Gaspé 22 x 19 $200
1940 116 Old cabs, Montreal $200
1941 134 Bonsecours Market $250 T42-37
1943 86 Harbour scene, Glace Bay $250
1945 151 Fishing boats, Glace Bay $200
152 Village, Cloridorme $125 T46-33
1946 85 Grande Rivière, Gaspé $150
1947 126 Newport harbour $225 T48-28
127 Beach scene $175
1949 64 Ause Chapados, Gaspé $200

MOUNTCASTLE, CLARA H.
b Clinton, Ont fl 1868-98 H Mo98
1888 237 Spoils of the table wc Montcastle, mispr

MOYER, STANLEY GORDON
22 Dec 1887, Mildmay, Ont M
Addr: 1924, Dominion Bank, Yonge & Cottingham Sts, Toronto; 1925-31, 1178 Yonge St, Toronto
1924 279 Miss Jocelyn Taylor sanguine
280 Roy Mitchell, Esq sanguine
1925 168 Miss Florence Mieville
310 Norman F. Read sanguine
1926 193 Miss Erie Harvey sanguine
1927 162 Mme Lugrin-Fahey
163 Marguerita
316 Miss Violet Audras charcl
1930 122 Old Dutch woman $150
1931 203 Portrait of a man $1,000
1940 117 Self portrait nfs

MUELEN, EMIEL see VAN DER MUELEN, EMIEL

MUELLER, ERNST see MULLER, ERNST

MUHLSTOCK, LOUIS
23 Apr 1904, Narajow, Poland AGO CC1 M NGC WWA47
Addr: 1925, 1171 St Dominique St,

Montreal; 1927-34, 3997 St Dominique St, Montreal; 1935-7, 3414 Ste Famille St, Montreal
1925 311 Study of an old lady charcl
1927 317 S. Muhlstock drwg
318 1st pilot, Q & O charcl
1931 204 Vue sur le Parc Monsouris, Paris $200
205 Boulevard Jourdan, Paris $100
414 Czechoslovakian woman charcl $50
415 Sketch charcl $50
1932 252 Frustration charcl $50
253 Mrs Ida Massey charcl $35
1933 308 Indian girl drwg $50
309 Indian woman of Caughnawaga drwg $50
1934 220 European youth charcl $100
1935 332 Young east-side girl charcl $50
333 Nude charcl $50
1936 150 Ste Famille Street, Montreal $75
151 Back yard $75
1937 160 M. Isaac Levine nfs 1938-164 T39-41
1950 103 Eva, spring. 1947 36 x 30 $400
104 Trees, rocks and moss, Isola. 1947 30 x 26 $350

MULLER, ERNEST (Ernst Mueller)
fl 1876-96 H
Addr: 1896, 45 Church St, Montreal
1896 118 Still life

MULLIGAN, C.W.
ARCA 1880-5 Architect
Addr: 1880-5, Hamilton

MUNN, ADELAIDE
Addr: 1936, 2096 Northcliffe Ave, Montreal
1936 152 The Lake of Two Mountains $100
1938 165 Rock garden $125
1944 101 Jungle flower $140 T45-31

MUNN, KATHLEEN JEAN
28 Aug 1887, Toronto ACO M
Addr: 1909M-11, 800 Yonge St, Toronto; 1913-23, 320 Spadina Rd, Toronto
1909M 90 Girl's head
91 Portrait
1909N 104 The forge
105 Three souls with but a single thought
1910 146 The stilly night
1911 127 A bank on the sea shore
128 The sun sprites
1913 223 A Spanish dancer S4-100 $200
224 Study
1914 150 Old age
151 A woodland dream
1915 162 The unknown
163 An interior
1916 173 Arrangement
174 Evening glow
1919 209 and 210 Drawing
1923 127 The dance

MUNRO, JEAN ELIZABETH COCKBURN (Mrs Gordon Munro)
1869, Orillia, Ont d 1945 CNS36 M
Addr: 1919, 100 Walmer Rd, Toronto; 1921, 31 bis rue Campagne Premiére, Paris; 1926, 100 Walmer Rd, Toronto; 1927-37, 222 Redfern Ave, Westmount, Que
1919 120 St Jean-du-Doigt, Finistère
121 Spring morning in old Paris, Boulevard Edgar Quinet
1921 115 Vimy qui renait
116 Rèverie illus
1926 107 Bay of Douranenez, Brittany
1927 64 Revery
1929 161 The road to the sea, Percé, Quebec $250 1930-123
1929 S7, Calgary
116 Farm by the sea, Percé $180
117 The Ramparts, twilight, Quebec $60
118 Sunday on the beach, Percé $250
1930 124 Winter landscape, Quebec $250 1931-206 $200
1931 207 Canal and Marble Bridge, Venice $200
1932 145 Village on a tidal river, Quebec $250
146 Spring time, lower Montreal $250
1933 168 Chicoutimi Basin, Quebec $250 T34-58
1934 141 Winter in the city of Westmount $200 T35-52
1936 153 Nova Scotian fishing village $150

1937 161 Early morning, south shore, Nova Scotia $175 T38-38

MUNRO, L.
Addr: 1895, 10 Main St, Hamilton, Ont
1895 51A Westminster Abbey

MUNRO, SARAH JEAN see MACLEAN, SARAH JEAN

MUNTZ, B.W. (Miss)
Addr: 1918, 600 Sherbourne St, Toronto; 1919, 221 Lonsdale Rd, Toronto
1918A 197 Portrait of a boy plaster 1918N-216
198 Tony plaster
1918N 215 La silencieuse plaster
1919 186 Fidgets plaster

MUNTZ, LAURA ADELINE (Mrs C.W.B. Lyall)
18 Jun 1860, Radford, Warwicks, Eng
9 Dec 1930, Toronto AGO B CC1 H M Mo12 NGC TB3 W78
ARCA 1895 Painter
Addr: 1893-8, Paris; 1899-00, 16 Rusholme Rd, Toronto; 1901-5, Yonge St Arcade, Toronto; 1906-12, 6 Beaver Hall Sq, Montreal; 1913, 4205 Dorchester St W, Westmount, Que; 1914, 310 Grosvenor Ave, Westmount, Que; 1915, Toronto; 1916-19, 24 Bernard Ave, Toronto; 1920, Toronto; 1921, 221 Lonsdale Rd, Toronto; 1922, Torontoo; 1923-8, 24 Bernard Ave, Toronto; 1929-30, Toronto
1893 108 A fairy tale $500 F1-83
1898 185 The gleaner wc
186 Violets wc
187 The brass kettle wc
1899 94 The widower and his daughter
95 Mother and child
96 On the river, Holland
97 Lullaby
215 At the ferry wc
216 In the doorway wc
1900 81 Child, with roses
82 Eventide
83 Feeding the goat
84 By the river
152 The handmaiden wc
1901 77 Music from the reeds
78 Girl knitting F2-53
79 Waiting for the boats
182 The lullaby wc F2-54
183 A little maiden wc
1902 122 The little scribe 1904-120 F4-58
123 Inspiration
124 The hyacinth
125 The Japanese fan
126 The worker
226 Daily bread wc
227 A daughter of Eve wc
228 Innocence wc
1902 F3, Rochester
132 The spirit of the pines illus $600
1903 80 My neighbour's child 1904-119
81 April comes
82 Sissy in the wood
83 The dark ladye
173 The little red head wc
1904 118 Mother and daughter
235 The Angel, from 'The reaper of the flowers' wc F4-108 F6-131 $300 nfs
236 Mother and babe wc F4-109
237 The dream wc F4-110
238 An elf wc F4-111
1905 123 Forbidden fruit
1906 136 The passing dream F5-125 $250
137 A study
138 Mother and child F6-132 $150 1909M-81
139 A young girl
140 The lullaby
1906 F5, Halifax
126 Study of a child $150
127 The first daffodil $150
1907 F6, Sherbrooke
130 The pansy boy $150
133 A little girl $150
1909M 79 The ghost story 1909N-106 S2-80 S3-117
80 In the woods
1910 147 A daffodil (NGC)
148 Child with cherries
1912 S3, Winnipeg
118 Study
119 Lady in black
120 In the woods wc
121 Girl in white wc
1913 225 Portrait of a child S4-101 $250
226 Madonna with angels S4-102 $300 nfs. Purchased by National Gallery
227 Madonna with bird
228 Meditation
1914 S5, Patriotic Fund
55 Girl with seagulls illus
1916 Lyall, to 1929
145 Madonna and children

146 Madonna and child
1918A 109 Iris illus
110 Rebekah
1919 105 Maternity illus
1921 98 A sea anemone
1923 109 Mother and child
110 A young girl wc
1925 144 The enchanted pool
1926 87 Cathie and her cat
88 A madonna illus S7-101 $550
1927 132 A lullaby
1928 103 Summer time $550
1929 S7, Calgary
100 Portrait of a child $300

MURPHY, CECIL see BULLER, CECIL

MURPHY, J. HERBERT
Addr: 1937, 356 St Antoine St, Westmount, Que
1937 289 Whistling boy sculp nfs
1938 240 Laughing boy sculp nfs
1939 258 Master Robert Bell sculp nfs

MURPHY, ROWLEY WALTER
28 May 1891, Toronto 4 Feb 1975, Toronto AGO CWW64 M NGC WWA47
ARCA 1941 RCA 1974 Sr 1962 Council
Painter
Addr: 1930, 172 Simcoe St, Toronto; 1934-5, 118 Lakeshore Ave, Ward's Island, Toronto; 1936-7, c/o Ontario College of Art; 1942-71, Toronto
1930 125 Old and new Toronto wc $200
1934 142 Freighters laid up wc $150 T35-53
1935 194 In Reilly's Bay $200 T36-56
195 Docks in winter $200
1936 154 North shore, lower St Lawrence $200
155 HM schooner Nancy, 1789-1814 wc $150
1937 162 Cape Hopewell $200
1938 166 On the beach, Huntsport wc $150
1938 S8, Toronto
167 Sanctuary window des, by OCA students, assisted by Rowley Murphy. Margaret Park, Leon Masoure, Suzanne Schwartz, Jenny Morris, Aileen Meldrum, Helen Chisholm, Victoria Barber, Jean McLeod
1939 170 Island landscape $150
171 Coal dock wc $100
1940 118 Dry dock in wartime $200 T41-38
1941 135 On deck, Canadian destroyer, 1940 wc $200
136 Dry dock $100 T42-38
1941 S9, Toronto
46 Dutch tramp $15
1942 99 Convoy in rough weather illus $150 T43-30
100 Searchlights, eastern Canadian port $150 1943-88 $250
101 Minesweeper and Fairmiles, night wc $100
1943 Lieut R. Murphy, RCNVR
87 HMCS Moose Jaw ramming U 501 $300
142 The Fairmile officers off watch drwg $100
143 HMCS Ottawa refitting before being torpedoed drwg $100 T44-39
1944 102 Ship breakers, Huntsport wc $150
159 Young Canadian seaman charcl $100
1945 153 Canadian destroyer in heavy weather $300
154 The dockyard car, Esquimalt $300 T46-34
155 Camouflage composition $200 1952-67 $150 T53-23
1946 86 Abandoned wc $100
87 Winter, Lake Superior $100 T47-38
1947 128 HMS Mary Rose fitting out wc $100
129 Waterside house $150 T48-29
1950 105 Below Brooklyn Bridge 36 x 34 $150
1951 134 Unloading a Hurricane at Halifax Dockyard drwg $100
1953 59 Church at Sydney, Cape Breton wc $125
1954 61 Water Street, Halifax wc 18 1/2 x 26 1/2 $150
1956 32 South Water Street, Halifax $200
1957 48 Docks in winter $150
1958 61 Dockyard composition $500
1959 63 The anchor winch 24 1/2 x 31 $300
1960 58 Wreckage of HM topsail schooner Tecumseth, Penetanguishene 18 x 21 1/2 $200
DW 1974 Schooner Marie Stewart refitting at Yarmouth,

Nova Scotia. 1939 36 x 39 1/2

MURRAY, GRETA P.
Addr: 1913, 20 McTavish St, Montreal
1913 368 A grey day pastel

MURRAY, JAMES ALBERT
2 Jul 1919
ARCA 1968 Architect
Addr: 1969-71/79, Toronto
1964N Murray & Fliess
145-7 Eastdale Vocational School. General view, exterior. Interior view with stairs. Model

MURRAY, ROBERT DONALD
1970 242 Cover, University of Waterloo telephone directory
1971 57G and 58G Poster, University of Waterloo

MURRAY, ROBERT GRAY
2 Mar 1936, Vancouver AGO B CC1 IO M
RCA(e) 1973 Sculptor
Addr: 1979, New York

MUSGROVE, ALEXANDER JOHNSTON (ALEC)
22 Nov 1882, Edinburgh 31 Jan 1952, Winnipeg CC2 M
Addr: 1923-4, 409 Nokomis Bldg, Winnipeg; 1927-37, 310 Assiniboine Ave, Winnipeg
1923 128 Near the lake shore wc
1924 152 The blue jar
153 Near the city
281 Sketch crayon
1927 165 An interior
1929 162 Road makers $400
163 Fish houses, Snake Island wc $50
1931 208 Old houses, Winnipeg wc $100
1933 169 The man with the bananas $375
1937 163 Fish houses, Lake Manitoba $100 T38-39
1939 172 Fishing haven, north Manitoba $250
173 The green sweater $250
1940 119 The wayside vendors $600 T41-39
120 The farm by the river $350
1945 247 Head of a woman pencil $25

MYERS, BARTON
6 Nov 1934, Norfolk, Va Co
RCA(e) 1976 Architect
Addr: 1979, Toronto

MYERS, JOSEPH
Addr: 1933, 6173 Durocher St, Outremont, Que
1933 170 Genevieve pastel $50

MYLES, BEATRICE see BANTING, BEATRICE

MYRAN, FREDA
1939 298 Mallards linocut
299 Tufted drakes linocut

N

NAIRN, RONALD F.
see KERR, K.E. ROBERT, 1971

NAKAMURA, KAZUO
13 Oct 1926, Vancouver CC2 CWW79 M NGC TB3 WWA59
1953 60 After snowfall $100
1964J 48 Conic structures 50 x 40 $925
1964N 41 Inner structure 48 x 37 $775
42 Square infinity 50 x 40 $925

NANTON, J.R.
H
1895 71W Bay of Gravan wc

NEDDEAU, DONALD FREDERICK PRICE
28 Jan 1913, Toronto CWW79 M WWA56
RCA(e) 1976 Painter
Addr: 1936, 80 Lawton Blvd, Toronto; 1979, Toronto
1936 156 Willow grove $75
1948 116 Civic holiday, Oshweken $200
1950 106 Boys fishing 25 x 29 1/2 $200
1951 67 The sea #2 $300
1953 61 L'Eglise de l'Immaculée Conception, du paroisse de l'Enfant Jesus $200
1954 62 Death in the afternoon 28 x 34 $350
1955 60 Bait nets $200
61 Waiting village, east coast $200
1956 33 L'Anse, Ainimé, Gaspé $125 T56-25
1957 49 Bridge at Barachois $150

50 Quiescent quay $200
1959 64 Pour la pêche 22 x 27 $200

NEIL, FRANCES BARBARA
9 Nov 1909, Wolverhampton, Eng
1949 65 Herring boats $200
1950 107 St George 24 x 30 $200
1951 68 By the pepper tree $100

NEILSON, HENRY IVAN
27 Jun 1865, Cap Rouge, Que 26 Apr 1931, Quebec AGO H M Mo12 NGC PMC TB3
ARCA 1915 Painter
Addr: 1906, 634 St Catherine St, Montreal; 1911-12, Valcartier, Que; 1913, 286 Major St, Toronto; 1914-18, Cap Rouge, Que; 1919, c/o McKenzie & Co, 86 King St W, Toronto; 1920-1, Cap Rouge, Que; 1922-23, Ste Geneviève Ave, Quebec; 1924-7, Quebec; 1928-9, 260 Grand Allée, Quebec; 1930-1, Quebec
1906 141 Herring market, east coast, Scotland
142 Shrimpers, St Monan's, Fife, Scotland
143 When the kye comes hame
1906 F5, Halifax
131 The bonnie Muirland $125
132 Where gushing floods roar over the Lynn $125
1911 129 An autumn morning
130 Lakeside pastures
131 Where gushing floods roar
1912 174 The end of the portage, Lake Helen
175 Quebec sunrise wc
274 Schooners, Quebec harbour etch
275 Sous le Cap Street, Quebec etch
1913 229 An evening reverie S4-103 $250
230 Where ocean breakers kiss the silver sands
369 Deepening of the St Charles River, Quebec etch S4-156 ǂAGOǂ
370 The old wood bridge, Rivière-au-Pin, Quebec etch S4-157 $20
1914 152 An October evening
153 A September day
1914 S5, Patriotic Fund
5 An October day illus
1915 164 Dawn, Grand Lac Hélène, northern Quebec
165 An October pastoral, Cap Rouge, Quebec illus ǂNGCǂ
1916 175 An October day, Cap Rouge River
176 Seal Islands, lower St Lawrence
177 Automne, Rivière du Cap Rouge
178 Le chemin de St Augustin
303 Le Calvaire de St Augustin etch
304 The centre span, Quebec Bridge etch
1918A 128 Spring's garland ǂNGCǂ
129 Autumn's woodlands
130 Dawn
259 Old mill, St Nicholas, Quebec etch
260 Ice carters, Cap Rouge etch
1918N 142 Golden autumn
1919 122 An October day, Cap Rouge Valley, Quebec
123 The ice bridge, St Charles River, Quebec wc
124 The Basilica, winter evening, Quebec wc
211 Quebec from south, Levis etch
212 Sardine fishermen etch
213 Basse-ville, Crane Island etch
214 Ecureuil village, Quebec etch
1920 185 The guardian of the north, Cap Brûlé 1921-119
186 A June woodland
187 A summer breeze
188 A souvenir of Scotland
328 The old blacksmith shop etch
329 Quebec from the east etch
1921 210 Dufferin Terrace, from Bishop Laval Rampart, Quebec etch
1922 269 Dufferin Terrace, from Bishop's Gardens, Quebec etch S6-120
270 Louise Basin, Quebec etch S6-121
1923 129 Cap Brûlé, Côte Nord wc
130 Cap Trinité, Saguenay wc
218 The farm yard etch
219 Old saw mill, Petite Rivière etch
1928 216 Wayside chapel, St Pierre, Ile d'Orléans, Que etch $70
217 Prescott Gate, Quebec etch $80

218 Old church, Tadousac etch $100
219 Les Ecureuils, Que etch $70

NELSON, JAMES
1831, Belfast d 1913 Mo12
ARCA 1880-09 Architect
Addr: 1880-09, Montreal

NELSON, MARION HOPE (Mrs Frank W. Hooker)
27 Mar 1866, Richmond, Va 29 May 1946, St Catharines, Ont AGO H
Addr: 1903-4, St Catharines, Ont; 1905-6, 5 Race St, St Catharines, Ont; 1909N-14, Selkirk, Man
1903 93 Market scene at Crécy en Baie
94 At Bettws-y-Coed, north Wales
1904 121 Portrait
122 The blacksmith F4-59
123 An orchard
1905 131 The brook
1906 F5, Halifax
Hooker, to 1914
133 Beth and her pets $100
1909N 70 The village smithy
1912 S3, Winnipeg
249 Royal Mail from Norway House
250 Old fire place
1914 S4, Winnipeg
173 The village smith $85
174 Evening in Holland $25

NESBITT, JOHN
7 Oct 1928, Montreal M
ARCA 1966-74 Sculptor
Addr: 1967-8, Montreal; 1969-71, New York
1964J 79 P. sculp 68h illus $1,200
1964N 82 Two verticals sculp 26h $325

NEUMANN, ERNST
27 May 1907, Budapest 1955, Venice M TB3
Addr: 1927, 757 Bloomfield Ave, Outremont, Que; 1931, 2015 Decarie Blvd, Montreal; 1933, 1070 Bleury St, Montreal; 1935, 1178 Phillips Pl, Montreal; 1936-7, 1215 Greene Ave, Westmount, Que
1927 319 The demolition of St Andrews litho Newman mispr
320 The new bridge, Montreal litho
1931 416 Rabbi J. Stern drwg Newman mispr
417 Unemployed litho $12
1933 310 Unemployed #4 litho $12
311 Unemployed #5 litho $12
1935 290 Head of a girl plaster nfs
334 Street scene litho $12 1936-246 $10
1936 245 Seated nude etch $10
1937 324 Self portrait drwg nfs
1939 174 Harry Shane, Esq nfs
300 Hon Chief Justice Greenshields litho
1941 137 Artist and model, portrait of Goodridge Roberts $1,500
138 M. Dickstein, Esq nfs
1943 89 The Martello Tower $150 T44-30

NEWCOMBE, WILLIAM JOHN BERTRAM
18 Jul 1907, Victoria Aug 1969, London, Eng M TB3 WWA53
1938 167 Oil refinery $250
1947 130 Sitting women and the wall $350 T48-30
1949 66 Summer time $300 T50-14
1950 108 Albertan mood 12 x 30 $150
1953 62 Root synthesis wc $125

NEWFELD, FRANK (b Neufeld)
1 May 1928, Brno, Czechoslovakia CWW79 M
ARCA 1971 Council Designer
Addr: 1979, Scarborough, Ont
1970 243 Catalogue, Picasso
244 Book, This rock within the sea

NEWLANDS, A.F.
Addr: 1914, 29 1st Ave, Ottawa
1914 230 Pippa passes illum
231 Arrowhead illum

NEWMAN, JOHN BEATTY
6 Apr 1933, Toronto IO M WWA76
RCA(e) 1973 Painter
Addr: 1979, Toronto

NEWMAN, SHEILA
1965 54 On flight coll 25 x 20 1/4 nfs

NEWTON, ALISON HOUSTON LOCKERBIE (Mrs Stanley Newton)
23 Jan 1890, Leith, Scot 1967, Toronto M
1941 139 House on Hargrave Street wc $50

NEWTON, FRANCIS American
30 Jun 1873, Lake George, NY 27 Sep 1944, East Hampton, NY AAA29 B TB WWA36
Addr: 1936, Fulling Mill Farm, LI, NY
1936 157 In the Painted Desert, Arizona #2 $600
158 Japanese grapes $700

NEWTON, LILIAS TORRANCE (Mrs Francis G. Newton)
3 Nov 1896, Montreal 10 Jan 1980, Cowansville, Que AGO CC1 CNS36 CWW61 EC M NGC TB2 WWA47
ARCA 1923 RCA 1938 Sr 1967 Council
Painter
Addr: 1916-18, Lachine, Que; 1920, 616 St Joseph St, Lachine, Que; 1921-3, 32 Lincoln Ave, Montreal; 1924, 119 St Matthew St, Montreal; 1927-9, 20 de Casson Rd, Westmount, Que; 1930, 43 Trafalgar Ave, Montreal; 1932, 4100 Côte des Neiges Rd, Montreal; 1933-5, University Tower Bldg, 660 St Catherine St W, Montreal; 1937, 522 Pine Ave W, Montreal; 1938-71, Montreal
1916 Torrance, to 1920
224 Girl in blue
225 Portrait sketch
317 Sketch charcl
1918A 165 Head of a child
166 The red scarf
1920 246 Portrait
1921 117 The little sisters ◊NGC◊
118 Marcelle, portrait 1922-154 illus S6-67
1922 155 Denise
1923 220 The refugees drwg
221 Nude drwg
1924 154 Rev Francis G. Newton
155 Stewart Torrance, Esq
1927 166 Dr C.S. Fosberry, LLD FRCO, Head Master, Lower Canada College
167 Mrs John Savage illus
168 Mrs Arthur Kittson
1929 164 Winkie, portrait 1930-127
1929 S7, Calgary
119 Mme Lily Valty $500
1930 126 Mrs W.J. Northgrave
1932 147 André Illiashenko illus $400
1933 171 Robert Mackay, Esq $250
172 Fanya T34-59 $250
1934 143 Frad, portrait
144 Still life, lilies and roses
221 Edwin Holgate drwg
1935 196 Hon Vincent Massey nfs
197 Mrs Vincent Massey nfs
1937 164 Dr H.M. Tory (Research Council, Ottawa)
165 Mrs A.H.S. Gilson nfs
1939 F11, New York
52 Louis Muhlstock 24 x 25 1/4 DW 1940 T51-31 1954 Retro Sec 45
1940 121 T.F.M. Newton illus nfs T41-40
1941 140 Rev F.H.E. Cosgrave, DD LLD, Prov, Trinity College, Toronto illus nfs
1942 102 W/C W.R. MacBrien, RCAF nfs T43-31
1944 103 Mrs Walter Gordon nfs
1946 88 Margaret Morrison nfs
89 Dr Charles Camsell, CMG FRRC nfs
1947 131 W.M. Birks, Esq, CBE LLD illus nfs
132 Lt Col W.H. Clarke Kennedy, VC CMG DSO ED nfs
1949 67 Gen, the Hon A.G.L. McNaughton nfs
1950 109 Dr N.A.M. Mackenzie 50 x 50 illus nfs ◊University of British Columbia◊
110 Margaret Andrew 25 x 20 nfs
1951 69 Hon W. Ross Macdonald, KC, Speaker, House of Commons nfs
1952 68 FM, Rt Hon, the Earl Alexander of Tunis, KG illus
1953 Travelling exhibit
24 Derek and Hildy $500
1954 63 Dr R.W. Wallace, FRSC CMG 50 x 60 nfs
64 Justice Martineau 24 x 30 illus nfs
1956 34 A.E. Grauer, Esq illus nfs
1957 51 HM Queen Elizabeth II illus nfs
52 HRH Prince Philip, Duke of Edinburgh illus nfs
1958 62 HRH Prince Philip, Duke of Edinburgh, study for portrait illus nfs
63 Victor Drury, Esq nfs

NEWTON, W. PARKER
fl 1885-93 H
1885 4 Near Pawtucket, RI $30
84 Browley Brook, Maine $30
136 Homeward bound $40

1888 92 Landscape $30
135 Solitude $20
163 Toronto, from Kew Beach $50
166 Meadow road $20

NEWTON, WILLIAM
1970 245 Booklet cover, Educational planning: papers of the International Conference, March 20-2 1967
246 Booklet cover, Women returning to the labour force: 1st report Women's Careers Centre
247 Book, Living and learning
1971 59G Magazine, Task, Ontario Dept of Labour
60G Annual report 1969, Metropolitan s. s. Board
61G Poster, folder, Bauhaus. Society of Graphic Designers of Canada
62G Report, Task force, Dept of National Health & Welfare

NEYLAND, HARRY A. American
1877, Erie, Pa d 1958 B TB
Addr: 1909M, Hamilton, Ont
1909M 96 Breakfast time

NICHOLS, JACK
16 Mar 1921, Montreal AGO B CC2 CWW64 M TB3 WWA47
ARCA 1951 Council Painter
Addr: 1952-71/79, Toronto
1951 70 Mother with children on paper illus nfs
1955 62 Encounter at dusk illus $500
1965 55 Clown and assistant litho 19 x 26 $100 S10-55
56 Spectator litho 16 1/8 x 25 1/2 $100 S10-56
1966 46 Perruque litho 25 1/4 x 19 1/4 $110
47 Winged presence litho 21 x 27 1/4 $110

NICOL, PEGI (MARGARET KATHLEEN NICHOL) (Mrs Norman MacLeod)
17 Jan 1904, Listowel, Ont 12 Feb 1949, New York AGO CC1 M NGC TB2 WWA47
Addr: 1926-7, 356 2nd Ave, Ottawa; 1931, 1201 Dorchester St W, Montreal; 1932, 356 2nd Ave, Ottawa
1926 108 Portrait in the evening Pegi Nichol ◊NGC◊
109 Paugan Creek
1927 169 Nancy Twoyoungmen, Stoney Indian girl
170 Alice Garbutt
1931 209 Spears of iris $100
1932 148 Ice and snow $150

NICOLET
1938 S8, Toronto
Nicolet & Southam Press
348 3 folders, CPR
349 Calendar illustration

NICOLET, FRANK LUCIEN
b 1887
Addr: 1932-4, YMCA, 1441 Drummond St, Montreal
1932 149 Northern lights at Labelle, Quebec wc $250
1934 145 Last leaves wc $150

NICOLETTI, RODOLFO (RUDI)
10 May 1914, Toronto M
1944 104 Nebula $150

NICOLL, JAMES MCLAREN
1892, Fort Macleod, Alta M
1938 168 Self portrait nfs
1939 175 Uncle Arch nfs
1948 117 Marion nfs

NICOLL, MARION FLORENCE S. MACKAY (Mrs James McLaren Nicoll)
11 Apr 1909, Calgary CC1 M
RCA(e) 1976 Painter
Addr: 1979, Calgary
port: by James M. Nicoll, 1948-117

NIVERVILLE, LOUIS DE
7 Jun 1933, Andover, Eng CC1 Co IO M TB3
RCA(e) 1973 Painter
Addr: 1979, Toronto

NOBBS, PERCY ERSKINE LLD
11 Aug 1875, Haddington, Scot 1963, Montreal CWW61 Mo12 NGC PMC TB3 WWC21
ARCA 1909 RCA 1920 Sr 1955 Council Architect
Addr: 1904-7, Montreal; 1908-10, McGill University, Montreal; 1911-18, 49 Beaver Hall Hill, Montreal; 1919-25, Phillips Sq, Montreal; 1926-30, Montreal; 1931-7, 38 Belvedere Rd, Westmount, Que, res,

1240 Phillips Sq, Montreal, office;
1938-63, Montreal
1904 285 Design for decoration of Byzantine church
286 Clock Tower at Vernoa
287 Set of stair newels photo
1907 334 Christ Church Cathedral, proposed general decoration
1908 159 McDonald Engineering Bldg, McGill University
160 McGill University Union, built 1906
1909M 155 House, Belvedere Rd, Westmount
156 Proposed front to old Medical Bldg, McGill University
1910 222 Proposed building, Art Association of Montreal competitive des
1911 201 New Birks Bldg, Montreal
1912 250 House, Dr Todd, Senneville, Quebec
251 The University Club, Montreal
1920 282 Proposed Saskatchewan War Memorial. Hall of Honour drwg
283 Memorial window, University Club drwg
284 Memorial window, Medical Bldg, McGill University drwg
1921 185 Garden in Westmount des
186 War memorial chapel, Sherbrooke des
187 6 minor war memorials photos
1922 237 Residence gatehouse, Westmount
238 New buildings, McGill Stadium
239 Proposed war memorial, Regina, interior S6-114
1931 210 The dining room wc $110
211 In a garden wc $90
212 In Labrador, after rain wc $130
1934 146 West Indian harbour wc $120 T35-54
147 From Brimstone Hill, St Kitts wc $150
148 Carribean clouds wc $120
1935 335 The Royal Arms dec panel
1938 S8, Toronto
380 Wallpaper design. Hon mention, Canadian Wallpaper Manufacturers Limited
Nobbs & Hyde, to 1939
1913 342 Macdonald Park, McGill University S4-143 $500 nfs
343 University of Alberta, river front S4-144 $20
344 House, near Montreal
1919 193 War Memorial Museum, Regina plaster model
194 Proposed Students' Residence, Macdonald Park
1925 247 Monument to the missing
248 Proposed development, Belvedere Terrace, Westmount
1933 245a-b Proposed hotel, Antigua, BWI
1937 252 Proposed Rood Cross, Christ Church Cathedral
253 Altar, Church of the Visitation, Château Richer
254 Reconstruction of Hawthornden, Georgeville, Que
255 Stencils, nave roof, Christ Church Cathedral
1939 279 St Paul's Church, Gaspé col drwg nfs
280-1 Erskine and American United Church. Pulpit and choir. Antependium, embroidery
DW 1932 New wing, Royal Victoria Hospital, Montreal des temp drwg 19 1/2 x 27

NOBLE, HAROLD B.
1948 118 Fall sketch $100
119 Landscape sketch $100

NOEL, JEAN GUY
1971 Zeuzere de Zegouzie film screened 14 Apr

NOICE, YVONNE
1938 S8, Toronto
380 Wallpaper design. Hon mention, Canadian Wallpaper Manufacturers Limited

NOLIN, ALICE
Addr: 1922-4, 266 Sherbrooke St E, Montreal; 1931, 860 Sherbrooke St E, Montreal
1922 227 Tête de femme plaster
1924 234 Betty sculp
1931 334 Mlle Jacqueline D. bust $200

NOORDHOEK, HARRY CECIL
10 Feb 1909, Moers, Germany M
ARCA 1968 Sculptor
Addr: 1969-71, Dorval, Que; 1979,

Carrara, Italy

NORFIELD, CLAYTON see MASSEY, HART

NORGATE, ROBERT MAXWELL
18 Jun 1920, Toronto 24 Sep 1956, Toronto M
1948 173 Steel worker lead $200

NORMAN, A.
H
1880 124 Romsdalfiord, Norway (Allan Gilmour)

NORMANDEAU, PIERRE AIME
5 Nov 1906, Outremont, Que 3 Nov 1965, Montreal M
1939 259 M Jules Bazin ter cot nfs
1946 143 L'indifférente ter cot nfs

NORRIS, GEORGE ALEXANDER
Dec 1928, Victoria M
RCA(e) 1974-8 Sculptor

NORRIS, LEONARD MATHESON
1 Dec 1913, London, Eng M WWA78
RCA(e) 1974 Illustrator
Addr: 1979, Vancouver

NORWELL, GRAHAM NOBLE
11 Dec 1901, Edinburgh 20 Jun 1967, Val David, Que AGO M NGC TB2
Addr: 1921, Truro Apts, Albert St, Ottawa; 1922-3, 197 Sparks St, #41, Ottawa; 1924, Aitken Dott, S Castle St, Edinburgh; 1926, Aylmer Apts, Ottawa; 1933, 1441 Drummond St, Montreal; 1937 c/o Johnson Art Galleries, Montreal
1921 120 Water pattern, Chelsea Falls
121 Afternoon Ottawa valley
1922 156 Bridge at Rockcliffe (Col J.W.Woods) S6-68
157 Birches, early winter
1923 131 Gatineau ◊AGO◊
132 Laurentians
1924 156 Cramond Bridge, Scotland gouache
157 Thames, London wc
1926 110 Landscape, Italy wc
1933 173 Winter, Ottawa valley $150
1937 166 Dead trees $300
167 From Mont Tremblant wc $300
1939 176 Lake Timiskaming $350
177 Winter wc $150
1939 F11, New York
53 Laurentian landscape 28 x 25 $300
1941 141 Laurentian winter $250
1943 90 Winter nfs
144 Bonsecours Market conté & wc drwg nfs

NUGENT, JOHN CULLEN
5 Jan 1921, Montreal M WWA78
RCA(e) 1976-9 Sculptor

NUGENT, WALTER
1970 106 Lounge chair, Walter Nugent Designs Limited

NUTT, ELIZABETH STYRING
5 Sep 1870, Ouchan, Isle of Man
c 25 Mar 1946, Sheffield, Eng M
NGC TB2
ARCA 1929 Sr 1940 Painter
Addr: 1923, School of Art, Halifax; 1924, 24 George St, Halifax; 1925-36, Nova Scotia College of Art, Halifax; 1937-46, Halifax
1923 133 Sunshine
1924 158 Where sunlight falls
1925 169 In bluebell time, England
170 June, Herring Cove, NS
1926 111 Evening sunlight
112 The North West Arm, Halifax, NS ◊NGC◊
1927 171 Froggatt Bridge, Derbyshire, England
172 Winter, North West Arm, Halifax, NS
1928 115 A south Yorkshire cottage $750
1929 165 The old cottages, Baslow, England $750
166 On the North West Arm, Halifax $350
1930 128 Autumn on the North West Arm, Halifax $500
1931 213 Above the city $750
214 Derelicts $275
1932 150 A moorland bridge $500
151 A moorland stream $400
1933 174 Conksbury Bridge, north Derbyshire, England $550 T34-60
1934 149a Sanctuary $400
1935 198 Winter nfs
199 Symphony $150
1936 158a The grain elevator $500
1939 178 Spring on the North West Arm, Halifax, NS $540

O

O'BRIEN, LUCIUS RICHARD
15 Aug 1832, Shanty Bay, Ont 13 Dec 1899, Toronto AGO B EC H M Mo98 NGC TB W78
RCA 1880 Council Painter
Addr: 1880-2, Toronto; 1883, Yonge St, Toronto; 1884-6, Toronto; 1887, 36 Yonge St, Toronto; 1888-92, Toronto; 1893-9, 20 College St, Toronto

1880 37 Moonlight at Bishop's Rock, Grand Manan
39 Capes Trinity and Eternity
69 Northern Head of Grand Manan (Hon George Brown)
97 Low tide on Bay Chaleur
115 Sunrise on the Saguenay, Cape Trinity 1882-268 DW c 1882 34 1/2 x 49 1/2 T51-32 1954 Retro Sec 4
241 The Laurentian Range from Isle aux Fleurs wc
242 A glimpse of Lake Ontario wc
243 Good Harbour Beach, Massachusetts wc
244 Cape Rouge from Isle aux Fleurs wc
245 First tint of autumn wc
246 In the gloaming wc
247 Cape Tourmente in an easterly gale wc

1881 10 Tower archway, Parliament Buildings, Ottawa wc $50
38 A bastion, Quebec wc $60
51 Falls on the Chaudiere River, near Quebec wc $75
107 Rosey Point, Lake Simcoe wc
108 Grande Rivière, Sainte Anne wc
110 Ashburton Cliffs, Grand Manan wc
111 Fort Chambly, Quebec sketches wc
113 Our boat, near Cape Salmon wc
114 St John's suburb, from the Ramparts, Quebec wc
127 Near Ange Guardien Indian ink $30
128 Autumn leaves wc $25
129 A street in Château Richer, Quebec wc $25
130 Virginia creeper, autumn tint wc $25
131 North Channel, from Two Head Island wc
132 At Point Lévis, Québec wc, with proof engr
137 Camp in the woods wc $30
142 On the Ramparts at sunrise, Quebec wc $20
242 Quebec from Point Levis. Painted for Queen Victoria
312 View from the King's Bastion, Quebec. Painted for Queen Victoria

1882 49 Kakabecank Falls, Kaministiquia River $500 1954 Retro Sec p36 Kakabeka Falls illus ≬NGC≬
145 In the marsh at Longue Point, a chance encounter wc $200
205 A sketch at St Maurice Forges, Quebec wc
243 View from Queenston Heights, Ont monoc
263 A pool on the Nepigon monoc $40
315 Quebec on the Queen's birthday (Marquis of Lorne)

1883 138 A bit of old Quebec wc $45
140 Point à Pic, Murray Bay wc $75
142 A Gaspé fishing boat wc $40
144 Mount Eboulement wc $200
164 Vache Caille Rapids on the Saguenay wc $50
165 On the beach Percé wc $150
182 Cliff at Percé wc $80
183 Cape Gaspé wc $90
191 In the hills of Gaspé wc $90
192 Lobster fishery wc $80
212 Murray Bay wc $35
215 A cove on the coast of Gaspé wc $125
218 Fraser's Falls, Murray Bay wc $30
227 La Roche, Percé wc $200
272 Elms wc $35
286 A colloquy on the beach wc $50
299 Salmon fishing on the Restigouche wc $50
302 Manor house, Rivière Ouelle wc $50
310 In Gaspé Bay, mackerel fishing wc $50

1884 103 Cottages on the cliff, Clovelly, north Devon wc (George Lewis)
106 A Devonshire woodland road wc $55 S1-51 $50
117 Bideford Bay, from the cliffs of north Devon wc $120
121 The Coast Guard, north Devon wc $250 S1-41 $200
129 Becalmed in Bideford Bay wc $50
134 Cape Trinity, September day on the Saguenay wc (George Lewis)
135 Twilight on the Thames wc $60
144 On the coast of north Devon wc $100 S1-37 $90
149 Signal of distress wc $100
152 In the Hamoaze, Plymouth, old England's walls wc $50
156 A Clovelly herring boat taking in the nets wc $100
161 Village green, Datchet, near Windsor wc $90 S1-33

1884 S1, Saint John
12 Near St Catherines wc $35
25 Morning after the wreck wc $90
32 Bideford Bay wc $100
45 The Thames, at Cusely wc $75
53 Early morning, Bideford Bay wc $90
62 Near Plymouth wc $50
65 Mill on the Mississippi wc $30
66 On the Genesee wc $30

1885 236 Return of the herring boats, Bideford Bay wc $40
249 The portage wc $60
257 Off Clovelly, drifting for herring wc
267 Windsor Castle wc $200
277 A tributary of the St Maurice wc $35
280 Lake Kakamosemi
293 Cape Trinity, from Eternity River wc $35
294 Grand'Mère, St Maurice River wc $80
298 Sunshine on the Saguenay wc $50
303 Weathering, Heartland Point, west Devon wc $90

1886 48 September on the Saguenay, first tint of autumn wc $300
50 A bastion of Fort Chambly, before the restoration wc $35
56 Sunrise on Lake St John wc $150
61 Isle Maligne, River Saguenay wc $200
65 Ouiatchowin Falls, St John wc $100
77 Portage at Chute au Diable, Peribonka River wc $200
83 La Tuque, St Maurice River wc $90
85 La Roche, Percé wc $100
86 Outlet of Lake St John, by the Saguenay wc $250
88 Indian summer wc $100
91 Lake Tsitagama, Peribonka River wc $100

1886 F1a, London, Eng
2010, artist number
Voyageurs on the St Maurice (L.P. Brueneau, Esq, Montreal)
September on the Saguenay (HE Marquis of Lansdowne)
Fort Chambly
Sunrise on Lake St John
Ile Maligne, River Saguenay
Quiatchowin Falls, Lake St John
Portage at Chute au Diable, Peribonka River (Col Oswald, Montreal)
Outlet of Lake St John, by the Saguenay (Col Oswald)
La Tuque, St Maurice River
La Roche Percé
Mount Ebouliment (C.H. Nelson, Esq, Toronto)
View of the St Lawrence from the Fort, Quebec (Queen Victoria)
Lake scenery, Cape Carleton, Quebec (Princess Louise)
Quebec (Queen Victoria)
Low tide in Bay Chaleur (Princess Louise)

1887 117 Valley of the Illecillewaet wc $250
123 Mountain trail wc $250
125 A last look at the prairie wc $100
130 Evening in the Rockies wc $150
133 Mountain road in British Columbia wc $250
148 Mount Hermit Glacier wc $250

152 Mount Sir Donald wc $250
155 The Glacier Mountains wc $125
159 The glacier of the Selkirks wc $350
161 The glacier, from the valley wc $125
166 Mount Hermit wc

1888 14 Mount Sir Donald, Macdonald Valley wc $150
30 Cloudland, view from the Terminal Mountain, from the Selkirk Glacier wc (Hon Sir D.L. McPherson)
34 In the Selkirk Mountains, Hermit Range wc $150
37 Salmon fishing in the Fraser Canyon wc $75
47 The peak, from the valley wc $60
49 Crest of the Rockies at the head of Bow River Pass wc (Hon Sir D.L. McPherson)
57 Yale, BC wc $200
62 A misty day, Burrard Inlet wc $100
63 Brockton Point, Vancouver harbour wc $60
65 On the Cariboo Road, BC wc $175
72 Mount Baker, Vancouver Island wc
257 Mount Cheops wc $75
270 Railroad and river, Fraser Canyon, BC wc $150
303 A prospector's camp wc $75 ǂAGOǂ
305 An October day, lower Fraser wc $60

1889 108 Arbutus tree, Vancouver Island wc $40
127 Sandy Cove, Howe Sound, BC wc $75
129 British Columbia forest wc $300 ǂNGCǂ
134 Home of the seal, Howe Sound, BC wc $150
135 A ford in the Selkirks, BC wc $500
138 Incoming fog, lower St Lawrence wc $100
141 Mount Inchekia, Howe Sound, Pacific coast wc $250
143 Mount Sir Donald wc $200
165 A sheltered bay, Pacific coast wc $300
168 At rest, Yale, BC wc $150

1890 188 Out into the night wc $500
189 Clovelly wc $250
190 On the beach at St Ives wc $250
191 Norman stairway, Canterbury wc $150
192 Herring boats in St Ives Bay, Cornwall wc $100
193 Church at Harbledown, Canterbury wc $150
194 An evening at Canterbury wc $150
195 A westerly breeze wc $125
196 Clovelly herring boats wc $125
197 Trawlers becalmed wc $30

1891 135 Valley of the Montmorency wc
136 After the gale wc
137 Sixteenth century Rye, Sussex wc
139 Windsor wc
140 September equinox wc
141 The Stour and West Gate, Canterbury wc
167 At the harbour's mouth wc
194 Footprints of an avalanche wc

1892 98 Mill pond at Blair wc $120
124 Canterbury Cathedral wc $250 1893-237 $225 F1-178
134 Windsor Castle, early morning wc $200
152 Grand Falls on the Saint John River, NB wc $125

1893 235 The Great Peak of the Selkirks wc $350 F1-176
236 Niagara wc $250 F1-177
238 Lake Memphremagog wc $200 F1-179
239 A grey day on the St Francis wc $150
240 The Grand River, at Dover wc $125 F1-180
241 Fat lands of Ontario wc $125 F1-181
242 Gathering hay on Cold Water Marshes wc $125 F1-182
243 Spring wc $50
244 Summer wc $50

1894 87 Darkening 1900-88
88 A morning gleam
180 A morning in June wc
181 Wind and weather wc
182 Salt marsh and sand dunes wc
183 A reminiscence of Rosseau wc
184 A bend of Shadow River wc

1895 89 Mackerel fishing, Bay of Fundy
90 Northern Head, Grand Manan
91 Ashburton Head, Grand Manan
92 Sunrise at St Clement's Port
93 A meadow by the sea
94 Off Saint John, Bay of Fundy
1896 119 Solitude 1897-104
120 Mackerel fishing
121 Towing barges on the Hudson River
122 Dahlias and sunflowers 1900-89
123 Wreckage
124 Interval Meadows, Saint John's, Newfoundland
125 The Long Reach, Saint John's, Newfoundland 1897-109
126 A mountain at Banff
127 Maritime Canada
243 Shadow River, Muskoka wc 1897-38W
1897 105 Fishing craft on George's Bank
106 Misty morning, return of the fishing fleet
107 Morning in the harbour, Saint John, NB
108 Montmorency Falls
39W The mouth of the Humber wc
40W Fishing boats, Bay of Chaleur wc
1898 191 On Lake Tadenac wc
192 Falls of the Moon River wc
193 Worcester wc
194 A channel among the islands, Georgian Bay wc
195 In the Credit Valley wc
196 Laurentian rocks wc
197 Northern waters wc
1899 193 Landing cove at Grand Manan 1900-86
217 The shortest day wc 1900-174
218 A day in June wc
1900 deceased
85 and 87 Marine
90 In the harbour at Saint John, NB
173 In the heart of Muskoka wc
175 Valley of the Don wc
176 On the Resevoir Creek, Don Valley wc
1902 F3, Rochester
134 Landscape $95
1907 F6, Sherbrooke
134 Autumn $150
port: by R. Whale, 1882-64; by W.A. Sherwood, 1896-152; bust, by H. MacCarthy, 1891-1S; photo, 1954 Retro Sec p37

O'BRIEN, PATRICIA DOROTHY GUNN (PADDY) (Mrs O'Brien)
13 Oct 1929, Surrey, Eng IO M
1953 63 The bathers $400
1954 65 Bathers changing 30 x 24 illus $150
1957 53 Rue des Saints Pères, Paris $150
1960 59 Storm in the mountains, Provence 30 x 36 $200
60 Road to Marseilles 30 x 36 illus $200
1970 55 The Sybil sequence 30 x 40 illus $500

O'DONNELL, MARGUERITE see SCOTT, MARGUERITE

OESTERLE, LEONHARD FRIEDRICH
3 Mar 1915, Bietigheim, Germany
IO M WWA62
ARCA 1962 RCA 1968 Council Sculptor
Addr: 1963-71/79, Toronto
1960 85 Mother with child sculp $325
1961 88 Mother with child sculp 17 1/2h illus $380
89 Kneeling woman stone 15 1/2 x 14 1/2 $450
1963 97 Couple bronze $400
98 Girl welded brass illus $750
1964J 90 Family group bronze 22 1/2 $400
99 Sculpture, main entrance, R.S. McLaughlin Collegiate and Vocational Institute, Oshawa. Gordon S. Adamson, architect
1965 90 Female figure bronze 31 1/2h $650
1966 85 Maquette sculp
DW 1969 Walking woman bronze 13h incl base

OGILVIE, WILLIAM ABERNETHY
30 Mar 1901, Stutterheim, S Africa
AGO CC2 CWW79 M NGC WWA47

ARCA 1970 Sr 1971 Painter
Addr: 1931, 210 Dundas St W, Toronto; 1932, 36 Avenue Rd, Toronto; 1971, Palgrave, Ont; 1979, Guelph, Ont
1931 215 African day wc $150 ◊NGC◊
1932 152 Xosa women washing $300
1950 111 Gannets at Gaspé 24 x 28 $250

OHE, DOROTHY KATIE VON DER (Mrs Harry Kiyooka)
18 Feb 1937, Peers, Alta M
RCA(e) 1979 Sculptor
Addr: 1979, Calgary

OILLE, ETHEL LUCILLE (Mrs Kenneth McNeil Wells)
8 Oct 1912, Toronto M
Addr: 1932, 69 South Dr, Toronto; 1936, 19 South Dr, Toronto
1932 218 Bon Evan sculp
1936 223 Arthur Tracy sculp nfs

OLIS, MARCEL (b Olislaeger)
17 Jun 1891, Paris
Addr: 1918A, 57 Queen St W, Toronto
1918A 131 Dancing girls, study

OLIVER, WILLIAM MURRAY
16 Jun 1929, Aurora, Ont
RCA(e) 1976 Designer
Addr: 1979, Toronto

ONLEY, NORMAN ANTONIO (TONI)
20 Nov 1928, Isle of Man AGO B CC1 M TB3 WWA73
ARCA 1963 Painter
Addr: 1964-71/79, Vancouver
1953 64 The iron bridge wc $50
1963 56 Polar #1 $700
57 Polar #23 $350
1964J 49 Polar #18 52 x 46 $600
1965 57 Lunar gesture 41 x 35 $450 S10-57
1966 48 Ancient stones 8 1/4 x 9 1/4 $95
49 Haunted field 20 x 26 $200
1967 50 Dream landscape 35 x 40 1/4 $400
1970 56 Dike 20 x 25 3/4 illus $300
57 Across the street 20 x 25 3/4

OONARK, JESSIE (SEEKANIK) E2-384
1906, Baker Lake, NWT ED M
RCA(e) 1975 Print maker
Addr: 1979, Baker Lake, NWT

ORENSTEIN, HENRY
13 Jan 1918, Midland, Ont M
1950 112 Tenement 29 1/2 x 24 $200

OSBORNE, ROSALYNDE FULLER
b Hamilton M
Addr: 1926-7, 7 Turner Ave, Hamilton; 1928, 25 Severn St, Toronto; 1929-31, 7 Turner Ave, Hamilton
1926 113 Bass Rocks wc
114 Honfleur, France wc
1927 173 Rock study wc
174 Norman stairs, Canterbury wc
1928 116 Ravello wc $25
117 In the Forum Romanum wc $25
1929 167 Lilium auratum wc $75
168 Lemon lilies wc $65
1931 216 Canterbury Gate wc $25
217 Zinnias wc $50

OSHOOWEETOOK "B" E7-1154
3 Oct 1923, Cape Dorset, NWT ED
RCA(e) 1973 Sculptor
Addr: 1979, Cape Dorset, NWT

OSTER, JOHN
Addr: 1920, 1848 Gouin Blvd, Montreal
1920 189 Portrait of my father

OUELETT, JEAN
26 Dec 1922, Rivière du Loup, Que
ARCA 1972 Architect
Addr: 1979, Montreal

OUTHET, RICKSON A.
Addr: 1908, New York Life Bldg, Montreal; 1909M, 3 Beaver Hall Sq, Montreal; 1909N, 54 Beaver Hall Hill, Montreal; 1922, 264 Beaver Hall Hill, Montreal
1908 156 Garden at Westmount Aouthet mispr
157 Garden, Tuxedo Park, NY
158 Gardens, Seattle, Wash
1909M 143a Grantham Hall, Drummondville Aouthet mispr
1909N 109 Granthorn Hill, Drummondville
110 Estate at Seattle
1922 159 A Laurentian swamp wc

OUVRARD, PIERRE
8 Feb 1929, Quebec
RCA(e) 1979 Book binder
Addr: 1979, Ile aux Noix, Que

OWEN, JOHN
fl 1874-1880 H
1880 384 Autumn leaves
385 Morning glories

OWENS, NINA M. (Mrs)
Addr: 1918N, 26 Summerhill Ave, Montreal
1918N 143 Summer morning

OXLEY, J. MORROW
12 Sep 1883, Halifax CWW55
see CHAPMAN, ALFRED, 1946

OXLEY, LOREN ARTHUR
18 Sep 1917, Ottawa CWW79
see SOMERVILLE, WILLIAM, 1964N

P

P G L ARCHITECTS
see PAPINEAU, LOUIS JOSEPH

PACEK, JOSEPH
25 Aug 1925, Paris, Ont
see SULLIVAN, JOHN, 1971

PAGE, FORSEY PEMBERTON B.
22 Sep 1885, Toronto 22 Nov 1970, Toronto CWW64
ARCA 1947 Sr 1955 Architect
Addr: 1948-70, Toronto
1952 103 St Joseph High School. Chapel fittings, holy water basin, sanctuary rail photos
1957 Page & Steele
103 Juvenile and Family Court, Toronto
104 Queen Elizabeth Building, Canadian National Exhibition
1961 99 Education centre
1966 Page & Steele
142-4 Montreal Trust Tower, Toronto. Arcade. Interior detail. Model

PALARDY, JOSEPH JEAN ALBERT
23 Sep 1905, Fitchburg, Mass
Addr: 1928, 822 Wilde Ave, Outremont, Que
1928 118 The arch, Percé Rock $75

PALEY, R.L.
fl 1886-8 H
1886 23a The lover's walk $30
204 Checked $300. Selected for Fla, not in Fla cat
1888 213 Scene on the Gatineau $60 Paily, mispr
224 A well contested game $70
228 A calm morning wc $10
281 A sugar house wc $10
282 Bluff Point, West Rideau Lake wc $10
314 Summer morning wc $11

PALIN, ETHEL
fl 1888-95 H
Addr: 1895, 13 Gloucester St, Toronto
1895 95 Waiting

PALM, OTTILLIE E. (Mrs Josef Jost)
13 Feb 1878, Hamilton, Ont March, 1961, Munich B M TB
Addr: 1909N, 19 Bold St, Hamilton; 1910, 234 John St, Hamilton; 1913, 2 Travancore, Cedar Ave, Montreal
1909N 111 The wooden bowl
1910 149 Carpo
1913 Jost
146 Peasant in Hartz Mountains, Germany
147 Marriage in Fussen, Bavaria

PALMA, ARMAND DE
1941 210 Mr Alessandro Donato sculp nfs

PALMER, HERBERT FRANKLIN (FRANK)
24 Nov 1921, Calgary AGO CC2 M TB3
ARCA 1960 RCA 1966 Painter
Addr: 1961-71/79, Calgary
1954 66 Water front wc 16 x 22 illus $60
1955 64 Sea piece illus $70 (AGO)
1957 54 Landscape $125
55 Rock forms illus $200
1958 64 Waterfront $100
1959 64 Low tide 30 x 38 illus $225
1961 64 Shore, west coast 38 x 36 illus nfs
1966 50 Sea wall 38 x 32 $270
DW 1967 Sea wall 43 1/2 x 42

PALMER, HERBERT SIDNEY
15 Jun 1881, Toronto 30 Nov 1970, Toronto AGO CC2 CNS36 CWW64 M NGC TB2 WWA47
ARCA 1915 RCA 1934 Sr 1951 Painter
Addr: 1907, Toronto; 1909M, 222 College St, Toronto; 1910, 322 Cottingham St, Toronto; 1912-16, 322 College St, Toronto; 1918, 2 Bloor St W, Toronto; 1919, 322 College St,

Toronto; 1920, 2 Bloor St W, Toronto; 1921-3, Toronto; 1924-35, 170 St Clements Ave, Toronto; 1936-70, Toronto

1907 150 Flitting shadows H.J. Palmer, mispr S3-123
151 A stormy evening
1909M 99 Autumn landscape 1909N-112
100 A passing shower 1909N-113
1910 150 October landscape
1912 176 Landscape
177 Grazing
1913 231 Down the valley
232 Above the falls, Eugenia S4-104 $250
1913 S3, Winnipeg
122 A Conestogo meadow
1914 154 Fall ploughing ǾNGCǾ
1914 S5, Patriotic Fund
28 In the valley illus
1915 166 Upland pasture illus
167 Shifting shadows
1916 179 The Lake, Eugenia
180 Sketch for 'On the hill side' illus ǾNGCǾ
181 Rocky pasture
1918A 132 An Ontario pasture illus 1918N-144 illus
133 A rainy day in the bush 1918N-146
134 The valley, near Belfountain, Ontario
135 Morning mists
1918N 145 On the hill top
147 Spring pasture
1919 125 November evening
126 Storm clouds
127 A Muskoka pasture
128 October pasture
1920 190 October in the sheep pasture 1922-159 S6-70
191 Lake of Bays, Ontario
192 Windy weather
193 A northern pasture
1924 159 The goat farm illus
1926 115 Gatineau Hill at Wakefield, Quebec illus
1927 175 Wakefield on the Gatineau, Quebec
176 Lingering snow, York Mills, Ontario
1927 F7, London, Eng
131 On the hillside (CNE)
1929 169 Across country, northern Quebec $450 S7-120
170 Sorting logs on the Gatineau $450
1930 F10, London, Eng
118 On the Gatineau River, Quebec $400
1931 218 November $450
1933 175 Rolling country $350 T34-61
176 Ontario pasture, Rice Lake $400
1935 200 Spring in the Gatineau valley $350
201 Lake Bernard, Ontario $200 T36-57
1938 169 The road by Maple Lake, Haliburton, Ont $200 T39-42
1939 179 The mill at Barrow Bay, Ontario illus $750
180 The golden pool $250
1939 F11, New York
54 The winding road 38 x 46 $400
1941 S9, Toronto
47 Under the maples $150
1943 91 Haliburton Hills $200 T44-31
1950 113 Farm near Barry's Bay, Ont 28 x 36 $450
1951 71 Early October, northern Ontario illus $750 1952-69
1955 63 Young conifers illus $450
DW 1935 Sumach Hill 38 1/2 x 44 T51-33 1954 Retro Sec 32
port: by C.P. Brady, 1918A-14; by F. Challener, 1919-22

PALUMBO, JACQUES GAETAN
16 Sep 1939, Philippeville, Algeria
M
Addr: 1976, Montreal
1976 S12, Montreal
163 Album Jacques Palumbo sérigraphie 26 x 20 illus

PANABAKER, FRANK SHIRLEY
16 Aug 1904, Hespeler, Ont CWW79
M PMC WWA47
ARCA 1942 Sr 1971 Painter
Addr: 1929-30, Hespeler, Ont; 1931, 59 Locust St, Burlington, Ont; 1933, Mountain View Apts, Hamilton; 1934-5, Hespeler, Ont; 1936, 166 Charlton Ave, Hamilton; 1937, 86 Charlton Ave E, Hamilton; 1942-71/79, Ancaster, Ont
1929 171 The fallen monarch $400
172 The goose family $200
1930 129 Morning gleam, Lake O'Hara $750
130 The homeward trail $400

1931 219 An abandoned farmhouse $500
220 Snow in the Rockies $400
1933 177 Evening surf, Cape Breton $800
178 Our mountain camp $300 T34-62
1934 150 Spring $350
1935 202 Wilderness Lake, Canadian Rockies $450
203 Above the valley, Baie St Paul $350
1936 159 Farlinger's Lane $225
160 Summer morning $125
1937 168 Pinnacle Mountain, Canadian Rockies $400
169 Moonlight, Nova Scotia $250 T38-42
1938 170 Mount Assiniboine $225
171 The Basilica, Hamilton $200 T39-43
1939 181 Old sailor, Nassau $150
182 The stream $150
1940 122 Late afternoon, Dundas Valley $350 T41-41
123 Still life $175
1941 142 A mountain farm, Quebec $300 T42-39
143 Bogey, Nassau boy nfs
1941 S9, Toronto
48 August, Dundas Valley $150
1944 105 Fall storm $450
106 September haze $175 T45-32
1945 156 Temagami $700
157 VJ night in Ancaster $500
158 Still life with egg plant $250
159 Early spring $250 T46-35
1946 90 The back door $300
1947 133 Dundas Valley $300
1948 120 Mallards $300
121 Spring, Georgian Bay nfs
122 Georgian Bay $225
1950 114 Highlands of Ontario 20 x 26 $250
1951 72 Church, South Bolton, Quebec $175
1970 S11, Halifax
28 Coast of Skye, Scotland. 1962 24 x 32 $600
29 Early spring. 1970 16 x 20 $275

PANCHAL, MANSARAM see MANSARAM, PANCHAL

PANILUK
Addr: 1976, Arctic Bay, NWT
1976 S12, Montreal
84 Abstract soapstone/saponite 10 x 8 1/2 x 7 illus

PANNETON, LOUIS PHILIPPE
10 Jan 1906, Trois Rivières, Que M
1946 91 Mr G. de Condé nfs T47-39
1947 134 Lorne H. Bouchard, ARCA 1948-123

PANTON, LAWRENCE ARTHUR COLLEY
15 Jun 1894, Egremont, Ches, Eng
20 Nov 1954, Toronto AGO CC2 CNS36 CWW49 EC M NGC TB2/3 W78 WWA47
ARCA 1934 RCA 1943 Council Painter
Addr: 1927-37, 65 St Germain Ave, Toronto; 1938-54, Toronto
1927 177 Early evening, Lake of Bays
1928 119 Muskoka winter $175
1929 173 Summer showers $400 F10-162
174 Evening sun $150
1929 S7, Calgary
121 June clouds $400
122 Tom $150
1930 131 Georgian Bay, August $450
132 Embroidery $250
1931 221 The readers $500 (NGC)
1932 153 Depression $500
154 Magnetawan $350
1933 179 Gold and grey $450 T34-63
180 Sullen earth $450 (AGO)
1934 151 Windsong $450 T35-56
152 The mill pool, Cheltenham $350
1935 204 Tawny autumn $300 T36-58
205 Sunlight and saffron $175
1936 161 Green cascade $350 T37-50
162 White hat nfs
1937 170 Ocean elegy nfs
171 Pomona nfs T38-43 $400
1938 172 Evening storm $400 T39-44
1939 183 Grey and white
1939 F11, New York
55 Spring storm 34 x 40 $450
1940 124 Woodland hilltop illus $225 T41-42
1941 144 Rock pattern $200 T42-40
1942 103 Morning, Little Cove illus nfs DW 1944 Morning, Little Cove, Grand Manan 28 x 32 T51-34 1954 Retro Sec 44
104 Pauline's Island temp & oil nfs T43-32
105 Falls on Madawaska wc $45
106 Saw mill road wc $45

1943 92 Northern river chute $150
1944 107 Languor temp & oil $400 T45-33
108 Landscape in yellow temp & oil $200 T45-34
109 The grove $100
1945 160 Northern morning temp & oil nfs T46-36
1946 92 Grandeur night to dust temp $550 T47-40
1948 124 Rock cluster, Nova Scotia landscape #3 temp
1949 68 Rock cluster, Nova Scotia temp $200
1950 115 The wave, Nova Scotia landscape 28 x 32 $450
116 Rock cluster, Nova Scotia landscape 20 x 24 $200
117 Wind and rock, Nova Scotia landscape 25 1/2 x 29 1/2 $400
1951 73 Ballet of fog and rock temp 1952-70 illus T53-25
74 Rock and surf temp illus
1953 65 Evening surf, Nova Scotia oil on temp illus $450
1966 S10, Charlottetown
58 Atlantic figure 29 1/2 x 33 1/2 nfs
69 Untitled $750

PAPINEAU, LOUIS JOSEPH
1976 S12, Montreal
PGL Architects: Louis Joseph Papineau, Guy Gerin-Lajoie, Michel LeBlanc
106 Mirabel Airport. Passenger terminal bldg 2 photos

PAPP, JOSEPH SULYOK DE
20 Sep 1897, Savjhely, Hungary
CNS36
Addr: 1937, 3446 Ste Famille St, Montreal
1937 217 Sunday $250 T38-53

PAQUETTE, MAURICE
1941 145 Nature morte $75 T42-41

PARADIS, JACQUES R.
Addr: 1935, 4211 Gouin Blvd W, Cartierville, Que
1935 336 Quebec linocut $10

PARADIS, JOBSON
1871, St Johns, Que 11 May 1926, Guelph, Ont H W78
Addr: 1904-7, Montreal; 1910, 458 Berri St, Montreal; 1920, 342 Somerset St E, Ottawa
1904 320 The chestnut tree b&w
321 On the river side b&w
322 Study of a head b&w
323 Study of trees b&w
1907 270 Old street, Montmartre wc
271 Across the valley, St Agathe wc
296 Rue St Vincent, Paris crayon
1907 F6, Sherbrooke
135 The Pont Marie, Paris drwg $25
136 Rue St Vincent, Paris $20
137 A street at Montmartre $20
138 Study of a head $10
1910 151 My home
1920 330 Le vieux châtaignier

PARENT, PIERRE OVIDE LUCIEN
29 Apr 1893, Montreal d 1956
ARCA 1936 Architect
Addr: 1937-56, Montreal
1938 Tourville & Parent
248 Monastery

PARIZEAU, MARCEL B.
6 May 1898, Montreal 15 Aug 1945, Montreal CNS44
1944 143 Chapelle du Petit Trainon
144 Une vue du vieux Menton

PARK, MARGARET
1938 S8, Toronto
167 Sanctuary window des, by OCA students, assisted by Rowley Murphy

PARKER, ARTHUR HENRY
b 1874
Addr: 1923, Mount Tolmie, Victoria
1923 134 Misty moon wc

PARKER, HARLEY WALTER BLAIT
13 Apr 1917, Fort William, Ont M
1939 184 Self portrait wc nfs
1941 146 Portrait of Helen $50
1951 75 Old bricks, new grass wc $150
1952 71 The red staircase wc $150

PARKER, JOHN ALLEN
1947 135 Night check-up wc $30

PARKIN, JOHN CRESSWELL CC
24 Mar 1922, Sheffield Co CWW79

ARCA 1954 RCA 1965 Council Architect
Addr: 1955-71/76/79, Toronto
1953 106 Central Collegiate Institute, Oshawa, Ont photo
107 Humber Memorial Hospital, Weston, Ont photo illus
1954 122 Lawrence Avenue, Service Building, Simpson's Limited, North York photo #138-1
123 Headquarters bldg, Ontario Association of Architects photo #138-3
1955 93 National Headquarters, Salvation Army, Toronto
1957 John B. Parkin & Associates, to 1959
105 Parking garage, Dundas Square, Toronto
106 Imperial Oil, Engineering Bldg, Sarnia, Ont
1958 101 Pitney-Bowes of Canada Limited, office bldg, Toronto
102 Ortho Pharmaceutical Corp (Canada) Limited, Don Mills, Ont. Factory and offices
1959 102 Bank of Nova Scotia, Don Mills, Ont
1960 101 Adams Brands Limited, Scarborough, Ont photo
102 Primrose Club, St Clair Ave W, Toronto photo
1961 100 Sun Life Assurance Company of Canada, office bldg, University Ave, Toronto
101 Religious school, Holy Blossom Temple, Toronto
1963 119 Imperial Oil Limited, Ontario Regional Office Bldg,
1964J John Parkin & Associates, to 1967
113-16 Imperial Oil Limited, Ontario Regional Office Bldg, Don Mills, Ont. Exterior, 2 views. Entrance. 1st floor plan
117-19 Thomas Lipton Limited, plant and offices, Bramalea, Ont. Exterior, 2 views. Interior
1964N 148-9 Sifto Salt, mill and warehouse. General view. Exterior
150-2 H.J. Heinz Company of Canada Limited, Leamington, Ont. General exterior view. Exterior view with bridge. Exterior view
153-61 International Airport, Malton, Ont. Administration, tower and aeroquay. Administration building, general view illus. Interior view of lobby. Plaza, exterior. Aeroquay, exterior view with sculpture. Exterior view, night. Overall site plan. Enplaning floor, 2nd floor. Control tower. General view, exterior. Interior view
1965 136-42 Bata Limited, world headquarters. Exterior rear view. Exterior entrance. Exterior, end view. Interior conference hall. Plans, A, B and C
143-7 St Marks Presbyterian Church, North York. Interior. General view. Plan. Section
1966 145-8 McKinnon Industries Limited. Facade, general view. Exterior. Board room. Section
149-51 Warner-Lambert Research Institute. Main entrance. View from Hadwin Rd. Site plan
1967 130-4 Ottawa Station, Ottawa. A.Northwest elevation B. Passenger concourse,showing massive concrete column C. Helicoidal ramp leading to underground tunnel and tracks D.Floor plan E.Detail of two-way main truss and pin connection
1976 S12, Montreal
Parkin Architects Planners
107 Art Gallery of Ontario. Stage 1. 2 photos
DW 1965 Toronto International Airport photo 23 7/8 x 20
see also, Rowland, Douglas, 1968, 1971

PARLOW, MAIDA DORIS (Mrs Arthur Raymond Knowles) (Mrs Donald French)
5 Aug 1891, Toronto CC1 CWW61 M
Addr: 1914, 288 Sherbourne St, Toronto; 1915, 755 Yonge St, Toronto; 1918-24, 288 Sherbourne St, Toronto
1914 155 Minuet in G
1915 168 The sybil
169 Coming storm
1918A 300 One, braver than the rest
301 The very top

300-1, Trustees, National Gallery of Canada, Travelling scholarship competition
1919 129 Flying kites
130 The village tenement
1923 Knowles, to 1924
101 Forbidden fruit 1924-119
1924 120 The pearl fishers

PARR, NUNA
Cape Dorset, NWT
Addr: 1976, Cape Dorset, NWT
1976 S12, Montreal
85 Bear ivory 4 1/2 x 1 3/4 illus

PARRISH, STEPHEN American
9 Jul 1846, Philadelphia 15 May 1938, Windsor, Vt AAA29 B F H TB WWA36
1882 43 Gloucester harbor $250
246 In port, Gloucester harbor, Mass monoc $7
247 Portsmouth, NH monoc $12
251 Rocks, Cape Ann monoc $12
252 Low tide, Bay of Fundy monoc $18
257 Fishermen's houses, Cape Ann monoc $18
258 Old farm near the sea monoc
260 Carlton, NB, Bay of Fundy monoc $12
273 On the Saint John, NB monoc $12

PARTRIDGE, DAVID GERRY
5 Oct 1919, Akron, Ohio AGO CC1 M TB3 WWA76
ARCA 1962 RCA 1979 Council Painter
Addr: 1963-8, Ottawa; 1969-71, London, Eng; 1976/79, Toronto
1949 69 The welder $100 1950-118 18 x 24 $150
1951 76 London street market wc $100
135 Long rest etch $10
1964J 50 Yellow orb 48 x 60 $600
80 Standing configuration sculp $275
1966 90 Circular sculp 24 x 24 $300
1967 80 Thorned configuration sculp 72 x 16 $525
1970 89 Untitled sculp 60 x 48 $1,500
1976 S12, Montreal
86 Large crevassed woods & nails 24 x 72 illus
DW 1979 A flight of mountains wood & nails, acry reflector, steel base 107 x 48 x 24

PARTRIDGE, R.B.
Addr: 1933, 6079 Terrebonne Ave, Montreal; 1935, 1104 Beaver Hall Hill, Montreal
1933 181 Studio interior $250 T34-64
1935 206 Interior $1,800
337 Head of a girl drwg $50

PASSET, JEAN POL
Addr: 1976, Montreal
1976 S12, Montreal
171 L'immigrant film 16mm b&w/n&b 5 mins

PATERSON, GEORGE
1939 185 Portrait study of a young lady in black nfs

PATERSON, ROBERT ALLEN
26 May 1936, Unity, Sask
1963 58 Hero form $600

PATON, J.B. (Mrs)
H
1898 81 Out of work

PATRICIA, HRH PRINCESS VICTORIA PATRICIA HELENA ELIZABETH (d Duke of Connaught) (Lady Patricia Ramsay, m Hon Alexander R.M. Ramsay)
17 Mar 1886, Buckingham Palace
12 Jan 1974, Windlesham, Surrey, Eng
Addr: 1912-16, Rideau Hall, Ottawa
1912 52 Indian houses and totem poles, Alert Bay
53 Ottawa, from Government House
54 A Stockholm sunset
55 Morning at Lake Louise 1913-69
1913 70 Oriental study S4-33
71 Highland stream near Balmoral, Aberdeenshire, Scotland S4-34
1914 42 A woodland glade
43 Hyacinths and porcelain
1914 S5, Patriotic Fund
26 White narcissus illus
1915 49 Ottawa River at sunset
50 Lilies and silver
1916 42 Ice breaking up in early spring on the Ottawa River

PATRICK, MARTHA A.
H
Addr: 1898, Ottawa; 1900, 29 Victoria Ave, Ottawa
1898 79 Portrait of a lady
80 Chrysanthemum study
1900 92 Portrait of a lady
93 Study of a head

PATRICK, N. WILSON (Mrs)
1938 173 Miss Jessie Wilson nfs

PATTERSON, ANDREW DICKSON
30 Jun 1854, Picton, Ont 31 Jul 1930, Montreal AGO EC H Mo12 NGC TB3 W78
ARCA 1882 RCA 1887 Ret 1915 Council
Painter
Addr: 1883, 46 King St W, Toronto; 1884-6, Toronto; 1887, 46 King St W, Toronto; 1888-9, Toronto; 1890-3, Ottawa; 1894, Medical Council Bldg, Toronto; 1895-6, 33 Canada Life Bldg, Toronto; 1897-02, Elmsly Pl, Toronto; 1903-5, Toronto; 1906, 316 St James' Chambers, Toronto; 1907-8, Toronto; 1909M, 316 St James' Club, Montreal; 1909N, Toronto; 1910-14, 4160 Sherbrooke St W, Westmount, Que; 1915, Montreal; 1916, 4162 Sherbrooke St W, Westmount, Que; 1917-18A, Montreal; 1918N-21, 241 Beaver Hall Hill, Montreal; 1922-7, 451 Sherbrooke St W, Montreal; 1928-30, Montreal
1880 7 F.W. Jarvis, Sheriff, York County
1882 71 Roses
74 Late A.J. Smith, Esq
99 Mrs F.L. Osler
105 Rev F.L. Osler
1883 49 Children of W.B. McMurrich, Esq
91 Mrs S. Massey, Montreal
114 Lily pond on the Humber $150
134 Mr Lodd, ex-alderman
1885 7 Mr Alderman Saunders
14 Sisters
22 Late Mrs Leuty
116 Portrait
173 A setting sun should leave a track of glory in the skies $125
287 A child no more, a maiden now
326 and 327 Portrait chalk $25 each
1887 106 Dorothy DW 1887 28 1/2 x 20 1/2
1888 91 Sir John A. Macdonald, 1886 1890-65
167 Col Gzowski, ADC to the Queen
1891 107 Mrs Robert Cassels
108 Late Robert Cassels, Esq
1892 86 My mother
92 My father
1894 90 Sir Wm. Howland, KCMG
91 Late Toussaint Trudeau, Esq
92 Portrait
1895 96 Mr John King, QC
1896 128 Hon Mr Justice Burton
129 Rev Wm. Shortt
130 Wilfred, son of Prof Mavor
131 Homer Watson, RCA
132 L'allegro
133 Il penserosa
1897 110 Sir Frank Smith
111 Late Sir Daniel Wilson, Toronto University
112 Mrs Stewart
113 Portrait of a lady, period 1870
114 Prof Chapman, PhD, Toronto University
1900 93a Late Sir George A. Kirkpatrick, KCMG (Government House, Toronto)
1901 88 Dr Watson
89 Portrait study F2-55
1902 127 E.D. Armour, KC
128 Mrs Frederic Nicholls
129 His Hon Sir Oliver Mowat, GCMG
1904 F4, St Louis
60 My mother in a garden hat 1905-133
61 The string of beads 1905-134 S2-81
62 The bookworm
1905 135 Study of a man reading
136 George N. Morang, Esq
1906 144 Little Miss Grace (J.C. Grace, Esq)
1907 152 Prof W.R. Long, Toronto University
1908 106a Portrait of my mother
1909M 98 Miss Mary I. Robertson
1910 152 Mrs Albermarle Annesley crayon
153 James Ross, Esq crayon
154 Hilda Ross crayon
155 Master Jimmie Ross crayon

1910 S2, Liverpool
82 Dr R.A. Stevenson
1914 232 Nell Gwyn, after Sir Peter Lily crayon
1916 305 Drawing, after painting by Hoppner
306 Drawing, after painting by Matthew Maris
307 Drawing, after painting by Reynolds
308 The artist's mother
1918N 246 John Ogilvy, Esq crayon
247 Mother of Géricault crayon
248 Crown Prince of Belgium crayon
249 Isobel, daughter of P.M. Robertson, Esq crayon
1920 194 and 195 Portrait pastel
1922 160 Homer Watson (1898) S6-71 ◊NGC◊
271 Sir Vincent Meredith, Bart drwg
272 Sir Frederick Williams Taylor drwg
1924 282 Countess of Haddington crayon
1925 312 J. Rawson Gardiner, Esq drwg
313 David Pottinger, Esq drwg
314 Dr E.F. Cleveland drwg
315 Lady with a bridal veil drwg
1927 321 Mrs Wm.H. Humphrey drwg
322 Miss Virginia Walthour drwg
323 Edith, daughter of Mrs de Kay Sloan drwg
324 Peggy drwg
1929 273 Late Bliss Carman, Canadian Laureate drwg $200
274 Wm.D. White, Esq drwg
275 A lady of Virginia drwg $150
276 Girl with goats, after Matthew Maris drwg $50

PATTERSON, EDITH LALANDE RAVENSHAW
(Mrs Andrew Dickson Patterson)
b East Sheen, Surrey, Eng DBA G
Addr: 1901, Toronto; 1902, 10 Elmsley Pl, Toronto; 1903, 95 Yonge St, Toronto; 1904, Toronto; 1905, c/o McKenzie & Co, Toronto; 1914, London, Eng; 1915, 66 Cathcart Studio, Redcliffe Rd, London, Eng; 1916-22, 17 Cathcart Studio, 34 Redcliffe Rd, London, Eng
1901 E.L. Ravenshaw, Mrs A.D. Patterson
206 Scotch landscape wc
1902 229 On the Yare, Norwich wc
230 The old town, Norwich wc
231 Landscape, evening wc
232 A summer fantasy wc
1903 188 Early morning wc
1904 241a Landscape pastel
241b Poplars pastel F4-112
288 Screen stencil des
1905 137 Morning, Rye, Sussex pastel
138 Evening, Rye, Sussex pastel
1914 233 Il monte, rosa col etch
234 Black mill, Winchelsea etch
1915 280 The three graces col print
281 The river mezz
1916 E. Lalande, to 1918A
292 The Long Water, Hampton Court aqua
293 The archway, Winchelsea etch
1918A 245 St Maclou, Rouen etch
246 Sunningdale Golf Links, Berkshire etch
1921 211 Wax wings col print
212 Phlox and butterfly col print
213 Evening mezz
214 A backwater mezz
1922 161 Looking towards Ben Lomond wc

PATTERSON, FREEMAN W.
25 Sep 1937, Long Reach, NB
RCA(e) 1975 Photographer
Addr: 1979, Clifton Royal, NB

PATTERSON, WILLIAM JOHN
21 Aug 1916, Belfast AGO
Addr: 1936, 145 Hazelwood Ave, Toronto; 1937, 5 Lipton Ave, Toronto
1936 163 Tommy $150 T37-51
164 Pauline $150
1937 172 Referie $200
173 One of the cast, a pose $200

PATTISON, ALBERT MEAD
1887, Clarenceville, Que 26 Nov 1957, Hudson, Que M
Addr: 1913, 96 Durocher St, Montreal; 1924-9, 202 Lazard Rd S, Town of Mount Royal, Que

1913 233 Place d'Armes Square wc
234 Inspector Street wc
1924 160 Charing Cross Bridge, London wc
161 Bastille Day, Rouen wc
1929 277 The new harbour bridge, Montreal pencil $25
278 Church of St Andrew and St Paul pencil $25

PATTULO, MARY FRANCES (Mrs W.D. Gregory)
fl 1889-90 H
1889 40 Student's table $100

PAUL, GREGORY PRESTON
18 Mar 1933, Toronto M WWA56
1953 66 Half Mile Hill $150

PAUL, LOUISE
b Fort William, Ont 11 Aug 1961, Oakville, Ont M
1948 174 Gina Mallow as 'Ophelia' sculp $100

PAULL, ALMOND E.
1824, Cornwall, Eng 26 May 1902, Toronto
ARCA 1880-5 Architect
Addr: 1880-5, Toronto

PAVELIC, MYFANWY SPENCER (Mrs Donald Campbell) (Mrs Nikola Pavelic)
27 Apr 1916, Victoria
RCA(e) 1975 RCA 1976 Painter
Addr: 1979, Sidney, BC
DW 1976 Herbert Siebner acry & oil 35 x 34

PAVITT, D.A.J.
Addr: 1934, 220 Elm Ave, Westmount, Que
1934 153 Winter wc $30
222 Reed pen drawing $25

PAYETTE, DANIEL
1971 Pitié pour les étranges film screened 7 Apr

PAYNE, GORDON EASTCOTT
16 Oct 1890, or 1891, Payne's Mills, Ont AGO M
Addr: 1925, Ingersoll, Ont
1925 171 Phlox
172 Rockport
port: by Manly MacDonald, 1925-147

PAYZANT, CHARLES ST G.
Addr: 1931, 61 Oxford St, Halifax
1931 222 The yellow awning wc $40
223 Forty love wc $40

PEACOCK, DONALD K.
b 1920 M
1966 86 Torso walnut 13 1/2h $130

PEARSON, JOHN ANDREW
22 Jun 1867, Derbyshire, Eng 11 Jun 1940, Toronto CWW36 NGC TB3 WWC21
ARCA 1929 RCA 1936 Sr 1937 Architect
Addr: 1930-40, Toronto
DW 1936 Peace Tower, Ottawa pencil drwg 24 3/4 x 12
port: by, E.W. Grier, 1936-86
see also Darling, Frank, 1893-53A

PEARSON, LEE S.
1945 161 Lake McArthur wc $75

PEARSON, PETER
1970 Best damn fiddler from Calabogie to Kaladar film screened 19 Feb

PECK, ESMOND H. (Mrs)
1949 70 Studio view $250

PECK, HUGH A.
5 Dec 1888, Montreal M
Addr: 1925-33, 1 Belvedere Rd, Westmount, Que
1925 249 Small residence, Westmount, Quebec
1933 182 Evening light $150

PEDEN, FRANK
fl 1900-45
Addr: 1907, Montreal
1907 Peden & McLaren
337 Mount Royal Avenue Church. Perspective
338 Picton Public Library. Perspective

PEDERY, DORA DE see HUNT, DORA

PEEL, MILDRED (Lady, m Sir George William Ross)
b 1856 d 1920 H Mo98/12 M
1889 47 Le déjeuner pour Marie $100

PEEL, PAUL
7 Nov 1860, London, Ont 11/12 Oct 1892, Paris AGO B EC H M NGC TB W78
ARCA 1882 RCA 1891 Painter
Addr: 1881-2, London, Ont; 1883-4, c/o John Peel, Esq, London, Ont; 1885-92, London, Ont
1881 266 Interior of church at St Vehac $125
284 The young musician $150
285 Le déjeuner $250
294 The botanist (W.T. Peel)
295 Fish from Bay of Fundy $100
1882 73 The spinner $125 (MMFA)
80 Mud Creek, Paris $65
1883 5 The meadow $100
9 Breton's cabin in December $75
10 Sardine fishery of Cape Finistère, France $700
31 Return of the flock $450 Fla-2011
75 Un étude $100
78 Rainy morning, return from market $125
1884 23 Near London, Ontario $30
51 Young mother $350
53 The market at London, Ontario $150
1885 8 Good-bye 1886-133 $35 Fla-2011
77 The anxious moment
186 Painting
1886 2 Covent Garden Market, London, Ontario $150 Fla-2011
109 Awaiting his return $75 Fla-2011
119 Admiration $75 Fla-2011
182 Return of the harvesters $1,000 Fla-2011
194 Return of the flock $200 Fla-2011 S2-83
198 Papa's boat $125 Fla-2011
1888 84 Two friends $100 1889-10 $75
127 Father will return $350
130 Mother's little help $100 1889-54 $75
169 The meadow lark $100
1889 48 The young gleaner $100
56 Landscape, snow scene $50
59 The young botanist $200
81 Landscape $50
83 Papa gone $300
93 The Arab $200
98 Fisherman's wife at home $300
1893 deceased
109 The Venetian bather $1,500 F1-84 (NGC)
1907 F6, Sherbrooke
139 Landscape in Brittany $300 nfs (E. Whaley Esq, Toronto)
1910 S2, Liverpool
84 The milk maid
DW not presented

PEGY, W.
H
1885 212 Flowers wc

PEHAP, ERICH KONSTANTIN (ERIC)
10 Apr 1912, Viljandi, Finland IO M WWA59
1954 98 Disquietude print 18 x 32 illus $40
1961 65 Dancers print 20 x 24 illus $50
1968 39 One entrance of the house of the magician, Kabah 23 1/2 x 19 $55

PELL, AUGUSTUS J.
fl 1859-85 H
Addr: 1884, Notre Dame St, Montreal
1882 178 In the hills, Vermont wc $60 A.J. Peel mispr
200 Below Sorel, St Lawrence River wc $60
1884 168 The far west wc $150

PELLAN, ALFRED (b Pelland)
16 May 1906, Quebec AGO B CC2 CWW79 M NGC TB2 WWA47
ARCA 1971 Painter
Addr: 1979, Auteuil, Laval, Que

PELLETIER, PIERRE YVES
15 Dec 1938, Montreal
RCA(e) 1978 Graphic designer
Addr: 1979, Montreal

PEMBERTON, SOPHIE THERESA (Mrs Arthur Beanlands) (Mrs Deane Drummond)
15 Feb 1869, Victoria 31 Oct 1959, Victoria CC1 DBA DVP G M
ARCA 1906-8 Painter
Addr: 1904, London, Eng; 1905-8, Victoria; 1909N, c/o H.M. Lamb, Windsor Hotel, Montreal
1904 124 Un livre ouvert F4-63
1905 132 A Chelsea pensioner 1909N-4

1907 Beanlands, to 1909
13 Penumbra

PENFOLD, KATHERINE S.
Addr: 1896, 515 Clarke Ave, Westmount, Que
1896 134 La tricoteuse
135 A sketch

PENSON, SEYMOUR R.G.
fl 1880-91 H
1885 52 Near the eagle's nest, Lake Rosseau $30
1888 261 In the woods wc $30
1889 147 Lake Rosseau wc $50
1891 146 Bridge at the Narrows wc
231 Gorge, Muskoka River

PENTZ, DONALD ROBERT
18 Sep 1940, Bridgewater, NS M
RCA(e) 1976 Painter
Addr: 1979, Regina

PEPPER, GEORGE DOUGLAS
25 Feb 1903, Ottawa 1 Oct 1962, Toronto AGO CC1 CWW58 M NGC TB2 WWA47
ARCA 1942 RCA 1957 Council Painter
Addr: 1925-7, 239 Frank St, Ottawa; 1928, 88 Carlton St, Toronto; 1931, 16 Torrington Pl, Ottawa; 1932, 441 Walmer Rd, Toronto; 1935-7, Studio Bldg, 25 Severn St, Toronto; 1943-62, Toronto
1925 173 Sunflowers
316 The beech tree wd cut
317 Pastorale wd cut
1926 194 Winter linocut 1927-328
1927 325 A street in Hull pen & ink
326 Ontario homestead pen & ink
327 January linocut
1928 120 Winter morn wc $50
1929 S7, Calgary
123 A street in Hull $250
1931 224 Indian smoke houses $200
225 Grey day, Lake Superior $175
418 Portrait sketch pencil $20
419 Sketch of a boy pencil $15
1932 155 Sketch, Blue Rocks, NS $75
1935 207 Winter, St Urbain $75
208 Green fields, grey day $50 T36-59
1936 247 An old man drwg $10
248 The woodcutter drwg $10
1937 174 The golden crop $80 T38-44
1938 174 Negro boy $65 T39-45 1939-186 $40
1940 125 St Hilarion wc $20
126 Barns wc $20
1941 147 Figures $400 T42-42
148 Card game at night $150
1941 S9, Toronto
50 December in Quebec $80
1942 107 Saturday afternoon nfs T43-33
1946 93 Lake in the mountains $60
1948 125 Figure composition $550
193 Composition chalk drwg $25
1949 71 The dispossessed $350 T50-15
1950 119 Waterfront, Dieppe 27 x 40 $400
120 Rock girt lake 16 x 20 $75
1951 77 A Newfoundland harbour wc $100
78 Newfoundland cove wc $100
1952 72 Labrador Eskimo $100 T53-26
73 Hebron, Labrador wc $100
1954 67 Newfoundland outport wc 14 x 21 illus $100 ◊LAG◊
1955 65 Mending nets, Grand Banks illus $250
1956 35 White village illus $200
1957 56 Spanish village illus $450 DW 1958 31 x 37
57 Welcome to the Sultan of Morocco $350
1959 66 Mountain village, Andalucia 28 x 36 illus $500
1960 61 Emergence 20 x 36 illus $500
1963 59 Trawling off the Grand Banks (rose fish) 44 x 55 illus $1,800

PEPPER, JOHN ROBERT
1905, Prescott, Ont M
Addr: 1931-2, 38 Barton Ave, Toronto
1931 226 Street scene, Quebec $150
1932 156 Giants at rest $150

PEPPER, KATHLEEN see DALY, KATHLEEN

PERCIVAL, GERTRUDE
Addr: 1924,328 Mackay St, Montreal
1924 239 Joseph W. Percival sculp

PERCIVAL, PHYLLIS M. REYNOLDS (Mrs Albert C. Percival)
b USA CNS40

Addr: 1929-35, 220 Percival Ave, Montreal West
1929 175 A corner of Bonsecours Market $35
1931 227 Spring at St Martin, Quebec $65
228 At Caughnawaga $50
1932 157 Unloading, Lunenburg $100
1934 154 Rising tide, Ogunquit $125 T35-57
1935 209 The green hills $125
210 A sunlit village $175
1938 175 Off Pointe Claire $400
176 Motif #1, Rockport, Mass $300
1941 150 Sherbrooke Street near Guy $150 T42-44

PEREHUDOFF, WILLIAM
21 Apr 1919, Langham, Sask M WWA76
ARCA 1968 Painter
Addr: 1970-1/79, Saskatoon
1967 51 Zephrus series #1 69 x 83 $900
1968 39a Color improvisation 60 x 64 $800

PEREIRA, SWYNFEN
Addr: 1900, Ottawa
1900 177 The red bridge wc

PERKINS, GRANVILLE American
16 Oct 1830, Baltimore 18 Apr 1895, New York B Gr TB
Addr: 1883, New York
1883 275 Jersey coast, Ashbury Park wc (R.F. Gagen, ARCA)

PERRAULT, GERARD
b 1903
1938 S8, Toronto
205 Book, L'Isle d'Orléans. English buff colored morocco, mosaic des
206 Book, Maria Chapdelaine. Blue English morocco, mosaic des
207 Book, Québec la double provence. Half leather, with rag mat
208 Book, La Gaspésie. Half calfskin & imitation wood

PERRAULT, SUZANNE PARENT (Mrs)
28 Mar 1924, Montreal M
Addr: 1976, Laval, Que
1976 S12, Montreal
148 Transparence rideau tissé/woven curtain 42 x 41 illus

PERRE, HENRI
1828, or 1821, Strasbourg 1890, Toronto AGO EC H M NGC W78
ARCA 1880 RCA 1882 Council Painter
Addr: 1880-2, Toronto; 1883, 14 King St W, Toronto; 1884-90, Toronto
1880 89 Pennsylvania landscape
150 On the Wirrihaten, Pennsylvania wc
152 The first frost wc
155 and 158 Pennsylvania landscape wc
156 On the Schuylkill wc
1881 264 A mountain stream $90
299 A rifted cloud $50
320 Rainstorm $80
1882 5 View of Toronto from Scarboro' $75 A. Perre, mispr
34 Evening in Colorado $100
79 Landscape $200 DW 1882 24 1/2 x 31 1/2 DW 1880 date error 1883-18
1883 26 Rainy day, New Brunswick $75
32 Rapids near Intercolonial Railway, Quebec $150
43 Cottage near Point Levis, Quebec $35
59 Boulder on the St Lawrence, near IR $100
110 Rocky road on the St Lawrence, IR $300
126 Village of Bic, on the IR $200
129 The great cut at Bic, on the IR $150
137a Old pirate cave, on the St Lawrence, near IR $300
175 Landscape near IR, Quebec wc $60
178 Morning on the Metapedia wc $40
200 Boulders on the St Lawrence wc $60
204 Natural mountain path near IR wc $60
209 High tide on the St Lawrence wc $50
228 Groups of spruce trees wc $60
265 Near the St Lawrence, Quebec wc $40
287 In the Credit Valley wc $35
301 A little village on the

IR, early morning wc $40
303 Rapids, on IR wc $40
1884 S1, Saint John
40 Spruce trees wc $40
90 Autumn $30 1885-102 $45
108 Return from the hunt $100
119 Hazy afternoon $25
123 Metapedia $25
125 In the Alleghany Mountains $40
131 In Colorado $25
133 In Lower Canada $25
1885 1 Willows on the Schuylkill, Pennsylvania $75
27 Pasture, Eastern Townships $35
40 Near New Market, Ont $45
63 Under the oaks $120
115 Tranquility $45
170 Old French Canadian mill $50
201 Landscape wc $15
213 Stormy day wc $25
1886 128 Canadian oak, early autumn $125 F1a-2012
162 The double-leaf pine $45
180 Canadian willows $60
1886 F1a, London, Eng
2012, artist number
At London, Ontario (J. Griffiths Esq, London, Ont)
River scene (Princess Louise)
1888 13 Bic Falls wc
312 The Pirate's harbour, St Lawrence

PERRIGARD, HAL ROSS
3 Jan 1891, Montreal 23 Apr 1960, Montreal M NGC PMC TB2
ARCA 1924 Painter
Addr: 1915-22, 747 St Catherine St W, Montreal; 1923-4, 269 Old Orchard Ave, Montreal; 1925, 220 Mountain St, Montreal; 1926, 269 Old Orchard Ave, Montreal; 1927-37, 418 Claremont Ave, Westmount, Que; 1938-60, Westmount, Que
1915 170 Reflections
171 On River St Francis
1916 182 The Magog River
309 One night on the Richelieu b&w
310 Three trees, viewpoint b&w
1918A 261 The coal trestle b&w
302 At Hull
303 Breaking for the tunnel ≬NGC≬
302-3, Trustees, National Gallery of Canada, Travelling scholarship competition
1918N 148 Melting time
149 The Cliff, Magog, Quebec
250 When snow holds sway b&w
251 Winter, above the Magog b&w
1919 131 Sun glow and winter velvet pastel
132 The Tower of Babel, Valley of the Ten Peaks, Canadian Rockies pastel
215 Fire trail charcl
216 Above the trailing clouds, Canadian Rockies charcl
1920 196 Mount Assiniboine, Canadian Rockies
197 Sous le Cap, Quebec
331 Fire trail b&w
332 Cold b&w
1921 122 Home
1922 162 Cathedral Peak, Canadian Rockies S6-72
1923 135 An old mill and his friend the tree
136 Sand dunes of Annisquam
1924 162 Low land silence
163 The shore
1925 174 In harbour
175 The distant glow pastel
176 January day
1926 116 Reflections pastel
1927 178 The little red house on the hill
179 Light on sails pastel
180 Alone pastel
1929 176 The old standby $160
177 Green banks $500
1929 S7, Calgary
124 Late summer $250
1931 229 Cathedral $925
230 In old Quebec $400
1933 183 Old settler's home $400 T34-65
184 The old news shop $350
1935 211 Old stone boats at low tide $400
212 The old road $150 T36-60
1937 175 Stream in the Rockies $350
176 A bit of old Gloucester $350 T38-45
1938 177 Hell's Gate, Canadian Rockies $350 F11-56 27 x 22 $500
1938 S8, Toronto
380 Wallpaper design. Hon

mention Canadian Wallpaper Manufacturers Limited
1939 187 Sunday quiet $350
188 Around the bridge $250
1941 151 Springtime in the country $200 T42-45 1942-108 $250
152 Blacksmith's holiday $275
1944 110 Motif in the hills $175
1945 162 Beginning of spring illus $350 T46-37
163 December snow $225
1946 94 Near the docks, Gloucester $500
1947 136 Impressions of a spring day $350
137 Pete's place, winter sun $400 T48-31
1948 126 Snow blanket $425
1951 79 Pattern in the gorge $400
1952 74 Abandoned quarry, Pigeon Cove, Mass $600

PERRY, ALFRED LESLIE
30 Sep 1896, Lachine, Que
Addr: 1920-2, 340 Oxford Ave, Montreal; 1924, 341 Côte St Antoine Rd, Westmount; 1927, 1190 University St, Montreal; 1929-33, New Birks Bldg, 620 Cathcart St, Montreal; 1935-7, 1405 Bishop St, Montreal
1920 202 Waterfront, Longue Pointe, Quebec wc
285 St Vincent de Paul, Que
1922 163 Hart House, Toronto wc S6-73
1924 283 Lincoln Cathedral, England
284 Fountain, Trinity College, Cambridge
1933 185 Winter sunset $35
1935 213 Reflections, Lake Tremblant $35
214 Winter scene, Morin Heights $200
1939 189 Quebec farm buildings $45
1949 109 Union Church, Ste Anne de Bellevue
1927 Perry & Luke, to 1935
249 Residence, Westmount, Que
250 Club house, Knowlton, Que
1929 232 St Luke's United Church, Montreal
233 Residence, Mr H.M. Banks, Westmount
234 Residence, Mr F.W. Sharp, Westmount model
1931 373 Quebec Golf Club, Boischatel, Que pencil
374 Residence, Westmount, Quebec pen & ink
1933 246 Residence, Westmount, Que
1935 268 Residence, Col G.W. Birks model
269 Residence, Mr H.M. Long
1937 Perry, Luke & Little, to 1939
256 Rosemere Golf Club
257 Residence, Mount Bruno, Quebec
1939 282 Garneau cottage, St Marguerite
283 Ogilvie cottage, St Agathe

PERRY, FRANK
15 Jan 1923, Vancouver WWA76
RCA(e) 1974 Sculptor
Addr: 1979, North Vancouver
1957 82 Seated figure sculp $100
1964J 81 Head bronze illus $650
1967 81 Wall and door sculp 18 x 5 x 12 $1,000
1970 90 Reclining soldier sculp 39 x 30 x 14 $3,000

PETCHEY, WINIFRED see MARSH, WINIFRED

PETER, FRIEDRICH GUNTHER
23 Feb 1933, Dresden, Germany WWA78
RCA(e) 1974 Calligrapher
Addr: 1976/79, North Vancouver
1976 S12, Montreal
126 Psalm cal Chinese ink/encre de chine illus

PETERS, GORDON
17 Jul 1920, Edinburgh IO
RCA(e) 1973 Painter
Addr: 1979, Caledon East, Ont
1965 58 Ontario relic 15 x 22 $150
59 Winter silence 15 x 22 $150

PETERS, LLOYD A.
Addr: 1937, 2 Thora Ave, Toronto
1937 325 Rustic charm dry pt $18
326 Home lane dry pt $18
1938 261 The apple pickers dry pt $18
262 Hay for sale dry pt $18

PETERS, SUSAN M.
1884 S1, Saint John
142 A domestic breeze $75

PETLEY-JONES, LLEWELLYN
23 Aug 1908, Edmonton AGO CWW79
1950 121 Les trois françaises 40 x 32 1/2 illus $550

PFEIFER, BODO
15 May 1936, Dusseldorf WWA73
1966 51 Untitled 84 x 90 $800

PFEIFFER, GORDON EDWARD
10 Oct 1899, Quebec CNS44
Addr: 1927-31, 208 Bougainville Ave, Quebec; 1932-6, 4 McMahon St, Quebec
1927 181 Logging on Lake Beauport
1931 231 Le départ, Charlesbourg, Quebec $85
1932 158 Le four abandonné $300
1933 186 Laurentians $195 T34-66
1936 165 Nude resting $100
166 Nude, Saguenay $1,000
1940 127 Rainy Sunday $150 T41-43
1947 139 After rain $250
1952 75 Soft winter weather $300

PFEIFFER, HAROLD SAMSON
4 Apr 1908, Quebec
1945 231 Portia White sculp nfs
1946 144 Judy plaster in bronze $300
1947 216 William Primrose, Esq, violinist plaster nfs
1949 122 Mrs E. Ross Willmot, Ottawa plaster for bronze nfs
1957 83 Old Willya, Port Harrison Eskimo sculp $400

PFLUG, CHRISTIANE SYBILLE SCHUTT (Mrs Michael Pflug)
20 Jun 1936, Berlin 4 Apr 1972, Hanlan's Point, Toronto Island
1964J 51 On the balcony 47 x 39 1/2 illus nfs
1964N 43 With the last snow 39 1/2 x 47 1/2 illus $600
1965 60 The window at night 55 1/4 x 50 1/4 illus nfs

PHELPS, HELEN WATSON American
1859, Attleboro, Mass 6 Feb 1944, New York TB1/3
1909M 100a A young girl

PHILLIPS, JOHN KENNETH
20 Apr 1909, Toronto AGO
Addr: 1934-6, 45 Charles St E, Toronto
1934 155 Marie Cecilia Guard $400
1936 167 Self $100

PHILLIPS, MARY MARTHA
1856, Montreal d 1937 H Mo12
Addr: 1893-5, Victoria School of Art, Montreal; 1897-8, 2270 St Catherine St, Montreal; 1903, c/o Johnston & Copping, Montreal
1890 198 Citadel, Quebec wc $15
1892 122 Virginie wc $15 1893-245 $20
137 An old salt wc $15
1893 246 Gloucester harbour wc $25 F1-183
1895 72W Roses wc
73W Idleness wc
1897 36W Laval courtyard, Quebec wc
1898 200 An oyster boat wc
201 Laprairie houses wc
1903 77 Hay field by the sea
1904 242 The hayfield pastel

PHILLIPS, WALTER JOSEPH
25 Oct 1884, Burton-on-Humber, Eng 5 Jul 1963, Victoria AGO B CC1 CWW61 EC NGC PMC TB2 W78 WWA47
ARCA 1921-30 Painter 1931-3 Engraver RCA 1934 Sr 1954 Engraver
Addr: 1914-16, 110 Bannerman Ave, Winnipeg; 1918A-23, 32 Bannerman Ave, Winnipeg; 1924, Wylye, Wilts, Eng; 1925-6, 104 Wellington Cr, Winnipeg; 1927, 730 Wolseley Ave, Winnipeg; 1928, 629 Wolseley Ave, Winnipeg; 1929-36, 729 Wolseley Ave, Winnipeg; 1937, 501 River Ave, Winnipeg; 1938-40, Winnipeg; 1941-8, Calgary; 1949-61, Banff; 1962-3, Victoria
1914 156 Evening on the Winnipeg River wc
157 Winnipeg River wc
1915 172 The last snow, Kenora wc
173 Autumn night wc
1916 183 The lake, evening wc
184 Afterglow, Norman Bay, Lake of the Woods wc
311 The lake etch
1918A 136 The quiet lake wc
137 Snow bound wc
262 Rosie col print
263 The golden hour col print
1918N 150 Sunset, Lake of the Woods wc
151 Twilight, Lake of the Woods wc
252 Afternoon etch
253 Sunset col print
1919 217 Vilas Park, Madison col print

218 Winnipeg River at Minaki col print
1920 198 Two lakes wc 1921-215
199 A water baby wc ◊NGC◊
333 Rushing river col print
334 Willow Drive, Madison col print
1921 123 Summer idyl wc
124 The edge of the lake wc
216 Holiday time col print
1922 164 Lake of the Woods wc S6-74 ◊AGO◊
165 The stump wc
166 A lake homestead wc
273 The dock col print
274 Evening col print S6-122
275 Long Bay, Keewatin print S6-123
276 Burnt lands col print
1923 137 The raft wc
138 A place in the sun wc
139 Vista wc
222 The bather
223 St Andrews. frontispiece, 'Women of Red River'
224 Norman Bay #2 col print
1924 164 A group of birches wc
1925 177 Cottages at Wylye wc
178 Water nymphs wc
318 Wylye Mill Bridge col wdcut
319 Summer col wdcut
320 The batwing sail col wdcut
321 Morning col wdcut
1926 195 Mountain torrent col print from wd block
196 Mountain larch col print from wd block
1927 182 Siwash house posts temp
183 Lake McArthur wc
329 Jim King's wharf, Alert Bay, BC col wdcut ◊AGO◊
330 The beach col wdcut
331 Mount Schaeffer col wdcut
332 A Gloucester village col wdcut
1928 121 Siwash house posts, Karlukwees, BC wc $150 F9-87
122 The shady beech wood wc $165
220 Tulips col print $25
221 Nasturtiums col print $15
222 Zinnias col print $25 ◊AGO◊
1929 178 The picnic wc $250
279 Mamalilicoola, BC col wdcut $35 ◊AGO◊
280 Karlukwees, BC col wdcut $30 ◊AGO◊
281 Bredon village col wdcut $25
1929 S7, Calgary
125 Birches wc $200
126 Margaret wc $150 ◊EAG◊
1930 133 La Salle, Manitoba wc $175
134 The clothes line, Mamalilicoola, BC wc $175 ◊AGO◊
135 Approaching storm, Moraine Lake, Alberta $150
136 Silver Plains, Manitoba wc $175 ◊NGC◊
215 April in the Cotswolds col print $16.50
216 Moraine Lake wd engr $10
1931 232 York boats wc $150
233 Pacific coast wc $200
420 Poplar Bay col wdcut $30
421 Rushing river wd engr $10
1932 159 Lac Lu wc $150
160 Karlukwees, BC wc $150
254 Moon and mist wd engr $12.50
255 Cook's Creek wd engr $12.50
1933 187 Margaret in Rumanian dress wc $250 T34-67
312 Vista Lake wd engr
313 Simon, BC wd engr $12.50
314 Kincome, BC wd engr $12.50
315 Alert Bay, BC wd engr $12.50
1934 156 Prairie town wc $150
223 Hnausa col wdcut $45 DW 1934 17 1/4 x 12 T35-58
224 Gimli col wdcut $25
225 Headingly wd engr $12.50
1935 338 Howe Sound, BC col wdcut $27.50 ◊AGO◊
339 Gerran's Bay, BC col wdcut $22.50 T36-61
340 Gimli #2 col wdcut $17.50 ◊AGO◊
341 Hanging Rock Island, Lake of the Woods wd engr $12.50
1937 177 Mount Biddle wc $150 T38-46
178 Summer at Muskoka wc $150
327 Simoon, BC col wdcut $20 ◊AGO◊
328 Mistaya Valley wd engr $7.50
1938 178 Wenkchemna wc $250 T39-46
179 York boats wc $150
1940 128 Star Lake, Man wc $175

129 The golden west wc $200
171 Jack pine col print $15
172 Lake Louise col print $10
1941 154 Rainbow Falls wc $175
243 Leaf of gold wdcut $28
1942 111 Mount Rundle from Vermilion Lakes wc $250 T43-34
112 Trail from Skoki wc $200
177 Mountain road col wdcut $25
1943 146 Ski lodge col wdcut $15
147 Prairie elevator col wdcut $20
1944 160 Beaver Lodge col wdcut $20
1945 164 Saanich maples wc $175
165 Under the maple wc $250
248 Above Lake Louise col wdcut nfs
1946 95 Johnson's Creek, near Banff wc $250 ◊NGC◊
1947 140 Falls on Gold Creek, Revelstoke wc $450
141 Falls under Mount Lefroy wc $450
1949 72 At Columbia Ice Fields wc $250
1952 117 Indian Days, Banff col wdcut $35
118 Sharp's dock, Pender Harbour, BC col wdcut $30 1953-129
1953 67 Lake Minnewanka wc $250
1955 66 Split rail fence, Ontario $250

PHILLIPS, WALTER N.
1938 S8, Toronto
380 Wallpaper design. Hon mention Canadian Wallpaper Manufacturers Limited

PICARD, FRANCOISE
17 Apr 1923, West Sheffield, Que TB3
1947 142 Tête de femme gouache
1949 73 La Seine en bleu, Paris '48 gouache $45

PICHER, CLAUDE
30 May 1927, Quebec AGO CC2 NGC TB3 WWA78
ARCA 1960 Painter
Addr: 1961-71, Quebec; 1979, Matane, Que
1945 166 Grove at Ste Pétronille $50

PICHET, ROLAND (b Pichette)
4 Jul 1936, Montreal
RCA(e) 1978 Painter
Addr: 1979, St Sauveur des Monts, Que

PICKERING, BERNARD M.
8 Feb 1903, Toronto
Addr: 1930, 24 Thyra Ave, Toronto
1930 137 Clay castle $150

PICKERING, DAVID
b 1941
Addr: 1976, Kingston, Ont
1976 S12, Montreal
87 Bronze mound bronze 9 x 21 x 21 illus

PIGOTT, MARJORIE
6 Jan 1904, Yokohama IO WWA76
ARCA 1971 RCA 1974 Painter
Addr: 1979, Toronto
1970 59 Through a window curtain 28 1/4 x 20 1/4 $600
DW 1974 Lyrical fantasy. 1973 wc 16 1/2 x 28

PILOT, ROBERT WAKEHAM MBE DCL
9 Oct 1898, St John's 17 Dec 1967, Montreal AGO CC1 CNS36 CWW64 EC NGC TB2 W78 WWA47 WWB54
ARCA 1925 RCA 1934 Council Painter
Addr: 1913-15, 3 Beaver Hall Sq, Montreal; 1920-6, 67 Ste Famille St, Montreal; 1927-8, c/o Watson Art Gallery, 679 St Catherine St W, Montreal; 1929-37, 3531 Ste Famille St, Montreal; 1938-67, Montreal
1913 235 Sketch
1915 174 Grey day, winter
175 Early morning
1920 200 Twilight, Les Eboulements
201 Montreal, from Mount Royal
1922 167 Concarneau, Brittany S6-75
168 L'Eglise Saint Gervais, Paris S6-76
277 Canal, Chartres etch S6-124
278 Vieille ruelle, Concarneau etch S6-125
1924 165 Man with lantern
166 Cab stand, Lévis illus
285 The white house, Concarneau etch
286 Richelieu Church, and dam etch
1925 179 Snow carts, Lévis

180 Quebec from Levis illus (NGC)
322 The cathedral and trees etch
323 The gateway, Chartres etch 1926-200
324 The river at Chartres drwg
1926 117 The coast of Grand Manan
118 The arched rock, sun effect
119 Swallow-Tail lighthouse, Grand Manan, NB
197 Quebec from Point Levis etch 1927-333
198 Cape Diamond, Quebec etch
199 Habitant farm, Chambly etch
1927 184 View of Toledo, Spain
185 Arab town, Morocco
334 French Canadian farm etch
1928 123 Sunset, Quebec from Levis $400 F9-177
124 Market place, Tangiers $200
125 Silk Market, Tetuan $200
1928 F8, London, Eng
103 Shipyard, Lunenburg $200 S7-127
1929 179 The harbour, St John's, Newfoundland $450
180 Lifting fog, Newfoundland $480
1929 S7, Calgary
128 View of Quebec $500
1930 138 View at Percé, Quebec $500
139 Swallow-Tail Cape, Grand Manan, NB $500
1931 234 Parliament Buildings, Quebec $500
235 Church, St Michel, Quebec $250
236 Sillery, Quebec $250
1933 188 Winter twilight, Levis, Quebec $450 T34-68
189 The flying canoe mural dec (John H. Molson, Esq)
1934 157 Parliament Buildings, Ottawa $1,200
158 Country road, Chambly
159 The Beauport Road, autumn
1935 215 The blue house, Chambly nfs (MMFA)
1936 168 St Sauveur, Quebec $300 T37-52
1937 179 Out-door oven, Baie St Paul $275
180 October, St Urbain, Que $1,000
1939 F11, New York
57 Farm, St Urbain 19 x 25 $400
1941 155 Early spring, St Sauveur, Quebec nfs
1946 96 March, Piedmont $600 T47-41
97 Grey day, Simon River, Quebec $350
98 March, Piedmont, Quebec $350 T47-42
1947 143 Quebec, from Point Levis $1,200
144 March day, Lac Supérieur, Quebec illus $750
1949 74 Snow Dome Glacier, Columbia Ice Fields $900 cat #79 mispr for 74
75 Sunwapta Gorge, Columbia Ice Fields illus $900 1950-123 30 x 40 illus
1951 80 The schooner, Baie St Paul, winter illus $600
81 Winter, Baie St Paul $700
1952 76 Kingston from the waterfront illus $800 1953-68 nfs
1953 69 Dufferin Terrace, Quebec illus $900
1953 Travelling exhibit
27 Schooner in the ice, Baie St Paul $600
1954 68 Twilight, Dufferin Terrace, Quebec 22 x 28 illus $600
69 The tuna wharf, Wedgeport, NS 22 x 28 $600 1955-68 $450
48 Retro Sec. Columbia Glacier, Sunwapta Valley
1955 67 Rue des Jardins, Québec $700 1956-36 22 x 28 illus (NGC)
1956 37 Autumn,Sacré Coeur on the Saguenay $800
1957 58 The glacier $600
59 The Narrows, St John's, Newfoundland illus (MMFA) S10-61
1958 65 Twilight, Dufferin Terrace, Quebec illus $700
66 Place d'Armes, Quebec $700
1959 67 Rue des Jardins 22 x 28 illus $800
1960 62 Notre Dame de Paris 24 x 32 illus $700
1963 60 Lower town, Quebec $1,500
1966 S10, Charlottetown
60 The Governor's Garden, Quebec nfs (AGH)
DW 1935 Twilight, Levis 30 x 40

1954 Jubilee year, text
1958 Horatio Walker, Memorial sec, biog

PINHEY, H. EARDLEY
Addr: 1913, 65 blvd Arago, Paris
1913 236 Old Moret wc S4-105 $20
237 Stacking seaweed, Brittany wc S4-106 $20
1925 Late H. Eardley Pinhey, c/o Mrs Pinhey, Hudson Heights
325 Crypt of a church at Provins drwg
326 Interior, Chartres Cathedral drwg

PINHEY, JOHN CHARLES
24 Aug 1860, Ottawa 7 Sep 1912 EC H Mo12 NGC TB3 W78
ARCA 1885 RCA 1897 Council Painter
Addr: 1885-90, Ottawa; 1891-2, Montreal; 1893-11, Hudson Heights, Que
1885 2 The leisure hour
105 Portrait
114 Les vielles
178 A senator
194 In the forest of Fontainebleau
1886 41 The unexpected return $75
120 A summer day $50
122 Portrait
148 The leisure hour, a portrait
195 Tribute to the dead $275
#195 Selected for Fla, not in Fla cat
1887 45 Tranquility $125
1889 19 The lone pine $40
58 The village belle $60
61 and 70 Portrait
92 The lost children $100
1890 11 In the old Chartreuse $75
67 A legend of the Ottawa River $300
1891 236 An interrupted siesta, Mexico
1892 4 The trysting place $50
23 Christ in the wilderness
54 Why don't you play? $75
89 Faith $25
1893 110 Summer is over $175
111 Jael $175 F1-85
112 Imperia nfs
1894 94 Constantia
95 Wild flowers
96 Sunset in winter
97 Iris
1895 97 The mower
98 Clio
99 Vivian
100 Stella
1897 115 La penserosa DW 1897 19 1/2 x 24 3/4 Reverie mistitle
1900 91 John Christie, Esq
1901 90 A father in Israel F2-56
1903 91 Study of a head
92 A Roman maiden
1906 145 Oaks in September
146 The prodigal's return
1907 153 A Moss Trooper
154 An old mill
155 An old mill dam S2-85
156 Boy fishing
1908 107 A woodland glade
108 An old sluice gate
109 An old bridge 1909M-101
110 Old mill
1909M 102 Storm and sunshine
1910 156 Early spring
157 Marshy land
158 Old trees by the river
1910 S2, Liverpool
86 The haunted mill

PINKERTON, CONSTANCE C.
Addr: 1913, Montreal
1913 238 and 239 Landscape, Knowlton, Quebec

PINKERTON, H.L.
1938 S8, Toronto
R.G. McLean Limited
203 6 pieces, Goodyear truck tire campaign
204 10 pieces, Goodyear automobile tire campaign

PINNEO, GEORGIANNA PAIGE
26 Mar 1896, Nova Scotia flg 1974
1943 95 Le bureau de poste, Bic, Québec $50
1947 145 Rocks and sea wc $75 T48-32

PINSKY, ALFRED
31 Mar 1921, Montreal WWA56
1954 70 Mount Royal 23 x 48 $200

PIPON, FLORENCE MACDONALD (Mrs)
Addr: 1931, c/o Bank of Montreal, Halifax
1931 237 South shore, Nova Scotia $150
238 Herring Cove, Nova Scotia $100

PITSEOLAK E7-1100
c1900, Nottingham Island, Hudson Bay, NWT ED
RCA(e) 1974 Print maker
Addr: 1979, Cape Dorset, NWT

PITTS, GORDON McLEAN
see MAXWELL, WILLIAM S, 1927-1937

PLAMONDON, ANTOINE SEBASTIEN
28 Feb 1804, Ancienne Lorette, Que
4 Sep 1895, Neuville, Pointe aux Trembles, Que AGO B EC H NGC W78
RCA Hon Member 1880 Ret 1881 Painter
Addr: 1880-95, Quebec
1954 1 Retro Sec. Still life (NGC) 1970 cat listed, in error, as DW 1880 Still life with apples and grapes

PLAMONDON, MARIUS GERALD
21 Jul 1919, Quebec 3 Oct 1976, Quebec WWA59
ARCA 1959 Stained glass designer
Addr: 1960-71, Quebec

PLASKETT, AILEEN ANNE
16 Jan 1905, London, Eng
Addr: 1928-35, 188 James St, Ottawa
1928 126 Marigolds $60 Aileen Q. Plaskett, mispr
1929 181 Mirrored zinnias $85
1931 239 Miss Betty Young $100
240 Peonies $125
1933 191 Elise $50
1935 216 Billi nfs

PLASKETT, JOHN MAYSEY
1873, London, Ont
Addr: 1924-33, 188 James St, Ottawa
1924 167 The cloudburst
1931 241 Portrait
1933 190 Portrait

PLASKETT, JOSEPH FRANCIS
12 Jul 1918, New Westminster, BC
AGO CC2 NGC TB3
RCA(e) 1978 Painter
Addr: 1979, Paris

PLAYFAIR, CHARLES GREGORY PAUL
19 Apr 1917, Hagersville, Ont TB3
1948 127 Six dancers: construction on a theme from 'Burnt Norman' $400
1949 76 Three swimmers $125 T50-16
1951 82 The bathers $400

PLETZER, GEORGE ARNOLD
1 May 1907, Orangeville, Ont
Addr: 1925-9, 377 Pacific Ave, Toronto; 1930, 162 Caledonia Rd, Toronto; 1932, 2 Failsworth Ave, Toronto
1925 181 Evening lights
1929 182 Beside the Grande $100
1930 140 Afternoon $100
141 Scraps $175
1932 161 Tretheway Park, winter $200

PLIMSOLL, FANNY GRACE English
b London, Eng fl 1891-14 DBA H
Addr: 1893, 464 Guy St, Montreal; 1894, YMCA Bldg, Montreal; 1896, 32 rue Poucelet, Paris; 1899, 20 rue Bayen, Paris; 1902, 29 Ontario Ave, Montreal; 1912, Osborne Hotel, London, Eng
1893 113 An after dinner pipe $125 F1-86
114 Les petit poisson pour souper $39
115 Japonicas $30
247 The village well wc $55
248 Street sketch, Montreal wc $20
1894 89 Studio interior
185 Poplars wc
1896 136 The weary spinner, Barbizon
137 Dutch interior
138 Sea shore, north Holland
139 Windmill near Alkmaar
1899 104 Dutch landscape
1902 264 Head, Friesland peasant min
265 Reverie min
266 Une Parisienne min
1912 178 Laitière
179 La dentellière de Bruges

POIRIER, NARCISSE
19 Mar 1883, St Felix de Valois, Que flg 1972
Addr: 1925, 4902 St Denis St, Montreal; 1927-37, 4908 St Denis St, Montreal
1925 182 Nature morte
1927 186 Etude de pommes
1929 183 Chrysanthèmes $250
1931 242 Dans le vieux Montmartre, Paris $400
1933 192 Nature morte $100
1935 217 Nature morte $125
1937 181 Paysage Laurentian $300

POJAR, BRETISLAV
1971 Psychocratie film screened 21 Apr

POLLOCK, DAVID RAYMOND
17 Jun 1926, Toronto
1944 111 Self portrait $200 T45-35

PONG, CHARLES
Addr: 1921, Toronto
1921 125 Sketch

POOLE, FREDERICK VICTOR English
b Southampton, Eng fl 1890-37 B DBA F G TB
Addr: 1912, 62 Wolfrey Ave, Toronto
1912 180 Idle moments
1912 S3, Winnipeg
124 Betty
125 Autumn morning
216 The last satyr dec des
217 Prehistoric pig-sticking

PORTEOUS, C.E.L.
fl 1880-96 H
Addr: 1884, Lindsay, Ont
1883 250 Study, River bank, Scugog River wc $50
282 Wheat field, Sussex Vale, NB wc $50 S1-70
293 Sunset 'Against the eastern sky, lay the embers of the day' wc $50
1884 111a On Gull Creek, a study of rocks $40
131a Black Creek wc $40 S1-27
170 Indian summer wc $40
180 Scugog River wc $35
1884 S1, Saint John
14 In Maremma wc $50
23 Cinderella wc $150
43 Portrait wc $50
47 Evening wc $50
58 On the Scugog River wc $50
1885 159 OEnone (water) $80
222 Fiammetta wc $20
307 Can the story be true? wc $50
319 In doubtful mind wc $60
port: by E. Dyonnet, 1902-46

PORTEOUS, FRANCES ESTHER DUDLEY
10 Sep 1896, Ste Petronille, Que
Sep 1946, Montreal
Addr: 1929, 3493 Atwater Ave, Montreal
1929 184 Peonies, flower study $100
185 White lilac, flower study wc $40
1940 130 Bermuda fruit and flowers $85

PORTEOUS, PIERCY EVELYN FRANCES (Mrs George Robert Younger)
25 Feb 1907, Montreal
Addr: 1927, 670 Sherbrooke St W, Montreal
1927 335 Le Père Blouin etch
336 Church of Ste Famille, Ile d'Orléans etch
1947 Younger
187 The bridge, Island of Orleans $125 T48-42

PORTER, MARY MARGUERITE see ZWICKER, MARY MARGUERITE

PORTNALL, FRANCIS HENRY
3 May 1886, Caterham Valley, Surrey, Eng CNS29
Addr: 1935, 109 Angus Cr, Regina
1935 219 My hunting partner wc nfs

POTTERTON, GERALD
dates not on file
RCA(e) 1974 Film maker
Addr: 1979, Westmount, Que

POUSSIN, NICOLAS French
Jun 1594, Villers, France 19 Nov 1665, Rome B TB
1880 20 Androcles and the lion (W. Kingsford, Esq)

POWELL, CHARLES B.
1880 302a Card receiver des

POWER, EDITH ALICE MORTON (Mrs Joseph William Power)
1854, Brockville, Ont H
Addr: 1900-9, 72 Sydenham St, Kingston, Ont
1900 178 Macdonald Park by moonlight wc
1909N 114 Wood near Rice Lake

POWER, JOSEPH WILLIAM
c 1852 25 Aug 1925, Florida
ARCA 1891-09 Architect
Addr: 1891-08, Kingston, Ont; 1909M, Merchants Bank Chambers, Kingston, Ont
1891 204 Residence, King St W, Kingston des
205 St Andrew's Church,

Kingston des
1908 161 St George Cathedral, Kingston, and interior
162 Residence, G.T. Oliver, Cobourg, Ont, and interior
163 Residence, Mrs C. Donnelly, Cobourg, Ont, and interior
1909M 157 City buildings, proposed new dome
158 Banking building, remodelled
159 Bank interiors
160 Biological buildings, Queen's University

POWER, L. JOHN
1816-82
ARCA 1880 Architect
Addr: 1880-2, Kingston, Ont

POWER, NORA
Addr: 1929, 6661 de St Vallier St, Montreal
1929 282 Sous le Cap, Quebec etch $7

PRAGNELL, BARTLEY ROBILLIARD
20 Jun 1908, Moose Jaw, Sask 1966, Calgary
1939 190 From church wc $35

PRATT, CHARLES EDWARD
15 Jul 1911, Boston, Mass
ARCA 1958 RCA 1966 Architect
Addr: 1959-71, Vancouver; 1979, West Vancouver
1966 Thompson, Berwick, Pratt & Partners
171-3 Totem Park Residence, University of British Columbia. Exterior, 3 views
174-5 Henry Angus Building, University of British Columbia. Exterior, 2 views
DW 1967 Koerner House, University of British Columbia photo 14 x 48 1/4
see also Thom, Ronald, 1964N; Thompson, Charles 1964N

PRATT, JOHN CHRISTOPHER
2 Dec 1935, St John's B CCI CWW79
ARCA 1965 Council Painter
Addr: 1966-70, St John's; 1971, St Mary's Bay, Nfld; 1979, Mount Carmel, Nfld

PRATT, MARY FRANCES WEST (Mrs John Christopher Pratt)
15 Mar 1935, Fredericton WWA78
RCA(e) 1976 Painter
Addr: 1979, Mount Carmel, Nfld

PRENT, MARK GEORGE
23 Dec 1947, Montreal WWA78
RCA(e) 1979 Sculptor
Addr: 1979, Montreal
1971 6S His final statement sculp 12 x 24 x 24 $500

PREVOST, ROBERT
c 1927
RCA(e) 1978 Set designer
Addr: 1979, Montreal

PREVOT, EDITH
Addr: 1918N, St Eustache, Que
1918N 152 Vieux moulin, St Eustache

PREVOT, MARIE
Addr: 1915-16, 1880 Clarke St, Montreal
1915 176 Sketch
1916 185 Sketch

PREZAMENT, JOSEPH
3 Jan 1923, Winnipeg WWA59
1958 67 Anna nfs
1967 52 Archaic garden 22 x 40 $350

PRICE, ADDISON WINCHELL
12 Sep 1907, Port Credit, Ont
ARCA 1948 Painter
Addr: 1928, Port Credit, Ont; 1930, Stave Bank Rd, Port Credit, Ont; 1948-71/79, Port Credit
1928 127 July thunderstorm $400
1930 142 Spring's awakening $300
1940 131 Spring reveries $150 T41-44
1941 S9, Toronto
49 Voices of spring $100
1942 113 Fountain of sunshine $125 T43-35
1944 112 Spring time $125 T45-36
1947 146 A sunny intermission $250
1948 128 April caprice $250
129 Call of spring $250
1949 77 Silver strains $250 T50-17
1951 83 Spring $300

PRICE, ARTHUR DONALD
22 May 1918, Edmonton IO WWA59
ARCA 1960 RCA 1973 Sculptor
Addr: 1961-70, Cyrville, Ont; 1971/79, Ottawa

1955 115 The blackboard sculp nfs
1957 84 Bird on sidewalk sculp $300
85 Reclining figure sculp nfs
1958 92 Coat of Arms, City of Ottawa sculp
1959 92 Birds of welcome maquette 16"long $300
1960 88 Prudential Assurance Company of England. Family group bronze 103 x 114 x 60
89 Family group bronze maquette illus $1,200
1963 99 Masked Venus at the polling booth bronze $1,500
1968 62 Vertical habitat sculp 19 1/4h $475
1970 91 Interlude 78h $5,000
DW René sculp 9h base 4 1/2h

PRICE, WINCHELL see PRICE, ADDISON WINCHELL

PRINCE, RICHARD EDMUND
6 Apr 1947, Comox, BC WWA76
RCA(e) 1978 Sculptor
Addr: 1979, Vancouver

PRINGLE & BOOTH LIMITED
Addr: 1938, Toronto
1938 S8, Toronto
J.T. Harris and Bruce Milne
209 Photomontage decoration
210 Group of photographs

PRINGLE, ANNIE WHITE GRIEVE (Mrs James B. Pringle)
6 Mar 1867, Leith, Scot 12 Dec 1945, Smith Falls, Ont CNS36 H
Addr: 1931, 13 Brooke Ave, Westmount, Que; 1937, 2080 Marlowe Ave, Montreal
1931 243 Eleanor 1937-182 nfs

PRITTIE, MARY ELIZABETH
17 Nov 1908, St Catharines, Ont
1950 124 Reflections 20 x 24 nfs
1964J 52 Poppies coll 48 x 60 nfs

PROCTOR, FLORENCE EVELYN KEMP (Mrs)
17 Jan 1886, Montreal
Addr: 1934-6, 3 Beaumont Rd, Toronto
1934 160 Winter $850
161 England $850 T35-59
1935 220 The garnet tree $500
221 Poppies $350
1936 169 Harvest $300
170 Picnic $300
1938 180 Lake Rosseau $300

PROCUNIER, MAY V.
Addr: 1937, 797 Indian Rd, Toronto
1937 183 Tulips $100

PROULX, JOSEPH ONESIME
b 1890
Addr: 1920, 2821 Bordeaux St, Montreal
1920 335 Drawing

PROVIS, ALFRED English
fl 1846-86 B DBA G
1880 48a Wait a while (Maj de Winton)

PROWSE, N. English
fl 1884-8 DBA H
1888 22 Harvest field wc $25
54 Afternoon sunshine, brocoli field wc $40
284 Tide out, St Ives wc $110

PRUS, VICTOR MARIUS
24 Apr 1917, Minsk Mazowiecki, Poland
ARCA 1971 Architect
Addr: 1971/79, Montreal
1968 115-18 Metro, Bonaventure, Montreal. A.Plan B.Boarding platform C.Skylight D.Interior

PRYNE, ROLFE EDMUND
30 Jun 1914, Toronto IO
Addr: 1976, Mississauga, Ont
1976 S12, Montreal
38 The Mennonite egg temp 30 x 36 illus

PUJOL, C.
1882 301 A good story (loan)

PURCELL, JOSEPH DOUGLAS
21 Oct 1927, Halifax
1949 78 The launch way wc $100

PURDY, HENRY CARL
6 Nov 1937, Wolfville, NS
RCA(e) 1978 Council Painter
Addr: 1979, Parkdale, PEI

PURVES, ROSS
1938 S8, Toronto
Saturday Night Press
337 and 338 Book, Canadian Industries Limited. Ross

Purves, Carl Mangold
339 Booklet, Imperial Oil
340 Booklet, Service Station Equipment Limited
342 Booklet, Automatic Oil Heat

PYE, WILLIAM English
fl 1881-08 B DBA G H
Addr: 1884, Weymouth, Dorset, Eng
1884 158 Village of Hadleigh, Essex wc $75
159 Village of Benfleet, Essex wc $40

Q

QUILTER, FLORENCE THOMPSON (Mrs)
1950 125 Alas, poor Yorick! 24 x 28 $125
1951 84 Rocks and pools $125

QUIN, DE LISLE
Addr: 1927, 619 Avenue Rd, Toronto; 1929, 592 Sherbourne St, Toronto
1927 187 Low tide at La Malbaie, Quebec wc
1929 186 Cape Ann, Mass wc $25

QUINAUX, JOSEPH Belgian
29 Mar 1822, Namur, Belgium 25 May 1895, Brussels B TB
1882 306 Old mill near Treves, evening (loan) T. Quinaux mispr

QUINN, HUGH SUMMERVILLE
c 1872, Ottawa 25 Aug 1948, Ottawa
Addr: 1916, 205 Daly Ave, Ottawa; 1918N-24, 116 Osgood St, Ottawa
1916 186 Summer time
187 An autumn sunset
1918N 153 Fields
1924 168 Landscape near Ottawa

R

RABB, ERNEST
1926, Komarno, Czechoslovakia
1953 124 Christ sculp $200

RABINOWITCH, DAVID GEORGE
6 Mar 1943, Toronto B CWW79 IO WWA76
RCA(e) 1973 Sculptor
Addr: 1979, New York

RADFORD, JOHN A.
1860, Devonport, Eng 24 May 1940, Vancouver H
Addr: 1894, Toronto; 1898, Mail Bldg, Toronto; 1904-9, Toronto
1894 199 Home in Sherbourne Street, Toronto
200 Mantel
201 G.P. Magannis, stable, Parkdale
202 Cottage on Lake Ontario
203 A county club house
1898 202 When autumn blushes at verdant summer wc
235 Gothic doors des
236 Sketch for mantel
1904 289 Art gallery, perspective sketch
290 Sketch designs
1909M 102a One of the old regime

RAE, BARBARA
Addr: 1938, Toronto
1938 S8, Toronto
380 Wallpaper design. Hon mention. Canadian Wallpaper Manufacturers Limited

RAGINSKY, NINA
14 Apr 1941, Montreal
RCA(e) 1976 Photographer
Addr: 1979, Victoria

RAICUS, ETHEL
1901, Toronto IO
1963 61 Untitled wc $150

RAILTON, RICHARD REGINALD
12 May 1895, Croyden, Surrey, Eng
Addr: 1919, Brockville, Ont; 1922, 85 St Paul St, St Catharines, Ont
1919 133 The last gleam wc
1922 279 Old Victor Mission building, Toronto etch

RAINE
1908 Mitchell & Raine
167b Baronial hall

RAINE, HERBERT
2 Dec 1875, Sunderland, Durham, Eng 24 May 1951, Montreal AGO NGC TB2
ARCA 1916 Architect 1924 Etcher
RCA 1925 Sr 1947 Council Etcher
Addr: 1914-23, New Birks Bldg, 10 Cathcart St, Montreal; 1924, 1016 Drummond Court Apt, Montreal; 1925-

6, New Birks Bldg, 10 Cathcart St, Montreal; 1928-36, New Birks Bldg, 620 Cathcart St, Montreal; 1937-51, Montreal

1914 221 Residence, Lorne C. Webster, West Crescent Heights, Westmount, Que
222 Residence, W.G.M. Shepherd, Esq, West Crescent Heights, Westmount, Que

1915 282 Evening, the Canal, Montreal etch
283 Caudebec-en-Caux, France etch 1916-313

1916 265 J. Fulford Memorial Fountain, Brockville, Ont
266 Church of St Columba, Notre Dame de Grâce
312 Old courtyard, St Vincent St, Montreal (2).The fisher folk at Kamouraska, Quebec. Spring, Lake St Louis. 4 etch
313 Interior of Reims Cathedral, France. West entrance, Louviers Church, France. 2 etch

1918A 264 The wayside Cross, St Joachim, Quebec etch
265 Old farm house, St Joachim, Quebec etch
266 Bank of Montreal, Montreal etch
267 The pilgrims, Ste Anne de Beaupré etch

1918N 154 Old farm house, St Joachim, Quebec wc
155 A grey day, Beaupré, Quebec wc
156 Island of Orleans, from Beaupré wc

1919 219 Place Jacques Cartier, Montreal etch
220 Notre Dame Church, Montreal etch
221 The Church of Bonsecours, Montreal etch
222 Old buildings, St Paul Street etch

1920 336 Old houses in a courtyard, St Vincent St, Montreal etch
337 Château de Ramezay, rear view, Montreal etch
338 Château de Ramezay, Montreal etch
339 Bonsecours, Montreal etch
340 Champlain Market Square, Quebec drwg
341 Notre Dame Street, Montreal drwg
342 Commissioners Street, Montreal drwg
343 The Grove, Beaconsfield, Quebec drwg

1921 217 A farm house, St Joachim, Quebec etch
218 The Ramparts, Quebec dry pt
219 Nearing St Joachim, Quebec dry pt
220 Les Eboulements, Quebec dry pt
221 Houses in a courtyard, St Vincent Street, Montreal drwg
222 Schooners, Quebec drwg
223 The stone cottage, Beaconsfield, Quebec drwg
224 The Island ferry, Quebec drwg

1922 280 Sous le Cap, Quebec etch S6-126
281 Champlain Street, Quebec etch S6-127
282 Old yard, L'Assomption, Quebec etch S6-128
283 Corner of Côté and Craig Streets, Montreal etch
284 The sword-fisher, Gloucester, Mass drwg
285 Lobster pots, Gloucester, Mass drwg
286 The derelict wharf, Gloucester, Mass drwg
287 Rockport, Mass drwg

1923 225 Albi Cathedral etch
226 Faded palaces, Albi etch
227 Old bridge, Albi etch
228 Market place, Carcassonne etch

1924 287 Fish wharf, Gloucester, Mass drwg
288 Gloucester, Mass drwg
289 Stirling Castle, Scotland dry pt
290 Côté Street and Bank of Montreal, Montreal etch

1925 327 Whitby, Yorks, Eng etch
328 St Féréol, Quebec etch
329 Morlaix, France drwg
330 A street in Coutances, France drwg

1926 201 Mary Arches, Exeter, England dry pt
202 Champlain Street, Quebec etch
203 Trees, St Guilmiliau, France dry pt

204 Evening, Les Eboulements, Quebec dry pt
1928 223 Lake O'Hara, the Rockies etch $50
224 Mount Robson, BC etch $50
225 Stepcote Hill, Exeter, England $30
1928 F8, London, Eng
20 Old houses in a courtyard, St Vincent Street, Montreal etch $40
1929 283 Cathedral Square, Courtrai, Belgium etch $40
284 Old farm house, Baie St Paul, Quebec dry pt $35
285 Bruges, Belgium dry pt $35
286 Market place, Dol, Brittany dry pt $25
287 The mast menders, Gloucester, Mass drwg $30 F10-12
288 Boats in the offing, Gloucester, Mass drwg $30
1930 217 St Michael's, Ghent etch $35
218 Notre Dame des Victoires, Quebec etch $35
1931 422 The McKenna house, corner of Hébert and Ste Famille Streets, Quebec dry pt $40
423 Lévis, Québec dry pt $30
424 Corner of Hébert and Ste Famille Streets, Quebec etch $25
425 Champlain Market, Quebec dry pt $25
1932 256 Aspetogan, from Chester, NS dry pt $35
257 Silver birches, Aspetogan, NS dry pt $35
258 A misty day, Chester, NS dry pt $35
1933 193 Afternoon, Boule Rock, Métis Beach, Quebec wc $30
194 Boule Rock, Métis Beach, Quebec wc $30
316 Canal scene, Ghent dry pt $23
317 The Piggery, Gloucester, Mass etch $28
318 The Convent of Marie Bourgeois, Verdun etch $34
319 The osprey, Métis Beach, Quebec dry pt $34 1935-343 $27.50
1934 226 Villa Maria Convent, Montreal etch $28
227 Old courtyard, St Vincent Street, Montreal etch $23
1935 342 St Damase, Quebec dry pt $28.50
344 Sandy Bay, Quebec etch $28.50
1936 249 Late afternoon, Métis Beach, Quebec dry pt $35
250 Boule Bock, Métis Beach, Quebec dry pt $35
251 Street scene, Quebec $29
1938 263 The Piggery, Gloucester, Mass etch $25
264 Farm buildings, St Joachim, Quebec etch $22.50
265 Street scene, Albi, France etch $25
266 Old house and yard, L'Assomption, Que dry pt $22.50
1944 161 The Grove, Beaconsfield, Quebec drwg $35
162 The Campus, Dartmouth College, NH drwg $35
DW 1926 Notre Dame, Montreal etch

RAINNIE, HEDLEY GRAHAM JAMES
29 Jul 1914, London, Eng d 1961
WWA47
ARCA 1945-53 Painter
Addr: 1946, Toronto; 1947-53, New York
1941 156 Negro boy $150
1942 114 Les calèches, Québec $100 T43-36
1944 113 Portrait of a Chinese girl $500 T45-37
1945 167 Is the love healer working $350 T46-38
168 Portrait of a young girl nfs

RAINNIE, URSULA (Mrs)
1942 115 Study wc $30
1944 114 Flower piece $100 T45-38

RAKINE, MARTHE DE (Mrs Boris de Rakine)
b Moscow AGO B CC2 NGC TB2
1950 126 Still life 19 1/2 x 23 $350
1951 85 Still life $300
86 In the garden $250
1953 70 The blue lake $450
1954 71 Children's art class 26 x 33 $450

RAMER, NOAH HUBERT
5 Oct 1860, Markham, Ont c 15 Apr 1931, Hamilton, Ont H

Addr: 1926-8, 175 Jackson St W, Hamilton, Ont
1926 120 Still life
1928 128 Still life

RAND, PAUL (b Otto Schellenberger, c 1940 Rand)
27 Nov 1896, Bonn, Germany 27 Jan 1970, Vancouver
1942 116 Mount Whistler, BC $300 T43-37
1944 115 Zucca harvest $500 T45-39
1945 169 Clay banks, Penticton, BC $300

RANEY, SUZANNE BRYANT (Mrs)
7 Oct 1918, London, Eng WWA59
1952 77 The city $35

RAPHAEL, DIANA English
(Mrs R. Raphael)
1941 157 Portrait in a mirror $75

RAPHAEL, SHIRLEY
29 May 1937, Montreal
1970 70 Up and down series 28 1/2 x 36 1/2 illus $80

RAPHAEL, WILLIAM
1833, Prussia 15 Mar 1914, Montreal EC H Mo98/12 NGC W78
RCA 1880-97 Council Painter
Addr: 1880-2, Montreal; 1883, 123 German St, Montreal; 1884-6, Montreal; 1887, St Catherine St, Montreal; 1888-92, Montreal; 1893-8, 2204 St Catherine St, Montreal
1880 51 L'habitant
63 Preparing for a smoke
68 Indian encampment at lower St Lawrence (William Scott) 1881-322 Indian encampment on the lower St Lawrence DW 1880 23 1/4 x 41 1/4 S1-75 1954 Retro Sec 5
73 Pointe au Pic, Murray Bay
1881 261 Morning effect on the River St Lawrence $125
313 R. St Charles $100
1882 102 A chance shot $100
1883 105 Sketch from nature $65
1884 19 The gipsy $50
34 The labourer $25
1885 21 Path through the woods $200 1886-131 $150
80 Sketch from life $50
100 Potatoes in bloom $100 1886-142
1886 19 An amateur $50
23 L'enfant du sol $60
139 The changing of the leaf $100
143 Autumn tints $40
144 October $40
164 Never too late to mend $60
183 The golden season $40
184 In the woods $30
1887 18 An afternoon idyl $200
32 A bad case nfs
1889 21 Homeward bound $60
24 Woodland scene $40
1890 68 A midnight jaunt $250
69 The hay field $50
1891 72 The mill
74 Two friends
75 The tramp
1892 35 The oat field $60 1893-119 $75 F1-89
62 Harvest time $200 1893-117
66 Abandoned $200 1893-116 $250 F1-87
91 Mill dam $50
1893 118 A potato plot $125 F1-88
1895 105 Sunset
106 In for a swim
1896 140 Le rendezvous
141 Winter
1898 93 A difficult problem

RAPIN, AIMEE Swiss
1869, Payerne, Switzerland B TB
Addr: 1922, 17 rue Necker, Genève; 1925, Quai des Eaux Vives, Genève
1922 169 Nature morte pastel S6-169 Still life
1925 183 La gitane

RASTRICK, FREDERICK JAMES
b West Bromwitch, Eng 13 Sep 1897, Hamilton, Ont
ARCA 1880-1 Architect
Addr: 1880-1, Hamilton, Ont

RAVENSHAW, EDITH LALANDE see PATTERSON, EDITH LALANDE

RAWLINSON, LIONEL, LIMITED
1938 S8, Toronto
211 2 single beds, unfinished, solid walnut, Chippendale des, combining groove effect with his crown and ball des
212 Dressing table, unfinished, solid walnut illus
213 Chest of drawers, solid

walnut illus
214 Sermon on the Mount
wd carv by late Mr W.A.
Allen

RAWSTRON, ALICE DELPHINE
16 Feb 1924, Montreal
1959 68 John David 20 x 24 $150

RAYMENT, COLLIN
Addr: 1938, Montreal
1938 S8, Toronto
215 Magazine advertisement

RAYMOND, MAURICE
23 Jul 1912, Montreal NGC WWA47
RCA(e) 1978 Painter
Addr: 1979, Montreal
1943 96 Les pommes de terre $100
(MMFA)

RAYNER English
1880 330 Aberdeen church (Col
Bernard)

RAYNER, GORDON
14 Jul 1935, Toronto AGO CC1 IO
1960 63 Detour 48 x 36 $150

RAYNSFORD, LOUIE K. (Mrs)
Addr: 1934, 35 Barat Rd, Montreal;
1935, 6 Springfield Ave, Montreal
1934 162 Helen min
163 Hugh Harkness min 1939-
191 nfs
1935 222 Sue min nfs
223 Joan min nfs
1939 192 Mrs Fraser MacIver min
nfs

REA, KENNETH GUSCOTTE
24 Jun 1878, Montreal d 1941
WWC21
Addr: 1907, Montreal
1907 339 The Chapel at West Point
340 New office building, Montreal Light Heat & Power Co

READ, ADELE
Addr: 1926, 119 Grand Ave E, Chatham, Ont
1926 163 An old man sculp

READ, GEORGIE B.
1938 181 Hills $45
182 Landscape with sheep $45

REDINGER, WALTER
6 Jan 1940, Wallacetown, Ont B
WWA76
RCA(e) 1973 Sculptor
Addr: 1979, West Lorne, Ont

REDMAYNE, GLADYS
Addr: 1907, Montreal
1907 297 A study in charcoal

REDSELL, PAULINE HAZEL DAISY (Mrs
William Fediow)
1908, Toronto Mar 1980, Toronto
Addr: 1931, Lorne Park, Ont; 1932-3,
481 Shaw St, Toronto; 1935, 32 St
Joseph St, Toronto
1931 426 The beggar woman linocut
$8
427 The stern oar linocut $5
1932 259 Head of a young man
charcl $50
1933 320 Whistling Charlie linocut
$12
321 Seven base fiddles pen &
ink $30
1935 345 Evening over Derwent
Water wash drwg nfs
346 Skiddaw, Cumberland
wash drwg $35
1942 172 Mother and child sculp
$75
173 Margaret sculp $60
1943 136 Tony sculp $75
1944 152 Fountain figure sculp
$150
1948 175 Maggie, portrait head
sculp $150
1957 86 Douglas Campbell, actor
plaster $600
87 Frances Hyland, as Ophelia
plaster $500
1958 93 Prof Barker Fairley in
bronze $1,500
1960 Fediow, to 1964
76 Head of a dancer, Naomi
sculp $300
1964J 70 Folk singer plaster $350

REED, TORQUIL ARNOLD SARGENT
b 1927
1947 147 Early breakfast $150

REEVE, JOHN
30 Nov 1929, Barrie, Ont
RCA(e) 1979 Ceramist
Addr: 1979, Halifax

REEVE, WILLIAM GORDON
9 Aug 1898, Clarksburg, Ont

1954 72 Old meeting house 22 x 30 nfs

REEVES, JOHN ALEXANDER
24 Apr 1938, Burlington, Ont WWA78
RCA(e) 1975 Council Photographer
Addr: 1979, Toronto

REFORD, WILLIAM
d 1895 H
Addr: 1884, Toronto
1883 260 Mud banks, Charles River, tide out $25
1884 56 On a lea shore $50
1884 S1, Saint John
95 Red cow $20
1885 59 Sunset study $25
71 Summer morning $50
110 Taking a rest $50
200 Off Sandy Hook wc $10
244 Old farm house wc $10
281 On the Don wc $25
286 Fishing wc
308 Cloudy day, Lachine Canal wc $25
323 Becalmed, mouth of the Delaware wc $10

REHN, FRANK KNOX MORTON American
12 Apr 1848, Philadelphia 6 Jul 1914, Magnolia, Mass AAA28 B H TB Y
1882 62 High tide, Old Orchard Beach $125
253 Entrance to Gloucester harbour, Mass monoc

REICHERT, DONALD KARL
11 Jan 1932, Libau, Man AGO WWA73
RCA(e) 1974 Painter
Addr: 1976/79, Winnipeg
1976 S12, Montreal
39 Blue passing acry 50 x 50 illus
40 Night walk acry 50 x 50 illus

REID, BILL see REID, WILLIAM RONALD

REID, DANIEL LEIGH
26 Jun 1951, Oshawa, Ont IO
Addr: 1976, Oshawa
1976 S12, Montreal
88 Tripartus m med 90 x 18 x 27 illus

REID, GEORGE AGNEW
25 Jul 1860, n Wingham, Ont 23 Aug 1947, Toronto AGO B CC1 EC H Mo98/12 NGC PMC TB1/2 W78 WWA47
ARCA 1885 RCA 1890 Sr 1936 Council Painter
Addr: 1885-6, Toronto; 1887, King St E, Toronto; 1888-92, Toronto; 1893-00, Yonge St Arcade, 95 Yonge St, Toronto; 1901-7, 435 Indian Rd, Toronto; 1908-18, Wychwood Park, Toronto; 1919, 26 Wychwood Park, Toronto: 1920-9, 62 Wychwood Park, Toronto; 1930-7, 81 Wychwood Park, Toronto; 1938-47, Toronto
1885 75 Meditation $50
94 The last load $200 1886-25
127 Among the antiques $50 1886-32
134 From the milking $300 1886-200 $250. Selected for Fla, not in Fla cat
146 Twilight $20
152 The rehearsal $50
168 Where the crane feeds $25 1886-27 Fla-2014
196 Landscape $100
1886 22 At the Custom House, Venice $35
1887 5 The spinner $40
15 At the fountain, Florence $75
29 The flute player $150
36 Evening $75
72 Portrait of a gentleman nfs
75 A Roman resting place $40
97 Portrait of a lady nfs
104 Venezia $75
1888 77 Sunshine and shadow $100
86 Calves $35
89 Alone $35
90 Study of a girl's head $50
100 Portrait of the artist
116 Gossip $500 ◊AGO◊
144 At sunset $35
156 Marine $40
170 Drawing lots $300
185 Studio interior $50
206 At the window $150
288 Deserted house wc $30
300 Green pastures and still waters wc $30
301 Portrait of the artist wc
302 Early morning wc $30
1889 11 Cabbage patch $40
45 A corner of a courtyard $20
74 The lake, Montsouris Park, Paris $25
1890 70 Mortgaging the homestead $2,000 DW 1891 50 1/2 x 83 1/2

71 The other side of the question $100
72 Dreaming $800 ◊NGC◊
73 On the Seine, below Paris $50
74 Notre Dame, Paris $50
75 Haymaking $50
76 Old bridge at Poissy on the Seine $50
1891 16 In the Bois de Boulogne
24 Twilight, Toronto
25 Mountain pasture
26 Family prayers
27 Sunlight and shadow
29 In autumn, near Paris
30 Moonlight
31 Portrait
33 In the Luxembourg Garden
1892 50 The foreclosure of the mortgate $3,000 1893-120 F1-90 1901-93
1893 121 The visit of the clock-maker nfs F1-91
122 Lullaby $300 F1-92
123 A mountain village $75 F1-93
249 Late afternoon pastel $100 F1-184
1894 98 Harvest dec panel
99 Life's twilight
100 Tristesse
101 Nightfall 1900-97 1904-127
102 Autumn sunlight
103 A grey day
104 Summer sunshine
105 Andante
1895 108 Rest dec mural
109 Miss Vickers
110 Miss Caro Adams
111 Portrait
112 Mist
113 In a daisy field
114 Autumn
115 In the orchard
116 A hot day
1896 142 Mother and child
143 Child's head
144 Busy
145 Blossoms
146 Daisies
245 Reverie pastel
246 Neighbours pastel
1897 116 Court of Lions, Alhambra
117 Aqueduct of the Alhambra
118 Old musician
119 Twilight 1899-109
120 A mountain village
121 Evening
122 Among the daisies 1904-130
123 A modern madonna
45W Snow wc
1898 82 The foot bridge
83 In the old orchard
84 A trout brook
85 Mowing
208 Entrance hall, new city building dec mural study wc
209 Night wc
210 Twilight wc
1899 106 Summer dec panel illus
107 Evening star
108 Child's head
110 The rye field
111 Portrait
1900 94 Music dec panel 1902-130
95 Reading pastel
96 The cloud
1901 94 Summer dec panel F2-58
95 Mother and child, from 'Pioneers' panel, City Hall, Toronto F2-59
96 Portrait F2-60
97 Rising moon
1902 233-6 Twilight effect wc (4)
1903 95 Landscape
96 Study in white
97 Across the valley
98 Twilight in the park
99 Autumn
100 Child's head
1904 125 Music F4-64
126 The twilight of life F4-65 F5-136 $800
128 Mother and child
129 Afterglow 1907-159 1908-115 ◊NGC◊
131 Evening clouds
131a A new day F4-66
243 After sunset wc
244 Twilight wc
245 Evening wc
1905 148 May dec panel
149 Prof Pelham Edgar
150 Youth and age F5-137 $500 F6-142
151 In the sunlight
1906 153 Spring F6-140 $1,000
154 Iris F5-134 illus $1,000 1907-157 F6-145 illus $2,000 1908-113 1909N-115 S2-89
155 A study in green
156 A castle in Spain F5-135 $200 1907-161 F6-144 $150
157 Reading pastel
1907 158 Tranquility

160 and 162 Portrait
272 A harmony in browns wc
273 The brook wc
1907 F6, Sherbrooke
141 A Canadian girl $300 S2-88
143 The new moon $100
146 May $500
1908 114 Spring dec panel
116 Sun and shade
1909M 109 The arrival of Champlain at Quebec 1910-160
110 Brown and gold 1909N-116
111 Woodland at sunset
1909N 117 Early spring
1910 159 The evening star
161 Mother and child
162 The reader
1910 S2, Liverpool
87 The homeseekers S3-126
1911 132 Portrait
133 The stream dec panel
#134 not in catalog
135 Afternoon sunlight, autumn
136 Willows in spring
137 By the North Sea
1912 181 The coming of the white man
1913 240 The mountain top S4-107 $500
241 Burning weeds
242 Summer clouds
243 The carpenter's shop S4-108 $100
244 The cloud
245 Winter morning pastel S4-109 $75
1914 158 The village in the valley ◊NGC◊
159 The shady path
160 Still life
1914 S5, Patriotic Fund
49 In the cellar window illus
1915 177 An idyl illus
178 Clearing after rain
179 The dark entry, Canterbury
180 Vacant lots ◊NGC◊
1916 188 A winter sunset
189 A village byway
190 The sunlit valley
191 The winding stream
1918A 138 Ave Canada mural dec study
139 Early morning, Canterbury
140 Afternoon, Wychwood Pond illus
1918N 157 Spring
158 Study for picture '1917'
1919 134 The blue print illus ◊AGO◊
135 Early spring
1920 203 The quiet river
204 Autumn afternoon
1921 126 Spring dec panel
127 July
128 Portrait
129 The fountain pastel
1922 170 Spring illus S6-78
171 Dawn S6-79
1923 140 Welcome to Champlain, 1608
141 The pond
142 Reverie pastel
1924 169 Dawn, replica of panel for Weston Town Hall
170 The edge of the hill 1925-186
1925 184 The discovery of Niagara
185 Past, present and future
187 Morning illus
1926 121 The Agawa Canyon
122 An Algoma waterfall
123 A lake in the hills illus 1927-188 illus F7-158 $550
205 Earlscourt Library, dec panel des
1927 189 A northern river
1928 129 A Canadian lake $1,000
130 Mrs F.K. Morrow
131 The valley stream $250 1929-188 $300 F9-112
1929 187 The dark canyon $750 S7-131 1933-196 $800
189 Saw mill interior wc $250
1929 S7, Calgary
129 Castle in Spain $750
130 Evening, Montreal River $300
1930 143-4 The discoverers. Jarvis Collegiate Institute, left & right panels dec frieze
145-6 Jarvis Collegiate Institute dec panels studies
1930 F10, London, Eng
216 Quiet water $400
1931 244 Champlain dreams of the way to Cathay $1,000
245 Rippled water $400
246 Winter sunset $150
247 Evening Timagami $150
1932 162 Ottawa valley, road builders $1,000
1933 195 Gold $1,200
197 Lake Timagami $350 T34-69

1934 164 Prof C.T. Currelly, portrait study pastel
164a Autumn sunshine and showers $300 T35-60
1935 224 Prof C.T. Currelly nfs 1947-149
225 Ontario pioneers logging $500
1936 171 Self portrait nfs T37-53 ◊AGO◊
1937 184 Harmony in blue and gold $800
185 Agawa Canyon $250 T38-47
1939 193 Hope Bay, Bruce Peninsula $350 1940-132 T41-45
301 Northern lake drwg $15
1939 F11, New York
58 The path of light 40 x 30 $300
1941 158 Autumn on the Indian trail $250 T42-46
1941 S9, Toronto
51 Sunset, Lake Timagami $150
1942 117 In the rye field $150 T43-38
1944 116 The wayside apple tree $250
1945 170 Agawa Canyon, Algoma $200
171 Reverie nfs T46-39
1946 99 Harrowing, York County $100
1947 Late G.A. Reid, RCA
148 Agawa Canyon nfs T48-33
port: by Marion Long 1938-133

REID, ISOBELLE CHESTNUT (Mrs)
27 May 1903, Fredericton AGO
Addr: 1936, 197 Elizabeth St, Toronto
1936 172 Still life wc $40 T37-54

REID, LAURA EVANS (Mrs R.M. Reid)
15 Feb 1883, Guelph, Ont Nov 1951, Vegreville, Alta
1950 127 Alberta town in winter 24 x 30 $200

REID, LESLIE MARY MARGARET
8 Feb 1947, Ottawa IO
RCA(e) 1978 Painter
Addr: 1976/79, Ottawa
1976 S12, Montreal
41 Tancredia acry 64 x 87 1/4 illus

REID, LORNA FYFE
8 Jul 1887, London, Ont NGC TB2
Addr: 1916-18A, Studio Bldg, 25 Severn St, Toronto; 1920, 30 South Dr, Toronto
1916 192 The wind flower ◊NGC◊
1918A 143 Air castles 1920-205
1920 206 Deep sea fisherman

REID, MARY AUGUSTA HIESTER (Mrs George Agnew Reid)
10 Apr 1854, Reading, Pa 4 Oct 1921, Toronto AGO B CC2 EC H Mo12 NGC TB3 W78
ARCA 1893 Painter
Addr: 1887, King St E, Toronto; 1893-00, Yonge St Arcade, 95 Yonge St, Toronto; 1901-7, 435 Indian Rd, Toronto; 1908-18, Wychwood Park, Toronto; 1919-21, Toronto
1886 35 Church of the Salute, Venice $15
36 Grand Canal, Venice $15
108 A study $15
1887 55 A youthful art lover $40
74 Still life, 100 years ago $40
86 View of the Coliseum $25
1888 79 Study of peacock feathers $20
98 Daisies $10 ◊AGO◊
103, 106 and 159 Roses $15, $45, $30
104 Winding the clock $75
124 Guitar player $50
146 Fruit $15
151 Daffodils $25
165 Study of fruit $15
1889 46 In the cloisters $15
66 From my window $30
103 Roses $12
1890 77 Before Communion $150
78 Panel $100
79 Jacqueminot roses $75
80 Still life and roses $30
1891 20 Playmates
21 Roses
22 A roadside cottage
28 Panel
1892 17 Roses and still life $100
68 Carnations $15
69 Chrysanthemums $35 ◊NGC◊
77 Roses and antique vase $25
1893 124 Roses and still life $150 F1-94
125 Chrysanthemums $100 F1-95 nfs
126 October sunshine $50 F1-96
127 A sunset rose $35
1894 106 At close of day

107 Roses on antique chest
108 The long seam
109 Yellow roses
110 October sunshine
111 Pansies
112 Roses
113 First autumn leaves
114 Mermet roses
115 Daisies
1895 117 Early autumn
118 Gray weather
119 Midsummer 1896-147
120 Violets
121 Sunset roses 1897-130
122 Studio interior 1896-148
123 October
124 A study
1896 149 Sunflowers
1897 124 Harvest field
125 Gate of Justice, Alhambra
126 Towers of the Alhambra
127 Yellow daisies
128 Roses in the ginger jar
129 Roses in antique vase
131 Pansies
132 Mermet roses
1898 86 Yellow roses
87 Twilight in June
88 Moonrise 1899-113 1902-133 1903-101 1904-137 1905-144 F6-147 $100 S2-90
89 A rose
90 Early autumn
91 Evening
92 Moorish bridge, Ronda
1899 112 Panel
114 Interior 1900-104
115 Roses
116 Carnations
117 Pansies
118 Chrysanthemums 1900-103
1900 98 Roses, Lady Dorothea 1901-101 F2-63 1902-131
99 A poppy garden
100 A verandah 1901-99
101 Full moon, July
102 Looking east 1901-98 F2-61 1908-119 ◊NGC◊
1901 100 Roses, President Carnot F2-62 F3-145
1902 132 Winter morning 1903-105 1904-138
134 Burning bush
135 Twilight
136 Carnations
137 Snow, morning effect
138 August moon
139 October
1903 102 November
103 Effect of moonlight
104 Dawn 1904-136 F4-70
106 Roses
1904 132 The hunter's moon F4-67
133 Winter twilight F4-68 1908-120
134 After sunset
135 Moonlight
1904 F4, St Louis
69 Winter morning
1905 142 Spring evening
143 A meadow in bloom F6-149 $60
145 The last traces of snow
146 Blossoms at evening
147 Autumn on the hills
1906 147 The cloud 1907-163 1908-117
148 Afternoon sunlight
149 First traces of snow
150 Spring twilight
1906 F5, Halifax
138 Roses $25
139 Hills in autumn $25
140 Roses, Golden Gate $100
1907 164 Night's approach
165 Snow clouds
166 Late afternoon
167 The new moon
168 After rain 1908-118
1907 F6, Sherbrooke
148 Daisies $50
150 Autumn in the hills $75
1909M 112 Lowlands 1909N-118
113 A misty evening
114 An arrangement
115 Pines at sunset
1909N 119 Indian summer
120 A misty evening, October
121 Spring
1910 163 Nightfall S2-92
164 November
165 The coming shower
1910 S2, Liverpool
91 Roses
1911 138 At twilight 1912-182
139 Flowers
140 October sunlight
1912 183 Still life
184 The old apple tree
185 The joy of summer pastel
1912 S3, Winnipeg
127 Hunter's moon
128 Roses
129 Interior
130 In an English garden

1913 246 Morning sunshine S4-110 $300 nfs Purchased by the National Gallery
247 A study in grays ◊AGO◊
248 The old chest
1914 161 Michelmas
162 A garden in August
163 Chrysanthemums
1914 S5, Patriotic Fund
18 Carnations illus
1915 181 Late summer
182 An orchard in May
1916 193 Marshy woods, November
194 Twilight
195 Autumn fires ◊AGO◊
1918A 141 Past and present, still life illus 1918N-159 ◊AGO◊
142 Birch in autumn 1918N-161
1918N 160 A creek in October

REID, MARY EVELYN see WRINCH, MARY

REID, ROBERT
dates not on file
ARCA 1971 Graphic designer
Addr: 1978, Montreal (1979 addr unknown)

REID, ROBERT R.
1970 248 Poster, War theatre. Robert R. Reid, Beverly Leach

REID, RUSSELL JAMES
22 Dec 1920, Leeds Village, Que
1947 150 Autumn climax $350

REID, WILLIAM RONALD (BILL)
12 Jan 1920, Victoria
RCA(e) 1973 Sculptor
Addr: 1979, Vancouver

REILLY, NELSON GERALD
b 1931
1956 38 Two undercover illus $200 T56-26

REINBLATT, MOSES MARTIN (MOE)
20 Jun 1917, Montreal 24 Aug 1979, Montreal AGO CC1 TB2 WWA47
1942 118 Joe nfs Remblatt mispr
1954 99 Women with skeins drwg 10 x 18 $20
1964N 44 October dance etch $45
1967 53 Landscape 50 x 30 $700
1970 61 Autumn tree 18 x 14 3/4 $65

RELIABLE TOY COMPANY LIMITED
1970 112 Toy cement mixer

RELIANCE ENGRAVERS LIMITED
Addr: 1938, Toronto
1938 S8, Toronto
216 4 pieces of dot etch, deep etch, litho plates, produced in 4 colors 'Alaska', proof from painting by Charles W. Simpson

RENO, VERNON
Addr: 1920, 1942 Hutchison St, Montreal
1920 207 Golden autumn
208 An old fashioned cottage

REPPEN, JOHN RICHARD
17 Jul 1933, Toronto 2 Jun 1964, Toronto AGO CC2 W78
1963 62 Miguel courtyard 48 x 48 illus $465
1964J 53 Indications of yesterday 48 x 48 $485
54 Many nights ago 48 x 48 $485

REUSCH, KINA (Mrs Boris Tomachevsky)
Addr: 1976, Montreal
1976 S12, Montreal
149 Abstract calligraphy #1 gobelin, wool 35 x 72 illus

REVELL, WILLIAM
1830-02 H
ARCA 1880 Painter
Addr: 1880-2, Toronto; 1883, Dept of Crown Lands, Toronto; 1884-92, Toronto; 1893-01, 618 Ontario St, Toronto; 1902, Toronto
1880 177 Pickings wc
287 Wall paper, hepatica des
293 Paper hanging, balsam weed des
294 Paper hanging, Canada coffee and balsam des
388 Illumination
1881 42 Labour's trophies $60
50 Gardener's pride wc $75 S1-24 $80
62 Foxgloves wc $35
80 Petunias wc
1882 174 Apple blossoms wc $36
1883 95 Rest $25
96 Earth's tribute $75 S1-156 $100
173 Iris wc $30

1884 82 Chinese immigrants $20
91 Easter's tribute $75
1884 S1, Saint John
61 White lilies wc $30
1885 132 Just gathered $20
133 From the orient $20
227 On the Maitland River wc $20
302 and 317 Flowers wc $40 each
330 Sketches drwg
1886 45 Summer snowballs wc $50
76 Red hawthorne wc $30
1888 20 Fruit wc $50 1889-121
287 Smoky day, Credit Valley wc $100
1891 118 Canada's fruit wc
1892 103 Crossed by shades and sunny gleams wc $100 1893-250 1901-204
117 A bit of the old homestead wc $40
121 Canadian fruit wc $100 1893-252 F1-186
1893 251 Sketch on the canal, Brantford wc $30
1895 79W In the forest wc
80W Evening near Ashbridge's Bay wc
81W In the barnyard wc
1897 41W On the Little Humber wc
42W Rose Hill, Ottawa wc
43W Accasia Avenue wc
44W Near Toronto wc
1898 203 In East Toronto wc
204 Woods in autumn wc
1901 205 On the marsh, east of Toronto wc

REVILL, W.
1938 S8, Toronto
Roden Bros Limited
239 Silver deposit decanter

REYNOLDS, E.W, & COMPANY, LIMITED
Addr: 1938, Toronto
1938 S8, Toronto
217 6 scratchboard drwgs, advertisements, Magazine Publishers Association. H. Macdonald Hassell
218 Cylinder carton, Simms lather brush. J.M. Bowman, H. Macdonald Hassell

REYNOLDS, JOS (Miss)
fl 1891-6 H
Addr: 1895, Toronto
1895 107 Day dreams

REYNOLDS, JOSHUA (Sir) English
16 Jul 1723, Plympton, Eng 23 Feb 1792, London B DBA G TB
1880 125a Miss Stuart (J.W. Harper, Esq)
1883 34 Portrait (Harper, Esq, Ottawa)

RHODES, KATHERINE J.
Addr: 1920, St Louis Rd, Quebec
1920 209 Portrait
210 The bathers

RHYN, GEORGE A.
1947 151 Houses by the water $300
1949 79 Landscape with cornfield $300

RICHARDS, CECIL CLARENCE
5 Jan 1907, Rinsey, Cornwall, Eng
AGO
ARCA 1957 RCA 1967 Sculptor
Addr: 1937, 1109A Bay St, Toronto; 1958-67, Winnipeg; 1968-71/79, Lakefield, Ont
1937 290 Forbes Maclean sculp $200
1954 111 Woman marble 19h illus $500
1955 116 Evening sculp illus $500
117 Protection sculp $500
1956 52 Abraham and Sara sculp $300
1957 88 Siren sculp $200
1963 100 Sacrificial ram bronze $600
101 Ruth bronze $300
1964J 82 Flight bronze 19 x 27 $1,150
1965 91 Lazarus at the rich man's gate bronze 12 x 7 $600
92 The sacrifice bronze 20 x 7 $1,000
1967 82 Jonah is thrown to the big fish sketch for fountain bronze 13 x 13 $1,000
83 Sacrificial ram bronze 13 x 20 illus DW 1968
1968 63 Dancer changing 20h $700

RICHARDS, FRANCES ELWOOD (Mrs William Edwin Rowley)
1852, Brockville, Ont 1934, Glassonby, Cumbld, Eng B DBA H
ARCA 1882-5 Painter
Addr: 1882-7, Ottawa
1882 245 Italian model monoc

249 and 265 Portrait monoc
254 Study monoc $10
264 and 269 A French Canadian monoc $10 each
1887 11 Yseult $60
23 Une habitante $200
121 Evelyn wc $75
126 Yachting wc $35
154 In the park $35
162 Come for a stroll wc $35

RICHARDS, IDA
H
1882 4 Peignan Indian (Marquis of Lorne)
35 Study of a woman's head $30
59 John McLennan, MP
60 Miss Nelia L.
86 Mrs H.J.M.

RICHARDSON, DORIS K.
1958 68 Yoe girl $175

RICHARDSON, FREDERICK
b Brockville, Ont fl 1863-04 H
Addr: 1895, Belleville, Ont
1880 24 Cattle yard
1891 235 Animal subject
1895 125 Great expectations
126 Sunset

RICHARDSON, MARGARET W. (Mrs)
1939 194 Joseph Lee, Esq min nfs
195 Mrs Joseph Lee min nfs

RICHMOND, JOHN RUSSELL
25 Oct 1926, Toronto IO
RCA(e) 1978 Council Illustrator
Addr: 1979, Claremont, Ont
1953 71 Jesus is condemmed $400
1954 73 The converted orchard 16 x 24 illus $200
1955 69 The Fifth Station $250
1961 66 Market Hall, Peterborough 36 x 48 $300

RICHMOND, LORRAINE see SURCOUF, LORRAINE

RICHSTONE, BELLE C.
Addr: 1931, 4250 Marcil Ave, Montreal
1931 248 Flowers $60

RICKARD, H.P.
Addr: 1938, Toronto
1938 S8, Toronto
219 Mahogany corner cabinet with carved frieze, glazed door banded with tulip wood
220 Mahogany serpentine fronted chest of drawers
221 Mahogany chest of drawers faced with burr elm, banded with sycamore

RICKERSON, GENIA TSERETELLI
19 May 1901, St Petersburg
1956 39 September mood $75 T56-27
1958 69 Corn $150

RICKETTS, HARRY E.G.
b 1901
Addr: 1933, 444 Moffat Ave, Verdun, Que; 1937, 212 Kindersley Rd, Town of Mount Royal, Que
1933 198 Fine and cold wc $65
1937 186 Autumn sunshine, Ahuntsic wc $85
187 Owl's Head, Nova Scotia wc $35
1947 152 Falling leaves wc $100
1952 78 Morning mood wc $100

RIDGE, FREDERICK C.
Addr: 1936, 5612 Queen Mary Rd, Montreal
1936 173 Silver Lake, Laurentians $60

RIDOUT, EVELYN M. (Mrs Fellowes)
1882, Toronto
Addr: 1901, 46 Cecil St, Toronto; 1902-5, 86 St Albans St, Toronto; 1909N, 84 Forest Hill Rd, Toronto
1901 91 Study of a dog
92 Study of a horse F2-57
1902 140 A fresh team, Herts
141 The Queen of Spades
142 The wicked cease from troubling
1904 139 The innocents at home
1905 141 The smithy
1909N 122 The mill team, Muskoka
123 The little housewife

RIDPATH, DREW
1971 121 Waste containers. Clayton, Ridpath Associates

RIDPATH, J.I., LIMITED
Addr: 1938, Toronto
1938 S8, Toronto
222 6 pieces, oak dining room furniture

RIGOLO, STANISLAV DINO
19 Aug 1924, Porcia, Italy
1946 100 On a sideroad wc $50
101 Little sister wc $50

RIMMER, DAVID MCLELLAN
20 Jan 1942, Vancouver WWA76
1970 Migration film screened 20 Feb
1971 Variations on a cellophane wrapper film screened 7 Apr

RINFRET, JEAN CLAUDE
3 Sep 1929, Shawinigan, Que
RCA(e) 1979 Set designer
Addr: 1979, Montreal

RIOPELLE, JEAN PAUL
7 Oct 1923, Montreal AGO B CC1 CWW79 NGC TB2
RCA(e) 1975 Painter
Addr: 1979, Paris

RIORDAN, JOHN ERIC BENSON
5 Dec 1906, St Catharines, Ont 23 Dec 1948, Montreal CNS36 CWW48
ARCA 1946 Painter
Addr: 1937, 4801 Grosvenor Ave, Montreal; 1947-8, Montreal
1937 188 December, day's end, North River $175 T38-48
1938 183 The still hour of early morning, Laurentide Park $150
1939 196 March evening, St Sauveur $175
197 God's country, Yoho Valley, Rockies $175
1941 Lieut E. Riordon, RCNVR
159 Morning sun, Mulet River $85
1942 Lt Comm E. Riordon, RCNVR
119 God's country, Yoho Valley, Canadian Rockies $175
1943 97 Ahead to the eastward lies the dangerous night $300
1944 117 Eastbound to Britain, RCN frigate $200
1945 172 Clearing weather, March $400
173 Sinister night, 1941 $250 T46-40
1946 102 Eventide, St Sauveur illus $400 T48-43
1947 153 An October afternoon, Laurentians $700
154 The evening hour $500
1948 130 October afternoon, St Sauveur $300

RIORDON, MARY KATHLEEN (Mrs Gordon Forbes)
1939 71 They are concerned with matter hidden $200

RISTVEDT, MILLY (Mrs Handerek)
9 Nov 1942, Kimberley BC IO
1966 63 Untitled 66 x 89 $350
1967 54 Color form #21 63 x 63 $400

RITCHIE, SAMUEL DOUGLAS
26 Jan 1887, Three Rivers, Que d Nov 1959
ARCA 1937 Sr 1957 Architect
Addr: 1937, 2048 Union Ave, Montreal; 1938-59, Montreal
1937 Shorey & Ritchie
258 Terminal building, Provincial Transport, Montreal
259 Farm house, Mrs Margaret Doorly, Montecello, Que

RIVARD, LOUIS ANDRE
1970 249 Announcement, Fine feathers, National Film Board

ROBB, CHARLES see BUSH, CHARLES

ROBB, GEORGE ALEXANDER
15 Mar 1923, Toronto
1971 23A-6A Summer residence, Georgian Bay, Ont. Wide view, exterior. Near view, exterior. Interior with view. Plan and section

ROBERT, GILLES
25 Apr 1929, Montreal
RCA(e) 1974 Council Graphic designer
Addr: 1979, Montreal
1970 Gilles Robert & Raymond Bellemare, to 1971
250 Book cover, Refuse de la femme
251 Letterhead, Youville Stables
252 Letterhead, Théâtre de Capricorne
253 Poster, Design Canada, Concrete awards 1967
1971 63G Symbole, Secrétariat d' Etat Gouvrement du Canada
64G Symbole, une maison d' édition, Didier International

65G Symbole, manufacturier de vêtements féminins, Joseph Ribkoff Limited
66G Carte du Nouvel An, Gilles Robert & Associés Inc
67G Affiche pour un cinéma, Société Micro-Film Inc

ROBERTS, GOODRIDGE see ROBERTS, WILLIAM GOODRIDGE

ROBERTS, THOMAS KEITH
22 Dec 1909, Toronto CNS40 CWW79 IO WWA56
ARCA 1945 Painter
Addr: 1930-1, 663 Oriole Parkway, Toronto; 1934-7, rear 18 Grenville St, Toronto; 1946, Toronto; 1947-69, Port Credit, Ont; 1970-1/79, Mississauga, Ont
1930 219 Jake's place linocut $10
220 Deserted mill linocut $10
1931 428 Northern pine col linocut $10
429 In the lagoon col linocut $8
1934 165 Mountain side, Baie Fine wc $35
1936 174 Old mill, Delta, Ont $150
1937 191 Morton, mill pond wc $45
1938 184 Afternoon shadows wc $35
1941 160 Grain boats, Collingwood $85
1942 120 St Lawrence Market $250
121 Afternoon light $250 T43-39
1943 98 Waiting for the ferry wc $35
1944 118 Potatoe harvest $275
119 The road to Orangeville $200
1945 174 June night at Orlando's $200 T46-41
1946 103 City lights $350 T47-44
104 Cloud shadows, Coventry $275
105 Landing the big one $275
1947 155 East wind $275 T48-34
156 Logging, Gatineau River $275
1948 131 Below the dam illus $375
132 Departing storm $275
1949 80 Cataract $400
1950 130 Quebec school children 28 x 36 $400
131 Landscape 24 x 30 $300
1951 87 Varennes, Quebec $400
88 Mont St Hilaire, Que $400
1952 81 Mennonites after church $400 T53-29
1954 76 St George 24 x 30 $350
1955 71 Rowboats, St Maurice River $400
1957 61 Wash day, Sous le Cap $400
1958 71 High day at Killaloe $450
1959 69 Noon 28 x 36 $450
1960 65 A la douce memoire 26 x 24 illus $500 S10-62
1961 69 Winter, Quebec 24 x 48 $650
1967 55 That day in spring 36 x 49 $950

ROBERTS, WILLIAM GOODRIDGE LLD
24 Sep 1904, Barbados 28 Jan 1974, Montreal AGO B CC2 CWW55 NGC TB2 W78 WWA47 WWB56
ARCA 1952 RCA 1957 Sr 1972 Council Painter
Addr: 1937, 1843 Dorchester St W, Montreal; 1953/71, Montreal
1937 189 Buildings, Montreal wc $100
190 Market building wc $50
1950 128 Still life with azelias 20 x 24 $350
129 Road in Eastern Townships 20 x 24 $300
1952 79 Squaw Island $700 T53-28
80 Georgian Bay landscape $500
1953 72 Blue water, Georgian Bay $475
1954 74 Books, flowers and fruit 32 x 36 illus $485
75 Lake in the mountains 24 x 36 $475
1955 70 Georgian Bay #2 $600
1957 60 Laurentian landscape $700 DW 1958 32 x 48 1/2
1958 70 Laurentian stream $700
1960 64 Still life with apples 60 x 48 illus $1,200
1961 67 Seated nude 48 x 36 illus $800
68 Cedars 48 x 24 $650
1964J 55 Eastern Townships, Quebec 36 x 48 $800
port: Artist and model, portrait of Goodridge Roberts, by E. Neumann, 1941-137

ROBERTS, WILLIAM GRIFFITH
25 Jul 1921, Nelson, BC AGO NGC TB2 WWA62
ARCA 1957-65 Painter
Addr: 1958-63, Roxdale, Ont; 1964-

5, Milton, Ont
1952 82 Morning paper wc $75
1953 73 Laundry day in Spain wc $100
1954 77 Spanish buildings 21 x 33 illus $100
1955 72 The girl with the red rose $100
1956 40 The Pendeen Light #2 illus $100 T56-28
1957 62 Meditation by the sea $250
1958 72 Cathedral of the sea illus $200
1959 70 Canadian north #3 20 x 39 $200
1960 66 The secret wall and field 52 x 39 illus $550
1963 63 Painting of an old portrait 34 x 28 illus $350
64 Retarded boy $500
1964J 56 Canadian land shapes 24 x 46 $375

ROBERTSON, AGNES MUIR (Mrs)
Addr: 1918A, 193 St George St, Toronto
1918A 268 Old buildings in the old country pencil

ROBERTSON, BEATRICE see HAGARTY, BEATRICE

ROBERTSON, HUGH DOUGLAS
11 Jan 1900, Hamilton, Ont IO
Addr: 1931-7, 36 Herkimer St, Hamilton, Ont
1931 251 Il Redentore, Venice wc $40
252 Pines against a blue sky wc $75
1933 200 White caps wc $50 T34-70
201 Black Rock Point wc $30
1934 167 Christian Islands, Georgian Bay wc $50 1936-176 $70
1935 227 Fog at New Harbour, NS wc $65
228 Peggy's Cove, NS wc $65 T36-62
1936 175 St Jovite, Quebec wc $70 T37-55
1937 194 Road with stump fences wc $80
1938 186 Late afternoon, Georgian Bay wc $75
1939 199 Blue water, Georgian Bay wc $75
200 Farm houses wc $35
1940 133 Nassau boatman wc $100
134 Courtyard, Nassau wc $100
1941 161 Farmyard in March wc $120
162 Stream in early spring wc $40
1943 99 Fresh breeze, Bahamas wc $100

ROBERTSON, JAMES (Mrs)
Addr: 1904, Montreal
1904 312 Ada Robertson min

ROBERTSON, S.
fl 1895-04 H
Addr: 1904, Montreal
1904 140 and 141 Landscape

ROBERTSON, SARAH MARGARET ARMOUR
16 Jun 1891, Montreal 6 Dec 1948, Montreal AGO CCI NGC TB2/3 WWA47
Addr: 1920-6, 284 Mackay St, Montreal; 1927-34, 1470 Fort St, Montreal
1920 211 The spae-wife
1921 130 The red feather
131 La vendeuse
1922 172 Neighbours
1923 143 Murray Bay village
144 Village, Ile d'Orléans, Quebec wc
1925 188 The blue sleigh
1926 124 Le repos illus ◊NGC◊
1927 190 Foster village
191 Autumn stores
1934 168 Zinnias dec wc $25
169 Petunias dec wc $25

ROBERTSON, SYBIL
Addr: 1920, 4156 Dorchester St W, Westmount, Que
1920 212 Miss Taylor

ROBINS, WILLIAM
fl 1895-05 H
Addr: 1895, c/o Roberts & Sons, Toronto; 1903, 51 King St W, Toronto; 1904-5, Toronto
1895 101 Percé Bay
102 On the beach at Black Cape, Bay Chaleur
103 Fish wier, near St Luce, St Lawrence
104 Morning near Grand River
1898 211 The wintry sea wc
212 Royal autumn wc
213 When the crust is on the snow wc
214 The lonely shore wc
215 Morning wc

1903 108 Good-bye, sweet day
109 When earth wakes from her winter sleep
1904 142 Autumn
246 'Twixt night and day wc
1905 152 Brown autumn
153 Evening

ROBINSON, A. BEVERLEY (Miss)
H
1898 241 Design for a fan

ROBINSON, ALBERT HENRY
2 Jan 1881, Hamilton, Ont 7 Oct 1956, Montreal AGO CC1 CWW49 EC Mo12 NGC TB3 W78 WWA47
ARCA 1911 RCA 1921 Sr 1951 Council
Painter
Addr: 1909N-15, 10 Phillips Pl, Montreal; 1916, Main St, Longue Pointe, Montreal; 1920-9, 158 Vendome Ave, Montreal; 1930-3, 3568 Vendome Ave, Montreal; 1934-56, Montreal
1909M 103 Ste Agathe des Monts
1909N 124 Morning, Montreal harbor
125 Jacques Cartier market
1910 166 Rising mists, Montreal harbor
167 Sunset along the docks
1910 S2, Liverpool
93 Montreal harbor
94 Old houses, Montreal
1911 141 Sunny afternoon on the Ottawa
142 Evening at Prescott
143 Old houses in Montreal
1912 186 Leaving port, St Malo, night effect
187 Montreal, from St Helen's Island
188 Sunset over Dinard 1914-166
189 The sea at St Malo
1912 S3, Winnipeg
131 Sunset, Montreal
132 Laurentian village
220 Logging on the Gatineau b&w
1913 249 Murky morning on the Thames S4-113 $300
250 Nice
251 The Thames at Westminster S4-114 $150 nfs. Purchased by National Gallery
252 Old fishing boats, Nice
253 Early morning, Nice harbor
254 Moonlight, St Servan S4-115 $200
1914 164 Fisherfolk's dwellings, Dieppe
165 A grey day
167 Fresh breezes, Dinard
1914 S5, Patriotic Fund
31 Village gossips illus
1915 183 Sunlit seas illus
184 Chiesa della Salute
185 The night boat, St Malo
1916 196 Seascape
197 In harbor
198 Old sea wall, St Malo
199 Old market place illus
1920 213 March sunshine
214 The blue freighter
215 Old homestead, Lower Lachine Road
216 October afternoon
1921 132 Winter afternoon on the St Lawrence
133 Lower St Lawrence, March DW 1922 30 1/2 x 40 1/2
134 Village on the gulf ≬NGC≬
1922 173 St Joseph de Lévis S6-80
174 Winter afternoon, Lauzon S6-81
175 Village by the St Lawrence S6-82
176 On the road to Lévis illus
1923 145 The open stream
146 Melting snows, Laurentians ≬NGC≬
147 Return from Easter Mass ≬AGO≬
148 Church in moonlight ≬NGC≬
1924 171 Morning at Quebec
172 Evening at Quebec illus
173 Old house, lower Quebec
1925 189 Noontime in the hills illus ≬NGC≬
190 CGS Arctic at Quebec
1926 125 La Mal Baie
1927 192 Goelettes in the ice, La Mal Baie
193 Sunday in the country illus ≬NGC≬
1928 133 Spring freshet $500
134 Village in the hills $500 F9-101
1929 191 Charny, Quebec $400
192 Cottage in the hills $200
1931 253 Hillside farm, Bolton, Quebec $600
1933 202 Winter evening $700 T34-71
1939 F11, New York

58 Winter, Baie St Paul, Que
33 x 27 (MMFA)
1954 31 Retro Sec Early spring
(Continental Galleries)

ROBINSON, KATHERINE MARY DAY ROSS
(Mrs Robinson)
9 Jan 1928, Trenton, Ont
1952 119 Portrait of Suki etch $20

ROBINSON, KATHLEEN B.
Addr: 1905, 449 Ontario St, Toronto
1905 222 Group of miniatures,
modelled

ROBSON, ALBERT HENRY
7 Jan 1882, Lindsay, Ont 6 Mar
1939, Toronto EC
1938 S8, Toronto
Ryerson Press
272 Book, Canadian landscape
painters

ROCH, ERNST
8 Dec 1928, Osijek, Yugoslavia TB3
WWA76
RCA(e) 1974 Graphic designer
Addr: 1976/79, Montreal
1970 254 Portfolio, Art in medicine
255 Desk calendar, National
Arts Centre
256 Advertisement, announcement of new trademark, Kruger Pulp & Paper Limited
257 Postage stamps, regular
issue, Canada Post Office
258 Advertisement, Quebec
Steel Products
259 Poster, Canadian Pulp and
Paper Association, Expo 67
260 Symbol, New Brunswick
Telephone Company
261 Symbol, Simtec Limited,
firm manufacturing equipment for nuclear detection
262 Symbol, Creative Photographics Limited
1971 33G Symbol, IMASCO Limited
Ernst Roch, Rolf Harder
68G Symbol, Pharmacie Centre
69G Postage stamp, Canada
Post Office
1976 S12, Montreal
127 Montréal 1976 poster
illus
128 Henderson Steel Construction, trademark illus

ROCKETT, PAUL ARTHUR
1 Nov 1919, Toronto
RCA(e) 1979 Photographer
Addr: 1979, Vancouver

RODEN BROS. LIMITED
Addr: 1938, Toronto
1938 S8, Toronto
237-40 Sterling ware, tea
set, dresser set, tableware #237-40 N. Morland,
W. Revill
241 Exhibition medals
242 Cut crystal stemware

RODMELL, KEN
16 Feb 1934, Biggar, Sask
1970 263 Invitation, Noel Martin
264 Magazine, Imperial Oil
Review, August 1965
265 Editorial spread, The
kids kept the peace
1971 70G and 71G Article, Canadian
Magazine

RODOCANACHI, HYPATIA English
1872, London, Eng G
Addr: 1913, 3 Park House, Cambridge
St W, London, Eng
1913 333 Madeleine Gregory bas rel
334 Helen, daughter of W.E.
Gladstone bas rel

RODRIK, PAUL (b Paul Rodman Johnston)
22 Jun 1915, Toronto
1958 73 Northern town $900

ROGERS (Mrs)
H
1888 293 Halifax, Nova Scotia wc
297 Near Halifax, NS wc

ROGERS, G.E.
1938 S8, Toronto
Macmillan Company of Canada
G.E.Rogers, Hugh Eayrs
176 Book, Family portrait
177 Book, Manitoba essays
178 Book, Saucy again
182 Book, The speeches of
Thomas D'Arcy McGee

ROGERS, OTTO DONALD
19 Nov 1935, Kerrobert, Sask CC2
WWA73
ARCA 1970 Painter
Addr: 1971/79, Saskatoon

1970 62 Spanish sun 60 x 60 $800
63 Sea and storm 60 x 60 illus $800

ROGERS, WILLIAM A. LIMITED (CANADIAN)
Addr: 1938, Toronto
1938 S8, Toronto
66 8 piece silver tea service illus

ROHRLICK, MORRIE
1967 65 Number landscape 48 x 36 $200

ROLLAND PAPER COMPANY LIMITED
Addr: 1938, Montreal
1938 S8, Toronto
243 Book and text papers

ROLLO, ANDREW English
b 1877 29 Nov 1951, Edinburgh
Addr: 1908, 47 Victoria Ave, Toronto
1908 164 Sketch, St Machas Cathedral, old Aberdeen
165 Sketch, Elgin Cathedral, east end

ROLPH, SMITH & COMPANY
Addr: 1886, Toronto
1883 339-79 Christmas cards, Canadian subjects, for Rolph, Smith & Co des competition prizes
1886 Fla, London, Eng
2032, artist number
Wood engravings

ROLPH, ERNEST ROSS
21 Jan 1871, Toronto 4 May 1958, Toronto CWW48 Co TB2
ARCA 1922 Sr 1940 Architect
Addr: 1920-1, 36 North St, Toronto; 1923-58, Toronto
1920 286-7 Hart House, Toronto. View from southeast. South end of Great Hall, corner of Quadrangle
1921 188 Mausoleum photo
189 Bishop Ridley College drwg
see also Sproatt, Henry, 1923

ROLPH, JOSEPH THOMAS
8 Sep 1831, London, Eng 13 Jun 1916, Toronto H
ARCA 1880 Painter
Addr: 1880-1, Toronto; 1883, 26 Wellington St E, Toronto; 1884-92, Toronto; 1893-6, 158 St George St, Toronto; 1897, 618 St Joseph St, Toronto: 1898, 618 St George St, Toronto; 1899-05, 158 St George St, Toronto; 1906, 292 Lake Shore, Centre Island, Toronto; 1907, Toronto; 1908-15, 26 Chestnut Rd, Toronto
1880 167 Fruit wc
1881 249 Apples, pears and grapes $30
265 Pears, peach and grapes $25
300 Pineapple, grapes and peaches $50
1883 202 Rosedale Creek, looking east wc $30
211 Fruit, grapes wc $25
234 Ellis' Road, Grenadier Pond wc $30
243 Early spring, Louiseville, Ky wc $15
300 On the Don River wc $15
1884 163 Fall scene on the Humber River, Ont wc $40
1885 211 Passing shower wc $25
229 Autumn afternoon wc $35
230 Side line, Mimoco wc $35
232 Side line, Lambton wc $20
250 Mr Howard's workshop, High Park wc $25
283 and 300 Side line, Islington wc $35 each
305 Don River Creek wc $30
310 Old mill race wc $20
1887 153 Entrance to Sparrow Lake wc $30
167 Old foundry near Lambton wc $30
1888 6 Near Rathnally, Toronto wc $50
67 Old mill on the Humber River wc $30
71 Bay of Quinte wc $30
73 Road through High Park wc $35
229 Old house, Lake of the Mountain wc $20
231 Coming shower, Bay of Quinte wc $30
248 After the shower, Lake of the Mountain wc $30
269 Dusty lane, early spring wc $40 J.J. Rolph mispr
310 Late November, High Park wc $35
315 Street in old Bath wc $30

1889 170 Pigeons wc $50
1890 199 Vale of Avoca, Moore Park, Toronto wc $40
200 Brandy Creek, Muskoka, after the shower wc $40
1891 151 Howard Park, Toronto wc
155 Humber Bay wc
170 November morning, Austin Park wc
173 In the Queen's Park wc
174 Cool day in spring, Poplar Plains Road wc
192 Morning on the Commons wc
1892 96 Old Canadian cottage wc $50
146 The old Baldwin homestead wc $50
150 A woodland scene wc $50
159 Cloudy day wc $50
1893 253 Birch trees, coast of Maine wc $50 F1-187
254 Sluice gate, near West Goldsboro wc $50 F1-188
1895 74W Showery weather, Don River wc
75W Spring time, Don Creek wc
76W On Toronto Island wc
77W On the Commons, North Toronto wc
78W Near Burleigh Falls wc
1896 247 Hayes Common, Kent wc
248 Lloyd's Lane, Kent wc
249 Near Keteran Valley, Surrey wc
1897 46W River Wandle, Wandle, Kent wc
47W Reddington, Kent wc
1898 205 A lane in Kent, Eng wc
206 Toronto Island wc
207 The crown of the hill wc
1899 219 A hillside at Weston, Ont wc illus
220 A bit of Toronto Island, looking east wc
1900 179 Old willows, Cape Ann, Gloucester, Mass wc
180 Willows, Centre Island, Toronto wc
1901 201 After the shower, Gloucester, Mass wc
202 Shadows wc
203 Sand banks, Bloor Street, Toronto wc
1902 F3, Rochester
149 Digby Basin, Digby, NS $75
1903 191 Digby shore, NS wc
1904 247 Where the boats come in wc
248 A glimpse of the ocean wc
1905 156 Digby Heights, NS
157 Trees and rocks, coast of Maine
158 Mouth of the Kennebunk River
159 A sentinel, coast of Maine
1906 158 Kennebunk Point, Maine coast
1906 F5, Halifax
142 In the midst of life $75
1907 274 Queen's Park, 1900 wc
275 Doubtful weather, Maine coast wc
1908 123 Late afternoon, Kennebunk Park, Maine
124 Springtime, Braemore, Davenport Road, Toronto
1909M 107 Old trees, Gloucester, Mass wc
108 Quaint trees, York Beach, Mass wc
1909N 126 Road to Pikwauket Mountain, NB
127 Late afternoon, near York Beach, Maine
1910 168 A lane, Nantucket
169 Old wharf, Nantucket
1911 144 On the coast of Maine
1912 190 Fog lifting, Gloucester, Mass wc
1913 255 Where they build the yachts, Gloucester, Mass wc
256 Early morning start, Sparrow Lake, Ont wc
257 Old porch and chickens wc
258 October day, North Toronto wc
1914 168 Old boat house, Rocky Neck, Gloucester wc
1915 186 On Mimico Creek, Toronto wc
187 Early morning, near Gloucester wc

ROMANOW, WILLIS
13 Jan 1940, Canora, Sask
1963 65 The bathtub illus $400

RONALD, WILLIAM (b William Ronald Smith)
13 Aug 1926, Stratford, Ont AGO CC1 CWW79 IO NGC TB3 WWA73
RCA(e) 1975 Painter
Addr: 1979, Toronto
1951 89 The stirrup casein $170
1953 74 My garden duco & casein $650

1964N 45 Davan 50 x 80 $2,700
1970 30A National Arts Centre, Ottawa, mural. Lebensold, F.D, architect

RONALDS ADVERTISING AGENCY
Addr: 1938, Montreal
1938 S8, Toronto
65 16 page magazine insert, Canadian Industries Limited
245 4 folders. Charles Fainmell

RONALDS COMPANY
Addr: 1938, Montreal
1938 S8, Toronto
246 9 de luxe books, complete production Ronalds Company
247 Normandie Roof folders, menu and book
248 Folders
249 Label bands
#247-9, Stan Engel

RONNER, ALICE
Addr: 1919, 14 Madison Ave, Toronto
1919 136 Roses
137 Asters

ROSAIRE, ARTHUR DOMINIQUE
17 Jan 1879, Montreal Feb 1922, Los Angeles NGC W78
ARCA 1914 Painter
Addr: 1907, Westmount, Que; 1908, 4302 St Catherine St W, Westmount, Que; 1910-13, 4323 Montrose Ave, Westmount, Que; 1914-16, 296 Mountain St, Montreal; 1918-19, Montreal; 1920, 2224 4th Ave, Los Angeles
1907 169 Laurentian stream, 9 pm
170 Homestead on the hill
171 Cross country, Laurentian Mountains
1908 111 Le soir
112 Sugar bush
1910 170 Birches
1910 S2, Liverpool
95 Sand hills
1911 145 Midsummer, Mount Royal
1912 191 Goat herd
192 Old mill, Lachine
1912 S3, Winnipeg
133 Mount Royal Park
134 Gypsies arrival
1913 259 Profile, Miss H.
260 Old Lachine Canal S4-116 $200
261 Sunset, Lachine S4-117 $250 ◊NGC◊
1914 169 The old silo
170 The evening visit
1914 S5, Patriotic Fund
74 A Laurentian river, winter illus
1915 188 Mulet River, Laurentian Mountains illus ◊NGC◊
189 Logging, Laurentian Mountains
190 The new building
1916 200 The play hour illus ◊NGC◊
201 Solitude
202 In the silence of the moon
1920 217 The old mission, California

ROSAMOND, MARY
1941 163 Florida negress $100 T42-47

ROSEN, BERNARD
5 Sep 1933
1964N Rosen, Caruso & Vecsei
162-6 Fraternity House, McGill University. Exterior, front facade. Exterior, rear. Ground plan, 2nd and 3rd floor plans

ROSENBERG, HENRY MORTIKAR
28 Feb 1858, New Brunswick, NJ 24 Dec 1947, Citronelle, Ala H
Addr: 1905, Victoria School of Art, Halifax; 1918N-21, Tramway Bldg, Halifax
1905 139 Sons of the sea
140 Twilight on Nova Scotia coast
1906 F5, Halifax
143 A dreamer illus $100
144 Reveries $100
145 The hills of Petite Rivière, Nova Scotia $150
146 In the shadow $175
1918N 162 Doing his bit
163 Harbour at Halifax, war time
1919 138 The Japanese jar
1921 135 The swamp trail

ROSENTHAL, JOSEPH (JOE)
15 May 1921, Kishinev, Romania IO
RCA(e) 1978 RCA 1979 Sculptor
Addr: 1979, Toronto
1966 52 Figure #1 18 x 24 $175
DW 1979 Standing Kensington Market woman sculp

ROSS, FREDERICK JOSEPH
12 May 1927, Saint John TB2 WWA76
1957 63 Boys playing in graveyard $300
1958 74 Still life $200
1961 70 Dark landscape 27 x 36 $125
1970 64 Girl with mirror 30 x 24 nfs

ROSS, GEORGE ALLEN
24 Oct 1878, Montreal d 1946
CNS27 Co PMC WWC30
Addr: 1920, 1 Belmont St, Montreal
1920 Ross & Macdonald
288 Qu'Appelle Hotel, Regina
289 Railway station, Halifax Ocean Terminals, Halifax

ROSS, J.J.
Addr: 1907, Montreal
1907 364 Dr Osler rel J.J. Ross, MD

ROSS, JEAN
1947 157 Path in woods wc $50

ROSS, MARGARET
H
1891 97 Study of shells

ROSS, PHYLLIS G.
Addr: 1922, 355 Mountain St, Montreal
1922 228 A nymph plaster

ROSS, ROBERT
29 Dec 1902, Toronto AGO
Addr: 1928, 1351 Queen St W, Toronto; 1930, 119 Scollard St, Toronto; 1936, 68 Grenville St, Toronto
1928 135 Portrait in gold and green
226 Anne charcl
227 Miss Black charcl
1930 221 Portrait charcl $30
1936 177 Veronica $200
1951 124 Daria cer $300
1955 96 Girl's head drwg $60

ROSSI, ALBERTO Italian
8 Aug 1858, Turin B TB
Addr: 1893, Cairo
1893 128 A street merchant in Cairo $80

ROSTAND, MICHEL
9 Aug 1895, Sadagore, Nice B WWA76
1964N 46 Au pays du sourire 8 x 10 $600

ROSTRICK, J.W.G.
1880 269 Medieval cabinet des

ROTH, GEORGE W.
1970 266 Brochure, Emily Carr
267 University of Waterloo, 1969-70 Academic calendar
1971 72G Booklet, University of Waterloo, Extension
73G Poster, Conestoga College, Communication arts

ROTHFELS, JOANNE see MANNING, JOANNE

ROUNTHWAITE, CYRIL FREDERICK THOMAS
16 May 1917, Sault Ste Marie, Ont
CWW79
1964J Rounthwaite & Fairfield
126 Town Hall, Whitby, Ont
1966 152-4 Sault Ste Marie Air Terminal Building. View from vehicular approach. View from landing area. 1st floor plan

ROUS & MANN LIMITED
Addr: 1938, Toronto
1938 S8, Toronto
250-60 books, 261-4 folders
250 The first Canadian Christmas carol
251 The maid of the mountains
252 The loyalist
253 A merchant's clerk in Upper Canada
254 War log of the Nancy illus
255 The Rebellion, 1837 illus
256 Tom Thomson illus
257 J.E.H. MacDonald illus
258 Cornelius Krieghoff
259 The Toronto Stock Exchange
260 Not here, Doctor
261 Colour tonic
262 Pellegrin's carol
263 Just to remind you
264 Behold! The walrus tooth

ROUSSEAU, MARIETTE (Mrs Claude Vermette)
29 Aug 1926, Trois Pistoles, Que
WWA73
ARCA 1972 Council Textile designer
Addr: 1979, Ste Adele, Que

ROWAN, WILLIAM
29 Jul 1891, Basle, Switzerland 30 Jun 1957, Edmonton W78
1945 232 Cougar plaster $500
249 Josephine silverpoint nfs
1946 145 Grizzly sculp rowanite $350

ROWBOTHAM, THOMAS CHARLES LEESON
21 May 1823, Dublin Irish
30 Jun 1875, London B DIA RSBA
1881 87 Carnarvon Castle wc (Lady Macdougall)

ROWLAND, DOUGLAS CHARLES
28 Dec 1921, Kingston, Ont
ARCA 1968 Architect
Addr: 1969-71, Don Mills, Ont; 1979, Toronto
1968 119-22 International Business Machines Limited, Toronto, Headquarters Building. A. Main entrance B.Foyer C.Exterior D.Shipping entrance John B. Parkin Associates
1971 27A-30A Shaw & Begg Limited, Toronto, office building. View from northwest corner at Huntley Street. Elevator lobby on typical office floor. Detail of exterior precast columns. Ground floor plan. Parkin Architects, Engineers, Planners

ROWLAND, EDITH English
fl 1901-40 DBA TB2 WWB34
Addr: 1925, Derby Rd, Woodford, Essex, Eng
1925 191 Portrait min

ROWLEY, FRANCES see RICHARDS, FRANCES

ROY, JEAN MARIE
8 May 1925, Standon, Que
RCA(e) 1978 Architect
Addr: 1979, Quebec

ROYDS, MABEL ALINGTON (Mrs E.S. Lumsden) English
fl 1899-40 DBA
Addr: 1906, Havergal College, Toronto
1906 151 A girl, some hens and an old canvas
152 Apples

ROYLE, JEAN
Addr: 1932, 47 Edward St, Halifax; 1933, 122 Morris St, Halifax
1932 164 The mouth of the cove $400
1933 203 Sunset at Prospect, Nova Scotia $400
204 Calm evening $250

ROYLE, STANLEY
12 Dec 1888, Stalybridge, Lancs, Eng 27 Apr 1961, n Sheffield, Eng
CC1 DBA NGC TB2 WBA WWB34
ARCA 1936 RCA 1942 Non-res 1945
Council Painter
Addr: 1931-2, Nova Scotia College of Art, Halifax; 1933, 77 Queen St, Halifax; 1935-7, Mount Allison University, Sackville, NB; 1938-45, Sackville, NB; 1946-61 Hitcham, Eng
1931 254 Baslow Bridge, Derbyshire, winter $350
1932 165 Evening light, Peggy's Cove, NS $1,500
166 Morning light, Peggy's Cove, NS $500
1933 205 Evening light, Prospect, NS $200
206 Evening light, Blue Rocks, NS $1,000
1935 229 Tranquillity, Peggy's Cove, NS $500
230 Rock pool, Peggy's Cove, NS $350 T36-63
1936 178 Lumber wharf, Halifax, NS illus $300 T37-56 F11-60 30 x 25 (MMFA)
1937 195 Derbyshire, England $500
1938 187 A winter's evening, old cottages, England nfs
188 James Marshall Palmer, MA LLD nfs
189 Mid-day, Atlantic coast, Nova Scotia $325 T39-47
1939 201 Evening light, Lake Morraine, Canadian Rockies illus $1,500
202 Morning light, Lake Morraine, Canadian Rockies $600
203 Rock formation, Atlantic coast, Nova Scotia $600
204 The stillness of dawn, Peggy's Cove, NS $350 DW 1942 25 x 30 T51-35
1940 135 Evening stillness, Prospect, NS illus $1,000
136 Still pool, Peggy's Cove, NS $600 T41-46
137 Reflections, Prospect, NS $300

138 Carolyn nfs
1941 164 Drowned fisherman temp $1,250
165 Percé illus $600 T42-48
166 Saint John River, NB $600
167 Sky study nfs
1942 122 Fisherman and girl illus $1,000
123 Morning sunlight, Percé, Quebec $225
124 Grey day, Percé, Que $65
1943 100 Norman, Nova Scotian fisherman $150 T44-32
101 Old Quebec, looking from the Château Frontenac $125 T44-33
1944 120 Bedford Basin, Halifax, 1943 (W.H.C. Schwartz)
121 Frances nfs
122 Rocks at Peggy's Cove $250
1945 174 An English village $1,500

ROZA, GUSTAVO URIEL DA
24 Feb 1933, Hong Kong CWW79
RCA(e) 1973 Architect
Addr: 1979, Winnipeg

RUEL, WILLIAM H.
fl 1880-94 H
ARCA 1882-94 Painter
Addr: 1881, Bedford, NS; 1883, Liverpool, Eng; 1884-5, Wooton, Eng; 1886, Ryde, Isle of Wight; 1887-9, Wooton, Eng; 1900-1, Isle of Wight; 1892-3, Porchester, Hants, Eng
1880 77 Barnstaple Bay, Bristol Channel
1881 101 HMS Atlanta (M. Chiconi)
226 Painting
307 Going ashore
309 Taking a pilot $40
1882 1 Sniffing the breeze $50
11 October squall on the coast
48 Winter voyage off the Straits of Belle Isle $50
1883 98 Near Percé, Gulf of St Lawrence $45
125 Showery weather $100
128 A friendly race $40
130 Ebb tide $75
1885 15, 158 and 191 Painting
55 On the banks $25
1886 24 Digby harbour $10
30 Marine $15
1886 F1a, London, Eng
2015, artist number
View of Halifax
A Quebec timber ship
1889 101 Marine sketch, fishing $15
1890 81 French lugger leaving for home $25

RUELLER, GEOFREY see KNELLER, GODFREY

RUETER, WILLIAM
4 Aug 1940, Kitchener, Ont
RCA(e) 1976 Graphic designer
Addr: 1976/79, Toronto
1970 268 Announcement, Ruari McLean talk
269 Booklet, inside spread, '100 books since 1471'
1976 S12, Montreal
129 Book, Laurels for the third muse illus
130 Book, Seer illus

RUSSELL
1880 133-42 Leaves, modelled from nature sculp

RUSSELL, GEORGE HORNE
18 Apr 1861, Banff, Scot 25 Jun 1933, St Stephen, NB AGO B CC2 EC H Mo12 NGC PMC R2 TB1/3 W78
ARCA 1909 RCA 1918 Council Painter
Addr: 1893-6, 55 Church St, Montreal; 1902-5, 25 Durocher St, Montreal; 1908-16, 6 Beaver Hall Sq, Montreal; 1918A-26, 360 Beaver Hall Sq, Montreal; 1927-32, 1158 Beaver Hall Sq, Montreal
1893 255 Mount McDonald, Selkirk Range wc $300
1896 250 Evening, Purcells Cove, NS wc
251 Herring Cove, NS wc
1902 143 Charles Alexander, Esq; late Charles Alexander 1909M-105 1909N-128 S2-96
144 Evening
145 A lonely shore
146 An old home
1903 107 Under the willows ◊NGC◊
1904 143 Under the birches
144 The last load
1905 160 A meadow stream
1906 F5, Halifax
147 Fall ploughing $125
1907 172 Marguerite and Geraldine, daughters of Wm. C. Hodgson
173 Homeward
174 A by-way

276 The Muchalls Canal, Scotland wc
1907 F6, Sherbrooke
151 Cooling waters $500
1908 121 W.R. Baker, Esq, Sec'y CPR, Montreal
122 Early spring, Scotland
1909M 106 Rev J.B. Silcox, sketch portrait
1910 171 Mrs W.R. Baker
1911 146 Portrait
1912 193 Mrs Russell
1912 S3, Winnipeg
135 Mrs A.J. Mackenzie
1913 262 F.W. Molson, Esq
263 In Montreal harbour
264 Calves S5-41 illus
265 The little gooseherd S4-118 $200
1914 171 Old benignity
172 Barges on the Thames
173 The sheep barn
174 The flock
1915 191 H.R. Charlton, Esq
192 Gull Rock, Grand Manan New Brunswick
193 Anchored illus
194 Eastport
1916 203 The clam diggers illus
204 Fog, St Andrews harbour, New Brunswick
205 Seal Cove, Grand Manan ◊NGC◊
1918A 144 Miss Janet, daughter of Norman Wilson, Esq
145 James Carruthers, Esq, Montreal illus
146 Evening, St Andrews, New Brunswick ◊AGO◊
147 Foggy weather, Eastport, Maine
1918N 164 C.R. Hosmer, Esq
165 2nd Lieut Norman W. Russell, RAF illus DW 1919 47 1/4 x 32
166 On the beach, St Andrews, New Brunswick
167 Carting seaweed ◊AGO◊
1919 139 Singing Beach, Manchester
140 Rockport harbour
1920 218 Dr Perrigo
219 J.C. Noseworthy, Esq illus
220 Homeward
221 Stonehaven harbour, Scotland
1921 136 Clam diggers illus
137 Boys digging clams
138 At Grand Manan
139 Grandfather
1922 177 Edmond Dyonnet, RCA illus S6-83 F8-100 $525
178 Evening mist, St Andrews, NB S6-84
179 Blue Rocks harbour, NS S6-85
180 Clam diggers at St Andrews, NB S6-86
1923 149 E. Alexander, Esq
150 Surf, Monhegan
151 Evening, Monhegan harbour
1924 174 Carting seaweed, St Andrews, NB
175 A wayside model
176 Dr Frank D. Adams, PhD, late Dean, Faculty of Applied Science, McGill University illus
177 Anna, daughter of Mr and Mrs N.F. Wilson, Ottawa
1925 192 Hayter Reed, Esq illus 1926-126
193 On the beach, St Andrews
194 The clam digger, St Andrews, NB
1926 127 The duck pond
128 The clam digger
1927 194 Rev Hugh Pedley, DD illus
195 Marine, Nova Scotia
196 Clam diggers, St Andrews
1927 F7, London, Eng
112 Anchored $525
1928 136 A fisherman's home, Blue Rocks, NS $500
137 Breezy day, Nova Scotia coast $850 F9-116 1929-193
1929 194 Seining the weir $1,000
195 Oxen on the shore, Nova Scotia $600
1929 S7, Calgary
132 On the Maine coast $600
133 Rockport harbour, Mass $400
1930 148 Hon Senator Carrine Wilson
1930 F10, London, Eng
165 Coast of Nova Scotia $500
1931 255 Green Point Light, La Tête, NB $1,000
256 Crescent Beach, NS $600 ◊MMFA◊
257 Leaving port $400
258 Fishing village, Grand Manan, NB $400
1932 167 Point Lepreaux, NB $1,200

1933 Late George Horne Russell
207 Evening tide, Point Lepreaux $600 T34-72
208 The breakwater, Seal Cove, NB $500
209 Lords Cove, Deer Island, NB $350
210 Clam digger, St Andrews, NB $375
port: bust, by H.Hébert, 1916-248

RUSSELL, GYRTH
30 Apr 1892, Dartmouth, NS 8 Dec 1970, England AGO B CWW64 NGC TB1/2 WWB34
Addr: 1918A, England
1918A 269 Nuit d'été etch
270 Le Boul' Mich etch

RUSSELL, JOHN ALONZO
28 Oct 1907, Hinsdale, NH 3 Dec 1966, Winnipeg CWW64
ARCA 1965 Architect
Addr: 1966, Winnipeg

RUSSELL, JOHN WENTWORTH
28 Aug 1879, Binbrook, Ont 5 Nov 1959, Toronto AGO B CC1 CWW58 Mo12 NGC TB1/3
Addr: 1905, 14 Leader Lane, Toronto; 1909N, 54 Queen St S, Hamilton; 1911, 394 Yonge St, Toronto; 1915, 1 Breadalbane St, Toronto; 1918A, 54 Queen St S, Hamilton, Ont; 1919, 30 College St, Toronto
1905 154 Frederick Holmestead, Esq
155 Portrait
1909N 129 Archibald Browne
130 Curtis Williamson, RCA
1911 147 His Hon Lieut Gov J.M. Gibson
1915 195 Rt Hon Sir Wilfrid Laurier, GCMG illus
1918A 148-9 Matron Elizabeth Russell, RRC; a life of devoted service to hospital and Red Cross work ◊AGO◊
1919 141 Grandmother and child
142 Still life arrangement illus

RUSSWORM, GLEICHEN see GLEICHEN-RUSSWORM, HENRICH

RUSTON, HILDA SOPHIA MARQUETTE
(Mrs Alfred Ruston)
22 Sep 1912, Kitchener, Ont
1945 176 Gypsy house nfs
1947 158 Mennonite rigs $100
159 Mennonite church $125
1948 133 Mennonite escorts $150
1949 81 Mennonite study $45
82 Old bridge, Conestogo, Ont $100
1950 132 Prayer meeting 20 x 24 $125
1951 90 Mennonite market illus $150
91 Tin roofs $150
1957 64 Mennonite church $450

RUTHERFORD, R.W. (Capt)
fl 1877-88 H
1885 156 Lt Col Montizambert

RYDER, JOHN
H
1881 219 Harrow-on-the-Hill (Alex McLeod)

RYERSON PRESS
Addr: 1938, Toronto
1938 S8, Toronto
265 Selected poems by Sir Charles G.D. Roberts. C.D. Ellinger
266 Snobs and spires. Frank Carmichael
267 West by east, poems by J.E.H. MacDonald. Thoreau MacDonald illus
268 Poems by Francis Sherman. Thoreau MacDonald
269 Pens and pirates. Frederick H. Varley
270 This is Ontario. Frank Carmichael, map by Stanley Turner
271 Our great ones, Jack MacLaren
272 Canadian landscape painters, Albert H. Robson
273 The neighing north. J.W. G. Macdonald
274 Canada's past in pictures, Charles W. Jefferys

SADOWSKA, KRYSTYNA KOPCERYNASKA
(Mrs Konrad Sadowski) (Mrs Stefan Siwinski)
2 Jun 1918, Lublin, Poland CWW79 IO TB2
1954 100 God Pan ink & oil 25 x

19 illus $30
1955 97 Evening nfs
1958 75 Kiss with moon $100

SAFDIE, MOSHE
11 Jul 1938, Haifa CWW79
ARCA 1972 Architect
Addr: 1979, Montreal

SAILA, CLEMENT P.I.
Addr: 1930, 169 Birch Ave, Toronto
1930 149 The haunted house wc $100

SAINT CHARLES, JOSEPH
10 Jun 1868, Montreal 26 Oct 1956, Montreal CC2 CNS36 Mo12 PMC TB2
ARCA 1901 Sr 1938 Painter
Addr: 1895, YMCA Bldg, Montreal; 1899-01, Montreal; 1902, 34 Labelle St, Montreal; 1903, 14 Phillips Sq, Montreal; 1904-5, Montreal; 1906, 473 St Hubert St, Montreal; 1907-8, Montreal; 1909N, 801 St Hubert St, Montreal; 1910, 314 St Catherine St W, Montreal; 1911, 801 St Hubert St, Montreal; 1912-14, 591 St Catherine St W, Montreal; 1915-18, 502 St Catherine St E, Montreal; 1920, 801 St Hubert St, Montreal; 1922, 706 St Catherine St E, Montreal; 1923-56, Montreal
1895 127 The grinder
128 My portrait
1899 122 Petite tête de femme
123 Study of a head
124 Petite mendiante
125 Scene, interieure
1901 114 Mr Alf Laroque
115 Woman playing mandolin F2-68
116 Red man, Cameriere F2-69
117 Mrs S, portrait
1902 147 Lieut Gov Jetté
148 Mr L. de M.
149 Hon L. Gouin
279 M. de M. pastel
280 Maj Pelletier crayon
1903 38 Mr Philippe Hébert, sculptor
39 Jeune femme à la fenétre
1904 145 Mousquetaire lisant F4-71
146 Jeune italienne
147 Petite italienne
148 Femme drapée F4-72
149 Un regard au dehors F4-73
150 Hon Judge Champagne F4-74
151 Mlle L.J. Tarte
324 Dr B. b&w
325 Mr R. b&w
1906 F5, Halifax
154 A member of the Red Cross $60
1907 280 and 281 Tête de vieillard pastel
282 Tête de femme pastel
1907 F6, Sherbrooke
159 Study pastel $60
160 Study $100
1909M 180 Femme en plain air
180a Italienne en priere 1909N-141 Italian at prayer
1909N 142 Mrs C, portrait
1910 172 Miss Y.
173 Model at rest
1911 161 Portrait de femme
162 Femme lisant
1912 208 Young girl 1913-268 S4-119 $100
209 Portrait of the artist
1913 266 Lieut Gov Sir François Langelier
267 Reverie
269 Child with apple S4-120 $50
270 Profile pastel S4-121 $50
271 Child with red tuque pastel S4-122 $25
1914 S5, Patriotic Fund
52 Young girl's head pastel illus
1915 205 Coin de ferme, Berthier
287 Tête d'étude crayon
288 Tête de jeune fille crayon
1918A 159 Portrait of the artist
276 and 277 Drawing
1918N 179 Lt Col L. Leduc
180 Calm evening at Pont-rouge, Quebec
181 In jail, 1792
182 Suzanne pastel
1920 222 Jeune bohémienne pastel
223 Jeune fille, tête
1922 194 Tête de jeune fille
195 Montréal, vu de Longueuil S6-94
1938 207 Jeune fille des Laurentides pastel $400
1939 303 Mme J. Saint Charles charcl nfs

SAIT, GWENDOLYN L.
Addr: 1933, 4134 Old Orchard Ave, Montreal
1933 211 August day, Caughnawaga $200

SALADA TEA COMPANY OF CANADA LIMITED
Addr: 1938, Toronto
1938 S8, Toronto
275 Posters, 3 original drwgs
Charles Comfort

SAMILA, DAVID JOHN
26 Mar 1941, Winnipeg IO
1965 61 Agreed pencil 30 x 22 $135

SAMPSON MATTHEWS LIMITED
Addr: 1938, Toronto
1938 S8, Toronto
H.V. Shaw
276, 278, 280-1, 283-6, Wampoles bottle labels & cartons
287 Softone can illus
288 Glassite varnish can illus
292-3 Rose brand bottle labels illus
295, 300 Shirriff jar and bottle labels
298 Lushus cartons
309 Tuckett tobacco tin illus
311-12, 314, 316, Neilson chocolate boxes
318 Neilson chocolate bar wraps illus
323-5 Tuckett newspaper & magazine advertisements
327 Tooke Bros, 2 folders
335-6, Canada Packers containers
A.J. Casson
277, 279, 282, Wampoles bottle labels and cartons
289, 291, McCormick's Fiddlesticks and Bix cartons illus
294 Rose brand marmalade tin label
299 Fancy free carton
301-8, 310, Tuckett cigarette and tobacco cartons illus
313, 315, 317, Neilson chocolate boxes illus
319 Neilson Bitter sweet, Butter toffee, Jersey milk
320 Birks-Ellis-Ryrie booklet
321 Buntin Reid folders
326 Provincial Paper, Supertext folder
328 Provincial Paper, blotter
329 Canada Life, 2 folders
330 Terminal Warehouse, booklet
331 Shirriff, Lushus showcard
332 Shirriff, Lushus and Fancy free magazine advertisements, produced for Cockfield Brown & Company Limited
334 Canada Packers, Biscot shortening tin
J.G. Gauthier
290 McCormick's Krackers carton illus
296-7 Shirriff, jar labels
J.E. Sampson
322 Buckingham, 3 newspaper advertisements
J.S. Hallam
333 Goodyear, tire card

SAMPSON, JOSEPH ERNEST
11 Jul 1887, Liverpool 29 Oct 1946, York Mills, Ont AGO CNS36 NGC ARCA 1939 Painter
Addr: 1913, Arts and Letters Club, Toronto; 1921-5, 72 St Leonard Ave, Toronto; 1936-7, 10 Forest Glen Cr, Toronto; 1940-45, Toronto
1913 272 The boudoir
273 The doll
1921 140 The artist
1925 193 Over the hill
1929 S7, Calgary
134 Maligne Lake $750
1936 179 Day dreams $500
1937 196 Jeanne nfs F11-61 40 x 40 1944-123 1945-177
1938 S8, Toronto
Sampson Matthews Limited
322 Buckingham, 3 newspaper advertisements
1939 205 Sisters nfs
1940 139 The essential man $750 T41-47
1942 125 Hon N.O. Hipel, Speaker, 1935-1938 nfs
1945 178 Lily pond $250
1946 In memory of Joseph E. Sampson, who died 29 Oct 1946
106 Maligne Lake, Jasper Park
107 The Throne, Jasper Park
108 Backwater, Canoe Lake
109 Sundown, Rockport
110 The harbor, Rockport
111 Northern tapestry ◊AGO◊

SAMUEL, EDITH MARY THORNTON
b 1935
1960 67 Trees 48 x 32 $225

SAMUELS, H.S. (Miss)
H
1891 84a Mandarin oranges

86 Grapes

SANBORN, MARGARET JANE
26 Jul 1861 H
Addr: 1893, 5 Close St, Montreal; 1896-9, 5 Essex Ave, Montreal; 1904, Montreal; 1907, Westmount, Que; 1910-23, 566 Roslyn Ave, Westmount, Que
1893 129 Portrait nfs
256 Before twilight wc $20
1896 252 Spring wc
253 A hillside wc
1899 129 Pike River
221 Case of miniatures wc
1904 313 and 314 Portrait min
1907 359 2 miniatures
1910 174 Mount Titlis, from Lucerne
1913 274 Hester Halliday wc on ivory min
1915 284 Late Col Sweeny min on ivory
285 Mrs Sweeny min on ivory
1916 206 Mrs James S. Graham, Ottawa min on ivory
207 At dusk wc
1923 152 Capt Bennet's boat wc

SANDHAM, HENRY
24 May 1842, Montreal 21 Jun 1910, London, Eng AGO B DBA EC Mo98 NGC TB W78
RCA 1880 Hon Non-res 1883 Council
Painter
Addr: 1880, Montreal; 1881-2, Boston; 1883, c/o Notman Photo Co, Park St, Boston; 1884, 219 Tremont St, Boston; 1893-5, 152 Boylston St, Boston; 1896-9, 154 Boylston St, Boston; 1900-5, Boston; 1906-9, London, Eng
1880 35 Fish nets, Bay of Fundy
60 On Mount Royal, Montreal
94 Beacon Light, Saint John harbour DW 1880 30 1/4 x 16 1881-271
117 Gathering sea wrack (Geo. Hague, Esq) Fla-2016 Gathering seaweed (Geo. Hague, Esq, Montreal)
238 Study of rocks wc
239 Gulf of St Lawrence wc (William Notman)
240 Montreal wharf, sketch wc
1881 334 Hon Joseph Howe
337 Hon Judge Strange Johnston
1882 138 Canada in winter, a trip on snowshoes $110
1883 161 Swoop her up wc $100
220 The meadows of St Ann wc $150
1884 10 Low tide $150
21 An old homestead $100
27 On the western plains $60
44 Point au Pic, Murray Bay $100
60 The old subdued and slow $225
61 Call to sunrise mass $400
137 Close quartered wc $60
141 A 'corner' in marbles wc $50
169 Storm wc
1886 78 and 97 Tobogganing wc $20 each
79 A snow storm wc $20
154 Un habitant $150 Fla-2016
1886 Fla, London, Eng
2016, artist number
Tobogganing
1887 171 An attractive girl wc $175
1891 95 In the potato field
138 Water babies wc
1893 130 The founding of Maryland, March 27th 1634 $8,000 F1-97
1894 120 Portrait of an ancestor
121 Self satisfaction
186 The fall of the leaf wc
187 Château Frontenac wc
1895 131 Cleopatra
132 The summer girl
82W Crow's Nest, Monoghan, Maine wc 1896-255
1896 150 'Standing with reluctant feet, where the brook and river meet'
151 A toiler of the sea
254 The fisherman's home wc
256 When Greek meets Greek wc
1899 126 A Canadian oven
127 A modern Magdalene

SANKEY, LLOYD PHILIP
see DONALDSON, JAMES MILLER, 1968

SAPP, ALLEN (SAPOESTAKEN)
2 Jan 1929, Red Pheasant Reserve, Sask
RCA(e) 1975 Painter
Addr: 1979, North Battleford, Sask

SATURDAY NIGHT PRESS
Addr: 1938, Toronto
1938 S8, Toronto
337 Book, Canadian Industries Ltd. R. Purves, C. Mangold

Ross Purves
338 Book, Canadian Industries Ltd
339 Booklet, Imperial Oil Ltd
340 Booklet, Service Station Equipment Ltd
342 Booklet, Automatic Oil Heat
Orme Payne
341 Letterhead, Saturday Night Press
Carl Mangold
343 Letterhead, Canadian Industries Ltd

SAVAGE SLOAN LIMITED
1970 107 Flush valve. Stuart Sales Engineering Company Limited

SAVAGE, ANNE DOUGLAS
27 Jul 1896, Montreal 25 Mar 1971, Montreal AGO CC1 CNS40 NGC TB2 WWA47
Addr: 1918A, 52 Trafalgar Ave, Montreal; 1918N-29, 20 Highland Ave, Montreal; 1931, 4090 Highland Ave, Montreal
1918A 150 The snow spirit
1918N 168 The Pied Piper
169 Ville Marie
1920 224 October
1921 141 Belmont Street
1922 181 Lake Wonish S6-87
182 Dusk
1923 241 Fortis et veritas. Mural decorative painting competition
1925 196 Des monts
197 September
1927 197 Kitwanga Hills, BC
198 Rocher de Boule, Kispayax, BC
337 Kitwancool drwg
338 Kitsyguclos drwg
1928 138 Hills on the Skeena $350
1929 196 Shacks at Percé
1931 259 Lake Wonish $200

SAVARD, CLAUDE
1971 Fête de nuit film screened 7 Apr

SAWAI, NOBORU
18 Feb 1931, Honmach, Takamatsu, Japan WWA76
Addr: 1976, Calgary
1976 S12, Montreal
164 Signs of Zodiac wdcut & copper etch/gravure sur bois et cuivre 26 x 20 illus

SAWCHUCK, GEORGE
1927, Kenora, Ont
RCA(e) 1978 Sculptor
Addr: 1979, Vancouver

SAWYER, WILLIAM
1820, Montreal 9 Dec 1889, Kingston, Ont H NGC W78
1883 113 An old student $95

SAXE, CHARLES JEWETT
1870, St Albans, Vt PMC
ARCA 1911-22 Architect
Addr: 1896, 37 St Luke St, Montreal; 1902, Montreal; 1903, 107 St James St, Montreal; 1907-22, Montreal
1896 275 Residence, plan
276 Residence, elevation
277 Country residence
1902 Saxe & Archibald, to 1907
254 Residence, A.H. Scott, Esq
1903 199-01 Residence, Jas. Shearer, Esq. Exterior. Reception hall. Entrance hall
202 Residence, Arthur H. Scott, Esq, Montreal
1907 341 Residence, Alex Falconer, Esq
342 Residence, Shirley Ogilvie, Esq, MacGregor Street
343 Residence, James Reid Wilson, Esq, Lacolle
344 Fairmount Methodist Church
345 Residence, W. St Pierre
see also, Archibald, John, 1899

SAXE, HENRY
24 Sep 1937, Montreal B WWA78
RCA(e) 1975 Sculptor
Addr: 1979, Tamworth, Ont

SCHAEFER, CARL FELLMAN
30 Apr 1903, Hanover, Ont AGO CC2 CWW79 NGC TB2 WWA47
ARCA 1949 RCA 1965 Sr 1971 Council Painter
Addr: 1932, 103 Snowdon Ave, Toronto; 1935, 100 Bain Ave, Toronto; 1950-71/79, Toronto
1932 168 Dark cedars $200
1935 231 Before rain, Parry Sound wc $65 ‖AGO‖
1948 134 Fallen tree wc $125

135 The Parade Square, Fort Henry, Kingston $125
1949 83 View of Barry's Bay wc $125
1950 133 View of Kingston Penitentiary, Portsmouth 16 x 23 $250
1952 83 Fields with evening sky wc $175 1953-76 $185
1953 75 Mill ruin at Ayr wc $185
1955 73 Still life, yellow illus $185 ≬AGO≬
1958 76 Wheat field and the Pinnacle $275
1959 71 The great oatfield 22 x 30 illus $600
1961 71 The square piano, Brittania Road West 15 1/2 x 22 1/2 illus $200
1966 54 Pine stump and field weeds 22 x 30 $375 S10-64
1966 S10, Charlottetown
63 Destruction of the square piano $300
1967 57 Wind in the woods 22 x 30 $600
1968 40 The great plain near Bamberg, Waterloo County 22 x 30 illus $600
DW 1966 Oatfield, Waterloo County wc 15 x 21 3/4
port: by C. Comfort, 1948-34 and 1970-13

SCHAFLEIN, JOHN EDWARD American
1894, San Diego
Addr: 1925, c/o Brigdens, Winnipeg; 1929, 610 Castle Bldg, Montreal; 1930-1, 2177 Comte St, Montreal
1925 198 The pioneers illus
199 Noontime
1929 197 Youth $500
1930 150 By the well $400
1931 260 The veteran $750

SCHEEPERS, MALVINA see COBURN, MALVINA

SCHELL, FRANCIS H. American
1834, Germantown, Pa 31 Mar 1909, Germantown, Pa AAA28 B Gr TB
1882 271 Lumberman's stable, St Maurice River monoc

SCHELLENBERGER, OTTO see RAND, PAUL

SCHENK, V. (Mrs)
1939 302 The nave of All Saints Cathedral etch $12

SCHLACTER, JOHN N.
22 Oct 1906
1947 160 The raft nfs
1948 136 July morning $30

SCHLASSER, C. see SCHLOESSER, CARL

SCHLEEH, HANS MARTIN
9 Oct 1928, Koenigsfeld, Germany CWW79
RCA(e) 1976 Sculptor
Addr: 1979, Dorval, Que
1963 107 Lute player sculp $750
108 Human soul sculp $700

SCHLIENGER, OSCAR
25 Oct 1905, Basel, Switzerland
1945 179 Mist over Port Credit wc $150
180 After the bath wc nfs
1951 92 Gray spring day $150

SCHLOESSER, CARL BERNHARD (KARL SCHLÖSER) German
21 Jun 1832, Darmstadt, Germany 1914, London, Eng B DBA DVP G TB
1880 61 The first sickness (W. Kingsford) Schlasser mispr

SCHMIDT, MARIANNA
1928, Hungary
1967 60 Plastogome #6 24 x 24 illus $300

SCHOELER, JEAN PAUL RENE
29 Oct 1923, Toronto
RCA(e) 1973 Architect
Addr: 1976/79, Ottawa
1976 S12, Montreal
Schoeler, Heaton, Harvor & Menendez
108 Ecole Secondaire, Charlebois 2 illus
see also Harvor, Stig, 1971

SCHOENAUER, NORBERT
2 Jan 1923, Reghin, Romania
RCA(e) 1978 Architect
Addr: 1979, Montreal

SCHOENMAKERS, WILLEM
19 Mar 1922, Rotterdam IO
1961 72 Figure 35 x 63 illus $850

SCHREIBER, CHARLOTTE MOUNT BROCK MORRELL (Mrs Weymouth George Schreiber)

1834, Woodham, Essex, Eng 1922, Paignton, Devon, Eng EC H Mo98 NGC W78
RCA 1880-6 Painter
Addr: 1880, Toronto; 1881-3, Deer Park, Toronto; 1884, Streetsville, Ont; 1885-6, Toronto; 1893-8, Springfield-on-Credit, Ont
1880 6 Friends
26 The croppy boy; confessions of an Irish Patriot DW 1880 35 1/2 x 30 1881-239 S1-135
30 Of what is she thinking? portrait
31 Joan of Arc praying before battle
76 Olivia, 'Vicar of Wakefield'
1881 246 Duck on nest $10
252 He sees it $20
260 Messenger of mercy $100
274 A box on the ear (Ontario Society of Artists)
283 Foster mother, a scene from real life $100 1882-44
292 Domestic bliss $60
293 Christabel
305 Goldilocks
1882 7 After tea $80
46 The white doe of Rylstone $400
51 An autumn bouquet, portrait
76 A trial of patience $80
101 A day's sport spoilt $100
1883 1 Christmas morning $300
6 Priscilla and John Alden $275
54 Relics $75
60 Little King Cole was a merry old soul $25
99 See the conquering hero come $275
115 Little fairy, Muriel $30
118 Little gipsy, Gwendoline $30
1884 22 Weary, friendless and forlorn $35 S1-102 $75
30 Amy and her kitten $35
37 An ideal head $35
42 My love has golden hair $35
87 A comforter $100
92 Mischief $35
1884 S1, Saint John
109 A cuff on the ear $75
1885 74 This is my chair $35
95 Absorbed $30
123 A parting look $35
137 Portrait $35
141 Robin Adair $150
145 Study of an Arab
157 O loosen the snood in your hair, Janet $150
183 Baby Louise $35
197 Enjoying the vacation $25
1886 28 A cold day $40
29 Mary with the flaxen hair $35
147 Stumping in Canada $130 Fla-2017
163 Sophia visiting her father in prison, 'Vicar of Wakefield' $130
208 Statute labor, girls in the way $130. Selected for Fla, not in Fla catalog
1888 75 Bo-peep $35
113 Mother's darling $40
115 A valiant hero $35
225 Excelsior $50
1893 131 Christobel $500 F1-98
1898 98 Rebekah and Abraham's servant

SCHREIBER, JOHN
31 Jul 1921, Brzozno, Poland
1971 31A-4A Ballantyne residence, Tibbits Hill, Brome, Que. Conversion and addition. Dining room. View from rear. Approach to house. Site, upper level, main level, lower level plans

SCHREIER, HILDE
19 Jun 1926, Austria IO
Addr: 1976, Ottawa
1976 S12, Montreal
150 Court group, celebration sisal, knotted & wrapped/ sisal, noué et enroulé 90h illus

SCHWARTZ, SUZANNE
1938 S8, Toronto
167 Sanctuary window des, by OCA students, assisted by Rowley Murphy
1939 206 Winter evening $40

SCHWOB, DORIS
1970 270 Announcement, Pas de deux

SCIORTINO, FRANCESCO SAVERIO
12 Nov 1875, Citta Rohan, Malta
1 Sep 1958, Oka, Que PMC
ARCA 1921-39 Sculptor

Addr: 1915, 75 Sherbrooke St W, Montreal; 1918N, c/o T. Carli, 316 Notre Dame St E, Montreal; 1920-5, 210 St James St, Montreal; 1926, 276 St Urbain St, Montreal; 1927-31, Montreal; 1932-3, 272 King St E, Toronto; 1934-9, Toronto
1915 244 Fun plaster bust
245 Dames de l'Ile de Malte bas rel
1918N 217 Hon Beaubien bust
1920 276 Weight of dissolution plaster 1921-181 1924-240 illus
1921 182 In Jerusalem, from the Calvary plaster
1923 190 Dames de l'Ile de Malte bronze 1924-243
191 Fountain, detail model plaster
192 Church memorial tablet fragment plaster
1924 241 Fountain, detail sculp
242 Permanent smile sculp
1925 273 Marguerite Bourgeois sculp
1926 164 Tabernacle plaster model
1932 219 Motherhood plaster $150 bronze $500
1933 268 Motherhood dec panel plaster $500 bronze $700

SCLATER, GILBERT TURNBULL
9 Dec 1908, Edinburgh d 1939
Addr: 1932, 89 Glen Rd, Toronto; 1935, 128 Park Rd, Toronto
1932 169 Mont Carmel, Quebec $125
1935 347 The mill race wd engr framed $5.50

SCOBIE, MARGARET
Addr: 1916, 50 Forest Hill Rd, Toronto; 1918A, 600 Sherbourne St, Toronto
1916 258 Faun plaster
1918A 199 Girl with a lamp plaster
200 Portrait of a lady plaster

SCOTT (Miss)
1882 226 and 227 Panel dec des

SCOTT, ADAM SHERRIFF
18 Jul 1887, Galashields, Scot 23 Oct 1980 CNS36 NGC TB2
ARCA 1935 RCA 1942 Sr 1957 Council Painter
Addr: 1927, 725 St Catherine St W, Montreal; 1931-5, 3531 Ste Famille St, Montreal; 1937, 3615 Lorne Cr, Montreal; 1938-71, Montreal; 1979, Ste Anne de Bellevue, Que
1927 199 The valley, Ste Marguerite, Quebec
1931 261 Maj J.M. Morris
262 Study $300
1933 212 Summer afternoon $1,000
1934 170 Alfred Laliberté, RCA illus $1,000 T35-62 1935-232
1935 233 Mrs Ross Clarkson
1937 197 After the shower, Georgeville, Que $175 T38-49
198 Laid aside $75
199 Mr A. Murphy nfs
1939 207 Maj J.C. Routledge, Black Watch nfs
1939 F11, New York
62 After the shower 28 x 18 $175
1940 140 Mrs R.W. Steele nfs
1941 168 C.C. Jennings, Esq, MA MC nfs 1942-126
1943 102 Alan Maclachlan, Esq nfs
103 Sgt Maj Hugh Craig, Black Watch nfs
1945 181 Grandmother's wedding dress, Miss Elaine Scott nfs
1946 112 Miss M.K. Holt nfs
113 Corp John Reford nfs T47-45
1947 161 H.W. Molson, Esq nfs
162 John Bassett, Esq, nfs
163 Dr Albert Le Sage nfs
1954 37 Retro Sec. Study in black and grey (St James Club, Montreal)
DW 1943 A visitor to the studio 36 x 28 1/4 T51-36

SCOTT, CHARLES HEPBURN
29 Nov 1886, Newmilns, Scot 28 Jun 1964, Vancouver CC1 CWW61 EC TB2 WWA47
ARCA 1940 Sr 1956 Painter
Addr: 1926, 6212 Balaclava St, Vancouver; 1932-6, 590 Hamilton St, Vancouver School of Art, Vancouver; 1937, 6212 Balaclava St, Vancouver; 1941-64, Vancouver
1926 129 Twilight
1932 170 Al fresco $500
260 Smuggler's Cove drwg $25
261 Evening in the cabin drwg $25
1933 213 Ships of Yule T34-73
1937 200 Winter in the garden $100 T38-50

1938 190 Canadian youth illus $400
191 The Massive Range wc nfs
1939 208 Western pioneer $300
209 Come wind, come sun $400
1941 169 Cariboo landscape $350
170 Light and form wc $40
1946 114 Early spring in the garden $150 T47-46
1948 137 The merry jetty $400
1952 85 Quiet woods, BC wc $150

SCOTT, COLIN ALEXANDER
fl 1889-94 H
Addr: 1893-4, Ottawa
1889 158 Cascade, Muskoka wc $15
1890 201 Spring wc $35
202 Summer wc $35
203 Autumn wc $35
1891 52a Mackenzie's Avenue, Ottawa
103 The north shore
191 Landscape wc
200 Bark canoe wc
1892 78 November $20
109 South Harpswell, Maine wc $25
158 Murray Bay wc $20
1893 132 Une calêche $25
257 Bush, meadow wc $30
258 Goldenrod wc $50
1894 125 A cup of tea
188 Cattle wc
189 A study wc

SCOTT, CYNTHIA MYRA
28 Apr 1939, Winnipeg
RCA(e) 1974 Council Film Maker
Addr: 1979, Uxbridge, Ont

SCOTT, GERALD W.
30 Sep 1926, Carlton, NB AGO
1948 138 Paul Borzos nfs
139 Fritz Alexander nfs
1960 68 Self portrait 22 x 28 nfs

SCOTT, LILLIAN
Addr: 1927, 1104 Ouellet Ave, Windsor, Ont
1927 200 Old Etaples, Canadian Headquarters, France wc
339 Chartres, France drwg

SCOTT, MARGUERITE (Mrs O'Donnell)
Addr: 1937, 80 St Louis St, Quebec
1937 201 Market horses, Quebec wc $15
202 After a storm, Quebec wc $60
1938 267 and 268 Study drwg $75 each
1939 260 Foal plaster $20
261 Neighing stallion plaster $60
1941 171 Canadian foal nfs
1943 O'Donnell
145 Foal drwg $25

SCOTT, MARIAN MILDRED DALE (Mrs Francis Reginald Scott)
26 Jun 1906, Montreal AGO B NGC TB2 WWA47 WWB58
ARCA 1972 RCA 1975 Painter
Addr: 1918N-27, 552 Pine Ave W, Montreal; 1929, 22 Highland Ave, Montreal; 1976/79, Montreal
1918N Dale, to 1927
38 Night
1927 42 Sketch
1929 198 Piedmont Hills $75
1950 134 Field 24 x 20 $100
135 Stone and protoplasm (1) 24 x 22 $100
1966 55 Structure #1 34 x 36 $300
56 Structure #2 58 x 54 $600
1967 58 Untitled #1 44 x 50 $600
59 Untitled #2 58 x 62 $800
1970 65 Artifact #6 58 x 64 $1,000
1971 37 Artifact #M 60 x 60 illus $1,000
1976 S12, Montreal
42 Undercurrent #1 acry 58 x 58 illus
43 Undercurrent #2 acry 60 x 55 illus
DW 1975 Artifact. 1970 60 x 60 acry on duck

SCOTT, MARION see ALFSEN, MARION

SCOTT, MARY S.
H
1889 75 Lemons $40

SCOTT, R. STUART
9 Feb 1904, Nanaimo, BC
Addr: 1936, 1804 W 14th Ave, Vancouver; 1937, 1806 W 14th Ave, Vancouver
1936 180 Precipitation wc $50
1937 203 Halibut boats, Vancouver wc $50

SCOTT, SIMON
Addr: 1976, Vancouver
1976 S12, Montreal
89 Generation alum 14 x 6 x 2 illus

SCOTT, THOMAS SEATON
16 Aug 1836, Birkenhead, Eng 15 Jun 1895, Ottawa NGC W78
RCA 1880 Council Architect
Addr: 1880-95, Ottawa
1880 347 Union Station, Toronto
1881 23 Tower, West Block, Departmental Bldg, Ottawa des DW 1881, Tower, West Block, Parliament Building, Ottawa drwg 39 x 17 1882-237 Mackenzie Tower, Ottawa
1882 202 Campagna, Rome wc sketch
234 St Louis Gate, Quebec des
240 Kent Gate, Quebec
241 The Grand Canal, Venice sketch

SCOTT, W.P.
fl 1883-9 H
Addr: 1887, Montreal
1887 56 Foggy morning, Point au Pic
61 Autumn tints
87 Mill dam at Cowansville
105 An October day

SEARLE, JAMES ELMHURST
13 Jun 1929, Winnipeg CWW79
see SMITH, ERNEST, 1964J-1967

SEARS, HENRY
30 Oct 1929, Toronto
RCA(e) 1978 Architect
Addr: 1979, Toronto

SEATH, ETHEL
1879, Montreal 10 Apr 1963, Montreal AGO NGC TB2 WWA47
Addr: 1906, 9 University Ave, Montreal; 1907, Montreal; 1909M, 870 St Catherine St, Montreal; 1913-25, 329 Victoria Ave, Westmount, Que; 1927-32, 9 Seaforth Ave, Montreal; 1934-7, 3570 Côte des Neiges Rd, Montreal
1906 148 Sketch pen & ink
1907 298 Women weaving pen & ink
299 Girl reading etch
300 The knitter etch
301 Toodles etch
1909M 164 Interior, Christ Church Cathedral, Montreal
1913 275 Old quarry, Outremont
1915 196 Moonlight, barns at Beaupré
1916 314 Fairy cobweb drwg
315 The singing lesson drwg
1918A 271 Snow elves drwg
272 A tempting morsel drwg
1919 145 Purple cineraria
1920 225 The green boat
344 Knives and scissors to grind drwg
1921 142 A bit of China
143 On the Canal, Montreal
1924 178 The Canal, Montreal
1925 200 Fish house, Percé
1927 201 Clearing snow
202 Flower study
1929 S7, Calgary
135 Old house, Côte des Neiges $80
1931 263 Houses in winter $40
1932 171 Street corner, Montreal $80
1934 171 The pink fruit dish $45
172 Sun flower $35
1935 234 The pineapple $75
1936 181 The shell $100 T37-57
1937 204 The window 1938-193 T39-48
1938 192 Shell pattern #2 $50

SEAVEY, JULIAN RUGGLES
1857, Boston 1940, Hamilton, Ont H
Addr: 1898, 9 Main St, Hamilton, Ont; 1909N, Hamilton, Ont
1882 40 Ebb tide, Massachusetts Bay $70
1885 104 A bite $120
1888 139 Hamlet $60
155 Belle $30
173 Plums $35
1891 119 Head wc
178 Pomegranates wc
227 Musical instruments
229 In the doctor's study
1892 21 Still life, grapes $75
162 Still life wc $25
1898 95 Old stone bridge, Geneva Lake, Wisconsin
96 Raspberries
220 New York harbour wc
1909N 131 Mrs B.

SEBAG, NANCY see MONTEFIORE, NANCY

SECORD, JAMES EDWIN
b 1917 4 Aug 1979, St Catharines, Ont
1964N Secord & Herzog
187-8 Band stand, Niagara Falls. General view. Detail

SEELEY, FLORENCE
H

Addr: 1886, New York
1886 33 Nonquitt Beach $20
105 Daffodils $20
110 Micmac wigwam $100
118 Roses $15
1886 Fla, London, Eng
2018, artist number
Roses (HE Marquis of Lansdowne, Ottawa)
1888 158 Nova Scotia's emblem $16
Serly, mispr
160 The old well $20

SEGAL, A.J.
Addr: 1933-5, 3668 Durocher St, Montreal
1933 269 D.A. Brandon, Esq sculp nfs
1935 291 Ruth sculp nfs

SEGSWORTH, FLORENCE E.
Addr: 1905, 635 Ontario St, Toronto
1905 177 October

SEGUIN, TUTZI see HASPEL, TUTZI

SEIDEN, REGINA (Mrs Eric Goldberg)
4 Jul 1897, Rigaud, Que NGC WWA47
Addr: 1916-18A, 169 Park Ave, Montreal; 1918N-20, 152 Park Ave, Montreal; 1922-4, 27A McGill College Ave, Montreal; 1925, 257 Peel St, Montreal; 1927, 682 St Catherine St W, Montreal
1916 210 Portrait
211 A girl in pink
1918A 151 Girl in blue
1918N 171 Portrait
1919 146 Portrait illus ◊NGC◊
1920 226 Summer
1922 183 Old woman illus S6-88 ◊AGH◊
184 Fiesole S6-89
1923 153 Dora ◊NGC◊
154 Old houses, Paris
1924 179 French Canadian kitchen
1925 201 Une polonaise
1927 203 Argentine girl
204 Fisherman's house, St Tropez
340 Boats on the Seine drwg

SEKIDO, YOSHIDA
Addr: 1923, 197 Sparks St, Ottawa
1923 155 Near the lake wc

SELLMAN, E. ELLA
Addr: 1928, 12 Earl St, Toronto
1928 139 Study of a head pastel

SELWYN, WINIFREDE
1888, Brandon, Man
Addr: 1924, 545 Gilmour St, Ottawa; 1926, 128 Stewart Ave, Ottawa
1924 180 Near the San Fernando Valley, California wc
181 On the beach at Santa Monica, California wc
1926 130 The end of the road wc

SEMAK, MICHAEL WILLIAM
9 Jan 1934, Welland, Ont WWA76
RCA(e) 1974-9 Council Photographer
Addr: 1976/79, Pickering, Ont
1976 S12, Montreal
180 Moscow USSR/1975 silver print 9 1/2 x 7 1/2 illus

SEMPLE, MARGARET HUNTER DOTY (Mrs Howard Mitchell Semple)
3 Mar 1900, Yarmouth, NS
1942 127 Still life nfs
1947 164 Morning, Peggy's Cove $100
165 Boats in fog wc $50
1951 92a Spring ice, Lake Moraine wc $200

SETON-THOMPSON, ERNEST see THOMPSON, ERNEST EVAN SETON

SEVIER, GERALD LESLIE (GERRY)
25 Jan 1934, Hamilton, Ont IO
RCA(e) 1976 Illustrator
Addr: 1979, Toronto
1965 62 Figures in action #2 49 x 61 $500
1966 57 Flowers in reverse 36 x 30 $250
1967 61 Principle 36 x 48 $475
1968 41 TW1, combination #3, 2 units 48 x 23 $575
42 TW1, combination #6, 2 units 48 x 23 $575
1970 66 Ancient symbol #3 51 x 45 $625

SEXTON, DONALD
1938 269 The rebellion ink drwg $20
270 The refugees ink drwg $15

SEYMOUR, MUNSEY
1837, Mint, Calcutta 1912, Barton, Vt H NGC
Addr: 1893, Montreal

1882 128 Buffalo wallow, twilight wc $60
206 On Memphremagog, windy wc $225
1893 133 Evening on the Carron, Easter Ross, Scotland $225 F1-99

SHABAEFF, VALENTIN
c 1891, Russia AGO B NGC TB2
Addr: 1931, 3531 Ste Famille St, Montreal
1931 266 Hunting in XVI century in Russia $185 Shebaeff, mispr
267 Russian old fisherman $75
1947 217 Three Kings cer panel $1,500
218 Sacred dance cer rel $300

SHACKLETON, KATHLEEN English
5 Feb 1884, Dublin DBA
Addr: 1931, 1188 Phillips Pl, Montreal
1931 264 Rex Patterson, Esq pastel
265 Mme E.P. Benoit pastel
1938 195 Eskimo girl, Aklavik, NWT pastel $250
1939 210 Arctic trading store pastel $100
1941 172 J.P. Vinette, lineman, CPR pastel nfs

SHADBOLT, JACK LEONARD
4 Feb 1909, Shoeburyness, Eng AGO CC2 CWW79 NGC TB2 WWA47
1941 244 A red shed drwg $18
245 A country church drwg $18
1942 128 Signature piece $125 T43-40
1964N 49 Amulet, red into white 60 x 48 $500

SHADLOCK, FRANK
Addr: 1932, 46 Balmoral Ave N, Hamilton, Ont; 1933, 83 Sandford Ave S, Hamilton, Ont
1932 172 The musicians, still life $200
173 Brazen laughter, still life $75
1933 214 Portrait of my daughter

SHARP, DOROTHEA
Addr: 1913, Braeleigh, Forden Ave, Westmount, Que
1913 276 Daisies and babies S4-123 $120

SHARPS, ROBERT G.
1938 196 Self portrait nfs

SHAW, AUSTIN
Addr: 1920, 28 College St, Toronto
1920 227 Miss Catherine Proctor
228 Master Galt Austin Shaw

SHAW, AVERY MAYNARD
27 May 1907, St Martin, DWI 17 Feb 1957, Saint John
Addr: 1936-7, 66 S Park St, Halifax
1936 182 Old barn wc $35
183 Green squash $50
1937 205 Backyards wc $35

SHAW, HAROLD VAIL
c 1902, Toronto
1938 S8, Toronto
Sampson Matthews Limited
276, 278, 280-1, 283-6, Wampoles bottle labels and cartons
287 Softone, can
288 Glassite varnish, can illus
292-3 Rose brand bottle labels
295, 300, Shirrif, jar and bottle labels illus
298 Lushus cartons
309 Tuckett tobacco tin
311-12, 314, 316 Neilson chocolate boxes
318 Neilson chocolate bar wrappers
323-5 Tuckett newspaper and magazine advertisements
327 Tooke Bros 2 folders
335-6 Canada Packers containers

SHAW, JOHN W.
see BANZ, GEORGE, 1968

SHEA, FELIX JAMES
b 1896
Addr: 1927, 364 Dorchester St W, Montreal; 1928, 648 Dorchester St W, Montreal; 1931, 1188 Phillips Pl, Montreal
1927 341 In the reeds wd cut
1928 228 Nude study wd cut $10
229 The flight wd cut $8
1931 430 Early flight wd cut $12
431 Snipe wd cut $12

SHELDON-WILLIAMS, INGLIS
25 Dec 1870, Elvetham, Eng 30 Nov

1940, Tunbridge Wells, Eng DBA
Addr: 1914, 1721 Scarth St, Regina
1914 174 Hon ex-Chief Justive E.L. Wetmore, Chancellor, University of Saskatchewan
176 Hon J.S. Sheppard, MLA, Speaker, Saskatchewan Legislative Assembly

SHENNAN, DAVID
17 Jan 1880, Dumfries, Scot 27 May 1968, Montreal
ARCA 1948 Sr 1953 Architect
Addr: 1949-68, Montreal

SHEPARD, S.
H
1888 311 Sleighing party wc

SHEPHERD, CHARLES GREY
17 Jan 1926, St Catharines, Ont
ARCA 1971 Council Industrial designer
Addr: 1979, Oakville, Ont

SHEPHERD, HELEN PARSONS (Mrs Reginald Shirley Moore Shepherd)
16 Jan 1923, St John's
RCA(e) 1978 Painter
Addr: 1979, St John's

SHEPHERD, M. CECILIA
Addr: 1907, Victoria
1907 277 Study of an old man's head wc
278 Study of a boy's head wc

SHEPHERD, REGINALD SHIRLEY MOORE
28 Mar 1924, Portugal Cove, Nfld TB3
RCA(e) 1976 Painter
Addr: 1979, St John's
1951 93 The Cathedral, St John's, Newfoundland wc $175

SHEPPARD, PETER CLAPHAM
21 Oct 1882, Toronto 24 Apr 1965, Newmarket, Ont AGO CWW58 NGC TB2 W78 WWA47
ARCA 1929 Sr 1952 Painter
Addr: 1915, 65 Summerhill Ave, Toronto; 1916, 63 Summerhill Ave, Toronto; 1919, 22 Cornish Rd, Toronto; 1920-2, 101 1/2 King St W, Toronto; 1923-4, 39 Clair Ave E, Toronto; 1925-30, 70 Oakwood Ave, Toronto; 1931-3, 48 Oakwood Ave, Toronto; 1934-5, 68 Kendal Ave, Toronto; 1936-7, 48 Oakwood Ave, Toronto; 1938-65, Toronto
1915 197 The water trough
198 The two engines
1916 212 The bridge builders, Bloor Street Viaduct, Toronto
1919 147 Old house, April
148 Down by the way
1920 229 The side show illus
230 Lake traffic (NGC)
1921 144 Lower New York illus 1922-185 S6-90
145 The hillside
1923 156 Pioneer
1924 182 Waterfront, Toronto
183 The storm
1925 202 The blue sleigh
1926 131 Fairbank
1927 205 Midwinter (NGC)
206 Commerce
1928 140 Rapids, Whetstone River $350 S7-136
1929 199 Ice bound $500
200 Hazy days $500
1930 151 Lowtide $350
152 Sea port illus $350
153 The green boat $300
1931 268 Fishing boats $500
269 After the storm $300
270 Sea port $350
1932 174 Three old houses, Louisa Street illus $300
175 Rostance as Vincent Crummels $100
1933 215 Fruit market $300
216 Queen Street, West, Toronto $300
217 Ocean freighter $350 T34-74
1934 173 Hamilton Market $225
174 Laid up $300
175 Cab stand, Place Viger $225 T35-63
1935 235 Harbour scene, Halifax $350
236 Bay of Fundy $350 T36-64
237 Saint John River $450
1936 184 Edge of town, early spring $150 T37-58
185 June $350
1937 206 City docks, Toronto $400 T38-51 F11-63 35 x 44
207 Fruit boat $150
208 Evening $300
1938 197 Waterfront $450
198 Credit Forks $150 T39-50
199 Don Valley $250
200 Winter $250

1939 211 Market day, Quebec $300
212 Northern village $450
213 Freighters, Montreal $350
1940 141 Grain field $150
142 The visit $150 T41-48
1941 173 Repairing the ship $300 T42-49
174 Autumn $300
175 Old town $300 1942-129 T43-41
1941 S9, Toronto
53 Edge of the lake $85
1943 104 Caledon farm $350 T44-34
105 Builders $150
106 Fair for Britain $400
1944 124 Edge of the town $300 T45-40 1945-182 T46-42
125 Mill at Barberton $300
1945 183 Fall fair $600
184 Autumn pattern $250
1946 115 Small craft $350 T47-47
1947 166 After rain, Brooks Falls $400 T48-35
167 Summer pasture $150
1948 140 Coming storm $300
1949 84 Georgian Bay $350 1950-136 30 x 36
1951 94 Farm, Combermere $350
1952 86 Farm, north country $350
1953 78 Mill town $350
1954 78 Ocean port 24 x 34 $400 1955-74 illus $350

SHERBECK, M. CARMEN (Mrs)
1947 168 Sunday afternoon $200

SHERRIFF-SCOTT, ADAM see SCOTT, ADAM SHERRIFF

SHERWOOD, WILLIAM ALBERT
1 Aug 1855, Omemee, Ont 5 Dec 1919, Toronto AGO H Mo98/12 W78
ARCA 1891-13 Painter
Addr: 1892, Toronto; 1893, 54 Arcade St, Toronto; 1894-01, Yonge St Arcade, Toronto; 1902, 124 Victoria St E, Toronto; 1903-8, 2 1/2 Queen St E, Toronto; 1909M, Russell House, Toronto; 1910-13, Toronto
1885 78 Prof Boys
324 and 325 Portrait pastel
1888 121 Dr McAlpine
132, 192 and 253 Portrait
210 Study of a head $25
247 Flirt wc $30
1889 42 John Gordon, Esq
63 Alexander McLachlan, poet
1890 82 His lordship sitting in state $30
83 Rev Henry Scadding, DD Cantab nfs
84 Jacko
1891 102 F.M. Bell-Smith, RCA
115 W.A. Sherwood, portrait
1892 13 and 15 Portrait
32 An Alpine warder $75
1893 134 Comrades $125 F1-100
135 The negotiation F1-101
1894 126 Life's eventide
127 Miss May Patterson, Sydney 1895-138
190 A head pastel
1895 136 Meditation pastel
137 Portrait of a lady
139 Mr J.S. Fitch
140 Tired out
1896 152 L.R. O'Brien, RCA
153 P. Parks, Esq
154 Portrait of the artist 1897-144 1901-112
155 Summer's night, Hanlon's Point, Toronto
156 Bright summer days
1897 140 Dr Davies
141 Little newsboy
142 The morning paper
143 Strayed or stolen
1898 106 In the rushes
107 The Bit, Ingle
108 Mr W.H. Wallbridge
217 St Bernard wc
1899 121 Portrait of J.S.
1900 110 Miss D, Los Angeles, Calif
1901 113 In the leafy wood F2-67 1902-150
1903 111 The backwoodsman
1904 152 Late Dr Scadding
152a A Canadian backwoodsman F4-75
153 Miss Patterson F4-76
1905 161 The westerner
1907 177 J. Lavine, Esq
279 Lake Louise wc
1908 134 Dr Barnhardt
1909M 120 The mirror of the forest
121 Stolen fruit

SHINE, ANTHONY
see BLAND, JOHN, 1964N
LE MOYNE, ROY, 1964N

SHKLAR, LOUIS
Addr: 1931, 3575 St Lawrence St, Montreal
1931 335 My mother sculp

SHONIKER, CLAIRE MARIE (Mrs Viktoras Brickus)
12 Sep 1931, Toronto IO
1961 75 English ivy 30 x 40 $200
1964N 50 Orchard 30 x 40 $300
1965 63 Orchard 22 x 28 $160
1966 58 Spring apple 22 x 28 $165
1968 43 Begonia 72 x 48 $1,000

SHORE, HENRIETTA MARY
b Toronto B TB2 WWA36
Addr: 1907, Toronto; 1908, 28 Toronto St, Toronto; 1909N-12, Yonge Street Arcade, Toronto; 1916, 1216 Hollingsworth Bldg, Los Angeles
1907 178 Girl with doll
179 Child of the ghetto
1908 131 Girl in blue
1909N 132 Miss Phyllis Sanford
133 Winter
1910 175 Child with fruit
176 The blue cape
1910 S2, Liverpool
97 Girl in brown
1911 148 Sisters S3-136
149 Water lilies
150 In the park S3-137
151 Lady in white waist
1912 194 Woman in black
195 Dahlias
196 Little girl in green
197 At the zoo
1916 213 Mother and child
214 The promenade

SHORE, LEONARD ELDON
13 Jul 1902, Clarksburg, Ont
ARCA 1960 RCA 1968 Council Architect
Addr: 1961-71/79, Toronto
1958 Shore & Moffat, to 1959
103 Etobicoke Civic Centre illus
104 Collingwood District Collegiate Institute
1959 103 Municipal buildings, Township of Vaughan
1960 103 Physics and Mathematics Building, University of Waterloo photo illus
104 British American Oil Company Limited, Clarkson, Ont. Entrance area of office building photo
1961 Shore & Moffat, to 1971
102 Gate house, Page-Hersey Tube Limited
1963 120 Sir Alexander Campbell Building, Ottawa
121 Imperial Oil Limited, Sarnia, Research Laboratory
1964J 120-1 Sir Alexander Campbell Building. View from courtyard. Exterior
122 Cayuga Technical and Commercial High School. Exterior
1964N 167-9 West Haldimand Hospital. Exterior view. Exterior view with landscaped court. Overall 1st floor plan
1965 148-51 C.W. Jefferys Secondary School. Interior. Interior, classroom. Exterior, showing driveway. Entrance with steps
152-5 Board of Trade, Country Club. Interior looking out on courtyard. Exterior with stairway. Interior of hall. Interior showing fireplaces and conference table
1966 155-9 Arts Library Building, University of Waterloo. General view illus. Cantilevered arcade at 1st floor level. Library. South elevation, final stage of Arts Library. 2nd and 3rd floor plans
160-4 Research and Development Centre, British American Oil Company Limited. View showing laboratory and administration office. Exterior view. Engine testing laboratory. Dynamometer test area. Plot plan
1968 123-6 Central Services Building, University of Waterloo. A.Perspective B.Interior C. Exterior, entrance D.Exterior, rear view
1970 45A-50A Georgian Bay Secondary School, Meaford. View from northeast. View along Eliza Street, looking west. Foyer and sculpture gallery. View from main entry. Plot plan. Ground floor plan. one illus
1971 35A-8A Research Centre, Shell Canada Limited, Oakville. View looking southeast to staff entrance and main service penthouse. Main entrance stair to library. View looking north to main en-

trance. Main floor plan
DW 1969 Arts Building, University of Waterloo photo
15 x 56 3/8

SHOREY, HAROLD EDGAR
see RITCHIE, SAMUEL, 1937

SHRAPNEL, EDWARD SCROPE
c 1847, Gosport, Hants, Eng 25 Sep 1920, Oak Bay, Victoria H
ARCA 1880-8 Painter
Addr: 1880-3, Orillia, Ont; 1884-8, Whitby, Ont
1881 65 Sheep wc $35
257 Dead game $30
1884 S1, Saint John
29 Still life wc $35
1885 118 Lake Couchiching wc $35
192 Visitors in the backwoods $35
1886 121 Canadian game $200
1887 58 A trout stream in Muskoka $25
69 A brace of speckled trout $25
137 Indian camp on Crozier Lake wc $15
138 A brush camp at night wc $15
1888 137 Speckled trout
217 Moonlight $10
313 Return from the hunt wc
1889 20 Dead game $50

SHUTTLEWORTH, EDWARD BUCKINGHAM
7 Jun 1842, Sheffield, Eng d 1934
H Mo98/12
ARCA 1880-92 Painter
Addr: 1880-92, Toronto
1883 101 A rough morning at the island $20
1885 86 Marine $50

SIDDALL, JOHN WILSON
4 Sep 1861, Yorkshire, Eng 26 Jun 1941, Toronto
Addr: 1895, Toronto
1895 Siddall & Baker
54A-5A Messers A & S Nordheimer's premises. King Street, Toronto. Colborne St, Toronto
56A Government office, British Columbia des
57A English church at Louisville Siddal mispr

SIEBNER, HERBERT JOHANNES JOSEF
(VOM SIEBENSTEIN)
16 Apr 1925, Stettia, Germany CCI
WWA76
RCA(e) 1973 RCA 1976 Painter
Addr: 1979, Victoria
DW 1976 Fairyvale col wd cut
17 x 22
port: by M. Pavelic, DW 1976

SILVERMAN, BEN
Addr: 1927, 3903 Clarke St, Montreal
1927 342 Bonsecours Market drwg
343 Harbour view, Montreal drwg

SILVERSLETH, MARGRETHE
23 Jul 1897, Christiansholm, Denmark
Addr: 1931, 2070 Union Ave, Montreal
1931 432 Textile, wool des $200

SILVESTER, ROGER
1939, Gillington, Kent, Eng
1971 39 Arise my love and come away. Song of Solomon series $95

SIMCIK, HANS
b Vienna
1970 271 Symbol, Canada, Dept of Regional Economic Expansion
272 Package, Dyazide, pharmaceutical

SIMMONS LIMITED
Addr: 1938, Toronto
1938 S8, Toronto
344 Metal furniture, bedroom suite

SIMOENS, LEOPOLD R.
5 Aug 1934, Bruxelles, Man
1970 273 Catalogue, Eleventh Winnipeg Show
274 Poster, Fourth annual exhibition, Art Directors Club
275 Poster, The rainmaker

SIMONS, LUCIE
1959 72 Playground 30 x 36 $125
1960 69 Spring in Montreal 36 x 30 $100
1961 76 Interior with window sill 24 x 36 illus
1964N 51 Florist's showcase 48 x 36 $250
1967 62 Birds escaping from a bag 35 x 47 1/2 $300

SIMPKINS, HENRY JOHN
16 Jan 1906, Winnipeg CNS40 WWA73
ARCA 1936 Council Painter
Addr: 1930-1, 1549 Mackay St, Montreal; 1932, 848 6th Ave, Verdun, Que; 1933, 1481 Sherbrooke St W, Montreal; 1934-5, 3534 University St, Montreal; 1936-7, 5206 Decarie Blvd, Montreal; 1938-51, Montreal; 1952-71/79, Dorval, Que
1930 154 Tadousac $375
155 The beer parlor $500
1931 271 Laurentide Park $300
272 The Ouareau River wc $125
1932 176 A logging river wc $125
1933 218 The white pine $275
219 Autumn wc $100
1934 176 A sunlit glade wc $125
177 Splitting cod wc $125
1935 238 Peggy's Cove, NS wc $150
239 The camp wc $150
1936 186 At ease wc illus $150 T37-59
187 The old bridge, St Sauveur wc $125
1937 209 The mill, Brébeuf wc $150 T38-52
210 Under the willows wc $150
1938 201 Bonsecours Market wc $150 T39-51
202 Mid-winter wc $150
1939 214 Circus grounds wc $125
215 Laurentian rock wc $125
1940 143 The lumber camp wc $125
1941 176 Mother wc nfs
177 The stream wc $125
178 March sunlight wc $50
1943 107 Getting the hay in wc $125
1946 116 The blacksmith's shop wc $100
1947 169 The blower wc $175 T48-36
1948 141 The log drive wc $200
1954 79 Boy with trumpet 22 x 28 $300
1955 75 Sheila nfs
1957 65 Maj W. Baldwin nfs

SIMPSON, CHARLES WALTER
16 Apr 1878, Montreal 16 Sep 1942, Montreal CC2 CNS36 EC NGC PMC TB2 W78
ARCA 1913 RCA 1920 Council Painter
Addr: 1909-10, 302 St Nicholas Bldg, Montreal; 1911-15, 214 Park Ave, Montreal; 1916-17, Montreal; 1918A-19, 305 Pine Ave W, Montreal; 1920-7, 65 McGill College Ave, Montreal; 1928-35, 2049 McGill College Ave, Montreal; 1936-7, 2054 Victoria St, Montreal; 1938-42, Montreal
1909N 134 Hollyhocks
1910 177 Noontime
178 Golden October
1911 152 Quebec from the Beauport Heights
203 Group of 3 etchings
214 Coal barges, Montreal harbour etch
215 Montreal harbour etch
1912 198 Winter quarters ◊NGC◊
199 Wolfe's Cove, Quebec
276 Frame of etchings:
Sous le Cap, Quebec
Chapel of the Grey Nuns, Quebec
Cape Diamond, Quebec
1912 S3, Winnipeg
138 Ploughing
221 Etchings in oval frame:
Sous le Cap, Quebec
Sous le Fort, Quebec 1914-235
King's Bastion, Quebec
1913 277 The cradle S4-178 $300 S5-20 illus
278 The afterglow
279 Before the dawn
371 Frame of etchings:
Place Youville, Montreal S4-159 $20
Notre Dame, Montreal S4-160 $20
Hôtel Blanchard, Quebec 1914-236 S4-161 $18
1914 177 Indian summer
178 Sunlight and shadow
179 The tide wave
237 An oratory, Notre Dame etch
1915 199 From Levis Heights
200 Winter in the harbour ◊NGC◊
286 The temple etch
1918A 152 The Citadel, Quebec 1918N-172
153 The tow path
154 On the canal illus
1918N Capt C.W. Simpson
173 Old French house, Beaupré, Quebec
174 St Joachim, Quebec
175 Isle Visitation
1919 149 Mid-ocean 1920-231
1920 232 Fishermen, Gloucester illus
233 Gloucester harbour

234 Lumbering in British Columbia
1921 146 The end of the season, Montreal harbour illus F7-122 $1,000 S7-137 $800
147 The wayside shrine
148 Low tide, Gloucester
1922 186 The farm by the river S6-91
187 Incoming tide illus S6-92
1923 157 The white fan
158 The blue shawl
1924 184 Miss Margaret Coughlin illus F8-96 $785
185 Miss Olga Guilaroff
186 Decoration, autumn leaves
1925 203 Miss Kathleen McCombe
204 The riverside farm
205 Village street, Beauport
1926 132 Kathleen
1928 141 Chinese lanterns $750 1929-201 F9-182
1929 202 Shadows $100
203 Noontime $100
1929 S7, Calgary
138 The yellow gown $800
1930 F10, London, Eng
217 The blue cup $775
1931 273 Lake O'Hara $400
274 October afternoon, Montreal $500
275 1831-1931, Montreal $500
276 The Cavalier house, St Martin $100
1932 177 Grace $500
178 Broken ice illus $500
1933 220 Le temps des fêtes, Christmas day $1,000 T34-75
221 Incoming tide $100
222 The golden pathway $100
1934 178 On the beach $500 T35-64 1935-240 $750 1939-216
1935 241 August, noontime $85 T36-65
242 Sunset, St Eustache $85
1936 188 The hillside farm, Isle Jésus $500 T37-60 1937-211 F11-64 40 x 40 $750
189 The face of the cliff, Ogunquit $500
1938 203 Thin ice $750 T39-52
204 The frozen pond $750
1938 S8, Toronto
216 Alaska. 4 pieces of dot etch, deep etch litho plates produced in 4 cols, proof from the painting. Reliance Engravers Limited, Toronto
345 Book cover, Empress of Britain
346 2 magazine advertisements, Canadian National Railways
1940 144 The beach at Ogunquit $600 T41-49
1941 S9, Toronto
54 March thaw $150
1942 Late Charles W. Simpson
130 Journey's end unfinished T43-42
131 Evening breakers $75
132 Flowing tide $75
DW 1921 Indian summer, Montreal harbour 30 x 40 T51-37
1954 Retro Sec 21

SIMPSON, MINNIE A. (or R.)
H
1888 117 Monguilt Beach Minnie R.
143 Study of onions $30 Minnie A.
222 After a storm $25 Minnie
240 Summer Minnie R.

ROBERT SIMPSON COMPANY LIMITED
Addr: 1938, Toronto
1938 S8, Toronto
347 6 piece bedroom suite in wheat maple, Imperial Rattan Company Limited

SINCLAIR, ROBERT A. (or R.)
fl 1883-9 H
1888 122, 192 and 223 Portrait R.A.
179 Portrait R.R.

SINCLAIR, ROBERT WILLIAM
9 Feb 1939, Saltcoats, Sask
RCA(e) 1976 Painter
Addr: 1979, Winterburn, Alta
1971 38 Distant mountain 9 x 12 $80

SINGER, DANNY
1970 Seata film screened 12 Feb

SINGER, SYLVIA ROBERTA (b Sylvia Roberta Weininger)
26 Mar 1930, Montreal TO
1965 71a Sound and fury etch $55

SINKINS, AUDREE LUCILLE
22 Feb 1911, Toronto
Addr: 1932, 56 Colborne St E, Orillia, Ont

1932 220 Mrs Kenneth Wells sculp

SISE, HAZEN
see AFFLECK, RAYMOND, 1964J-1968

SISLER, REBECCA JEAN
16 Oct 1932, Mount Forest, Ont AGO IO WWA78
RCA(e) 1973 RCA 1979 Council
Sculptor
Addr: 1979, Toronto
1957 89 The miracle sculp $200
1959 93 Pilgrim sculp 30h $500
1960 90 Bereaved mother sculp $1,500
1964N 84 Woman with infant sculp 15 x 12 x 8 nfs
DW 1979 Arches. 1972 sculp oak 43 x 70 x 13.5 metric

SIVERSLETH, MARGRETHE see SILVERSLETH, MARGRETHE

SIWINSKI, STEFAN
1970 108 Lounge chair, Stefan Siwinski Designs

SKELTON, LESLIE JAMES
27 Apr 1848, Montreal 10 Jan 1929, Colorado Springs AAA29 B F H NGC TB
Addr: 1896-7, Colorado Springs
1890 85 Old mill, Lachute nfs
86 Adirondack solitude nfs
1896 157 York harbour, coast of Maine
1897 134 Winter in Colorado
135 Quiet waters

SLIPPER, GARY PETER
27 Apr 1934, Calgary
RCA(e) 1977 Painter
Addr: 1979, Bantry, Co Cork, Eire

SLOAN, CHARLES WILLIAM
20 Jun 1929, Toronto
RCA(e) 1974 Industrial designer
Addr: 1979, Toronto

SLOAN, JOHN
29 Apr 1891, Aberdeen, Scot 31 Dec 1970, Hamilton, Ont
ARCA 1936 Sr 1961 Sculptor
Addr: 1924, 88 Clyde St, Hamilton, Ont; 1925, 29 Myrtle Ave, Hamilton, Ont; 1931-5, 80 Graham Ave S, Hamilton, Ont; 1936-7, 39 Sherman Ave S, Hamilton, Ont; 1938-57, Hamilton, Ont; 1958-70, Dundas, Ont
1924 244 John Sloan Gordon, ARCA bust
1925 274 Nude. Rest sculp
1931 336 Kelpie plaster $200
1933 270 Pan sculp
1934 206 Flute player sculp $150
1935 292 Salome sculp $400
1936 224 A hewer of wood, a drawer of water plaster $200 stone $500
225 Sketch group for memorial 'There is no truth more than death' plaster $350 stone $750
1937 291 The awakening plaster $400 stone $800
1938 241 Late Homer Watson, RCA plaster $200 stone $300
242 Valerie plaster $100 stone $200 S9-55 plaster $50
1939 262 Steel sculp $300
1943 137 War worker $300 stone $500

SMARDON, KATE I.
fl 1888-96 H
Addr: 1896, Montreal
1896 257 Water lilies

SMART, EDMUND HODGSON English
1873, Alnwick, Northld, Eng 14 Nov 1942 DBA TB WBA WWB34
Addr: 1911-14, 444 Guy St, Montreal; 1915, 3608 Euclid Ave, Cleveland, Ohio; 1927, 12 Lawrence St, Chelsea, London, Eng
1911 153 Miss Mispelblom Beyer
1912 200 Harmony, portrait of Miss Augusta Schmidt
201 Frank W. Ancott, Esq 1914-180
1913 280 Mrs J.A. Brook
281 Wm. Drysdale, Esq S4-125 $500 nfs
282 The prodigal's own portrait
1915 201 The price of victory
1927 207 Sir Robert Borden
208 Gen Sir Arthur Currie
207-8 copyright

SMART, LESLIE E.
20 Aug 1921, Emsworth, Hamps, Eng
RCA(e) 1975 Graphic designer
Addr: 1979, Toronto
1970 276 Book, Crown jewels of Iran

277 Book, Call them Canadians
278 Poster, Queen Victoria's ear
1971 74G Symbol and stationery, Norm Scudellari Photography

SMART, PHILIP
b 1950
1970 279 Announcement, Colour on colour

SMEDLEY, G.
H
1882 248 Horticultural gardens, Toronto monoc

SMITH, CARVOLTH see SMITH, G.W. CARVOLTH

SMITH, CHARLES ALEXANDER see ALEXANDER, CHARLES

SMITH, CLARICE E.
Addr: 1926, 48 Earnscliffe Apts, Toronto
1926 133 Peacock feathers wc
1938 205 Petunia wc nfs

SMITH, DOROTHY SEELY
Addr: 1927, Wolseley Barracks, London, Ont
1927 209 Drying sails

SMITH, E. GORDON
Addr: 1928, 106 Hazelton Ave, Toronto
1928 142 Needles Pass, South Dakota $250

SMITH, EDITH AGNES
1867, Halifax d 1954 H
Addr: 1932, Ladies' College, Halifax
1932 179 Fog at Blue Rocks, NS $300

SMITH, ERNEST JOHN
17 Dec 1919, Winnipeg WWA76
ARCA 1967 RCA 1973 Council Archirect
Addr: 1968-71/79, Winnipeg
1964J Smith, Carter, Searle Associates, to 1967
123-5 School of Architecture, University of Manitoba. Main entrance, illus. Library, from court. Main floor plan
1965 133-4 Manitoba Telephone System, administration building. South and east elevations
135 Canadian Wheat Board Building. Front elevation
1966 168-70 Liquor Control Commission, and warehouse, Winnipeg. Facade and main entrance. Exterior west wall. Basement, 2nd floor plans and section
1967 135-7 Pan American Swimming Pool. A.West elevation and public approach B.Diving platform C.Plan, seating level and press box
DW 1973 School of Architecture, University of Manitoba, Fort Garry Campus. 4 photos mounted 27 1/8 x 29 7/8 overall size

SMITH, FRANCIS HOPKINSON American
23 Oct 1838, Baltimore, Md 7 Apr 1915, New York AAA28 B Gr H
Addr: 1883, New York
1882 137 Old dock, Long Island wc $100
1883 139 The Sand Market, on the Seine, Paris wc $225
147 Ponte di Soupi, Venice wc $250

SMITH, FREDA PEMBERTON
2 Apr 1902, Montreal
Addr: 1922-34, 42 Windsor Ave, Westmount, Que
1922 188 Study pastel
1925 206 Head of a girl pastel
1927 210 A hair pulling pastel
1929 204 A Czechoslovak girl $35
1930 156 Portrait of a girl $50
1931 277 Moon peonies and jack-o-lanterns $100
1933 223 The glass house, Westmount $150
322 Portrait drwg
1934 179 Old house, Notre Dame de Grâce $50 T35-65
1938 206 Elizabeth reads in bed $75
1939 217 The old buggy $75
1940 145 Portrait of a lady pastel nfs
1941 179 Portrait of a lady nfs
180 Three boats $50
1942 133 Celia wears blue $150
1943 108 House under construction, Kingston, 1943 $50
1950 137 Bear Track Bay, Lac Tremblant 28 x 34 $200

1953 80 Vers les eboulements, Ile aux Coudres $150
1961 74 Spring garden 34 x 28 $500

SMITH, FREDERICK MARLETT see BELL-SMITH, FREDERICK MARLETT

SMITH, G.W. CARVOLTH
1953 81 The outer bay $150

SMITH, GEORGE F.
H
ARCA 1881-2 Engraver
Addr: 1881-2, Toronto
1880 387 Illumination
1881 122, 123, 125 and 126 Proof engr, after W.H. Gibson
124 Proof engr, after O'Brien
133 Frame of proof wd engrs
1882 277 Proof wd engr

SMITH, GORDON APPELBE
18 Jun 1919, Hove, Sussex, Eng AGO CC1 CWW79 NGC TB2 WWA59
ARCA 1959 RCA 1967 Council Painter
Addr: 1960-71, Vancouver; 1979, West Vancouver
1959 73 Red landscape 34 x 48 illus $300
1963 66 Near the sea 44 x 44 illus $450 S10-66
67 Summer night $450
1964J 57 Sea insect 44 x 44 illus $450
58 Beach pools at night $400
1964N 52 Night form 45 x 50 illus $500
1965 64 Clouded yellow 40 x 40 $450 S10-65
1966 59 Red wizard 49 x 44 illus $450
60 Journey in green 32 x 36 $375
1967 63 Summer painting 55 x 55 $700
64 Painting #2 65 x 55 illus $750
1968 44 Untitled #1 20 x 24 $85
45 Untitled #2 20 x 24 $85
1970 67 Easter green 55 x 55 illus $700
68 Untitled 24 x 37 $150
1970 S11, Halifax
30 Double fold. 1970 acry 44 1/2 x 40 1/2 $400
31 Untitled. 1970 acry 44 1/2 x 48 1/2 $400
DW 1968 Black diamond 50 x 55

SMITH, GORDON HAMMOND
8 Oct 1937, Montreal CC2 CWW79 IO WWA73
ARCA 1967 Sculptor
Addr: 1968-71, Arundel, Que; 1979, Ashburn, Ont
1963 102 Thrust #2 bronze $375
103 Existance 2 welded steel $325
1964J 86 War welded steel 19h $325
1964N 89 Growth summer '64 sculp 76h illus $2,000
90 #1 Cor-ten sculp 76h $525
1965 93 On different ground sculp 23h $375
1968 64 Relief sculp 48 x 72 illus $1,500
1970 92 Optic screen #2 sculp 53 x 30 $1,700

SMITH, HARRY LESLIE
26 May 1900
Addr: 1935-7, 1104 Beaver Hall Hill, Montreal
1935 243 Portrait sketch $75
1937 212 The back yard wc $35
213 Summer kitchen wc $35
1939 218 Ninth Avenue 'El' wc $75
219 New York sky line wc $25
1941 181 Country station wc $100
1944 126 The farm house wc $50
1945 185 Mine shaft wc $75
186 Asbestos, Thetford Mines wc $75
1946 117 Winter landscape wc $75
1947 170 Country kitchen wc $150 T48-37
171 Interior with figure wc $150
1948 142 The artist wc $150
1949 85 Musician $400
1951 95 Hazy day, Quebec $150

SMITH, HENRY WALTER
16 May 1917, Hamilton, Ont NGC TB2
1951 91 Christmas tree wc $95

HOWARD SMITH PAPER MILLS LIMITED
Addr: 1938, Montreal
1938 S8, Toronto
146 2 calendars
147 House magazine, Paper on parade
148 Miscellaneous mailings
149 Trade paper advertisements
150 Page layout, Paper on parade

151 Calendar pages
152 Letterhead
153 Folders
146-53 des by G.S. Bagley

SMITH, JAMES AVON
22 Apr 1832, Macduff, Banffs, Scot
10 May 1918, Toronto H NGC W78
RCA 1880 Council Architect
Addr: 1880-2, Toronto; 1883, 31 Adelaide St E, Toronto; 1884-92, Toronto; 1893, 80 Summerhill Ave, Toronto; 1894, 26 Bank of Commerce Bldg, Toronto; 1895-8, 80 Summerhill Ave, Toronto; 1899-17, Toronto; 1918A, 81 Woodlawn Ave, Toronto
1880 341 Metropolitan Church, Toronto
344 Deaf and Dumb Institution, Belleville
348 St James Presbyterian Church, Toronto DW 1880 pen & wc drwg 18 x 33 1/2 1881-90
349 Knox College, Toronto
1881 Smith & Gemmell, to 1882
179 Parliament Buildings, Toronto. South front competitive des
197-8 Parliament Buildings, Toronto. East and north fronts
1882 232 Parliament Buildings, Ontario 5 drwg des
1883 73 Propeller 'Quebec' in a gale on Lake Superior $25
232 Approach to Mount Cennis Tunnel wc $20
235 HMS Northampton, and tenders, Halifax harbour wc $25
253 Becalmed, near Halifax wc $15
1884 138 Becalmed off Stag Rocks, English Channel wc $40 S1-8 $25
1885 260 Breakwater, Saint John, NB wc $40
284 Fishing boat, Devil's Cove wc $50
1886 71W Round the buoy on the home stretch wc
1887 14 Midland Rover aground off the Fort, at Toronto $80
1888 11 Off the Island, Toronto wc $25
61 On the Humber Bay wc $25
235 Thistle and Volunteer race wc $75
1889 67 Spanking breeze $30
1890 204 Waterloo Bridge and Parliament Buildings, London wc $50
1892 115 Sails against steam wc
126 The coming squall wc
1893 136 Herring boats leaving Wick harbour $150
1894 119 Westminster Bridge and Parliament House
1895 129 Sunset on the sea shore
1896 158 The shore, MacDuff, Scotland
258 Sunset on the Humber, Toronto wc
1898 94 The Macassa, in Toronto Bay
1918A 155 A naval training brig for boys
port: by J. Lawson, 1886-185; E.W. Grier, 1908-60

SMITH, JOHN IVOR
28 Jan 1927, London, Eng AGO CC2 IO WWA62
RCA(e) 1973 Sculptor
Addr: 1979, Piedmont, Que
1963 104 Sleeping family sculp $850
1964J 84 Torse with hose wood 62h $2,000
85 Head cast stone 18h $350
1964N 83 Patrician head sculp 23h illus $350
1965 94 Wozzeck cast stone 10h $450

SMITH, JOHN MEREDITH see MEREDITH, JOHN

SMITH, JOHN ROXBURGH
10 Aug 1883, Greenock, Scot 12 Jul 1975, Montreal CNS51 CWW64 NGC
ARCA 1947 RCA 1952 Sr 1957 Council Architect
Addr: 1916, 216 Hutchison St, Montreal; 1920, 511 St Catherine St W, Montreal; 1928, 85 Osborne St, Montreal; 1947-71, Montreal
1916 215 Paestum, Italy wc
216 Venetian quay wc
316 Quebec pencil
1920 235 Old house, Chambly Canton, Quebec wc
290 Suburban cottages
291 Sketch in Verona, Italy
1926 162 Outremont War Memorial, Henri Hébert, sculptor,

base, H. Hébert, J.R. Smith
1928 143 Alley in Quebec wc
186 Proposed garage for C. Forbes, Esq, Montreal
187 Proposed residence, Outremont, Que
1953 McDougal, Smith & Fleming
110-13 Redpath Library, McGill University, extension. Tyndale Hall, looking north, illus. From the north. From lower campus. From the east photo
1957 Fleming & Smith, to 1960
107 Montreal Children's Hospital. New medical and surgical wing
1960 105-6 Engineering Building, McGill University. Entrance from campus. University Street front photo
DW 1952 School of Nursing, Jewish General Hospital, Montreal wc & conté drwg des 18 x 22

SMITH, JOSHUA
1880, or 1881, London, Eng 26 Mar 1938, Toronto CWW36 W78
Addr: 1922, 278 Bloor St W, Toronto
1922 189 Case of miniatures

SMITH, KATE ADELINE (Mrs Frank Hoole)
10 May 1878, Rotherham, Yorks, Eng
Addr: 1921, 7626 Heather St, Vancouver
1921 149 The barn
150 Mid-day rest

SMITH, LAWRENCE
Addr: 1932, 55 Hepbourne St, Toronto
1932 180 Portrait, Georgian Bay $250

SMITH, LESLIE VICTOR
1880, Simcoe, Ont 23 Mar 1952, Toronto
Addr: 1908-9, 341 Sherbourne St, Toronto; 1910-13, 4 Linden St, Toronto
1908 125 The window seat
126 Miss Edith Ellis
1909M 123 A nocturn
124 Portraits min
1909N 137 Old Mermaid Inn, Rye, Sussex
138 The Béguinage, Bruges 1912-203
1910 179 Pont du Cheval, Bruges
180 Impromptu
1911 154 Recollections 1919-202
1913 283 Fading light S4-126 $150 nfs

SMITH, LEWIS EDWARD
1 Aug 1871, Halifax d 1926
Addr: 1918A, 583 Belmont St, Belmont, Mass
1918A 273 Une corbeille de fleurs, Paris etch

SMITH, MARIANNE LEE see LEE-SMITH, MARIANNE

SMITH, MARJORIE THURSTON
Addr: 1933, 2180 St Luke St, Montreal
1933 224 La chanteuse $100

SMITH, MURRAY STUART
8 Nov 1925, London, Ont
1953 79 Jane Allport nfs

SMITH, ODRIC (Mrs)
1951 97 Trudy nfs
1952 87 Fair beau $300

SMITH, OTTIE (Miss)
1881 159 Wallpaper, maple leaf des

SMITH, WILLIAM RONALD see RONALD, WILLIAM

SMITH, WILLIAM SAINT THOMAS
30 Mar 1862, Belfast 18 Feb 1947, St Thomas, Ont H Mo12 NGC PMC TB2 ARCA 1902 Sr 1937 Painter
Addr: 1901, St Thomas, Ont; 1902-3, 95 Yonge St, Toronto; 1904, Montreal; 1905-14, St Thomas, Ont; 1915-27, 85 Stanley St, St Thomas, Ont; 1928-47, St Thomas, Ont
1901 118 On the North Sea F2-70
207 Battleship in a gale off Plymouth Sound wc F2-66, in cat following #70
208 Dog's head wc
1902 237 Rough sea, coast of Cornwall wc
238 Low tide, Katwyk, Holland wc
1903 110 The storm wc
194 Fisherman's return, Magdalen Islands wc

195 Homeward wc
196 Old English church, St Thomas wc
1904 249 Newfoundland trout stream wc
250 Misty morning at sea F4-113
251 Newfoundland fisherman's home wc
252 Moonlight at sea wc F4-114
1905 162 A sunker
163 Rock-bound coast
164 Sunset, Newfoundland
165 Sunrise at sea
166 Waves and rock
1906 159 Sunset at sea F5-149 $300
160 Fishing boats making Anstruther harbor
1908 127 Misty morning
128 Snow storm
1909M 125 The restless sea, Newfoundland
126 Autumn day at sea
1909N 135 Evening, Firth of Forth
136 Stormy sea
1910 S2, Liverpool
98 Restless sea
99 Squally weather
1911 155 Trawler in a storm wc
156 North Sea breakers wc
157 Flying spray, Orkney wc
158 On the Orkney coast wc
1912 204 The stormy Pentland Firth wc
205 Orkney waters wc
1913 284 Breakers, Orkney wc S4-127 $500
285 Rough weather, Orkney wc S4-128 $300
1914 181 Sunset on the North Sea
1914 S5, Patriotic Fund
17 Stormy sea, Orkney illus
1915 202 October day wc
203 North Sea breakers wc
1916 217 Orkney trawlers wc
218 Twilight wc
1919N 176 October day wc
177 Early summer wc
1920 236 Orkney home wc
237 Orkney coast wc
1921 151 The old mill, Bear River, NS wc
1922 190 Stormy coast, Orkney S6-93
1924 188 A crofter's home, Orkney
189 Rocky coast, Orkney
1927 211 Rocky coast, Island of Ransag, Orkney wc

SNOW, JOHN HAROLD THOMAS
12 Dec 1911, Vancouver AGO CC2 WWA 59
ARCA 1965 Graphic designer
Addr: 1966-71/79, Calgary
1966 61 Adcage litho 16 x 20 $75
1967 65 Blue jug litho 22 x 16 $80
1968 46 Crete 18 x 14 $90
1970 69 Brookgreen 18 x 14 illus $90

SNOW, MICHAEL JAMES ALECK
10 Dec 1929, Toronto AGO B CC1 CWW 79 DMS IO TB3 WWA76
RCA(e) 1973 Painter
Addr: 1979, Toronto
1964J 59 Black and white walking woman 60 x 65 $700
1964N 53 Four grey panels and four figures 4 panels 60 x 20 $2,000
1971 Standard time film screened 31 Mar

SOHNS, G. FREDERICK Scottish
fl 1868-1901 DBA H
Addr: 1881, Scotland
1881 98 On the River Earn, Perthshire wc $25
102 Strathearn wc $25

SOLOMON, R.
1880 80 Marine view (D. Brymner)

SOMERS, JOAN
Addr: 1976, Toronto
1976 S12, Montreal
44 The meeting place III 38 x 28 illus

SOMERVILLE, WILLIAM LYON LLD
5 Aug 1886, Hamilton, Ont 14 Apr 1965, Toronto CWW61 NGC PMC TB2
ARCA 1928 RCA 1939 Sr 1957 Council
Architect
Addr: 1928-34, 2 Bloor St W, Toronto; 1935-6, Toronto; 1937, 30 Bloor St W, Toronto; 1938-65, Toronto
1928 188 McMaster University, preliminary study for group of buildings
189 Residence, Oriole Parkway, Toronto photo
1929 235 Parish Hall, St Jude's Anglican Church, Toronto

1930 180-1 Residence, Dr N.S. Shenston, Toronto. Residence. Entrance door
1932 208 Sketch for country residence
1934 209 Residence, Mossom Road, Toronto
210 University Hall, McMaster University, Hamilton
1937 260-2 Residence, R.F. Unsworth, Toronto
1939 284 Design for a national gallery of art for Canada
1943 119-20 Canadian approach to Rainbow Bridge, Niagara Falls photo
1946 155-6 Canadian approach to Rainbow Bridge, Niagara Falls. Pedestrian entrance, Carillon Tower. Bus terminal waiting room photo
157 Red Cross Lodge, Westminster Military Hospital, London, Ont photo
1947 195 St Joseph's Hospital, Hamilton. Main entrance
1948 186-8 Oakville-Trafalgar Memorial Hospital, Oakville. Entrance, pencil sketch. Plexiglass model 2 photos
1951 Somerville, McMurrich & Oxley, to 1966
111-12 David B. Mills Memorial Library, McMaster University. Entrance. Library. Associate architects, Bruce Brown & Brisley
1964N 170-3 McGregor College Chapel, Nigeria. Front elevation, 2 views, one illus. Decorated front floor elevation. General interior
1966 165-7 Provost Cosgrave-Seager Men's Residence, Trinity College, University of Toronto. Passageway to Quadrangle, Trinity College. Bronze lion, sculptor Harold Stacey
DW 1940 Ontario Hospital, St Thomas wash drwg 12 x 20

SORBONNE, NOEL
Addr: 1931, 5940 Sherbrooke St W, Montreal; 1933, 4360 St Denis St, Montreal
1931 337 Etude de vieille italienne sculp
1933 323 Tête de l'artiste crayon

SORBY, THOMAS CHARLES English
fl 1856-84 DVP G
Addr: 1884, 162 St James St, Montreal
1884 197 Town Hall, Bromley, Kent, England
198 Midland Railway Station and Hotel, St Pancras des

SORENSEN, DAVID
1937, Vancouver
Addr: 1976, Montreal
1976 S12, Montreal
45 Untitled #1 acry 71 x 82 illus

SORLEY, QUEENIE see GILVERSON, QUEENIE

SOUCY, JEAN BAPTISTE
1 Jul 1899, St Antonin, Que WWA53
Addr: 1929, 7448 St Denis St, Montreal
1929 205 Rampes conduisant au Pincio wc $150

SOUCY, JOSEPH ALFRED ELZEAR
18 Nov 1876, Onémisme, Que d Feb 1970
Addr: 1915-20, 255 Bleury St, Montreal; 1929-37, 1199 Bleury St, Montreal
1915 246 La prière sculp
1918N 218 Dollard des Ormeaux plaster
1920 277 Méditation plâtre
1929 250 Dr L.J.V. Cléroux sculp
251 Madonna statuette walnut
1931 338 Le pélerin sculp $350
1933 271 Master Jean, Misses Andrée and Denise Duquette sculp
1935 293 L'Hon N.A. Belcourt, LLD PC plaster $150 bronze $225
1937 292 Bishop of early Christian age sculp $200

SOUTHAM PRESS
Addr: 1938, Montreal
1938 S8, Toronto
348 3 folders, CPR
349 Calendar illustration
348-9 Nicolet & Southam Press

SPENCE, D. JEROME
see FINLEY, SAMUEL, 1902-1907

SPENCER, MYFANWY see PAVELIC, MYFANWY

SPERBER, MAURICE
1947 230 Portrait of a boy drwg nfs

SPICKETT, RONALD JOHN
11 Apr 1926, Regina AGO CC1 CWW79 TB3 WWA73
ARCA 1965 RCA 1968 Painter
Addr: 1966-71/79, Calgary
1953 83 Beside the midway illus $150
1956 76 Squaw chorus illus $200
1966 62 Tossed river 60 x 60 $850
63 Red rider 60 x 60 illus $850 S10-67
1966 S10, Charlottetown
68 Tossed rider 60 x 60 $850
1967 66 Aspect of the wipeout 60 x 84 $1,200 DW 1969

SPIEDEL, CHARLES
1970 280 Menu cover, The Coffee Shop
281 Menu cover, Horizon Room

SPIERS, HENRY (HARRY) American
15 Oct 1869, Selsea, Sussex, Eng
B F TB WWA36
Addr: 1895, 10 1/2 Adelaide St, Toronto; 1898, Yonge Street Arcade, Toronto; 1905, Toronto
1895 83W A master workman wc
1898 216 A study wc
1905 178 Young fisherwoman

SPOONER, JAMES
fl 1854-04 DVP G H
1888 45 Mid-day shade, first change of the leaf wc (Jas. Spooner)

SPRACHMAN, MANDEL CHARLES
15 Jan 1925, Toronto
RCA(e) 1978 Architect
Addr: 1979, Toronto
1968 138-40 Forest Valley Day Camp. A.Main entrance B.Exterior C.Floor plan

SPRATLEY, KEITH
27 Jul 1930, Toronto
ARCA 1968 Architect
Addr: 1970-71/79, Toronto
1971 Spratley, Adamson & Assoc
39A-42A St Lawrence Centre for the Arts, Toronto. View from west. View from north. Upper theatre lounge, illus. 1st floor plan

SPROATT, HENRY
14 Jun 1866, Toronto 4 Oct 1934, Toronto CNS27 Co EC NGC PMC R2 TB2 WWC21
ARCA 1909 RCA 1914 Council Architect
Addr: 1907-13, Toronto; 1914-21, 36 North St, Toronto; 1923, 1162 Bay St, Toronto; 1924-34, Toronto
1907 346 Residence, Toronto
347 Suburbs of Toronto
348 Summer quarters, RCYC, Toronto
1914 223 Burwash Hall, Victoria College, Toronto DW 1915 wc drwg 18 3/4 x 52
224 Hart House, University of Toronto. Southeast corner
225 Bishop Strachan School, Toronto
1920 292-4 Hart House, Toronto. Music room. Music room bay, view of Quadrangle through arch. Detail view of Great Hall
1921 190 Memorial tablets, Toronto University
1923 Sproatt & Rolph
183 Hart House, Great Hall interior photo
port: by F. Lessor, 1921-91
see also Darling, Frank, 1895

SPURR, GERTRUDE see CUTTS, GERTRUDE

STACEY, H. OSWALD
Addr: 1934-6, 1037 Bathurst St, Toronto
1934 180 Lac d'Or $125
1936 190 Autumn gold $100
1944 190 January thaw
1945 127 Summer storm $200

STACEY, HAROLD
Addr: 1938, Toronto
1938 S8, Toronto
350 Pewter vase
351 4 piece pewter tea set
352 Pewter cream and sugar
350-2 one illus, 3 pieces
353 Pewter cigarette box
354 4 piece sterling silver flatware
355 Silver brooch set with lapis lazuli
356 Silver cuff links, 2 pairs
1966 167 Bronze lion, Trinity Col-

lege, University of Toronto.
W.L. Somerville, architect

STALKER, GEORGE FREDERICK
11 Mar 1845, Edinburgh 23 Aug 1895, Ottawa G H
Addr: 1884, 51 O'Connor St, Ottawa
1884 199 Facade for concert hall and assembly room
200 The Pends, north entrance, St Andrew's Cathedral, Scotland $12
201 The Pends, south entrance $12
1889 179 City hall, competitive des
180 YMCA building, Ottawa, competitive des

STANFORD, J. HENRY (J. Henry Stanford-Szewlinski)
Addr: 1903, 712A Sherbrooke St, Montreal; 1912, Winnipeg
1903 113 Evening in Buckhaven
114 Campfire in the forest
1909M 117 Souvenir of Versailles
117a Pont St Michel, Paris
1912 S3, Winnipeg
255 Notre Dame de Paris

STANISZKIS, JOANNA KATARZYNA KILKANSKA (Mrs Thomas Staniszkis)
10 Apr 1944, Czestochowa, Poland
RCA(e) 1979 Textile designer
Addr: 1979, Vancouver

STAPLES, OWEN P.
3 Sep 1866, Stoke-sub-Hamdon, Eng
5 Dec 1949, Toronto AGO CNS36 H Mo12 NGC PMC TB2 WWA47
Addr: 1893-5, 39 McGill St, Toronto; 1897-01, 7 Maitland Place, Toronto; 1903-4, Toronto; 1905-37, 69 Hogarth Ave, Toronto
1888 78 Captivity $40
1891 36 Portrait of a King Charles spaniel
1893 139 The last load $100 F1-104
1894 116 The log barns
117 The love song
118 Autumn
1895 130 Mother and child
1897 133 Tom
1898 99 The last gleam
100 Barry, Irish setter
101 Winter
102 Evening
1899 222 Chatham market wc
223 Hollyhocks wc
1900 105 The smithy
1901 102 Late afternoon F2-64
103 End of the day
1902 F3, Rochester
165 Peacocks $120
1903 112 Quebec from Point Levis
192 Cutting corn wc
1904 159 Hoeing turnips
160 Haymaking F4-78 F5-152 $50
253 The first snow pastel F4-115
1905 170 Winter
171 Haying
172 Day dreams
1906 161 Rapids
162 Light of eventide
1907 186 Breaking the sod
187 September
188 Dying embers
1907 F6, Sherbrooke
153 The horsepower, thrashing $100
154 Summer $75
155 Eventide $200
156 Reverie $50
157 October $75
158 Niagara $75
1908 129 Spring ploughing
130 Pines in winter
1909M 118 Quay at Clovelly
1909N 139 Sunrise in August
140 A road through the Caledon Hills
1910 181 Construction of Toronto General Trusts Building
182 Autumn landscape
1910 S2, Liverpool
100 Light at eventide
101 Spreading flax
1911 159 For of such is the kingdom of heaven
160 The lumber mill wc
1912 206 Market garden wc
207 The duckling wc
1912 S3, Winnipeg
139 Building a sky scraper
140 Autumn wc
222 Construction of a bridge b&w
223 A railway cutting b&w
1913 286 The river valley wc S4-286 $150
1914 182 Late Dr William Brodie
183 Dorothy
1915 204 Construction of the Viaduct, Toronto wc
1916 219 The forest
220 The elm wc

1918A 156 Maple leaves wc
157 The Upper Credit wc
274 Doorway, University of Toronto etch
275 Bridge at Belfountain etch
1918N 178 Knitting
1919 150 Arrival of the Prince of Wales at the Royal Canadian Yacht Club
1920 238 New Year's eve
239 Portrait study, Maud
1922 192 The settler's cottage wc
193 The old well wc
288 University door, Toronto etch
289 Evening on the bay etch
1923 160 St Louis St, Quebec wc
1924 190 Chelsea Falls, Gatineau wc
291 Doorway, University of Toronto etch
1925 207 A sunny garden wc
208 Frenchman's Bay wc
1926 206 The Rotunda, University College etch
1927 344 Doorway, University College, Toronto etch
345 Great Hall, Hart House, University of Toronto etch
1928 230 Quadrangle, Hart House, University of Toronto etch $12
231 Chapel, Hart House, University of Toronto etch $12
1929 206 Bay Street, Toronto wc $100
1931 278 Ships loading, Nova Scotia wc $250
1932 181 Building castles wc $75
1933 324 Ships, Nova Scotia col etch $15
325 Doorway, Royal Ontario Museum etch
1935 244 Peonies wc $80
245 Killarney Mountain wc $100
1936 191 Silver sands $500
192 Stormy weather wc $100
1937 214 Nicholas wc nfs
1940 146 Harmony $100
1948 143 The music room $100

STAPLETON, ARCHIBALD BRUCE
19 Jul 1910, Stratford, Ont
1946 118 R. Thomas Orr nfs T47-48

STARK, MURIEL E.
Addr: 1911, 76 Yonge Street Arcade, Toronto; 1926, 538 Sherbourne St, Toronto
1911 163 A study
1926 134 An Alsatian village wc

STARK, WILLIAM REDVER
1885, Toronto
Addr: 1911-21, 538 Sherbourne St, Toronto
1911 164 Study of a bloodhound
1914 184 Sea coast
1918A 158 Sketches from France wc
1919 151 Village street, Wambaiux
152 A cavalier of 1918
223 On the Somme, France etch
224 The chateau driveway etch
1921 152 Winter sunlight

STARON, GENOWEFA (GENNY) (Mrs)
b Poland
1964J 87 Kneeling woman cement fondu 60h $1,000
1965 95 Salome cement fondu 18 x 25 x 6 illus $300
96 Iona III cement fondu 40 x 33 x 12 $700

STAUNTON, HELEN (Mrs)
Addr: 1934, 265 Queen St S, Hamilton
1934 181 Self portrait

STEEGMAN, JOHN OBE
10 Dec 1899, London, Eng 22 Apr 1966, Coffinswell, Devon, Eng
CWW55 TB2 WWB34
1954 80 Church in Kensington, London wc 17 x 21 $80
1955 77 Kensington Gardens, London $75

STEELE, A.D.
d 1890, England
ARCA 1881 Architect
Addr: 1881-90, Montreal
see also Hutchison, Alexander, 1884

STEELE, HELEN FITZGERALD see FITZGERALD, HELEN

STEELE, R.W. (Mrs)
Addr: 1937, 65 Forden Ave, Westmount, Que
1937 215 August, McGoun's Point, Quebec $30
216 September still life $40

STEELE, SYDNEY (Mrs)
1945 188 St Brigid anemones wc $35

STEELE, W. HARLAND
b Toronto CWW64
see PAGE, FORSEY, 1957, 1966

STEFFAN, JOHANN GOTTFRIED Swiss
13 Dec 1815, Waedenswil, Switzerland
16 Jun 1905, Munich B TB
1880 125 Mountain storm (Allan Gilmour)

STEGEMAN, CHARLES
5 Jun 1924, Ede, Netherlands AGO
1963 68 Blue torso $275

STEGEMAN, FRANCOISE see ANDRE, FRANCOISE

STEIGER, FREDERIC
21 Oct 1899, Solwutz, Romania CWW79 TB2 WWA76
1938 208 Forgotten $650
1940 147 The letter $500 T41-50
1941 182 Saskatchewan $500 T42-50
1945 189 I remember $500
190 Mrs 'Awkins $500 T46-43
1948 144 The patriarch $500
145 Ginny $500

STEINER, PETER
Addr: 1976, Montreal
1976 S12, Montreal
131 Analyse de la fonctionnalité pédagogique livre/book illus

STEINHOUSE, TOBIE THELMA DAVIS (Mrs Herbert Steinhouse)
1 Apr 1925, Montreal B WWA73
ARCA 1972 Print maker
Addr: 1979, Westmount, Que
1958 77 Lumière de printemps, Montréal $500
1968 47 Claire de lune 14 x 16 $90
1970 70 Mid-summer night's dream 12 x 15 $105
1971 40 Songes en equilibre 12 x 18 $115

STEPHENS, FRANCES E.
Addr: 1931, 1371 Pine Ave W, Montreal
1931 279 Study in green and yellow

STEPHENS, PAUL
1970 282 Poster, Rouse Institute 10 x 10
283 Poster, Ontario College of Art

STEVENS, DOROTHY (Mrs Reginald de Bruno Austin)
2 Sep 1888, Toronto 5 Jun 1966, Toronto AGO CWW64 NGC TB2 W78 WWA 47
ARCA 1931 RCA 1949 Sr 1958 Painter
Addr: 1911, 17A Harbord St, Toronto; 1912-19, 2 Spadina Gardens, Toronto; 1925, 192 Glenrose Ave, Toronto; 1928, 79 King St E, Toronto; 1930-6, 7 Rosedale Rd, Toronto; 1937-66, Toronto
1911 206 Odalisque etch S3-228
207 Coppelia etch
208 Repose etch
209 Ponte Veechio, Florence etch 1913-372 S4-162 ◊AGO◊
1912 277 Nude etch
278 The coal dump at Quebec etch
279 Firenze etch S3-224 Florence
1912 S3, Winnipeg
141 Bridge at Florence
225 Overlooking Florence etch
226 New bridge across St Lawrence, at Quebec etch
227 Boats at Quebec etch
229 The coal chute at Quebec etch
1913 287 Beneath the fairy light that kissed her golden hair S4-130 $450
288 Study in red
373 Le quai etch S4-163
1914 185 La jeune Lisette
186 Visiting
1915 206 Dolores
207 Cynthia smiles illus
1918A 160 Miss A. Cassidy
161 The young widow
278 Jack etch
279 Paddy etch
1919 225 Railroad shops etch
226 The old fashioned child etch
1925 209 Florence Proctor
1928 144 Miss Dora Creed
1930 157 Miss Patricia Watson
1931 280 Mrs George Ross
281 Amy, picanniny $500 ◊NGC◊
433 Prof Pelham Edgar dry pt
434 Picanniny dry pt $15
1932 182 Mrs Minerva Elliot
183 Colored nude illus $600 ◊AGO◊
1933 225 Nudes and pineapples $600 T34-75

1934 182 Mrs G.M. Merrick
183 The mauve decade $750 T35-66
1935 246 Autumn fantasy $250
247 Nude in sunlight $500 T36-66
1936 193 Mrs Hugh Eayres nfs
1938 209 My studio window $500
1939 220 Ballet, portrait of Janet Volkoff $600
1939 F11, New York
65 Conversation piece of Rody Kenny Courtice 43 x 44 $600
1940 148 Musical arrangement $250 T41-51
1941 183 Lieut Comm Kaakon Jorgensen, Royal Norwegian Air Force nfs T42-51
1941 S9, Toronto
56 Street in Baie St Paul, Quebec $35
1942 135 Miss Josephine Barrington, portrait study $250
1944 128 Portrait group of Lorraine, Barbara and Billy Weiss nfs
1946 119 Gloria illus $500 T47-49
120 Coloured child in banana grove $400 T47-50
1947 172 Two Lakes, Laurentians $150 T48-38
1948 146 San Miguel de Allende $200
147 Jose $200
1949 86 Mexican mother and child $400 DW 1950 32 x 28 1954 Retro Sec 38
1952 88 Spice Island, BWI illus $150
1953 83 Frank Erichsen-Brown illus ‡AGO‡
1954 81 Santa Tomas Chichi Castenango 25 x 25 $200
1955 78 Mexican mother and child $300
1957 66 Jamaica illus $250
1959 74 Mexican mother and child 25 x 27 $300

STEVENSON, M.S.
Addr: 1931, 1545 Drummond St, Montreal
1931 339 Mary sculp

STEVENSON, MARGARET A.
1938 210 Case of miniatures nfs

STEVENSON, RUSSELL
H
1880 319b Gate house, Killyleigh Castle wc
319c Killyleigh Castle, County Down wc
322 and 323 Sketch wc

STEVENSON, W.S.
Addr: 1928, 117 14th Ave E, Calgary
1928 145 Afternoon wc $50

STEWART, CLAIR
20 May 1910, Kenton, Man CWW64
RCA(e) 1974 Council Graphic designer
Addr: 1979, Toronto
1938 S8, Toronto
McLaren & McCaul Limited
190 2 menu covers, T. Eaton Co Limited
191 Mailing folder
192 2 mailing folders, Boats
191-2 Buntin Reid Co Limited, Toronto
193 Spring and summer announcement folder, Cook Clothing Co Limited
195 3 newspaper advertisements, National Trust
196 China booklet
197 Gift book, Caravanserai
198 De luxe jewellery book, 1936
196-8 Birks-Ellis Ryrie Limited, Toronto
200 House organ booklet, Canada Ink Company
202 Business forms, letterhead, office stationery, labels, McLaren & McCaul Limited

STEWART, DAVID MURRAY MCCHEYNE
12 Dec 1919, Toronto
1955 79 Jolly Miller Skating Rink $500

STEWART, DONALD CAMPBELL
22 Nov 1912, Hamilton CNS44 CWW79 WWA47
ARCA 1943-55 Sculptor
Addr: 1936, 258 Hess St S, Hamilton; 1944-54, Toronto; 1955, Vancouver
1936 226 Green torso sculp $100
1938 243 Fiona sculp nfs
1941 223 Phyllis Gummer plaster nfs
1945 233 Maya plaster $1,000
234 Orpheus plaster $300

STEWART, ELVA
Addr: 1976, Urbana, Ill

1976 S12, Montreal
46 Patchwork pythagoras canvas/toile 48 x 48 illus

STEWART, H.G.
H
1892 74 Flowers, chrysanthemums

STEWART, MICHAEL
8 Apr 1940, Toronto
RCA(e) 1973 Industrial designer
Addr: 1979, Toronto

STEWART, MURRAY see STEWART, DAVID MURRAY

STEWART, WILLIAM
1832, Toronto 15 Dec 1907, Hamilton
ARCA 1880-3 Architect
Addr: 1880-3, Toronto

STIKEMAN, ANNIE English
fl 1880-96 DBA DVP H
Addr: 1896, 949 Dorchester St, Montreal
1896 259 The fish market, Folkstone wc

STIRLING, D.
6 Dec 1822, Galashiels, Scot d 1887
ARCA 1880-5 Architect
Addr: 1880-5, Charlottetown

STOCK, THOMAS REUBEN
23 Feb 1907, Essex, Eng
Addr: 1935, 1441 Drummond St, Montreal
1935 248 Prospect Cove, NS wc $20
249 Idle dreams wc $30

STOKES, PETER JOHN
27 Mar 1926, London, Eng
ARCA 1972 Architect
Addr: 1979, Niagara-on-the-Lake, Ont

STOKVIS, BETTY see BLACK, BETTY

STONE, AMY BLANCHE
18 May 1887, Bristol, Eng CNS40
Addr: 1936, 18 Severn Ave, Westmount, Que
1936 194 The last trilliums of spring wc $50
1938 211 Cyclamen in pot wc $75
1939 221 Peonies wc $75

STONE, THOMAS ALBERT
14 Nov 1894, Fownhope, Herefords, Eng AGO
Addr: 1923, 623 Bathurst St, Toronto; 1925-6, 4 Grange Rd, Toronto; 1930-6, 2 Yorkville Ave, Toronto
1923 161 Cedar Valley F.A. Stone mispr
1925 210 Sparrow Lake
1926 207 The pine in the moonlight aqua
1930 158 Storm, north of Orillia $200
1931 282 Falls, South River $100
1932 184 Passing storm, Parry Sound $200
1933 226 Bracebridge $300 T34-77
1934 184 Blue Glacier, Mount Robson $125
1935 250 Cutting ice at Haliburton $200 F11-66 30 x 40 $250
1936 195 Heavy snowfall, Haliburton $125
1938 212 Winter morning, Burk's Falls $250
1941 184 The Gatineau Hills $150 T42-52
1941 S9, Toronto
57 Atlantic fishing boats $60
1942 136 Miss Phyllis Lee temp & oil nfs T45-44
137 Miss Peggy MacPherson temp & oil nfs
1943 109 Resting $150 T44-35

STORM, W.G.
c 1885 d World War I
Addr: 1907, Toronto; 1909M, 100 Pembroke St, Toronto; 1910, 64 St Ann's Rd, Toronto
1907 189 Secluded spot
1909M 122 Solitude
1910 183 The river's edge

STORM, WILLIAM GEORGE
29 Oct 1826, Burton-on-Stather, Lincs, Eng 1892, Toronto Co H NGC W78
RCA 1880 Council Architect
Addr: 1880-92, Toronto
1880 337 Toronto University DW 1880 wc drwg 24 x 48 1/2 1881-208
338-9 Toronto University. Views from north, and southeast
342 Edinboro Ass. Co, office. View from northeast
346 Toronto University, Convocation Hall, interior 1883-340

352 St James' Cathedral, Toronto, from northwest
359 Normal School, Toronto, from southeast
365 Osgoode Hall, Toronto, from southwest
1883 341 Osgoode Hall, Library
354 Osgoode Hall, atrium
355 University Library, Toronto
365 Atrium
1888 320 Old St Andrews, Toronto wc
1891 214 Victoria College, Queen's Park des

STORMS, MARY
1938 S8, Toronto
380 Wallpaper des. Hon mention Canadian Wallpaper Manufacturers Limited

STOUGHTON, ARTHUR ALEXANDER
1867, New York American
1955, Mount Vernon, NY CWW49
Addr: 1923, 640 Westminster Ave, Winnipeg
1923 184 House, Armstrong Point, Winnipeg pencil sketch
229 Behind the barn etch
230 Agrigentum etch
231 St Germain l'Auxerrois, Paris drwg
1924 250 Monument to Chief Peguis, base, A.A. Stoughton, Marguerite Taylor, sculptor photo
1927 272 War Memorial, Prince Albert, Sask, base, Prof A.A. Stoughton, Marguerite Taylor, sculptor photo

STOVEL, REX
Addr: 1895, 173 King St W, Toronto, listed as exhibitor, no work listed in catalog

STOYAN, PETER (b STOYANOFF)
29 Jun 1900, Macedonia, Greece
Addr: 1925, 266 Coxwell Ave, Toronto
1925 331 The old willow trunk dry pt
332 Before spring dry pt

STRANGE (Maj Gen)
1882 280 Scene in Grenada wc

STRASMAN, JAMES COLIN
8 Nov 1937, Penticton, BC
RCA(e) 1976 Architect
Addr: 1979, Toronto

STRATTON, LILY
fl 1901-40
Addr: 1901-2, 224 Cooper St, Ottawa
1901 104 Portrait study
105 Study of pigeons
1902 154 Portrait

STRATTON, MAY
b Peterborough, Ont 1 Oct 1940, Peterborough, Ont
Addr: 1901-2, 224 Cooper St, Ottawa; 1906, 237 Bank St, Ottawa; 1920, 224 Cooper St, Ottawa
1901 106 Study of grapes
1902 155 Brunette
1906 163 Portrait
1920 240 Egg study

STREET, WILLIAM
see CHETWYND, ARTHUR

STRICKLAND, WALTER REGINALD
Aug 1841, Lakefield, Ont 6 Feb 1915, Lakefield, Ont
ARCA 1880-5 Architect
Addr: 1880-5, Toronto; 1895, Front St, Toronto
1889 Strickland & Symons, to 1895
183 House, Rosedale, Toronto
184 St Simon's Church, Toronto
1890 227 House, Rusholme Road, Toronto
228 House, A.T. Todd, Esq
229 St Matthew's Church, Toronto
1891 202 Church des
211 St Simon's Church, Toronto
1895 52A Union Station, Toronto

STRONG, RICHARD ALLEN
26 Sep 1930, Chardon, Ohio
RCA(e) 1978 Landscape architect
Addr: 1979, Toronto

STRONG, WILLIAM A.
see CRAIG, JAMES S, 1965, 1967

STRUTT, JAMES WILLIAM
8 Jan 1924, Pembroke, Ont

RCA(e) 1978 Architect
Addr: 1979, Lucerne, Que

STUART, LOUIS (or LEWIS)
Addr: 1901, 17 Main St, Hamilton
1901 111 Among the roses Lewis
211 Shore at old Brunswick, England wc

STUDHAM, RICHARD LYNN
30 Jun 1936, Stanley, Durham, Eng
Addr: 1976, Montreal
1976 S12, Montreal
90 Temporal dolmen cer 20 1/2 x 6 x 50 illus

SUGINO, SHIN
5 Mar 1946, Osaka IO
RCA(e) 1976 Photographer
Addr: 1979, Toronto

SULLIVAN, ALAN
1953 84 Still life $75

SULLIVAN, BEATRICE
fl 1899-38
1938 213 Girl with dog nfs

SULLIVAN, JOHN STANLEY
22 May 1922, Cardiff, Wales
1971 Sullivan & Pacek
43A-6A Timberbank Junior Public School. View from west gulch. Entrance court. Staircase graphics. Ground floor plan

SULLY ALUMINUM LIMITED
Addr: 1938, Toronto
1938 S8, Toronto
357-63 Cast aluminum kitchen utensils. Triplicate set. Oval roaster. Coffee pot. Double frypan. Small tea kettle. Preserving kettle. Griddle illus

SULYOK DE PAPP, JOSEPH see PAPP, JOSEPH SULYOK DE

SURCOUF, LORRAINE JOY (Mrs John Richmond)
21 Jul 1933, Winnipeg IO
1961 77 Civilized mountain 24 x 36 $400
1963 69 Beachscape $1,000
1964J 60 Beachscape dye on linen 65 x 68 $500

SURREY, PHILIP HENRY HOWARD
8 Oct 1910, Calgary AGO B CC2 NGC WWA47
RCA(e) 1978 Painter
Addr: 1979, Westmount, Que

SUTHERLAND, FANNY English
fl 1858-89 B DBA DVP G H TB
1885 19 Hark! Hark! The lark! $350
61 Miss Minnie Magrath
85 Miss Lucy Harris
1886 211 Drowned land. Selected for Fla, not in Fla cat
1889 43 Dorothy Vernon staircase, Haddon Hall $200
55 Golden autumn $200
166 Tapistrical looking-glass at Hardwick Hall wc $200

SUTHERLAND, FLORENCE M.
H
1888 254 Anemony wc $15

SUTHERLAND, FREDERICK WILLIAM
b 1860 d c 1920 H
Addr: 1918, Humber Bay, Ont
1918A 280 Bronxdale house wd engr
281 Country house, New Jersey wd engr

SUZOR-COTE, MARC AURELE DE FOY
5 Apr 1869, Arthabaska, Que 27 Jan 1937, Daytona Beach, Fa AGO B CC1 EC Mo12 NGC TB2
ARCA 1911 RCA 1916 Council Painter
Addr: 1896, 153 St Denis St, Montreal; 1897, Montreal; 1902, 39A Dubord St, Montreal; 1906, 125 Berrie St, Montreal; 1907, Paris; 1909N-10, Arthabaska, Qùe; 1911, 222 Berrie St, Montreal; 1912-14, Montreal; 1915, 26A Victoria St, Montreal; 1916-17, Montreal; 1918-26, 67 Ste Famille St, Montreal; 1927-8, 3531 Ste Famille St, Montreal; 1929-31, Montreal; 1932, c/o Scott & Sons, Montreal; 1933-4, Montreal; 1935-7, Daytona Beach, Fa
1896 Coté, to 1902, 1907-11
24 Un chemin creux, en Bretagne
25 Les bords de la Rivière Nicolet
26 Noix
1897 27 Un ravine sur la Colline
28 L'entrée du Bois St Michel
29 Le chemin, Montant
30 Le mirage, soir d'été

1902 35 Un coin abandonné
36 La clairière du Bois Boisseau
37 L'etang des vaux à Cernay, soleil couchant
272 Soir d'orage pastel
1906 F5, Halifax
155 State life $75
156 Cernay, la ville $125
157 Bay of Margot $125
1907 46 Le tournant de la rivière
47 Coucher de soleil, sur les Brugères, Bretagne
48 Bretonne en prière
49 Commencement de dègel au Pont Rouge
1909N 31 The road to the saw mill 1911-30 S2-30 S3-144
32 The settlement on the hillside ◊NGC◊
1910 42 A typical Arthabaska settler
43 A street in Arthabaska, winter 1912-213
1910 S2, Liverpool
28 Canadian stream in winter
29 Primitive sugar camp S3-145
1911 32 The knitting girl
33 The pond
34 Winter scene
1912 210 Old French Canadian pioneer
211 The birch grove, Lake Nicolet
212 Radiant September afternoon
214 Sunny winter afternoon, Arthabaska
215 A grey winter day, Nicolet River
1912 S3, Winnipeg
142 Cattle grazing
143 Moonrise in September
1913 289 Youth and sunlight ◊NGC◊
290 Old St Louis Street on a dull winter day
291 Scene on the Magog River, Sherbrooke S4-131 $600
292 The settler's daughter S4-132 $500
293 Sunset in March
374 Portrait of a habitant charcl S4-164 $50 nfs
1914 187 The founder of my village (Senator Wilson, Montreal)
188 My old model, Normandy, France (F.H. LeMay, Montreal)
189 The Nicolet River in April (Arthur Coté, Montreal)
238 French Canadian type charcl
1914 S5, Patriotic Fund
44 March evening, a thaw illus
1915 208 Melodies illus
209 Golden glow
247 The old pioneer bronze 1919-187 Vieux pionnier canadien ◊NGC◊
1918N 183 Paysage de fin d'hiver, Rivière Gosselin, Arthabaska, Québec illus
184 Lever de lune en octobre
185 Soir d'automne
186 Type canadien, étude
219 La compagne du vieux pionnier bronze illus 1919-188
220 Le retour du faucheur bronze
1919 153 L'approche du printemps, Arthabaska, Québec
154 Vieux paysan canadien-français illus
155 La boucherie
189 Faucheur las bronze
227 Paysan fusain et sanguine
228 Femme indienne allant à la ville fusain et sanguine
229 Bucheron fusain et sanguine
230 Paysan sanguine
1920 241 La bénédiction des erables, vieille coutume canadienne-française disparue
242 Jeune paysan canadien
243 Paysage vu d'une fenêtre en hiver
244 Paysage de fin mars
345 Tête de vieux paysan canadien fusain
346 Jeune indienne de Caughnawaga fusain
347 Le bûcheron fusain
348 Etude de nu des col
1921 153 Nude
154 A boy
155 Thaw
156 Spring
225 By the fireplace charcl
226 A peasant breakfast charcl
227 and 228 Study of an old man charcl
1922 196 and 197 Etude du nu pastel
198 Le Père Cholette pastel

199 Jeune bohémienne pastel
229 Louis Graveure, chanteur sculp S6-111
230 James A. Wright sculp S6-112
290 Pierre Denault fusain
291 Etude de nu fusain
292 Etude pour un tableau fusain
293 En costume 1860 fusain
1923 162 Alleghany hills in winter, near Arthabaska, Quebec
163 Golden September, Arthabaska, Quebec
164 and 165 Nude pastel
193 The nun plaster
194 The Chapdelaine couple plaster
195 The portageur plaster ◊NGC bronze◊
196 The country doctor plaster
232 Windy October charcl
233 Breton woman charcl
234 Head of a man charcl
235 Evening clouds charcl
1924 191 Magdalena
192 The old willow illus
193 Despondency pastel
194 Nude study pastel
245 Indian women, Caughnawaga sculp F7-177 $450 ◊AGH AGO MMFA NGC VAG◊
246 Hauling logs, Arthabaska sculp 1926-165 Logging in winter, Quebec illus ◊NGC 15 x 61 1/2 bas rel◊
247 A man of sorrow sculp
248 Bacchante sculp
292 Head of an old man praying charcl
293 Head of an old man charcl
294 Head of an old Métis woman charcl
295 Head of an old woman charcl
1925 211 Symphonie pathétique 1926-135 illus
212 Eté
213 Sérénité illus 1926-136
214 Bleu et or
275 Maria Chapdelaine sculp 1926-168 1928-175 $180 ◊AGO◊
276 La canadienne sculp
277 Explorateur canadien en 1670 sculp
278 Je me souviens sculp
333 Vieillard charcl
334 Vieille femme charcl
335 Paysan canadien charcl
336 Angoisse (Hon A. David)
1926 166 Gentleman pioneer of the French regime sculp
167 Démangeaison sculp
208 and 209 A Quebec peasant charcl
210 The moaning of the wind charcl
211 Mrs Cresser-Gaskins, pianist charcl
1927 212 Coureur de bois chassant
213 Dégel, fin de mars (Prov de Québec)
214 Fondation du Séminaire de Joliette, 1860 equisse déc (Prov de Québec)
215 Harmonie du soir equisse pour panneau déc (Prov de Québec)
266 Le vieux fumeur bronze illus 1928-172 The old smoker $220
267 L'appel à l'original bronze
268 Le bûcheron bronze ◊AGO◊
269 L'essoucheur bronze ◊AGO◊
270 L'evêque plâtre
346 Chef Montour, Caughnawaga fusain (Prov de Québec)
347 Indien de Caughnawaga fusain (Prov de Québec)
348 Etude pour défricheur fusain (Prov de Québec)
349 Etude pour l'essoucheur fusain (Prov de Québec)
350 Approché de l'orage fusain (Pierre Masson)
1928 146 The lone house $800 S7-139
147 Sérénité $1,000
148 J.B. Cholet, old pioneer $800 F9-132
149 Blue and gold, landscape $1,000
173 Calling the moose sculp $230 S7-165 ◊EAG◊
174 Gentleman pioneer sculp $200
232 November evening in the Brulé charcl $250
233 Old man praying charcl $100
234 The blind man charcl $100
235 Joe Lavallière charcl $100
1929 S7, Calgary

166 The trophy bronze $300 ◊EAG◊
1932 185 French Canadian peasant $600
186 Thaw in March, Arthabaska $700
187 Son of the pioneer $350
188 Boy from my village pastel $500
221 The bishop bronze
222 Coureur de bois, the explorer bronze $225
262 The old habitant drwg $200
263 Study of a head drwg $200
264 The old pioneer drwg $200
1954 15 Retro Sec. Scene d'hiver, Québec (Musée du Québec)
DW 1916 Coin de mon village, Arthabaska 24 x 34

SVARRE, GRACE CIPPARONE (Mrs)
c 1936, North Bay, Ont
1966 124 Beth Israel Synagogue, Peterborough, Ont, tapestry for the Ark. Craig, Zeidler & Strong architects

SVENDSEN, SVEND V. Norwegian
1864, Christiania, Norway B H TB
1886 7 Ice boating on Toronto Bay $300

SWARTZMAN, ROSLYN SCHEINFELD (Mrs Monte Swartzman)
17 Aug 1931, Montreal WWA76
RCA(e) 1973 Print Maker
Addr: 1979, Montreal
1964N 54 Les hautes roches etch 10 x 20 $40
1967 67 La grande arbre 18 x 24 $75
1970 71 Legend I 22 x 20 $95

SYER, JOHN English
17 May 1815, Atherstone, Eng 26 Jun 1885, Exeter, Eng B DBA DVP G H TB
1882 319 Leander Valley, Wales (loan)

SYMINGTON, J.F.
H
1882 2 On the hillside $75
173 Champagne wc $75

SYMONS, BEATRICE see FRY, BEATRICE

SYMONS, WILLIAM LIMBERY
1862, Stoke Gabriel, Devon, Eng
17 Feb 1931, New York
ARCA 1891-6 Architect
Addr: 1891-6, Toronto
see also Strickland, Walter, 1889-1895

SZILASI, GABOR
3 Feb 1928, Budapest
RCA(e) 1977 Photographer
Addr: 1979, Montreal

T

TABER, RUSSELL
1946 121 Sketching, Burleigh Falls nfs T47-51
1947 173 Lil illus nfs T48-39
174 Studio study nfs T48-40
1948 148 Old farm, Lake Vernon $200
149 Trunk driftwood $300

TACHE, EUGENE ETIENNE
24 Oct 1836, St Thomas de Montagny, Que 13 Mar 1912, Quebec H
ARCA 1880-6 Designer
Addr: 1880-6, Quebec

TACK, LEIGH
Addr: 1932, 3683 Hutchison St, Montreal
1932 223 Jobless sculp $50

TACON, PERCY HENRY
2, or 18 Jul 1902, London, Eng
Addr: 1934-7, 352 Aberdeen Ave, Hamilton, Ont
1934 185 A corner of our kitchen T35-67 nfs
186 Calla lilies
1936 196 Still life $100 T37-61
1937 218 Queen Anne's lace $175 T38-54
1938 215 Fruit $175 T39-53
1950 138 Composition 40 x 30 $250
1960 70 Composition 41 x 37 $350
port: bust, by E. Holbrook, 1948-166

TACONIS, KRYN
7/5/1918, Rotterdam 12 Jul 1979, Toronto
RCA(e) 1976 Photographer
Addr: 1976/79, Toronto
1976 S12, Montreal

181 Hutterites 16 x 20
2 photos illus

TAHEDL, ERNESTINE (Mrs Richard Ian Ogilvie)
12 Oct 1940, Vienna WWA78
RCA(e) 1977 Stained glass designer
Addr: 1979, Mont St Hilaire, Que
1966 64 Composition 101 45 x 65 $600

TAIT, SYLVIA (Mrs Eldon Grier)
20 Mar 1932, Montreal
1964N 55 Departure 40 x 37 $300
1965 65 The siren's attack 30 x 48 $450
1967 63 Homage to McLuhan 20 1/2 x 26 $150

TALBOT KELLY, GILES
26 Oct 1929, Rugby, Eng
RCA(e) 1975 Graphic designer
Addr: 1979, Middlesborough, Eng

TANABE, TAKAO
16 Oct 1926, Prince Rupert, BC AGO CC2 NGC TB2
ARCA 1967-79 Council Painter
Addr: 1968-71, West Vancouver; 1976/79, Banff
1971 41 Painting 96 x 48 $1,200
1976 S12, Montreal
47 The land 3/74-75 acry 32 x 56 col illus

TANNAHILL, ROBERT E.
Addr: 1927, 542 Bourbonière Ave, Montreal
1927 216 Market day

TANNENBAUM, RUTH
Addr: 1938, Montreal
1938 S8, Toronto
364 Newspaper advertisement
365 Original fashion drawing

TARDIF-COTE, THERESE
13 May 1926, Lachine, Que
1964N 57 Ecrin despoir 40 x 50 $200

TASCONA, ANTONIA (TONY)
16 Mar 1926, St Boniface, Man AGO WWA73
ARCA 1970 Painter
Addr: 1971/76/79, St Boniface, Man
1963 70 Two worlds $275
71 The collision $250
1964N 56 An ancient rite 44 x 48 illus $600
1965 66 Radiation 44 x 48 $600
1968 48 Converging tri-cycle 36 x 72 $950
1970 72 Special re-entry 36 x 72 $1,200
1971 42 A sonar device 48 x 72 $14,000
1976 S12, Montreal
48 Inverted apex lacq on alum 60 x 48 illus

TATA, SAMUEL BEJAN
30 Sep 1911, Shanghai
RCA(e) 1976 Photographer
Addr: 1979, Montreal

TATE, JAMES RICHARD
18 May 1882, Buxton, Eng 21 May 1960, Toronto
Addr: 1930-7, 88 Quebec Ave, Toronto
1930 159 The barn yard
1933 227 Little freighter, Quebec harbour $75
1934 187 Hydrangea flowers $125
1935 251 Still life nfs
252 In studio mirror nfs
1936 197 Bill nfs T37-62 1939-223
1937 219 Mr Oliver Ingram nfs
1938 216 F. Rostance as the Guardsman nfs
217 A bit of England nfs
1939 222 Nedibus Clarkibus: Ned Clarke nfs
1940 149 Land's End, England nfs
150 Sergt Malcolm UCCB nfs T41-52
1941 185 Rt Rev Dom Pacôme Gaboury, Lord Abbot, Cistercian Monastery, La Trappe, Que nfs
1941 S9, Toronto
60 Algonquin waters $100
1943 110 The propellers, 1943 nfs
1948 150 Flight to Egypt nfs

TATOSSIAN, ARMAND
26 Sep 1948, Alexandria, Egypt WWA76
RCA(e) 1973 Painter
Addr: 1979, Montreal

TATTERSALL, JOE
1947 175 Vera $350
176 Yorkshire springtime $250

TATTERSFIELD, PHILIP

17 Jun 1917, London, Eng
RCA(e) 1976 Landscape architect
Addr: 1979, West Vancouver

TAVERNIER, ANDREA Italian
23 Dec 1858, Turin 15 Nov 1932, Grottaferrata, Italy B H TB
Addr: 1893, Rome
1893 140 The return of the fishing boats on the Adriatic coast

TAYLOR, ANDREW THOMAS (Sir)
Oct 1850, Edinburgh 5 Dec 1937, London, Eng CWW36 H Mo98/12 NGC TB1/3
ARCA 1885 RCA 1890 Hon Non-res 1910 Ret 1913 Council Architect
Addr: 1884-92, Montreal; 1893-03 43 St François Xavier St, Montreal; 1904-5, Montreal; 1906-15, 21 Lyndhurst Rd, Hampstead, London; 1916-37, London
1884 193 Glasgow Municipal Building, 1883. 2nd premiated des A.T. Taylor & Henry Hall
194 2 semi-detached residences, Ontario Ave, Montreal
195 The Cathedral, Malines, Belgium
1886 Taylor, Gordon & Bousfield Bourfield, mispr
187 Houses, Prince Arthur St, Montreal
1887 174 Near Dalmally, Argyleshire, Scotland wc
184 Bank of Montreal, interior des
1888 241 Old English church wc $25 E. Taylor, mispr
268 Murray Bay wc $25 A.J. Taylor, mispr
275 The mills, Chambly wc $35
316 House in Ottawa, interior sketch wc T. Taylor, mispr
319 House to be erected in Montreal wc
1889 106 Siena Cathedral wc $20
107 Scene in Peregia wc $20
181 Almshouse at Chiselhurst
182 St Laurent, Rouen, Normandy
1890 205 Sunset over the marsh wc
230 Entrance corner of residence, Montreal des drwg
1891 205 Residence des
206 View in Ghent, Belgium
210 Bank of Montreal, West End Branch
213 Macdonald Technical Building, McGill College, Montreal DW 1890 pen drwg 32 3/4 x 20 1/2 1892-167
1893 278 New building, Bank of Toronto, Montreal
279 New building, Bank of Montreal, Vancouver, BC
1894 197 Peter Redpath Library, McGill College, Montreal 1895-67A
1895 68A Bank of Montreal, Notre Dame Street Branch
69A Art Gallery, Montreal, new wing
70A Bank of Toronto, branch, Montreal
71A English church, Chambly
72A Atlantic City, the Promenade
73A Scene in Ghent
1896 260 Old houses and wharves, Quebec, evening wc
261 Sillery Church, near Quebec wc
278 Diocesan Theological College, Montreal
279 St Peter's Church, Sherbrooke
280 Bank of Montreal, Seigneurs St, Montreal
1897 53W Leaves from an architect's sketch book wc
1898 218 A seaside cottage, Magnolia wc
234 Jubilee Nurses' Home, Montreal General Hospital
1899 256 Santa Maria delle Fiore, Florence, with Giotto's Tower
257 Macdonald Chemistry and Mining Building, McGill University, Montreal
258 Molson's Bank Building, Vancouver, BC
1901 238 Marchants Bank Building, Winnipeg, in course of construction
239 Bank of Montreal, Sydney, Cape Breton, in course of construction
240 Medical Faculty, McGill College, additions in course of construction
1902 255 Summer residence, Lake St Louis
1903 206 New Maternity Hospital, Montreal

1904 291 Bank of British North America, new building, Winnipeg
292 Bank of Montreal, East End Branch, Montreal
293 Isolation Pavilion, Royal Victoria Hospital
294 Bank of Montreal, interior perspective, new banking room
295 Merchants Bank, Winnipeg
1906 167 Doorway of an old house
168 Borgo San Jacopo, Florence
1907 349 A street in San Gimiano, Italy
350 In a garden
1908 166 Vienna at sunset, from San Domenico
166a The Abbey Square, Middleburgh, Holland
1912 252 St Bavo, Haarlem, Holland
1915 267 Christ Church Priory, Hants
268 Interior, Santa Maria Novella, Florence

TAYLOR, FREDERICK BOURCHIER
27 Jul 1906, Ottawa AGO B NGC TB2 WWA47
ARCA 1948 RCA 1967 Council Painter
Addr: 1932-4, 451 Wellington St, Ottawa; 1937, 4136 Dorchester St W, Westmount, Que; 1948-60, Montreal; 1961-71/79, San Miguel de Allende, Mexico
1932 265 Medieval house, Compiègne-sur-Oise, France pencil $25
266 Monastic chapel, Fiesole, Italy pencil $25
1933 326 Morning on the river aqua $6.50
327 Government and industry etch $11
1934 228 Tower Bridge, Thames litho unfrmd $10
1937 329 We took it straight etch unfrmd $12.50 frmd $15
1939 224 Prof Ramsay Traquair nfs
225 Portrait of an Austro-Italian Canadian $125
1940 151 Miriam $1,250
1941 186 Student nfs
187 Zotique Marcellin nfs T42-53
1942 138 McGill undergraduate, 1942 $500 T43-45
139 Canada's reaction to war, 1939-1942 $500
1943 111 The spirit of total war nfs
112 The moulders $75
1944 129 Welding kiln sections $250
130 Hull rivetting, a high rivet $250
1945 191 Miners drilling at a grizzily, Noranda, Que $350
192 Miners waiting at a shafthead for the cage, Noranda, Que $250 T46-44
1946 122 Rebellion on Plessis Street, at Notre Dame Street East, Montreal $500 T47-52
123 Back galleries, St Antoine Street, Montreal $350
1947 177 Dead Man's Bend, Montreal $250
1948 151 Alexander Brott nfs
152 Old house, Park Avenue, Montreal $150
1949 87 Notre Dame de Bonsecours, Montreal $750 1950-139 40 x 30
1950 140 Findlay Market, Quebec 30 x 30 $350 ◊BAG◊
1951 98 Rooftops, Quebec illus nfs
1952 89 St Norbert Street, Montreal illus $450 T53-30
1953 86 Dr David L. Thompson
1954 82 Looking up St Cecile Street, Montreal 40 x 21 $450
1955 80 Fur workers fleshing sheepskin $250
1956 42 Self portrait $1,500 T56-30
1958 78 Hélène $700
1959 75 Overlooking San Miguel de Allende 24 x 30 $400
1964J 88 Head of a young Mexican Indian woman bronze $300
1964N 58 Mexican market 24 x 30 $425
1965 67 Fishing boats, Torremolinos, Spain 30 x 50 $750 S10-69
1967 69 Approach to the bull ring, Mijas, Spain 32 x 47 $750
DW 1968

TAYLOR, HERB
1971 Breams at Stratford film screened 14 Apr

TAYLOR, IRENE
1950 141 Figure study 20 x 25 $100

TAYLOR, JAMES D.
1970 284 Brochure cover, 'Ink'

Provincial's Paper Vol 29 #3 1964
1971 75G Annual report, Abel-Black Corp Limited
76G Promotion booklet, Abitibi Provincial Paper Limited
77G Booklet, The Group of Seven 50th anniversary, Globe Envelope Products Ltd

TAYLOR, JOCELYN (Mrs Roy Mitchell)
29 May 1899, Toronto WWA56
RCA(e) 1975 Painter
Addr: 1979, Oakville, Ont
1949 88 Kingston Market wc $50
1951 99 Grande Rivière $75
100 Mal Anse II wc $50
1953 85 Mont St Louis wc $85
1954 83 Mal Bay, Gaspé wc 18 x 24 $85
84 Drowned land wc 18 x 24 nfs
1959 76 Fish houses, Gaspé 24 x 30 $200
1964N 59 Reflections 24 x 30 illus $250

TAYLOR, JOHN BENJAMIN
12 Jun 1917, Charlottetown 15 Sep 1970, Edmonton
1958 79 Badlands $400
80 Glacier $425
1959 77 Valley of the Ten Peaks 20 x 24 $400

TAYLOR, KATE LIVINGSTONE
Addr: 1918A, 9 Saline St, St Catharines, Ont; 1921, 123 Howland Ave, Toronto
1918A 162 Bombardier Ross Malcolm Taylor min on ivory
163 Baby Mary min on ivory
1921 157 Miniature of a child

TAYLOR, LILA see KNOWLES, LILA

TAYLOR, M.P.
fl 1890-03 H
1890 206 St Giles Cathedral, Edinburgh wc

TAYLOR, MARGUERITE JUD (Mrs Hilliard Taylor)
23 Jul 1886, Paris 8 Apr 1964, Winnipeg
Addr: 1920-1, 108 Linden Ave, Norwood, Winnipeg; 1922-5, 105 Ruby St, Winnipeg; 1927-31, 607 Broadway, Winnipeg
1920 275 Lieut Alan McLeod, VC RAF bust
1921 183 Late Lieut Gen Sir Sam Hughes, KCB sculp
1922 231 Study of a head of an old man sculp
1923 197 Soldiers' Relatives, Memorial, Winnipeg sculp photo
1924 249 Chief Peguis bust photo
250 Monument to Chief Peguis, base by A.A. Stoughton photo
1925 279 Meditation statuette plaster
1927 271 Canada bronze figure photo
272 War Memorial, Prince Albert, Sask, base by Prof A. A. Stoughton photo
1931 340 Jeunesse sculp $30

TAYLOR, RICHARD LIPPINCOTT DENISON
18 Sep 1902, Fort William d 1970
Addr: 1928, 1121 Bay St, Toronto
1928 150 Dorothy Veronica temp

TAYLOR, ROBERT ROSS
16 Jun 1940, Toronto
RCA(e) 1978 Photographer
Addr: 1979, Winnipeg

TAYLOR, WILLIAM HUGHES
23 Dec 1891, Port Stanley, Falkland Islands NGC TB2
Addr: 1918A, 5287 Western Ave, Montreal; 1918N, 307 Craig St W, Montreal; 1919-21, 185 Oxford Ave, Montreal; 1922, 30 Benoit St, Montreal; 1925-6, 211 Girouard St, Montreal; 1927, 597 Harvard Ave, Montreal
1918A 164 Girl in black, study
1918N 187 Sunlit window-shade pastel 1919-157
188 Sunrise and mist, Beaupré, Quebec
1919 156 Caughnawaga
1920 245 Portrait
349 Melting snow, Craig Street, Montreal b&w
1921 158 The Gypsy costume
159 Schooners waiting for cargo, Quebec ◊NGC◊
1922 200 Steamer Arctic at Quebec pastel S6-97
201 Portrait
1925 215 Old house, Concarneau
216 Fishing boats, rising tide, Concarneau
337 and 338 Etching

1926 137 The fish quay, Rockport, Mass
138 Fishing boats, Concarneau
1927 217 Old bridge, Rapallo
218 Quebec
1945 193 September afternoon, Lac Quenouilles $300 T46-45
1952 90 October, the North River $400
1954 85 August noon, Fox River, Gaspé 24 x 32 $400
1956 41 The Canal, Montreal $400 T56-29

TEITELBAUM, MASHEL ALEXANDER
2 Feb 1921, Saskatoon AGO CCl
1964J 61 White jazz 76 x 68 $800

TEMELA, NAWLIKNIK
Addr: 1976, Lake Harbour, NWT
1976 S12, Montreal
91 Bear soapstone/saponite 13 1/2 x 12 x 7 illus

TEMPEST, JOHN SUGDEN
11 Jan 1864, Keighley, Yorks, Eng
Addr: 1928, 3904 4th St W, Calgary
1928 151 Pipestone Pass wc $100

TEMPLAR, ALBERT EDWARD
3 Oct 1897, London, Ont
1942 140 Mother, portrait nfs

TEMPLE, KATHLEEN
Addr: 1909M, Toronto; 1909N, Havergal College, Toronto
1909M 130b St Paul, from south side
130c Chioggia
1909N 143 Florence, from Piazza Michelangelo

TEMPORALE, LOUIS LUIGI
27 Oct 1909, Maiano, Italy IO WWA 62
RCA(e) 1974 Sculptor
Addr: 1979, Port Credit, Ont
1954 112 Negro head sculp 15h $900
1958 94 Dark Venus sculp $1,200

THACKER, ALFRED DENNIS
12 Jan 1879, Walsall, Staffs, Eng CNS29
Addr: 1913, 104 Union Ave, Montreal
1913 345 Pair of semi-detached cottages, Ste Anne de Bellevue

THEPOT, ROGER FRANCOIS
18 Feb 1925, Landeleau, France B CWW79 IO TB3 WWA47
ARCA 1972 Ret 1976 Painter
Addr: 1976, Toronto
1965 68 Apollon Musagéte 57 1/2 x 42 $1,200
1966 65 Prism #2 30 x 30 $400 1967-70 $450
1968 49 Contradiction of a red 44 x 36 $700
1970 73 Geometrical extension #2 51 x 57 $1,200
1971 43 Composition en trois coleurs 35 x 45 5/8 $700

THEROUX, EMILE ANDRE
26 Feb 1938, Crabtree Mills, Ont
RCA(e) 1979 Graphic Designer
Addr: 1979, Montreal

THOM, RONALD JAMES
13 May 1923, Penticton Co WWC77
ARCA 1972 Architect
Addr: 1976/79, Toronto
1964N Thompson, Berwick, Pratt & Partners, Ron Thom in charge
174-7 Massey College, University of Toronto. Exterior view with entry. Exterior view of court. Interior view of refectory. Ground floor plan
1971 47A-50A Thomas J. Bata Library, Trent University, Peterborough, Ont. Exterior view with University Court. View from bridge across the Trent Canal. View of Bata Library and the Canal, illus. Floor plan 3rd level
1976 S12, Montreal
Thom Partnership
109 Lester B. Pearson College, Pedder Bay, Vancouver Island photos 2 illus
see also Thompson, Charles, 1964N

THOMAS, ALICE BLAIR POLLARD (Mrs Adolphus George Thomas)
fl 1897-1916 d c 1945, Los Angeles H
Addr: 1904, Toronto; 1916, Blenheim Court, Apt 300, Jervis St, Vancouver
1901 211 Marine wc
212 Passing shower wc
1904 254 Old cedar tree wc

1916 221 In the Olympics
222 Fir trees

THOMAS, LIONEL ARTHUR JOHN
3 Apr 1915, Toronto AGO CC2 NGC TB2 WWA73
ARCA 1960 Designer
Addr: 1961-71, Vancouver; 1979, West Vancouver
1960 91 St Mark and the lion, St Mark's College, University of British Columbia sculp photo
92 Symbols from the cuneiforms, Vancouver Public Library mosaic mural photo
1970 93 Natures own forms. The seven basic forms sculp photo 16 x 20 nfs
94 The Nootka whaling scene, Victoria Provincial Museum photo 16 x 20 nfs

THOMAS, MAURICE
Addr: 1937, 4932 Coolbrook Ave, Montreal
1937 220 Grey day in Gaspé $25

THOMAS, WILLIAM TUTIN
d 26 Jun 1892, Montreal Co
ARCA 1881-4 Architect
Addr: 1881-4, Montreal

THOMPSON, CHARLES J.
1964N Thompson, Berwick, Pratt & Partners
189-91 Commissary Kitchen, University of British Columbia. Exterior front view. Exterior view with bridge. Main floor plan
see also, Pratt, Charles, 1966; Thom, Ronald, 1964N

THOMPSON, ERNEST EVAN SETON
14 Aug 1860, South Shields, Durham, Eng 23 Oct 1946, Seton Village, Sante Fe, NM AGO B CC2 CWW38 EC H Mo98 TB W78
ARCA 1893-4 Painter
Addr: 1893-4, 86 Howard St, Toronto
1893 F1, Chicago
105a Awaited in vain, an incident in the Pyrennes
1894 131 The hunter's mit
132 The old ford with a new face
191 Study of a lion's head wc

THOMPSON, GRATTAN D.
Addr: 1922, 304 University Ave, Montreal; 1925, 65 McGill College Ave, Montreal; 1927-31, 2048 McGill College Ave, Montreal
1922 240 Dr W.G. Turner, proposed residence
241 Alva House, alterations
1925 250-1 Roddick Memorial Gates, McGill University
1927 251 Interior of store, W.G. Heaney & Co
1931 375 Residence in Westmount photo
376 Film Trade Building col photo

THOMPSON, MARGARET COLLINS DUNCAN
(Mrs R.R. Thompson)
10 Dec 1884, Brooklyn, NY
Addr: 1933, 487 Argyle Ave, Westmount, Que
1933 228 Arran, from Ayrshire coast, Scotland wc $30

THOMSON, GEORGE
10 Feb 1868, n Claremont, Ont 21 Jul 1965, Owen Sound, Ont AGO CWW 61 NGC WWA47
Addr: 1918N, 194 Winthrop Ave, New Haven, Conn; 1919, 789 Elm St, New Haven, Conn; 1929-37, 591 8th St E, Owen Sound, Ont
1918N 189 An October landscape
190 Early snow
1919 158 Willows
1929 207 The brook in sunlight $400 Thompson mispr
208 Autumn on the Georgian Bay $300
1930 160 River in autumn $400
1931 283 April ice, Georgian Bay $400
284 Autumn sunlight $400
1932 189 Lingering snow $400
190 Radiant stream $300
1933 229 Spirit of the Georgian Bay $400 T34-78
230 Birches in summer $400
1934 188 Georgian Bay in summer $400 T35-68
189 Below the falls $300
1935 253 An October breeze $400 T36-67
254 Among the heights $300
1936 198 Tête à tête $400
199 Niagara $400
1937 221 An early snow fall nfs

222 Morning among the islands $300 T38-55
1939 226 Rocky highlands $350
227 North shore in autumn $350
1940 152 Whitefish Falls $350
1941 S9, Toronto
58 Muskoka River $80
1943 113 Breeze from the northwest $325
1944 131 In the highlands $225
1945 194 Breeze from the south $325
195 A Muskoka farm $225
1948 153 Spring at Lake of Bays $325
1950 142 Clearing in the west 28 x 36 $325

THOMSON, THOMAS JOHN (TOM)
4 Aug 1877, n Claremont, Ont 8 Jul 1917, Canoe Lake, Ont AGO B CC1 EC NGC R1 TB W78
Addr: 1914-16, Studio Building, 25 Severn St, Toronto
1914 190 A lake, early spring
191 Frost after rain
1914 S5, Patriotic Fund
21 In Algonquin Park illus
1916 223 The hardwoods
1938 S8, Toronto
Rous & Mann Limited
256 Book, Tom Thomson, Canadian artists series illus

THOMSON, WILLIAM JAMES
28 May 1858, Guelph, Ont 25 May 1927, Toronto AGO EC H W78
Addr: 1912, Toronto; 1918A, 11 Bleecker St, Toronto
1885 226 Weather bound wc $20
306 Fair weather wc $20
1912 S3, Winnipeg
all etchings
230 Muggy night, Lake Ontario
231 Zero weather
232 The Ridge Road
233 Old canal, St Catharines
234 The grip of winter
1918A 282 The hub of Detroit etch
283 The river at Detroit etch

THORNE, JAMES EDMUND
12 Apr 1908, Toronto
1944 132 Pumpkin field wc $65

THORNTON, MILDRED VALLEY STINSON
(Mrs John Thornton)
1890, Dresden, Ont 27 Jul 1967, Vancouver
Addr: 1932, 1955 Robinson St, Regina; 1934, Regina
1932 191 In the Touchwood Hills, Saskatchewan $350
1934 190 Foreclosed $600
191 Bulwarks of the prairie $300
1941 188 Dominie Jack, Okanagan Indian $200

THORNTON, PETER MUSCHAMP
8 May 1916, Edmonton TB2
ARCA 1957 RCA 1968 Council Architect
Addr: 1958-71/79, Vancouver
1953 Gardiner, Thornton & Partners
108 Westminster Abbey, BC, general view drwg
109 British Empire Games swimming pool, Vancouver drwg
1960 Gardiner, Thornton, Gathe & Associates, to 1965
107 St Mark's College, University of British Columbia, exterior
1963 122-3 Benedictine Motherhouse
1964J 102 Convent of the Good Shepherd, and St Euphrasia's School, interior photo illus
1965 123-6 Loyola Retreat House, Guelph, Ont. Chapel interior, sculpture by Robert Wegstein, Vancouver; windows by Gerald Tooke, Toronto. View of patio. General views, 2
DW 1968 Sacred Heart Church, Williams Lake, BC photo 12 x 63 1/2

THURSTON, EDWIN
fl 1898-09 H
Addr: 1909N, Meadowvale, Ont
1909N 144 The meadow path
145 Summer

TIBBLES, RALPH
1970 285 Book, Nancy
286 Letterhead, Canadian Society of Professional Journalists

TIDEMAND, ADOLPHE Norwegian
14 Aug 1814, Mandal, Norway c 25 Aug 1876, Christiania, Norway B G TB
1882 325 The bridal crown (loan)

TIKTAK

RCA(e) 1973 Sculptor
Addr: 1979, Rankin Inlet, NWT

TILL, ERIC STANLEY
24 Nov 1929, London, Eng CC2
RCA(e) 1978 Film maker
Addr: 1979, Toronto

TIMMAS, OSVALD
17 Sep 1919, Tartu, Estonia WWA73
ARCA 1972 RCA 1974 Painter
Addr: 1979, Toronto
1967 71 Armour relic 40 x 26 $275
1968 50 Homage to iron ore 40 x 26 $275
51 Southern frontier 40 x 26 illus $275
1970 74 Keystone 40 x 26 illus $350
DW 1974 The primitives I. 1973 wc 40 x 26

TIMMERMAN, GRANT
1947 178 Lighthouse at Lachine $100
179 Montreal harbour wc $50

TINNING, GEORGE CAMPBELL
25 Feb 1910, Saskatoon TB2 WWA47
ARCA 1953 Council Painter
Addr: 1954-71/79, Montreal
1938 228 Noon at McGill, November wc $150
229 Demolition wc $50
1955 81 Barn interior $250

TISON, HUBERT
16 Mar 1937, Montreal
RCA(e) 1978 Graphic designer
Addr: 1979, Montreal

TOLGESY, VICTOR
22 Aug 1928, Miskolc, Hungary 6 Jan 1980, Ottawa CC1 TB3 WWA59
ARCA 1972 Sculptor
Addr: 1976/79, Ottawa
1967 84 Vibrant vertical. Waterloo Lutheran University award. alum 108 1/2 x 12 illus
1970 95 Grand courtesan sculp 45h $750
96 Karakorum sculp 32h $500
1971 7S Cosmic invention, Eridanus the river sculp 80 x 56 illus $1,500
1976 S12, Montreal
92 The acrobat's horse plywood/contre-plaqué 84 x 84 x 24 col illus

TOMMEV, FOTO SPIRO
c 1899, Zhelevo, Greece
Addr: 1923, 96 Tecumseth St, Toronto
1923 166 The summer pasture

TONDINO, GENTILE
3 Sep 1923, Montreal CC2 NGC TB2
ARCA 1962 RCA 1969 Council Painter
Addr: 1963-71/79, Montreal
1964N 60 Figure brushing hair illus $300
61 Figure resting $350
1966 S10, Charlottetown
70 Mother and child $700
1967 72 Landscape 36 x 48 illus $700
1970 75 Women at the window 44 x 38 $700
DW 1969 Paysage 48 x 36

TONNANCOUR, JACQUES GODEFROY DE
3 Jan 1917, Montreal AGO B CC2 NGC TB2 WWA47
ARCA 1971-6 Council Painter
Addr: 1976, Paris
1950 143 The queen of spades 40 x 30 $350

TOOKALOOK, A.
Addr: 1976, Belcher Island, NWT
1976 S12, Montreal
93 Tellelayo soapstone/saponite 6 x 17 x 2 1/4 illus

TOOKE, GERALD ERNEST
27 Jun 1930, London, Eng
ARCA 1966 Graphic designer
Addr: 1967-71, Toronto; 1979, Ottawa
1965 123 Windows, Loyola Retreat House, Chapel, Guelph, Ont Peter Thornton, architect
1968 65 Satellite sculp 12 x 12 x 14 $350
1971 8S R.Q. #3 sculp $850

TOPHAM, FRANCIS WILLIAM WARWICK
1838, London, Eng English
25 May 1924, n Guildford, Eng B
DBA DVP G TB WBA
1880 321 Haymaker wc (Thos. Reynolds)
332 Angels whisper wc (Thos. Reynolds) 'Topham' in cat, ptb F.W.W. Topham

TOPHAM, WILLIAM THURSTON
23 Jul 1888, Spondon, Derbys, Eng
11 Mar 1966, Montreal H
ARCA 1944 Sr 1958 Painter
Addr: 1918N, 51 Victoria St, Montreal; 1919, 84 St François Xavier St, Montreal; 1923-4, 358 Beaver Hall Hill, Montreal; 1926-7, 533 Phillips Sq, Montreal; 1929-35, 1237 Phillips Sq, Montreal; 1937, 2047 Victoria St, Montreal; 1944-66, Montreal
1918N 191 Troops bathing in the Ancre, Viviers Mill, moonlight
192 Behemoth, a tank at Montauban wc
1919 159 'Who died for us.' Crucifix at Crucifix Trench, Contalmaison Road, night of 8th July 1916
1923 167 The House of Usher wc
1924 196 The turquoise necklace wc
197 Forest fire
1926 139 The moonlit portal, Maison Mère des Soeurs de la Congrégation, Montreal 1928-152 $350 S7-141
1927 219 New Year's eve, Christ Church, Montreal
1929 209 Laurentian landscape $300
1929 S7, Calgary
140 Silver winter, Black Lake $150
1931 285 Dawn, Mont Tremblant $250
1932 192 The rock pool, autumn sunlight $250
1933 231 Old house, l'Assomption, Quebec, winter night $300
1935 255 Roseate dawn, Mont Tremblant $450 T36-68
1937 223 Lost River Valley $300 T38-56
224 Moonlight, Lake MacDonald $250
1939 230 The Basilica of St James, Montreal wc $150
231 The intruders $150
1940 153 Laurentian farm $300 T41-53
1941 189 North River, showery weather $350 T42-54
190 Moonlight, MacDonald Lake, Quebec wc $150
1943 114 Fishing in the Gorge, Mont Rolland $200 T44-37
1944 133 The last of the snow $150
1945 196 September, Rivington, Rouge River, Quebec $300
197 Daybreak, North River, Val David $200 T46-46
198 The fisherman, Ste Marguerite, Quebec $250
1947 180 Rapids at the river bend $250
1949 89 North River rapids $200
1950 144 Spring flood, North River 22 x 30 $400
1952 91 The Condor Rock, Mount Condor, Val David, Quebec $300

TORONTO CARPET MANUFACTURING COMPANY LIMITED
Addr: 1938, Toronto
1938 S8, Toronto
366-9 Rugs, Barazak, 6'x9' two, Orienta 4'6"x7'6" two. one illus

TORONTO RATTAN COMPANY LIMITED
Addr: 1938, Toronto
1938 S8, Toronto
370-5 Chair, ottoman, fernery, chair, settee, table illus

TORRANCE, ADA see BRUCE, ADA

TORRANCE, LILIAS see NEWTON, LILIAS

TOULMIN, MARGARET
2 Oct 1916, Filton, Bristol Co, Eng
RCA(e) 1973 Sculptor
Addr: 1979, Ganges, BC

TOUNISSOUX, FRANCOISE
17 Jul 1947, Montreal
Addr: 1976, Montreal
1976 S12, Montreal
49 Tensions acry 40 x 40 illus

TOUPIN, FERNAND
12 Nov 1930, Montreal
RCA(e) 1977 Painter
Addr: 1979, Anjou, Que

TOURVILLE, R.R.
see PARENT, LUCIEN, 1938

TOUSIGNANT, CLAUDE
23 Dec 1932, Montreal CC1 CWW79 WWA70
ARCA 1972 Painter
Addr: 1979, Montreal
1971 44 Tryptique, 3 elements 24 x 20 illus $4,800

TOVELL, VINCENT MASSEY
29 Jul 1922, Toronto
RCA(e) 1978 Film maker
Addr: 1979, Toronto

TOWN, HAROLD BARLING LLD
13 Jun 1924, Toronto AGO B CC2 CWW 79 NGC TB2 WWA66
ARCA 1958 Painter
Addr: 1959-71/79, Toronto
1950 145 Don Quixote 36 x 44 nfs
1951 101 Two nudes $300
136 Bathers monot $45
1959 78 Heather & Grandmother 20 x 25 nfs
1963 72 Entrance of the tyranny of the corner illus $2,000
73 Tyranny of the corner, Persian set $2,000
1964J 62 Departure of the tyranny of the corner 81 x 74 illus $2,000 S10-71 illus $2,600
1970 S11, Halifax
32 Stretch #7. 1969 oil on lucite & canvas 48 x 48 $2,240
33 President's shape. 1969 oil on lucite & canvas 74 x 74 $3,800

TOWNSEND, HARVEY
1966 87 Metropolis sculp 25 1/4 h $300

TOWNSEND, HORACE
1880 257 Canal scene in Hamburg drwg
258 La rue de la Grosse Horloge, Rouen drwg
259 and 260 Sketch by Chalon drwg
261 Details of a cabinet des
264 Cabinet des
277 Sideboard des

TOWNSEND, PAULINE E.
Addr: 1896, Montreal
1896 165 Farm building, Ste Anne de Bellevue

TOWNSEND, SAMUEL HAMILTON
1856, Toronto 27 Mar 1940, Toronto
ARCA 1891-09 Architect
Addr: 1892-4, Toronto; 1895, Gerrard St, Toronto; 1896-02, Toronto; 1903, 15 Gerrard St, Toronto; 1904-9, Toronto
1891 216a Residence des
1892 164 Kentville church
165 Residence, St George St, Toronto
166 Sarnia Collegiate Institute
169 A $4,000 house, Brampton
170 Residence, James Hedley, Esq
1895 60A A $4,000 cottage
61A and 66A House, Pembrooke St, Toronto
62A Cottage, Nassau St, Toronto
63A A country church
64A Church of St Saviour, Queenston
65A A $3,000 cottage, Niagara Falls
1903 207 Residence, Park Road, Toronto

TOZER, MARJORIE HUGHSON
24 Jul 1900, Halifax
Addr: 1927, 35 Fenwick St, Halifax
1927 220 St John's, Newfoundland

TRACY, ARTHUR JOHN
20 Feb 1910, South Mymme, Midd, Eng
Addr: 1928, 117 Melville Ave, Toronto; 1932, 75 St George St, Toronto; 1936, 246 Brunswick Ave, Toronto
1928 176 Renie, portrait medln $50
177 Bruce, portrait medln $50
1932 224 Dick sculp
1936 227 Rosemary sculp nfs
1948 176 Maureen marble $700
177 Joan Michener ter cot

TRAQUAIR, RAMSAY
29 Mar 1874, Edinburgh d 1952
CWW49 PMC
Addr: 1918N-32, McGill University, Dept of Architecture
1918N 228 First Church of Christ Scientist, Edinburgh photo 1919-195 1920-296 1924-225
1920 247 The voyage of the ship Argo wc 1921-160
295 House of Skirling, Peebleshire, Scotland, for Lord Carmichael Skirling
1921 161 The Chinese horseman wc 1922-202
1922 203 The gods of the mountain wc 1923-168
294 The Water Gate, York wd cut 1923-236

1923 237 The salmon pool wd cut 1924-296 1925-340 (McGill University)
1924 297 Arisaig, Scotland wd cut 1925-339
1927 251 The landing, Guysborough wd cut
1932 193 The Barrens, Nova Scotia wc $50
port: by F.B. Taylor, 1939-224; bust, by F. Chambers, 1931-308

TRAVERS, CYRIL JOHN
2 Oct 1887, Manchester
Addr: 1938, Toronto
1938 S8, Toronto
376 Metal inkwell and pen holders
1942 142 The coal yard wc $50

TREMBLAY
see BLOUIN, ANDRE, 1968

TREPANIER, RACHEL
1946 146 Léon, portrait

TREVETT, WILLIAM E.
1938 S8, Toronto
Cooper & Beatty Limited
75 Foundry type specimen book
76 Proof envelope

TREVOR, LESLIE J.
1907, England
RCA(e) 1979, Graphic designer
Addr: 1979, Toronto

TREWEEK, G.E.
Addr: 1907, Plymouth, Eng
1907 283 Sundown, Cornish coast wc
284 Near Newquay, Cornwall wc
285 Lizard Head and Kynance Cove, Cornwall wc

TROTTIER, GERALD MATHEW
9 Sep 1925, Ottawa AGO CC2 IO NGC TB2
1964J 63 Resurrection 72 x 84 illus $1,500
1966 66 A tribute to rivers at western 84 x 72 $1,500
67 Self portrait tableau 68 x 27 nfs

TRUDEAU, CHARLES ELLIOT
see LE MOYNE, ROY, 1964N

TRUDEAU, YVES
3 Dec 1930, Montreal CC2 DMS WWA73
RCA(e) 1974 Council Sculptor
Addr: 1976, Montreal; 1979, Outremont
1976 S12, Montreal
94 Mur fermé et ouvert #38a alum 36 x 66 illus

TRUEMAN, J.A. (Mrs)
Addr: 1931, Mount Allison University, Sackville, NB
1931 435 Chelsea, old church etch

TRUEMAN, LAURA
H
1886 67 The old town of San Remo, Italy wc

TRUSTER, SOLOMON
Addr: 1938, Toronto
1938 S8, Toronto
380 Wallpaper design. Hon mention, Canadian Wallpaper Manufacturers Limited

TRYON, DWIGHT WILLIAM American
13 Aug 1849, Hartford, Conn 1 Jul 1925, South Dartmouth, Mass AAA28 B F H TB
1890 87 A pasture $375

TUCKER, LILLIAN
fl 1894-01 d 1939 H
Addr: 1896, 4211 Dorchester St, Montreal; 1899, 4203 St Catherine St, Montreal
1896 167 Old street at Boucherville
168 Pauline
1899 130 Miss Tucker

TUDIN, TONY
3 Feb 1930, S Africa IO
RCA(e) 1979 Textile designer
Addr: 1979, Toronto

TUDOR-HART, ERNEST PERCIVAL
27 Dec 1873, Montreal 8 Jun 1954, Quebec B DBA NGC TB1/2 WBA WWB34
Addr: 1896, 50 ave Malakoff, Paris; 1902, France, c/o Ivan Wotherspoon, KC, Montreal
1896 Hart, to 1902
205 Cottage wc
206 Bonsecour at Rouen wc
207 Dinard wc
1902 91 A scene in Brittany
92 A spring day in Brittany

1943 115 Francis Richards, Esq, RNVR $2,200

TULLY, BERESFORD L.
Addr: 1895, Toronto
1895 77 News rack carv walnut
78 Dragon carv walnut
79 Lion's head, study pine
80 Clustrent leaf, study pine

TULLY, KIVAS
1820, Garrarucum, Queen's Co, Ireland 24 Apr 1905, Toronto Co H Mo 98 W78
Addr: 1895, Parliament Bldg, Toronto
1895 58A Asylum for the insane, Brockville
59A Trinity College, Toronto, erected 1851
port: by S. Tully, 1892-73; bust, by H. MacCarthy, 1898-242

TULLY, SYDNEY STRICKLAND
10 Mar 1860, Toronto 18 Jul 1911, Toronto AGO CC1 H Mo12 NGC W78
ARCA 1890 Painter
Addr: 1891-2, Toronto; 1893-5, 61 Prince Arthur Ave, Toronto; 1896, 132 Sloan St, London, Eng; 1897, Toronto; 1898, Brunswick Ave, Toronto; 1899-01, 176 Roxborough Ave, Toronto; 1902-3, 27 Wellington St E, Toronto; 1904, Toronto; 1905-6, 36 Toronto St, Argyle Studio, Toronto; 1907-8, Canadian Bank of Commerce, Lombard St, Toronto; 1909M-10, 36 Toronto St, Toronto
1888 110 Meditation $25
125 Un hollandais 1889-44 $150
186 Study of a head
1889 37 Boy's head, a study $80
77 Arab study, a quiet smoke $275
167 and 175 Study in red chalk $10 each
1890 88 Miss Louise LeFevre nfs 1893-142 F1-106
89 Miss Francie Dumoulin nfs
90 Peeling apples $25
91 Study of a head of a Flemish girl
1892 31 Still life, oysters and lemons $50
51 Sketching $60
64 Tessa $30
73 Mr Kivas Tully, OAA
1893 141 Le vieux curé $80 F1-105 S2-103
262 Anticipation wc $20
263 Study wc $20
1893 F1, Chicago
192 Anticipation pastel
193 Study pastel
1894 128 Within sound of the sea
129 When the tide is low
130 Portrait of Miss X pastel
1895 141 Motherhood
142 Spring. A suggestion for decoration
143 Sketch
144 Miss Mabel Cartwright
145 Lieut Col Bolton, Prince of Wales Dragoons
146 Marjory, daughter of F. Arnold, Esq nfs
1896 169 'Auld Minnigaff', Newton Stewart, Galloway
170 Scotch mist, Minnigaff, NB
171 Glen Trool, Galloway
1897 136 A clearing shower
137 Korrali, a study
50W The task wc
51W Ebb tide wc
52W St Breludes, Jersey wc
1898 109 Jeanne
110 Windy weather, Rye, Sussex
111 Shipping, Rye, Sussex
112 Uriah Kempet's Lane, Rye, Sussex
113 Misty morning, Rye, Sussex
221 Cottage doorway, Talham wc
222 Meditation wc
223 Phoebe wc
1899 131 Twilight of life, illus, 'Evening of life' F2-71 1904-161 F4-79 S2-102 ◊AGO◊
132 George White Fraser, Esq
133 Fading light of day
134 Autumn
135 Après l'orage
224 Study in red chalk
1900 110a Poplars, afternoon effect
110b Evening dec panel
110c French Canadian interior
110d Niagara ferry
110e At the loom
110f Monday morning
1901 120 Breezy morning, Lower Canada F2-72 F3-175 $600
121 Mrs Aemilius Jarvis
122 One of the Heliades
123 Francis Tate
1902 156 Lady in black and white
157 A breezy morning, Cap à l'Aigle

281 The lady and the dragon pastel
282 The last load pastel
1903 120 Mrs Hayter Reed nfs
121 The sisters
122 Study of a child's head
123 The ford, Meadowvale
124 Twilight, Dymchurch, Sussex, England
1904 162 High tide, Cape Cod
163 Noontide
255 Mrs Hayter Reed pastel F4-116
256 Babette pastel
257 En japonaise pastel
1905 179 Enchanted forest pastel ◊AGO◊
180 Mrs John Cawthra pastel
181 Zaida pastel
182 Amid the sand dunes
1906 169 The green chair pastel F5-158 $200
1907 F6, Sherbrooke
161 Dalton M'Carthy, Esq $300 nfs (Toronto Hunt Club)
162 Head $100
163 Poplars $75
1908 135 Knalhaven, Dordrecht ◊NGC◊ Kualhaven, mispr
136 Mother and child, Holland
137 Barges, Holland
1909M 131 Peaseblossom
132 Klumper maker #133 not in catalog
134 Evening
135 Dutch interior
1909N 146 Peaseblossom, from 'Midsummer night's dream' pastel
147 Misty morning, Holland
148 Evening pastel
1910 184 Lady in white pastel ◊NGC◊
185 Twilight
1911 Late Miss Sydney S. Tully
134 Group of four pictures #134 following #164 in cat

TULVING, RUTH
23 Dec 1932, Estonia IO
RCA(e) 1977 Painter/print maker
Addr: 1979, Toronto
1966 68 Nude and window coll 36 x 48 $350
1968 52 Old doll 18 x 17 $80
53 Bull and horse 18 x 22 $80

TUNIS, RON
1970 The house that Jack built film screened 12 Feb

TURNBULL, ANDREW WATSON English
1874, England DBA DVP TB2 WBA WWB 34
Addr: 1929, 21 Sheen Rd, Richmond, Eng
1929 289 Trinity University, Dublin etch $30
290 Queen's College, Belfast etch $30

TURNER, JANICE FLOOD
Addr: 1976, Lacolle, Que
1976 S12, Montreal
95 Untitled/Sans titre m med 50 x 24 x 24 illus

TURNER, JOSEPH MALLORD WILLIAM
23 Apr 1775, London English
19 Dec 1851, Chelsea, London B TB
1883 88 The Rialto, Venice (R.F. Gagen, ARCA)

TURNER, PHILIP JOHN
1876, Stowmarket, Eng 13 Aug 1943, Montreal CNS36 CWW36 Mo12 PMC
Addr: 1913, 116 Board of Trade Bldg, Montreal; 1916, 49 Beaver Hall Hill, Montreal; 1930-7, 1100 Beaver Hall Hill, Montreal
1913 346 Residence, Glen and Sherbrooke Sts, Westmount photo
1916 267 'Coolegreane', Philipsburg, Quebec
1930 Turner & Maw Associates
182 St Philip's Church, Montreal West
1937 263 Pulpit, Christ Church Cathedral, Montreal
264 Children's corner, St Matthias Church, Westmount
1939 285-6 Christ Church Cathedral, Montreal. Children's corner. Reredos

TURNER, RICHARD JULIAN
22 Feb 1936, Edmonton AGO CCI
ARCA 1966-77 Sculptor
Addr: 1967-71, Vancouver
1964N 84 Foetus form cement & steel 109 x 50 x 18 illus $2,000

TURNER, STANLEY FRANCIS
1 Aug 1883, Aylesbury, Bucks, Eng
3 Jun 1953, Toronto AGO CNS36 CWW 49 TB3 WWA47
ARCA 1930 Painter

Addr: 1921-33, 159 Redpath Ave, Toronto; 1934-53, Toronto
1921 229 Interior etch
230 Curtain etch
1922 204 Emigrants
295 Chinese player col print
1923 169 Beaver Hills, Saskatchewan
242 Western pioneers. Mural decorative painting competition
1923 S6, Hamilton
98 Immigrants
1924 198 Summertime illus
199 September snow in the Rockies
298 University Tower, Toronto etch
299 Queen Street, Toronto etch
1927 221 September snow in the mountains
352 West entrance, University of Toronto etch
353 The monks of Oka etch
1930 161 Easter, Quebec temp $125
162 The Basilica, Ste Anne de Beaupré temp $125
222 Court House, Gettysburg etch $20
223 Tulip poplars, Mount Vernon etch $20
1931 286 New Basilica, Ste Anne de Beaupré wc $125 1933-233 $100
287 Lower Town, Quebec wc $125
288 Château Richer wc $75
289 Baude Street, Quebec wc $75
436 The new ship etch $20
437 Gettysburg etch $20
438 Mount Vernon etch $20
1933 232 Market, Quebec wc $100 T34-79
328 Château Richer etch
1938 S8, Toronto
270 Book, This is Ontario, map
1939 F11, New York
67 The immigrants 40 x 48 $500
1941 S9, Toronto
59 Quebec City $75

TURQUAND, HELEN ELIZABETH
17 Jun 1885, Hamilton
Addr: 1921, 949 West End Ave, New York
1921 162 Autumn woods temp
163 In the harbour

TUU'LUQ, MARION
c 1910, Back River District, NWT
RCA(e) 1978 Designer
Addr: 1979, Baker Lake, NWT

TWISSE, ARTHUR
1964N 85 Construction 5 sculp 25 x 29 $350
86 Rehearsal sculp 23 x 26 $350
1966 89 Nebula-nine sculp 36 x 46 $450

TYSON, J.F.
1970 113 Telephone set, Northern Electric Co, Limited. J.F. Tyson and S.M.K. Horne

U

UKPATIKA, ANOUHALLUQ
1976 S12, Montreal
165 Old woman silkscreen 31 x 21 1/2 illus

ULRICH, JAMES
1944, Lethbridge, Alta
Addr: 1976, Calgary
1976 S12, Montreal
50 Ch'i #5 acry 68 x 86 illus

UMHOLTZ, DAVID
1943, Pennsylvania
Addr; 1976, Saskatoon
1976 S12, Montreal
51 Empress of Saskatoon acry 44 x 60 1/2 illus

U'REN, JOHN CLARKSON English
fl 1880-20 DBA DBW G
Addr: 1907, Plymouth, Eng
1907 190 Sunset, Mullion Island, Cornwall
286 A peep from a Cornish cavern wc

URQUHART, ANTHONY MORSE (TONY)
9 Apr 1934, Niagara Falls, Ont
AGO B CC1 NGC TB2 WWA73
ARCA 1961-8 Council Painter
Addr: 1962-8, London, Ont
1955 82 The inn chairs $80
1957 57 Cape Jarney $250

1963 74 Allegory $600
1964J 64 Germinating woman 50 x 44 $500
1966 S10, Charlottetown
74 The yellow bride 80 x 48 $800
1967 85 Mountain/Cathedral sculp 8 x 12 x 10 $900
1970 97 Girder sculp 22h illus $600

USTINOV, PLATON CORNELIUS VON
21 Oct 1903, Jerusalem
1938 219 The end of False Creek, Vancouver, BC $150 T39-55
220 CPR tracks, Vancouver, BC wc $75
1939 304 Homo Britannicus drwg $25

UWINS, THOMAS English
25 Feb 1782, Pentonville, London
25 Aug 1857, Staines, Eng B DBW G TB
1881 220 Mid-day (H.F. George Twining)

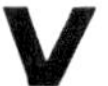

VACHELL, DESMOND see HARVEY, DESMOND VACHELL

VAITIEKUNAS, VINCENT
1971 Multiplicity film screened 31 Mar

VALE, FLORENCE GERTRUDE (Mrs Albert Jacques Franck)
18 Apr 1909, England IO
1951 36 Saturday night market $150

VALENTINE, A.C.
Addr: 1938, Montreal
1938 S8, Toronto
377 The Canadian market
378 Illustrated charts
379 3 folders

VALENTINE, LLEWELLYN FREDERICK
3 Feb 1939, Calgary
RCA(e) 1977 Architect
Addr: 1979, Calgary

VALENTINE, WILLIAM
1798, Whitehaven, Cumb, Eng 1849, Halifax H
1881 332 T.C. Haliburton (Sam Slick) artist not listed in catalog (loan)

VALLANCE, HUGH
Dec 1866, Hamilton, Ont 14 Mar 1947, Montreal NGC
ARCA 1925 RCA 1926 Sr 1936 Council Architect
Addr: 1924-7, 1070 Bleury St, Montreal; 1928-47, Montreal
1924 226-8 Crane Building, Beaver Hall Square, Montreal. Union Avenue elevation. Night view. Beaver Hall Square photo enlargements
1927 252 A suggestion des DW 1927 Extension to Sun Life Building, Montreal des pencil drwg 18 1/4 x 15 1/4

VAN ALSTYNE, THELMA SALINA AYLMA (Mrs E. Lloyd Van Alstyne)
26 Jan 1913, Victoria
RCA(e) 1977 Painter
Addr: 1979, Port Hope, Ont

VAN BUSKIRK, CAROLINE RUTH
17 Oct 1868, St Thomas, Ont
Addr: 1915, Gravel Rd, St Thomas
1915 210 Polperro harbour wc

VAN DAELE, JORIS P.
1921, Antwerp
Addr: 1976, Wyoming, Ont
1976 S12, Montreal
182 Sambuscus stem (x 270 mag) photo 11 x 14 illus

VAN DER MEULEN, EMIEL GEORGE
6 Oct 1928, Netherlands
RCA(e) 1976 Architect
Addr: 1979, Toronto

VAN DER WEYDEN, HARRY American
8 Sep 1868, Boston AAA28 B DBA F TB
Addr: 1919, Montreuil-sur-Mer, France
1919 164 The calm of evening

VAN GINKEL, BLANCHE LEMCO (Mrs Harmen Peter Daniel Van Ginkel)
14 Feb 1923, London, Eng WWA78
RCA(e) 1974 Architect
Addr: 1979, Toronto

VAN GINKEL, HARMEN PETER DANIEL
10 Feb 1920, Amsterdam
RCA(e) 1977 Architect
Addr: 1976, Montreal; 1979, Toronto
1976 S12, Montreal

135 Ginkelvan. Van Ginkel Partners col illus

VAN LUPPEN, FRANCOIS see LUPPEN, FRANCOIS VAN

VAN MARCKE, EMILE see MARCKE DE LUMMEN, EMILE VAN

VARLEY, FREDERICK HORSMAN
2 Jan 1881, Sheffield 8 Sep 1969, Toronto AGO B CC1 CWW64 EC NGC TB2 WWA47
ARCA 1921-39 RCA medal 1969 Group of Seven Painter
Addr: 1912, Toronto; 1914, 229 Oakmount Park, Toronto; 1919, Studio Bldg, 25 Severn St, Toronto; 1920, 401 Charlton St, Toronto; 1921-2, 11 Colin Ave, Toronto; 1923-4, 70 Lombard St, Toronto; 1925, 3461 Yonge St, Toronto; 1926-7, Vancouver; 1928, 3857 Point Grey Rd, Vancouver; 1929, Vancouver; 1930, 1087 Bute St, Vancouver; 1931-2, 3857 Point Grey Rd, Vancouver; 1933, BC College of Art, Vancouver; 1934, 1233 Georgia St W, Vancouver; 1935-9, Vancouver; 1940, Ottawa
1912 S3, Winnipeg
235 Tree study b&w
236 Colliers' wives b&w
1914 S5, Patriotic Fund
58 The hillside illus
1919 160 Prisoners illus. Painted for Canadian War Memorials
1920 248 Mr Chester D. Massey (Hart House, University of Toronto) illus
249 Self portrait ()NGC()
1921 164 Sir George Parkin (Sir George Parkin) illus
1922 205 Mr Irving Heward Cameron, MD LLD FRCS illus S6-99
1923 243 Immigrants. Mural decorative painting competition
1924 200 Decorative panel
1925 217 Portrait group illus
1928 153 The artist's wife
236 Sphinx chalk $50
237 Study of a head chalk $50
238 The sketchers chalk $75
239 Mountain forms, BC chalk $50
1929 S7, Calgary
142 Gypsy character $500
143 Vera charcl $75
144 Girl's head charcl $50
145-54 oil sketches $60 each
145 Copper Cove, BC
146 On the road to Garrow Bay, BC
147 A lonely beach, BC
148 Incoming tide
149 Romantic coast, BC
150 The sand bar
151 Coast Mountains, BC
152 Evening and quiet water
153 Tantalus Mountain from Black Tusk meadows, Garibaldi Park
154 From my studio window, Vancouver
1930 163 Vera $1,000 ()NGC()
1931 290 Portrait study $750
1932 194 Dhârâna $1,000 ()AGO()
195 Early morning wc $50
1933 234 Woman $250
1934 229 Head of a negress drwg $100
230 Marie drwg $50 ()AGO()
231 Woman drwg $50
1934 Travelling exhibit
80 Tranquil Valley wc $100
1938 S8, Toronto
Ryerson Press
269 Book, Pens and pirates
1941 191 Summer in the Arctic $1,000
192 Arctic sea $750
1942 143 Trooper, 1942 $600
port: bust, by F. Wyle 1922-234; bust, by L. Mol 1963-95

VARLEY, JOHN English
17 Aug 1778, Hackney, Eng 17 Nov 1842, London B DBA DVP G TB
1880 333 Warwick Castle wc (V. Clementi)

VARVARANDE, ROBERT EMILE
2 Jan 1922, Lyons, France AGO CC1 TB2
1954 86 La Bretone 24 x 18 $105
1964J 65 The offerings XII.63 30 x 36 $500

VAUX, EMMA PLIMSALL
b Brockville, Ont
Addr: 1908, Arlington Hotel, Toronto; 1909N, 5 Chestnut Park, Toronto; 1911, 3 Chestnut Park, Toronto
1908 138 Her pet
1909N 149 Dutch farm house
150 Christine

1911 165 and 166 Sketch from Luxembourg Garden
210 and 211 Drawing

VENABLES, ADOLPHUS ROBERT
fl 1833-73 G
1881 327 Gen Sir Hastings Doyle (loan)

VENNE, JOSEPH
14 Jun 1859, Montreal
Addr: 1913, 5 Beaver Hall Sq, Montreal
1882 233 Facade for a chapel
1913 Venne & Labelle
347 Mausoleum, a study
348 Church, Southbridge, Mass, perspective

VERMETTE, CLAUDE
10 Aug 1930, Montreal
RCA(e) 1973 Industrial designer
Addr: 1979, Ste Adèle-en-Haut, Que

VERMETTE, MARIETTE see ROUSSEAU, MARIETTE

VERNER, FREDERICK ARTHUR
26 Feb 1836, Sheriday, Ont 6 May 1928, London, Eng AGO EC H Mo12 NGC TB3 W78
ARCA 1893 Painter
Addr: 1883-4, 16 Edith Villas, Kensington, London, Eng; 1886, 2 Edith Villas, Kensington, London, Eng; 1887, London, Eng; 1893, Ontario Society of Artists, King St W, Toronto; 1894, 79 King St W, Toronto; 1895-8, 16 Edith Villas, Kensington, London, Eng; 1899-02, 39 Palace Terrace, Fulham, London, Eng; 1903, c/o McKenzie & Co, Toronto; 1904-5, London, Eng; 1906, 417 Palace Rd, London, Eng; 1907-09M, London, Eng; 1909N, 95 Yonge St, Toronto; 1910, 417 Fulham Rd, London, Eng; 1911, c/o McKenzie & Co, 95 Yonge St, Toronto; 1912-27, 417 Fulham Rd, London, Eng
1880 72 Canadian fruit
109 Sunset, Parry Sound
237 Camp on Nipigon River wc
1882 122 On the Detroit River wc $50
124 Burnham Church, twilight wc $50
182 Doune Castle wc $100
201 Advocates' Close, Edinburgh wc $100 ◊NGC◊
1883 20 A red sky at night is the shepherd's delight $250
219 Foreland, north Devon wc $30
239 Doune Church, Scotland wc $15
258 Misty morning, Nipigon River wc $50
269 Ojibwa camp, Fort Frances wc $15 Ojibbeway mispr
276 Wallace's Monument, near Stirling wc $50
284 Coomb Martin, north Devon wc $15
305 Plainstone Close, Edinburgh wc $75
312 Tide out wc $30
1884 16 The upper Ottawa $500
113 Buffalo in the marsh wc $60
130 Buffaloes, winter wc $60
160 Buffalo, afterglow wc $50
176 Buffalo, moonlight wc $50
1884 S1, Saint John
71 Buffaloes wc $50
1885 181 Pawing buffalo, winter $500
214 Bull frog wc $20
234 A shady nook wc $50
251 Cottage in Sark wc $50
262 On the Lynn, Devon wc $50
291 Yarmouth wc $30
1886 10 Nature's mirror $600 Fla-2020
49 Cottages in Jersey wc $50
62 Sunset o'er the glen wc $25
73 Stony Lake wc $35
111 A Dutch girl on the Lookout $50
157 Flushing harbour, Holland $100
1886 Fla, London, Eng
2020, artist number
Last of the herd
High water
Indian encampment
Wigwams on Rainy River
Elk at rest
Nipigon River
Parliament Buildings, Ottawa, from the river
Buffaloes
1887 19 Devon cottages $95
26 Dutch fishing boats $200
31 The red man's ranche $200

46 Nutting season, Burnham beeches $175
92 Sunset on the marsh $95
160 Still life wc $75
1888 18 Autumn wc $125
118 Blacksmith's shop $50
207 Cottage near the sea $75
245 120th Row, Yarmouth wc $75
259 St Nicholas Church, Liverpool wc $60
266 Buffalo grazing wc
278 October wc
1889 8 Monarch of the prairie $500 1893-146 $1,000 F1-108
15 and 17 Swans $50 each
130 Oak trees wc $100
1890 92 Alarmed, Wapiti deer $300
93 The leader of the herd $125
94 The afterflow, returning from the mill $60
207 An old beech tree wc $50
1891 160 Twilight wc
161 Buffalo wc
185 Ogeblana wigwams, Lake of the Woods wc
1892 39 Our cows $250
60 Jersey cattle in the Marsh Lake $250
149 Sunset on the prairie wc $60
157 Ice flow, Detroit wc $50
1893 143 Stampede $600
144 Milking time $600 F1-107
145 Hunting the elk $300
264 St Clair, March wc $350 F1-194 St Clair Marsh wc
265 Alarmed, Canadian elk wc $200
1894 192 Stonehenge wc
193 Ann Hathaway's cottage, Stratford-on-Avon wc
194 Shottery, Stratford-on-Avon wc
1895 147 On the Rainy River
148 Autumn, near Sandwich
84W Doon Castle, Scotland wc
85W Old cottages in Wiltshire wc
86W Homeward over the heather wc
87W A woodland way wc
88W Ojibwa camp wc Ojibewa mispr
89W Sunset, Norfolk wc
90W Group of birches wc
1896 262 Buffalo, twilight wc
263 Buffalo, evening wc
264 Buffalo, winter wc
265 Turkeys wc 1897-56W
266 Brendon, north Devon wc
267 Cheswick Church wc
1897 138 Group of buffalo
139 A shady pool
54W Lake Huron wc
55W Cottage by the sea, Jersey wc
57W In the backwoods wc
58W Cullercoats fishwives wc
59W Sunset, Burnham Common wc
1898 114 Buffalo
115 Cottage, Wimbledon
224 Ann Hathaway's cottage wc 1899-225
225 Cottages, Froome, Dorset wc
226 Evening, Wimbledon Common wc
1899 136 Buffaloes, early morning
137 Wapiti deer, misty morning
138 Wimbledon Common
139 Buffalo, evening
226 Ojibwa Indians, Lake of the Woods wc Ogibbawa mispr
227 Harvest time, Welford wc
228 Beech woods wc 1901-213
1900 182 Early morning, Parry Sound wc
183 Early autumn wc
184 Dutch maid wc
1901 125 American bison F2-73
126 Fog bound, Lake Superior
214 Sioux encampment wc
1902 159 Buffalo pawing
239 Herd of bison, evening wc
1902 F3, Rochester
176 'Twixt day and night $180
1903 126 Bison foraging
196a Wimbledon wc
196b Old beech tree wc
1904 165 Old trail, winter F4-80
166 Swans and cygnets
258 Fog bound, Lake Superior wc
259 Red River, sunset wc
1905 183 Bison, evening
184 Herd of bison, sunset
1906 F5, Halifax
159 Bison illus $300
1907 191 Bison, autumn afternoon
192 Sioux encampment 1908-139
287 November evening wc
1907 F7, Sherbrooke
164 Bison, morning mist $150

165 Oak and beechwoods $100
1909M 136 Herd of buffalo
137 Morning on the Dart
137a North shore, Lake Huron
1909N 151 Bison, mid-day
152 Bison pawing
1910 186 Bison foraging in a blizzard
187 Twilight, Burnham Common
1910 S2, Liverpool
104 Buffalo, mid-day
1911 167 Buffalo in a blizzard
1912 216 Buffalo in the marsh
217 Buffalo, sunset
218 Ojibwa Indians, fog bound wc Ojibbaway mispr
1913 294 Buffalo by the river
295 Wandering home wc S4-133 $200
296 Autumn sunset wc
297 Marsh, twilight wc
298 Evening wc
1915 211 Bison, Canadian
1916 226 Buffalo, winter evening
1918A 167 Bison, winter morn
168 Bison, leader of the herd wc
1920 250 Golf links, Sandwich wc
251 The last of the Mohicans wc
1923 170 Sioux teepees wc
1924 201 Canadian bison
202 Ojibwa Indians, Thunder Bay wc Ojibbawa mispr
1925 218 Bison in a blizzard wc
1927 222 Upper Ottawa River wc
223 Bison, winter evening wc

VERNON, MARY see MORGAN, MARY

VERNON, WILLIAM H. English
1820-09 DBA G H
Addr: 1881, Athol, NS
1881 318 Sunset on the Avon $50

VESCEI, ANDREW
see ROSEN, BERNARD, 1964N

VEZINA, EMILE
6 Jan 1876, USA 16 Jul 1942
Addr: 1915, 203 Montgomery St, Montreal
1915 212 Arabe de Tunis pastel

VICAJI, DOROTHY E. (Mrs Rustom Vicaji) English
fl 1915-30 DBA
Addr; 1924, 17 Holly Mount, Hampstead, London, Eng; 1925, Ritz Carlton Hotel, Montreal
1924 203 Mrs Norman Stines, California
1925 219 Elaine illus

VICAJI, RUSTOM English
fl 1918-27 DBA
Addr: 1925, 17 Holly Mount, Hampstead, London, Eng
1925 220 The canal wc
221 Le soir, Méditerranée wc

VICKERS, ALFRED English
10 Sep 1786, Newington, Eng 1868, London, Eng B G TB
1880 79 The Inn at Pontre Vyla, north Wales (D. Brymner)

VICKERS, H. MOODIE (Miss)
Addr: 1901-2, 172 Adelaide St, Toronto; 1904, Toronto; 1911, Paris
1901 215 Study of a head wc
216 Bedouin wc
1902 240 Reveries wc
1904 302 Death of Tecumseh bas rel
1911 168 The vegetable market
169 The flower market
170 The yard door

VIGNEAU, MARGUERITE
b Trois Rivières, Que
1951 125 Negro child ter cot $100

VINCELLETTE, ROMEO
b Verdun, Que
Addr: 1937, 4488A Des Erables St, Montreal
1937 225 Near Piedmont $150
1945 199 Laurentian winter scene $250
200 Late afternoon, Ste Adèle $200

VINEBERG, LOUISE (Mrs) (signs Louvin)
1964J 42 Europa #2 coll 40 x 30 $200

VISSER, JOHN DE
8 Feb 1930, Veghel, Netherlands
RCA(e) 1973 RCA 1976 Council Photographer
Addr: 1979, Port Hope, Ont
DW 1976 Toronto, autumn hues. Off Salvage, Newfoundland photos 1 b&w 1 col 11 x 14 each

VLETTER, FIONA DE
31 Mar 1927, Tjepoe, Java
1961 28 Rooster 10 x 24 $175

VOGT, ADOLPHE (ADOLF) American
1843, Liebenstein, Thuringia, Germany 1871, New York B H NGC TB
1880 5 Startled horses (Sandford Fleming)
9 Milking time (Sandford Fleming)
1883 136 Winter quarters (James Spooner)
1886 Fla, London, Eng
2021, artist number
Cow (J. Rankin, Esq, Montreal)
Cattle drinking (J.R. Wilson, Esq, Montreal)

VON DER OHE, KATIE see OHE, DOROTHY KATIE

VON HOLMFELD, EYVINO see HOLMFELD, EYVINO

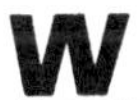

WAINWRIGHT, ORMA A.
Addr: 1938, Toronto
1938 S8, Toronto
380 Wallpaper design. Hon mention, Canadian Wallpaper Manufacturers Limited

WAINWRIGHT, ROBERT BARRY
29 Jun 1935, Chilliwack, BC B
RCA(e) 1976 Painter
Addr: 1976/79, Montreal
1976 S12, Montreal
52 Continental night rider acry 96 x 54 illus

WAKE, MARGARET EVELINE
16 Apr 1867, London, Eng 13 Oct 1930, Vancouver
Addr: 1921-6, 1834 Barclay St, Vancouver
1921 165 A Siwash Indian woman M.S. Vake mispr
1926 140 Sophie

WALDMANN, OSCAR Swiss
25 Jun 1856, Geneva B TB
Addr: 1930, 3 Passage Sabra, rue Gambetta, Malakoff, Seine, Paris
1930 192 Deer in summer sculp walnut $200

WALES, PHILIP
1866, Port Louis, Mauritius H
Addr: 1897, 395 Gilmour St, Ottawa
1897 150 Study of pines

WALKER, HORATIO
12 May 1858, Listowel, Ont 27 Sep 1938, Ste Pétronille, Que AGO B CC2 EC H Mo98/12 NGC TB WWA36
RCA 1913 Hon non-res RCA 1917 Ret 1929 Council Painter
Addr: 1909N-13, Ste Pétronille, Ile d'Orléans, Que; 1914-18, New York; 1919-38, Ste Pétronille, Ile d'Orléans, Que
1901 138 Spring pastoral
139 Lime burners, moonlight
1909N 153 Evening, Ile d'Orléans (Byron E. Walker, Esq) ◊AGO◊
1910 188 The first gleam, ploughing
189 Woman milking, morning
1911 171 Hauling the log (A.T. Sanden, Esq, New York)
1913 299 Man sawing wood
1914 192 Miss Ruth Johnston (R.R. Counsell, Esq)
1914 S5, Patriotic Fund
83 Painting
1915 213 Lime burners at night illus
214 An autumn pastoral wc
1916 227 Miss Pretty illus
1918A 169 Horses at the trough illus (N.E. Montross, Esq) ◊MMFA◊
170 A load of wood, winter
171 Autumn DW 1918 20 1/2 x 15 1/2 T51-40 1954 Retro Sec 11 1958 Memorial Sec
1921 166 Autumn illus
167 Mme Clarence A. Gagnon
1958 Memorial Sec. port (Ontario Society of Artists) biog essay, Robert W. Pilot
Evening, Ile d'Orléans 28 x 36 ◊AGO◊
Snow landscape 8 1/2 x 15 1/2 ◊AGO◊
Autumn 20 1/2 x 15 1/2 DW 1918
Mother and little white pigs 25 1/4 x 35 3/4 ◊NGC◊
Première neige sketch ◊NGC◊
Pétronille sketch ◊NGC◊
Horses at the trough 50 x 40
The ice cutters 21 x 38
The woodcutters 36 x 48

WALKER, JOLLIFFE

Addr: 1910, 100 Metcalfe St, Montreal
1910 190 Little Miss Muffet
191 Mrs Davidson Parker

WALLACE, GEORGE BURTON
7 Jun 1920, Sandy Cove, Dublin Co, Ireland AGO IO
RCA(e) 1975 Sculptor
Addr: 1979, Dundas, Ont

WALLCOUSINS, ERNEST English
fl 1912-28 DBA
Addr: 1912, Toronto
1912 S3, Winnipeg
237 and 239 Illustration b&w
238 Illustration col

WALLIS, KATHERINE ELIZABETH
1861, Peterborough, Ont 15 Dec 1957, Santa Cruz, Cal B H Mo12 NGC TB1/2
Addr: 1904-7, Paris; 1922, 309 Park St, Peterborough, Ont; 1927-30, 27 rue de Fleurus, Paris; 1931-5, 1379 Sherbrooke St W, Montreal; 1937, c/o Col Wallis, 5210 St Patrick St, Montreal
1904 303 Mignonne statuette
304 Dachschund bronze
305 La toilette sculp
1907 365 Mignonne bust marble
1922 232 Portrait rel S6-113
233 Dante Alighieri rel S6-114
1927 273 Faun's head bronze (Arthur Browning, Esq)
1930 193 La lutte pour la vie mahogany illus $4,000 ◊NGC◊
1931 341 Mother and child bronze cire perdue $225
342 A good boy bronze cire perdue $80
1935 294 Little Japanese sisters ter cot $80
1937 293 Blackbirds bronze cire perdue $90

WALSH, JOHN STANLEY
16 Aug 1907, Brighton, Eng AGO WWA 62
1944 134 Night scene, Montreal gouache $60
135 Naval gun plant, Vancouver wc $50
1945 201 New York night scene gouache $70
202 Victoria Lane, Montreal $70

1961 78 Canary Islands wc 15 x 20 $150

WALTER-HASLAM/INSURRECTION ART COMPANY
1971 45 L'evidence en art/L'art en evidence 2 pieces 96 x 48 illus nfs

WALTERS, EMILE
31 Jan 1893, Winnipeg TB1/2 WWA36
Addr: 1924, 47 5th Ave, NY
1924 204 Spring blossoms

WARD, DUDLEY see WARD, WILLIAM DUDLEY

WARD, FLORENCE E.
Addr: 1901, c/o H.J. Matthews, Yonge St, Toronto; 1902, 95 Yonge St, Toronto; 1904, Toronto
1901 249 Alma mater sculp F2-84
250 The coming of spring, the happy morning of life and of May sculp
251 Nereid sculp
252 A joyous sprite sculp F2-85
253 Maggie sculp F2-86
1902 291 Vesta sculp
292 Young Canada sculp
1904 306 Mischief cast
307 Reverie bronze
308 Ancilla Domini bas rel
309 Young Canada bas rel

WARD, WILLIAM DUDLEY BURNETT
19 Apr 1879, Graveley Bank, Staffs, Eng 1935, Montreal AGO
Addr: 1914, 110 Scarborough Rd, Balmy Beach, Toronto; 1918A, 70 Victoria St, Toronto; 1929, 887 Stuart Ave, Outremont, Que; 1931, 750 Bloomfield Ave, Outremont, Que
1914 193 The honeymoon wc
194 How very absurd wc
1914 S5, Patriotic Fund
57 The chaperone illus
1918A 172 Somewhere in fairyland
284 Illustration, fairy story
1929 211 Will he awaken? wc $75
1931 291 Woodfolk magic, presto wc $60

WARDELL, ARTHUR W.
see DUNLOP, DANIEL, 1970

WARDELL, DOROTHY WILMA

5 Dec 1910, Hamilton, Ont
1942 144 Artist's mother pastel nfs

WARE, L. GRAEME
H
1891 4 Daffodils
1892 82 Morning glories $30

WARKOV, ESTHER
12 Oct 1941, Winnipeg WWA76
RCA(e) 1974 Painter
Addr: 1979, Winnipeg

WARREN, PETER HAWORTH
10 Apr 1933, Toronto
RCA(e) 1975 Architect
Addr: 1979, Montreal

WARRENER, LOWRIE LYLE
1900, Sarnia, Ont
1939 233 Edge of clearing, BC nfs

WARWICK, SEPTIMUS
fl 1914-25
Addr: 1916, 84 St Mark St, Montreal
1916 268 and 269 House, Westmount des

WATERS, MACKENZIE
1 Oct 1894, Belleville, Ont 4 Sep 1968, Fa CNS36 CWW58 TB2
ARCA 1936 RCA 1952 Sr 1953 Non-res 1963 Architect
Addr: 1936, 96 Bloor St W, Toronto; 1937-62, Toronto; 1963-6, Florida; 1967, USA
1936 212 Residence, Maj Gen D.M. Hogarth, CB, Toronto
213 Distillery, W & A Gilbey Limited, New Toronto
DW 1952 not recorded

WATSON, ALEXANDER
17 Oct 1858, Saint John 1923, Saint John H
Addr: 1897-8, Saint John; 1900, 5 King St, Saint John; 1920, 105 Wentworth St, Saint John
1897 61W Violets wc
62W Salmon River, Saint John, New Brunswick wc
1898 122 At the pond
227 Old sheds in a fog wc
228 Stream in the meadow wc
1900 114 An evening sky
115 Waiting for the tea to draw
116 Landscape
189 Reading the story wc
1901 132 Memories F2-74
1920 252 Along the shore wc

WATSON, GENEVIEVE
Addr: 1912, 16 Wilton Cr, London, Eng
1912 219 St Bartholomew's Church, Smithfield, London wc
220 Sloth Fair, Smithfield, London wc

WATSON, GRACE
1939 234 Waiting for the fishing party, Gloucester $25

WATSON, HOMER RANSFORD
14 Jan 1855, Doon, Ont 30 May 1936, Doon, Ont AGO B CC1 EC G H Mo98/12 TB1/2 W78
ARCA 1880 RCA 1882 Council Painter
Addr: 1880-36, Doon, Ont
1880 29 The pioneer mill
1881 240 The stone road (Mr Bayley)
243 April day $100
250 On the Grand River, near Doon $100 [NGC]
287 The last of the drouth $300
304 Sunset (R. Gilmore)
1882 24 In the gathering gloom $500
56 Down in the Laurentides $200 DW 1882 25 1/2 x 41 1/2 1883-83 S1-98 T51-41 The Laurentides
69 In the clover $200
81 An old clearing $175
1883 41a Down the ravine $400
52 A land of thrift $400
71 After the rain $400 [BAG]
122 Cornfield $400 [NGC]
123 The day has been wet and weary $300
127 Fitful August $600
131 At noon $300
1884 50 Through the fields $200
54 The mill in the ravine $200
69 September dawn $200
84 The torrent $100
89 Near the close of a stormy day $500
1884 S1, Saint John
87 Moonlight $50
91 Twilight $50
92 At beginning of day $75
100 Over the plain $75

105 Clearing up $25
112 Sunset in the fields $25
114 A mountain lake $75
124 Woodland road $75
1885 6 Forest, field and valley $200
33 Grove at sunset $500
36 A torrent 1891-41
97 A grey day at the ford $200
1886 104 The saw mill $500 Fla-2022 1887-25 $400
114 Storm brewing on the hills $150
134 Gathering gloom after days of forest fires
1886 Fla, London, Eng
2022, artist number
Frosty morning in October (J. W.H. Watts, Esq, Ottawa)
Gathering storm (Geo. Haig, Esq, Montreal)
Ploughed field (J.W.H. Watts)
Landscape (J.W.H. Watts)
River torrent (Marquis of Lorne)
1887 10 Early spring $800
16 The hillside $150
35 The day's last gleam $150
40 Morning $150
50 May $500
63 A frosty morning $300
95 Twilight nfs
103 Before the storm $300
1888 81 Grey day in July $100
82 Sawmill $500
99 Moonrise $30
108 Road through the fields $100
129 Where the upland dips to the shore $250
147 The mill $40
211 Evening 1889-41 $100
1889 69 Under the beeches $40
80 A lowland burn $100
84 Stormy weather $40
86 Sultry weather $40
87 Spring day $40
96 Departing shower $100
1890 95 Woodland gleams $125
96 The silent mill $125
97 The hillside gorge $125 ØNGCØ
98 The meadow stream $125
99 The glade nfs
100 The braes of Fife nfs
101 A Berkshire road nfs
1891 42 A Fifeshire pasture
43 Over the common
44 Evening on the Thames
45 When the shadow creeps over the hill
47 In the maple forest
48 Heatherland
1892 8 October (R.B. Angus, Esq)
46 A kitchen corner in a humble home $80
53 From shelter to pasture $500
61 Road to the river $65
79 After the mists have lifted $400
80 Evening on the Thames $100
1893 147 Early spring, Grand River Valley F1-109
148 Storm passing the oak glade F1-110
149 Village of Kilrenny, Fife F1-111
1893 F1, Chicago
112 At the farm
1894 138 The farm
139 The woodcutters
140 Wood gathering in the glade
141 Among the beeches November morning
142 The hillside road
143 The wayfarer
144 The swineherd
145 The forest lane
146 Among the hay ricks
147 Path under the oaks
1895 154 God's acre
155 A March morning
156 A house in the glade
157 Hay making, last load
158 Cottage in the wood
1896 172 November evening
173 The village woods
174 The wayfarers
175 In the woods, autumn
176 The yeoman's path
177 Cloudy morning, April
178 The wayside inn
1897 149 The old mill
1898 116 The mill ford
117 River woodlands
118 Squally weather, fishing boats running to harbour
119 The dry creek
120 Over the hill
121 The shelter (W.D. Matthews, Esq)
1899 140 The old stone bridge
141 Crossing the ford illus

1901-133 (Andrew Wilson, Esq, Montreal) F2-77
142 Marine
143 Landscape with sheep
1900 111 November in the clearing
112 Over the hill
113 The dry watercourse F3-182 $720
1901 134 Moonlight (Andrew Wilson, Esq) F2-78
135 The meadow (John Payne, Toronto) F2-79
136 Through the woods (John Payne) F2-80
1903 128 The mill pool
1904 167, 168 and 169 Landscape
1904 F4, St Louis
81 The loggers (James Ross)
82 The floodgate (James Wilson) 1908-150 S3-146 1924-206 illus [NGC]
1905 207 Loading oats
208 Path through the willows
209 The fallow field
210 Souvenir of Devonshire
211 A gravel pit
212 Woodland
213 Evening
1906 178 The pit
179 The wheat field
180 Fighting the fire
181 The glade
1906 F5, Halifax
160 The crossing $1,000
161 Elm Tree ford $500
162 The wayside inn $1,000
1907 193 Polling the willows
194 Passing squall
195 A Devonshire cottage
1908 151 Rolling mists, Cape Breton coast
152 Crossing Grand River
1909M 140 Pioneers crossing a river
1909N 161 Wayside inn
162 The lock
1910 192 The source 1912-221 1913-301
193 The stronghold 1911-172
194 After the storm
195 Farm in the ravine
1910 S2, Liverpool
105 Pioneer crossing a river at sunset
106 Smugglers' Cave, coast of Nova Scotia
107 Lone cattle shed
108 The dry creek
1911 173 Rolling surf, Cape Breton
174 The maple wood, evening
175 The sap gatherer
176 Autumn drouth
177 The field oak
1912 222 The ravine farm
223 In the forest
224 After the storm
225 The glade of birch trees
226 Moonlight on the creek
1912 S3, Winnipeg
147 Crossing the river
1913 300 Evening after rain S4-134 $1,000 nfs [AGO]
302 The abandoned trawler
303 A woodman's home S5-10 illus
304 The ravine road S4-135 $700
1914 195 The grave of the derelict
196 Oak forest
197 Tree bank and rocky field
1915 215 The birth of an army
216 The review
217 The range
218 Woods in June illus
1916 228 March evening illus
229 December dawn
230 Sugar cabin
231 Breaking winter
1918A 173 Mill in the forest
174 Breaking winter, moonrise
175 Winter evening
176 Forest in autumn
1918N 193 Edge of the forest
194 April woods
195 October day
196 Passing wind storm
1919 161 Late autumn, northlands
162 The red oak illus [EAG]
163 Forest sun and haze
1920 253 Passage to the unknown illus
254 Out of the pit
255 The broken field
256 The farm in the ravine [NGC A ravine farm]
1921 168 Beechnutting time
169 Woods of Paradise Lake
170 The stone barn
171 Moonrise, Grand River
1922 206 North country landscape
207 Lifting fog, Cape Breton
208 Hill side S6-100
209 Dry weather, Grand River S6-101
1923 171 Valley of the Ridge 1924-205 1925-222
172 The Bush Inn, from study in 1880

173 A glacial stream, British Columbia
174 Early snow, evening
1924 207 Woods in June
208 Gleaning the wood lot
1925 223 Side road cabin
224 March evening, Grand River valley
1926 141 Pioneer cabin, Grand River country
142 Early winter in the forest
143 Wild apple tree in blossom
1927 224 Early morning sunrise
225 Farm lands in midwinter thaw
226 Flamboro township woodland
1928 154 In the shadow. Souvenir of the western desert
155 Thawing weather
156 Oak of the banks, Grand River
1929 212 The bridge at Greensville
213 Grand River cottage
214 Woodland glade by the river
215 A sketch in May
1930 164 Drouth at Boulder Creek
165 Old mill
166 Side road sketch in May
1931 292 Waning winter (NGC)
1932 196 Pioneer cabin of the drover, Plains Road
197 The brook oak
198 Ice break in March
1933 235 Drovers cabin in clearing weather T34-81
1934 192 Storm drift
193 Near twilight, British Columbia T35-69
1935 256 October moon $1,500
1936 Late Homer Watson, RCA
200 High water at Pine Bend
1954 8 Retro Sec. Landscape (MMFA)
port: by A.A. Patterson, 1896-131, 1922-160; bust, by J. Sloan, 1938-241

WATSON, PATRICIA
1970 The summer we moved to Elm Street film screened 10 Feb

WATSON, SUSAN
10 May 1949, Toronto
Addr: 1976, Toronto
1976 S12, Montreal
151 Untitled mop cotton/coton éponge 96 x 54 x 39 illus

WATSON, SYDNEY HOLLINGER
6 Apr 1911, Toronto CWW79 NGC TB2 WWA47
ARCA 1951 RCA 1955 Council Designer
Addr: 1951-71/79, Toronto
1942 145 Lower Town façade wc $100 T43-47
146 Rue Champlain wc $100
1944 136 Early birds $100
1948 154 St Peter altar panel nfs
1949 90 Cliff houses, Mesa Verde $125 T50-18
1950 146 Cliff houses, Mesa Verde 36 x 30 $300
1951 137 High altar, Mission of St Alban, Peterborough, Ont photo
138 Christus Rex altar panel illus
1952 92 City, back elevation illus $300
1953 87 Harbour illus $150
1953 Travelling exhibit
32 Mexican market $175
1954 87 The music shop 28 x 36 illus $350 DW 1956
1955 83 Still life in window illus $300
1956 43 Medieval city illus $250 T56-31
1957 68 Italian evening illus $350
1958 81 Reflections illus $350
1959 78 The cup 24 x 56 illus $400
RCA medal des, 1963 p2 illus

WATSON, WINNIFRED
Addr: 1931, 16 Sussex Ave, Toronto
1931 439 Bertha drwg

WATT, HENRY ROBERTSON (ROBIN)
26 Sep 1896, Victoria 11 Sep 1964, Cowansville, Que
ARCA 1952 RCA 1962 Painter
Addr: 1928-9, Linton Apts, Sherbrooke St W, Montreal; 1953-64, Montreal
1928 157 The artist's wife
1929 216 Mrs Norman Bethune
217 G. Hertzberg, Esq
291 Miss Helen Byers chalk
292 Master Malcolm Byers chalk
1929 S7, Calgary
155 Daisy Woo $1,500
1949 91 A. Murray Vaughan, Esq nfs T50-19
92 Roydan McConnell nfs
1950 147 Pamela, daughter of

Duncan Stewart, Esq 20 x 16 nfs
148 Lares et pénates 24 x 32 $750
1952 93 Dr H.P. O'Neill nfs T53-31
1953 88 Jeannine illus nfs
1954 88 Mrs Keith Henderson 36 x 28 illus nfs
1955 84 Mrs Robert W. Pilot nfs
1956 44 Rt Rev James S. Thomson, DD nfs
1958 82 Hélène nfs
1961 79 Gilbert Marion 36 x 28 illus nfs DW 1962 1964N-65a, in memorium, Robin Watt, RCA, MC and Bar, Croix de Guerre
1963 74 Visc Hardinge of Lahore nfs

WATTERSON, GRACE MARGARET VICTORIA WILSON (Mrs J.C. Watterson)
22 Apr 1906
Addr: 1935, 1525 St Mark St, Montreal
1935 257 Mrs J.N. Petersen min nfs

WATTS, ETTA (Mrs)
fl 1895-1900 H
Addr: 1895, 610 St Denis St, Montreal; 1896, Fraser Institute, Montreal; 1899, 459 Clarke Ave, Westmount, Que
1895 149 In mischief
1896 179 Moonlight on the Scottish coast
180 A spring morning
1899 148 Roadway near Beaupré, Que
149 Old mill, Bavaria
150 Twilight, Beaupré, Quebec

WATTS, JOHN WILLIAM HURRELL
16 Sep 1850, Teignmouth, Eng 26 Aug 1917, Ottawa H Mo98 NGC
ARCA 1880 RCA 1881 Council Designer
Addr: 1880-92, Ottawa; 1893-5, Dept of Public Works, Ottawa; 1896-8, c/o Wilson & Co, Ottawa; 1899-02, Ottawa; 1903-7, Sparks St, Ottawa; 1908, 33 Sparks St, Ottawa; 1909-12, Ottawa; 1913, 66 Roberts St, Ottawa; 1914-17, Ottawa
1880 256 Copper etch, 4 proofs
Church of the Recollet, Montreal
View from Ste Famille St, Quebec
Point Levis, Quebec
Parliament Bldgs, Ottawa
267 Cabinet des
274 Sideboard 2 des Silver medal award
284 Cloth cases for book bindings 2 des
292 and 296 Paper hanging des
353 Chimney piece
1881 149 and 150 Copper etch proof
151 Sketches of Quebec wc
152 Sketches from life wc
169 Cabinet des
170, 178 and 200 Interior des
177 and 201 Furniture des
181 Drawing room, interior dec
183 and 193 Parliament Buildings, Toronto, east, west, south fronts, competitive des
184 Church des
189 Interior staircase des DW 1882 pen drwg 15 x 11 1/2
194 Chimney piece des
1882 223 Fan des
225 Elizabethan staircase des
1883 319 Frontispiece to Lucile b&w $10
326 The curfew tolls the knell of parting day b&w $10
333 Wall decoration des
359 A nursery corner des
1884 108 The Glen, Shelburne, NH wc $50 S1-54 $35
202 Stained glass window, sketch
1886 161 Joe $40
165 Canadian homestead $40
1888 39 Winter wc $35
276 Old houses, Woodstock, NB wc $10 1889-145
279 Autumn wc $35
1889 57 On the Grand River near York $40
90 Old homestead near Ottawa $20
1890 102 On the road to Cantley $15
103 Morton Flats $20
104 Creek at Hones' Falls $15
105 Springtime $20
1891 52b Old mill near Lynmouth
116 Woodland pool
187 Autumn hillside wc
1892 100 Old windmill at Lachine wc $15
116 Burnham beeches wc $15
1893 150 A forest pool $20 F1-113
151 October $20 F1-114 nfs
152 Landscape $20 F1-115

1894 148 Fall ploughing
149 Spring time
1895 162 A hillside road
163 A misty morning
1896 181 Pier Rock at Bic, Quebec
182 Salt-hay stacks
183 Hillside at Bic
1897 63W Autumn glory wc
64W Chill October wc
65W Last of the leaves wc
66W Road scene wc
1898 229 November wc
230 In the woods wc
230a Larkspur wc
1900 190 Misty morning, Amherst Island wc
191 Autumn wc
1903 197 Red oaks at Amherst Island wc
198 After the storm wc
1904 170 October afternoon F4-83
1905 189 Hay making at Bic, Quebec
215-17 Small church 3 des
1906 189 On the road to Doon
190 October afternoon
1908 145 Harvest, at Bic, Quebec
1913 305 Fort Chambly
306 Dull November day, Driveway, Ottawa

WAY, ANNIE M.
fl 1899-15 H
Addr: 1899, Fraser Hall, 9 University St, Montreal; 1915, 31 ave de Rumine, Lausanne
1899 229 At Orta wc
230 The Matterhorn wc
1915 219 At Orta wc

WAY, CHARLES JONES
25 Jul 1835, Dartmouth, Eng 13 Feb 1919, Lausanne B DBA H Mo98/12 NGC TB W78
RCA Hon Non-res 1881 Ret 1913
Council Painter
Addr: 1881-92, Lausanne; 1893, Ospedaletti, Italy; 1894-6, c/o Masson & Cie, Pl St François, Lausanne; 1897-8, Lausanne; 1899-00, Fraser Hall, 9 University St, Montreal; 1901, c/o H.J. Matthews, Yonge St, Toronto; 1904-5, Lausanne, 1906-8, 14 Pl St François, Lausanne; 1909N-18, 31 ave de Rumine, Lausanne
1880 154 The morning catch wc
336 Birth of a torrent, Switzerland wc
336a A la fontaine, Suisse wc
1881 72 Approaching storm in the mountains wc $75
1882 126 Church of St Mark, Venice wc $150
135 Path to the glaciers wc $60
141 The clock tower at St Prex wc $40
146 The Perron, an Alpine peak near Mont Blanc wc $100 Artist's gift to National Gallery. 1970 cat listed, in error, as DW 1881. 15 x 21 3/4
152 The tinker, spring time in Swiss village wc $40
163 On guard, a study from life wc
166 The comrades, a study of larch and fir, the Matterhorn in the background wc $225
184 An Alpine bridge, near Zermath wc $125
191 Gate of Valuchois wc $25
1883 145 Boatbuilder's sheds, Venice wc $75
146 The Ghetto, Venice wc $40
162 Street at Estavayer, Switzerland wc $20
163 Chalets at Zinal wc $50
169 The Perron wc $75
180 An Alpine bridge wc $100
194 In the valley of the Zinal wc $200
222 Milking, Grand Cornier in the distance wc $100
288 Squally weather off Venice wc $40
1884 118 Twilight at Venice wc $60
122 Alpine gorge, view of Sans Fie wc $350
174 On the mountains, summer afternoon wc $100
1886 84a Madonna del Sasso, at Locarno wc $25
84b The brook wc $100
1888 68 Coal hulk at the mouth of the Dart wc $20
1889 169 A Devonshire fishing village, the sea fog coming in wc $200
171 A winter's morning at the foot of the Wetterhorn, Grundewald wc $300
174 A veteran wc $30
1890 208 Val Anzasaca wc $50
1892 112 Fisherman's home wc $30
1893 266 A pool in the valley of

the Rhone, Switzerland wc $300 F1-195
1894 195 Assunta da Cutigliano, a peasant wc
196 Children of the Apennines wc
1896 268 A basket maker of the Apennines wc
1899 231 Lady Franklin's Rock, Fraser River wc
232 Mount Van Horne, autumn sunset wc
233 On Orta's sacred mount wc
234 Victoria, BC, when east is west
235 Cattle ranch, near Mission wc
236 The coast of Devon wc
237 Approaching storm wc
238 Low tide, Victoria, BC wc
1900 185 The noonday gun at Quebec wc
186 The Falls of St Ann wc
187 Summer evening, Cap à l'Aigle wc
188 The Custom House, Quebec wc
1901 131 By the brook in autumn
217 By the shore of Lake Magog wc
218 Woodland road, autumn wc
219 Willow trees in Rosedale wc
220 An autumn afternoon, Lake Magog wc
221 One of the chapels, St Mark's, Venice wc
222 Monte Carlo, and Menton in the distance wc F2-76 F3-183 $60
1901 F2, Buffalo
75 Venice
1904 260 Port of London wc
261 The Tower Bridge wc
262 An autumn evening wc
1905 199 Autumn morning, Laggo Maggiore
200 The moon is up and yet it is not night
1906 176 By the shores of Maggiore
177 Fishermen's houses, Lake Maggiore
1907 288 Ruins of Tourbillon Sivre, Suisse wc
289 Fishermen's houses wc F6-166 $30
1907 F6, Sherbrooke
167 Path through the forest $130
1908 144 Evening, Tremezzo, Como
1909M 138 Rye, evening
139 In an English village churchyard
1909N 154 A Sussex road, near Winchelsea
155 Lake of Como, picking up chestnuts
156 Icklesham churchyard
157 Evening, Rye
1910 196 Entrance to Villa Carlotta, Como
197 Rain at Tremezzo, Como
1911 178 Menaggio, Lake of Como wc
1913 307 An old bridge in the Canton Tessin wc
308 The road to the village wc S4-136 $50
309 A Sussex stream wc
310 At Fittleworth, Sussex wc
311 Sussex meadow wc
1915 220 A mountain cascade wc
221 A mountain village near Orta wc
1918A 177 The mountain cascade wc
178 The Barbican Gate, Sandwich wc

WEBB, PETER JOHN
17 Apr 1927, Kent, Eng CWW79
1964N Webb, Zerafa, Menkès
178-82 Lothian Mews, Toronto. Exterior court, 2 views, and night view, one illus. Entry view. Ground plan

WEBBER, GORDON MCKINLEY
12 Mar 1909, Sault Ste Marie, Ont
1965, Montreal AGO CC2 TB2 WWA47
Addr: 1934-6, 142 Balsam Ave, Toronto
1934 194 Calm $40
1936 201 Portrait study $75

WEBER, KATHLEEN NICHOL (signs Kay Murray Weber)
5 Nov 1919, Ayr, Ont IO
RCA(e) 1977 Print maker
Addr: 1979, Toronto

WEBSTER, ADELAIDE DE LALLY (Mrs George Donald)
Addr: 1925-6, 131 Crescent St, Montreal; 1927, 1523 Crescent St, Montreal
1925 225 Jimmie 1926-144
226 The little Irish girl pastel

1927 227 The blue overall
1949 93 Mary Ann nfs
94 In the hill country, Jamaica $200
1959 80 John Neville 30 x 25

WEBSTER, JEFFREY C.
Addr: 1929, 57 Hallowell St, Westmount, Que
1929 293 Darwin Falls, Rawdon etch $15

WECHSLER, DORA HARRIS (Mrs John Wechsler)
12 Dec 1897, Ottawa 10 Dec 1952, Toronto
1946 147 And war came to an end cer $125
148 To-morrow's leaders sculp nfs
1948 178 A nine o'clock special cer $125
1949 123 'But Lot's wife looked back from behind him, and she became a pillar of salt' cer $250
1951 126 Why cer with silver leaf nfs

WEDIN, PETER
Addr: 1931, 3416 Peel St, Montreal
1931 293 Gossiping $40
294 In the evening $35

WEGSTEIN, ROBERT
1929, Bruges, Belgium
1965 123 Sculpture, Loyola Retreat House, Chapel, Guelph, Ont. Peter Thornton, architect

WEININGER, SYLVIA see SINGER, SYLVIA

WEISMAN, GUSTAV OSWALD
26 Apr 1926, Lithuania AGO
ARCA 1963 Council Designer
Addr: 1964-6, Toronto; 1967-71/79, Cedar Valley, Ont
1949 95 Firefighters nfs
1953 89 Through the little white doorway $125
1954 89 The farewell kiss wc 30 x 20 illus nfs
1957 69 Land and sky fragments $250
1964J 66 Night comes over the land 24 x 38 nfs
1964N 62 Near Hockley 24 x 38 $250
1966 177 Fluid cross leaded antique glass circular 32"

WERNER, CHARLOTTE
Addr: 1976, Winnipeg
1976 S12, Montreal
166 Interrupted flow system #1 ink on paper 30 x 42 illus

WEST, BENJAMIN (Sir) English
10 Oct 1738, Springfield, Pa 10 Mar 1820, London, Eng B G Gr TB
1881 336 Chief Justice Strange (loan)

WESTMACOTT, E.K. (Mrs)
fl 1874-90 d 1890 H
1885 88 Rhododendrons $50

WESTON, JAMES L.
c 1815 d 1896 H
ARCA 1880-5 Painter
Addr: 1880-5, Montreal
1880 33 Study of grapes
235 Market place, Dieppe, France wc
273 Mrs Scott-Siddons litho
1881 121 Title page des for competition
172 Iron railing des
173 Tankard des
174 Portfolio covers des
175 Vase des
176 Panel des for competition
247 The young home ruler $20
270 Killing time on a frosty night $80
276 A midnight alarm $200
291 Little sunshine and showers
326 Portrait plaque
1882 18 Meditation, portrait
26 Waiting for a job $60
30 The little scullery maid $45
94 Cedar Rapids, from St Timothy $95
98 Misty morning on the Mersey $100
129 The old York redoubt, Halifax wc $43
192 Point Levis toll gate wc $70
1890 209 Early morning, Chateauguay Island wc $25
210 Study wc $40

WESTON, WILLIAM PERCY
3 Nov 1879, London, Eng 20 Dec

1967, Vancouver CC2 CWW64 NGC TB2 WWA47
ARCA 1936 Sr 1949 Painter
Addr: 1930-7, 1045 West 15th Ave, Vancouver; 1938-67, Vancouver
1930 224 Solitude drwg $25
1931 295 Peaks of silence $450
296 Scrub pine, west coast $400
1932 199 Jotunheim $450
200 Winter solitude $450
1933 236 Desolation $400
1934 195 Castaways $450
196 Whytecliffe $400 T35-70
1935 258 Hollyburn Ridge $350 T36-69
259 Tangled beach $400
1936 202 The summit $350 T37-63
203 Gleneagles, BC $350
1937 226 Shadows, Grouse Mountain $350
227 The booming ground $350 T38-57
330 Windswept pen drwg $75
1938 221 Life force $350
222 Flood tide $350 T39-56
223 Winter phantasy $400
1939 235 Old age $350
236 Hill top $350
1939 F11, New York
68 Castaways, Vancouver Island 42 x 36 $400
1940 154 Horseshoe Bay $300 T41-54
1941 193 British Columbia coast $300 T42-55
194 Dead pine $300
1942 147 Yale, BC $300
148 The white church, Vancouver Island $200 T43-48
149 Spring $150
1943 116 Devil's club $150
117 Swamp $100 T44-38
1944 137 Foxglove $200
138 Close of the day $175 T45-41
1945 203 Glacier Mountain, thunder weather nfs
204 Cradle of the clouds $175
1946 124 Swamp lanterns illus $250 T47-53
125 Mount Denver, BC $200
1948 155 Golden Ears $300
1949 96 Defiance, west coast fir $300
1950 149 Anvil Island, Howe Sound 32 x 27 $300
1951 103 Drift logs, Kew Beach, BC $300
1952 94 Rock forms, Restmore, BC $300

WHALE, ROBERT REGINALD
13 Mar 1805, Altarnun, Cornwall, Eng
8 Jul 1887, Brantford, Ont H NGC W78
ARCA 1881 Painter
Addr: 1881-7, Brantford, Ont
1881 248 Portrait of a lady
1882 50 Dr J.Y. Brown
64 Lucius Richard O'Brien, Pres RCA
1883 133 Up in the White Mountains sold
1886 26 Canadian red fox $50

WHATMOUGH, GRANT ALAN
24 May 1921, Toronto IO
1963 106 Elan Vitale sculp wd $900
1964N 88 Prototype sculp 19 x 12 $500
1965 97 Minotaur mahogany 22 x 24 x 19 $900
1966 88 Determinate form sculp 20 x 21 x 16 illus $825

WHEELER, ALICE A.
H
1888 148 The mandolin $20

WHEELER, ORSON SHOREY
17 Sep 1902, Barnston, Que CWW79 NGC TB2 WWA47
ARCA 1939 RCA 1954 Sr 1971 Council Sculptor
Addr: 1931-7, 1441 Drummond St, Montreal; 1940-71/79, Montreal
1931 343 Audrey plaster bronze $200
1932 225 Rev Archd Scott bronze $300
1933 272 Fenya plaster
1934 207 Negro plaster stone $450
1935 295 Christopher plaster nfs
296 Hilda plaster nfs
1936 228 Louise plaster nfs
1937 294 Mrs Edward I. Frost plaster nfs
295 Sir Edward Beatty bronze nfs
1938 244 Archd Frederick George Scott plaster
1939 263 E.E. Boothroyd, Esq, MA DCL VP Bishop's University

plaster illus nfs 1940-163
1941 224 Portrait of my mother plaster nfs
1942 174 Robert J. Meekren, Esq plaster nfs
1943 138 Rt Hon Sir Lyman Duff, PC GCMG, Chief Justice of Canada plaster nfs
1944 153 Harry A. Norton, Esq plaster nfs
1945 235 Mary Johnson plaster nfs 1946-149
1947 219 Dr K.E. Norris, Prin Sir George Williams College plaster nfs
1948 179 Pauline Johnson plaster
1949 124 John T. Hackett, Esq KC LLD DCL plaster nfs
1951 127 Prof John Bland plaster nfs
1952 113 J. Harry Smith, Esq sculp nfs 1953-125
1955 118 Douglas Burns Clarke sculp nfs 1958-95
1959 94 Dr W.P. Percival sculp illus nfs
1961 90 Hugh M. Wallis sculp illus
DW 1955 Head of a girl bronze 13h

WHITE, GEORGE HARLOW English
1817, London, Eng 18 Dec 1887, Charter House, London, Eng AGO B DBA G H NGC TB W78
RCA Hon Non-res 1881 Painter
Addr: 1881-7, Charter House, London
1880 230 Fairy Glen, Foss Noddyn, north Wales wc (AGO)
234 The stepping stones, north Wales wc (Hon E. Blake)
236 In the Lledr Valley, north Wales wc
328 Windsor Castle wc (W. Kingsford)
1881 13 Bettws-y-coed, north Wales wc $35
54 Traus Afron, north Wales wc $50
82 Cripplegate Church wc (T. M. Martin)
230 Fruit $30
1882 139 and 189 The ferry, Windsor wc $20 each
155 Windsor, from Eaton playfields wc $20
209 Durham wc $14
1883 206 On the road to Harlech wc $50
251 Barmouth wc $20
255 Gothland, north Wales wc $40
257 Mawddack River, north Wales wc $20
274 Rye Church, Sussex, England wc $25
278 Covent Garden Market, London, England wc $15
285 Glan Rhyde wc $40
292 Stepping stones, River Conway wc $20
1884 102 Windsor Castle wc $25 S1-17
107 Streetly, Berkshire wc $20
116 Ruins of the old Roman bridge, Pandy, north Wales wc $20
133 Stirling Castle, Scotland wc $30
145 Mountain tops, Carnarvonshire wc $30 S1-16
147 On the Arthog Mountain wc $40
150 Stirling on the River Forth, Scotland wc $30 S1-10
153 Near Dolgelly, north Wales wc $50
155 Conway Castle, north Wales wc $50 S1-44 $30
157 Cell Faur, north Wales wc $50 S1-20 $25
167 Doune Castle, Scotland wc $30
172 Pangbourne, on the Thames wc $30 S1-11
178 Windsor Castle wc $20 S1-17 $25
1884 S1, Saint John
31 An old pine wc $20
1885 207 River Wye wc $22
208 Tunbridge, Kent wc $22
209 Kent Valley wc $22
210 River Medway wc $22
218, 240, 282 and 297 Landscape wc $22 each
1886 47 The Kent Valley wc $20
51 The River Wye wc $20
54 Kirting on the River Forth, Scotland wc $20
57 Fisherman's quarters, Hastings wc $20
60 Hastings, Sussex wc $20
82 Tunbridge, Kent wc $20
87 The Wye, Herefordshire wc $20
The River Conway, north Wales. Artist's gift to

National Gallery. 1970 cat listed, in error, as DW 1885 wc 15 1/4 x 34 3/4

WHITE, JOSEPHINE H.J.
Addr: 1926 c/o Roberts Art Gallery, 20 Grenville St, Toronto
1926 145 L'Ecole Maternelle, St Jean de Luz, France

WHITE, MARGARET E.
1950 150 Maple trees 18 x 24 nfs

WHITE, WALTER HARRY
14 Apr 1901, Toronto
Addr: 1923, 526 Clinton St, Toronto
1923 209 Autumn landscape

WHITE-BEAVEN, MARTIN H.
1964N 87 Subdivided sculp 34 x 39 $250
1965 69 Shoreline drwg 24 x 29 $75

WHITNEY, ELIZABETH
fl 1876-98 H
Addr: 1893, Victoria School of Art, Montreal
1893 267 Vase, imitation Royal Worcester nfs
268 Tray, autumn leaf dec in matt cols $10
269 Plate, imitation Royal Berlin nfs
270 Bon-bon plate, imitation Doulton dec nfs
271 Cup and saucer glazed cols $4
272 Dessert plate matt cols $6

WHITTOME, IRENE
5 Mar 1942, Vancouver WWA78
RCA(e) 1978 Sculptor
Addr: 1979, Montreal

WHITTON, GRACE
Addr: 1938, Toronto
1938 S8, Toronto
380 Wallpaper design. Hon mention, Canadian Wallpaper Manufacturers Limited

WHYTE, ETHEL A.
H
1898 233a Landscape wc

WHYTE, REGINALD F.
Addr: 1912-14, Winnipeg
1912 S3, Winnipeg
256 Winter in Manitoba
257 Sunset on the Assiniboine
258 Assiniboine River
259 River at Deer Lodge
1914 S4, Winnipeg
179 The ferry $30
180 The dying day $35
181 The bend of the river $25

WICKENDEN, ROBERT JOHN American
8 Jul 1861, Rochester, Eng 28 Nov 1931, Brooklyn, NY AAA31 B H Mo12 TB2
Addr: 1899, Montreal; 1902-5, 3 Beaver Hall Sq, Montreal; 1916, 88 Stanley St, Montreal; 1925, 1295 St Antoine Rd, Montreal
1899 144 G.M. Fairchild
145 Sunset on the Oise (Hon Mr Atwater)
146 Notre Dame
1902 160 Sleep, poppy-crowned Arthur J. mispr, addr R.J.
161 An Outremont sunset
162 Mrs George Fairchild, Jr
163 The ripening grain, plain of Anvers
1904 171 Autumn evening
326 Notre Dame de Paris b&w
1905 193 The queen of the night
194 The hayfield
195 La mère Pannecaye auto-litho
196 The pioneer auto-litho
1916 232 Portrait
318 Sir Thomas More, after A. Durer etch
319 Portrait crayon
1925 227 Moonrise, Blue Sea Lake

WICKSON, ALEXANDER FRANK
30 Mar 1861, Toronto 22 Dec 1936, Toronto PMC
see DICK, DAVID BRASH, 1895

WICKSON, PAUL GIOVANNI
1860, Toronto 2 Sep 1922, Paris, Ont H Mo12 R1 TB W78
ARCA 1890-01 Painter
Addr: 1881, London, Eng; 1884-01, Paris, Ont
1881 35 Waiting wc $50
60 In the Cliffwood, Yorkshire wc $15 1882-120
86 Wilton Grange, Yorkshire wc $15
92 A Yorkshire village wc $15

1884 38 The dawn of genius $200
79 One of many $100 S1-155
P.G. Wixon mispr
1885 62 The end of the week $125
67 Sound on the Goose $500
1886 12 Hiawatha $360
1886 Fla, London, Eng
2023, artist number
The young artist (Marquis of Lansdowne)
1888 131 A thorn in the flesh
1890 106 A Scottish borderer $100
107 Success $250
1891 219 Pick of the flock
228 Bensville smithy
1892 2 A professional opinion $250
76 The bridesmaid $500
1893 address listed, no work exhibited
1893 F1, Chicago
117 At duty's call
1894 133 Mrs Paul Wickson
1896 184 Startled

WIELAND, JOYCE (Mrs Michael Snow)
30 Jun 1931, Toronto AGO B CC1 Co IO WWA73
RCA(e) 1973 Painter
Addr: 1979, Toronto
1971 Watersark film screened 21 Apr

WIENS, CLIFFORD
27 Apr 1926, Glen Kerr, Sask
ARCA 1971 Architect
Addr: 1979, Regina
1964N 183-6 Mennonite Brethren Church. General exterior view. Front exterior view. General interior. Interior view, detail showing lecturn
1970 51A-6A St Mark's Shop, Lumsden, Sask. Valley view. Winter view. Interior views, 2. Tunnel view. Plan of candle shop and casting studio
1971 51A-4A Silton Chapel, Silton, Sask. View of chapel font. Early morning mass. View of chapel sanctuary. Floor plan and cross section of chapel

WIESENBERG, LOUIS
Addr: 1924, 39 Crescent St, Montreal
1924 210 The bridge, Laurentian Mountains

WIETHASE, EDGARD Belgian
31 Aug 1881, Antwerp 16 Apr 1965, Uccle, Belgium B TB2
Addr: 1910, Antwerp
1910 198 Floraison
199 Village sous la neige

WIGGINS, W.H.
1971 141 Barbeque. Candesign

WIGGS, HENRY ROSS
28 Dec 1895, Quebec CNS47 CWW79 PMC
ARCA 1943 Sr 1965 Council Architect
Addr: 1933, Architects Bldg, Montreal; 1937, 630 Dorchester St W, Montreal; 1938-71, Montreal; 1979, Hamilton, Ont
1933 247 Small stone house
248 French Canadian cottage
1937 265 Proposed residence, Bridgetown, Nova Scotia
266 Proposed residence, Town of Mount Royal, Quebec
1942 158 Buildings, Mont Tremblant Lodge, Mont Tremblant, Que 1943-121 photo
1943 122 Residence, G. Edwin Robertson, Esq photo
1945 241 Verney Mills, Granby, Que
242 Textile plant, Ormstown, Quebec

WILCOX, CHARLES RICHARD
Addr: 1928, 58 Queen St, Halifax; 1931, 58 Rosehill Ave, Toronto
1928 240 Old house, Halifax etch
1931 440 The hoist etch $10
441 Under the wharf etch $10

WILCOX, GEORGIE M. CRAWFORD (Mrs Howard Buell Wilcox)
b 1889 flg 1951
Addr: 1912, Winnipeg
1912 S3, Winnipeg
260 Still life

WILDMAN, SALLY
2 Aug 1939, Tynemouth, Eng
RCA(e) 1978 Painter
Addr: 1979, Claremont, Ont

WILKES, ELIZABETH
Addr: 1937, 9 Prince Arthur Ave, Toronto
1937 228 Orchids wc $25
1942 150 Dogwood bloom wc $25
151 Snow flurries wc $25 T43-49
1945 205 Snow pine wc $75

206 Pattern in white and gold wc $75

WILKIE, MARION E.
fl 1895 H
Addr: 1895, 132 Sherbourne St, Toronto
1895 91 A girl's head, portrait wc

WILKINS, LOUISA A.
fl 1879-06 H
Addr: 1906, Windsor, NS
1906 F5, Halifax
163 Daisy the young Guernsey $10

WILKINSON, JOHN CRAIG SEATON (JACK)
18 Dec 1927, Windsor, Ont
RCA(e) 1978 Painter
Addr: 1979, Victoria

WILKINSON, THOMAS HARRISON
1847, Bradford, Yorks, Eng 1929, Hamilton, Ont H
1888 263 Patras in the Gulf of Corinth wc $50
1891 195 Evening near McKeller, Parry Sound wc
198 Winter in Muskoka wc

WILLARD, ERNVA A.
Addr: 1923, 65 Spencer Ave, Toronto
1923 175 Sunlit shops

WILLIAMS, F.D.
H
1882 96 The facteur's cottage at Cernay $250

WILLIAMS, INGLIS SHELDON see SHELDON-WILLIAMS, INGLIS

WILLIAMS, IVOR
Addr: 1918, 930 Burnsill Ave, Collingwood E, Vancouver
1918A 285 The Lions, BC chalk
1918N 197 Evening sky pastel
254 Vancouver, city pencil

WILLIAMS, JOHN C.
1947 181 Portrait of Jean pastel nfs

WILLIAMS, JOHN G.
Addr: 1918A, 107 Ontario St, St Catharines, Ont
1918A 286 and 287 Illuminated manuscript

WILLIAMS, M. BERTHA
H
Addr: 1898, 724 Spadina Ave, Toronto
1898 232 White roses wc
233 Petunias wc

WILLIAMS, MARGARET ADELAIDE
6 Jan 1902, Fort Qu'Appelle, Sask
Addr: 1934, 1103 Robson St, Vancouver; 1936, 114 King's Rd W, North Vancouver
1934 197 Rocky coast $30
198 Lone tree $30
1936 204 Mountains of Lynn $30

WILLIAMS, RICHARD EMERSON
b 1921
1954 91 Mennonite with mooncake 24 x 30 illus $150

WILLIAMS, YVONNE
9 Sep 1901, Port of Spain, Trinidad TB2
ARCA 1957 RCA 1964 Sr 1971 Council
Designer
Addr: 1935, 81A Wellesley St, Toronto; 1958-71/79, Toronto
1935 348 The Nativity st gl des nfs
349 Jubilee window st gl des nfs
1960 71 Memory of Stratford st gl 28 x 24 $300
1970 98 Example of double glass installation st gl 18 x 41 $1,000
DW 1965 St Bernard's Hospital, Toronto. st gl window des col inks on plastic 23 1/2 x 23

WILLIAMSON, ALBERT CURTIS
2 Jan 1867, Brampton, Ont 18 Apr 1944, Toronto AGO B CCI H Mo12 NGC PMC TB2 W78
ARCA 1894 RCA 1907 Ret 1934 Council
Painter
Addr: 1894, Equity Chambers, Toronto; 1904, Toronto; 1905, 28 Toronto St, Toronto; 1906-13, Yonge St Arcade, Toronto; 1914-30, Studio Bldg, 25 Severn St, Toronto; 1931-44, Toronto
1894 134 On the way to the village
135 A Brolles interior (NGC)
136 Embers
137 Philomene

1904 172 Klaasje F4-84 1908-140 ◊NGC◊
173 Old gigs
174 Old Jaap
175 Toil and trouble F4-85
176 Sifting beans
177 The bachelor F4-86 1905-203 1906-174
178 A Dutch Granny 1905-202
179 Normandy peasant F4-87
180 Head of a hag
181 Old man in blue coat F4-88
1905 201 Cornelius
204 Normandy interior
205 Hungry Piet
206 J.S. Williams, Esq
1906 170 Little Dutch maid 1907-197
171 An aged clergyman 1907-199 Methodist minister 1908-141 Portrait of my great-uncle 1909N-158 S2-111 A pioneer preacher ◊AGO An old clergyman◊
172 Dutch witch
173 French landscape
175 Dutch interior
1907 196 Interior
198 Jantje
200 An impression, Newfoundland
1908 142 and 143 Interior
1910 S2, Liverpool
109 Study in scarlet 1912-229
110 Archibald Browne, Esq 1912-228
1911 179 Portrait
180 Study in black
1912 227 William Cruikshank, Esq, RCA 1916-233 illus
1912 S3, Winnipeg
148 Newfoundland landscape
149 Portrait, Mrs C.
1913 312 Colored girl
313 Colored woman
314 Winter twilight
315 Portrait study
1914 S5, Patriotic Fund
67 A Dutchman illus
1918N 189 A cynic 1919-165 illus ◊NGC◊
1919 166 Newton MacTavish, Esq
1921 172 Dr Alexander McPhedran, Medical Faculty (University of Toronto) illus
1924 211 Dr F.G. Banting illus
1927 228 Sir William Mulock, Chancellor, Toronto University
1930 167 George H. Locke
DW 1908 Dutch interior 27 1/2 x 23 1/2
port: by J.W. Russell, 1909N-130

WILLIAMSON, ELEANOR (Mrs)
1939 237 Harlem belles $40
1941 195 Lotus blossom pastel $75
196 Phyllis pastel nfs
1942 152 The buckskin jacket pastel $50
1947 182 Anne pastel $50
183 Study of an artist head pastel nfs
1948 156 Redhead pastel nfs

WILLIAMSON, JOHN
1971 78G Booklist, School volunteers program, Canadian Mental Health Association
79G Poster, Canadian Industrial Editors Asscoiation

WILLING, JOHN THOMSON
5 Aug 1860, Toronto flg 1931 AAA 30 B F H TB
ARCA 1884-8 Designer
Addr: 1885-8, Toronto
1880 283 Book covers des prize award Jas. T mispr
1883 318 Wood engraver at work b&w
328 Christmas cards 4 des $35

WILSON, ALAN DENT
5 Aug 1923, Toronto
1942 153 Canadian sea cadet wc $200 T43-50

WILSON, ARTHUR G.
Addr: 1920, 1 Belmont St, Montreal
1920 257 The girl with the white cat wc

WILSON, JAMES
c1855, Montreal 31 Aug 1932, Pickanock, Que H
Addr: 1894-5, Sparks St, Ottawa; 1896-18, 123 Sparks St, Ottawa; 1923-31, 108 Sparks St, Ottawa
1883 108 Sketch
116 On the river
1884 3 Soon cometh the winter with the iron hand $35
1884 S1, Saint John
75 Gatineau Lake $35
79 Solitude $20

1885 162 Woodland brook $35
164 Calm lakeside $35
165 Early spring $25
166 Landscape
179 Winter $50
182 Moonlight
1886 37 Sketch on the River Seine, Paris, France $20
145 Misty moonlight, Loch Katrine sold
153 The lone hillside $50
172 Winter make speed to come $50
1887 91 Sketch at eventide $15
1889 62 Twilight $35
71 A sea wave $15
1890 108 Woodland retreat $35
1891 57 Old trees on the banks of the Ottawa
175 The brook, Eddyville wc
1892 70 When the tide is low $75
144 Wild woodland stream wc $100
1894 150 Sunset
1895 151 At the decline of day
152 September day
153 Spring on the Ottawa
1896 185 On the St Lawrence at Bic
1897 147 Spring
148 A September day
1903 132 Morning after the storm
1904 263 In the silence of the night
1905 190 La nuit
1906 187 Spring, old beechwood
188 On the edge of the sea
1907 290 Mountain peaks, Upper Spray Valley wc
1909M 143 Peaks of the Rockies
1912 230 A grey morning, Meach's Lake
231 Valley of the Peaks wc
1913 316 Clearing after rain, Percé S4-139 $30 nfs
317 Sunshine and shadow, Island of Bonaventure
1915 222 The distant hills, Percé
1916 234 Tumbling sea, Isle Bonaventure
1918A 179 Tumbling sea
1918N 199 Gatineau woodland
200 The afterglow
1923 176 Clearing weather, Percé
1924 212 Moonrise, Bay des Chaleurs
1927 229 Corner of the beach, Percé
1929 218 Corner of the beach $125
1931 297 Moonlight, Percé
port: by E. Fosbery, 1930-53

WILSON, JOHN A.
Addr: 1902, Pope Bldg, Boston; 1905, 277 Jarvis St, Toronto
1902 293 South Africa plaster model
1905 191 The tugs rendezvous, Chicago River
192 A harbor slip, Chicago

WILSON, MARGARET ETHELREDA
b Irondale, Ont
Addr: 1934-6, 89 Breadalbane St, Toronto; 1937, 50 Gerrard St E, Toronto
1934 199 Laughing water dec panel $200
200 Summer phantasy dec panel $200 T35-71
1935 260 Winter arabesque $400
261 Haliburton pioneer $400
1936 205 Fun and frolic $600
1937 229 Frost jewelled morning $400 T38-58
1938 224 The cave of the gnomes $350 1939-239 $300
225 Elfin frolics $250
1939 238 A woodland sanctuary $400

WILSON, PERCY ROY
19 May 1900, Birmingham, Eng
ARCA 1937-68 Architect
Addr: 1931, 58 Belvedere Rd, Westmount, Que; 1935, 5021 Victoria Ave, Montreal; 1937, 42 Sunnyside Ave, Westmount, Que, res; 1050 Beaver Hall Hill, Montreal; 1938-57, Westmount, Que; 1958-68, Beaurepaire, Que
1931 377 Ponte Pietra, Verona pastel $20
378 Door of the quarry, Les Baux pastel $15
1935 262 Baths of Caracalla, Rome wc $25 1938-227 $30
263 Castle of the Scaligers, Verona wc nfs
1937 267 Far Hills Inn and Country Club, near Val Morin
Wilson & Auld
268 Proposed residence, Stanstead College
269-70 Residence, F.T. Parker, Esq, Westmount
1938 226 Pont Valentré, Cahors wc $60 T39-57

228 The tall timbers wc $50
1939 240 Church of St Francis Assisi wc $25 1940-155
289 Mill and Quebec gate, Museum Village
290 A community theatre
291 Library, King Hall, Compton
287-8 Residence, Mr and Mrs W.G. McConnell, St Marguerite, Quebec. Wilson & Auld
1940 165 Study for open air museum, Mount Royal
1947 184 On the trail wc nfs
196 Country house, Ralph C. Bulman, Esq
197 Remodelled façade, 1458 Crescent Street
1948 189 A.B. Thompson house, Chantecler Hills, St Adèle
190 Chancel redecoration, St Matthias Church, Westmount
1957 108 Tower, St Thomas Church, Montreal

WILSON, RONALD YORK
6 Dec 1907, Toronto AGO CC1 CWW79 IO NGC TB2 WWA47
ARCA 1945 RCA 1948 Council Painter
Addr: 1946-71/79, Toronto
1941 197 Welfare worker $350 T42-56
1944 139 Pie social at Willisville $350 T45-42
1945 207 Head table $400
208 The march past $400 T46-47 (BAG)
1946 126 Young dancer $350 T47-54
127 Indian Harbour illus $450 T47-55
1947 185 Beauty contest illus $450 T48-41
1948 157 Feheley nfs
1949 97 Dancing class illus nfs DW 1949 25 x 40 T51-42 1954 Retro Sec 52
1950 151 The mill 40 x 28 $400
1951 104 White figures of Acambay duco (AGO)
105 Guanajuato duco illus
1952 95 Toluca market duco
1953 90 Fez, Morocco pyroxalin illus $450
91 De Lall
1953 Travelling exhibit
33 Moroccan conversation piece $600
1954 90 Figure 48 x 32 illus $600
1955 85 Moroccans illus $600
1956 45 'Come unto me' illus
1957 70 Winter beginning illus $750
1958 83 Venice illus $500
1959 81 Caribbean port 30 x 40 illus $900
1960 72 Landscape 30 x 40 illus $900
73 Ontario abstraction 24 x 32 $600
1963 77 Dragozzi $1,800
1964J 67 Sailing Carthage 76 x 52 illus $1,800
1964N 63 Endymion 51 x 77 illus $1,800 S10-73
1965 79 The port, Honfleur 51 x 38 $1,200 S10-72
1966 69 King Christophe 76 x 51 $1,800
1967 73 Fiesta 75 x 45 illus $1,800
1968 54 Flight 51 x 63 illus $1,650
1970 76 Kabuki 40 x 80 illus $1,700
1971 46 Tribute to Lawren Harris 52 x 60 illus $1,700

WINDEAT, EMMA S.
b Brockville, Ont d 1926 H
ARCA 1887-08 Painter
Addr: 1887-93, Toronto; 1894-01, 46 Cecil St, Toronto; 1902, Toronto; 1903-5, Indian Rd, Toronto; 1906-7, Toronto; 1908, Indian Rd Cr, Toronto
1887 158 A corner of a studio wc $35 E.L. Windeal mispr
1894 151 Silver poplars
1895 159 Herring Cove
160 Near Shimicook
161 George Gordon
91W Sketch wc
1897 60W Interior wc
1898 123 Willows and pool
124 Summer afternoon
125 Reflections
126 On St Lawrence, near Berthier en Haut
127 Isle du Pas
231 Cloud effects wc
1899 147 Old mill, East Lyme, Conn
1901 128 Landscape
129 Rocky woodland, a study
130 Berthier en Haut
1903 127 Landscape
1905 197 A shady pathway
198 A morning in February
1907 F6, Sherbrooke
168 Landscape, Berthier en Haut $30

169 Cutting oats, Shediac $30
170 Marsh lands near Toronto $30
1908 147 The deserted mill
148 Willows
149 By the river

WINDEYER, RICHARD CUNNINGHAM
1830, Fort Amherst, Chatham, Kent, Eng 24 Mar 1900, Toronto
ARCA 1880-8 Architect
Addr: 1880-8, Toronto
1883 349 All Saints Church, Toronto

WINKLER, FRIEDRICH (FRED, FRITZ)
5 Sep 1898, Weimar, Germany d 1974
Addr: 1931, 12 Kew Beach Ave, Toronto; 1936, 6 Sherwood Ave, Toronto
1931 344 Sea gull bronze, silver galvanized $600 Fred Winkler
1936 229 Canadian goose, garden fountain, R.S. McLaughlin, Esq, Oshawa Fritz Winkler

WINSLOW, MARJORIE SCARTH (Mrs)
10 Dec 1907, Montreal
Addr: 1933, 3636 McTavish St, Montreal
1933 273 Under a fountain plaster $15
1939 264 P.S. Stevenson, Esq sculp nfs
1941 198 Out of joint wc $20
225 Brigadier Beeman sculp nfs
1944 154 André Bieler, ARCA sculp illus
1945 236 Gertrude Baskine sculp nfs
237 Robert sculp nfs
1947 222 Richard Jack, RA, RCA sculp

WINTER, WILLIAM ARTHUR
27 Aug 1909, Winnipeg AGO B CC2 CWW79 IO NGC TB2 WWA47
ARCA 1947 RCA 1954 Painter
Addr: 1948-71/79, Toronto
1945 209 Monday $200
1946 128 Bathers by moonlight $300 T47-56
1948 158 Brother and sister illus $300
1949 98 Winter on the Ottawa $250 T50-20
1950 152 Driftwood 20 x 32 $300
153 Souvenirs 20 x 32 $300
1951 106 Beginning of the day $275
1952 96 Midgets $400
1953 92 Tree fort illus $500
1953 Travelling exhibit
54 Stilts $350
1957 71 Paper flowers illus $300
1963 76 The tree 24 x 30 illus $400
DW 1955 Street scene 24 x 30

WINTERBOTTOM, FRED R.
1940 156 Peonies $250
1942 154 Mixed flowers $200
1944 140 Peonies nfs

WISE, JACK MARLOWE
27 Apr 1928, Centerville, Iowa
WWA76
RCA(e) 1978 Painter
Addr: 1979, Victoria

WISE, ROLAND
19 Jun 1923, San Francisco
1954 92 Communion 50 x 45 $200 Rolland Wise, mispr

WISEMAN, JAMES LOVELL
16 Feb 1847, Montreal 13 Jan 1912, Montreal H
Addr: 1886, 162 St James St, Montreal
1886 Fla, London, Eng
2033, artist number
Wood engravings, portraits, views, etc

WITHROW, WILFRED F.
Addr: 1936, 90 Ellerslie Ave, Willowdale, Ont
1936 206 Autumn, Haliburton wc $25
1938 229 The lake road, Haliburton wc $40
230 Ingoldsby farm, Haliburton wc $40

WOEST, HEINZ
1971 151 Rug, Harding Carpet Ltd

WOLFE, GEORGE English
11 Jan 1834, Bristol, Eng 1890, Clifton, Eng B DBW G TB
1881 33 Coast scene wc (Lady MacDougall) Wolfe

WOLFFEL, LILO R. (Mrs)
1953 93 Beach $280

WOLINSKY, EVA
20 Apr 1925, Budapest
1955 119 Pensive mood sculp $150

1957 90 The night is long sculp nfs

WOLSLEY, JOHN
1948 159 Tenby, south Wales wc $120

WOLTER, HENDRICK JAN Dutch
15 Jul 1873, Amsterdam 1952, Laren, Netherlands B TB1/2
Addr: 1899, Amersfoort, Holland
1899 151 A Dutch canal, early spring

WONG, PAUL C.
19 Oct 1933, Hong Kong
1967 76 Spirit 72 x 96 $1,200

WOOD, ALAN
1935, Widnes, Lincs, Eng
RCA(e) 1978 Painter
Addr: 1979, North Vancouver

WOOD, CANDACE
H
Addr: 1883, New York
1883 39 Little Bo-peep $125

WOOD, ELIZABETH WYN (Mrs Emanuel Hahn)
8 Oct 1903, Orillia, Ont 27 Jan 1966, Toronto AGO CC1 Co CWW61 EC NGC TB2 W78 WWA47
ARCA 1929 RCA 1951 Sculptor
Addr: 1926, Orillia, Ont; 1927-35, 32 Adelaide St E, Toronto; 1936-66, Toronto
1926 169 Head of a negress bronze ‖NGC‖
170 Mourning woman sculp tin
1927 274 Winnipeg War Memorial des photo
1928 178 Caesar George sculp
1930 194 Gesture marble $1,600
195 Narcisse bronze $1,800
1931 345 Narcisse Pelletier bronze $1,400
346 Circular relief limestone $800
1932 226 Linda sketch model tin $225
267 Islands crayon $30
268 Reefs crayon $30
269 Rock crayon $30
1933 274 Linda plaster des, bronze or alum $3,000
1934 232 Stump crayon $15
233 and 234 Stumps crayon $15 each
1935 297 Immigrant plaster, granite $500
298 Reef and rainbow tin $450 ‖AGO‖
299 Woman holding skein plaster, alum $600
1940 164 Girl with trillium plaster, alum $700
1941 226 Garden wall rel, working model, plaster nfs
1941 S9, Toronto
61 Woman with grain, Man with pine plaster pair $50
1944 155 Blizzard alum $700
1948 180 Saskatchewan, panel, Bank of Montreal, Toronto working model plaster for stone Marani & Morris architects
1951 129 Stephen Leacock memorial, Orillia Public Library, working model
130 Regeneration plaster illus marble $480
1956 53 Katerie Tekakwitha hydrocol $1,000
1957 91 Fountain CNIB. Austin Floyd landscape architect nfs photo
92 Queen Elizabeth Building, Theatre, CNE mural sculp Page & Steele architects
1963 105 Tree at night sculp $400
DW 1952 Torso tin 8 1/4 h

WOOD, FAITH
21 Sep 1917, Devon, Eng IO
1942 155 Mary Laura $150
1952 97 Barbara $150

WOOD, GEORGE W.
see HUTCHISON, ALEXANDER C, 1897, 1907

WOOD, MARSHALL English
d Jul 1882, Brighton, Eng B G TB
1880 145 Sir John A. Macdonald marble bust

WOOD, WILLIAM JOHN
26 May 1877, Ottawa 4 Jan 1954, Midland, Ont AGO CC2 TB2
Addr: 1931, 275 1st St, Midland, Ont
1931 298 At home $300
442 Eva etch $5

WOODCOCK, PERCY FRANKLIN
17 Aug 1855, Athens, Ont 1936,

Montreal B CCI H Mo12 NGC PMC TB1/2 ARCA 1883 RCA 1886 Ret 1934 Council Painter
Addr: 1883-6, Brockville, Ont; 1887-9, Montreal; 1890-2, Brockville, Ont; 1893, 162 E 48th St, New York; 1894-02, New York; 1903, c/o Scott & Son, Montreal; 1904-6, no addr; 1907, Brockville; 1908-10, no addr; 1911-14, New York; 1915-18, Windsor Hotel, Montreal; 1919, 99 Notre Dame St W, Montreal; 1920-4, Windsor Hotel, Montreal; 1925, c/o Scott & Son, Montreal; 1926-34, Montreal

1882 27 The page off duty $75
36 A winter's study $100
47 Mending nets $200
55 The young mother $250
67 A study
78 Reverie $700
113 In the sulks

1883 37 The late return $50
87 The facteur's cottage $50

1884 1 By the river in a French village
5 Home by the willows, France
6 Twilight, behind the village church, France
11 Italian boy
81 Evening at Cerna la Ville

1886 3 The disappointment $500
146 Returning from the well $500 DW 1886 43 1/2 x 33 1/2 Fla-2024 1954 Retro Sec 9
155 The abandoned nest $500 Fla-2024, artist number

1890 109 Fin du jour
110 The last ray on Mount Stephen
111 Glacier stream at foot of Mount Sir Donald $125
112 Glacier stream at foot of Green Glacier $125
113 Water Lily Bay $60 1891-13 1903-130
114 The first ray on Mount Field $75
115 Winter $50
116 October evening $60

1891 12 A lowery day
14 Italian street singer
15 Coming snow storm
17 Souvenir au Grand Noir
34 Souvenir de Freneuse
37 Snowed up
38 Among the Thousand Islands
39 Femme d'Orient
40 Canadian winter evening

1892 18 Cabbage garden $100
19 Mail carrier $100
33 Farmyard $100
36 The country in November $150
41 Old mill at St Hilaire $45
58 Early morning $50

1893 153 The creek $150 F1-116

1903 129 Golden rod
131 Summer evening

1907 201 A misty morning
202 A cloudy day

1914 S5, Patriotic Fund
50 Jones Creek, Brockville illus

1915 223 A bend of the river, St Germain, France illus
224 and 225 Landscape

1916 235 Côte des Neiges, winter illus
236 Landscape, near Kanawaki Golf Links
237 Landscape, from Outremont heights
238 A hazy day in the country, near Montreal

1918N 201 Canadian landscape illus 1919-169 1920-261
202 Canadian farm 1919-168
203 Landscape, farm near Waterbury, Vermont
204 Environs of Montreal

1919 167 The swimming pool

1920 258 Near Beaconsfield in October
259 Early autumn
260 Indian summer

1922 210 Landscape S6-102
211 Late afternoon S6-103

1924 213 Bend in the river illus
214 Canadian farmstead
215 The afterglow
216 A hazy day

1925 228 Afterglow illus
229 Late summer, Bethlehem, NH
230 Winter on the St Lawrence
231 Canadian winter

1927 F7, London, Eng
118 Afterglow, winter $1,000 F8-119 $680

1929 S7, Calgary
156 Landscape, Quebec $350
157 Summer afternoon $450

WOODFORDE, M.L. (Mrs)
Addr: 1911, 125 St Anne St, Quebec

1911 181 Le petit déjeuner
182 The Sillery Road, Quebec wc
183 The fir wood pen & ink

WOODHEAD, DORA KELSEY (Mrs Robert Charles Woodhead)
b 1916
1945 211 W/Comdr W.B.F. Mackay nfs
212 Ruth, portrait sketch nfs
1947 186 Lionel Fosbery nfs

WOODHOUSE, EDITH
H
Addr: 1899, 16 St Luke St, Montreal
1899 238a Case of miniatures wc

WOODMAN, FLORENCE
Addr: 1902, 480 Adelaide St, London, Ont; 1904, London, Ont
1902 164 and 165 Still life
166 Roses
167 Grief
1904 182 Roses
183 Sunset roses

WOODS, J.B.
1970 114 Fire hydrant, Canada Valve Limited

WOOLNOUGH, HILDA M.
11 Feb 1934, England
Addr: 1976, Charlottetown
1964N 64 Horse linocut 22 x 32 $100
65 Hanging man wd cut 44 1/2 x 7 $100
1965 71 Yellow horse linocut 30 x 21 $90
1976 S12, Montreal
152 Burning ship of the Northumberland Strait des by Woolnough, quilted by Bedeque Craft House PEI 96 x 72 illus

WOVERMANS, PHILIPS (WOUWERMANS)
24 May 1619, Haarlem Dutch
23 May 1668, Haarlem B TB
1880 48 Battle piece attr to Wovermans (Maj de Winton)

WRANGLE, GERALDINE see MAJOR, GERALDINE

WRIGHT, R.L.
Addr: 1929-36, 19 Sherwood St, Brockville, Ont
1929 219 Winter sunlight $75
1933 237 A March day $75
1936 207 Winter sunlight $90

WRIGHT, SAM L.
fl 1888-98 H
1888 190 Roadway in Muskoka $175
194 Evening near Weston $50
198 Garrison Common $200

WRIGHT, W.H.
1944 141 Church, Snow Road, Ont temp $90
1945 213 Lumberman's farm temp $90

WRINCH, MARY EVELYN (Mrs George Agnew Reid)
12 May 1877, Kirby le Soken, Essex, Eng 19 Sep 1969, Toronto AGO NGC TB2
ARCA 1916 Sr 1947 Painter
Addr: 1895, 607 Church St, Totonto; 1898-01, 619 Church St, Toronto; 1902-4, Toronto; 1905, 95 Charles St, Toronto; 1906, 346 Toronto St, Toronto; 1907, Toronto; 1908, 9 Rowanwood Ave, Toronto; 1909M, 36 Toronto St, Toronto; 1909N, 9 Rowanwood Ave, Toronto; 1911-19, 30 Wychwood Park, Toronto; 1920-2, 29 Alcina Ave, Toronto; 1923-9, 62 Wychwood Park, Toronto; 1930, Toronto; 1931-7, 81 Wychwood Park, Toronto; 1938-69, Toronto
1895 150 Old-time vanities
1898 128 Portrait study
129 Sunflower time
1901 137 Blue necklace
223 Case of miniatures
Folly 1902-270
Sir Percival's sister
The Holy Grail
Sunflowers 1902-267
Poppies
Stadacona, E.C.
Winnifred
A model
A French type 1902-269
224 Larkspur and roses wc
225 In an old garden wc
1902 268 Sir Galahad's sister min
271 Study in gray and yellow min
1904 184 The pumpkin patch
185 Cabbage time
315 Case of miniatures F4-117
1905 185 Reverie

186 The last glow
187 Row of elms on a grey day
187 Mrs G.W. Reid
187 Portrait study
1906 182 Chartres, Normandy
183 Street in Vitre
184 Case of miniatures
The pink beau F5-164
Portraits F5-164
1907 203 In the sapling wood
204 Bay of the yellow water lilies
1908 146 Sawmills in Muskoka
146a Case of miniatures
1909M 141 Wood interior
142 The Stony Brook village
1909N 159 A still pool
160 Case of miniatures
Portrait in fancy dress, Miss Marjorie Hope Stinson (Mrs McGivern)
Grace, daughter of A.D. Crooks, Esq (loan)
1910 S2, Liverpool
112 The Rideau valley
113 On Stone Lake
1911 184 Twilight
185 Autumn on the duck pond S5-34 illus
1912 232 A waterfall
233 Breaking sky
1912 S3, Winnipeg
150 Sunny winter morning
151 White birches
1913 318 Sunny morning in winter
1914 198 The first green of spring
199 The goldfish
1915 226 A white birch wood
1916 239 A sunny window
240 La bonne Sainte Anne
1918A 180 The shores of the St Lawrence illus
181 Snow magic ‖NGC‖
182 Canada geese in a maple sugar plantation
183 The end of the procession (Mrs A.A. Bowman)
1918N 205 Quebec, old and new
206 The River in Galt
207 Poppies and delphinium
1919 170 Flickering sunlight on a June garden
171 The quiet river
172 Mount St Anne, Quebec
1920 262 Levis, from the Plains of Abraham
1921 173 At the foot of Montmorency
174 Murray Bay village
1923 177 Glittering water 1924-217 1925-232
178 Circles
1924 218 Green and gold
219 Tea for two 1925-234 S7-159 $200
1925 233 Elms and the village
1926 146 Autumn colours
147 Mrs James Mavor min (Mrs J. Mavor)
1927 230 Sawmill in action S7-158 $500 F8-120
231 Chinese dolls
1928 158 Montreal River $250
1929 220 Temagami from the north wc $400
1929 S7, Calgary
160 Temagami forest reserve $50
1931 299 McDiarmid fishing village, Lake Nipigon $300
300 The top of the hill $250
1933 238 Limestone shore, Bruce Peninsula $300 T34-82
239 Scarboro Cliffs $300
1934 201 Sparkling water $250 1935-264a T36-72
1935 264 The old flume, Jumping Cariboo Creek $600
1936 208 Sawmill, Dorset illus $300 T37-64 F11-69 33 x 24
1937 230 Landlocked lake $300
1939 305 Wind clouds col wd cut $15
306 Scarboro col wd cut $15
307 The inquisitive pansies col wd cut $12
308 Spring time, grey day col wd cut $15
1940 157 The lake, afternoon $175 T41-55
1941 S9, Toronto
62 Flowers from the garden $60

WYANT, ALEXANDER HELWIG American
11 Jan 1836, Evans Creek, Ohio
29 Nov 1892, New York B Gr H TB
1882 270 A burnt district, New Brunswick monoc

WYKE, GEORGE
Addr: 1918N, 793 Querbes Ave, Outremont, Que
1918N 255 The log cabin b&w
256 The tunnel roads, Outremont b&w

WYLD (or WYLDE) (Miss)
H
Addr: 1881, Halifax
1881 212 Enamel on porcelaine Wyld
1882 228-30 Decorative tiles $12.50 each Wylde
231 Decorative tile $10

WYLE, FLORENCE
27 Nov 1881, Trenton, Ill 14 Jan 1968, Newmarket, Ont AGO CC2 CWW64 EC NGC TB2 W78 WWA47
ARCA 1920 RCA 1940 Sr 1951 Council
Sculptor
Addr: 1914-19, 114 1/2 Church St, Toronto; 1921-37, 110 Glen Rose Ave, Toronto; 1938-68, Toronto
1914 209 Rebirth plaster 1915-248 bronze
210 The fruit of war plaster
1915 249 Dancing boy sculp ≬NGC≬
1918A 201 Sun worshipper sculp ≬NGC≬
1919 190 The ducks girl sculp
1921 184 The pot of basil plaster
1922 234 Frederick H. Varley, ARCA plaster illus S6-115 ≬NGC bronze≬
235 Head of a young Jew plaster
1923 198 Carlos Buehler sculp
199 Boy with dolphin, fountain bronze
1927 275 and 276 Child with jug plaster
277 Portrait rel plaster
1928 179 Young mother bronze $800 marble $1,000
1928 F8, London, Eng
205 Indian mother plaster $50
1930 196 Torso marble $2,500 ≬NGC≬
197 Vincent Massey bronze $1,000
198 Portrait marble $1,200
1931 347 Study of a girl plaster marble, 1 of 3, $5,000
1932 227 Wall fountain plaster cement $350 stone $750 1933-275
1934 208 Bird bath bronze $1,500
1935 300 Seated torso stone $1,500
301 Baby fountain, boy stone, or bronze $1,000
302 Baby fountain, girl stone, or bronze $1,000 cement $500
1936 230 Girl plaster bronze $1,500
231 Young woman plaster bronze $1,500
1937 296 Young woman bronze $1,200 stone $1,500
297 Girl bronze $1,200 stone $1,500
1938 245 The cellist mahogany $225 DW 1941 14 3/4h
246 Harvester plaster bronze $1,000 marble $1,500
1939 265 Torso plaster marble $3,000
1941 227 Margot, portrait sculp $200 copy $10
228 Susan, portrait plaster nfs
229 Mrs Terence MacDermot sculp nfs
1941 S9, Toronto
63 Esquimaux pottery head $85
1942 175 Negress stone $3,000 1943-139 plaster illus
1944 156 Joan sculp nfs
1945 238 October wd $200
239 Torso plaster $60
1946 150 Reclining woman illus stone $1,200
1947 220 Reclining nude stone $1,250
221 Jamaican stone $750
1948 181 Diana, panel, Bank of Montreal, Toronto, working model plaster for stone Marani & Morris architects
181a Margaret Gould sculp nfs
1949 125 Justice plaster stone $1,200
1951 128 Susannah sumac carv $250
1953 126 Roland Hayes sculp nfs
1954 113 Atlas sculp 21h $300
1955 120 Madonna sculp $300
1956 54 October sculp $225

WYNNE-CLARKE, A.
Addr: 1927, 163 Wolverleigh Blvd, Toronto; 1928-9, 270A Lee Ave, Toronto
1927 232 J. Lickorish, Esq wc
233 The finishing touch wc
1928 159 Man with a frown
1929 221 T.A. Miller wc

Y

YANEFF, CHRISTOPHER
18 May 1928, Toronto
RCA(e) 1977 Graphic designer
Addr: 1979, Toronto

YARWOOD, WALTER HAWLEY
19 Sep 1917, Toronto AGO CC2 TB2
ARCA 1967 Sculptor
Addr: 1968-71/79, Toronto
1950 154 Still life, fish 16 x 26 $200

YOUNG, PAUL
1937, Toronto
1966 70 Untitled drwg 24 x 36 $120

YOUNGER, PIERCY see PORTEOUS, PIERCY

Z

ZACK, BADANNA BERNICE
22 Mar 1933, Montreal
RCA(e) 1978 Sculptor
Addr: 1979, Toronto

ZADOROZNY, ANDREI MICHAEL
27 May 1921, Borsziv, n Lvov, Ukraine
1958 84 Asleep in the camp $120

ZAHN, EMIL
fl 1879-80 H
1880 262 Pillar panel des

ZANDER, HANS
1971 80G Poster billboard and full color advertisement, Toronto Daily Star

ZEIDLER, EBERHARD HEINRICH
11 Jan 1926, Braunsdorf, Germany CWW79 TB2 WWA76
ARCA 1970 Architect
Addr: 1971/76/79, Toronto
1976 S12, Montreal
110 Ontario Place, Toronto 2 illus
see also Craig, James S, 1965-1967

ZELDIN, GERALD
1943, Toronto
Addr: 1976, Lynden, Ont
1976 S12, Montreal
172 IFCA, a preview 1/2" vtr b&w/n&b 27 1/2 min

ZELENAK, EDWARD JOHN
9 Nov 1940, St Thomas, Ont B IO WWA76
RCA(e) 1974 Sculptor
Addr: 1979, West Lorne, Ont

ZERAFA, BORIS ERNEST
20 Jun 1933, Cairo CWW79
RCA(e) 1975 Architect
Addr: 1979, Toronto
see also Webb, Peter, 1964N

ZOLDAS, LENA
Addr: 1914, Winnipeg
1914 S4, Winnipeg
182 Manitoba roses $15

ZOLTVANY, BELA
c 1892, Budapest 28 Sep 1956, Montreal
1949 126 St Jean Baptiste bronze nfs
1951 131 Pieta black walnut $300

ZOLTVANY-SMITH, A.
Addr: 1927-31, 7406 Henri Julien St, Montreal; 1933-5, 75 Sherbrooke St W, Montreal; 1937, 3572 Jeanne Mance St, Montreal
1927 278 The first sin plaster
1929 252 Study sculp
1931 348 Lady with flowers sculp
1933 277 Funerary monument bas rel plaster
1935 303 Ste Cécile and St Tharsitius sculp photo nfs
1937 298 Oscar DeLall bronze $300
1939 266 Rev J.G. Granger bronze B.Zoltvany-Smith mispr

ZUCCA, ALBERT
Addr: 1935, 2024 McGill College Ave, Montreal
1935 304 Two heads wd $100
305 Hieratic panel sculp nfs

ZWICKER, LEROY JUDSON
21 Jul 1906, Halifax TB2 WWA47
Addr: 1933, 120 Granville St, Halifax
1933 329 Hot air etch
1938 231 Brodder Keeler nfs
232 Oriental $50 T39-58
1941 199 Diana and the plant $100 T42-57
1942 156 East coast Canadian port $100 T43-51
157 Maritimes $100
1944 142 Water Street, Halifax $150
1945 214 Ingonish, Cape Breton $75
215 Black and yellow nfs T46-48

1946 129 Spires and tenements $200
1947 188 Taxco, Mexico $150
189 Fiesta in the market place $100
1949 99 The jetty $50

ZWICKER, MARY MARGUERITE PORTER
(Mrs Leroy Judson Zwicker)
b 1904
Addr: 1935, King St, Yarmouth, NS
1935 218 Birches $50 Marguerite Porter

Members of Council 1880–1979

Record of service on Council 1880 to 1969-70 is from the catalogues. Errors in catalogues have been corrected from annual reports. Councils for 1970-1 to 1979 are from the minutes.

Only Academicians served on the Council from 1880 to 1935-6. The Council consisted of the officers - president, vice-president, secretary and treasurer - and twelve members, six elected each year for two-year terms.

From 1936-7 to 1949-50, one, or two, ARCA members served as an Associates Advisory Council, for one or two-year terms, without voting privileges. From 1950-1 to 1972-3 there were four ARCA members, two elected each year for two-year terms.

Under the 1973 revised constitution the executive consists of the president, vice-president, treasurer, and twenty voting members, ten elected each year for two-year terms. All members are eligible to be elected to the Council.

A Associate C Council HT Hon-Treasurer P President RVP Regional Vice-President S Secretary ST Sec-Treasurer T Treasurer VP Vice-President

ADAMSON, G.S: A 1950-2; C 1960-3; VP 1963-4; C 1964-70
AFFLECK, R.T: C 1969-71
ALFSEN, J.M: A 1957-9
ALLEN, R: C 1974-6
ALLWARD, H.L: C 1946-8, 1951-2; VP 1953-4; P 1954-7; C 1957-63
ALLWARD, W.S: C 1921-2, 1936-42
ARBUCKLE, G.F: C 1947-9, 1951-3; VP 1955-6, 1957-60; P 1960-4; C 1964-70, 1973-5
ARTHUR, E.R: A 1963-5
BAIRD, R.A: C 1978-
BARNES, A.G: C 1937-45, 1946-52
BARNES, W.M: A 1942-6
BAYEFSKY, A: A 1964-6, 1968-70
BEAMENT, T.H: C 1949-55; HT 1957-60; ST 1960-1; VP 1961-4; P 1964-7; C 1967-9, 1970-2
BEAMENT, T.H.(TIB): C 1978-
BEATTY, J.W: C 1914-17, 1919-21, 1924-6, 1928-32, 1933-9
BEAUCHEMIN, M: A 1970-3
BELL-SMITH, F.M: C 1887-8, 1889-91, 1893-5, 1897-9, 1901-3, 1905-7, 1908-10, 1913-15, 1918-20, 1922-3
BICE, C: VP 1966-7; P 1967-70; C 1970-1, 1973-5
BIELER, A.C.T: C 1975-7
BLACKWOOD, D.L: VP 1978-
BOUCHARD, L.H: A 1957-8, 1959-61
BOURASSA, N: VP 1880-5; C 1885-6, 1891-2
BRIGDEN, F.H: A 1936-8, 1939-40; C 1940-2
BROWN, M: A 1945-7
BROWNE, J.A: C 1920-4, 1925-7
BROWNELL, P.F: C 1897-9, 1901-3, 1905-7, 1909-11, 1913-15
BRYMNER, W: C 1886-9, 1891-3, 1896-8, 1900-2, 1904-6; VP 1906-9; P 1909-18
CAISERMAN, G: A 1961-3; C 1978-
CAPPER, S.H: C 1901-3
CARMICHAEL, F: C 1939-43
CASSON, A.J: C 1942-3; VP 1943-8; P 1948-52; C 1952-67, 1971-3
CATTELL, R.V: A 1969-72; VP 1974-6
CHALLENER, F.S: C 1902-4, 1905-7, 1909-11, 1913-15, 1918-20, 1924-6, 1927-35
CHAMBERS, J.R: C 1973-5
CHAPMAN, C: C 1974-6, 1977-9
CLARK, P: A 1963-5
CLOUTIER, A.E: A 1954-5; C 1959-60; HT 1960-5
COBURN, F.S: C 1929-31, 1933-41
COLLIER, A.C: A 1957-60; C 1962-5; HT 1965-72; C 1973-5
COMFORT, C.F: C 1946-54; VP 1954-5, 1956-7; P 1957-60; C1965-7,

1968-70, 1973-7
CONNOLLY, J: C 1888-90, 1891-3
COPPOLD, L.G.M: A 1950-1, 1960-1
CORMIER, E: C 1943-5; T 1946-8; C 1949-51, 1969-71
COSGROVE, S.M: A 1955-7, 1967-8
CRESSWELL, W.N: C 1881-5, 1886-7
CRUIKSHANK, W: C 1895-7, 1898-00, 1903-5, 1907-9, 1912-14, 1917-19
CULLEN, M.G: C 1909-11, 1914-16, 1919-21, 1924-6, 1927-9, 1929-33
CURRY, S.G: C 1889-91
CURTIN, W.A: C 1977-9
CUTHBERTSON, G.H: C 1975-6; HT 1976-8
DALLEGRET, F: C 1974-5
DARLING, F: C 1888-9, 1910-12, 1915-17, 1920-2
DAUDELIN, C: C 1976-8
DAY, F: C 1882-3, 1884-6, 1888-90, 1892-4, 1896-8, 1900-2
DE LALL, O.D: A 1948-9, 1954-8
DICK, D.B: C 1894-6, 1898-00, 1902-4
DINGLE, J.A.D: C 1970-3
DUFF, A.M: C 1977-9
DUNLOP, A.F: C 1891-4, 1896-8, 1900-2, 1904-9; VP 1909-14; C 1917-19
DURNFORD, A.T.G: A 1950-2; C 1960-4; VP 1964-6
DYONNET, E: C 1903-5, 1906-8; S 1910-47
EDSON, A.A: C 1880-3, 1887-8
ERICKSON, A.C: C 1969-71
ETROG, S: C 1974-6
FETHERSTONHAUGH, H.L: C 1948-52
FILION, A: A 1950-1
FINLEY, F.J: A 1949-50; S 1952-7; ST 1957-60; C 1960-1; ST 1961-7
FISET, E: C 1970-1
FISHER, B.R: C 1976-8
FLEMING, A.R: C 1973-5
FORBES, J.C: C 1884-6, 1888-90
FORBES, K.K: C 1941-3
FOSBERY, E.G: C 1932-8, 1940-3; P 1943-8; C 1948-50
FOWLER, D: C 1880-3, 1885-7
FRASER, J.A: C 1880-1, 1882-4
FREIFIELD, E: A 1965-7, 1968-70
FRESCHI, B.B.: C 1975-7; RVP 1977-9
FULLER, T: C 1884-6, 1888-90, 1892-4, 1897-8
GAGEN, R.F: C 1915-17, 1920-2
GANGON, C: C 1976-8
GAGNON, C.A: C 1923-5, 1937-41
GAUCHER, Y: A 1970-3
GERIN-LAJOIE, G: C 1976-8
GLADSTONE, G: C 1975-7
GOTTSCHALK, F: C 1975-7
GREGOR, H.F: C 1976-8, 1979-
GRIER, E.W: C 1895-7, 1899-01, 1903-6, 1908-10, 1913-15, 1918-20, 1923-5; VP 1926-9; P 1929-39; C 1939-41
GRIFFITHS, J: C 1880-1, 1882-4, 1885-7, 1890-1, 1894-6
HAHN, E.O: C 1932-4
HAHN, G: C 1906-8, 1911-13, 1916-18, 1921-3, 1926-8
HAINES, F.S: C 1934-7; VP 1937-9; P 1939-42; C 1942-6, 1948-50
HAMEL, J.A.E: C 1880-1
HAMMOND, J.A: C 1894-6, 1898-00, 1902-5, 1906-7, 1908-12, 1915-17, 1920-2, 1925-7
HARRIS, L.P: A 1964-6; RVP 1970-5
HARRIS, R: C 1880-1, 1883-4, 1885-7, 1889-91; P 1893-06; C 1907-9, 1911-13, 1915-17
HAWORTH, P: C 1957-9, 1960-2
HEBERT, A: C 1943-5
HEBERT, H: C 1923-5, 1930-2, 1935-7, 1945-7
HEBERT, L.P: C 1906-8, 1911-13
HEWTON, R.S: C 1945-53
HILL, G.W: C 1919-21, 1922-3, 1925-7
HODGSON, T.S: C 1974-6, 1978-
HOLGATE, E.H: C 1938-42, 1943-5
HOLMES, R.H: C 1922-4
HOPE, W.R: C 1903-5, 1906-8, 1911-13, 1916-18, 1921-3, 1926-8
HOPKINS, J.W: C 1881-5, 1887-9, 1891-3, 1895-7, 1899-01
HORNE, A.E.C: C 1953-60; VP 1960-1; C 1961-71
HORNE, M: C 1979-
HOUSSER, M.Y.M: C 1962-4, 1972-4
HOUSTOUN, D.M: C 1970-4
HOWARD, A.H: C 1885-7, 1889-91, 1893-5, 1901-3, 1905-7, 1908-10, 1912-14
HOWARD, H.B: C 1979-
HUBEL, V: C 1977; T 1978-
HUTCHISON, A.C: C 1883-4; VP 1885-6; C 1908-10, 1912-14; T 1914-19
JACKSON, A.Y: C 1921-3, 1926-32
JACOBI, O.R: C 1887-9; P 1890-3; C 1894-6
JEFFERYS, C.W: C 1928-30, 1934-40
JONES, H.G: C 1929-33, 1935-7; T 1942-6
KAHANE, A: A 1962-4
KAISER, R.J: C 1975-7
KEMBLE, R.I: C 1979-
KINOSHITA, G: C 1979-

KNOWLES, F.M.S.S: C 1899-01, 1903-5, 1907-9, 1912-14, 1917-19, 1922-4
KOLISNYK, P: C 1979-
KRAMER, B: C 1976-8
KUYPERS, J: C 1974-5
LALIBERTE, A: C 1923-7
LALONDE, J.L: A 1969-72
LANGLEY, H: C 1881-5, 1887-9, 1891-3, 1895-7, 1900-2, 1904-5
LEATHERS, W.L: C 1978-
LETENDRE, R: C 1974-6
LISMER, A: C 1950-2, 1954-6
LORCINI, G: C 1974-6
LORING, F.N: A 1941-3; C 1951-5
LUPPEN, F.V: C 1881-3
LYLE, J.M: C 1928-36, 1940-2
MACCARTHY, H.T.C.P: C 1892-4, 1896-8, 1901-3, 1905-7, 1909-11, 1913-15, 1918-20
MACDONALD, T.R: C 1967-9, 1972-4
MCEWEN, J: A 1967-9; VP 1970-2
MCLAREN, N: C 1973-5
MACLENNAN, I.R: C 1971-2; HT 1972-6
MCLOUGHLIN, M: C 1976-8
MARTIN, T.M: C 1880-4, 1885-8, 1890-2, 1894-6, 1898-00, 1903-5, 1908-10, 1912-14, 1917-18
MASSEY, H: C 1972-3
MATHERS, A.S: C 1945-7, 1955-7
MATTHEWS, M: S 1880-8; C 1888-9, 1891-3, 1895-6, 1899-01, 1904-6, 1907-9, 1912-13
MAXWELL, E: C 1910-12, 1915-17; VP 1917-20
MAXWELL, W.S: C 1916-18, 1921-3, 1926-8; VP 1929-37
MAYHEW, E: C 1977-9
MENSES, J: C 1977-9
MILLAR, C.B: C 1974-6; VP 1976-8
MITCHELL, J: C 1978-
MOLINARI, G: C 1975-7
MOSS, C.E: C 1899-01
MURPHY, R.W: A 1943-4
NEWFELD, F: C 1974-6
NEWTON, L.T: C 1941-51, 1954-6, 1957-8
NICHOLS, J: A 1966-8
NOBBS, P.E: C 1920-22, 1923-4, 1925-7, 1931-5, 1936-9; VP 1939-42; Acting P 1942-3
O'BRIEN, L.R: P 1880-90; C 1890-2, 1894-6, 1898-99
OESTERLE, L.F: C 1972-3
PALMER, H.S: C 1938-40, 1941-3, 1944-6; S 1947-52; C 1952-4
PANTON, L.A.C: C 1944-6, 1947-52; VP 1952-4
PARKIN, J.C: A 1962-3; VP 1967-70; P 1970-
PARTRIDGE, D.G: C 1977-9
PATTERSON; A.D: C 1887-8, 1889-91, 1893-5, 1897-9, 1902-4, 1905-7, 1909-11, 1913-15
PEPPER, G.D: A 1953-5; C 1958-60
PERRE, H: C 1884-6, 1888-90
PILOT, R.W: C 1935-40, 1947-8; VP 1948-52; P 1952-4; C 1954-62
PINHEY, J.C: C 1898-00, 1902-4, 1906-8, 1910-12
PRATT; J.C: C 1975-7
PURDY, H.C: C 1979-
RAINE, H: C 1927-9, 1945-7
RAPHAEL, W: C 1880-2, 1883-4, 1886-8, 1889-91, 1893-5
REEVES, J.A: C 1979
REID, G.A: C 1890-1, 1893-5, 1897-9, 1902-4; P 1906-9; C 1910-12, 1914-16, 1918-19; T 1919-21; C 1923-5, 1927-9, 1934-6
RICHMOND, J.R: C 1979-
ROBERT, G: C 1979-
ROBERTS, W.G: A 1952; C 1962-4
ROBINSON, A.H: C 1922-4, 1927-9, 1933-5
ROUSSEAU, M: C 1974-6
ROYLE, S: C 1943-5
RUSSELL, G.H: C 1919-20; T 1921-2; P 1922-6; C 1926-32
SANDHAM, J.H: C 1880-2
SCHAEFER, C.F: A 1949-50, 1958-62
SCOTT, A.S: C 1945-7
SCOTT, C: C 1978-
SCOTT, T.S: C 1880-2, 1883-5, 1886-8, 1889-91, 1893-5
SEMAK, M.W: C 1976-8
SHEPHERD, C.G: C 1977-8
SHORE, L.E: C 1972-4
SIMPKINS, H.J: A 1960-2
SIMPSON, C.W: C 1921-2; T 1922-41
SISLER, R.J: C 1976-8
SMITH, E.J: C 1974-6
SMITH, G.A: C 1970-3, 1975-7
SMITH, J.A: T 1880-8; ST 1888-10; T 1910-14; C 1914-16
SMITH, J.R: T 1954-7
SOMERVILLE, W.L: C 1941-8; T 1948-53; C 1955-7
SPROATT, H: C 1915-17; VP 1920-6; P 1926-9; C 1929-31
STEWART, C: C 1978-
STORM, W.G: C 1880-2, 1883-5, 1886-8, 1890-2
SUZOR-COTE, M.A.F: C 1917-19, 1923-5
TANABE, T: C 1976-8
TAYLOR, A.T: C 1892-4, 1896-8, 1901-3

TAYLOR, F.B: A 1955-7, 1958-9
THORNTON, P.M: RVP 1970-5
TINNING, G.A: A 1954-6, 1961-3
TONDINO, G: C 1968-9
TONNANCOUR, J.G: A 1972-3; C 1973-4
TRUDEAU, Y: RVP 1975-7
URQUHART, A.M: A 1966-8
VALLANCE, H: C 1931-3
VISSER, J: C 1974-7, 1978-
WALKER, H: C 1918-22, 1924-6
WATSON, H.R: C 1882-3, 1884-6, 1891-3, 1895-7, 1899-01, 1904-6, 1907-9, 1911-13; VP 1914-17; P 1917-22
WATSON, S.H: C 1957-68, 1972-4
WATTS, J.W.H: C 1882-3, 1884-6, 1888-90, 1892-4, 1896-8, 1900-2, 1904-6, 1907-9, 1911-13, 1916-17
WAY, C.J: C 1900-2
WEISMAN, G.O: A 1965-7
WHEELER, O.S: A 1946-8
WIGGS, H.R: A 1959-60
WILLIAMS, Y: A 1963-4
WILLIAMSON, A.C: C 1909-11, 1914-16, 1917-18, 1919-21, 1924-6
WILSON, R.Y: A 1947-9; C 1950-60, 1963-5, 1966-70, 1978-
WOODCOCK, P.F: C 1890-2, 1916-18, 1922-4
WYLE, F: C 1942-8

PRESIDENTS

O'BRIEN, L.R: 1880-90
JACOBI, O.R: 1890-3
HARRIS, R: 1893-06
REID, G.A: 1906-9
BRYMNER, W: 1909-18
WATSON, H.R: 1918-22
RUSSELL, G.H: 1922-6
SPROAT, H: 1926-9
GRIER, E.W: 1929-39
HAINES, F.S: 1939-42
NOBBS, P.E: Acting, 1942-3
FOSBERY, E.G: 1943-8
CASSON, A.J: 1948-52
PILOT, R.W: 1952-4
ALLWARD, H.L: 1954-7
COMFORT, C.F: 1957-60
ARBUCKLE, G.F: 1960-4
BEAMENT, T.H: 1964-7
BICE, C: 1967-70
PARKIN, J.C: 1970-

Exhibitions

This list shows the number of the exhibition, the year, the number of works exhibited, the site or sites, and the opening and closing dates when noted in the catalogues or in the minutes.

ANNUAL

1	1880	410	Clarendon Hotel, Ottawa, 6 Mar. Art Association of Montreal, Apr. Diploma works, Ontario Society of Artists, Toronto, May
2	1881	382	Legislative Building, Halifax, 5 Jul
3	1882	326	Art Association of Montreal, 11 Apr
4	1883	384	Educational Museum, Toronto, with Ontario Society of Artists, 23 May
5	1884	198	Art Association of Montreal, 15 Apr-4 May
6	1885	334	15 King St W, Toronto, with Ontario Society of Artists, 14 May
7	1886	224	Supreme Court Building, Ottawa, 2 Feb. #194-213 selected for Colonial and Indian Exhibition, London, England, 1886
8	1887	196	Art Association of Montreal, Phillips Sq, 20 Apr
9	1888	331	Granite Rink, Church St, with Ontario Society of Artists, 8 May
10	1889	188	National Gallery, Ottawa, 13 Mar
11	1890	231	Art Association of Montreal, 24 Apr
12	1891	243	Toronto Art Gallery, 6 Mar
13	1892	176	National Gallery, Ottawa, 30 Mar
14	1893	280	Art Association of Montreal, 1 Mar
15	1894	205	National Gallery, Ottawa, 30 Mar
16	1895	339	Art Gallery, King St W, Toronto, 15 Apr
17	1896	284	Art Association of Montreal, 12 Mar
18	1897	224	National Gallery, Ottawa, 9 Mar
19	1898	245	Ontario Society of Artists Gallery, Toronto, 3 Mar
20	1899	261	Art Association of Montreal, 7 Apr
21	1900	207	National Gallery, Ottawa, 15 Feb
22	1901	260	Ontario Society of Artists Gallery, Toronto, 12 Apr
23	1902	293	Art Association of Montreal, 20 Mar
24	1903	216	National Gallery, Ottawa, 16 Apr
25	1904	330	Art Association of Montreal, 17 Mar
26	1905	222	Ontario Society of Artists Gallery, Toronto, 12 May (Ontario Association of Artists, error on catalogue cover)
27	1906	206	National Gallery, Ottawa, 4 May
28	1907	352	Art Association of Montreal, 1 Apr
29	1908	181	Ontario Society of Artists Gallery, Toronto, 24 Apr
30	1909M	175	Archives Building, Sussex St, Ottawa, 6-21 May
31	1909N	160	Hamilton Public Library, Art Gallery, 25 Nov
32	1910	226	Art Association of Montreal, 24 Nov
33	1911	205	Art Museum, Toronto, 23 Nov (from Annual Report, Carnegie Public Library Building galleries)
34	1912	279	Victoria Memorial Museum, Ottawa, 29 Nov
35	1913	374	Art Association of Montreal, 679 Sherbrooke St W, 20 Nov
36	1914	239	Art Museum, Public Library Building, College St, Toronto, 19 Nov
37	1915	288	Art Association of Montreal, 18 Nov-18 Dec

38 1916 324 Art Association of Montreal, 16 Nov-16 Dec

39 1918A 303 Art Museum of Toronto, Grange Rd, with Ontario Society of Artists, 4 Apr. #228-03 Competitors for Travelling Scholarship offered by the Trustees of National Gallery of Canada

40 1918N 256 Art Association of Montreal, 21 Nov

41 1919 230 Art Gallery of Toronto, 25 Grange Rd, 20 Nov-20 Dec

42 1920 349 Art Association of Montreal, 18 Nov

43 1921 230 Art Gallery of Toronto, Grange Park, 17 Nov-2 Jan 1922

44 1922 300 Art Association of Montreal, 16 Nov-16 Dec

45 1923 248 Art Gallery of Toronto, 22 Nov-2 Jan 1924. #238-43 RCA Mural decorative painting competition

46 1924 299 National Gallery of Canada, Ottawa, 20 Nov-20 Dec

47 1925 344 Art Association of Montreal, 19 Nov-20 Dec

48 1926 211 Art Gallery of Toronto, 18 Nov-2 Jan 1927

49 1927 353 Art Association of Montreal, 24 Nov-2 Jan 1928

50 1928 240 Art Gallery of Toronto, 29 Nov-2 Jan 1929

51 1929 293 Art Association of Montreal, 21 Nov-22 Dec

51 1930 234 Art Gallery of Toronto, 8 Nov (Exhibition #51 repeated, to adjust to the Academy's 51st year)

52 1931 443 Art Association of Montreal, 19 Nov-20 Dec

53 1932 269 Art Gallery of Toronto, 4-30 Nov

54 1933 331 Art Association of Montreal, 16 Nov-17 Dec

55 1934 236 Art Gallery of Toronto, 2 Nov-3 Dec

56 1935 350 Art Association of Montreal, 21 Nov-22 Dec

57 1936 254 Art Gallery of Toronto, 6 Nov

58 1937 331 Art Association of Montreal, 18 Nov-17 Dec

59 1938 270 Art Gallery of Toronto, 18 Nov-18 Dec

60 1939 308 Art Association of Montreal, 16 Nov-16 Dec

61 1940 172 Art Gallery of Toronto, 11 Oct-11 Nov

62 1941 245 Art Association of Montreal, 6 Nov-4 Dec

63 1942 177 Art Gallery of Toronto, 6 Nov-6 Dec

64 1943 150 Musée de la Province de Québec, Québec, 5-26 Oct. Art Association of Montreal, 5-27 Nov

65 1944 162 Art Gallery of Toronto, 17 Nov-17 Dec

66 1945 250 Art Association of Montreal, 2 Nov-2 Dec

67 1946 160 Art Gallery of Toronto, 22 Nov-22 Dec

68 1947 231 Art Association of Montreal, 6-30 Nov. Musée de la Province de Québec, Québec, 16 Dec-27 Jan 1948

69 1948 195 Art Gallery of Toronto, Dundas St W, 19 Nov-12 Dec

70 1949 129 Montreal Museum of Fine Arts, 11-30 Nov

71 1950 154 Art Gallery of Toronto, 3 Mar-16 Apr. Exhibition of contemporary Canadian arts. Golden Jubilee of Gallery, 10 arts and crafts societies contributing. RCA, oils and pastels (154)

72 1951 139 Art Gallery of Toronto, 23 Nov-6 Jan 1952

73 1952 119 Montreal Museum of Fine Arts, 14 Nov-7 Dec

74 1953 174 Art Gallery of Toronto; 27 Nov-19 Jan 1954. J.W. Morrice Memorial section

75 1954 176 Montreal Museum of Fine Arts, 19 Nov-19 Dec. 75th Jubilee, with Retrospective section, and brief history of the Academy by Robert W. Pilot, President

76 1955 149 Art Gallery of Toronto, 25 Nov-2 Jan 1956. W.S. Allward Memorial section

77 1956 128 Montreal Museum of Fine Arts, 16 Nov-23 Dec. C.W. Jefferys Memorial section

78 1957 108 Art Gallery of Toronto, 15 Nov-15 Dec. Memorial Library, Halifax, 4-27 Feb 1958

79 1958 113 Montreal Museum of Fine Arts, 7 Nov-7 Dec. Vancouver Art Gallery, 27 Jan-22 Feb 1959

80	1959	103	Musée de la Province de Québec, Québec, 6-30 Nov. Winnipeg Civic Auditorium, 3-27 Jan 1960
81	1960	107	Art Gallery of Toronto, 26 Nov-2 Jan 1961. National Gallery of Canada, Ottawa, 9 Feb-5 Mar
82	1961	102	Montreal Museum of Fine Arts, 11 Nov-10 Dec. Sarnia Public Library and Art Gallery, 2-20 Jan 1962. Norman Mackenzie Art Gallery, Regina, 6-25 Feb
83	1963	123	Art Gallery of Toronto, 11 Jan-10 Feb. Divided in two for exhibits at Memorial University of Newfoundland, St John's, 25 Mar-20 Apr; Agnes Etherington Art Centre, Queen's University, Kingston, 5-28 Apr
84	1964J	126	National Gallery of Canada, Ottawa, 16 Jan-9 Feb. London Public Library and Art Museum, 6-31 Mar
85	1964N	192	Montreal Museum of Fine Arts, 6-19 Nov. Sarnia Public Library and Art Gallery, 8-30 Jan 1965
86	1965	178	Art Gallery of Hamilton, 12 Nov-12 Dec. Winnipeg Art Gallery, 1-21 Feb 1966
87	1966	156	Art Gallery of Ontario, Toronto, 28 Oct-27 Nov. National Gallery of Canada, Ottawa, 15 Dec-8 Jan 1967. Sarnia Public Library and Art Gallery, 14 Jan-7 Feb
88	1967	126	Montreal Museum of Fine Arts, 27 Oct-22 Nov. Saskatoon Gallery and Conservatory Corporation, 1-31 Jan 1968. Art Gallery of Greater Victoria, 27 Feb-18 Mar
89	1968	126	Art Gallery of Hamilton, 7 Dec-15 Jan 1969. Edmonton Art Gallery, 13 Feb-9 Mar
90	1970	316	National Gallery of Canada, Ottawa, 30 Jan-28 Feb. List of Diploma works 1880-1969. Selection from Diploma works to be in special section of exhibit, but not listed in catalogue
91	1971	225	Montreal Museum of Fine Arts/Musée des beaux-arts de Montréal, 25 Mar-25 Apr. Confederation Centre, Charlottetown, 1 Jul-31 Aug

SPECIAL

S1	1884	210	Owen Art Gallery, Saint John, summer
S2	1910	118	Walker Art Gallery, Liverpool, 4-23 Jul. Prepared for the Festival of Empire, Crystal Palace, London, 24 May 1910. Cancelled due to death of King Edward VII. Walker Art Gallery catalogue. (A catalogue was printed for the Festival of Empire exhibition but was not used)
S3	1912	275	Winnipeg Industrial Bureau, Winnipeg Museum of Fine Arts, 16 Dec-4 Jan 1913
S4	1914	184	Winnipeg Industrial Bureau, Winnipeg Museum of Fine Arts, 19 Jan-Mar
S5	1914	83	Patriotic Fund. Pictures and sculptures given by Canadian artists in aid of the Patriotic Fund. Opened in Toronto, 30 Dec, Art Museum at the Public Library. Circulated to Winnipeg, Halifax, Saint John, Quebec, Montreal, Ottawa, Hamilton, (London, cancelled) closed in Toronto.(1915 Annual Report)
S6	1923	128	Art Gallery of Hamilton, Jan. Selected from the 1922 annual exhibition
S7	1929	166	Calgary Exhibition and Stampede, 8-13 Jul. Edmonton Art Gallery, Jul. Canadian Pacific Exhibition, Vancouver, 7-17 Aug. Calgary catalogue
S8	1938	380	Canadian industrial arts, Art Gallery of Toronto, 4 Feb
S9	1941	63	Canadian Red Cross Society benefit exhibition and sale, Eaton's Fine Art Galleries, College St, Toronto, 21 Feb-1 Mar. Works given by the artists

S10 1966 74 Confederation Art Gallery and Museum, Charlottetown. The Academy in retrospect, 5 Jul-31 Aug

S11 1970 33 St Mary's University, Halifax, in co-operation with the RCA. Organized for the Atlantic Provinces Art Circuit, Dec 1970-May 1971. Beaverbrook Art Gallery, Fredericton, Dec. Memorial University Art Centre, St John's, Jan. New Brunswick Museum, Saint John, Feb. St Mary's University Art Gallery, Halifax, Mar. Moncton University Art Gallery, Apr. Centennial Art Gallery, Halifax, May

S12 1976 182 Spectrum Canada. RCA in conjunction with the Arts and Culture Program of the Organizing Committee 1976 Olympic Games. Complexe Desjardins, Montreal, 5-31 Jul

FAIRS AND EXPOSITIONS

F1a 1886 162 Colonial and Indian Exhibition, London, Eng, 4 May. Committee Chairman HE Marquis of Lansdowne, presidents of the RCA, Ontario Society of Artists, Art Associations of London, Ont, Montreal and Ottawa, with Robert Haris, RCA and Homer Watson, RCA. Official catalogue of the Canadian section, Group VII, Fine Arts.(2nd ed. Listed by artist number, works unnumbered)

F1 1893 196 World's Columbian Exposition, Chicago, 1 May-30 Oct. Committee, the RCA and representatives of the Ontario Society of Artists, and Art Associations of Montreal and Ottawa. The Canadian Department of Fine Arts catalogue

F2 1901 89 Pan-American Exposition, Buffalo, 1 May-1 Nov. Canada section, Canadian Art Gallery catalogue

F3 1902 28 Rochester Art Club, Rochester Chamber of Commerce Assembly Hall, 17-29 Nov. 20th Annual Exhibition, including paintings by the RCA. Syracuse Museum of Fine Arts, Nov. Rochester catalogue

F4 1904 114 Universal Exposition, St Louis, 30 Apr-1 Dec. Official catalogue of Exhibits, Department of Art, rev ed. Canadian section

F5 1906 164 Dominion Exhibition, Halifax, Sep. Fine Arts Department catalogue

F6 1907 174 Dominion and Provincial Exhibition, Sherbrooke, Quebec, Sep. Department of Fine Arts catalogue

F7 1927 14 Imperial Art Gallery, 12 Apr-30 Jun

F8 1928 16 Imperial Art Gallery, 2 Apr-30 Jun

F9 1929 16 Imperial Art Gallery, 6 Apr-29 Jun

F10 1930 14 Imperial Art Gallery, 5 Apr-28 Jun. 1927-30, Imperial Institute, South Kensington, London, Eng. Exhibitions of paintings, drawings, engravings and sculpture by artists residing in Great Britain ahd the Dominions

F11 1939 69 New York World's Fair. Canadian art exhibits under direction of National Gallery of Canada. RCA, 1 May-15 Jun

TRAVELLING

Catalogues for 1934-43. National Gallery of Canada lists for 1944-56. 1951, Diploma works only

1934	82	1941	55	1947	56
1935	72	1942	57	1948	42
1936	69	1943	51	1950	20
1937	64	1944	38	1951	42
1938	58	1945	42	1953	34
1940	58	1946	48	1956	32

www.ingramcontent.com/pod-product-compliance
Lightning Source LLC
LaVergne TN
LVHW010447080826
844660LV00027B/1226